PRODUCT
PHOTOGRAPHY

Nath-Sakura

PRODUCT PHOTOGRAPHY

LIGHTING, COMPOSITION, AND SHOOTING TECHNIQUES

rockynook

Product Photography
Nath-Sakura
www.nath-sakura.net
www.nath-sakura-formations-photo.fr

ISBN: 978-1-68198-929-7
1st Edition (1st printing, December 2022)

Original French title: Éclairer et photographier les objets
© 2022, Éditions Eyrolles, Paris, France
© 2022, Éditions Victoria/Nath-Sakura Factory
Translation copyright © 2023 Rocky Nook, Inc.

All images © Nath-Sakura
The photographs in this book were taken by Nath-Sakura at Studio B612, except
for the following photographs, which were taken by Yolan Lemaire, the studio's second photographer: pages 20, 22 (top), 31, 33, 35, 36, 38, 46 (bottom),
94 (bottom), 124, 127, 129, 130, 133, 134, 168 (top right), 174 (bottom right),
175 (top right), 177 (top), 178 (bottom right), 179 (bottom), 192 (bottom right),
195, 234, 235.

Rocky Nook Inc.
1010 B Street, Suite 350
San Rafael, CA 94901
USA

www.rockynook.com

Distributed in the UK and Europe by Publishers Group UK
Distributed in the U.S. and all other territories by Ingram Publisher Services

Library of Congress Control Number: 2022937116

Editor: Jocelyn Howell
Project manager: Lisa Brazieal
Marketing coordinator: Katie Walker
Translation by: Marie F. Deer
Layout and type: Danielle Foster
Interior design: Nord Compo
Cover design: Aren Straiger

ACKNOWLEDGMENTS
AND THANKS

The work that you now hold in your hands came close to never being finished. Of all the books I have written, this is the one that gave me the most trouble, as much because of the difficulty of the subjects I take on here as because of the challenge of making them easy to understand and fun to put into practice. Nevertheless, product photography is an exciting discipline, one that was worth my taking the necessary time to dedicate a truly useful book to it. Without the support and the many encouraging comments and questions that came from my faithful readers, I confess that I would never have been able to manage it.

This book owes a tremendous amount to Yolan, who works next to me as a photographer at Studio B612, and on whom I was able to rely for the production of certain shots; to Tao, who knew just what to do to support me and my business during the difficult writing of the chapters on optics; to Stéphanie, director of the photography division of the Eyrolles publishing company, who carefully reviewed and edited the [original French] book to make it perfect; and to Olly, my English setter, who insists on being on my lap when I am sitting at my keyboard (and an English setter is heavy!).

But above all, this book is dedicated to Victoria, my daughter, in her quest for perfection.

FOREWORD

Photographing objects always seems like a very easy thing to do until you start trying to do it, and then it can quickly turn into a nightmare if you underestimate how important it is to take the time to learn the basic concepts that govern light and the specific reflecting properties of each kind of material.

What could be more ordinary than a pair of glasses or a bottle of wine? And yet, photographing these objects can turn out to be a difficult task for anyone trying to light them and create a pleasant representation of them without a solid technical background.

It is impossible to figure out how many sources of light to use, how to position them, and how they work without first understanding Snell's law of refraction, the notion of families of angles on spherical surfaces, the management of direct and diffuse reflections, the difference between the reflections from glass and from metal, how to manage the intensity of light using a flash meter or exposure meter, and a host of other optic phenomena.

Lighting Concepts

Whatever camera you might be using, whether it is an analog camera made in the 1950s or one of the most modern and high-tech medium-format digital devices, in the final rendering of a photograph, everything depends on lighting, whose rules are as old as the physics of light (in other words, optics).

This book is not the kind of "recipe book for photography" that you will find flooding the market. Instead, it is meant to teach you the principles of light, and of lighting objects, in depth. Because even if you have read a book that goes into detail about how to illuminate a bottle of red wine, if you don't fully understand the laws governing the lighting of cylinders and the laws of reflection, it's a safe bet that it will take you a long time to figure out how to light the silk-screening or the gilded embossing on the label, with all the reflections in the right places; or worse, that you will find yourself at a total loss when you are faced with a bottle of rosé or whiskey.

It is better to take the time to grasp all of the principles that govern light, to deepen your comprehension of the phenomena that occur when light encounters matter, and to understand how you are going to be able to photograph an object, rather than embarking on making photographs that are doomed to fail because of a lack of knowledge of the issues that come into play.

I know how daunting this can seem to the amateur photographer, but I assure you that you will not be disappointed: by understanding what happens when you move your light source, why a reflection appears in an unexpected place, or why it continues to appear even when you have lowered the intensity of the light, you will understand a multitude of concepts that will be valid in all other photographic realms as well, from portraits to landscapes.

Themes and Examples

In this book, I have tried to establish a system of categories that will make it possible to cover product photography in its entirety: by reducing all the variables to questions of the condition of the surface, geometric forms, and reflectivity, we can apply the concepts we learn here to every class of objects, and thus determine the ideal kind and angle of lighting for photographing them.

Whether you're photographing a matte opaque plastic cylindrical object, such as a supplement bottle, or a clear glass trapezoidal object, like a perfume bottle, or an object made of mixed materials such as chrome, glass, and rubber, like a car, you will learn how to manage the appropriate lighting and perspective on all possible objects.

Asking the Right Questions

For every new object to be photographed, you always have to ask yourself the same questions: What material or materials is it made out of? Is the surface matte, satiny, or glossy? Is it smooth or rough? What is the expected result in terms of lighting, perspective, and positioning? What lighting options are impossible (generally having to do with the object's shape or reflectivity)? How is this class of objects usually lighted?

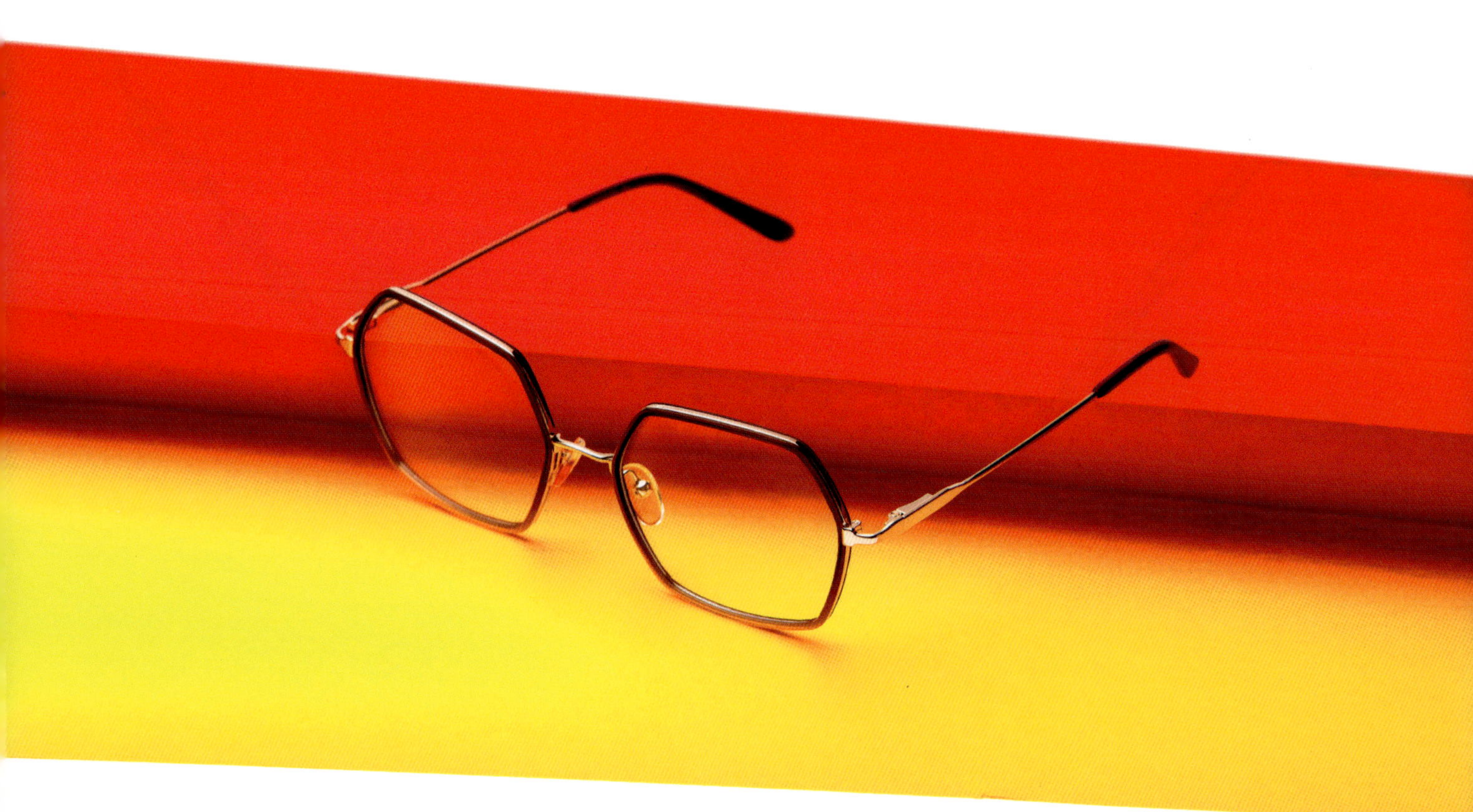

You will find answers to all of these questions in this book. Because the laws of optics always stay the same, once you have learned how to light clear glass, you will be able to photograph bottles, martini glasses, or any other object made out of clear glass. The same thing is true for all other kinds of materials, and all shapes. Even better, you will be able to use this knowledge to construct your own representations and to realize your own creative ideas.

Putting Myself in Your Shoes

Throughout the writing of this book, which I hope I've made as simple and as educational as possible, I asked myself whether the photography student that I was 20 years ago would easily understand the concepts that I discuss here. I use three methods of explanation—written, sketched, and through photographs—at the same time, each of which allows me to explain various aspects of lighting and perspective in a different and complementary way.

I have also tried to open artistic doors by using, for my illustrative examples, problems that I have encountered during my career as a commercial photographer. Of course, none of this will be of any particular interest unless you try to carry out your own take on each of these case studies, in order to create your own photographic universes.

CONTENTS

Foreword	VI
Absolute Rigor	12

THE LAWS OF OPTICS AND USING THEM FOR PRODUCT PHOTOGRAPHY — 15

Before You Start	16
The Basics of Light	18
The Amount of Light	18
The Quality of Light	19
Contrast	20
The Color of Light	21
The Roles of Light	22
Distance	22
Angle	23
Measurements With An Independent Exposure Meter	24
Measurement Methods	24
Which Light Should I Use?	28
Natural Light	28
Continuous Artificial Light	28
Flash Lighting	30

Shadow And Half-Light	31
Shadows And Shapes	37
Shadows And Space	37
Perspective	44
Showing Depth	44
The Behavior of Light	51
The Reflection of Light	60
The Condition of The Surface	61
Diffuse Reflection	61
Specular Reflection	62
Direct Reflection	63
Polarized Direct Reflections	65
Families of Angles	67
Families of Angles And Distances	70
The Inverse Square Law	74

SHAPE, TEXTURE, AND MATERIAL — 77

Light And Texture	78
Mixed Surfaces	81

Parallelepipeds 83

Complex Shapes 85

Spheres And Rounded Shapes 87

Cylindrical Shapes 92

Lighting Glossy Metals 96

Lighting Glass 98

LIGHTING
AND PRACTICE 105

Technical Implementation 106

Choosing a Background 108

Supporting Material 112

Tripods 114

Typology of Objects 116

Respecting Colors 119

Photo Editing 122

Bottles of Red Wine 124

Bottles of Rosé And White Wine 129

Frosted-Glass Bottles 132

Empty Bottles 134

Lighting a Painting 135

Lighting a Mirror 137

Lighting a Pyramid 139

Lighting Transparent Prisms 141

Lighting Parallelepipeds 143

Lighting Cylinders 145

Lighting Spheres 148

Eliminating Cast Shadows 151

Lighting Food 153

Lighting Electronics 158

Lighting Jewelry 160

Lighting Watches 164

Photographing Furniture 167

Photographing Eyeglasses 169

Make-Up And Perfume 173

Photographing Textiles 178

Photographing Clothing 180

Lighting Tableware 185

Lighting In An Aquarium 190

Lighting Sheet Metals 191

Lighting Plastic 192

Catalog Shots 193

Advertising Shots 196

Using Liquids 199

Composite Photographs 204

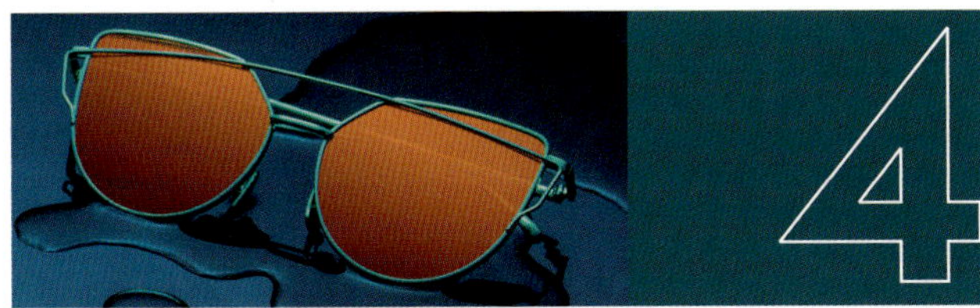

COMPOSITION
AND PROBLEM RESOLUTION 207

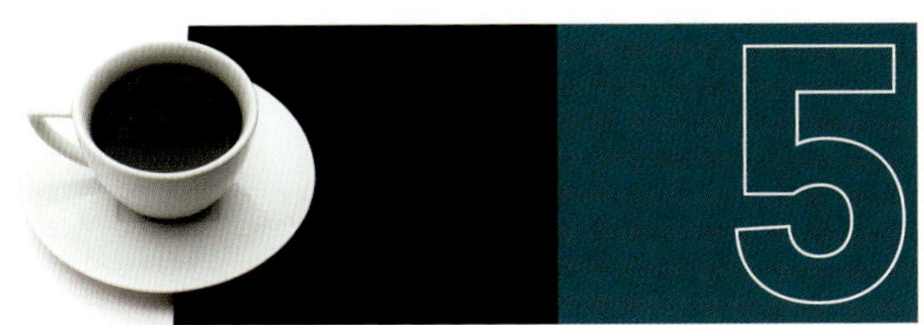

IMAGE ANALYSES
AND LIGHTING SETUPS 227

Composition And Contrasts **208**
Compositional Contrasts 208
Color Contrasts 209
Color Harmonies 211
Basic Rules of Harmony 211
Tone On Tone (Monochrome) 211

Staging **214**

Artistic Visions **217**

No Object Is Perfect **221**

Practical Exercises **228**
A Study of Rings 230
Sneakers Rock 232
Fragrance Diffuser 234
Flying Teacup 236
Waffles With Honey 238
Blue Orange 240
Into Orbit 242
Floating Perfume 244
Ants With Watch 246
Old Port 248
Freshness And Fruit 250
Jar of Moisturizing Cream With Splashes 252
Red Chili Peppers 254
A Watch And Its Impact 256
Anatomy of a Hamburger 258
Exploding Whiskey 260
Upside-Down Levitation 262

ABSOLUTE RIGOR

More than in any other realm of photography, the lighting and shooting of objects requires great precision, good working methods, and an excellent knowledge of the laws of optics.

If there is one field in which approximation is unacceptable, it is product photography. A faultless rendering is expected here, especially when we are dealing with manufactured items, using precise light metering and an exactitude to the nearest millimeter in the placement of reflections. Those who move too fast are condemning themselves to long hours of post-production digital editing.

Too Much Like Homework?

Given what I have just said, most amateur photographers who are reading this book will likely be tempted to run away! And yet, you will discover that while the subjects I discuss here do not allow for imprecision, it is actually not that hard to learn them, nor to set up lighting for your photography: it is usually a matter of applying simple geometrical principles, as in the case of families of angles, knowledge that will easily allow you to determine where reflections will or will not appear on a glossy object, or where nuances of lighting will appear on a matte one.

The understanding of optical phenomena that you will acquire over the course of reading this book will allow you to understand all aspects of your photography: the level of illumination for shadows and how they are propagated; the quality of reflections, their positioning on the object, and how they appear or disappear depending on the axis of your camera; the density and color of the objects that you are photographing; and so on.

Personally, I never made as much progress in photography as I did once I understood these concepts, which I was then able to apply to all aspects of lighting, ranging from lighting human beings to lighting photographs of objects.

About Thirty Basic Concepts

All optical phenomena can be reduced to about thirty basic concepts, which will allow you to take in the appearance of an illuminated object and know what the result will be once the camera shutter has been released. This means that you can avoid unnecessary "tests" and having to position your light sources from the outset, all while ensuring that you will be able to achieve a professional-level result. Of course, this will also require a lot of practice and a good measure of patience, but if you apply the methods presented here, you will make rapid progress.

Rigor and Working Method

What we are doing here is a far cry from leisure photography and guesstimating your shots. For this kind of photography, we have to hold ourselves to a precise method for preparing the objects, placing objects; of choosing light shapers and measuring the light; and to a set way of choosing the lens, the distance, and the angle of the shot.

In truth, none of the things that you will learn in this handbook are very complicated, but each action that is part of the process leading to the end result must be very precisely measured and prepared for.

In product photography, there is no place for rushing. You must make sure that the object is perfectly clean and the workspace carefully cleared of dust, and then place the object along an axis where all of its characteristics can be perfectly distinguished. From the laws of optics and the state of the object's surface you will determine the optimal lighting (in terms of number of light sources as well as quality, angle, and distance). You will then go on to add the necessary accessories that are required for your light sources, such as barn doors (lamp shields) or reflectors. Then you will carefully measure the quantity of light so that it conforms to the settings of the camera, and thus to the desired depth of field and image density, while optimizing the result so that it conforms to the dynamic range of your sensor. Finally, all that is left to do is to release the shutter and create a new universe.

❯❯ You can achieve this kind of shot without using Photoshop, by very carefully controlling the distances between the glass, the barn door, and the light sources, because all of this is only a question of optics and methodology.

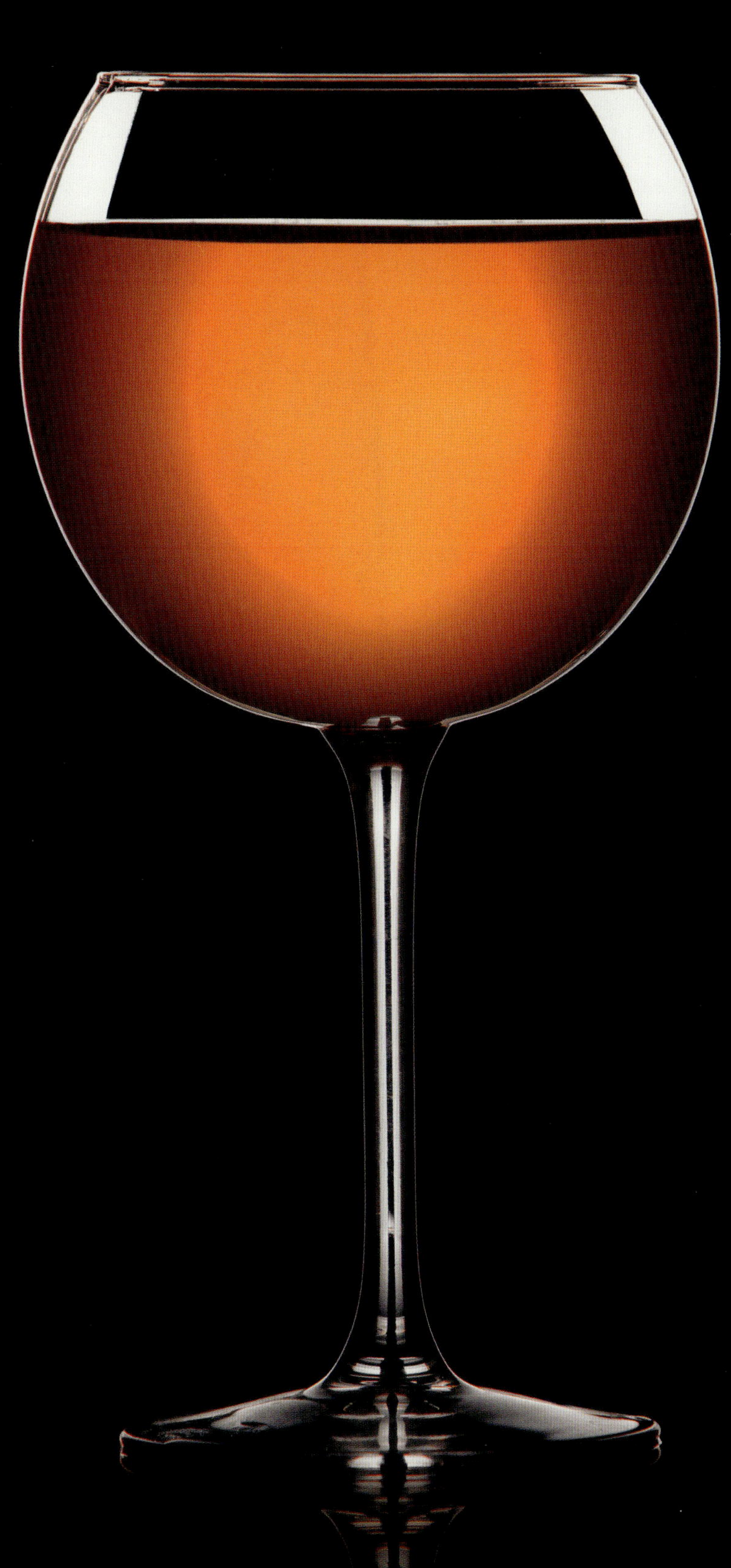

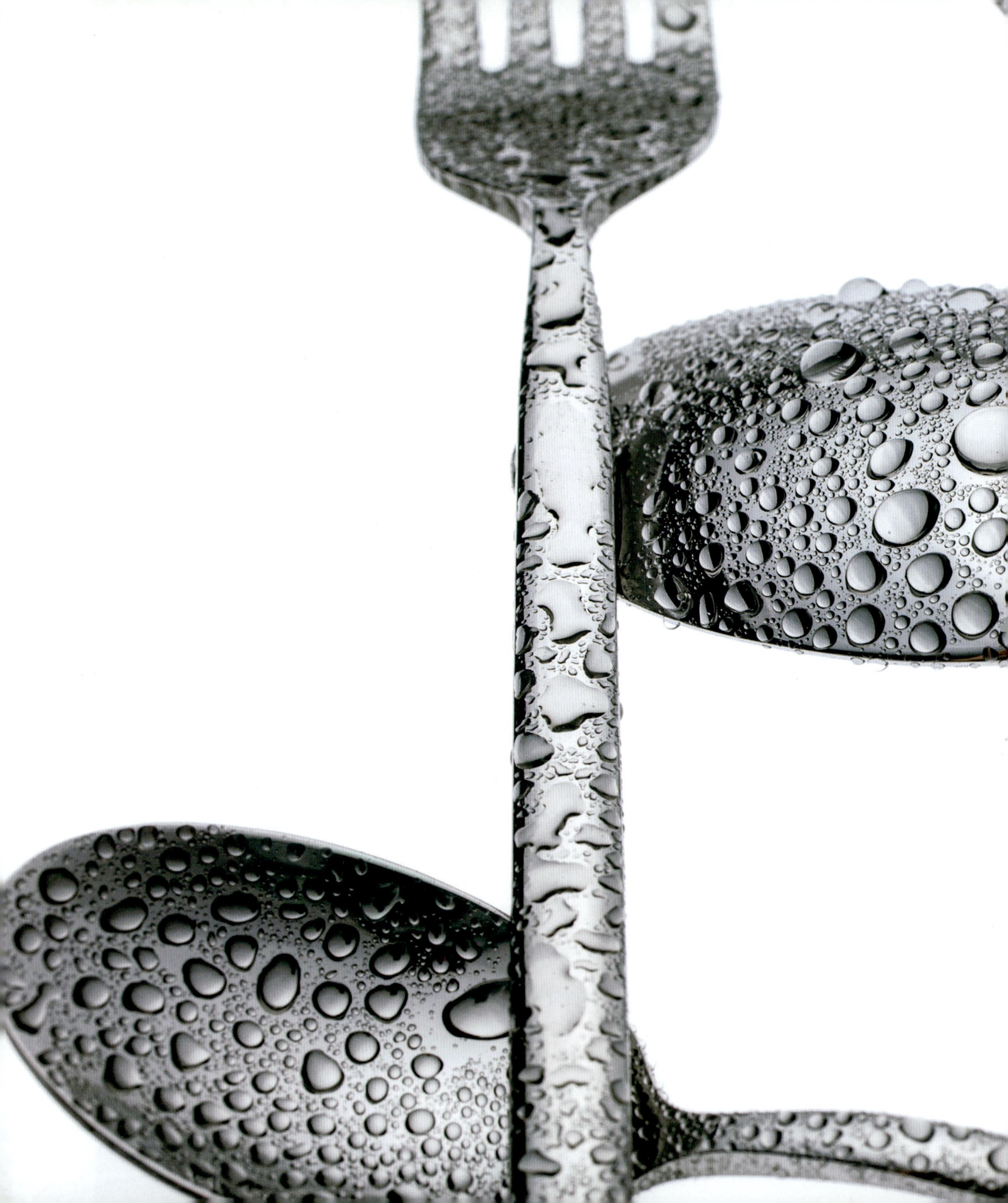

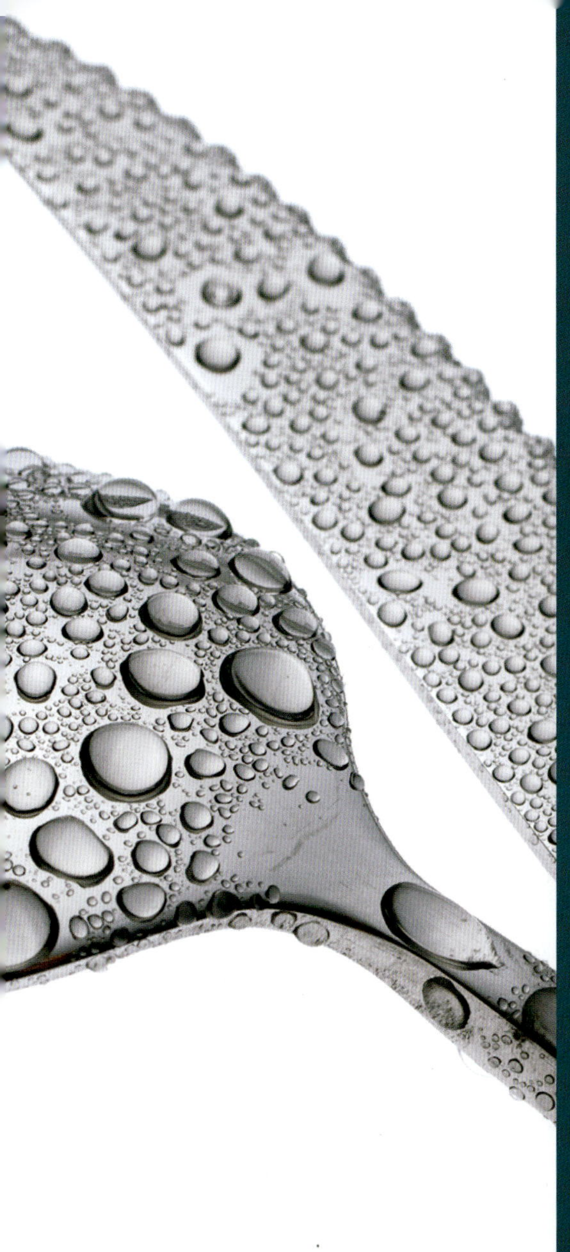

THE LAWS OF OPTICS AND USING THEM FOR PRODUCT PHOTOGRAPHY

1

» **16** Before You Start

» **18** The Basics of Light

» **24** Measurements with an Independent Exposure Meter

» **28** Which Light Should I Use?

» **31** Shadow and Half-Light

» **37** Shadows and Shapes

» **44** Perspective

» **51** The Behavior of Light

» **60** The Reflection of Light

» **65** Polarized Direct Reflections

» **67** Families of Angles

» **70** Families of Angles and Distances

» **74** The Inverse Square Law

BEFORE YOU START

Unlike for many types of photography, where inspiration and a sense of the present moment are precious qualities for the photographer, with product photography it is necessary to perform a precise review of one's entire working method.

When it comes to product photography, nothing is left to chance, and there is extremely limited space for improvisation. You must have a precise vision of the result that you want to achieve before you even start. And you must not neglect any detail.

Preparing the Objects and the Work Space

With an eagerness to start shooting, there is often one issue that photographers tend to consider a minor detail, but that could cause you to lose hours of your time to retouching work: the state and cleanliness of your work space. Thus, before you start, make sure to completely dust and degrease the spaces and mounts you will be using in your work, and set yourself up in a clean space. To eliminate most of the particles and prevent them from resettling during the shoot, I suggest using an anti-dust aerosol spray and antistatic dust cloths. Then, it's best to handle the objects you are photographing with antistatic gloves—usually made out of polyester, polyamide, or

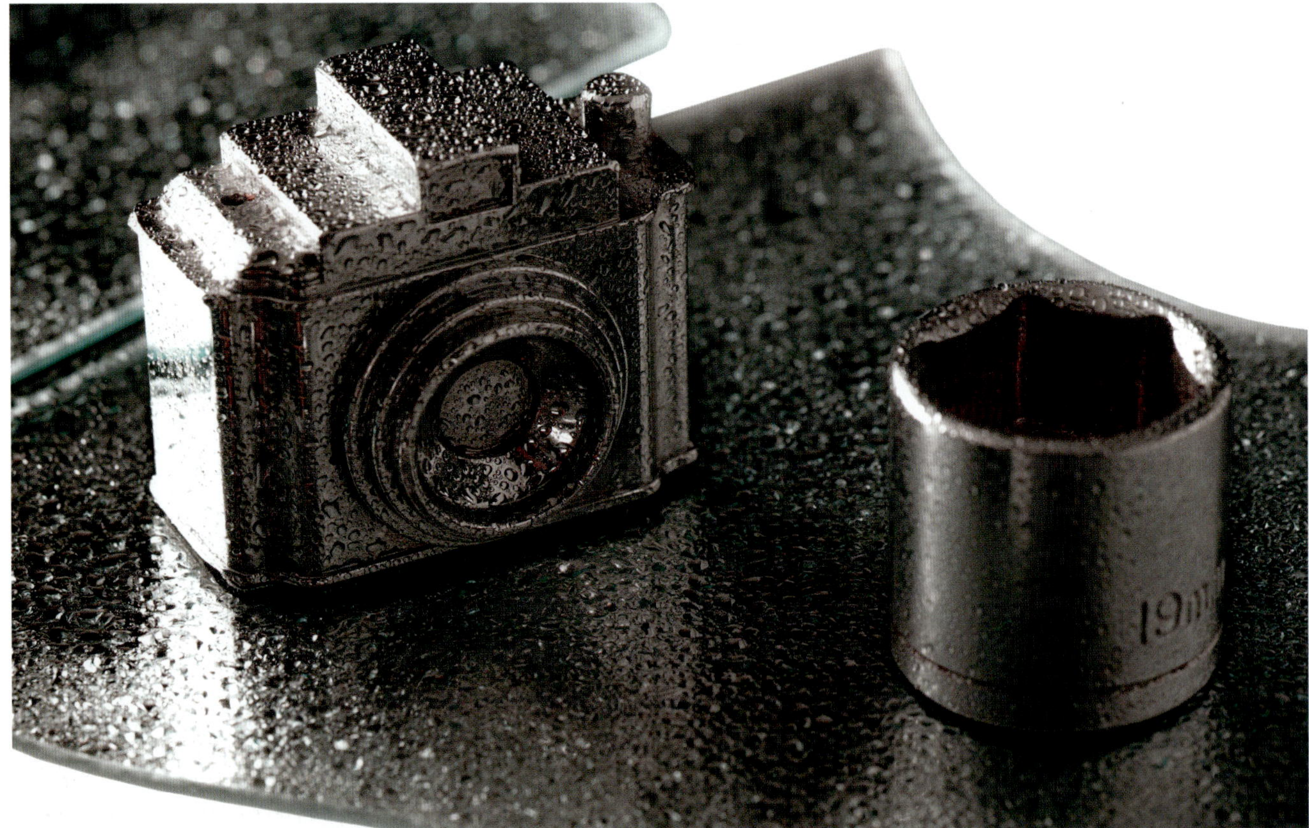

⌃ Meticulously preparing the objects is essential for the success of your product photography.

polyurethane—to avoid fingerprints, which are tediously difficult to remove in post-production.

Wedging Material

You will quickly learn that you need a large number of small wedges, of all sizes and shapes, to use in positioning objects and holding them in place at a particular angle. At Studio B612, we use a variety of shapes, ranging from small one- or two-millimeter props to bridges that measure in the tens of centimeters, made out of transparent plexiglass. They allow us to mount all kinds of objects along every axis that we might wish to use: lightly tilted, lying flat, angled to one side or another, as so on. The key is that the position of the object is maintained at a precise angle, without the support it is resting on being visible or creating awkward shadows. This may seem like a small detail, but the success of the shoot is dependent on it.

Lighting Equipment

There is no need to use expensive lighting equipment; for some objects—for example, for food or simple matte objects—you can even rely on natural sunlight through a window. But to be clear, it is impossible to properly photograph a bottle of wine or create an advertisement for perfume without having at least three adjustable artificial light sources. You can use continuous sources (such as HMI, tungsten, or LED) or flashes, the only difference in each case being lighting efficiency. Personally, I find it simpler and more comfortable to work with a flash, but the concepts that I discuss in this handbook will work with all types of lighting (natural light, continuous artificial lighting, and flash lighting).

To obtain the light that is best adapted to the object being photographed, it is necessary to use lighting modifiers/shapers, such as a large light box (like an octabox), a diffusing fabric, a zoom reflector, and, in some cases, a strip box (for bottles, for instance).

Finally, the use of an independent light meter or exposure meter is indispensable. It is the only instrument we have for precisely measuring the quantity of incident light; it also allows us to anticipate how the lighting will vary depending on the distance to and positioning angle of the object being illuminated. I know a lot of YouTubers and other tutorial authors will try to talk you out of using a light meter, but keep in mind that there is a reason why they are used in professional product photography: this tool allows us to save time, to obtain technically flawless photos beginning with the very first shot, and to ensure an optimal richness of tones.

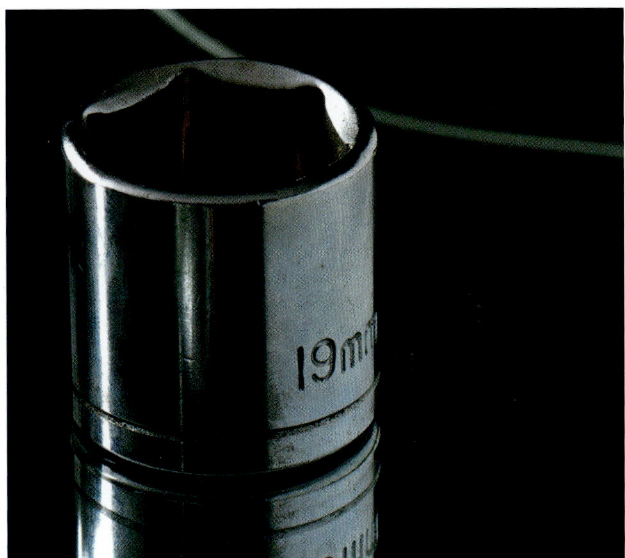

⌃ In this shot, the mirror was not dusted and the object was handled with bare hands, which explains the fingerprint that is clearly visible on the 19mm socket.

Shooting Equipment

The laws of optics require us to use lenses with very different focal lengths depending on the situation: telephoto lenses (from 100mm to 200mm) when we need to reduce the risk of problematic direct reflections, and wide-angle lenses (from 20mm to 35mm) for certain photographs where it is necessary to play with the perspective. The camera body itself is not that important, as long as it is easy to adjust manually. In addition, you will need a circular polarizing filter, a gray card, and, in some cases, a remote control to trigger the camera from a distance.

And Finally

A product photographer's studio is always cluttered with a large number of improbable accessories: spray bottles; boards made out of every imaginable material (wood, plexiglass, glass, cardboard) and color to serve as supports; aquariums and terrariums; powders; materials and textures for different kinds of staging; clamps, clips, and rods to hold the products and various decorations; wedges and a multitude of small elements for propping up the articles being photographed; tables of various sizes adapted to the setups needed for a variety of shots; and more.

As you read through these pages, you will discover the reasons for this accumulation of material.

THE BASICS OF LIGHT

You can only make serious progress in product photography if you truly understand how light acts and how we can intervene to transform it. Thus, let us first go back to the essential characteristics of light.

1. Without a measuring instrument, it is impossible to define how much actual light there is on an object.

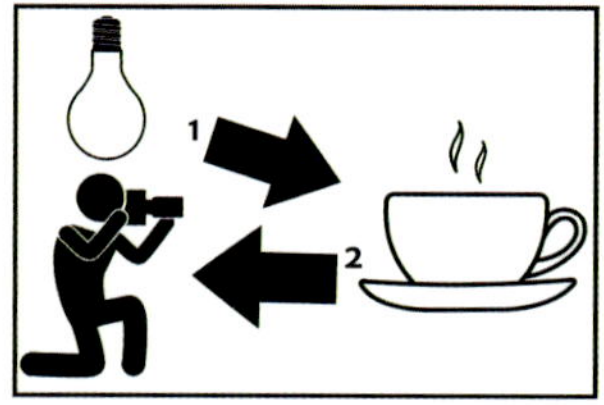

2. There are two kinds of measurable light: incident light (1) and reflected light (2).

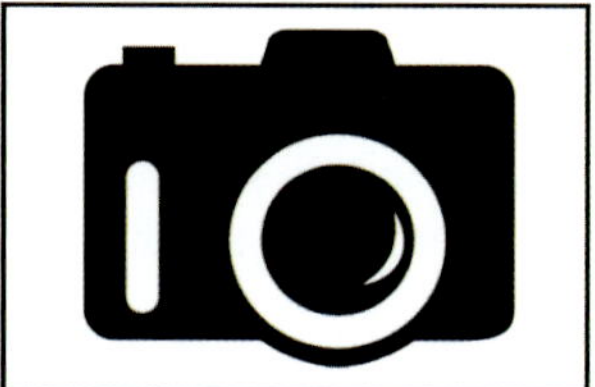

3. A light meter or spot meter built into the camera can only measure reflected light.

4. The quantity of light reflected by an object varies depending on its reflectance.

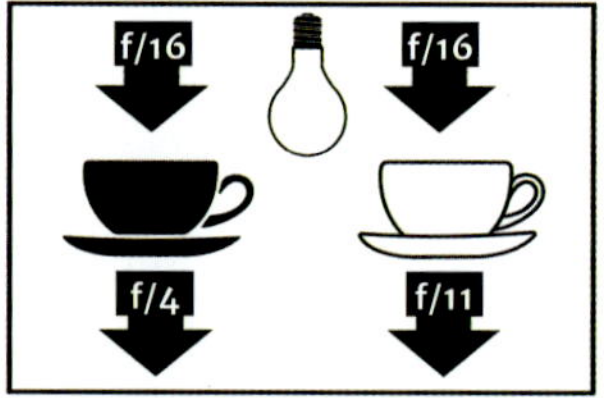

5. Measurements of reflected light cannot be precise because they vary according to the reflectance.

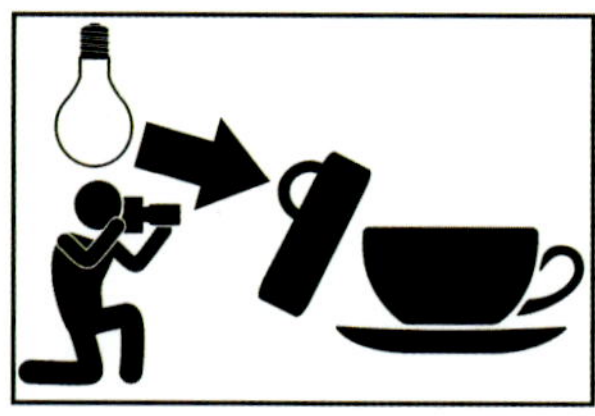

6. In order to obtain exact information, it is preferable to measure the incident light.

MEASURABLE LIGHT

As you will see over the course of these pages, the topics of shooting and lighting are intrinsically linked. Each of these concepts must be completely clear to you before you can begin producing high-quality images.

THE AMOUNT OF LIGHT

To precisely judge how to adjust your camera, you have to be able to determine how much light is present. The first mistake beginners make is to believe they can get this information just by looking at the camera screen or the photograph's histogram. However, these are not accurate measurements because, first, the image that appears on the camera screen is only a JPEG preview, compressed and transformed by the manufacturer's automatic demosaicing software, rather than the actual RAW file that you have created; and second, the data that is displayed, both in terms of over- or underexposure and in terms of color or density, is not data that you can use to clearly decide how to proceed. In other words, the histogram that you see is only a statistical presentation of the illumination levels and the RGB colors of the JPEG preview.

In order to be able to measure something, you need a measuring tool, and in photography, that tool is the light meter or exposure meter.

Incident Light and Reflected Light

We will start by drawing a distinction between illuminance (the amount of light that a given object receives, or "incident" light) and luminance (the amount of light that the object returns, or "reflected" light). We understand intuitively that the light is first projected by the light source and then reflected back by the object being photographed (see diagram opposite). In measuring reflected light (what ends up passing through the lens), we are not measuring the actual quantity of light from the light source, but rather what is left of it after some portion has been absorbed by the object. For the same amount of light falling on a black object and a white object, for instance, we will register different measurements—a pile of coal

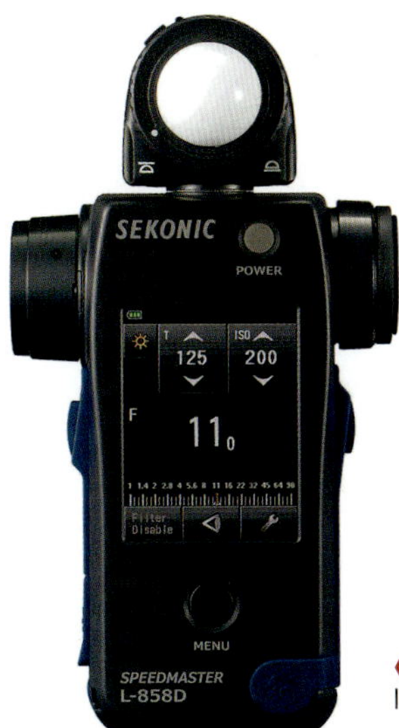

<< An independent exposure meter/ light meter/flash meter.

LIGHT QUALITY

Four factors determine the quality of the light. These need to be kept in mind at all times when you are executing your shots.

Apparent size: The larger the light source's apparent size, the softer the light. The smaller the apparent size, the harder the light.

Distance: The closer the light source, the softer the light; the farther away, the harder the light. But also keep in mind that the farther away the light source is, the smaller its apparent size will become.

Reflection: When light is reflected by a surface (such as a white wall), its beam will expand and the light will become softer.

Diffusion: Light that is diffused (such as by fabric or by a thick layer of clouds) is softer than direct light.

will reflect less light than a pile of snow. And you can determine the true measurement if you know each object's reflection coefficient (reflectance), but that requires keeping that specific information in mind for each different type of surface and making a compensatory calculation. It saves time to use a device that will allow you to measure incident light: an independent exposure meter/light meter.

Precision

The following section will address in detail how to use an independent exposure meter, but for now, keep in mind that this tool will allow you to know precisely how much light is being projected onto each part of the object, to measure its progressiveness, to determine the appropriate camera settings for your shot, and to estimate how much light needs to be added or, if necessary, removed. This is a simple and effective way to estimate the relative settings of the camera and the light source.

THE QUALITY OF LIGHT

On Earth, the quality of the light varies throughout the day and depending on the weather. On clear days, the light of the sun appears very hard, creating sharp shadows (with little half-light), whereas when it's overcast, the shadows become much softer and less dense (and there is much more half-light). These variations make up the qualitative aspect of the light.

I point out the idea of the penumbra—the half-light at the edges of the shadow, the transition area between shadow and light—because observing that is what allows us to deduce the quality of the light; it is this half-light that becomes larger or smaller when we change the lighting conditions.

The light quality itself has nothing to do with whether the shadow is light or dark: the luminance of the shadow depends on the luminance of the surface onto which it is projected, along with the quantity of light reflected by the environment. It will obviously be darker if it is projected onto a piece of gray paper than when it is projected onto a piece of white paper.

Four factors come into play in the importance of the half-light, and therefore of the light quality: the distance from the light source, its relative size, its diffusion, and its reflection.

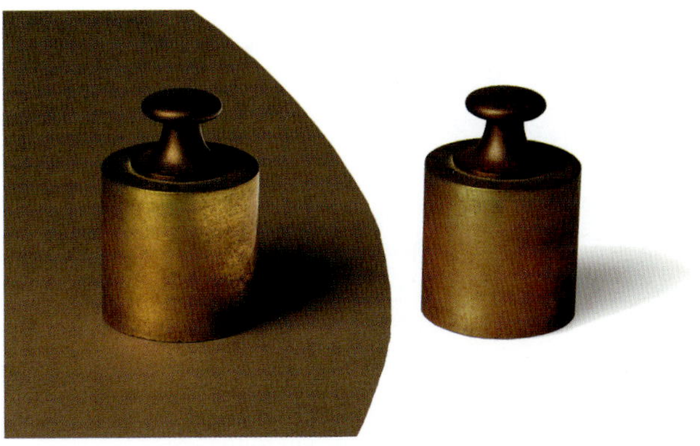

The object was lit in the same way for both shots, and the half-light is exactly the same in both, but it looks lighter or darker because of the different backgrounds.

To put it more simply, we can make the light softer by bringing it closer to the object, by using a larger shaper (such as a large octabox instead of a smaller bowl, for instance), by inserting a diffusing fabric between the light source and the object (such as a veil in front of the window), or by directing the light toward a reflective medium (such as a white wall).

In the studio, we can change the quality of the light by changing the size and distance of the light sources, by using softer shapers (light boxes or umbrella lights) or harder ones (zoom bowls or Fresnel bowls), or by choosing between reflected light and direct lighting. And we can use these same methods for continuous light, whether artificial or natural.

CONTRAST

To emphasize (or hide) textures on an object, we must manage contrast. Low-contrast lighting will give a sense of slightly flat homogeneity, which is ideal for shooting smooth-skinned fruit (such as apples or pears), for example, whereas high-contrast lighting will create ruptures and threshold effects that are perfect for photographing oranges and pineapples.

Let's start by doing away with the idea that hard light creates contrasts. What actually happens is that when we bring the light source closer, we increase contrast, and

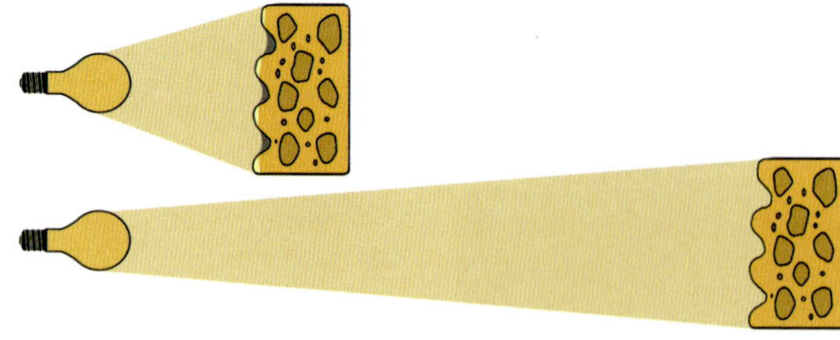

CONTRAST IS TIED TO DISTANCE FROM THE SOURCE

when we move the light source farther away, we "flatten" the image (see the photographs below).

The sharper the light beam's angle of incidence on an object, and the closer the light source, the more clearly we will see the smallest contrasts: they will create micro shadows in the hollows and slight climaxes at the peaks. Conversely, the farther away the light source, the less acute the rays will be and the more evenly all of the hollows and peaks will be lit. As you can see, this has nothing to do with the hardness of the light (which is one of its qualities, as we saw in the previous section).

Obviously, we can reinforce the sense of light contrast by acting on the object or on the composition, in particular by placing a light object against a dark background or by emphasizing one part of the shadow. But the representation of the state of the object's surface will not be affected by this.

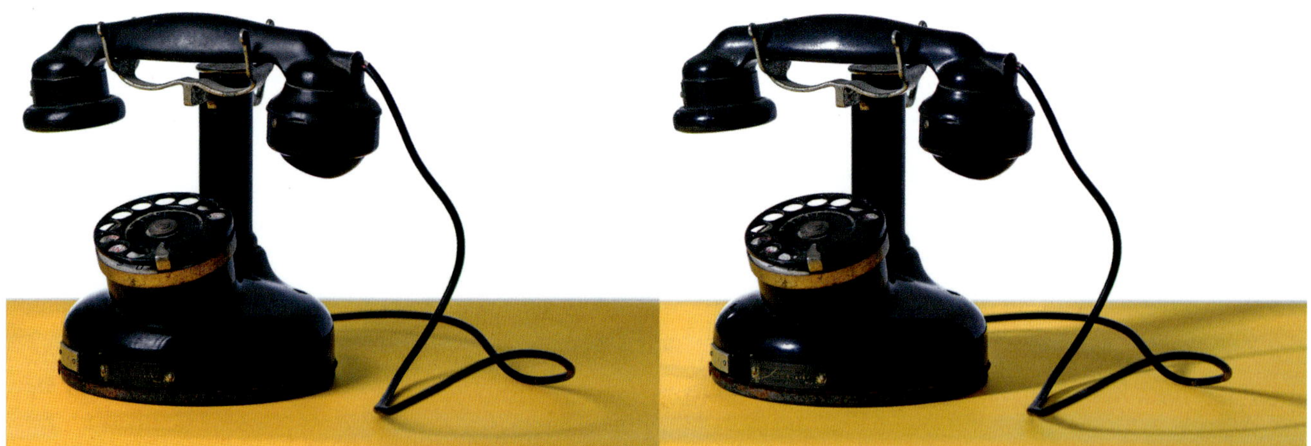

In the first photograph, the light source is placed about 8 inches away, whereas in the second, it is about 10 feet away. The flash was adjusted to send the same amount of light to the object.

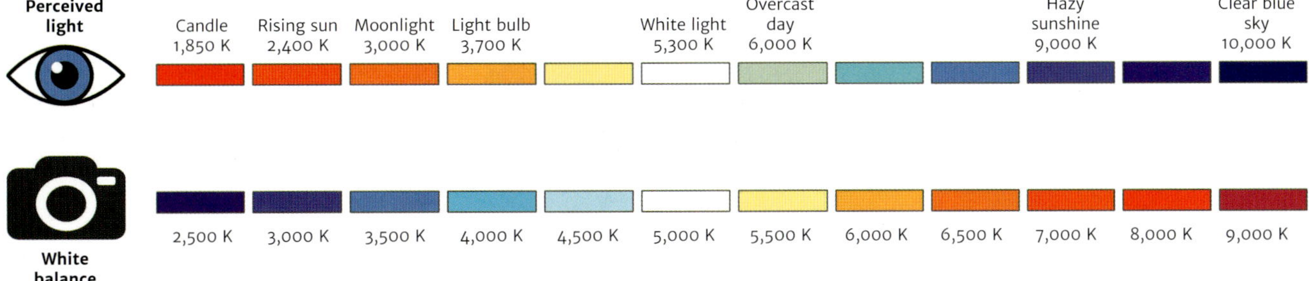

TEMPERATURES OF REAL COLORS AND WHITE BALANCE ADJUSTMENT

THE COLOR OF LIGHT

The correct white balance adjustment plays an essential role in the color rendering of a photograph.

Our brain is designed to automatically balance the colors that we perceive: if a bathroom with white walls is lit by an old incandescent bulb, we will see the walls as white—even if they would be distinctly yellow as measured by a light meter.

The Kelvin scale allows us to quantify the color of a light source: the lower the Kelvin temperature, the redder the source; the higher the Kelvin temperature, the bluer the source. We calibrate "white" light (the light of the sun at noon, in the middle of summer, on a clear day) at 5500K, and the "absolute" white standardized by the International Commission on Illumination (the CIE) at 6500K. By extension, lighting manufacturers offer "daylight" bulbs at a temperature between 5000K and 6000K.

This is why your camera needs to know about the real color of the light that is illuminating the object you are going to photograph. What we call "white balance" in photography and videography is actually "white compensation." Think about a candle. It emits a reddish-orange-colored light of about 1850K; if we adjust the camera's white balance using this value, we will get a very blue image, because the white balance adjustment is a correction. In order to get an image that is faithful to the color we actually perceive (neither reddish-orange nor blue) in the light of the candle, we will have to do the opposite, and add mostly blue, because of the white balance adjustment. In this particular lighting scenario, where we know the color almost exactly, we can adjust the camera to between 1800K and 2200K. But in order to be precise, we will customize the white balance, thanks to calibration with a gray card (see "Respecting Colors," chapter 3, page 119).

Of course, all cameras have an automatic white balance (AWB) management system (called AWB for Pentax, Sony, and Canon, or Auto for Nikon), based on an algorithm that intervenes depending on the proportion of red, green, and blue detected in the image, but it is not very effective for precisely defining what correction needs to be made for a given light. In order to be precise, you need to photograph a gray card in the same lighting that you will be using for the shot: this is the only way to ensure that the camera, and then the development software (via the eyedropper tool), will interpret the color perfectly. If you photograph a soda can that is Coca-Cola red, you cannot allow it to appear as carmine red: your client will reject the photo.

In order to correct the white balance for your photograph using a gray card, follow these steps:

1. Place the gray card in the same location and under the same lighting conditions as the object that you want to shoot.
2. Take a photograph, being careful to correctly expose the photo (using the value of the exposure meter or the flash meter).
3. Use the camera's "custom white balance" function (K) or the white balance selector (eyedropper tool) of the development software (e.g., Lightroom or Capture One) to select the gray of the photographed card as your basis.

THE ROLES OF LIGHT

The visual evidence of a single light source, consistent with the human experience of the sun as the sole source of illumination, is the basis on which the conventions of product lighting are built. This avoids the presence of contradictory or overlapping shadows. Nevertheless, even with only one heavenly body in the sky, an object can be lighted along several axes at the same time—for instance, when it is positioned near a reflective surface. In this case, the primary source works in harmony with the secondary, reflected source, the secondary one being weaker and softer. The entire language of lighting is in accordance with this idea.

- The primary source, corresponding to the sun, is called the *key light*: it has to be more powerful than all the others.
- The secondary source, corresponding to the reflection of a white wall, for example, must be situated opposite the primary light, while being weaker and more diffuse. This is called the *fill light*.
- If we place the key light behind the object, as is often done in food photography, we call it *backlight*. If it is positioned exactly opposite the object, so as to outline the object's edges in silhouette, we call it *rim light*.
- A light source that is directed toward the plane behind the object is called *background light*.
- And finally, the light source can be placed to illuminate the entire scene, or to give it a particular atmosphere, and this is called *ambient light*.

Even if there are several light sources present, the challenge for the photographer is to make it look as though there is only one, by playing with the intensities

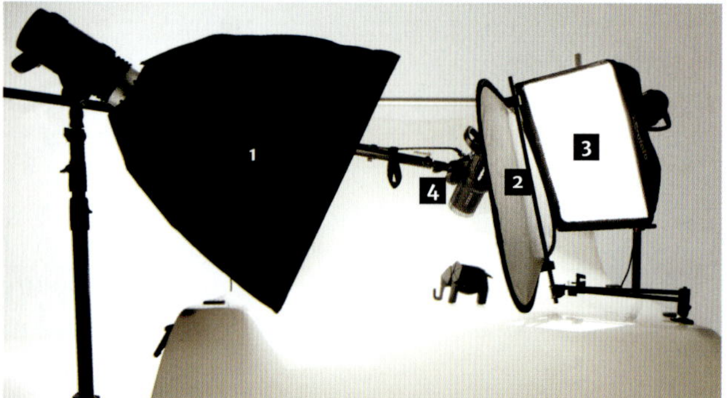

⌃ The roles of the light sources (both active and passive): (1) key light; (2) fill light (in this case, a reflector); (3) backlight; and (4) background light.

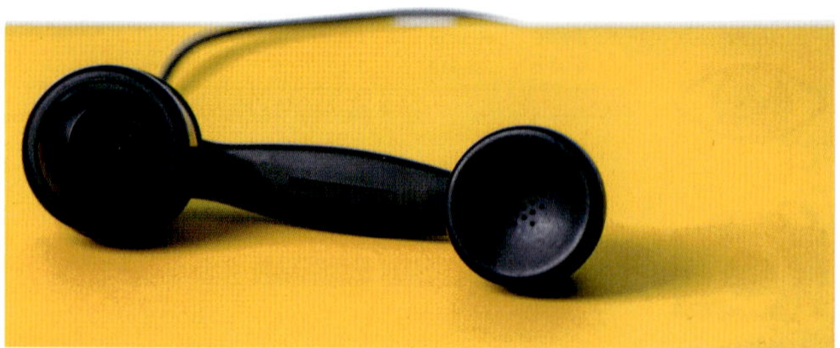

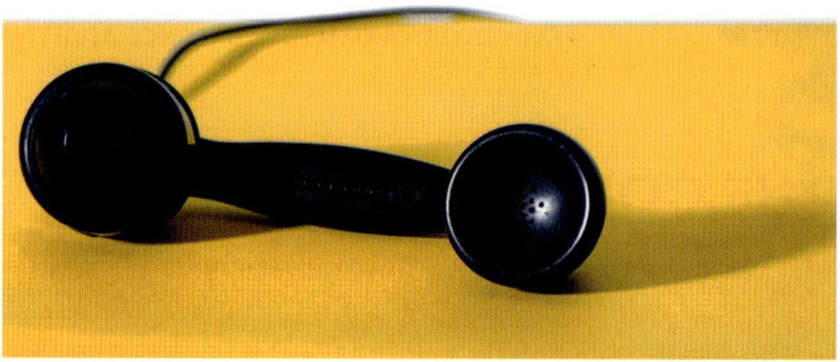

⌃ The same object, photographed with a light source of the same strength positioned one foot away (top) and thirteen feet away (bottom).

and qualities of the lights, while carefully choosing their angles as well. But as we will see throughout this book, most product-lighting arrangements require only one active light source, even though they may involve a large number of passive sources (reflectors).

DISTANCE

The distance of the light source, which is closely related to all of its other properties, has an effect on the quantity, quality, contrast, and role of the illumination. Whether you place a flash, measured at the same strength, one foot or thirteen feet from the object is not a trivial difference. Even if the quantity of received light is the same, the result will be completely different (as seen above): in the first case, the light will be much softer, with the contrasts more pronounced; in the second case, the light will be harder and the contrasts reduced. We can choose the distance at which we place the light source based on the size and number of objects we are going to photograph: the inverse square law formulated by Isaac Newton (but suggested forty-two years earlier by the French astronomer Ismaël Boulliau in his book *Astronomia Philolaica*) establishes that light decreases more and more slowly as one moves away from it. Let's imagine that we want to photograph two cars that are about three feet apart, and

Overexposure Warning

When you optimize your camera setting and the "Overexposure Warning" comes on, there is a high likelihood that the image you produce will start to flash. But don't let that make you believe that the image is burnt—that is not the case. It's just that the camera manufacturers intend their products for a wide variety of consumers, and this function is simply a safeguard for beginners.

And, in fact, it is easy to verify that the image presented as burnt (the correct term is *clipped*) by the camera is not by activating the same warning using Lightroom! The camera's built-in image analysis software sets up its alert rating to activate at 85% to 90% of the dynamic range, so there is still some margin left before there is a true loss of information in the light colors.

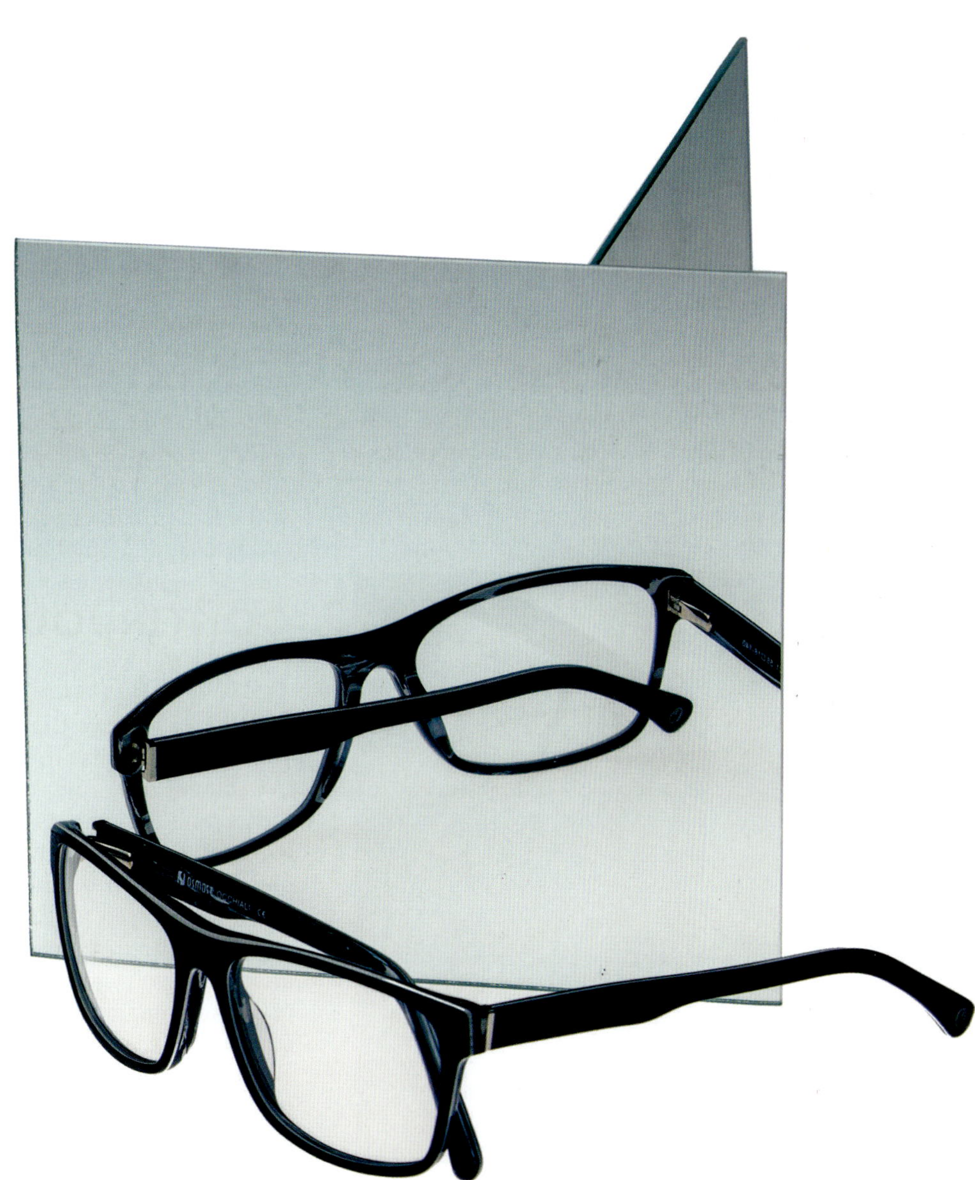

» This photograph was obtained without any retouching thanks to a precise measurement, using the manual flash meter, of the difference between the white background and the reflection in the mirror.

WHICH LIGHT SHOULD I USE?

Most novice photographers don't know what kinds of light they should use, and that is often because they aren't aware of the available options and of the relative advantages of using a flash as opposed to continuous light (whether artificial or natural). What follows is an overview.

Even though sunlight, the light of a desk lamp, and the light of a flash are different from each other in many respects, they all project a visible, measurable beam that is subject to variations in quality, quantity, contrast, color, and angle. The photographer who has grasped these concepts will be able to adapt each kind of light to their needs and preferences.

NATURAL LIGHT

Everyone starts by learning how to work with their camera using the sunlight or the overhead light in their room as the only source of light. In both cases, this is continuous light—used as the opposite of "discontinuous," which is what a flash emits, creating lighting on demand.

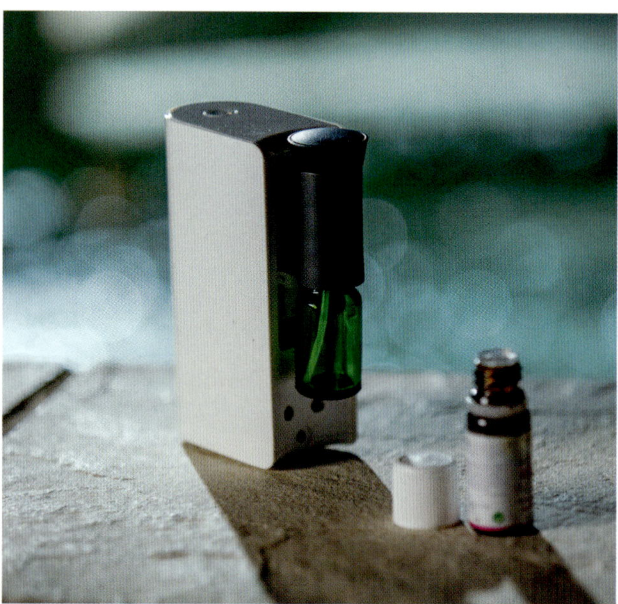

☆ A perfume diffuser photographed in natural light (behind a veranda at 6:00 p.m. in the summertime).

For all the other aspects of the lighting (measurement, quantity of light, quality of light, contrast, etc.), we proceed in the same way no matter what kind of light source we are dealing with. Of course, you can choose the sun as your light source, and you can make good use of it by measuring the light using an independent exposure meter and optimizing the exposure on the camera itself. But sunlight is hard to manipulate and transform—of course, you can decrease or increase how much light is diffused by varying the diaphragm aperture, the exposure time, and the sensitivity, and you can soften the light beam by positioning a diffusing fabric above the illuminated object, or change its angle by moving the camera, but all of this is still just a relative adjustment, without a lot of flexibility. You can't change the actual strength of the sunlight nor do anything about its distance.

CONTINUOUS ARTIFICIAL LIGHT

In order to achieve the exact image you have in mind, you will soon realize that you have to control your lighting sources very precisely in terms of distance, orientation, and strength. For example, it is very difficult to work when light from the sun is perpendicular to an object placed on a table. This is why you will quickly run into the need to use artificial light sources, whether continuous or flash. The need for light shapers will also arise when you want to shape the light and the shadows. Manufacturers offer a wide range of shapers to use with flashes, but the range is much more limited for use with continuous lights. Continuous light, which is simple to use, offers many advantages, one being that it is immediately visible and comprehensible to the human eye in terms of its strength—an aspect that flashes, which can offer infinitely greater lighting strengths, cannot provide. In addition, every kind of lamp has a color temperature

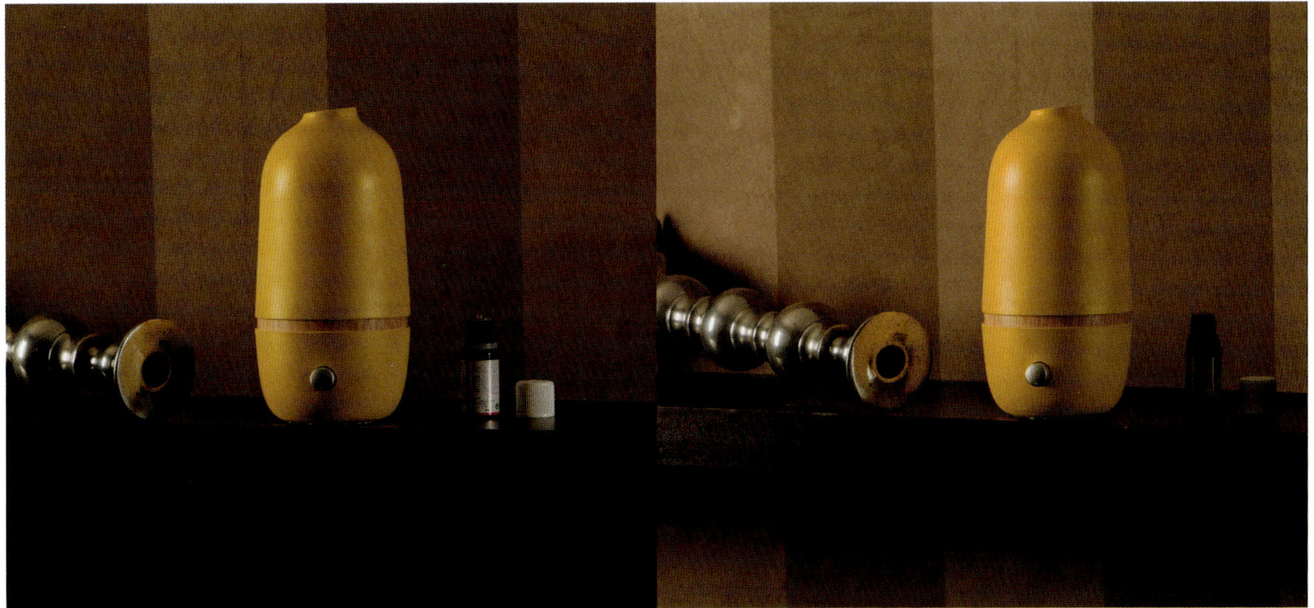

associated with its luminous efficacy. Incandescent and tungsten lights, for example, produce an orangish-yellow light, whereas HMI lamps calibrated to "daylight" produce a white light. Thus, you will have to adapt your white balance to the kind of lighting you're using, or else work with color gels.

Note that because they remain constant the entire time they are turned on, continuous light sources are absolutely necessary for video (provided they have a regular flicker frequency and don't produce a flicker effect).

Practical but Not Very Powerful

Continuous light is not able to reach the strengths released by flashes, which is one of the disadvantages of this kind of lighting for digital photography, which requires a lot of light. This means the photographer will have to work with higher sensitivities, larger apertures, and longer exposure times.

Aside from LED panels, which are energy-efficient and can run on batteries, other kinds of continuous light require a power connection.

Incandescent Lights

This old and inexpensive technology produces a very yellow light and a lot of heat, making it hard to use gels (which tend to melt). Food photography is impossible with incandescent lights because food will oxidize very quickly at high temperatures. These lights require a lot of energy, so their luminous efficacy is rather low.

Halogen Lamps

Halogen lamps were widely used in the 1980s for product photography, but they have now gone out of style. This kind of lighting offered a lot of advantages over incandescent lights, including: instantaneous ignition, identical light quality and quantity throughout its lifetime, 30% higher luminous efficacy, very good color rendering (color rendering index of 95–100), and a very white color temperature (5500K to 6500K).

The disadvantages include a short lifespan (2,000 hours), a very high temperature (which meant one could not bring the light too close to the objects being photographed), hypersensitivity to shocks, and high energy consumption.

HMI Lights

HMI (Hydrargyrum Medium-Arc Iodide) lights were first developed for use in the cinema. HMI technology was widely used in the early days of digital photography, when the digital backs of medium-format cameras split the image in scanning mode (for up to 2 seconds), making flashes unusable. With a light output that is three or

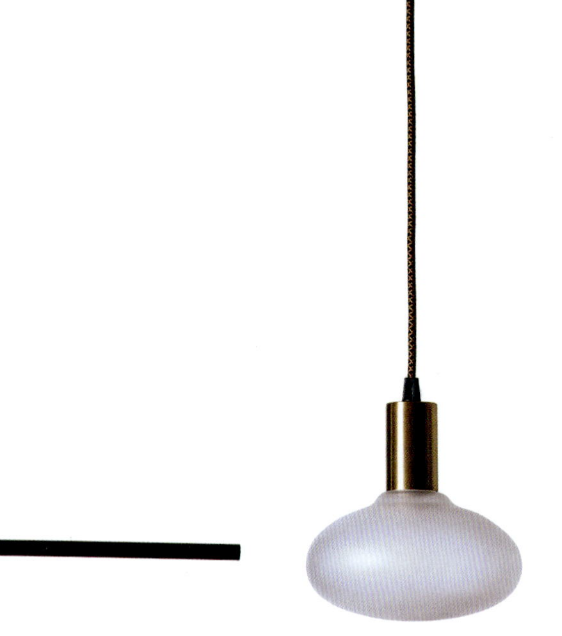

four times that of incandescent lights, HMI produces a white light with an efficient color index (the color rendering index varies from 80 to 95, with 100 being the maximum possible natural color rendition).

With color temperatures close to white (between 5000K and 8000K, depending on the ranges), this kind of lighting is still expensive and requires a lot of energy, especially since it works with ballast systems that are complicated to transport.

Fluorescent Tubes

Much less expensive than HMI, but also with poorer performance, fluorescent projectors have the advantage of not heating and of requiring little energy. On the other hand, their color temperature is unstable, which makes it hard to use them for product photography.

LED Lights

LED panels are the most recent kind of lighting to arrive on the market, and they are becoming more and more popular in photo and video studios thanks to their many beneficial qualities. They are convenient and light, require hardly any energy (which makes it possible to run them on batteries), last for tens of thousands of hours, and don't heat up. Some kinds of LED lights come equipped with dimmers that allow you to change their color and strength. The disadvantages include limited luminous strength, which means that the light sources have to be placed relatively close to the objects being photographed, and their conformation (panels that

are often quite wide), which means that zoom bowl shapers cannot be used with them.

FLASH LIGHTING

Because they are able to deliver considerable lighting strength (up to f/64 for a 1,000-joule flash placed one meter [about three feet] from the object) in a fraction of a second, flashes open up a very wide range of possibilities and adjustments for the photographer, with low sensitivities, short exposure times, and small apertures. Flashes only heat up for an instant (just for the length of the flash), and adapt very well to gels (as long as the pilot lights are not set to their lowest setting). In addition, there is a profusion of shapers available for shaping their light very precisely. This is the kind of lighting I prefer for my work.

There are several categories of flashes.

Speedlight Flashes

Speedlight flashes (hot-shoe flashes) are light and attach to the camera's hot shoe. They can also be positioned in remote mode and triggered with a synchronization cord or a radio transmitter. They work on batteries, which may mean a change in the color of the light that is emitted when they go off. And they are not very powerful compared to studio flashes, have a limited range of shapers that can be used with them, and are not equipped with the kind of guide lights that can help with product photography.

Studio Flashes

Studio flashes are capable of large luminous strengths (up to 2,500 joules) and are easy to adjust and direct. Their recycling time is much shorter than that of speedlight flashes. Depending on the brand, there are complete ranges of shapers that can be adapted to them. They are also very stable in terms of color temperature, give off a perfectly white light, and their luminous efficacy is unequaled (a thousand times greater than that of incandescent lights).

There are several kinds of studio flashes: speedlights or hot-shoe flashes (which integrate all of the electronics into one portable unit), pack-and-head system flashes (where the electronics are separate from the battery, allowing for a shorter recycling time), ring flashes (which encircle the lens), and monolights (all-in-one units equipped with an integrated battery; they are usually much more powerful than speedlights and are useful for outdoor photography).

SHADOW AND HALF-LIGHT

Shadow and half-light play a major role in the overall presentation of the photograph and the impression made by the object being presented.

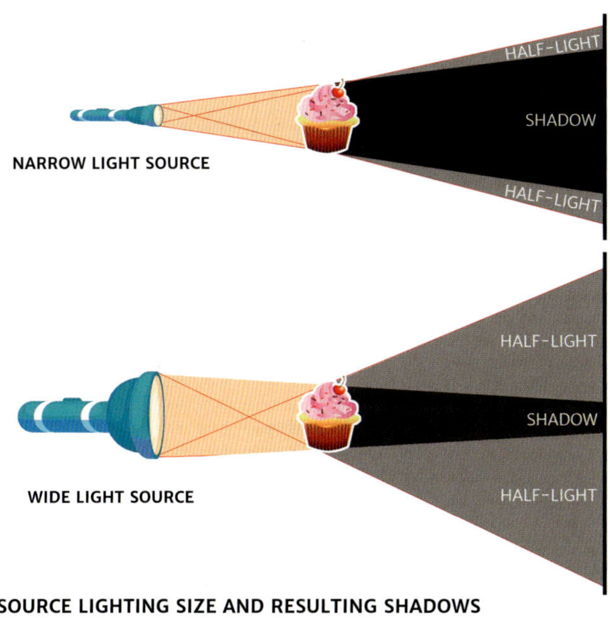

SOURCE LIGHTING SIZE AND RESULTING SHADOWS

The rendering of shadows, which is intimately linked to the quality of the original light and its distance from the object being photographed, greatly impacts the appearance of the final photograph. There are several important parameters that come into play.

All of the visual information generated by a light helps us to create a representation of the object. But this representation can be rendered very differently depending on the quality of the projected light: a hard light will anchor the object in the image, giving an impression of contrast and clarity, and will sculpt the surface of the object; a soft light will give the object a lighter and airier feeling, erase its physical disparities, and attenuate its contrasts.

The Four Factors

The difference between hard and soft light cannot be understood without distinguishing among shadow, half-light, and the illuminated area.

As we can see in the figure above, the shadow is the area that is not directly illuminated, as the cupcake blocks the passage of the light rays. As for the half-light, that is the area that is partially illuminated around the outside of the cupcake. The illuminated area is the area that receives the light with no obstacle in its way.

Thus, the narrower the light source (we usually call this a *point source*), the smaller the area of half-light—the transition from light to dark is rapid, creating hard, clearly defined shadows. And inversely, the wider the light source, the larger the half-light area will be as well—the shadows will be blurred, and we call this kind of light and these shadows "soft."

Four factors play a role in the quality of the shadows and the light: the apparent size of the light source, its distance from the object, the distance between the object and the background, and the kind of diffusion.

Make sure not to confuse the distinctions between hard and soft shadows and between light and dark shadows. The second issue—light versus dark shadows—depends on two factors: first, the density of the surface onto which the shadow is projected (if the shadow is projected onto a white background, it will obviously be lighter than if it is projected onto a dark background), and second, how much light is diffused by the nearby surfaces and objects.

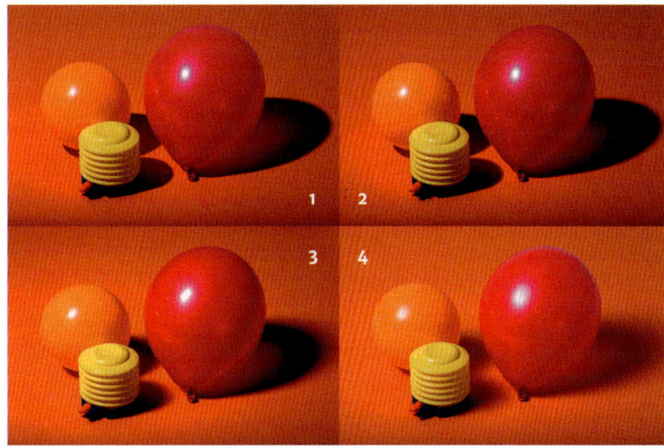

⏶ The same object, lit using different shapers, which generate different shadows. You can clearly see here the role that the half-light plays in the overall appearance of the object. (1) Naked flash; (2) flash equipped with a zoom bowl; (3) flash with a 30 x 40 cm light box; (4) flash equipped with a 150-cm-diameter umbrella.

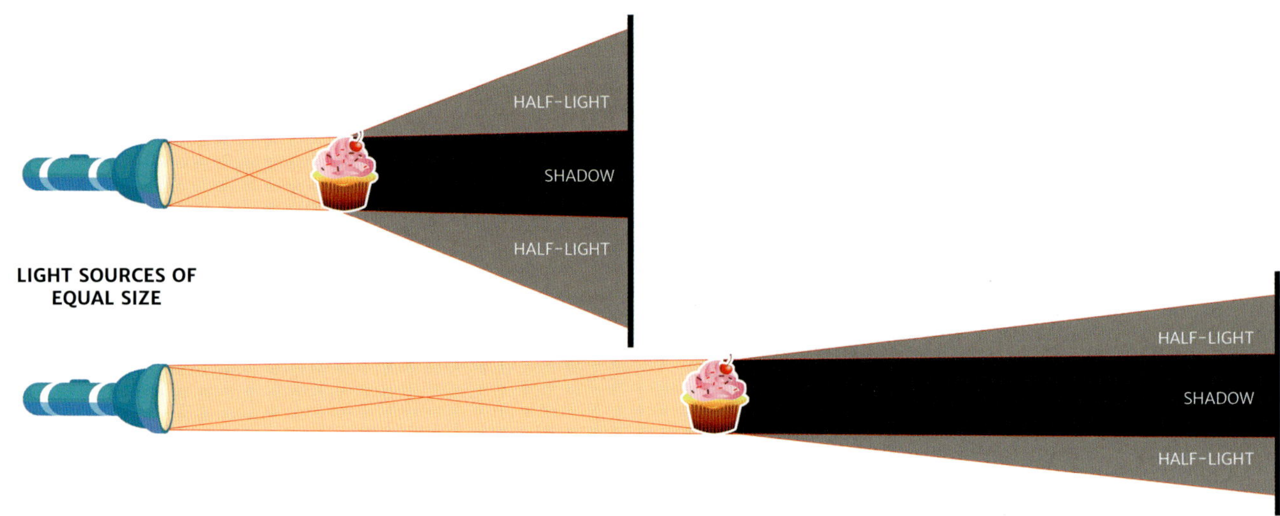

Apparent Size and Distance

The diagram on page 31 shows that the wider the light source, the larger the area of half-light, and the softer the shadows. But it is clear that what counts is the size from the point of view of the illuminated subject—in other words, the apparent size—of the light source.

From the point of view of the object, in fact, what really matters is the angle of illumination: depending on the distance at which the illuminating source is placed, it will be smaller or larger. And the larger it is, the larger the area of half-light will be and the softer the shadows will appear.

It also becomes clear that no matter what the actual size of the illuminating source is, moving it farther away will shrink its apparent size, attenuating the half-light and making the light harder. And from that, the following rule can be deduced: the farther away and/or the smaller the light source, the harder the light; the closer and/or larger the source, the softer the light.

Diffusion

There is another factor that affects the rendering of shadows, and also explains why sunlight seems harder at noon than at twilight, even though the apparent size of the sun and its distance hardly change at all over this short time period of just a few hours. A new parameter enters the equation here: diffusion. At noon, the sunlight travels through a thinner layer of atmosphere and its rays are more direct; at twilight, because the rays are coming at an oblique angle, the light encounters a larger number of air molecules, and a substantial portion of the light is

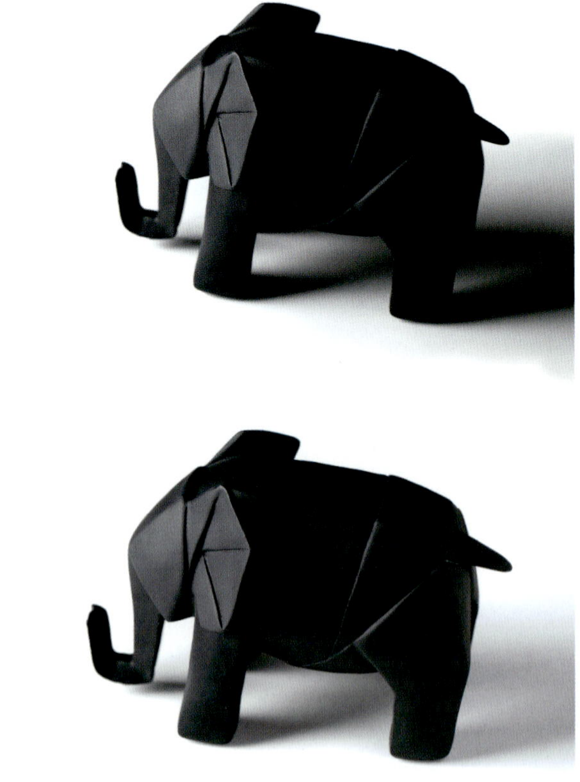

The same object, lit by the same source but placed at different distances; one meter (three feet) away for the first photo, four meters (thirteen feet) away for the second one.

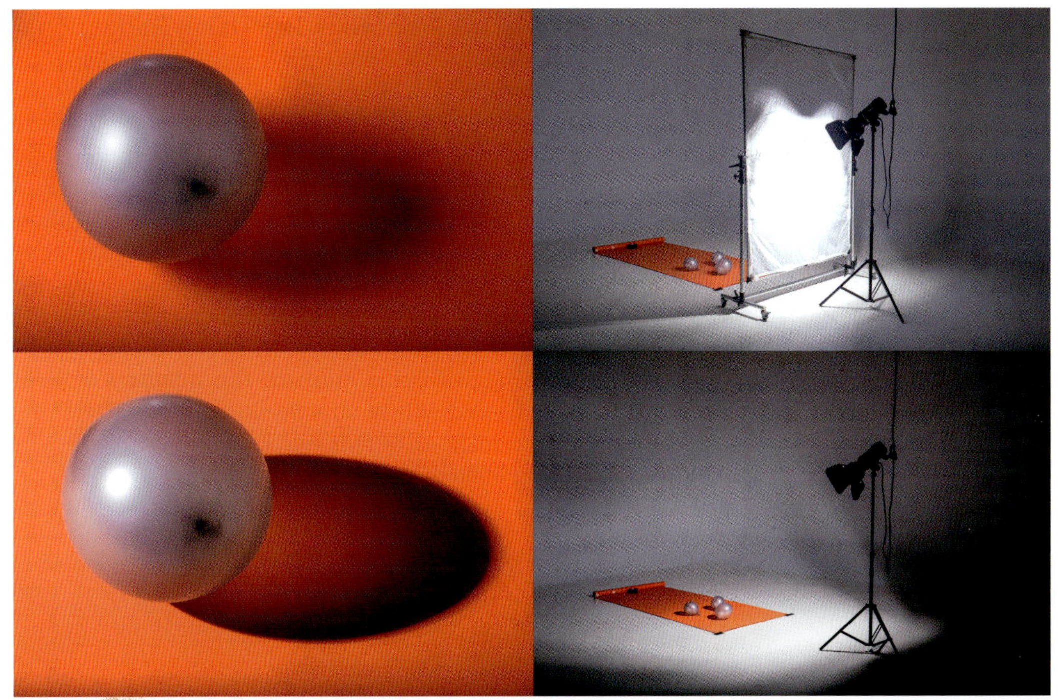

therefore reflected off into multiple directions. The same phenomenon takes place in cloudy weather, or if you compare taking pictures at sea level to taking them at the top of the Himalayas, where the layer of atmosphere is thinner and the light infinitely harder.

This third parameter plays an essential role. The difference between the two states presented here is connected to the diffusion of solar radiation by the atmosphere. The thicker and denser the atmosphere, the more light particles it absorbs and diffuses. The quality of the shadows varies according to the mediums that the light passes through. Thus, for product photography, we will often use diffuser panels that we insert between the object and the light source (see diagram below left).

Distance from the Background

Even though the quality of the light is not affected by the distance of the background onto which the object throws the shadow, the shadow itself will undergo considerable changes.

As we can see in the diagram on the next page, even though neither the apparent size of the light source nor the distance between the light source and the object has changed, the shadow that is thrown will appear more or less soft depending on how far away the background is. In the first example, the half-light area is one and a half times as large as the shadow area; in the second example, it is half the size of the shadow area. The shadow itself doesn't change, but the half-light gives the impression that the light has become harder, even though it is exactly the same on the object itself.

Note that at a certain distance, the area of half-light will appear so large that the shadow itself seems to disappear.

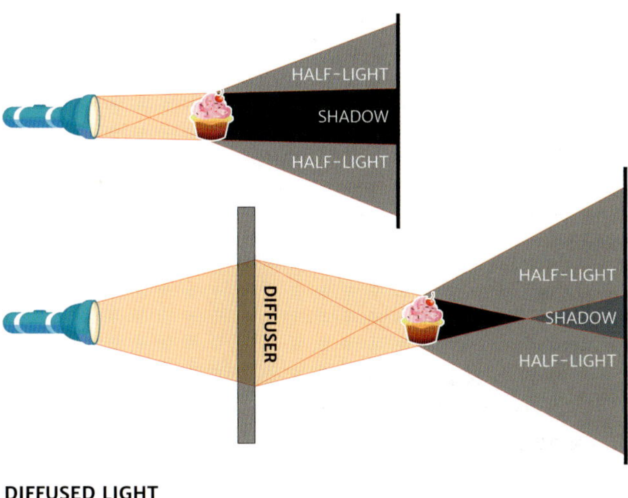

DIFFUSED LIGHT

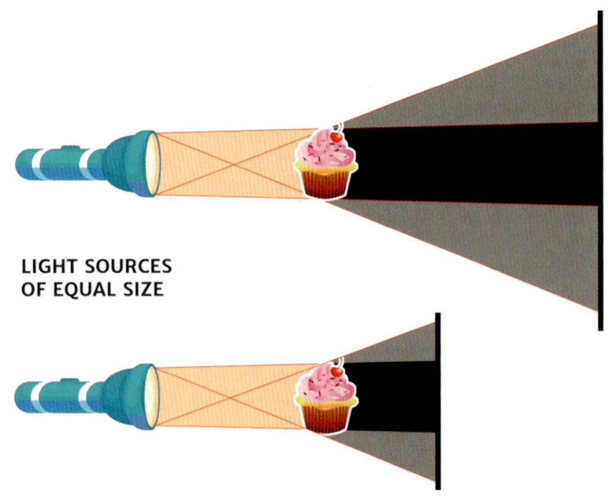

Increasing the Apparent Size Using Reflection

We have seen that the apparent size of the illuminating source plays a major role in the appearance of the light and shadows it produces. Aside from changing the size of the shaper (a large 150 cm octabox instead of a 50 cm softbox, for instance), or the distance from the light source, we can also use a reflected light, which will allow for a greater lighting angle and therefore a softer light. In the diagram on page 35, opposite, we have used a 25° angle in the case of the direct light, which becomes a 45° angle for the reflected light.

Of course, with this method, the quantity of light that is delivered will be drastically reduced. Therefore, we have to make sure that our light output is efficient and strong enough.

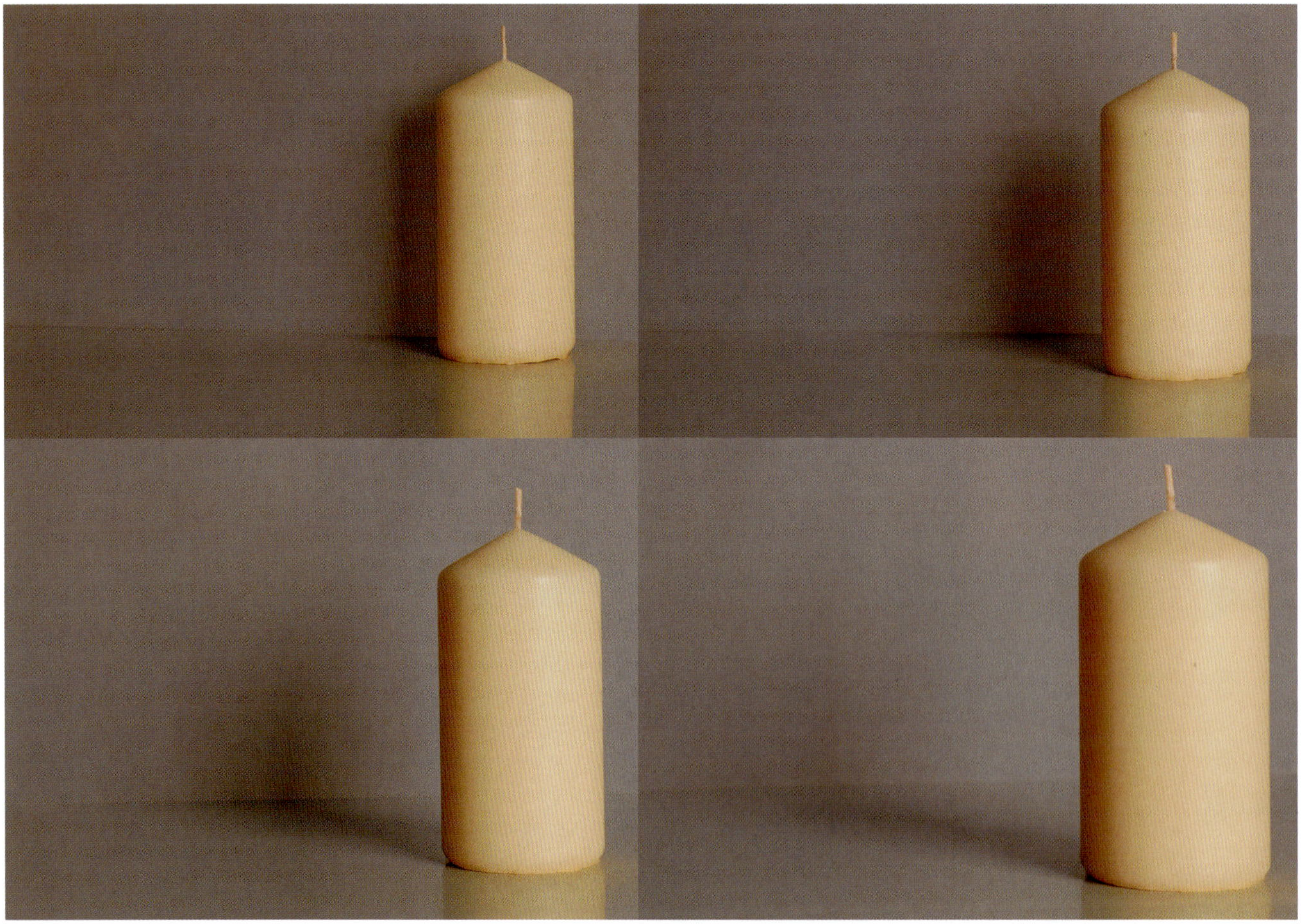

⌃ The first candle, which is closest to the background, is 2 cm away, the second one 10 cm away, the third one 20 cm away, and the fourth one 30 cm away. It's easy to see how the quality of the shadows changes as a function of the distance.

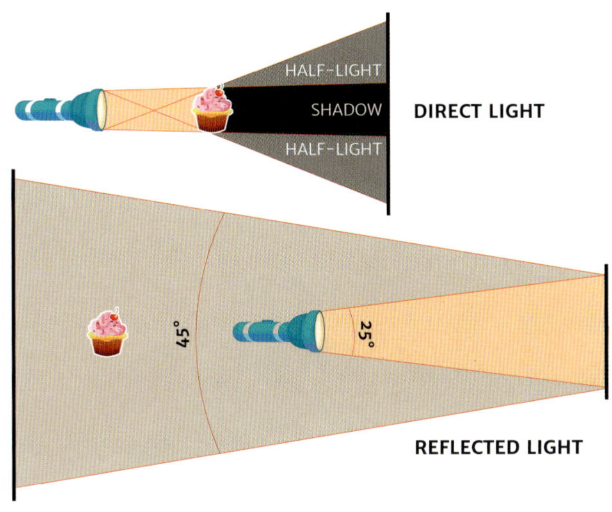

DIRECT LIGHT AND REFLECTED LIGHT

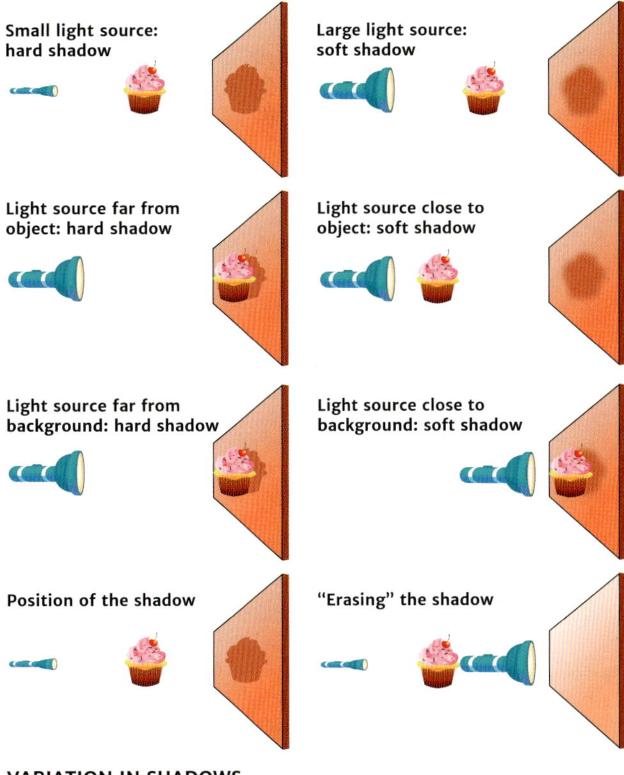

VARIATION IN SHADOWS

Eliminating Shadows

When creating product photographs for a catalog, we generally try not to have any shadows cast behind the subject, and to keep only a light trace of shadow below the object to anchor it in space. This is done, first, because otherwise it could make it harder to see the image itself, and also because the current standards for online sales sites require suppliers to use uniformly white backgrounds.

In this case, it is often difficult, if not impossible, to be satisfied with simply moving the object away from the background; that would just make the background look gray, which would not be appropriate. Thus, we move the object as far as possible from the background (depending on the size of the studio and the focal length we are using), and then we also light the background.

The distance is important because it is essential that the background be completely burned out (overexposed by at least 3 EV) in order for it to appear totally white; otherwise, it will look gray and the image will have to

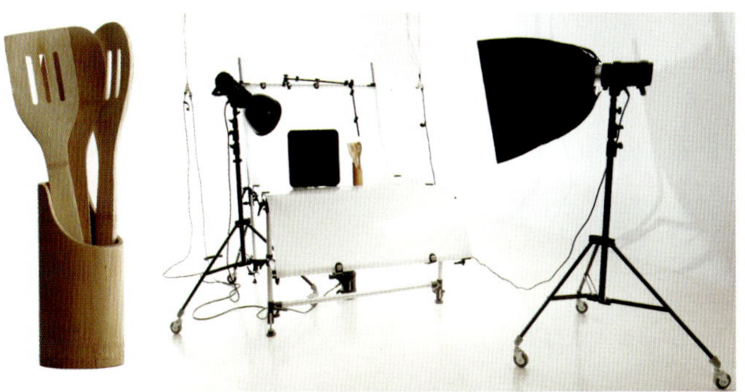

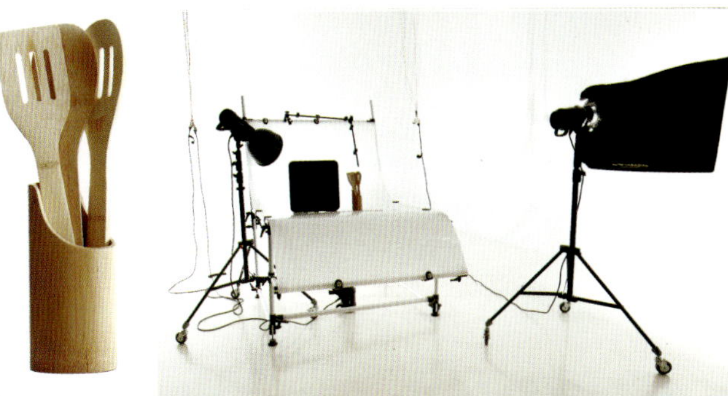

In the first photo, the light is direct (positioned six and a half feet away); in the second, it is directed at a white wall positioned thirteen feet from the object, which functions as a reflector.

be reworked in post-production. If the background is not far enough away from the object, part of the light will be projected onto the object, through reflection, and the edges of the photographed object will end up looking veiled and desaturated.

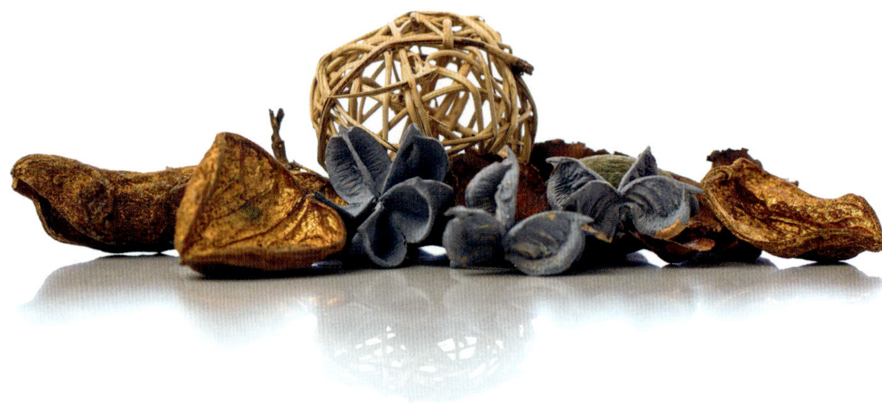

» In the first photo, the light that illuminates the background was measured so that its reflection onto the object would remain below +0.3EV, so that the edges of the object appear sharp. In the second photo, there is too much light reflected back by the background (+1.6 EV); this makes it look as though there is a veil over the edges of the object, and someone has run an eraser over the image.

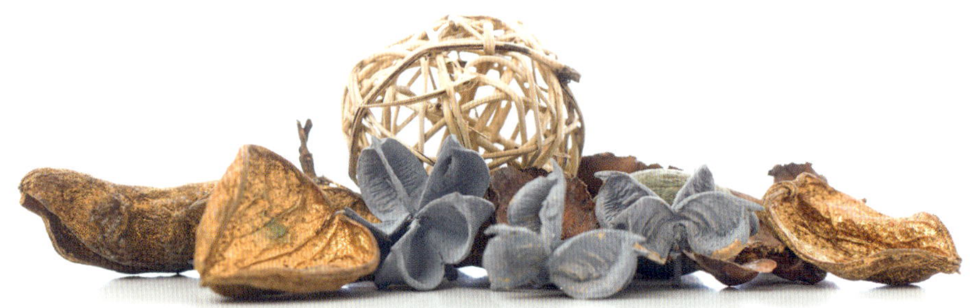

SHADOWS AND SHAPES

An object's geometry and shapes will appear more or less pronounced in an image,
eliciting a different impression, depending on the positioning and quality of the
shadows. For the representation to be effective, you need to anticipate all of the
phenomena at work.

Viewers easily understand the shape of a volume in space, the quality of its surface, and its color based on the distribution of shadows and light and of referential elements in the environment. Thus, we can give the impression that an object is glossy or matte, cubic or trapezoidal, light or dark, yellow or green, depending on the lighting, angle of view, focal length, exposure settings, and white balance that we have chosen.

SHADOWS AND SPACE

The study of shadows is probably the most crucial subject in photography when it comes to truly mastering light. And yet very few books address this topic in detail.

Having a good understanding of how shadows and half-light are spread, and along what axes, makes it possible to anticipate which light sources and tools you will need to use to get the photograph you want. This will allow the viewer to "see" the object in the way that you have chosen.

The Behavior of the Light

Before you start illuminating an object, you need to know that all light sources act according to the same immutable laws of physics. It is essential to understand that the position of the shadow will change based on all of the following:

- the orientation of the light;
- the angle of projection of the light;
- the geometrical features of the surface onto which the shadow is projected (a shadow will obviously appear differently depending on whether the surface it is projected onto is flat or uneven).

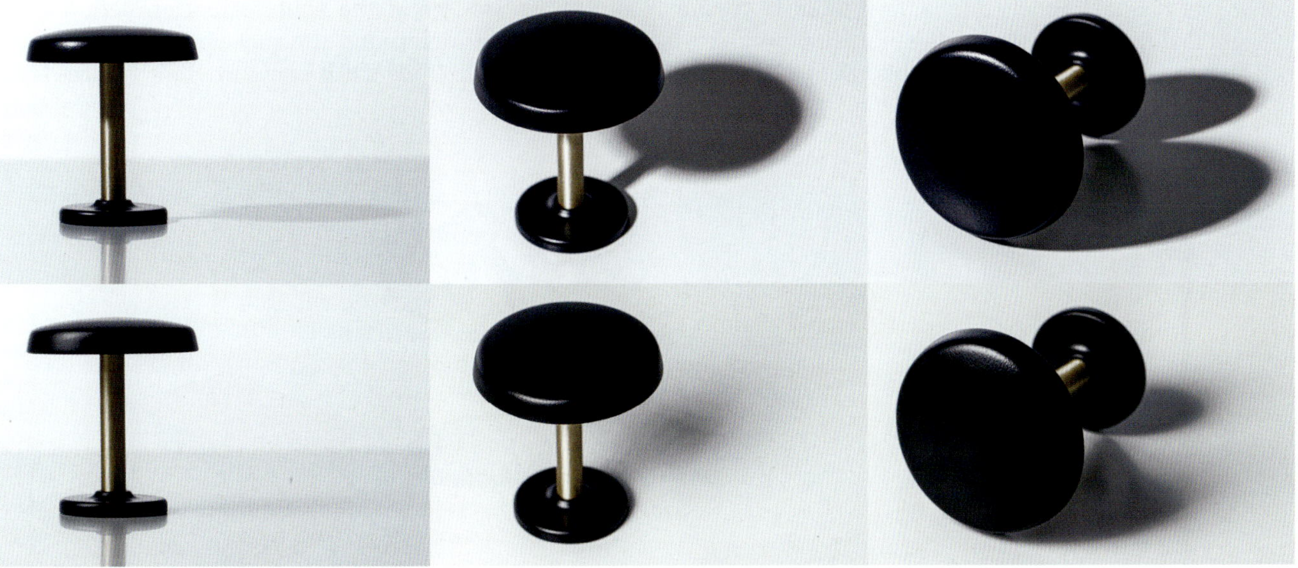

⌃ Lighted and presented differently, the very same object can elicit very different impressions. Depending on whether the light is hard (top row) or soft (bottom row), the nature of the shadow will vary greatly, whereas the direct reflections will vary to a limited extent. But the overall impression of volume that the object elicits will change considerably depending on how it is placed.

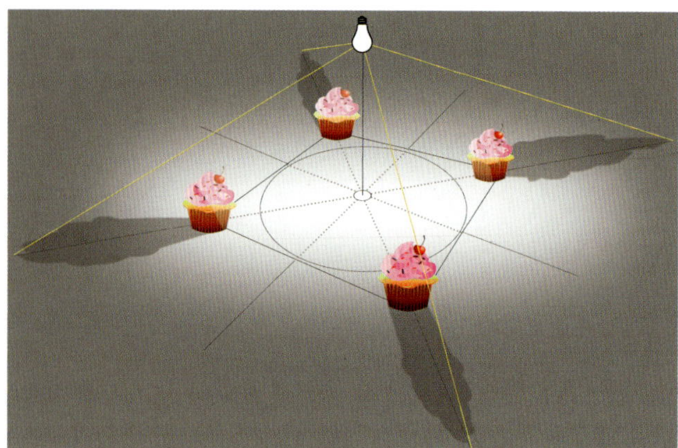

LIGHT AND PLACEMENT OF SHADOWS

In addition, the quality of the shadow (in other words the proportion of shadow to half-light) will vary depending on:

- the distance between the light source and the illuminated object;
- the apparent size of the light source from the point of view of the illuminated object;
- the diffusion between the source and the object;
- the reflection of the light according to the space in which the object is placed.

These variables allow us to predict the exact placement and quality of the shadows that will be produced. As we see in the diagram above, all we have to do is draw a straight line from the optical center of the light source to the highest point of the object (in this case the cupcake)

in order to predict exactly how long the shadow will be and along what axis it will be projected.

We can also see that the positioning of the light bulb in the center creates shadows in all directions. Thus, we can anticipate what effect it will have if we move the light source, whether vertically or horizontally. Using the same example, we can see that the shadows look hard (without any half-light) because the source is small.

Condition of the Surface onto Which the Shadow Is Projected

We obviously know that light is always spatially opposed to shadow. But intuitively, we are sure that we know that the shadow is exactly the same shape as the object that projects it, and that the shadows generated by the same light source will always be parallel. And yet, these two beliefs are both false, because they do not take into account the surface onto which the shadow is projected, nor the angle of incidence of the light. Thus, on a non-flat surface, such as desert sand dunes, the shadows can appear to be deformed and run at angles that would seem to be contradictory to the orientation of the light source.

Angle

In order to determine the size and axis of the shadow that is created by a particular light source, we have to determine the precise angle of the light with respect to the object.

As we can see in the photo at bottom left, we can rather easily determine the placement of the source that was used. If we don't know where it is placed (for

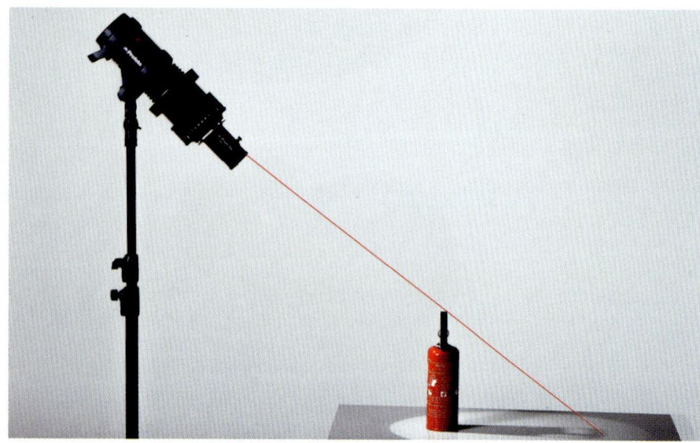

⌃ Using geometry, it's easier to understand how the shadow of the object is cast on the base behind it.

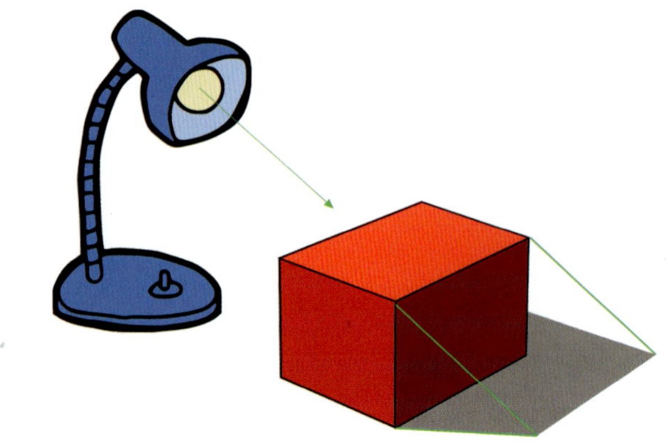

GEOMETRY OF PROJECTED SHADOWS

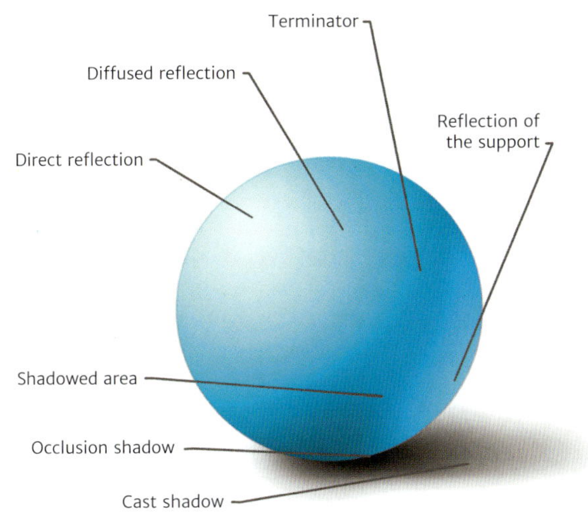

THE PROPAGATION OF LIGHT ON A SPHERE

instance, because it is positioned outside of the frame), then we simply have to draw a line from the shadow to the part of the object that is casting it; if we can draw at least two such lines, then the intersection point of the two lines will indicate the origin point of the light. If we know where the light is positioned, we just have to do the same thing by drawing a straight line between the source and the tangent points, and then we know exactly where the shadows will be.

Terminator

It will be extremely useful to understand the manifestation of shadows, the placement of light, and reflections on curved objects (spheres, bottles, etc.). You will notice that the harder the light, the more clearly delineated the terminator is (see diagram to the left; the terminator is the area where light transitions to shadow). This is one of the parts of the sphere's shadows that must be most closely observed: the terminator offers a wealth of essential information about the light that is being used.

From a strictly geometric point of view, it is important to know that the terminator always marks the beginning of the shadowed portion, while being tangent to the curve that it intersects—in other words, where light rays are tangent to the curve of the object (on every section of the plane).

Even without seeing the shadow that is cast, you can determine the quality of the light by observing how large the half-light is in the terminator area.

In the diagram opposite, it appears to be very gradual, which means that the light illuminating the object is a soft light. We can also determine that it is a small light source by observing the size of the direct reflection. By drawing a straight line perpendicular to that of

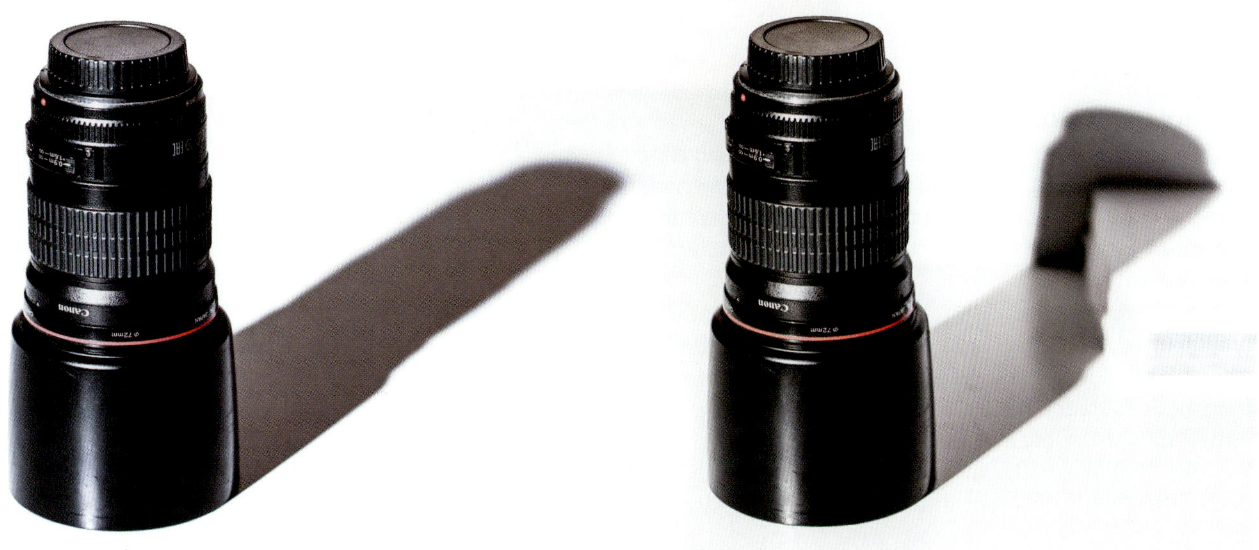

⌃ Geometry allows us to better understand how the shadow of the object is cast onto the base behind it.

the terminator, we can deduce the axis of the light, and determine how far away the light source is positioned by drawing a straight line from the high point of the cast shadow to the edge of the sphere. At the same time, a close observation of the cast shadow will give us valuable information about the distance between the object and the background against which the shadow is cast: the more pronounced the occlusion shadow, the closer the background. Here, it is very clearly drawn: thus, the sphere is sitting on a white plane. If there are no shadows at all, it means the object is suspended from above.

We can correlate this information with the size of the reflection of the background onto the object, which gives us information about the distance and the reflectance of the background.

Hard or Soft Shadows

In the previous section, I indicated that the quality of the shadow had only a tenuous relationship with the intensity of the dark areas. To put it very plainly, a hard shadow is not a darker shadow than a soft shadow. Depending on the case, a hard shadow might be light and a soft shadow might be dark; it will depend on the environment, any reflections that are present, the brightness of the base onto which it is being projected, and the quantity of light that is used. In a situation where the background is narrow and light, such as a hallway with white walls, the shadows that are cast will look lighter than if the walls were farther away or darker.

The space in which an object to be photographed is placed thus plays a considerable role in what the light and the shadows will look like.

Multiple and Contradictory Shadows

Even if several light sources are used, it remains crucial to never produce multiple or contradictory shadows (shadows that run along different axes), so that you maintain the impression that the object is being illuminated by only one source.

When two light sources are placed along different axes and directed toward the same object, they create different cast shadows. In the top diagram opposite, there are two hard light sources (distant zoom bowls) placed at 45° on either side of the back of the sphere. We can clearly see the two shadows, without any half-light, contradicting each other, with different luminances. We can also see the two terminators and the four areas that they delimit:
- the upper part is very light; it is where the light from the two sources overlaps;

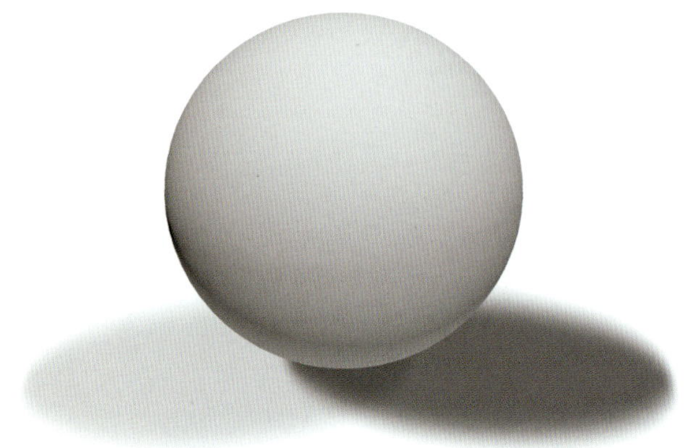

BEHAVIOR OF MULTIPLE SHADOWS

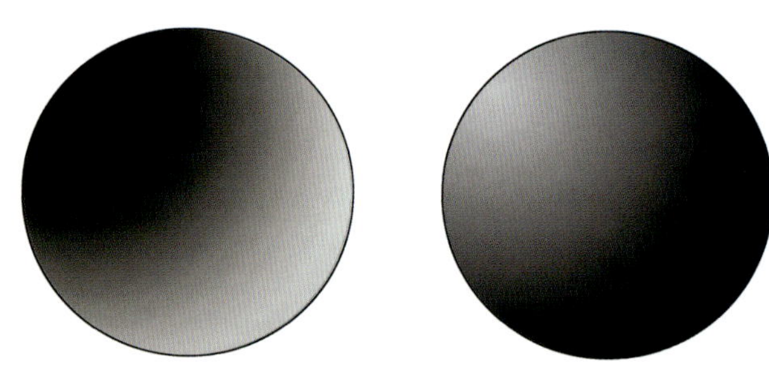

CONVEX AND CONCAVE

- the sides are slightly darker; each of them is lit only by one or the other of the two light sources;
- the underside is very dark; it constitutes the overlap of the two shadows.

We can also observe that the area where the two shadows overlap is much darker than either of them is individually. As with light, the shadows are additive. This notion must also be taken into account when placing backlights onto an object.

Light, Shape, and Illusions

Regardless of the concrete reality of what you are photographing, what matters is how it is presented to the viewers, and whether your shot matches the impression that you want to create. A white porcelain cup will look rounder or more elongated depending on the axis of your lens and the focal length that you use; it will look very white or more grayish depending on the light and the settings of your camera; and it will look as though it is posed, or levitating, depending on the placement of its shadow.

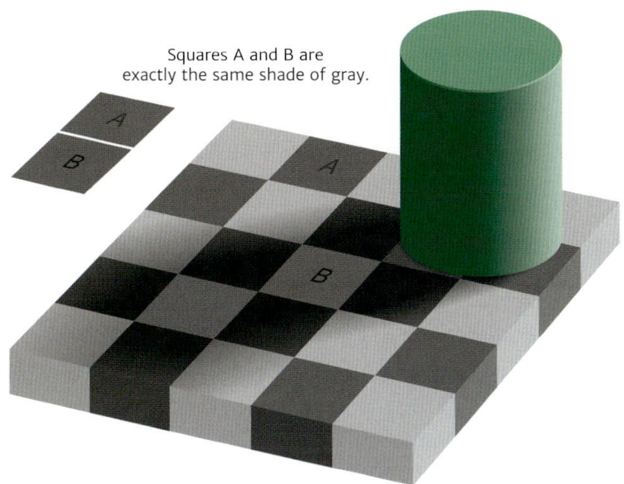

ADELSON'S CHECKER-SHADOW ILLUSION EXPERIMENT

In order to estimate a shape, our brain analyzes the placement of the shadows, their regularity, the variation in their hues, and the orientation of the light. For the bottom image on the previous page, I simply colored in two circles with a black-and-white gradient. For the first one, I placed the black above and the white below, and for the second one I did the opposite. Even though these are both two-dimensional representations, the viewer's impression is that the first circle is a concave surface and the second circle is a convex one. This is because, on the Earth, sunlight always comes from above, and our brain therefore interprets shapes based on this basic assumption. This is an essential data point to keep in mind when trying to create a "realistic" representation of the objects that we photograph.

In the same way, we analyze shapes based on their context. One of the best examples that has been given of this is Edward Adelson's famous "Checker-Shadow Illusion" (1995): it involves a checkerboard, on which a cylinder has been placed, which casts a shadow. Contrary to what we "see," it can be verified using image-analysis software that the squares A and B have the same shade and the same luminance.

This is an illusion based on contrast and context: we all understand the principle of the checkerboard, with its alternating light and dark squares, and we know intuitively that the areas that are placed in shadow appear to be darker than they are in reality. Thus, we look at squares A and B as though they were subject to different lighting and we interpret the image as a volume in three dimensions, thanks to the laws of perspective. We deduce from this that there is a light source placed behind the cylinder, and therefore we see square A as dark and square B as light.

Thus, for the photographer, it is a matter of working on the context in order to increase or decrease the contrasts, as required.

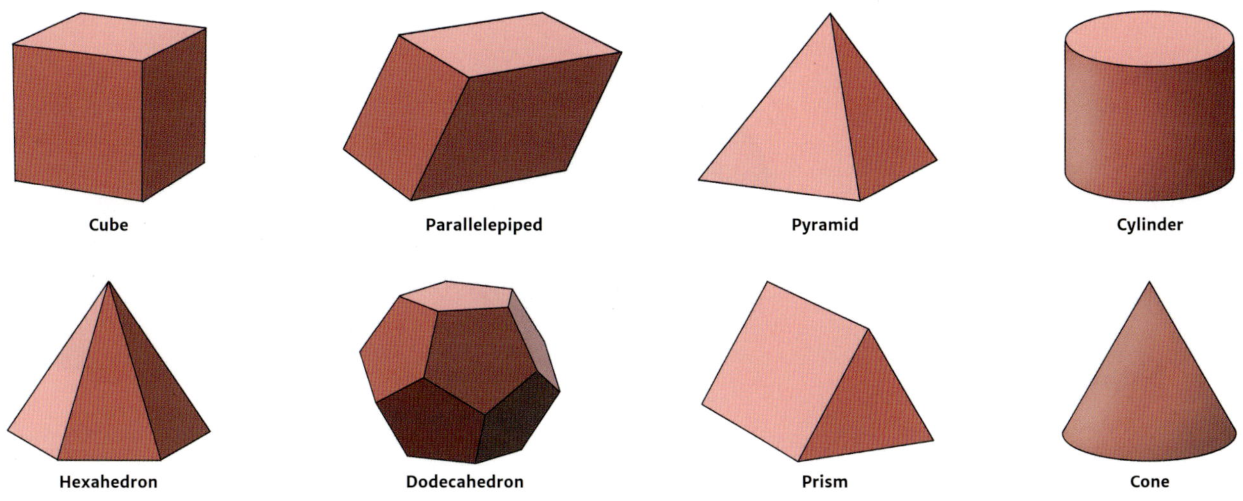

UNDERSTANDING SHAPES AND LEVELS OF ILLUMINATION

Representing Shapes

A cube photographed so that we can see only one of its faces will look like a square to the viewer, or like a diamond shape if the lens is placed at a very obtuse angle to the cube.

Whatever the object being represented, it belongs to a primitive modeling concept that we have integrated into our unconscious. A cubic object will not be understood correctly by the viewer unless we can see three of its faces, with a different luminance on each. Lighting that is placed an equal distance from each of the faces, with the same amount of light, will give the impression of a two-dimensional image, of a "flattened" cube.

Thus, as can be seen in the photos on page 43, moving the light source with respect to the object lends different characteristics to the shadows and the light, giving the impression of a greater or smaller volume and more or less density.

Representing the Condition of the Surface

When we look at a photograph, what allows us to determine whether an object is smooth or rough? Or whether it's glossy or matte? The reality of the object itself doesn't matter that much; it is the effect of the angle of the light and its quality that plays an essential role in the final photographic result. An irregular object, such as the surface of a sponge, will look very different depending on whether the light is placed in front of it or to the side. In the first case, the surface and the hollows will be illuminated in the exact same way, creating the impression

of a surface that is smoother than it is in reality; but in the second case, the hollows will appear darker and more textured, adding to the impression of irregularity on the surface of the object.

In the same way, as we can see in the images below, it is the quality of the reflecting light that gives us information about the condition of the object's surface: a sharp, clear reflection gives the sense of a smooth, glossy surface, while a soft, gradual reflection gives the sense of a matte surface. Just to be very clear, then: it is not as much a matter of the actual surface of the sphere as it is of the type of light that one uses. In the case of the three spheres shown below, for instance, these are all pictures of the same object (a glossy steel sphere), but it is lit in different ways.

- The first sphere was lit using a light box, placed sixteen and half feet away, and from which the diffusing fabrics were removed: the reflection is clear, the light is hard, the sphere looks glossy.
- The second sphere was lit by a light box placed at the same distance away, but using one diffusing fabric: the reflection is softened and gradual, and the sphere looks satiny.
- The third sphere was lit using a light box with both of its diffusing fabrics in place and with the light box positioned behind a large support equipped with a third diffusing fabric: the reflection is extremely soft, large, and gradual, and the sphere looks matte.

Of course, with a glossy metal sphere, this exercise was easy; with a matte sphere, it would have been

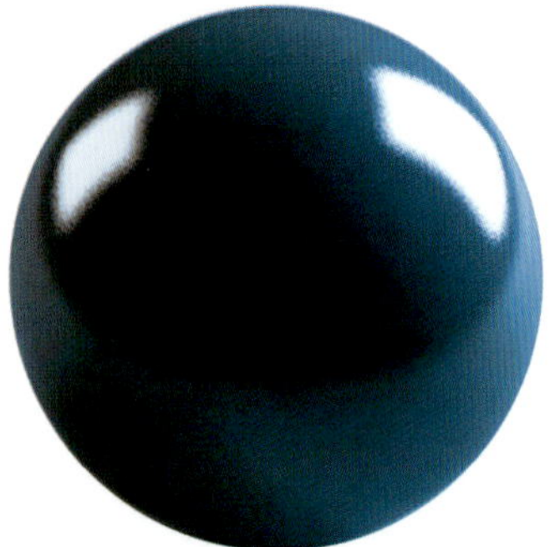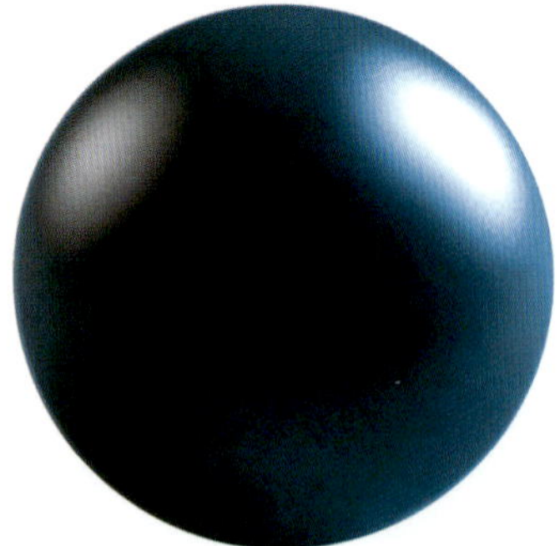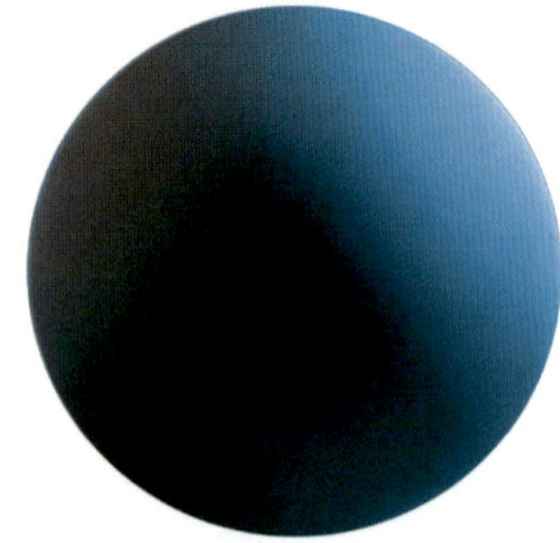

PERCEPTION OF THE CONDITION OF THE SURFACE BASED ON THE REFLECTIONS

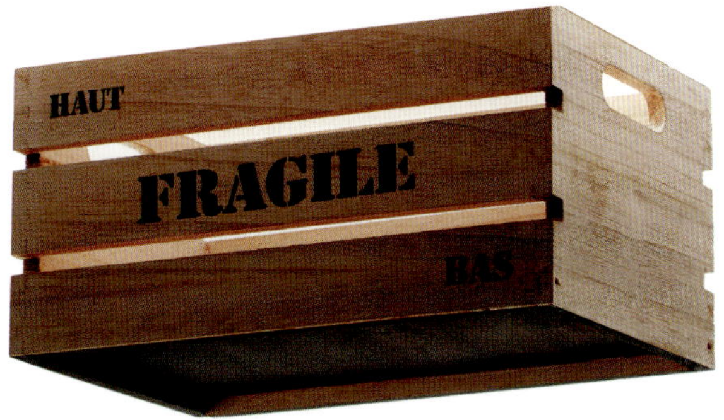

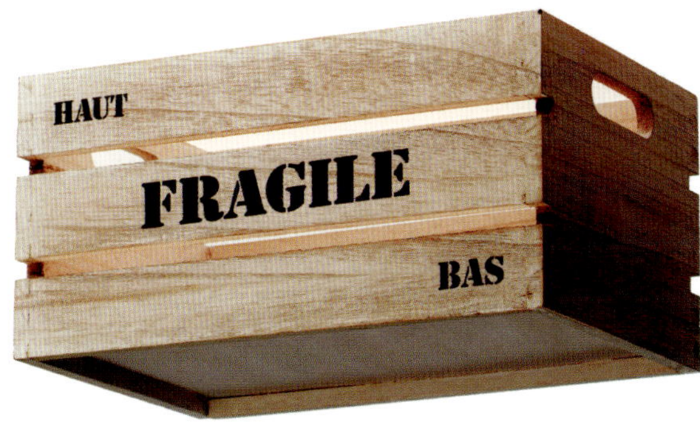

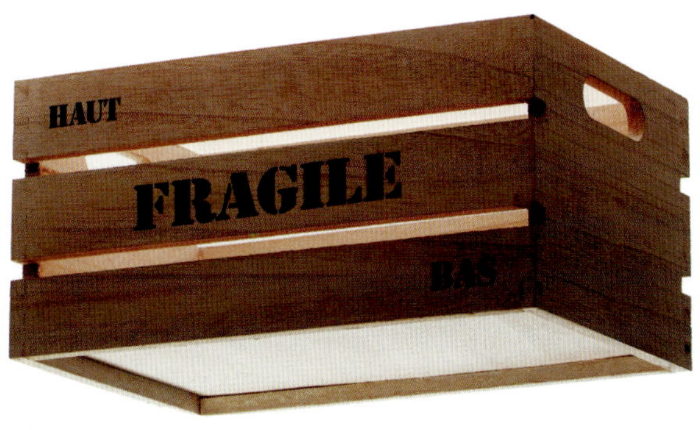

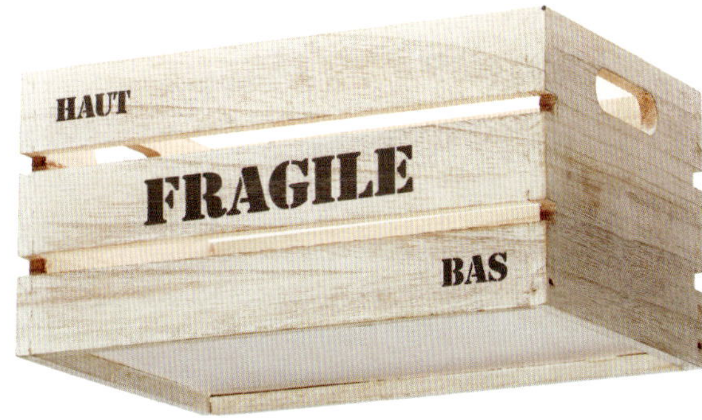

⌃ A wooden crate in the form of a parallelepiped, illuminated in four different ways. The object seems more "real" when the lighting gives each of its faces a different luminance.

impossible. Over the course of this book, we shall see that several other phenomena also come into play, such as the angle of incidence and the families of angles.

Before you start lighting something, therefore, you need to ask yourself what it is that you want to show. In terms of lighting, there is no such thing as a successful photo or a failed one; there are only photographs that have or have not achieved their aim. If the objective is to show a billiard ball, the first shot of the sphere on the previous page is good; if the idea is to show a frosted-glass bulb, it is the third shot whose lighting does the job.

Object and Reality

You will always be dealing with real objects, with irregularities and defects, even if they are brand-new manufactured products that have been delivered by your client. The ideal sphere or cube, perfectly smooth, and on which the light rests perfectly, does not exist.

If you want to avoid hours of retouching, it is absolutely necessary to place your light correctly and thoughtfully manage the illumination. Thus, you will have to anticipate all possibilities and determine in advance how you want the photographed object to look.

PERSPECTIVE

What allows us to grasp the real shape of an object is the variation in the tonalities of the light that illuminates it and the modifications in perspective. This phenomenon is related to the observer's distance from the object and the observer's position in relation to the horizon.

Compared to the reproduction of objects in two dimensions (like paintings), objects in three dimensions present an extra complication: representing depth. In order to make that happen, it is necessary to understand the laws of perspective.

SHOWING DEPTH

The representation of a shape implies, first, the representation of successive planes, under the principle that a nearby object is larger than a faraway object. A vanishing point is placed on the imaginary line (the horizon) that corresponds to the height of the gaze of the person viewing the image (or in this case, the height of the camera lens). All of the lines that go off into the distance converge toward the vanishing point(s), creating the effect that the farther away the forms are, the smaller they become. These are called the *vanishing lines.*

In linear perspective with one vanishing point (see top diagram, next page), also called *central linear perspective*, horizontal lines always stay horizontal and vertical lines are always vertical. This last point will be essential for the placement of the camera with respect to the objects being presented. With this kind of perspective, the vanishing point is generally placed in the center. For these representations, we neglect both vertical and lateral deformations—which is not all that important as long as the vanishing point is not too far removed from the center of the image; if it is rigorously kept on the central axis, then it is right for the horizontal lines not to converge.

In linear perspective with two vanishing points (see second diagram, next page), the perspective is called *oblique*: only the vertical lines remain parallel. In a "normal" view, the two vanishing points are positioned on the horizon line. The horizon line is the line that corresponds to the height of the camera lens. In this kind

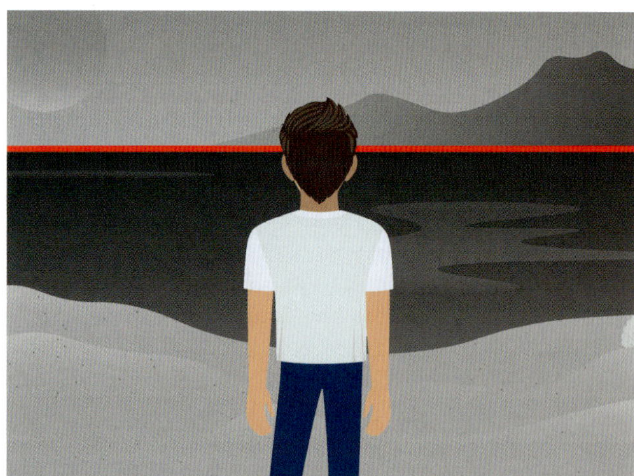

IT IS ONLY THE VIEWER'S HORIZON LINE THAT EXISTS

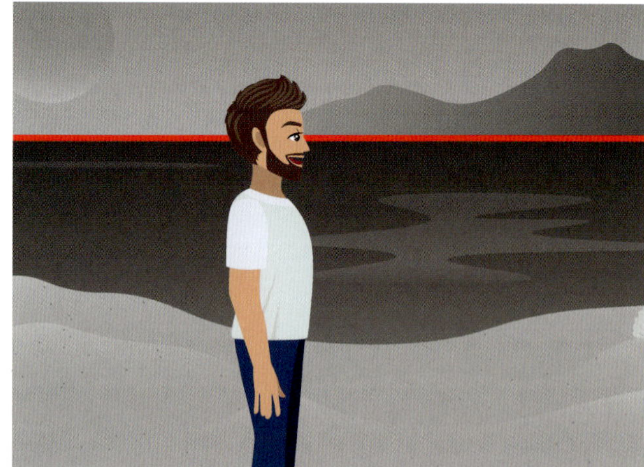

THE HORIZON LINE IS ALWAYS AT THE HEIGHT OF THE VIEWER'S EYES

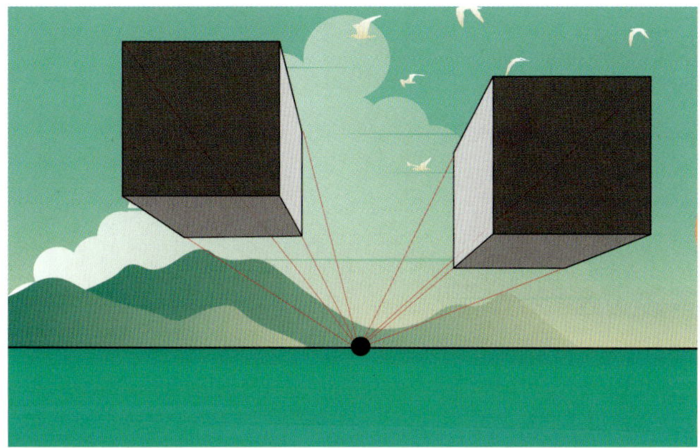

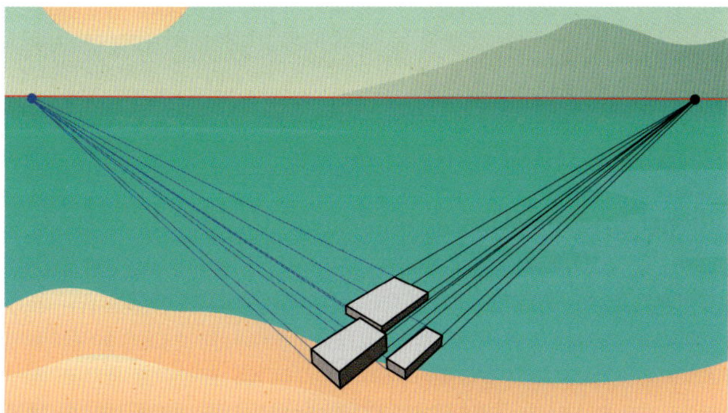

know that it's a cube is through visual cues related to perspective, which allows us to imagine depth. We can't forget that photography is a two-dimensional representation. It is clear, in the diagram below, that this representation of the cube gives very few visual cues to help us determine that it is a three-dimensional shape, whereas in the representation showing stacks of cardboard boxes, all of the visual elements necessary to understanding the shapes are present (perspective with three vanishing points; variations in tone connected to the presence of a light source that manifests in different illumination on each of the three visible faces; the presence of a shadow).

of representation, we ignore the deformations in height, which does not have that much effect on objects that are not very tall, but becomes problematic for large objects such as buildings.

We can also present an aerial perspective, which implies three vanishing points. In this case, the parallel lines of an object converge toward one of the three vanishing points. This perspectival axis is popular in commercial product photography, especially when presenting a line of products that includes a large number of different objects.

The Cube

Let's imagine a box in the shape of a cube. This is a shape that has six faces, only two or three of which are visible (depending on the angle). Without any information related to the variation in tones, the only way we can

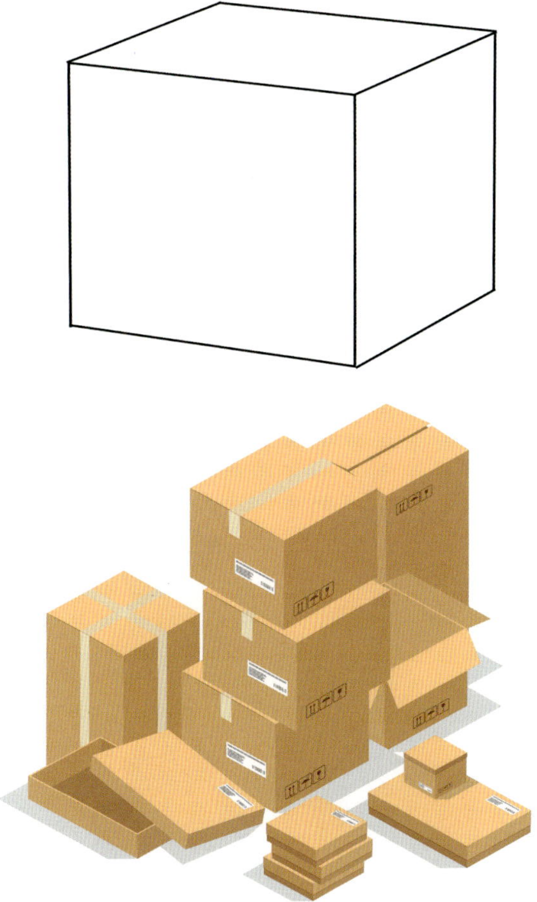

THE SENSE OF DEPTH IS OBTAINED THROUGH PERSPECTIVE, COLOR NUANCES, AND THE PRESENCE OF SHADOW

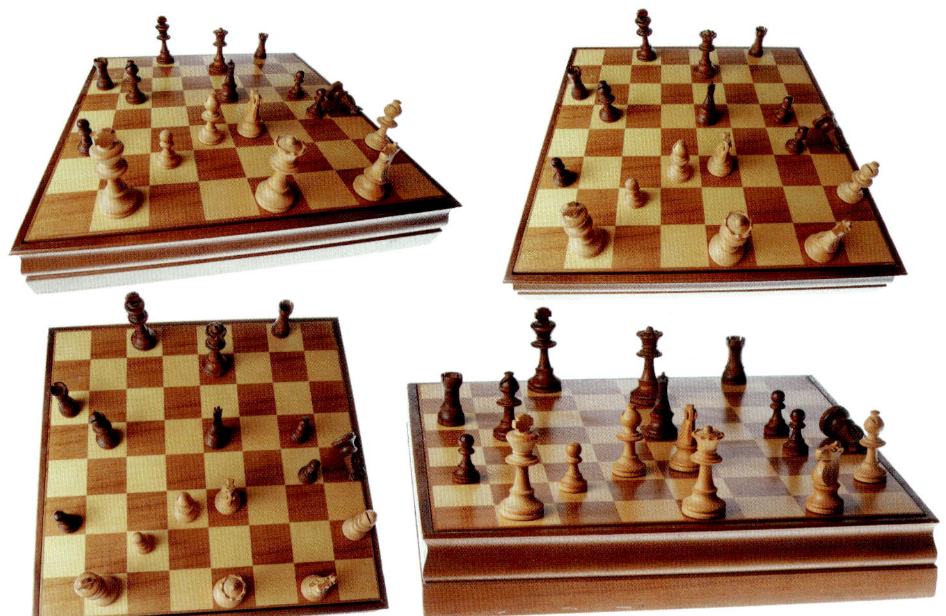

By definition, the twelve edges of a cube are exactly the same length, and the horizontal, vertical, and diagonal lines are all parallel to each other within each group. Using the laws of perspective, the lengths of the edges are different, as are the angles of the vertices, and the vertical, horizontal, and diagonal lines are no longer strictly parallel to each other.

Changing Perspective

It's the difference in size between objects in the foreground and objects in the background that most obviously demonstrates perspective to us. The same phenomenon occurs when we look at railroad tracks: we know that the rails are parallel, but their lines seem to be getting closer and closer together as they get farther away from us.

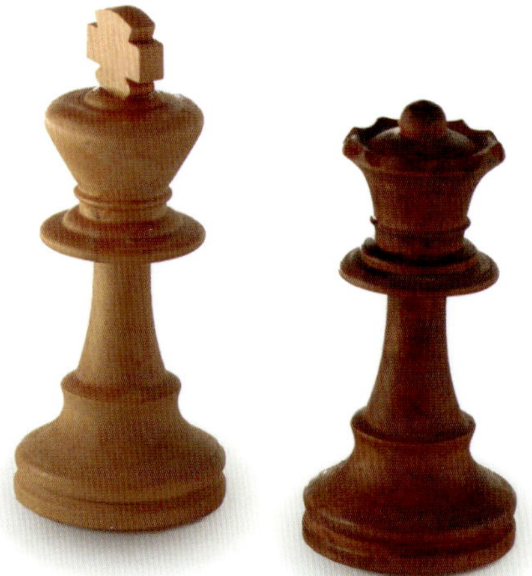

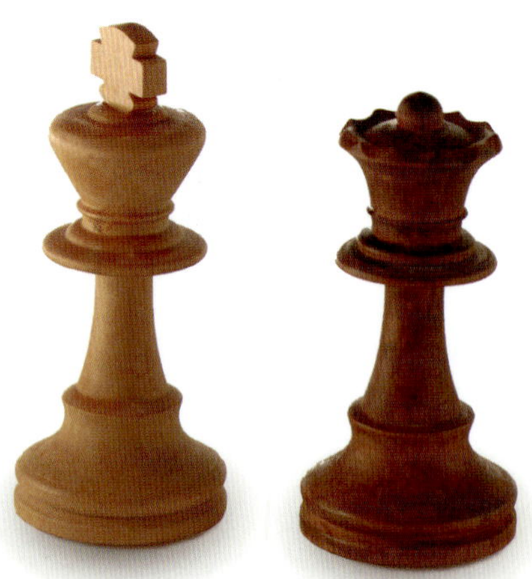

⌃ The same two objects, in both cases photographed from thirteen feet away, with the camera placed on a tripod so as to obtain the exact same point of view. For the first photo, a 200mm lens was used; for the second photo (cropped to produce the identical framing), it was a 16mm lens. The perspective is exactly the same in the two shots.

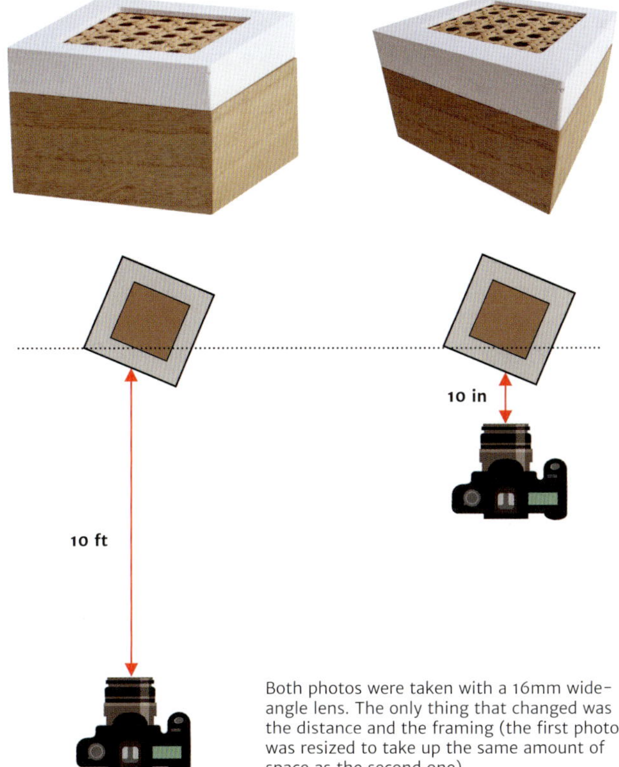

Both photos were taken with a 16mm wide-angle lens. The only thing that changed was the distance and the framing (the first photo was resized to take up the same amount of space as the second one).

THE EFFECT OF DISTANCE ON PERSPECTIVE

The effect of this can be clearly seen in the four photos of the chessboard shown on the previous page. Although these are photographs, printed in two dimensions, we can see the effect of depth in the first shot. We can also see that the closer we are to the object, the more accentuated the effect is of the receding lines converging, because the nearness renders them more oblique.

Shooting Distance

The closer the lens is to the photographed object, the greater the perspective and the sense of depth will become. This leads many beginners to confuse cause and effect, so they wrongly believe that wide-angle lenses "deform" reality.

The explanation is simple: In order to get the same framing as, for instance, a 200mm lens, a photographer using a 16mm lens has to get extremely close to the object being photographed, until they are just about touching it. Because the point of view is no longer the same, the horizon line and the vanishing point also change, which changes our perception of sizes.

But if we use these two lenses at the same distance, the perspective will appear exactly the same—even though, of course, the one taken with the wide-angle lens would have to be cropped to make the two images coincide (see the two photos at the bottom of the previous page). A wide-angle lens shows a wider area than our natural vision does, but also gives the feeling that the objects are farther away than they are in reality. In order to photograph an object, we will therefore have the tendency to get much closer.

Conversely, a long focal length shows us a much smaller area than our natural vision, but we are very far away, giving us the sense that the lines are not receding as much. This feeling is just the result, not the cause.

Levels of Lighting and Size

Our perception of sizes is intimately connected with the distribution of shadows and light in an image, as well as the presence of reflections (whether direct or diffuse). Whatever is well lit looks larger and nearer to us, and what is in shadow seems smaller or farther away.

Take the example of the wooden board reproduced below. It seems normal that if only one light source is used, the luminance values will look different on each of the three faces. The desired tonal differences in the placement of the light are thus: one face illuminated in full light; one face with an intermediate level, in half-light; and one dark face.

Of course, as we will see when we learn about lighting, the effect on the lighting of each face will not at all be the same if we use a large octabox (or if we work in natural light, with a cloudy sky) versus a small reflecting bowl (or daylight on a sunny day). The look of each of the faces will be different—large, and generating gradual shadows, in the first case; localized, and generating clear-cut shadows, in the second.

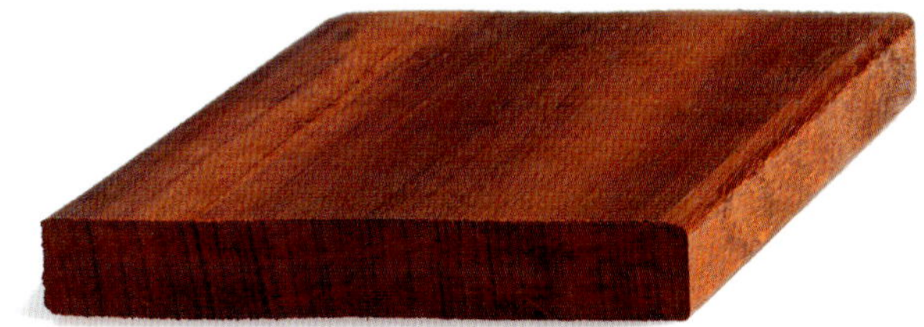

⌃ On this beveled wooden parallelepiped, we can clearly see the different levels of illumination on each of the three faces, and the beveling's very particular gradual shadow. This effect relates to the lateral placement of the illuminating source. Photo: YL/Studio B612

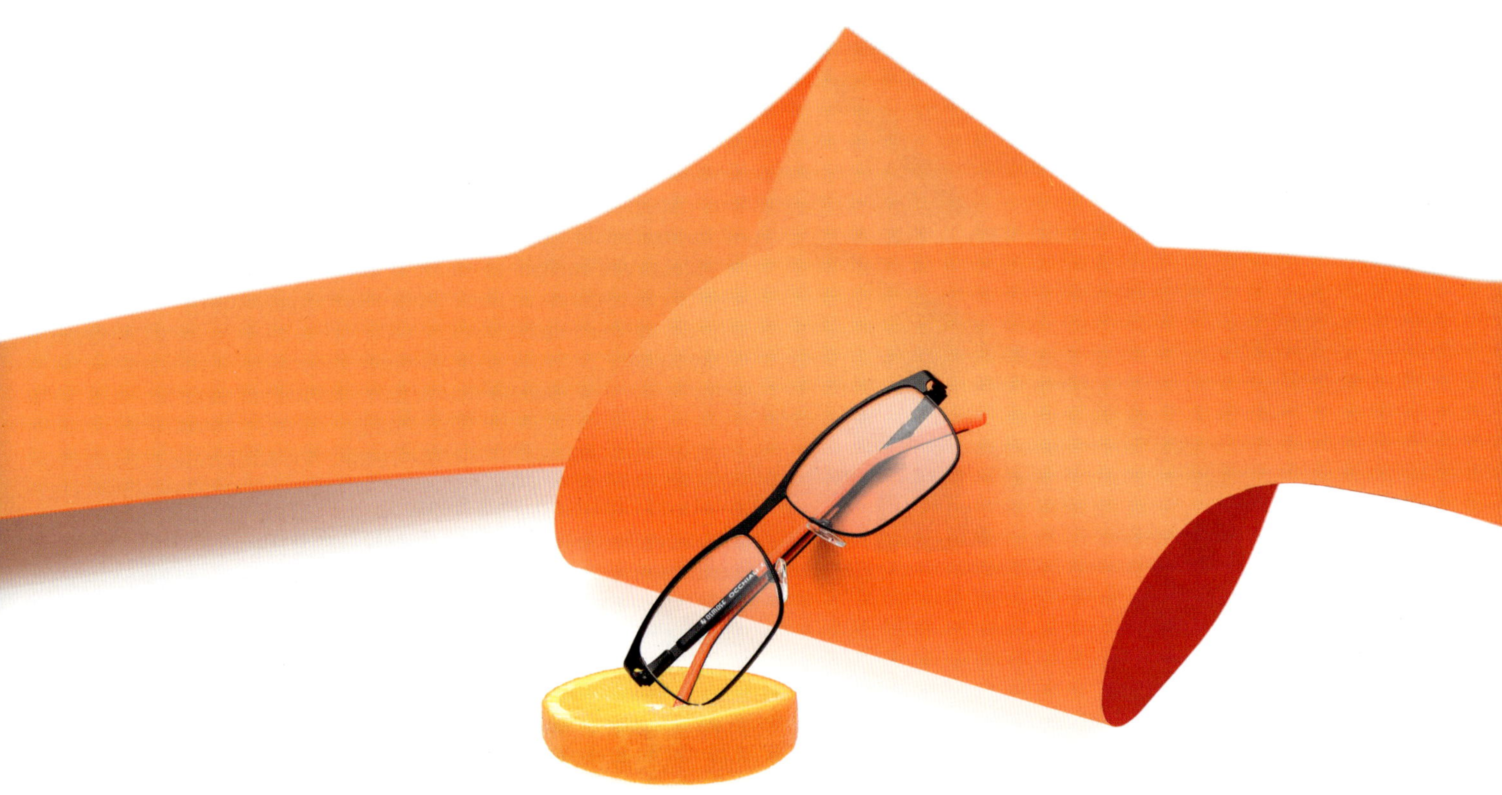

The lighting effects on the orange paper help the viewer understand that the part that the glasses are leaning on is rolled like a cylinder. The shadow cast under the part on the left allows us to see that the paper is slightly curved and is not entirely touching the white support underneath it.

Later, we will see that the ideal rendering of volumes differs according to their geometric shape. We would not light a sphere, a cylinder, and a cube in the same way, because every kind of lighting has the effect of giving visual clues to the real shape of the object: thus, a curve must present a gradual effect in terms of the level of lighting, and angles must present very different levels of lighting depending on which face is presented.

Horizon and Perspective

The overall look of the perspective and of how the objects are placed relative to each other changes dramatically based on the height of the lens compared to the objects. Changing the horizon level (in other words the vertical placement of the camera) will produce different relationships in the proportions of and relative distances between the objects.

In the diagram on the next page, we can see that the wine bottles are not all placed in the same position relative to the height of the camera. Let's look, for example, at the bottle on the right: its placement relative to the other bottles is very different when we move from the low-horizon shot to the high-horizon one. If we also tilt the lens, we can accentuate this phenomenon, which will have a large impact on the object's own relationships of proportion.

Rather than moving the camera, we can also sketch out the placement of an object at different heights with respect to the viewer (see the diagram at top-right on the next page) in order to see that the appearance of the same object (in this case, a cube) will vary quite a bit depending on its placement in space. Its geometry (especially the degree to which its lines do or do not recede) and its lighting will give us precise information about

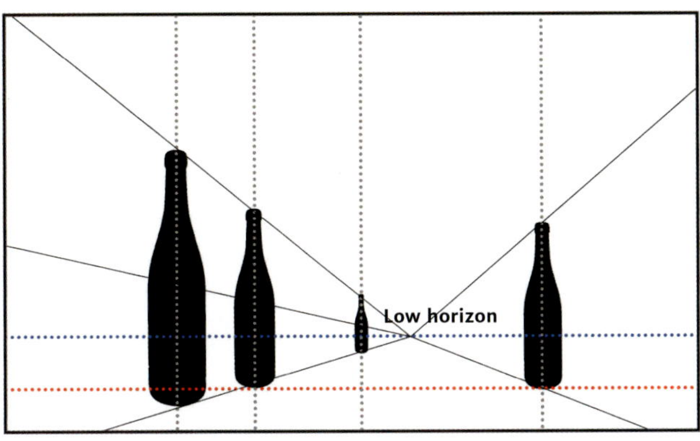

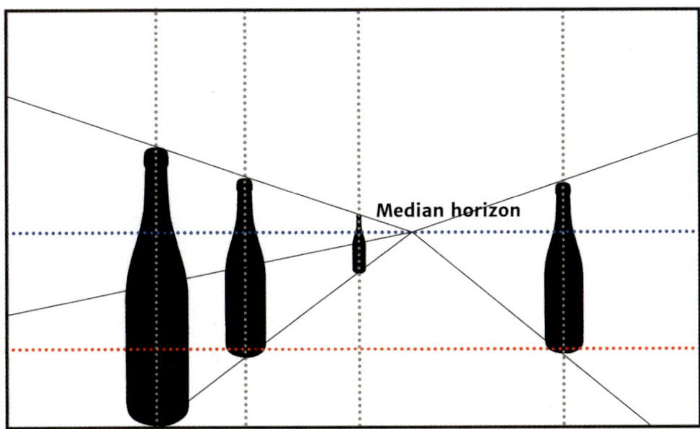

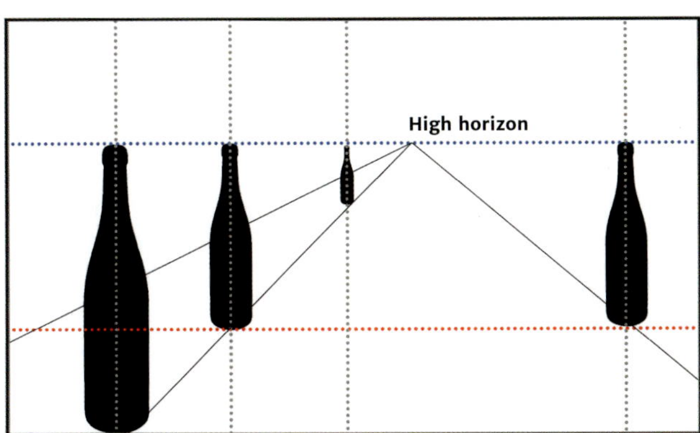

THE VOLUMES APPEAR IN DIFFERENT PLACES DEPENDING ON THE LEVEL OF THE HORIZON

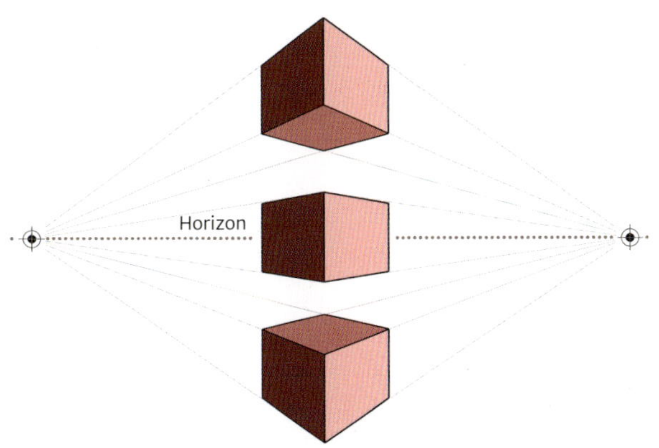

TRANSFORMATION OF THE SAME VOLUME DEPENDING ON ITS POSITION WITH RESPECT TO THE HORIZON

the height of the horizon with respect to the viewer, and about the distance of the shot.

Collapsing Planes

In terms of perspective, the farther away objects are, the closer they seem to be to each other. This impression is heightened when focal lengths are long—for instance, with telephoto lenses as compared to wide-angle lenses.

Of course, this phenomenon will be different depending on the respective distances between the objects: depending on the case, this phenomenon, which is called *collapsing planes*, will occur at various different distances.

As the viewer moves farther away, the object that is in focus will appear to grow smaller and will seem to be closer to faraway objects, which tends to make it harder

Size of the Object	Recommended Focal Length	Recommended Distance
12 in	135mm	5 ft
24 in	100mm	6.5 ft
36 in	90mm	7.5 ft
48 in	85mm	9 ft
60 in	75mm	11 ft
72 in	50mm	10 ft

In this table, the recommended focal length and distance based on the size of the photographed object are calculated using a 24 x 36 full-format sensor to maintain an average angle of view of 24°.

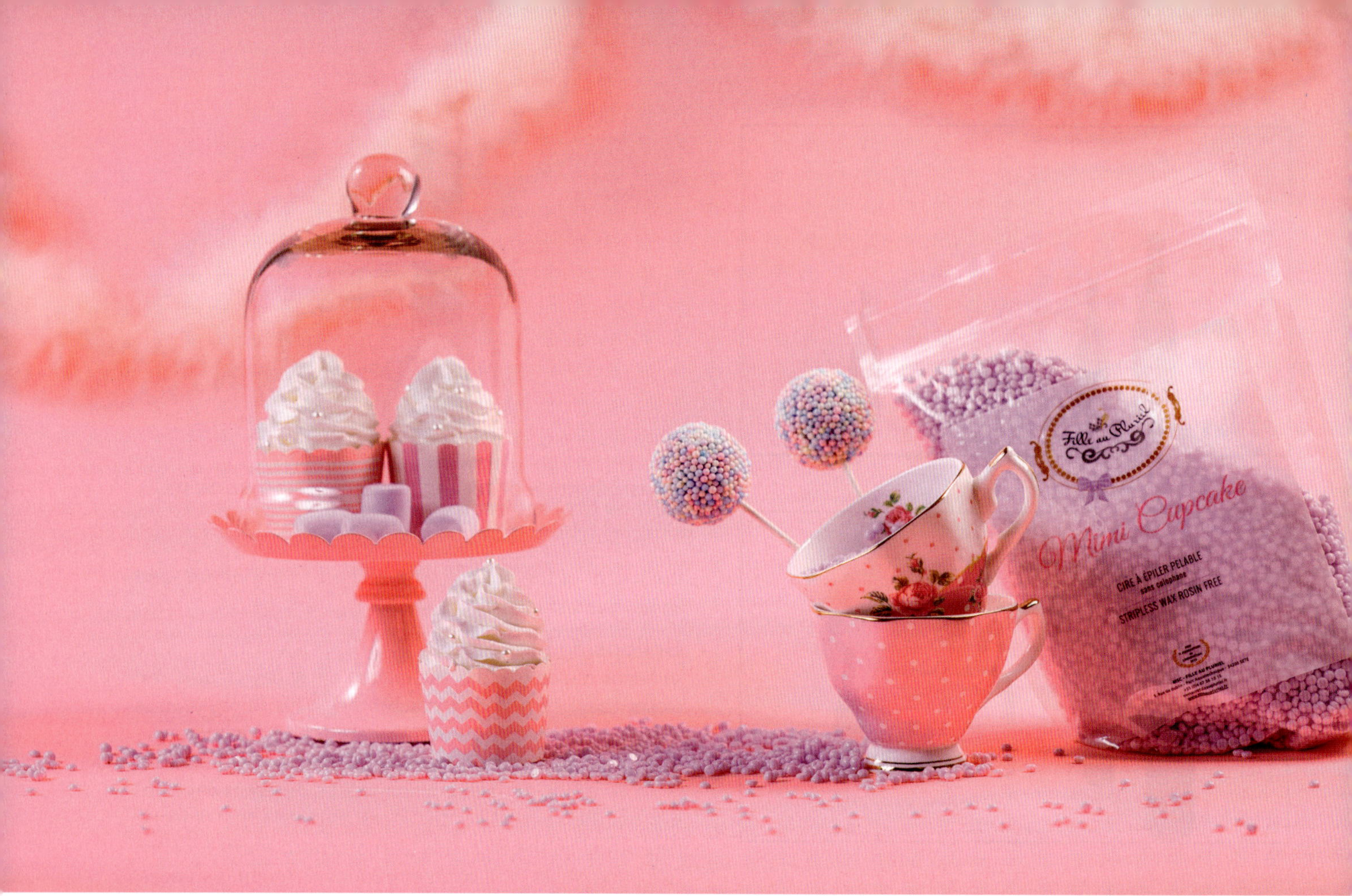

⌃ The objects making up this image were placed on different planes and along different axes to avoid the impression of the planes being collapsed.

to understand the image. This phenomenon occurs when, depending on distance, the object in the foreground is too far away from the one that was focused on: due to the combination of the rules of depth of field and perspective, the object in the background will look extremely different from the one in the foreground.

The general practice is to place yourself at a distance that allows you to maintain an average angle of view of 24° (see the table on page 49). The distance and the focal length will depend on the actual size of the object in question.

The point of maintaining an average angle of view of 24° is to avoid distortions due to perspective.

The method illustrated above is very practical when a product needs to be presented in a catalog, where you want to stay as realistic and as descriptive as possible.

For a maximally effective result, place the lens at the object's median height, with the lens perfectly horizontal, and make sure that the objects in the background are distributed more or less evenly around the space. However, don't think that this distance is an absolute imperative: depending on how far away the background is, what the focal length is, and any tilt that the object might have, the perspective can vary considerably. Even at ten feet, it can feel as though the planes are collapsed if the photographed object is placed in front of a forest.

THE BEHAVIOR OF LIGHT

In photography, it is not so much the light itself that interests us as it is the particular moment when the light meets the material. We will see that this meeting, in which the object plays an active role, can play out in several different ways.

In the preceding sections, we have seen the importance of the light beam's degree of concentration, luminance, and color in the illumination of objects. Depending on whether the light source is large or small, far away or nearby, diffused, reflected, or direct, the result can be radically different in terms of the distribution of shadows and half-light.

However, it is the object being photographed that plays the most important role: depending on whether it is transparent, translucent, or opaque, whether it is matte, satiny, or glossy, and whether it is polarizing or not, it will transform the light that it receives in many ways. An in-depth study of the possible scenarios is necessary to determine the best ways to light and photograph the object.

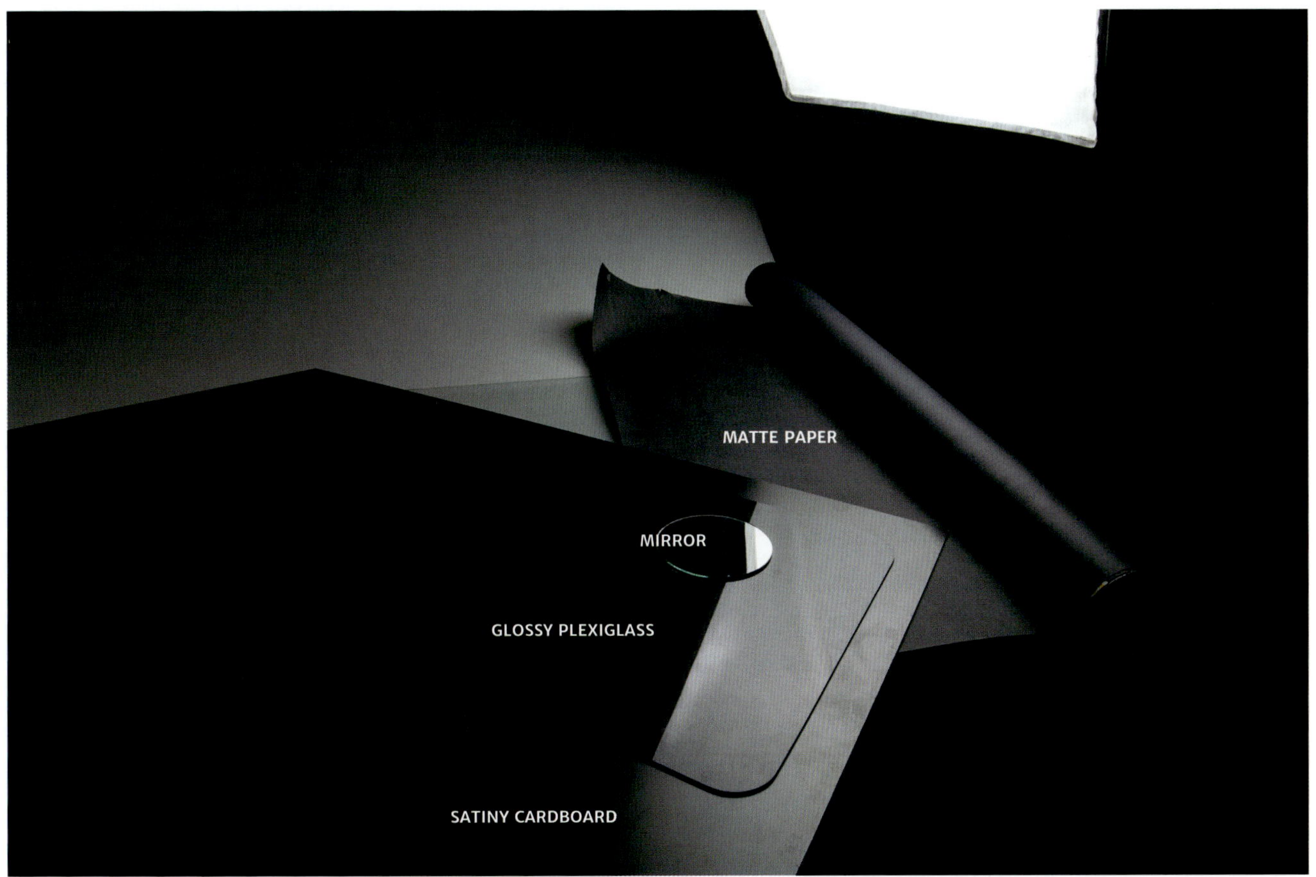

⌃ The characteristics of the objects being photographed—the condition of their surface, their material, their color, their density—play an essential role in how the light is distributed, sometimes radically transforming what they look like even if the light is identical.

The Light

It's been less than a century now that we've even had a precise idea of what light is, thanks to Max Planck, Louis de Broglie, and Albert Einstein. But we have known for a long time, thanks to Isaac Newton, Pierre de Fermat, René Descartes, and Augustin Fresnel, how light acts in space and how it interacts with matter. Light moves in a straight line in a vacuum, at a strictly fixed speed, but in other transparent or translucent mediums (such as water or glass), it moves more slowly, depending on the wavelength; in these cases, we speak of a dispersive medium.

Light can change its trajectory when it passes from one medium to another. Fermat's principle relates this change to the speed of light in each of the mediums. It also changes its trajectory when it encounters an opaque surface, and Snell's law explains precisely how. This law also describes how light is scattered by refraction, creating rainbows, for example.

We also know that light is not perceived by a receptor unless it is going directly toward it. Because science has finally proved that light is both an electromagnetic radiation and a particulate phenomenon, we can also explain other phenomena, such as polarization and diffraction. The photon, which has the characteristics of an elementary particle, does not exist unless it is moving at the speed of light. More precisely, when two electrically charged particles interact, they produce "packets" of elementary energy, and these "packets" are photons. The photons generate an electromagnetic radiation that is continuously variable, unlike the field of a magnet.

Nevertheless, as we have said, it is not the light itself that is interesting to the photographer, but how it behaves when it encounters matter. And there are then nine potential scenarios: absorption; selective absorption; polarization; dispersion; transmission; diffraction; diffusion; reflection; and refraction.

Absorption

Absorption refers to the physical process by which the light's electromagnetic radiation is transformed into energy—essentially, into heat—by meeting a nontransparent material (this is the Joule effect).

More precisely, it is the energy of the photon that is transmitted and that excites the atoms of the matter that the light encounters. The electromagnetic energy is

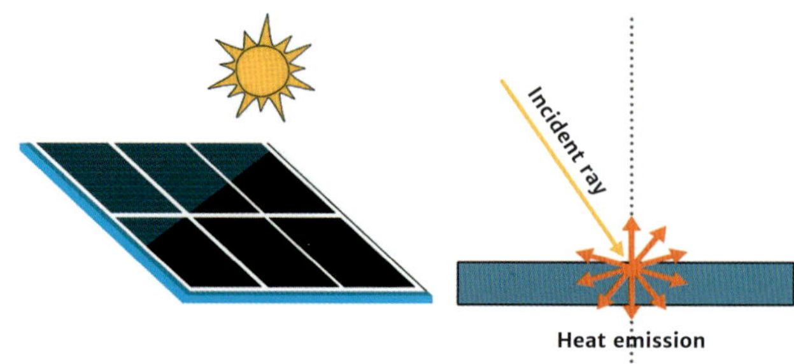

ABSORPTION

absorbed and transformed, according to the material that is encountered, into luminous energy, an increase in the speed of the particles (which translates, at the macroscopic level, into a rise in temperature), phonon (agitation of the crystal lattice in a crystal), or plasmon (the collective oscillation of electrons in a metal).

Each material has its own characteristic properties of electromagnetic absorption, depending on the wavelength of the light being used. A black material, of course, absorbs all wavelengths (converted into heat), whereas a white material reflects them.

This phenomenon, described by Edmond Becquerel as the *photovoltaic effect*, is used in particular for solar panels.

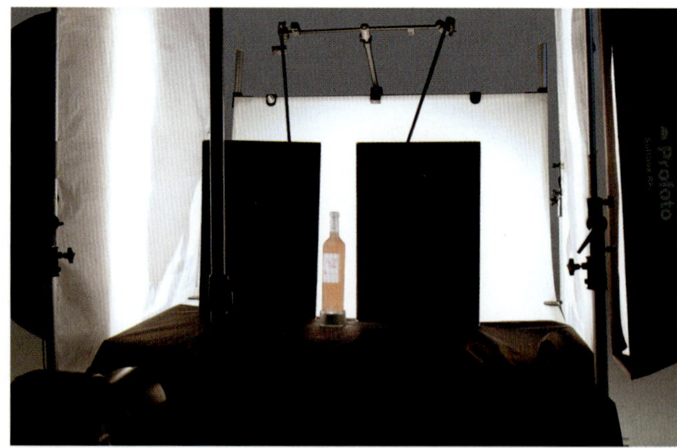

⌃ In photography, we can use black fabric or paper "barn doors" to absorb part of the light or limit the reflections (to achieve clear-cut edges on a bottle of wine, for instance).

When an ultraviolet photon hits the transition area of a semiconductor material (two layers of silicon, for example), it tears one electron away from the silicon atom, leaving a "vacuum" there. That electron, under the force of the electric field, moves, while the vacuum is "filled" with another electron. It is through this movement of electrical charges that an electric current takes place inside the crystalline material.

In photography, we use the phenomenon of absorption by setting up black "barn doors." They absorb part of the light that illuminates them, which has the effect of limiting the reflections on the objects. They can also be used when shooting in a location with walls that are too light, to limit the presence of highlights.

Selective Absorption

Have you ever wondered why a tree leaf looks green when the white sunlight shining on it is polychromatic? In reality, the green leaf absorbs all of the wavelengths of the white light except green, which it diffuses in all directions. This is why the leaf looks green to us. We call this phenomenon *selective absorption*—in other words, the absorption by the material of some of the wavelengths of the incident radiation. It varies according to the composition of the surface that is encountered and the wavelength of the radiation.

We can also perform the opposite experiment, illuminating the green leaf using a red light. Because it absorbs that wavelength, the leaf will appear somewhat black.

This is something that should be kept in mind when using colored light sources (whether LED or gels) to light objects.

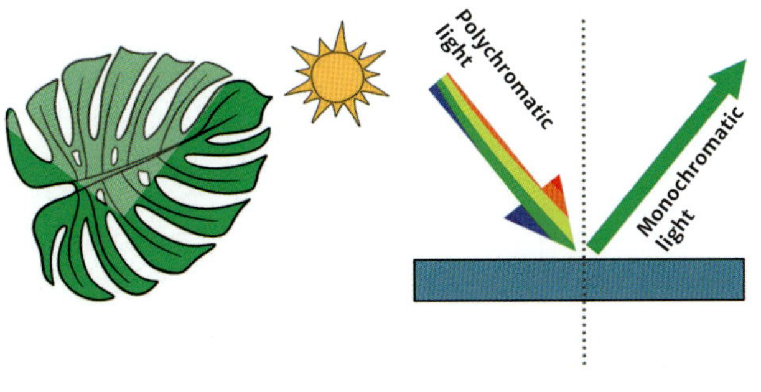

SELECTIVE ABSORPTION

Immersed in a blue liquid (which absorbs all wavelengths, except blue), a red straw looks black.

Polarization

The electromagnetic radiation that makes up visible light oscillates in several directions at once. The polarization of light allows for a privileged distribution of the orientation of the vibrations that make it up.

The polarization corresponds to the direction and magnitude of the electric field. For a non-polarized, or natural, wave, the electric field turns on its own axis randomly and unpredictably over time. Polarizing a wave means giving the electric field a definite trajectory. There are thus several kinds of polarization.

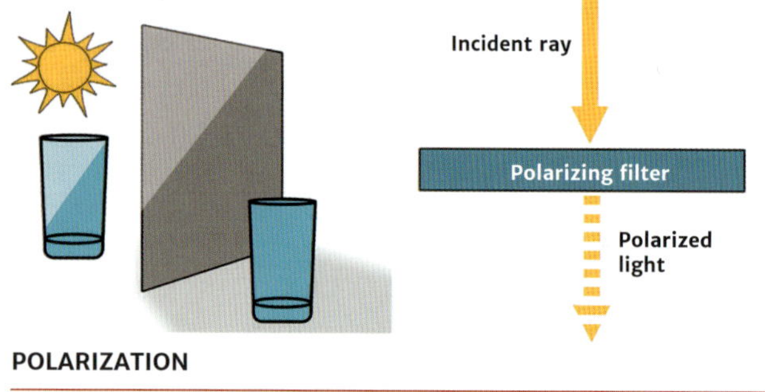

POLARIZATION

- Linear polarization: The electric field always goes in the same direction. The electric field and the magnetic field oscillate simultaneously in directions perpendicular to each other. By convention, the polarization of light describes the vibration of the electric field, and when the wave is linearly polarized, this field oscillates in one direction only.
- Circular polarization: The electric field rotates around its axis, forming a circle.
- Elliptical polarization: The electric field rotates around its axis and changes amplitude, forming an ellipse.

Polarization works similarly to the phenomenon of selective absorption. This is what a polarizing glass does when it absorbs all of the oscillations that are occurring in a direction other than the axis on which it is placed. For instance, if the polarizer's axis is positioned vertically, all other oscillations will be absorbed. This is why the polarizing filters that are installed on cameras are mobile and rotating.

In product photography, polarization is used to limit the presence of direct reflections on polarizing materials (such as metals, water, or glass).

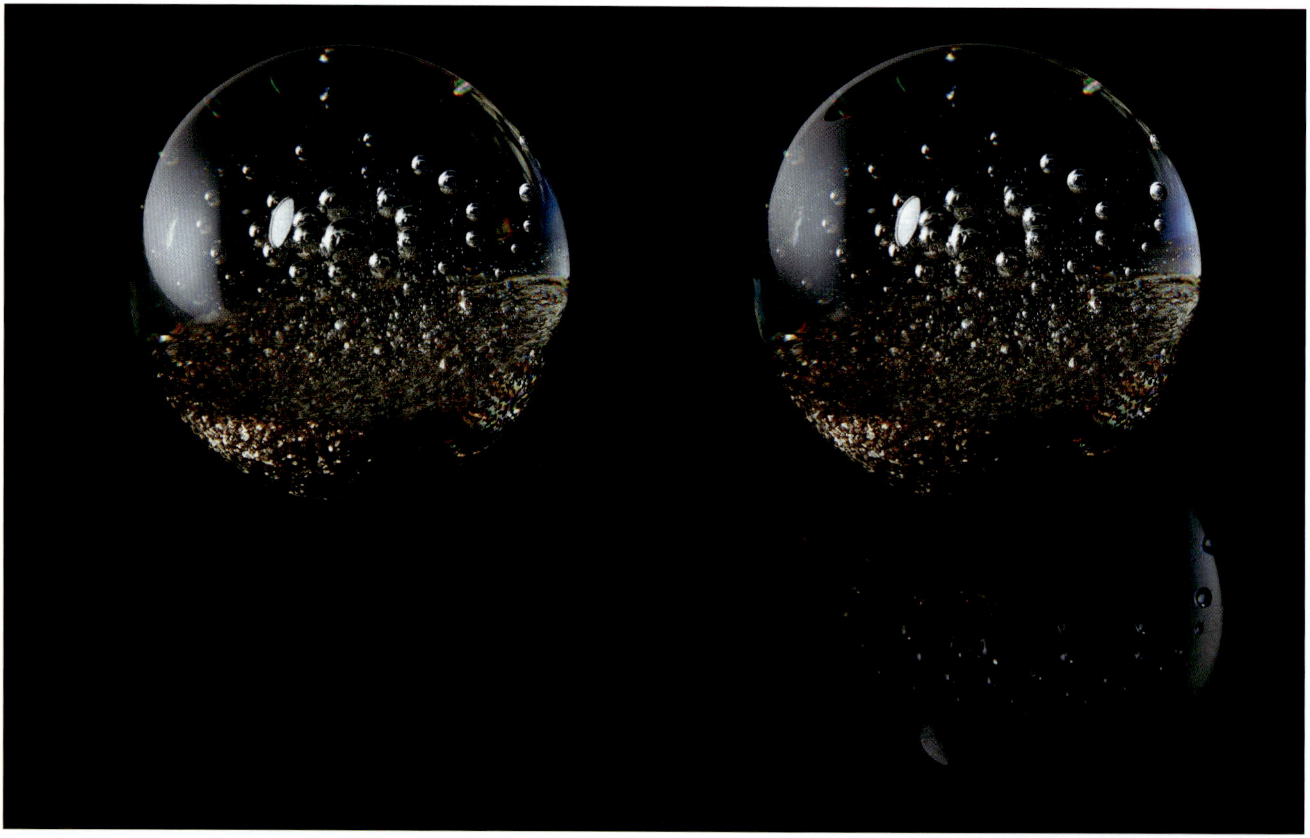

In the first photo, the light is polarized; in the second, it is not. The axis of the reflections plays the key role here: the reflections on the sphere remain almost identical, but the reflections on the glossy black plexiglass panel disappear with the polarization.

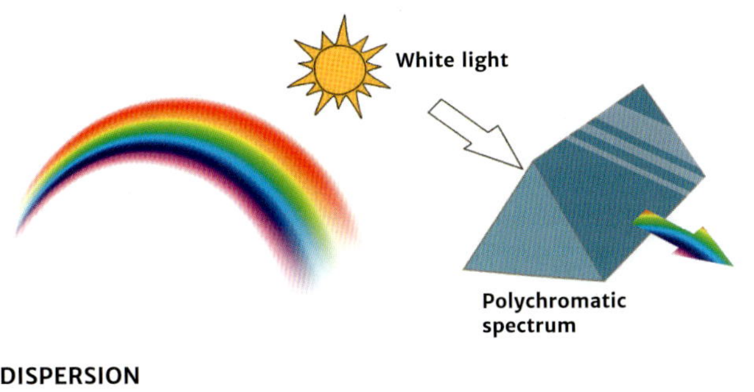

DISPERSION

Dispersion

A rainbow is a classic dispersion phenomenon that can be found in nature, where it is associated with the phenomenon of diffuse reflection on air and water molecules. Dispersion is the phenomenon that affects an electromagnetic wave that is moving through a "dispersive" medium—i.e., one in which the different wavelengths do not move at the same speed.

We can reproduce the same phenomenon using a prism. Discovered by Isaac Newton in 1666, the prism proves that white light can be broken down into a spectrum of colors (and recomposed, if one uses a second prism). White light is polychromatic. Traveling through the prism, because of refraction, the frequency of the radiation is broken down into seven monochromatic rays: red, orange, yellow, green, blue, indigo, and violet.

The difference in deviation is related to the fact that blue light has a higher refractive index than red light does when it passes through glass. The higher this index, the greater the deviation.

Transmission

The electromagnetic radiation that travels through a transparent material is "transmitted" by that material.

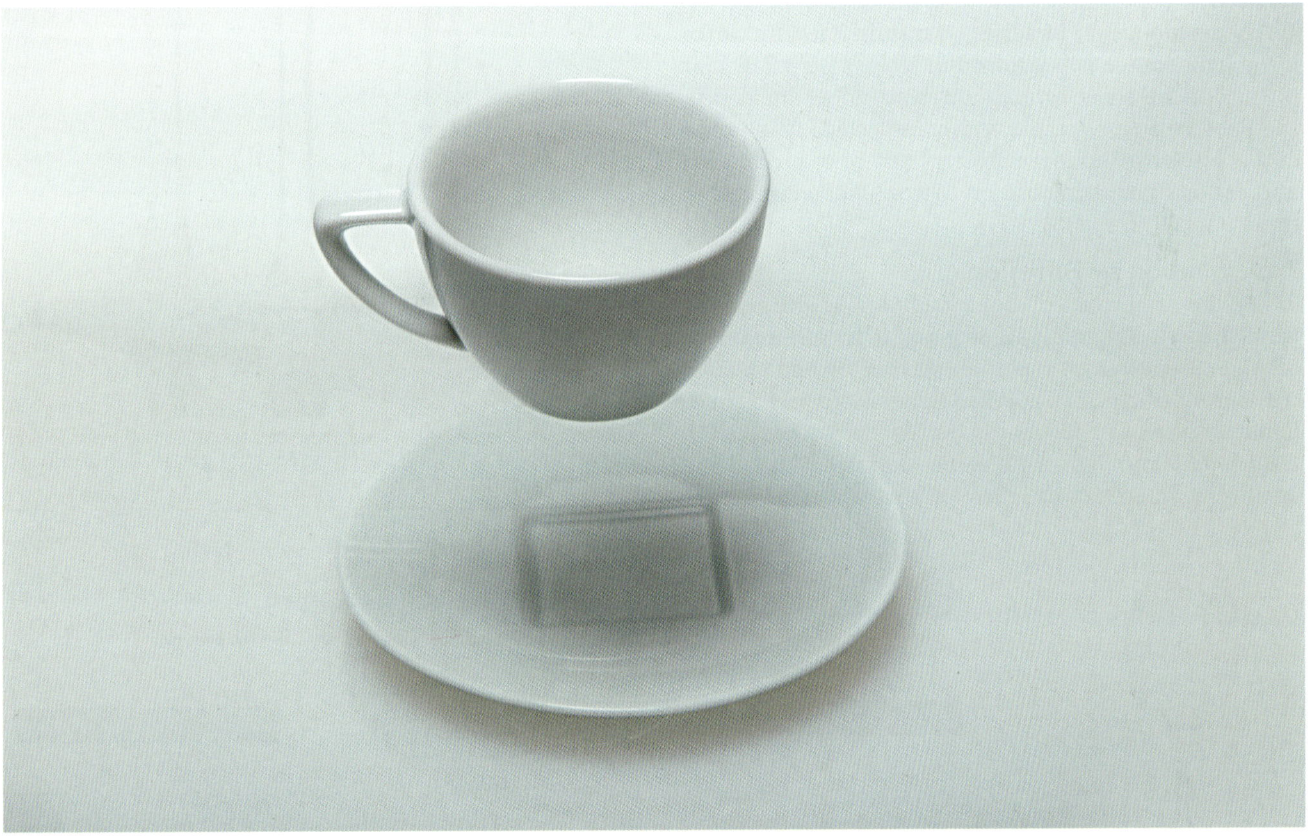

⌃ The phenomenon of transmission can lead to surprising photographs, without using Photoshop. In this case, the cup has simply been placed on a sheet of glass placed about four inches above the saucer.

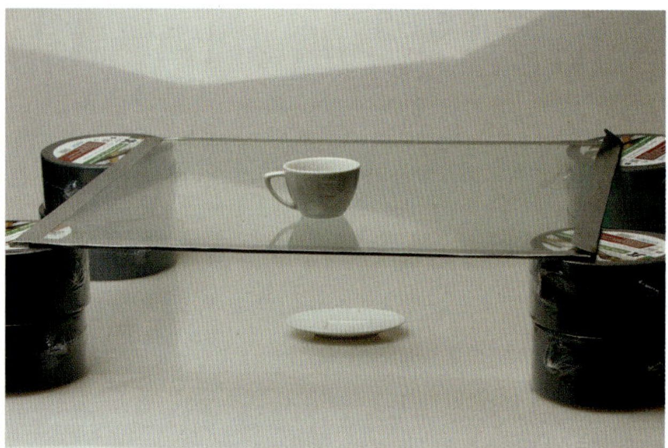

⌃ Setup for the previous photo

This is why a perfectly transparent medium, such as glass (as long as it is clean and perfectly flat) can't be shown in a photo: it transmits 100% of the light that is received.

The phenomenon of perfect transmission only works if the light source is positioned in an axis perpendicular to that of the sheet of glass. At every other incidence, the light will be refracted and/or reflected. This property is often used to make objects "fly" or to produce an impression of superimposition that would be difficult to make happen in reality.

Transmission by Diffusion

While the trajectory of light radiation is predictable through perfectly transparent glass, it is infinitely less so when it encounters materials such as frosted glass or translucent tracing paper. When light encounters a solid, liquid, or gaseous body that is translucent without being transparent, the light is randomly deviated. This is one of the characteristics of reflection that we shall address

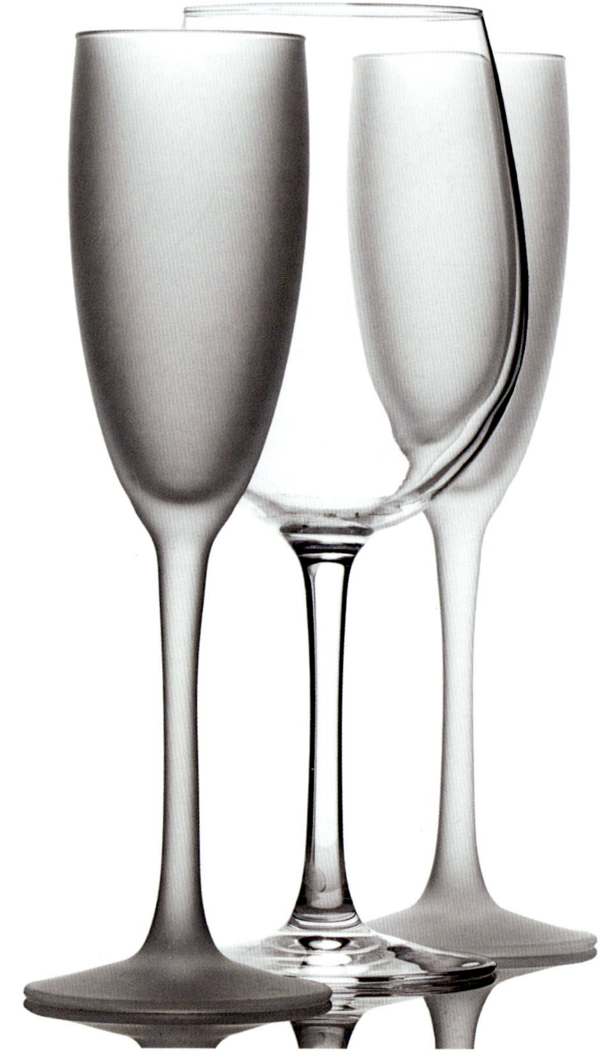

⌃ Transmission by diffusion can be better understood by watching what happens when you place frosted-glass goblets in front of and behind a transparent glass.

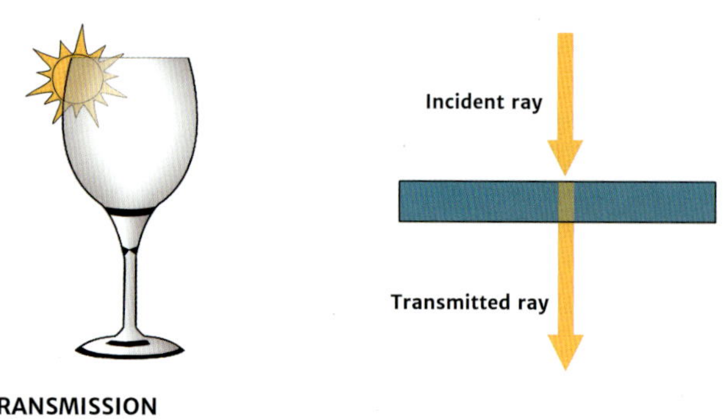

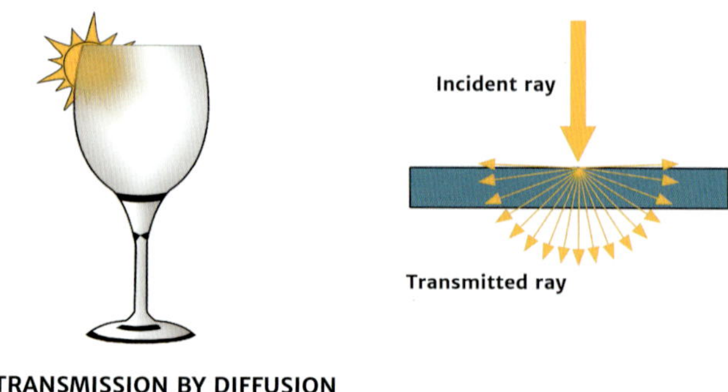

later, and that explains the look of the sky, where the light of the sun encounters gaseous molecules, each of which has different refractive properties. Depending on the angle of incidence of the sun's rays and the concentration of water and air in the atmosphere, the colors and appearance of the clouds can vary considerably.

Transmission by diffusion is also used a lot in product photography. By placing sheets of diffusing fabric in front of the light surfaces, one can increase the apparent surface of the illumination and the orientation of the rays, which has the effect of softening the light.

Translucent objects, for their part, have the property of absorbing part of the light received and reflecting the other part. They are therefore easier to light and to photograph than transparent objects.

Diffraction

When electromagnetic waves encounter an obstacle or a very narrow opening, they are diffracted. After the encounter with the material, the density of the wave is not preserved, contrary to the laws of geometric optics, and is distributed erratically. Diffraction systematically occurs when the wave encounters an object that hinders part of its propagation (typically the edge of a wall or the edge of the lens's diaphragm). It is then diffracted, and the closer to its wavelength the dimension of the opening it is crossing is, the greater the intensity of the diffraction. This is the phenomenon that, notably, results in the presence of the moiré effect in an image (a mesh fabric with very fine holes that causes an erratic repetition of the pattern, for example, which makes it very hard to photograph). Thus, it makes sense that a too-small aperture (such as f/22) will result in a loss of sharpness. But this can already start to be sensed at f/11 (most lenses have their maximum efficacy between f/4 and f/8). The same thing happens when you want to photograph the effect of a light coming through a small hole, or you want to catch a star-shaped sun by photographing it with the aperture closed: the electromagnetic waves are deflected as they strike the sides of the opening, some of the deflected waves bounce against the ones that are continuing on their path, and this creates interferences, just as when you throw two stones into a calm lake, a distance apart from each other, and their ripples intersect, creating new wave patterns.

This phenomenon is not used very often in product photography, but it allows us to explain moiré effects, as well as iridescence on the surface of DVDs or soap

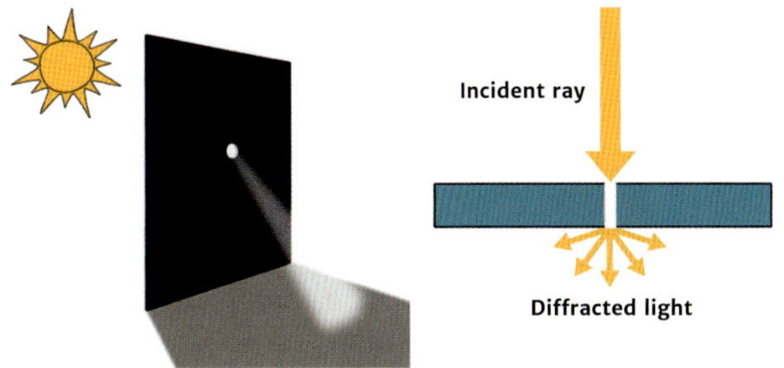

DIFFRACTION

bubbles, and serves as a good reminder that one should never close the camera's aperture too completely.

Most beginner photographers believe that sharpness can only be achieved with a great depth of field, and that the depth of field is only related to how far the aperture is closed. This approach is not completely wrong, but it overlooks several aspects of the issue. First of all, it must be noted that depth of field is a result of three other factors: focal length, focusing distance, and the size of the circle of confusion, all of which play an infinitely more crucial role than does the aperture.

Secondly, as of a certain aperture, the system is limited by diffraction, no matter what the optical qualities are. This critical aperture depends on the resolution of the sensor; for APS-C and 24x36mm sensors, the diffraction limit is just before f/8. After that critical aperture, closing the diaphragm just means reducing the optical quality. To get better resolution while still increasing the depth of field, *focus stacking* can turn out to be indispensable. This procedure consists of using Photoshop to combine several photographs whose focus is different (but all taken from the same angle of view), to create a greater depth of field.

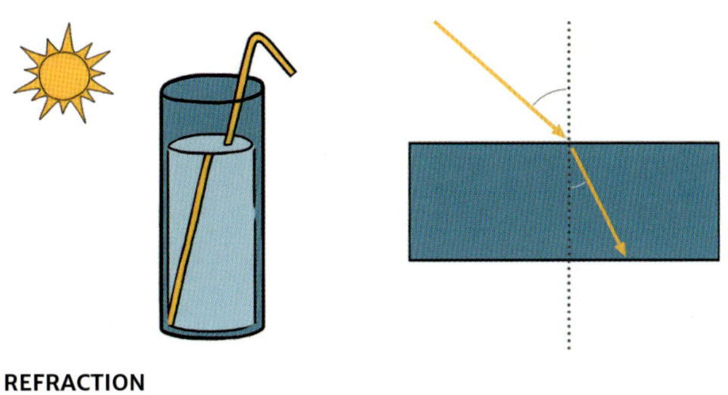

REFRACTION

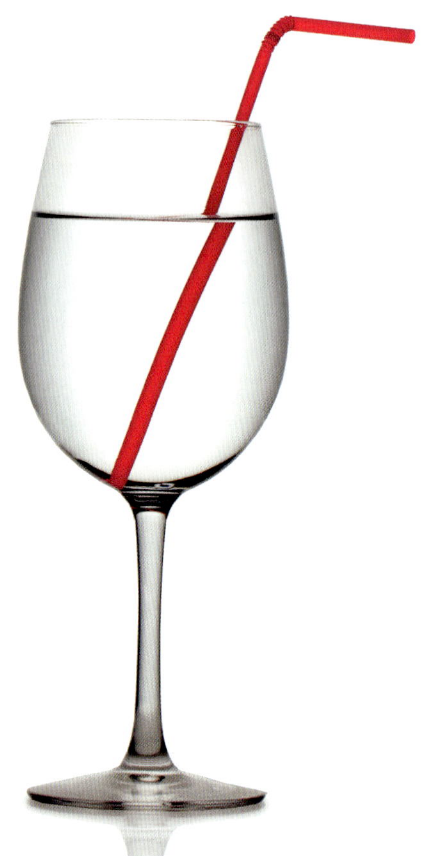

Refraction

Refraction is a phenomenon that deflects light from its path and changes its speed when it passes from one transparent medium to another one. Defined by Snell's law, refraction is manifested by a modification in the orientation of the propagation of the light waves.

It is the change in the speed of light, as a function of the medium that is encountered (because light does not travel at the same speed through air, glass, oil, water, or a diamond), that explains the deviation of a light ray. The *refraction index* is therefore defined based on the medium being traversed. We start from an absolute vacuum (where light travels fastest) as our base.

The lower the refraction index of a medium, the more quickly light will travel through it. Thus, light travels faster through ice than through a diamond. When light is traveling through various mediums, the deviation is more noticeable if the difference in their refraction indexes is greater: the higher the refraction index, the greater the deviation of the refracted angle.

This phenomenon is used, in particular, in lenses: when a light wave encounters a diopter (which is what we call the surface separating two homogenous mediums with different indexes), the light is refracted. Lenses (convex convergent and concave divergent) are the pairing of two diopters, which has the effect of applying two kinds of refraction to the incident light: the light rays that pass through the optical center of the lens are not refracted (direct transmission), while the others are.

We can observe this by filling a glass with water. The glass then acts like a converging biconvex lens: what we see through it is inverted, and the closer we get to the edge, the greater the angles of refraction of the light rays. This property will be particularly important when we need to photograph glasses of beer, for example.

Note that this phenomenon is completely reversed when the lens is immersed in water: the thin edges of the lenses, which converge when they are in the air, can diverge when they are in the water. Thus, the properties of a lens depend not only on its shape, but also on its environment. We will see several illustrations of this when we look at the photography of glass objects in an aquarium.

Reflection

Reflection is what we call the abrupt change in direction of a light wave when it encounters a glossy or opaque material. There are three kinds of reflection: diffuse reflection (or dispersion, see earlier); direct reflection; and specular reflection (from the Latin speculum, or mirror). Glass, mirrors, and the surface of water produce an almost specular reflection.

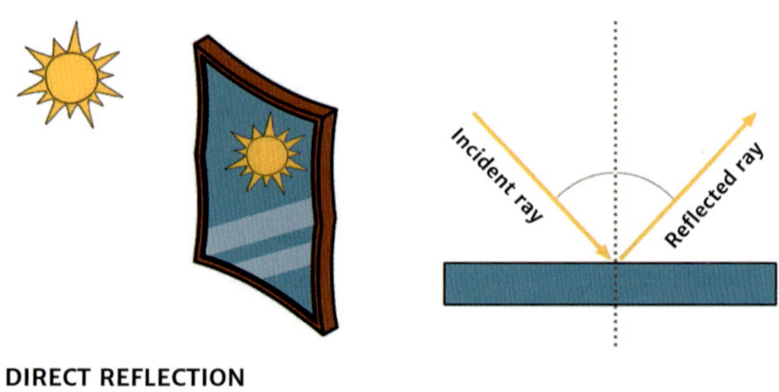

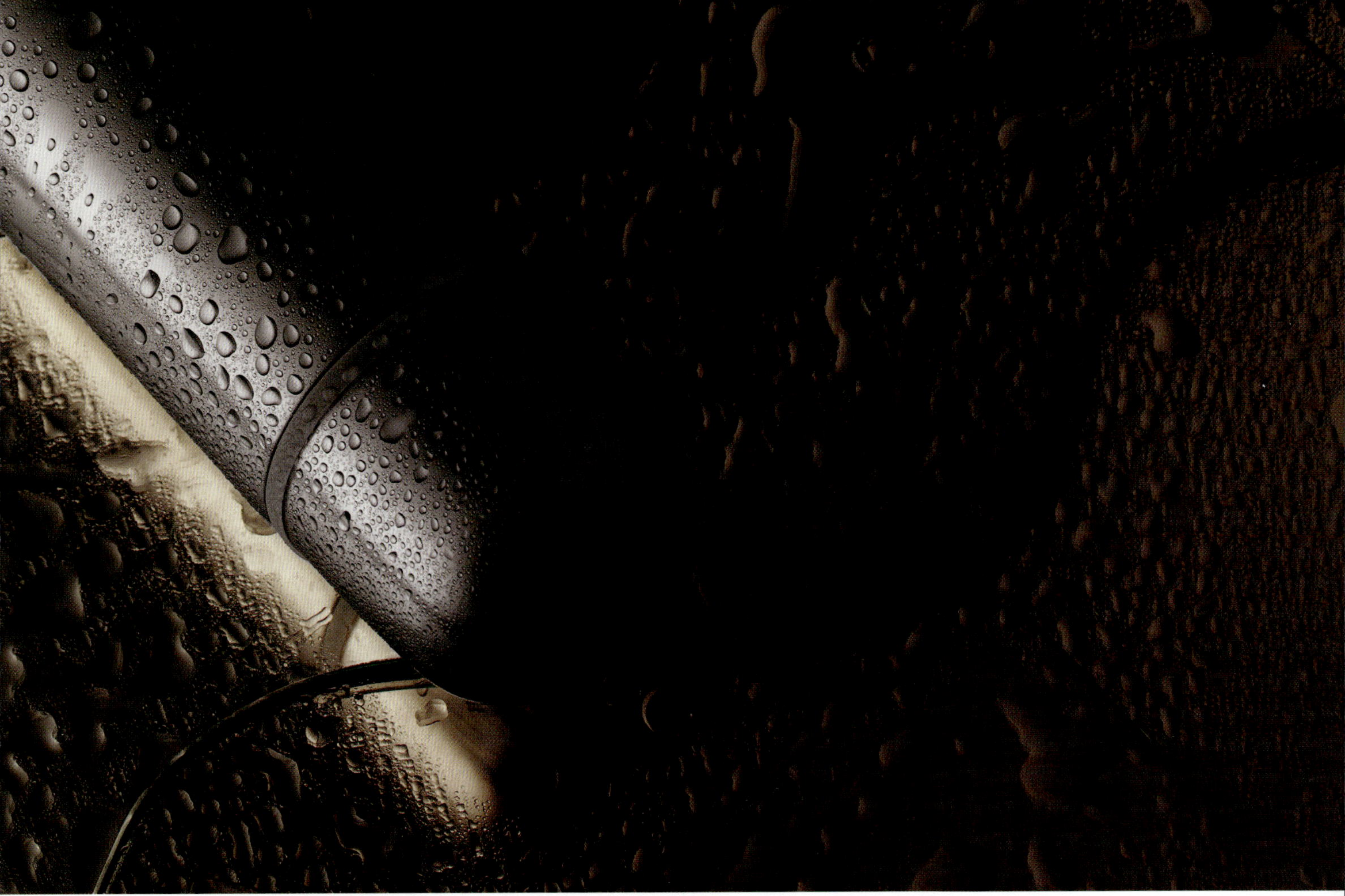

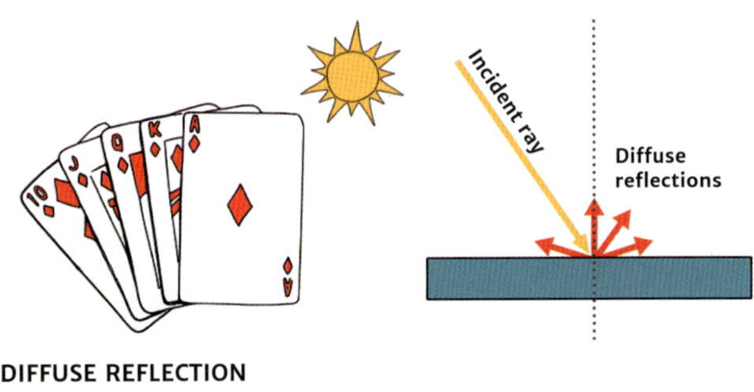

Reflection also obeys Snell's law, which establishes that the angle of incidence is equal to the angle of reflection. This means that if a light ray arrives at a 45° angle, with respect to the viewer, on a glossy object, its reflection will also appear at a 45° angle, on the other side.

Reflection is an essential concept in product photography, and the study of the phenomenon of reflection therefore merits an entire section (see the following pages) because it plays such a central role in this specialty. To begin with, without reflection, there would be no photography, and we would be blind: everything we see, and the way in which we see it, is the result of the reflection of light off of matter. It is not the objects themselves that we see, but a varying part of the rays that they reflect in our direction. In optical geometry, we call this *luminance*.

THE **REFLECTION** OF LIGHT

No matter what we want an object to look like—whether we want reflections to appear (or not), whether they should be sharp or diffuse, whether we want them to be placed in one particular place or another—we need a good understanding of the processes that come into play.

People don't expect to see the same kind of reflections on a transparent glass wine bottle as on a matte plastic bottle or flask. The quality and position of the reflections are what help us to understand what kind of material the object represented is made out of, and what shape it is exactly. It can also happen that the product needs to be presented without any reflections. Thus, we adapt the kind of lighting to the shape and material of the object we are photographing, as well as to the look we want to give it. But keep in mind that the object is not the only consideration: if a given material causes a certain kind of reflection, those reflections can still be made visible or

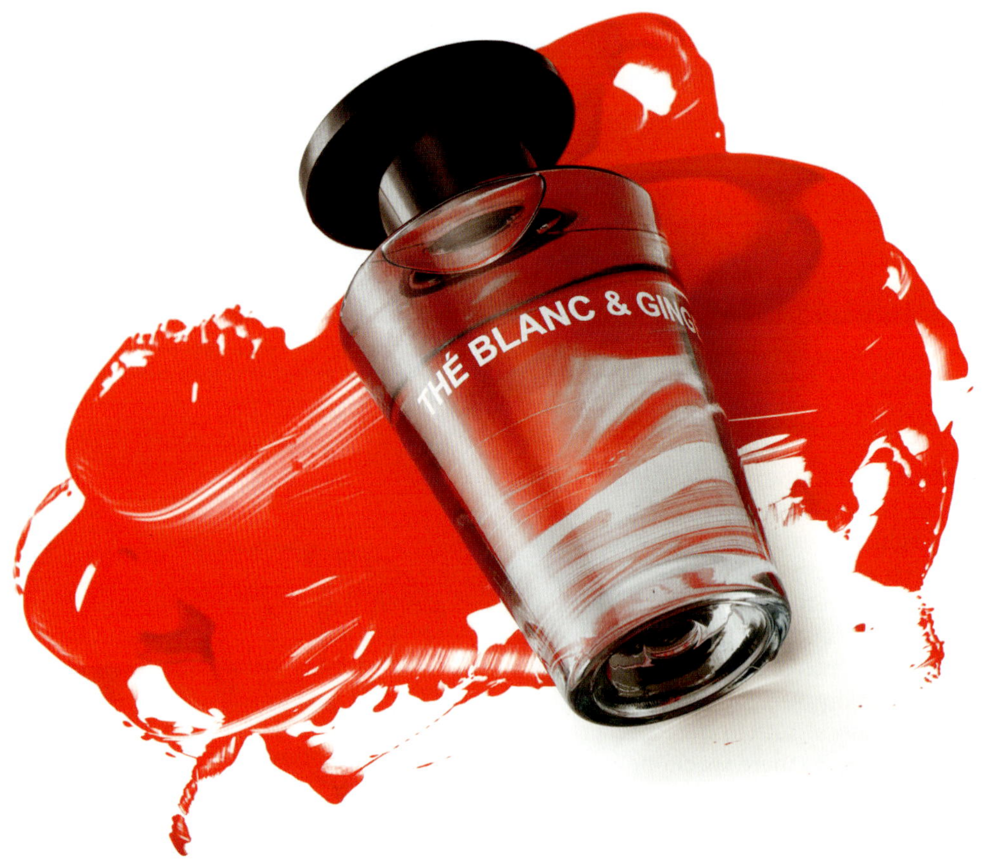

⌃ A good understanding of the laws of reflection allows us to achieve reflections that are appropriate to the photographed object and positioned in the right place, to help with a better visual understanding of the object. The difference in the reflections on the bottle and on the lid makes it clear that the bottle is made out of glass, while the lid is plastic.

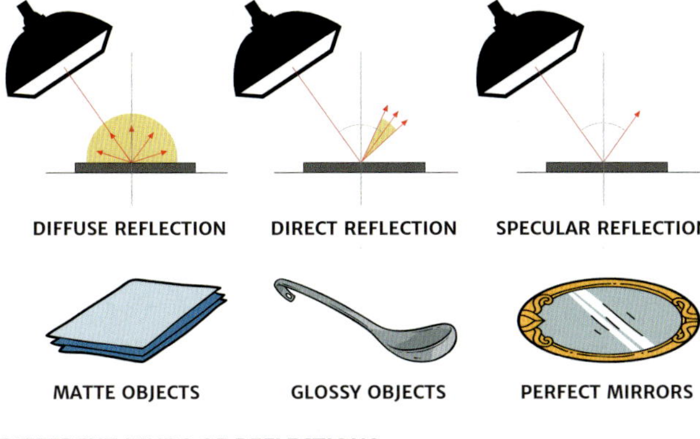

DIFFERENT KINDS OF REFLECTIONS

- We call an object *matte* when its surface is rough (even at the microscopic level, like a sheet of typing paper). This kind of surface produces mostly diffuse reflections. This is true for wood, paper, and matte plastics.
- We call an object *satiny* when its surface is smooth, but with some irregularities. This is the case for brushed steel, thin varnishes, and coated/glossy cardboard, like a pack of gum. This kind of surface generates direct reflections with very wide reflection beams.
- We call an object *glossy* when its surface is almost entirely smooth. This is true of mirrors, water, glass, or the blade of a new knife. This kind of surface generates direct reflections.
- *Specular* reflections, lastly, are reflections from objects whose surface is perfectly smooth–this is a theoretical definition, because no object has this perfect quality— however, the mirrors used in large astronomical telescopes and some very high-quality optical lenses (made by brands such as Zeiss and Schneider-Kreuznach) come close.

not, depending on where the picture is taken. We can also make the reflection appear pronounced or more diffuse by changing the quality of the light source.

Let's first look at the question of what kind of reflections the object itself produces; later on, we will address the question of the placement of the photographer (under the heading "Families of Angles").

THE CONDITION OF THE SURFACE

Even an object as matte as a sponge, for instance, becomes glossy when it is immersed in oil. Thus, what counts is not so much the material the object is made of as the surface: the smoother it is—and this is true when a film of water, varnish, or oil covers a rough surface— the more visible reflections it will produce.

The way in which a surface reflects light depends very much on its microscopic properties. A smooth surface will reflect the light in a well-defined direction (or bundle of directions), according to Snell's law, whereas a rough surface will disperse it into several different directions. The work of the physicists Lambert; Torrance and Sparrow; Phong and Blinn; and Bleckmann and Spizzichino has led to several ways to model this phenomenon. For our purposes here, there is no need to go into these mathematical models, but we can draw a number of technical lessons from them.

Let's start by sorting the condition of an object's surface into four categories: matte, satiny, glossy, and specular surfaces. (We will talk about glossy and transparent objects, like glass, in the following sections.)

DIFFUSE REFLECTION

When a light wave strikes an irregular surface, such as a sheet of typing paper, the reflection propagates in all directions, with the same luminance. Because it is the same no matter what the viewer's position is relative to the object, we don't perceive it as a reflection, but there is one (without a reflection, we would not see the object).

It is also diffuse reflection that causes the exposure on the object to remain constant no matter where it is photographed from. Even more interesting, this phenomenon takes place no matter what the angle of incidence of the light source is. We can prove this to ourselves by spreading out a piece of tissue paper in direct sunlight: no matter where we stand as a viewer, the tissue paper will always look the same. Diffuse reflection also takes place in the same way no matter what the size and quality of the light source are.

To better understand this, you can carry out a little experiment. Place a white sheet of paper and a mirror next to each other, then position a light source (such as your desk lamp) so that it lights both objects in the exact same way. Now move to a different position: the piece of paper will still look the same, no matter where you are while looking at it, but the mirror will look dark when you are anywhere other than at the angle of reflection, and it will look white when you are standing *at* the angle of reflection.

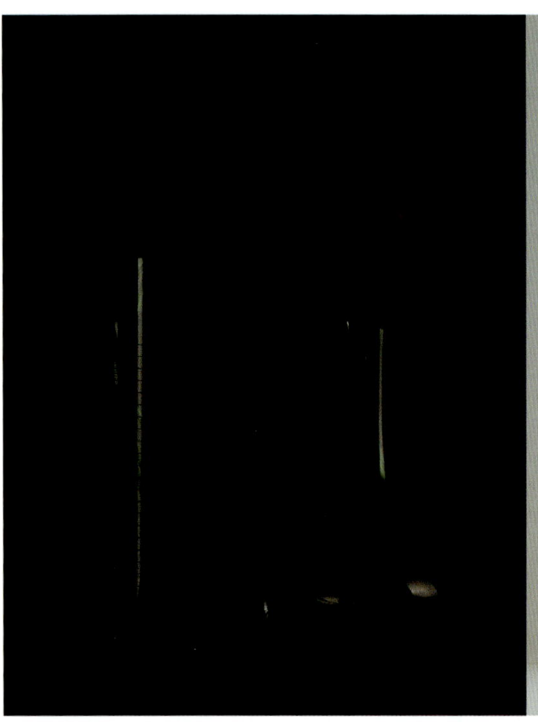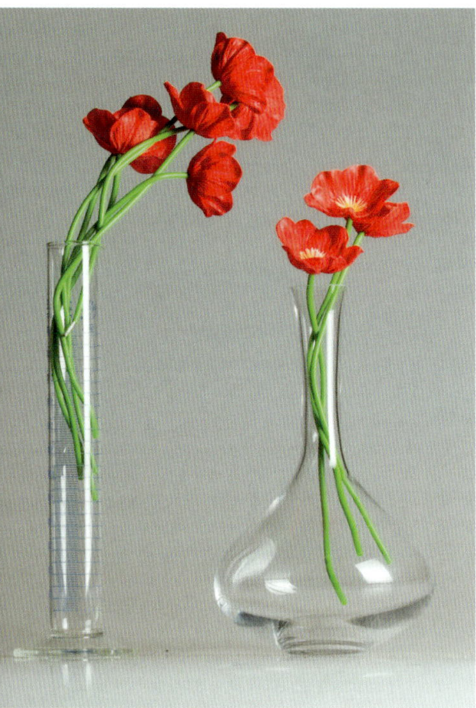

Once you have performed this experiment, move the light source: the piece of paper will certainly be less illuminated, but it will not change as you move around; in the mirror, on the other hand, the reflection will look smaller, and will appear or disappear depending on the position from which you are looking at it.

The only notable exception to this aspect of reflection on matte objects occurs when the object in question is black. In such a case, its luminance will vary depending on the viewpoint. This has less to do with the question of reflection than it does with the phenomenon of absorption, explained in the previous section: part of the light is absorbed as a result of the orientation of the object's irregularities, and thus of the placement of the photographer; the rest of it is reflected (because black is never absolute, and therefore not all of the light is absorbed), which explains the impression of glossiness that we can observe when the object is within a particular axis with respect to the light source.

SPECULAR REFLECTION

Specular reflection takes place when the incident ray gives rise to a single reflected ray, which is only possible when the light wave encounters no irregularities larger than itself (i.e., between 400 and 700 nanometers, the magnitude of the wavelengths of visible light) on the reflecting surface. In terms of physics, we can say that if the wavelength of the incident light is larger than the dimensions of the irregularities of the reflecting surface, the reflection is exactly within the reflected angle. This is a theoretical point, since it means that one hundred percent of the energy of the incident ray will be present in the reflected ray. In reality, part of the energy, even if it is an infinitesimal part, is always absorbed, diffused, or refracted by the surface of the object. This kind of reflection can therefore only take place with certain materials that guarantee that the light is only reflected by the surface and does not come from inside the object.

Nevertheless, this notion is useful for understanding how the reflection of a light is transmitted and where it can be photographed from. We will often use it for packaging shots, as a helpful tool in deciding how to photograph very glossy objects, such as mirrors, pure water, or flint glass and crown glass.

The reflections produced by this kind of surface are very precise: they look almost as if they were drawn on, and they appear exactly where expected. Thus, if a light source is placed at 45° to the left of a mirror, the specular reflection will appear exactly at 45° to the right. The angle of incidence is equal to the angle of reflection.

In reality, you will quickly realize that there is always at least a small portion of the light that is reflected along a slightly different axis, which means that reflections always seem to have a thin blurred border, because the objects that you photograph are not perfect theoretical objects—even if they seem to be perfectly smooth, even if you have taken the precaution of using nonwoven gloves in order to avoid leaving fingerprints, and even if there is no dust in your space. We can see an illustration of this in the sphere shown below. It was photographed brand-new, just taken out of its cardboard packaging, and handled with gloves, but the quasi-specular reflection at the left has a diffuse area in its lower part, which makes it into a direct reflection.

DIRECT REFLECTION

Direct reflection concerns all glossy objects whose reflective power is less than one hundred percent, which means, in reality, just about all glossy objects. These are objects whose surface includes irregularities that are larger than the wavelengths of visible light.

Snell's law applies again here: the angle of incidence of the light is equal to the angle of reflection, but the reflected light does not propagate at one single angle; a portion of the light is also reflected within a cone whose center is what is defined by that law. The greater the angle between the direction of observation and the theoretical direction, the less the quantity of observed light. The center of the reflection will be made up of a "specular peak," while in the rest of it the light intensity will decrease as a function of the angle of the cone axis.

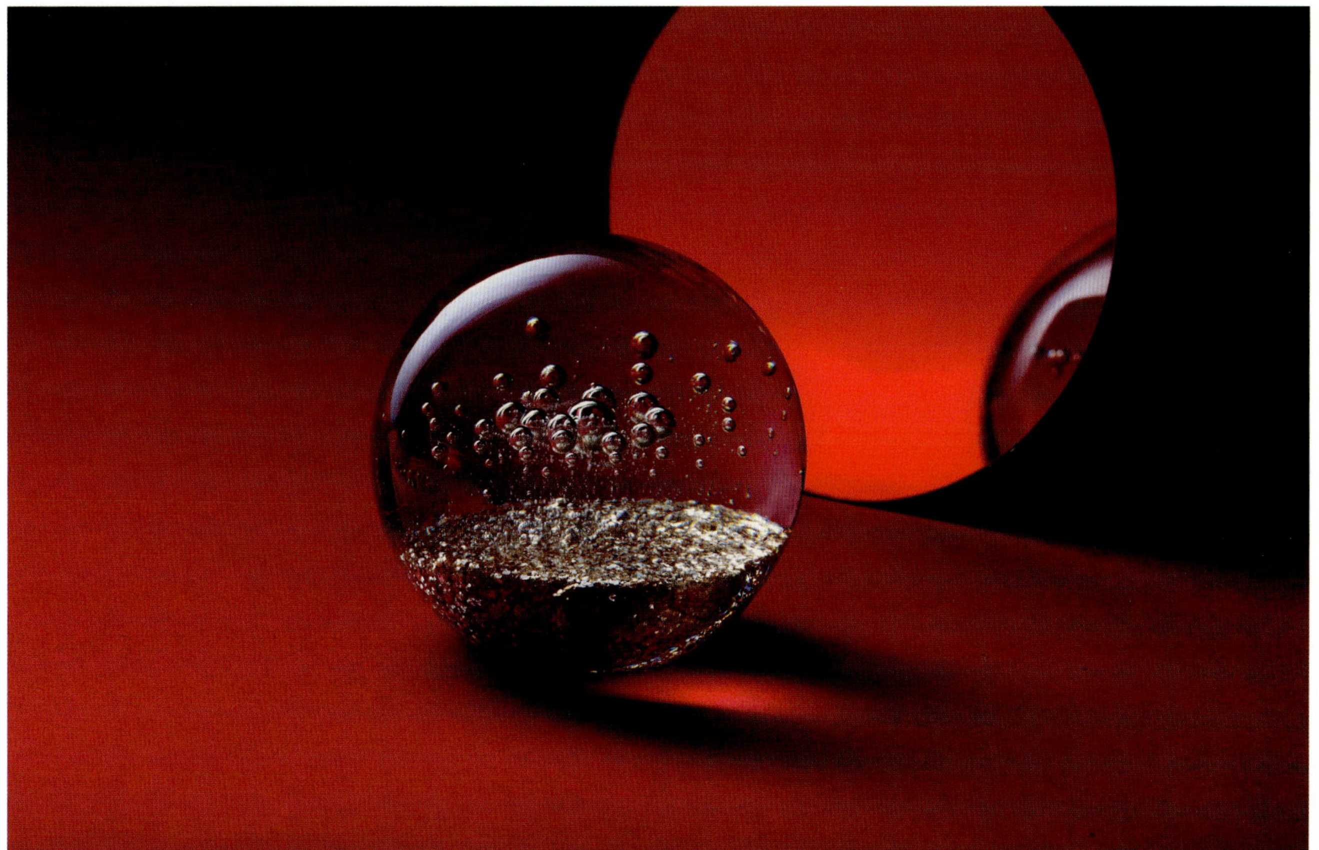

In this photo of a solid glass sphere and a mirror, placed on a sheet of matte red paper, we can clearly see that the light source (a flash equipped with an octabox, placed behind a five-foot by eight-foot diffusing fabric) causes a pronounced reflection on the sphere, which is perfectly reflected in the mirror, but that the paper is identical across the entire illuminated area.

We can understand the phenomenon at work here better if we place a glossy object (such as a new steel knife) underneath a light source. The four photos at right were taken under a large 5 x 8-foot diffuser.

- When the knife is placed exactly within the axis of the reflected light, the center of the specular reflection appears (photo no. 2) and the knife looks white. When the knife is lightly pivoted to one side or the other, it reflects the direct rays from the edge of the cone of diffusion, and the reflection looks bright, but grayish (photo no. 1).
- When we lift the back of the knife slightly, part of the object propagates the specular reflection while the rest of it reflects the direct light from the edge of the cone of diffusion: the knife looks partly white (specular reflections), partly gray (direct reflections connected with the cone of diffusion), and partly black (no reflections) (photo no. 3).
- Finally, when it is pivoted so as not to reflect the light at all, the knife looks black (photo no. 4).

Thus, we need to be completely aware of the results to be expected in terms of the presence (or absence) of reflections when we position the light source with respect to the object to be photographed.

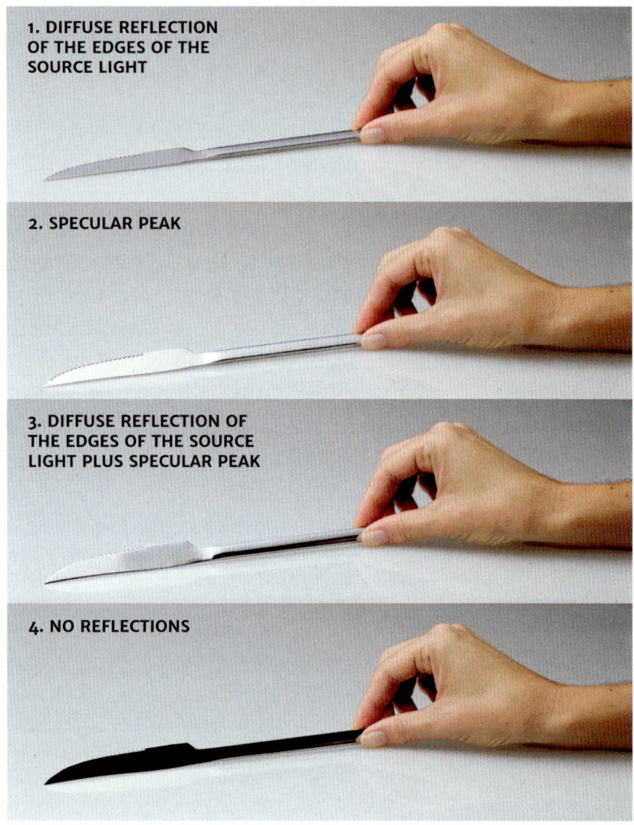

⌃ The appearance of the reflection on the knife changes considerably according to its position in relation to the incident light.

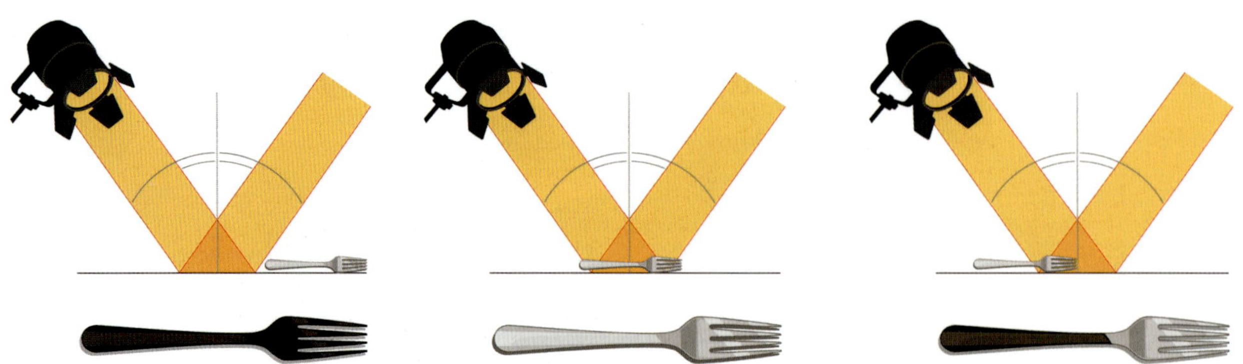

⌃ The photos above can be better understood by diagramming the placement of the object with respect to the light source.

POLARIZED DIRECT REFLECTIONS

Often confused with standard direct reflection, polarized direct reflections offer new opportunities for photographing.

We have seen that as a vibration of the electromagnetic field, light oscillates in all directions around the photon. Polarization forces this field to vibrate in one direction only; this is what a polarizing filter does, which is a filter of macromolecules that prevent the light from oscillating in directions other than its own polarization plane. With a vertical polarizing lens, only the vertical wavelengths will be retained; with a horizontal polarizing lens, it will be only the horizontal ones. If we superimpose a vertical polarizing lens with a horizontal polarizing lens, most of the rays will be blocked.

The Luminance of Direct Reflection
We have seen that standard direct reflection is always exactly as luminous as the source that causes it (when the source is moved farther away, the size of the reflection changes, according to the inverse square law, but not the luminance). This is not the case for polarized direct reflection, which is approximately twice as weak as a direct reflection coming from the same source.

Polarizing Materials
In reality, most materials produce polarized direct reflections, even if sometimes just locally, depending on how clean they are. Transparent and glossy materials partially reflect the light, which is more or less polarized depending on the angle of observation. Looking at it through a polarizing lens, we can see variations in the light intensity—this is the case for sunlight, which is also partially polarized, which is why when we photograph the sky using a polarizing filter, it looks darker and has more contrast. This is particularly visible at sunset. When we

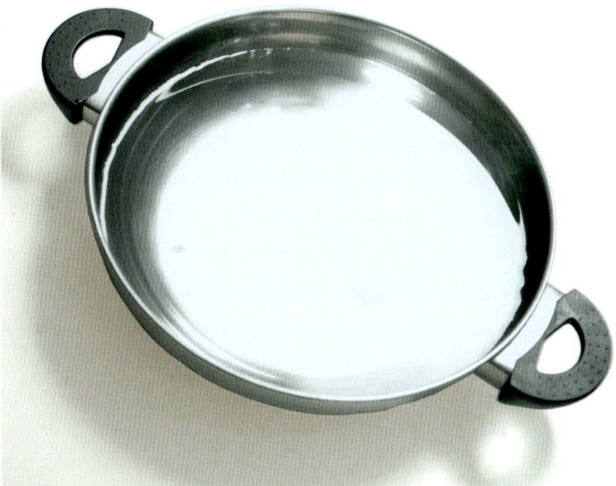
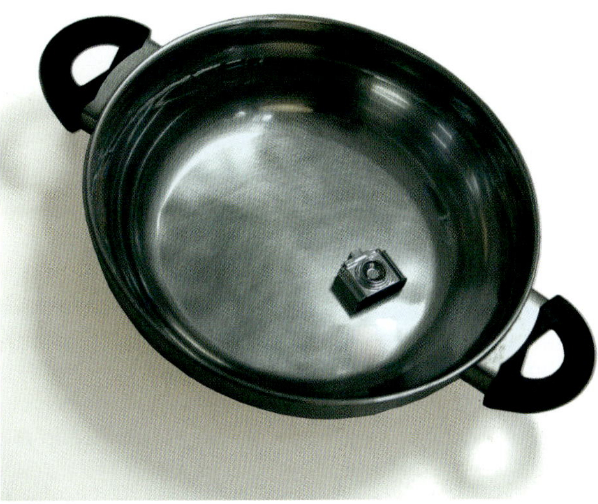

⌃ A stainless-steel wok filled with water, in which we have placed a small chrome-plated steel model of a camera, photographed using a large diffusing fabric lit by a flash. The shot was taken from within the family of angles. The photo on the left was taken without a polarizing filter and the model of the camera disappears; the photo on the right with a polarizer and the camera appears.

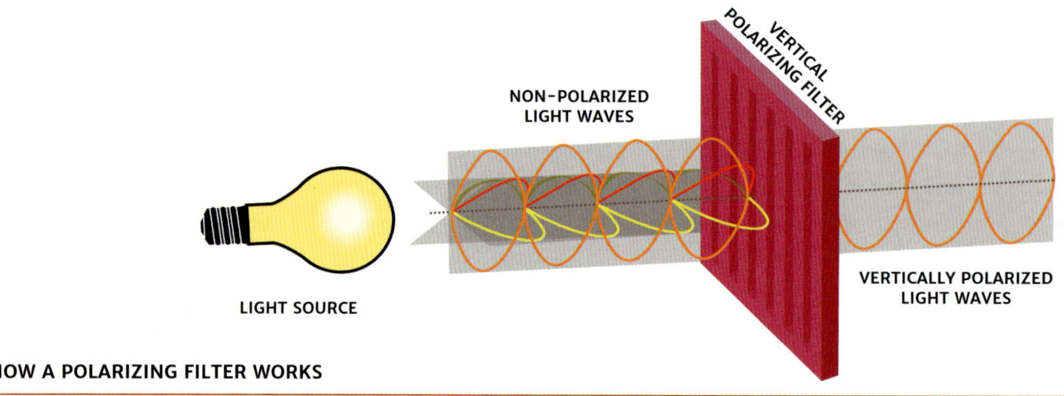

HOW A POLARIZING FILTER WORKS

are positioned at a 90° angle to a light source, the light is particularly polarized, but the phenomenon disappears when we face the source directly.

Moreover, the reflection on a horizontal surface (e.g., a lake, ice, a window) polarizes light horizontally. Eyewear manufacturers offer lenses with a vertical polarizing filter to protect your eyes from this kind of reflection. At Brewster's angle, the refracted ray and the expected direction for the reflected ray form a right angle; Snell's law allows us to easily predict Brewster's angle if we know the refraction index of each of the two mediums being traversed.

Finally, note that the polarization effect only appears on objects that produce glossy and specular reflections. Objects that produce diffuse reflections—in other words, matte objects—are not affected by polarizing lenses.

Polarized Reflections and Luminance

Because it loses some of the waves that made it up, a polarized direct reflection has less luminance than a standard direct reflection. Thus, when we polarize light, we get softer reflections (and as we get closer to Brewster's angle, we can even go so far as to eliminate them) and sharper contrasts. Rotating filters should be used so as to be able to carefully control the quantity of polarized reflections. Try the experiment shown in the photo on the previous page: with a polarizing filter placed horizontally over the lens, the surface of the water in the wok presents a direct reflection over its entire area; when the polarizing filter is placed vertically, it makes it possible to eliminate most of the reflection, and now we can see underneath the water, down to the bottom of the wok. Note that the filter also absorbs part of the non-polarized light and behaves like an ND filter, reducing the amount of incoming light.

With a polarizing filter, all direct reflections are transformed into polarized reflections, which can sometimes be very useful for reducing defects of glossiness, in particular for objects that have individual glossy spots, such as after being polished, for instance.

Note that polarization only takes place when one is within the axis of the light source, and that its maximum effect appears at a right angle to that axis.

It also needs to be noted that polarizing filters suppress part of the wavelengths and absorb a lot of light (up to 2 EV). Therefore, they cannot be used in the dark. They also tend to produce a slight vignette (a darkness around the edges) if they are too thick; be careful, therefore, to use only high-quality "slim" polarizing filters.

While simple polarizing filters can be used on mirrorless cameras without any problem, for SLR cameras you need circular filters. Like glass or the surface of water, mirrors polarize light. And SLR mirrors are oriented at about a 45° angle to the incident light: thus, with a simple polarizing filter over the lens, the light will be polarized along two different axes and no more light will be able to reach the sensor.

Polarizing filters for SLR cameras are made up of two filters: a linear polarizing filter and a rotating filter. The rotating filter allows you to adjust the light polarization over 90°.

Accentuating Reflections

In some cases, the direct reflections need to be accentuated in order to better highlight the photographed object. When the polarizing filter is turned to 90°, the polarized direct reflections reach their optimal intensity as an effect of the contrast, because part of the non-polarized light is absorbed.

FAMILIES OF ANGLES

Once you have assimilated Snell's law of reflection and how it applies—as a function of the medium that is encountered—to diffuse, direct, and specular reflection, the next step is to apply it to the reality of product photography.

So far, we have talked about one light wave, easy to schematize in the form of a straight line. In real lighting conditions, however, light takes the form of an infinite number of parallel waves that take up a specific amount of space (see diagram at right). Having a good understanding of the processes involved will make it easier to be precise in how you place the camera and the light with respect to the object, depending on whether (or not) it is desirable to see reflections on the object.

The Space Where the Reflection Is Visible

If we imagine a set of continuous and parallel straight lines (the light rays) leaving the source, and we apply Snell's law to them (the angle of incidence is equal to the angle of reflection), we can diagram a set of contiguous and parallel lines that are reflected.

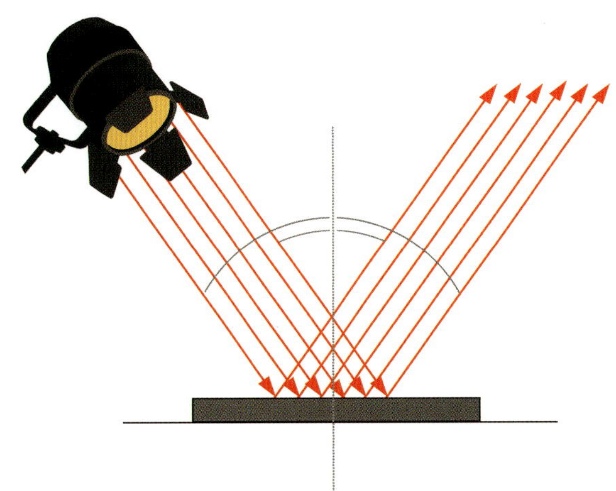

Reflections need to be understood as the juxtaposition of an infinite number of parallel waves.

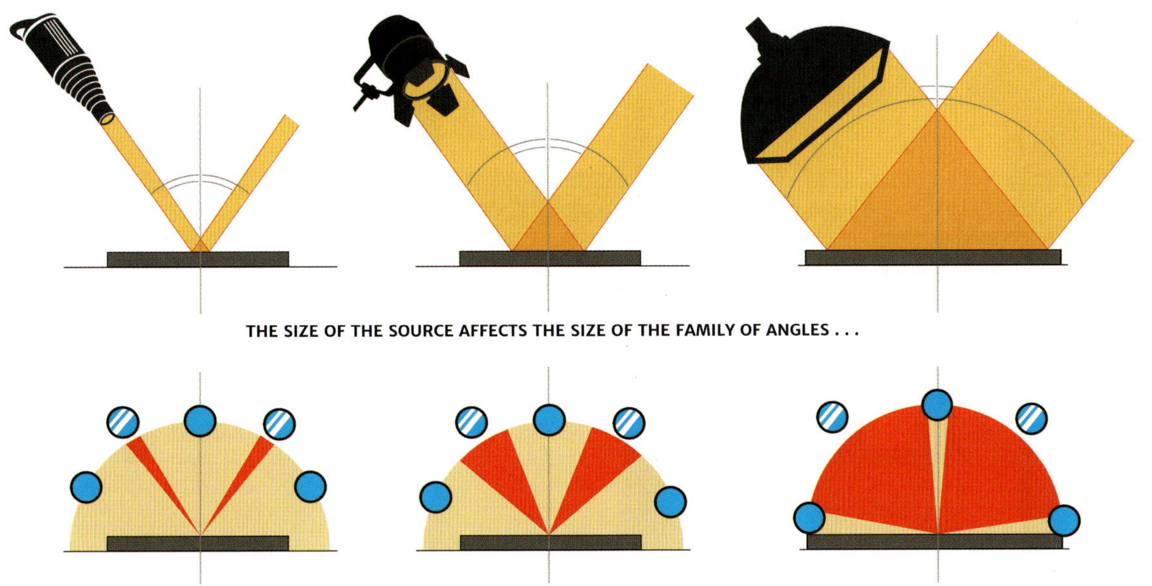

FAMILIES OF ANGLES AND SIZE OF THE SOURCE

This helps us understand why the reflection is only visible at a certain angle and invisible at all other angles, and also the fact that the space it occupies is intimately linked to the apparent size (and thus the distance) of the light source.

Let's take the portrait of my great-grandfather, pictured below, as an example. The portrait is placed within a matte wooden frame that includes a glass covering. The wood produces diffuse reflections and the glass produces direct reflections that are almost specular.

When my camera, which is placed facing the frame, is outside the family of angles generated by the light box (in the first photo, it is placed at a 45° angle to the frame), there is no reflection in the glass, and for good reason: my camera is outside the family of angles. On the other hand, when I move the light source so that the family of angles it produces is now in the camera's angle of view, the glass becomes white: the direct reflection occupies the entire space. Note that the appearance of the wooden frame has not changed at all, which makes sense, because the matte wood only produces diffuse reflections and its appearance therefore does not change depending on the orientation of the source light.

When we are illuminating an object, then, it is essential to determine, first, what kind of reflections will be produced by the materials that compose it, and second, what role we would like the direct reflections to play. Some objects are pleasing to the eye without reflections, such as when we are photographing a painting in order to create a facsimile of it; other objects, like chrome objects or wine bottles, require there to be some reflections that are carefully arranged.

Light Quality and Reflections

A reflection always has the same luminance as the source that produced it, and is therefore not influenced by the quality of the light that is used. What is interesting to us here is the border of the family of angles (the edges of the reflection): this is the area where the choice between a hard light and a soft light will make all the difference.

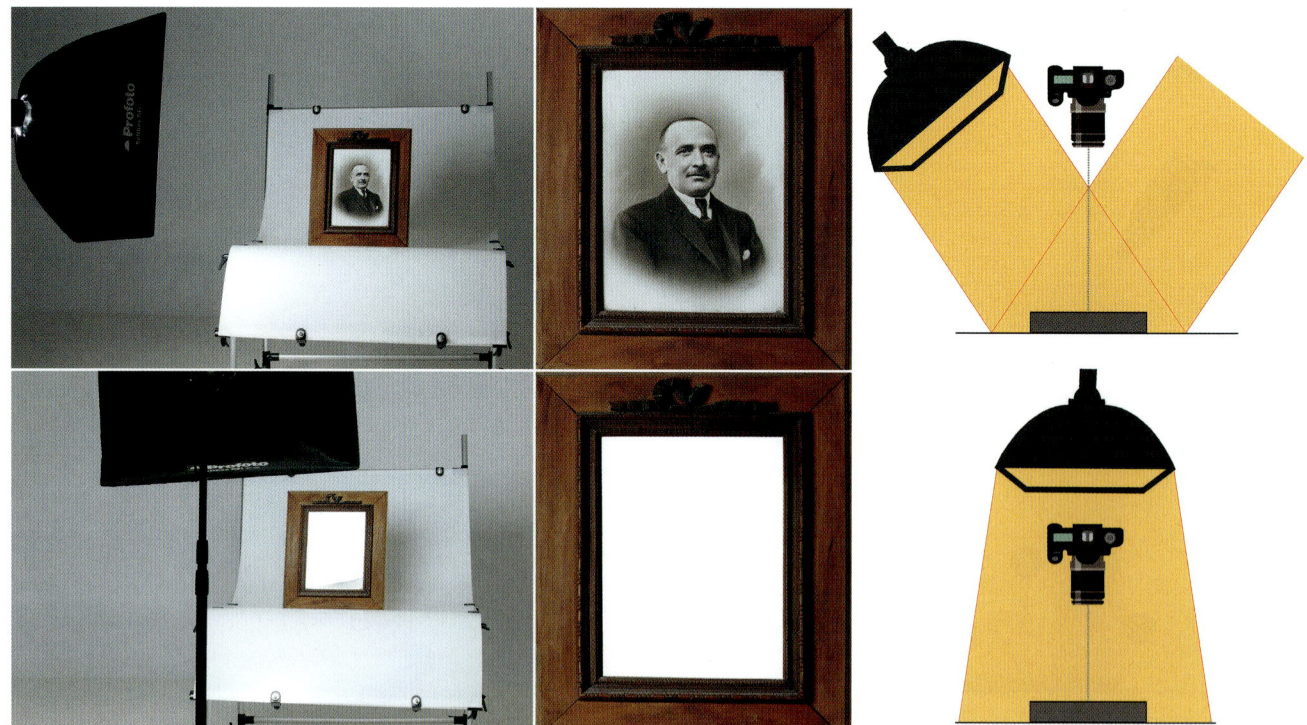

⌃ As we move the light source relative to the frame, the reflection in the glass appears only when the camera is placed within the family of angles. The wood of the frame, on the other hand, is not affected, because it only produces diffuse reflections.

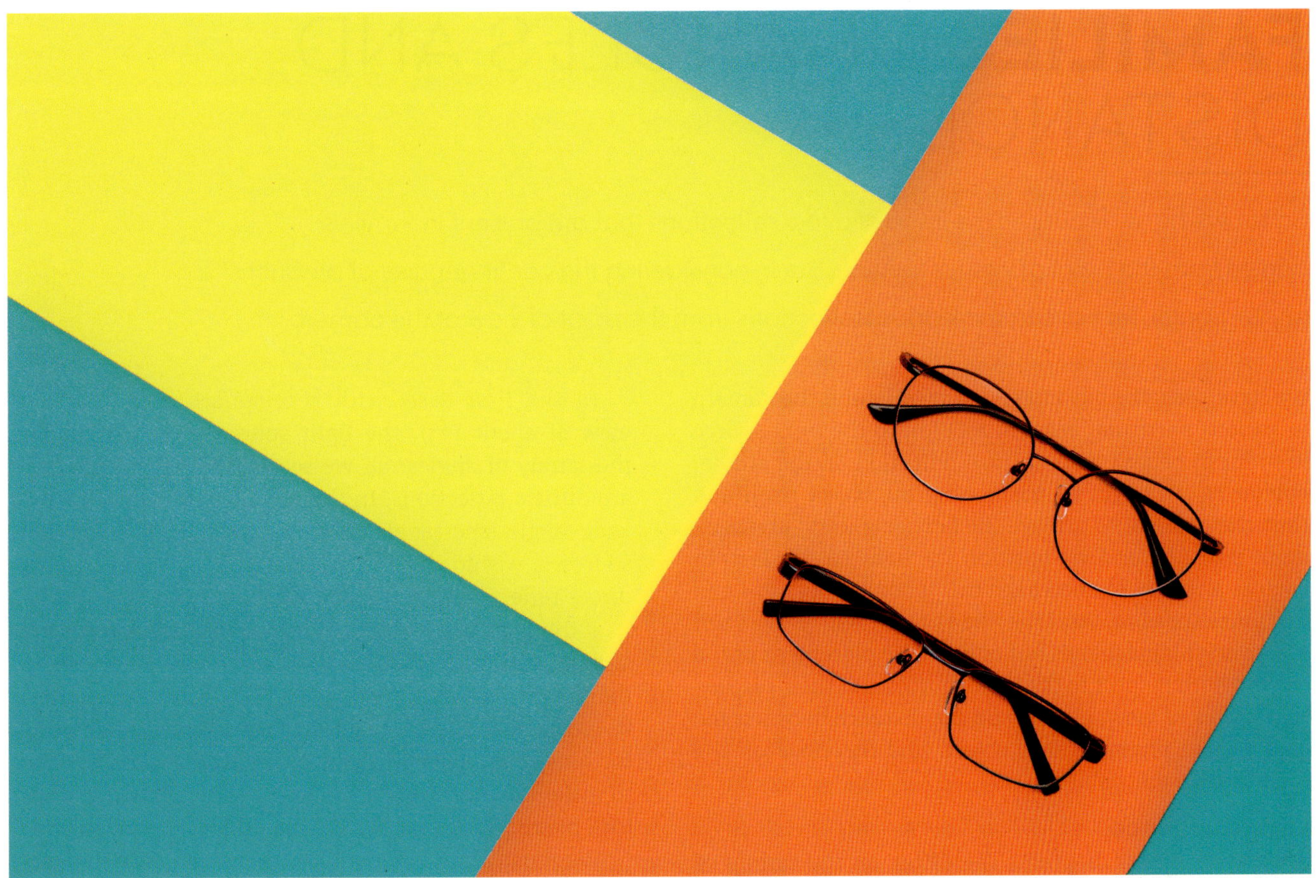

⌃ The absence of any reflections in the lenses of these glasses indicates that the light source illuminating the scene has been placed outside of the family of angles.

Some objects, such as chrome, liquids, varnished objects, and technological objects adapt very well to a hard light, with very clear and well-defined reflections. Such reflections will make the object look perfectly smooth, like oil. Other objects, such as high-end wines, certain foods, and luggage, work infinitely better with soft, smooth highlights.

The Total Family of Angles

For some objects, such as steel cutlery, we sometimes look for an overlapping reflection: in such cases, we use a very large light source (generally a diffusing fabric hung as close as possible to the object being photographed) to create a total family of angles. Because the reflection is present everywhere, this allows for a kind of lighting that molds itself to the shape of the object. A spoon, for example, reflects all sources at an angle of approximately 180°: if the source placed overhead is too small, or too far away, the reflection will not cover the entirety of the object and we will see a black margin (the area where there is no reflection), which will take away the "smooth" effect of the light. To address this, we can simply make the source larger and/or bring it closer, or else use a lens with a longer focal length. We will come back to this.

FAMILIES OF ANGLES AND DISTANCES

So far, we have discussed the issue of direct reflections that are present in families of angles from the point of view of lighting. But in considering the contingencies of product photography, we have to think about reflections from the point of view of the camera.

We have seen the advantages of positioning the camera in various particular ways in relation to the light source in order to benefit from diffuse reflection. In the studio, obviously, we begin by positioning the object itself and then the camera, to achieve the best geometric arrangement possible, and we position the light source last, in such as a way as to encourage the "good" reflections and minimize (or eliminate) the "bad" ones. But, as we shall see, everything depends not only on the placement of the camera with respect to the light sources and their respective angles of view, but also on the distance between the camera and photographed object, and therefore on the kind of lens that is used.

Light Incidence

The figure below diagrams the effect on the family of angles when the angle of view is changed, with the camera and a light source placed in the same positions with respect to the object in both examples.

In the first case, with a telephoto lens (angle of view of about 12°), the light source is clearly outside the family of angles: all we see on the pair of sneakers are diffuse reflections. In the second case, with a 28mm wide-angle lens (angle of view of about 75°), the light source is within the family of angles and there will be direct reflections on the pair of sneakers.

If this had been a matter of reproducing a flat document, such as a painting, the second example would have shown the direct reflection appearing as a "hot spot"—which would be unsightly and unacceptable for, say, a reproduction meant for a museum. But for a pair of sneakers, where we want to make the patent leather element show up and it would look matte without proper lighting, this is a good solution.

We must always remember, therefore, that the most important thing is the representation of the object's characteristics. Every object, depending on its volume in space, the specific state of its surface (matte, satiny,

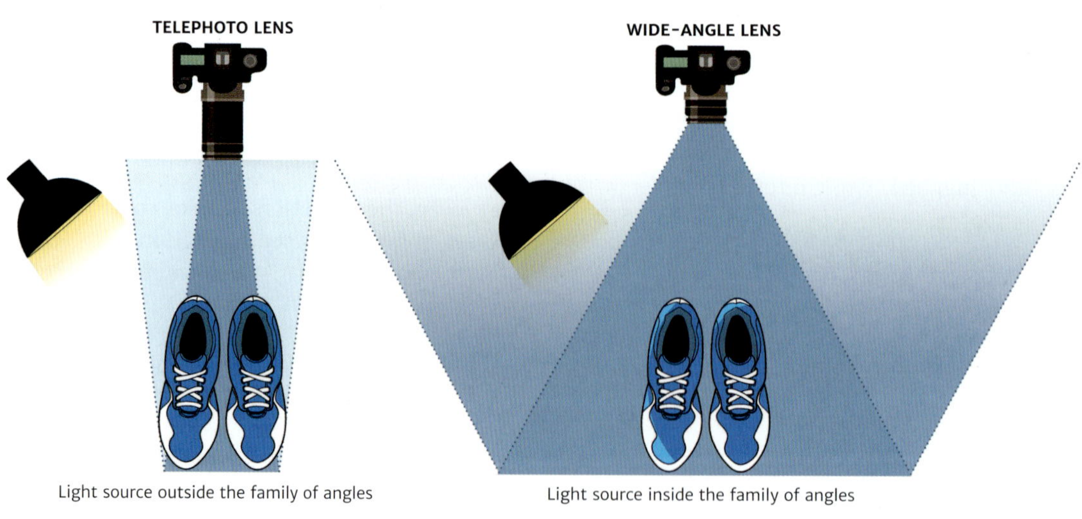

Light source outside the family of angles

Light source inside the family of angles

FOCAL LENGTH AND THE FAMILY OF ANGLES

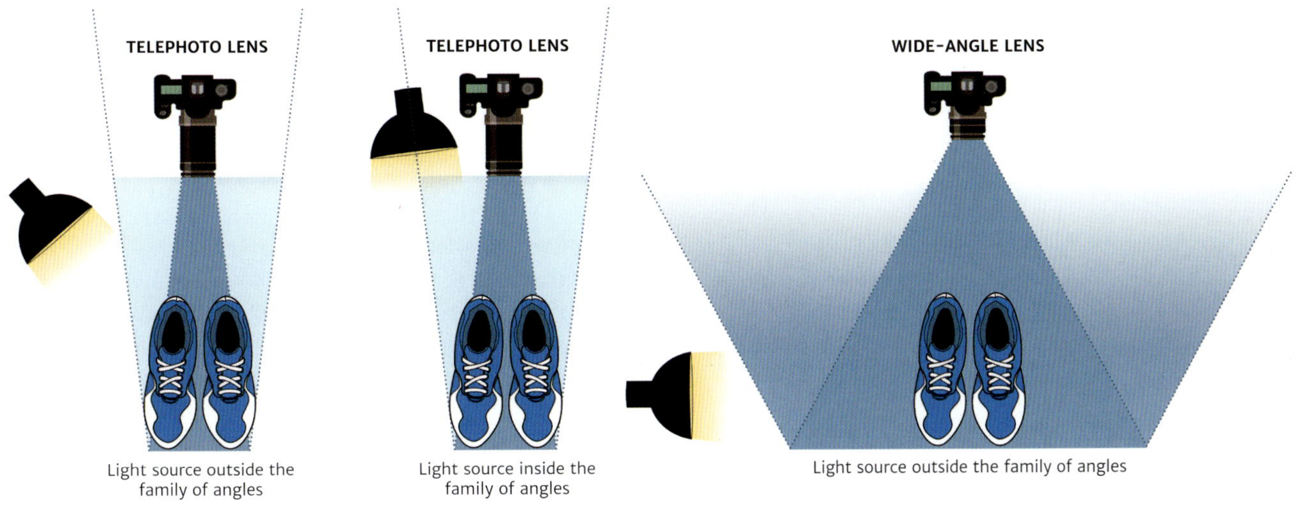

DIFFERENT LIGHT SOURCE PLACEMENTS

glossy areas), how it tends to be presented (also in terms of brands and fashions), and your own photographic intentions and goals, can be lighted to make various sets of diffuse and direct reflections appear. Or sometimes just one or the other.

But in all cases, the final factor remains the lens's angle of view: the larger it is (114° for a 14mm lens), the greater the risk will be that the lighting will be within the family of angles and that we will see direct reflections appear on the object. The smaller the angle of view (8° for a 30mm lens), the less chance there will be that the light source will be within the family of angles and that direct reflections will appear.

The situation can be easily managed in a large studio, where it is no problem to use a long focal length and place yourself a good distance away, but it is trickier in tighter spaces where you might feel the necessity for a wide-angle lens. In such a case, you will need to place the light source at a very oblique angle to eliminate direct reflections.

Camera-to-Object Distance

The challenge is to discover the ideal lighting angle, but as we have just seen, that will depend on the distance between the camera and the illuminated object. In fact, the farther away the camera (in other words, with a long focal length), the narrower the family of angles that will produce direct reflections. In this case, the placement of the light sources is much easier than when the family of angles is wider: when it is wider, the light sources will

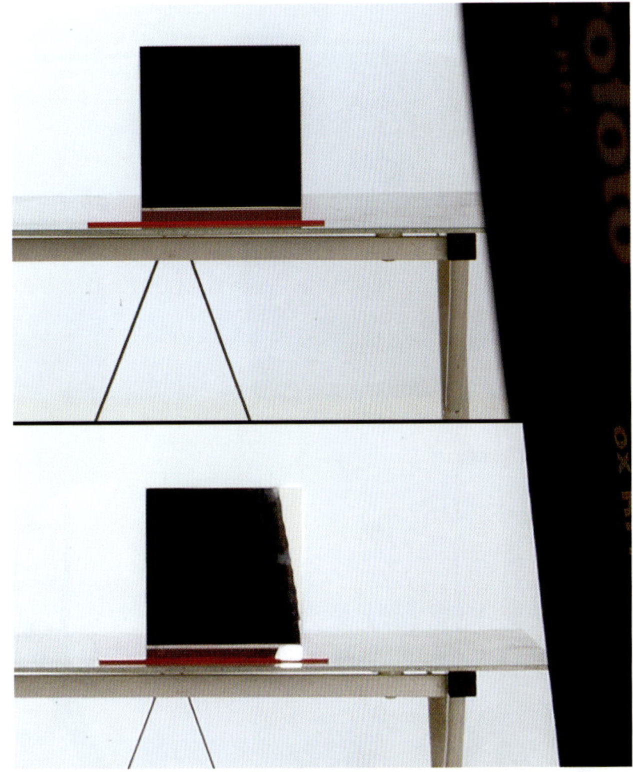

⌃ Two photos, taken from the same distance, with the light source in the same place, but with different focal lengths (16mm and 200mm), and the first image cropped to occupy the same space as the second one. In the second image, we can see the presence of direct reflections.

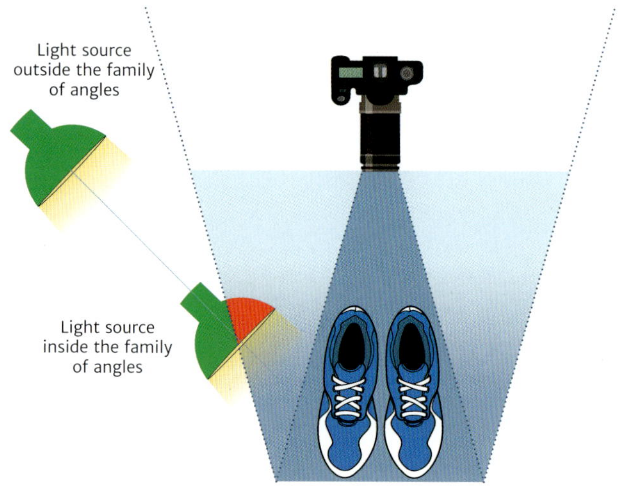

EXAMPLE OF LIGHTING PLACED AT 45°

have to be placed at a very oblique angle, and the surface of the object will not be illuminated in the same way everywhere, which will cause changes in luminance and hues that are liable to make the photograph look bad.

Thus, except in extreme cases (specifically, where the space doesn't allow enough distance or when the object forces a particular perspective), we always try to position ourselves far enough away (at least six and a half feet) from the object in order to be able to balance the direct and diffuse reflections as precisely as possible.

In terms of the lighting of flat objects (a painting, a notebook, etc.), the traditional method is to position two light sources, one on each side of the object, at 45°, in order to obtain even light that is conducive to creating a good facsimile reproduction: the diffuse reflections, luminance, and variation in hues will be identical across the

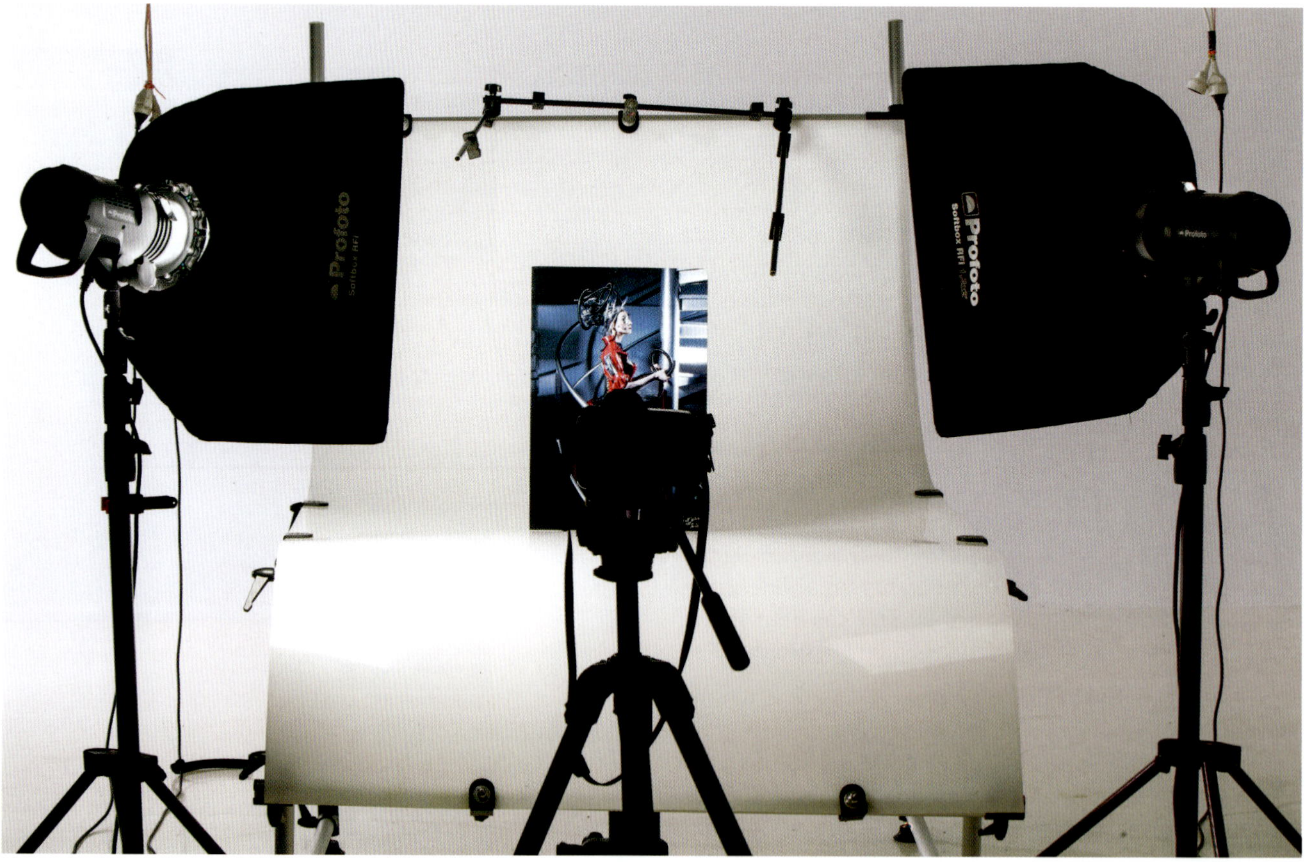

⌃ Traditional placement of light sources and camera for reproducing flat documents. The two sources are placed on either side of the object, at 45°, and the camera is placed six and a half feet away with a 135mm lens, perfectly horizontal at the level of the object's center, so as to maintain its exact proportions.

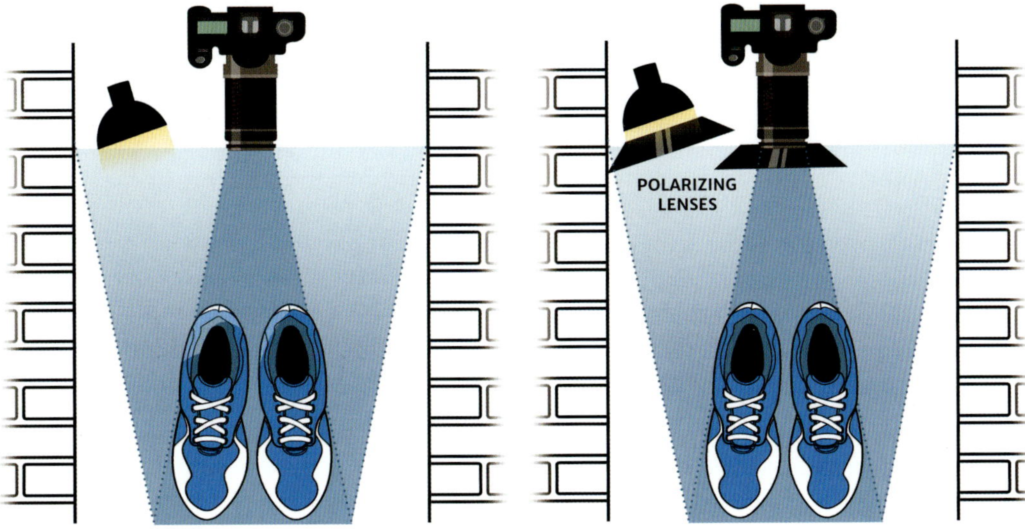

entire object. The preferred lens for this is a lens whose focal length is greater than 135mm, and you will need to place yourself at the shooting distance that allows you to maintain an angle of view of 24° (for a twelve-inch object, using a 135mm lens, that distance would be sixty inches; see page 49). The goal is to reproduce the object as faithfully as possible, without any perspectival effects; the lens needs to be perfectly horizontal (no bird's-eye view or low-angle effects) and placed exactly perpendicular to the object's center.

Object-to-Light-Source Distance

We have seen that the farther away the angle of the light source is from the family of angles, the lower the risk of obtaining direct reflections. Nevertheless, if the light source is at an angle that is too oblique (aside from the effect that it can have on the condition of the object's surface if it is too low-angled and the surface is not perfectly smooth), it presents a problem in terms of the distribution of the light quantities: you run the risk of having one part of the object be more illuminated than the other—which makes sense, because the illuminated part is closer to the light source than the other part is. This phenomenon increases as the light source is brought closer, because of the inverse square law (see next section). This problem can be resolved in two ways: either by choosing a less oblique angle for the light source, or by maintaining the angle but moving the light source as far away as possible.

Beyond ten feet, the decrease in light intensity with distance is very gradual (5% between ten and thirteen feet, 2% between thirteen and sixteen feet, etc.), which will be more than enough for small objects under twenty inches.

Observing the Object

In most cases, we want to show what the object really looks like, with direct reflections if the object is glossy, and diffuse reflections if it is not. In addition, the reflections need to be positioned in the right places on the object, and they should not interfere with how its hues and shape are presented.

The photographer must act very consciously in positioning the light sources and their shapers, and in choosing the distance and the angle of the shot as well as the focal length of the camera lens. We will see in the examples in the second chapter of this book that the possibilities are as various as the objects that are presented to us and as the photographic intentions that I had when I took the shots that I show. But the crucial question that you must ask yourself is always still about the presence or absence of direct reflections: should they appear, and if so, where on the object? The answer will allow you to determine how many light sources to use, their distance, their angle with respect to the object, and therefore also the distance and focal length to use for the shot.

THE INVERSE SQUARE LAW

We know intuitively that the farther away a light source, the less illuminated the objects will be. However, we have to quantify this when we address the photography of (large) objects.

The inverse square law, which was first suggested in 1645 by the French astronomer Ismaël Boulliau and then formalized by Isaac Newton in 1687 (apparently following a suggestion by Robert Hooke), applies to all energies and all waves. This physical law establishes that any physical quantity (electromagnetic radiation, energy, force, etc.) is inversely proportional to the square of the distance from its origin. It can be formulated as follows:

Intensity = $1/\text{distance}^2$

In terms of illumination, we can use the exposure meter to easily verify that light decreases with distance in a quantifiable manner. If at 1 foot I measure a light at f/11, at 2 feet I will measure f/5.6, the quantity of light having been divided by 4 (-2 EV), and at 3 feet I will measure around f/4.5 (-2.6 EV). This understanding of the proportions saves an enormous amount of time in positioning light sources with respect to the objects to be photographed and the desired result.

Squared

If we imagine the light rays leaving a particular point as a set of contiguous lines (see the diagram below), it's easy to see that the first cupcake, the closest one to the source light, receives most of the rays. The farther away they are from the light source, the fewer light rays the cupcakes get.

This decrease in the quantity of light is geometric. Imagine that at 1 foot, the quantity of light received is 100 (1/1); at 2 feet it is only 25 (1/4); at 4 feet it's 6 (1/16); at 8 feet it's 1.5 (1/64), etc. The luminance of the illuminated object decreases geometrically: very quickly in the first few meters, very slowly after that.

This is a key concept. Many beginners tend to believe that when you double the distance between the source and the object you halve its power. This is obviously false.

Implementation

Let's imagine that we want to illuminate a car. The photo that I show you on the next page has been composed to elongate the hood of the car; it measures 181 inches long. For the purposes of this book, I chose to place my main light (a 60-inch-diameter octabox) three feet from the front-right fender (to our left as we look at the car). You can see how quickly the light decreases from this side of the fender to the other side, about 70 inches apart (about -2.4 EV).

Obviously, if I had wanted the lighting to stay approximately the same over the entirety of the VW bug, I could have placed my light source fifteen feet ahead of the car (five times farther away). Then there would only have been a 3.8% drop in luminance between the two sides of the front fender (1/25 to 1/81), a difference that is hard to perceive with the naked eye.

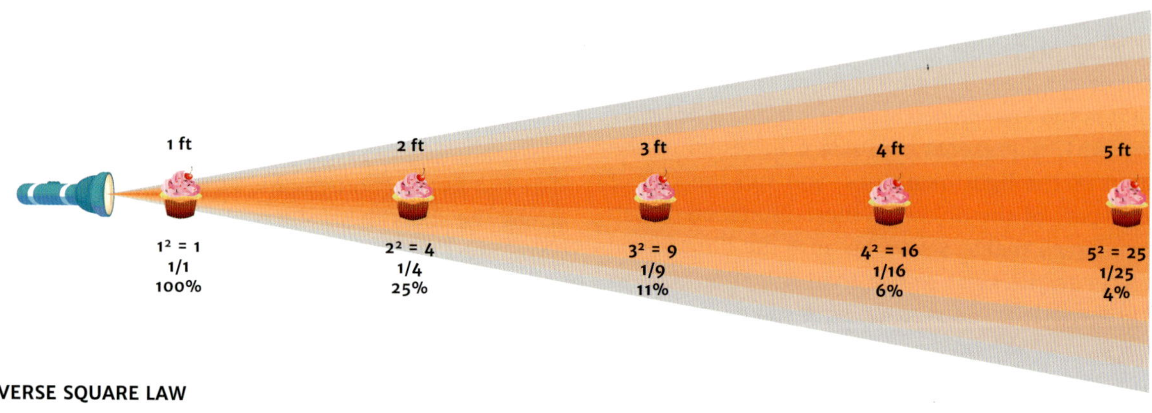

THE INVERSE SQUARE LAW

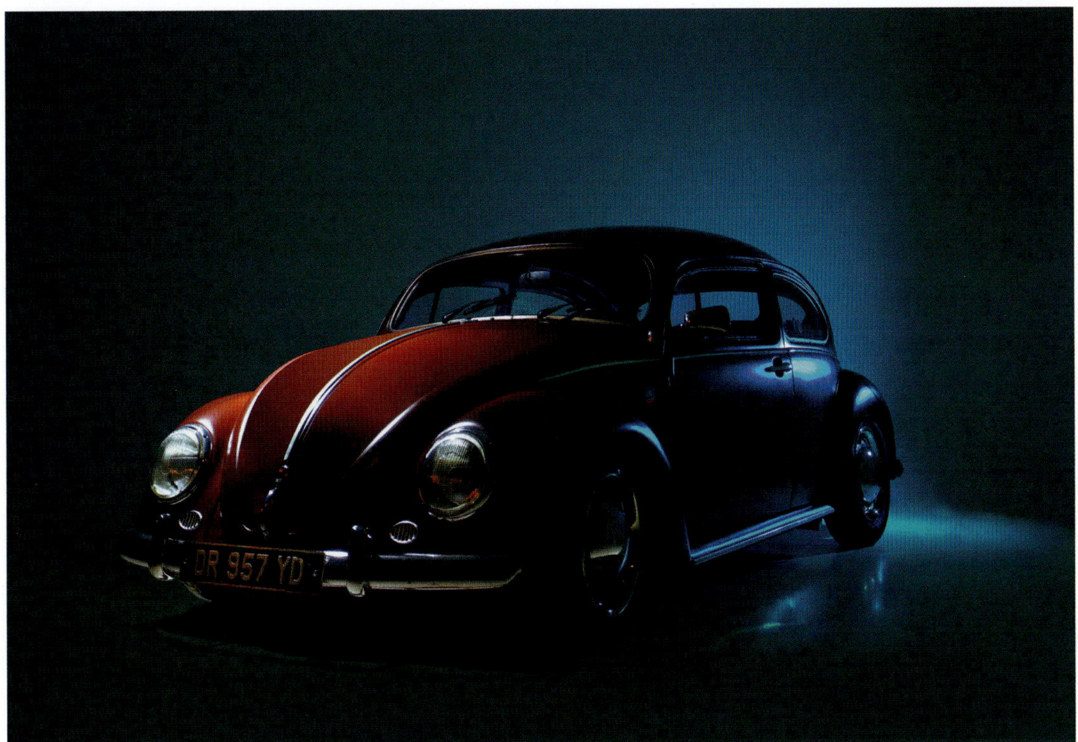

« The main lighting was placed on the frontmost part of the front-right fender (to our left as we look at the car), about three feet away. The luminance decreases rapidly between this area and, for example, the top of the front-left fender (to our right).

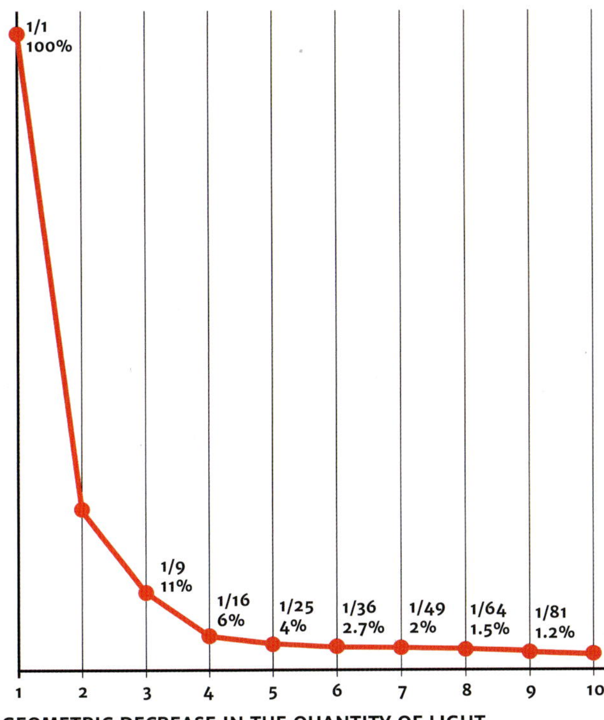

Direct and Specular Reflections

We saw earlier that direct and specular reflections are just as luminous as the source that lights them, and that is true no matter the distance. We can see a good illustration of this on the rear-left fender of the VW bug. In this shot, the source with cyan gel was placed at ten feet. But in spite of the weakness of the light projected there (–2 EV compared to the lighting on the front), the light on the back of the car and on the door on the left side of the car (on our right) shows a direct reflection that is almost clipped (blown out). I would have gotten a similar result in terms of luminance whatever the power of the flash, whether I placed it at ten feet or thirty feet. The luminosity of the direct reflection is in fact constant, no matter the distance from the source. This might seem like it contradicts Newton's inverse square law, but if we look more closely, we will see that even though the luminance doesn't change, the size of the reflection does. To be precise, the surface of the reflection changes according to the inverse square law: if at 1 yard the direct reflection measures 10 square inches, then with a source placed 2 yards away it will measure 2.5 square inches.

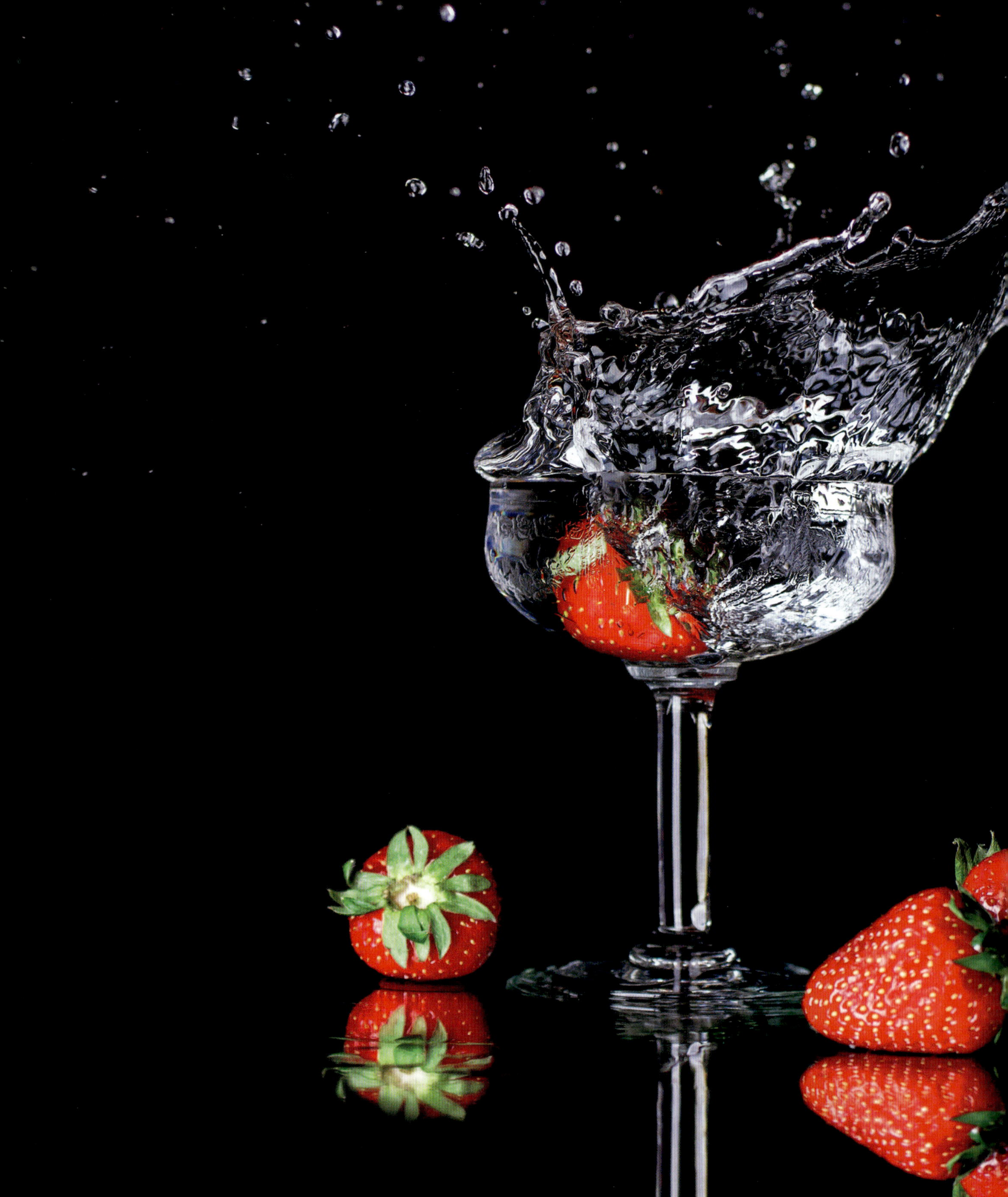

SHAPE, TEXTURE, AND MATERIAL

2

» **78**   Light and Texture
» **81**   Mixed Surfaces
» **83**   Parallelepipeds
» **85**   Complex Shapes
» **87**   Spheres and Rounded Shapes
» **92**   Cylindrical Shapes
» **96**   Lighting Glossy Metals
» **98**   Lighting Glass

LIGHT AND TEXTURE

So far, we have looked at objects with smooth, flat surfaces. But in most cases, objects have a texture that needs to be showcased.

If we don't make a point of illuminating it in a way that brings out the texture, a sponge will look like a brick, or like any old vaguely flat parallelepiped that produces diffuse reflections. It is the sponge's texture, made up of a multitude of variously sized holes, that allows us to identify it as a sponge. If it produced direct reflections, the angle of the lighting wouldn't matter: we would be able to discern the material through the reflections and shadows (because the texture of the sponge is oriented in all directions, some of them would be placed within the family of angles). But because this is a matte object, we have to use a different solution. For a sponge, as for all matte textured objects, it is the angle of incidence of the light rays that is most important.

Density and Orientation of the Source Light

When we are lighting the weft of textiles (except for satins and other glossy fabrics), raw leather, and any other matte textured surfaces, we don't have the advantage of being able to play with the reflections. This is because these objects produce only diffuse reflections, and so whatever the axis of the incident light, we will obtain a similar rendering, whether or not we are within the family of angles. Therefore, we need another strategy here.

What makes us appreciate a texture visually is the proximity of the juxtaposed light and dark areas, which define the object's peaks and valleys.

When placed directly in front of the object (see diagram opposite), the light will illuminate the peaks and valleys in the same way: the texture is completely erased, and the light and dark areas run into each other. If, however, we place the light source to the side, forcing the light rays into an oblique angle, the peaks will remain illuminated but will produce shadows in the valleys, which will be more or less pronounced depending on how deep the valleys are.

At a glancing angle, this side light bumps up against the high points of the sponge's surface, creating shadowed areas that our eye identifies as hollows, deeper or less so depending on their level of illumination.

Texture and Light Quality

We can emphasize the presence and density of shadows, and thus reinforce the texture of the object, by decreasing the proportion of half-light. Thus, it is a matter of producing a hard light: we can either use a small light source (a flash equipped with a zoom bowl, for example) or choose to move it farther away. This kind of lighting will emphasize the contrast between the light and dark areas.

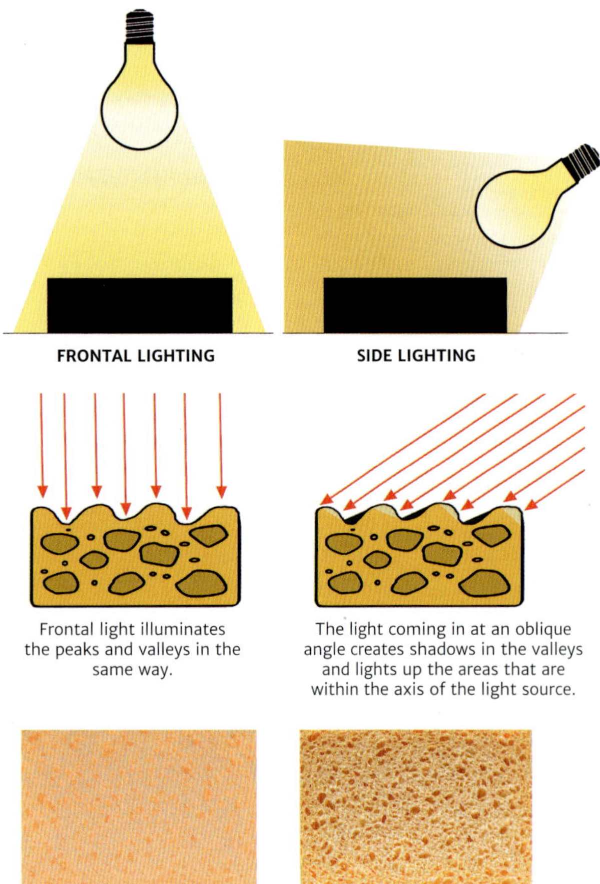

Frontal light illuminates the peaks and valleys in the same way.

The light coming in at an oblique angle creates shadows in the valleys and lights up the areas that are within the axis of the light source.

THE EFFECT OF SIDE LIGHTING ON A TEXTURED SURFACE

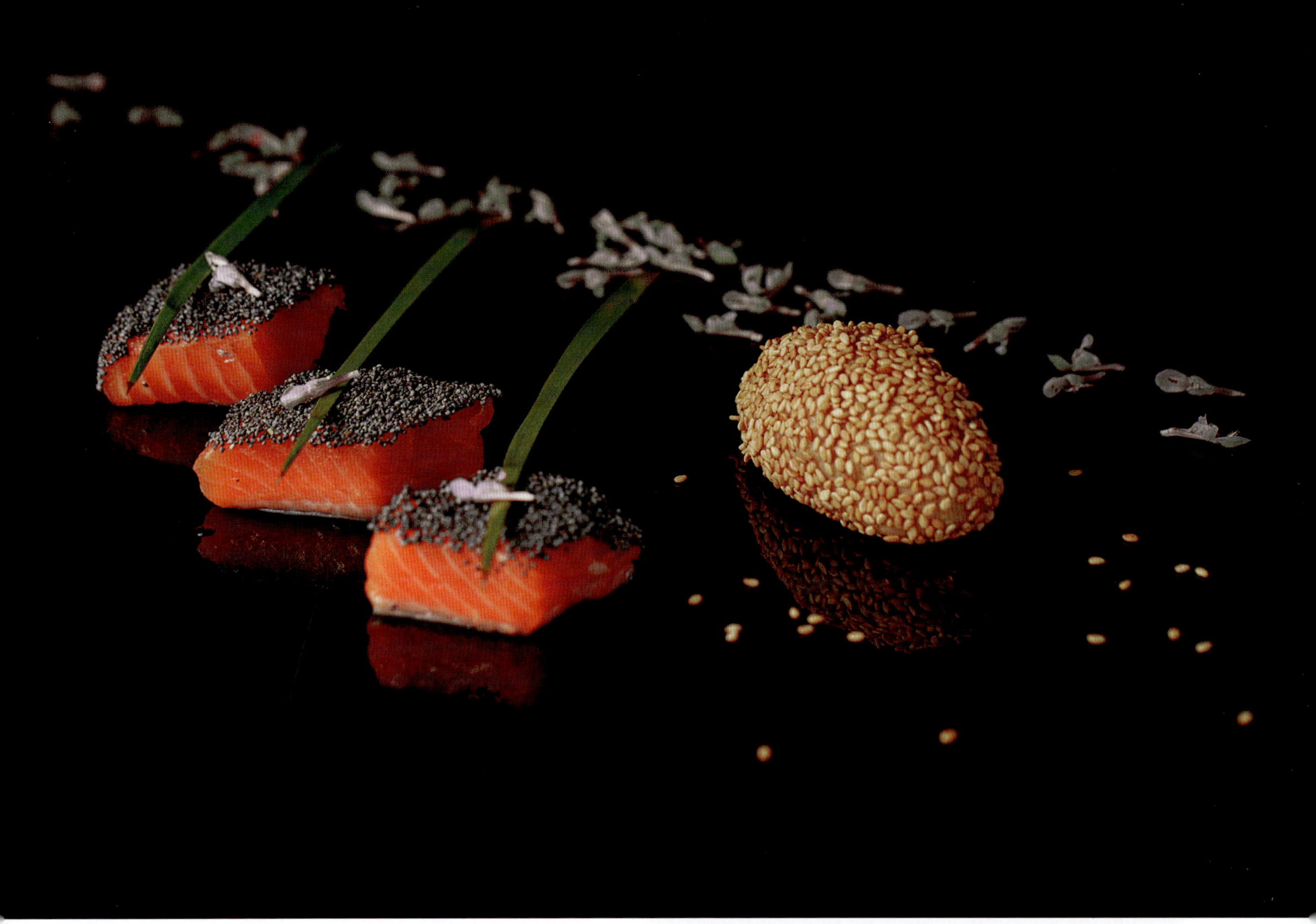

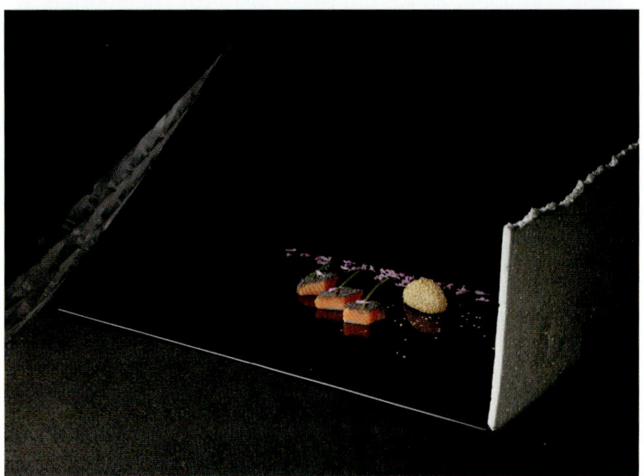

Moreover, because of the inverse square law and the oblique orientation of the source light, we could get different levels of luminance on the parts that are closer versus those that are farther away from the source; this is undesirable, and is not well suited to the object. Therefore, it is wisest to move the light source farther away (for a small sponge, six feet would be more than enough). This will inevitably cause a very pronounced shadow on the background, which is also not necessarily appropriate. We can get rid of that by using either a reflector or backlighting.

Texture, Direct Reflections, and the Object's Color

You might deduce that all textured objects should therefore be illuminated from the side. But as we will see, we also have to take their color into account. Let's photograph two notebooks, one made of black leather and

⌃ In order to highlight the chia seeds on the tuna sashimi and the sesame seeds on the hummus ball, we needed to place the light source at a very oblique angle.

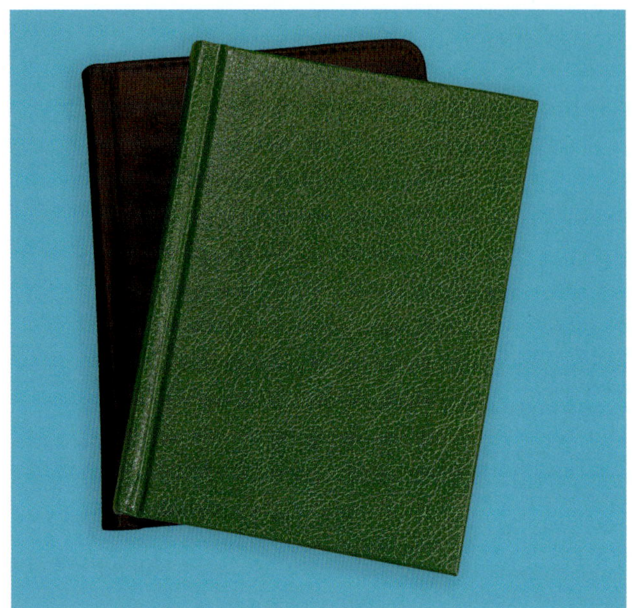

⌃ I've superimposed two leather notebooks of two different colors. The same lighting angle will not work to show the texture of both.

while the shadowed areas will merge with the color of the leather. We should note that because of the phenomenon of absorption, matte black objects reflect very little diffuse light. Glossy or satiny black objects, on the other hand, though they don't reflect diffuse light, do produce good direct reflections.

So this is the range we will have to look in. By placing the light source and the camera within the family of angles (in this case, a source tilted at 45°), we can finally make the texture appear, which will allow the viewer to better understand what the object is made out of and how it is made. Note that unlike with the sponge, for which a small, faraway source was appropriate, here we need a large, very diffuse source that covers the entirety of the object in order to capture how the cover really looks; I chose a large softbox placed at about twenty inches. A small or faraway source would have created overly pronounced direct reflections that would have given a very different impression.

the other of green leather, both of them slightly satiny. Although they are made of a similar material and have been placed under the same lighting, they each react differently to the light and generate different reflections: their textures, even though they are similar, are not oriented in the same way. If we place side lighting on the green notebook, as we did previously for the sponge, we will see the distinction between the shadows and the highlights on every ridge and inset; if we place the same light at the same angle on the black notebook, the highlights will disappear (because we are not within the family of angles that allows us to discern direct reflection),

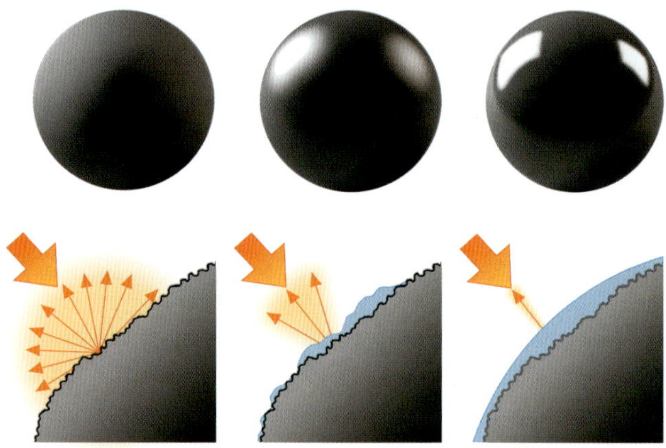

MATTE, SATINY, AND GLOSSY SURFACES

MIXED SURFACES

The life of a product photographer would be easy if all we had to do was photograph things with uniform surfaces, but that doesn't happen very often. Let's take a look at a case study.

So far, we have seen how to light and photograph objects that produce only one kind of reflection: diffuse reflections for matte objects, direct reflections for satiny objects, and specular reflections for objects that are very glossy and very smooth. But manufacturers often mix materials, colors, and textures: wood and glass, raw concrete and glossy plastic, highly textured leather and brushed metal. Thus, as always in photography, we have to make choices, because each kind of material requires its own particular lighting.

Which Method to Use?
For the photo at right, I chose to illuminate a perfectly cylindrical, entirely black vase with a lacquered flower pattern and a textured matte surface. The only simple solution to the problem of the mixture of materials was to allow only the diffuse reflections to appear, and I did this by illuminating the vase from outside the family of angles: at 45°, from above. This solution, although it

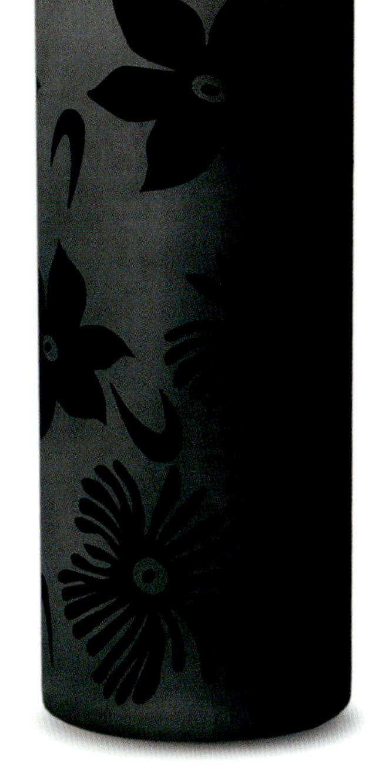

» A vase lit from below at a 45° angle in a lateral overhead shot to avoid direct reflections from the glossy black flowers and maintain the object's cylindrical appearance.

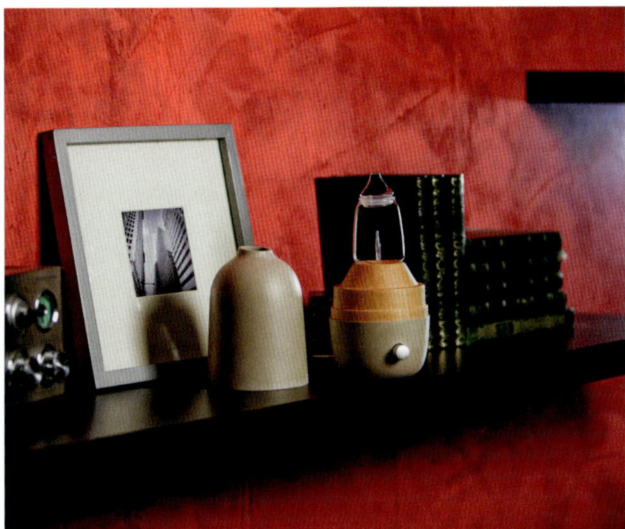

Setting up a shot for an essential-oil diffuser with a ceramic and satin-finished wood base and a transparent glass lamp that produces pronounced direct reflections.

was attractive, meant that one important aspect of the vase's appearance was sidelined—namely, the glossiness of the black flowers. I could have also played with direct reflections, but the cylindrical form meant that I needed to use a frontal source that was large enough to cover at least three quarters of one of the flowers, and the result was unsatisfactory because it took away the sense of the cylindrical shape (achieved by showing one side darker than the other).

This is all just to explain that, no matter how you approach the problem, it is technically impossible to resolve all of the opposing requirements of such an object with just one light. Thus, you have to choose to either ignore one of the aspects of the object (such as the glossiness of the flowers, in the case of this vase) or create a composite photo (several images, lit in different ways, which are then combined to make one photo at the end) to show all of them.

Composite Method
For another project, I had to stage a shot of an essential-oil diffuser with a ceramic and satin-finished wood base and a transparent glass lamp (see photo at left). As we will see in the section where I discuss this in detail, the method for illuminating transparent glass is completely different from the method for opaque objects, like this diffuser's

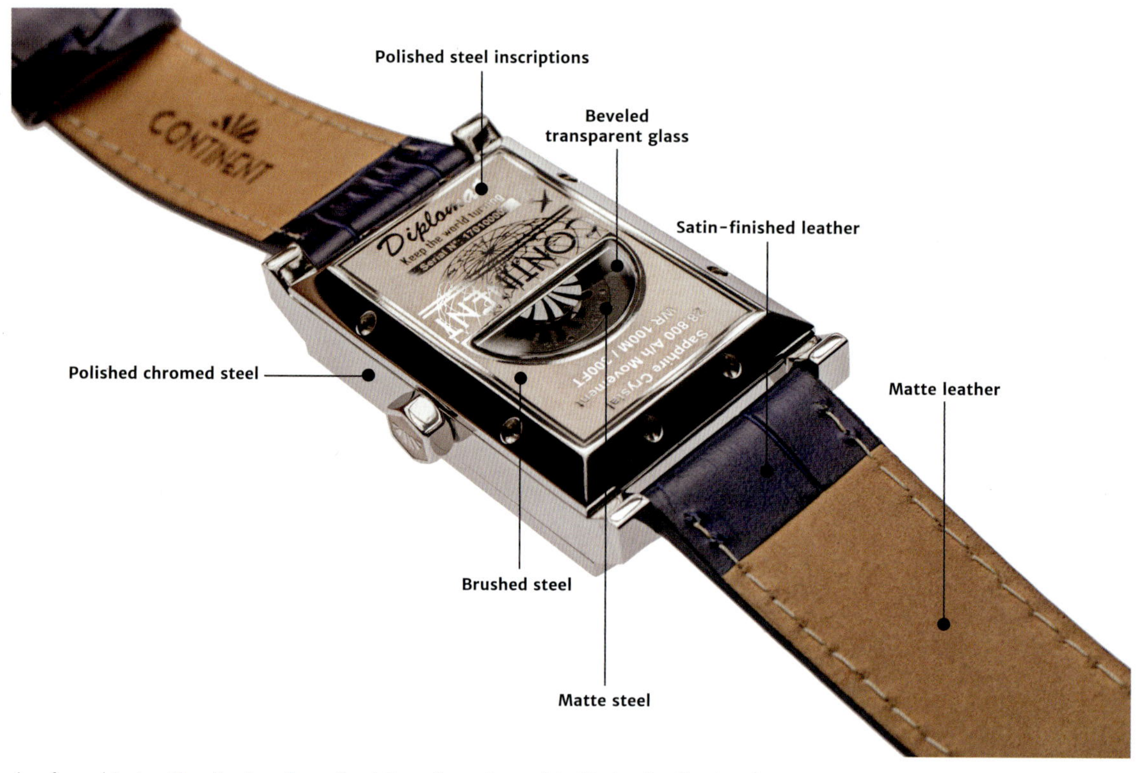

⌃ Example of an object with mixed surfaces (and therefore all possible kinds of reflections).

base. One major difficulty was that the object had to be staged on a shelf close to a wall, making it impossible to use backlighting, which would have been perfect for the glass lamp. In other words, there were irreconcilable constraints. Unless I wanted to plan for a long process of digital editing, the only way to manage this was to create two shots, with different lighting for each.

For the wood and ceramic base, the process was pretty simple: place a large light box (16 x 24 inches) directly in front of the diffuser, at 45°, and take advantage of the ceramic cover behind it to create a reflection emphasizing the cylindrical shape of the object. For the glass, on the other hand, I needed the reflections not to appear except on the sides. To make that happen, I took away the books, put a strip of black cardboard behind the glass, and set up a small Profoto B10 light (small enough to sit on the shelf) to create the reflection at the edge of the cylinder's family of angles. The two photos were both taken with the camera on a tripod, with the same camera settings, so that I would get the exact same angle and framing for each. Then I merged the two images together in Photoshop, keeping only the aspects of the light that I wanted and needed.

Discernment

Even though I've just presented an example where this was not true, do keep in mind that the issues of reflection can usually be solved using a single source. This is the case, for instance, with the watch back shown above. The object has six different kinds of surfaces, producing reflections that range from very diffuse (the matte leather part of the watchband) to highly specular (the transparent glass and the polished steel). A large octabox, placed at a 25° angle to the object, did the trick. Then, all I had to do was place a small wedge under the watch to anchor it at the exact angle where direct reflections appeared on part of the polished steel inscription and on the glass, while keeping the beveled portion of the polished chrome steel case outside the family of angles, in order to create a contrasting effect. All of this preparation required a lot of meticulous attention to detail, but you should know that you can solve most problems by observing the object and moving it in relation to the light source.

PARALLELEPIPEDS

Six-sided polyhedrons, such as cubes, cuboids, and rhombohedrons, can be presented and illuminated in many different ways. But there is only way that makes it possible to create a clear representation of their shape.

If you only present one side of the cube to your camera, all you will see in the picture is a square, and the viewer will have no way to clearly understand what kind of shape it is.

This is why it is customary to always present three sides, in what is called cavalier perspective, while making sure that each side occupies a different area from the other two. By establishing a hierarchy among the sides, using the position of the object and the position of the luminous intensity on each of the sides, we convey the weight of the shape in space.

Positioning Cubes

The ideal position of a cube in relation to the camera is what we see with the yellow cube in the illustration below. Its vertical square side is at a slight three-quarter view to the lens, which is at a slight bird's-eye angle so as to show a large part of the top-facing square side and an equal part of the second vertical side. It's clear to see, in comparison with the red cube, that this provides a clearer view of the shape and gives more density to the image.

The goal is to find a position that will allow the viewer to get the best possible sense of the shape, and the only way to do that is to establish a hierarchy of importance for the various sides of the cube, as much in terms of the space they take up as in terms of their luminance.

Positioning Cuboids and Rhombohedrons

Cuboids (rectangular parallelepipeds) and rhombohedrons (parallelepipeds whose sides are all lozenges) follow a more subtle rule than cubes. Here, we will take a less overhead perspective: it's a matter of de-emphasizing the top side and giving more importance to the vertical side that is next to the main vertical side we see. We will do the same with the lighting for each of the three visible sides.

Direct Lighting

Parallelepipeds can be lit using direct light (unless they create direct reflections, in which case we will either have to over-diffuse the source light by placing a diffusing fabric in front of it, or use backlighting by redirecting the light flux with reflectors, as we will see in the section on page 143). It is important that the light source be placed at a right angle to one of the three sides, in this case the one that we want to highlight. We will make sure that the lighting is optimized at +1.33 EV by measuring it with an independent exposure meter. The second side in the hierarchy should be lit by the edge of the source light; the third will be left in shadow. This is all reasonably easy to manage when the object is relatively large, but is more complex when it is small because there is a danger that the light source might end up lighting the other two sides too much from the side, creating very

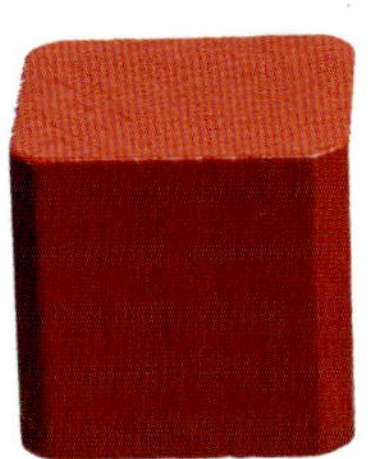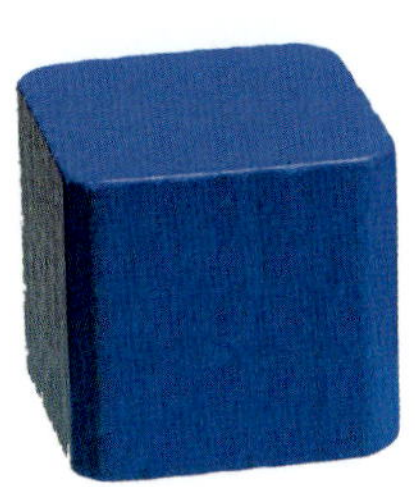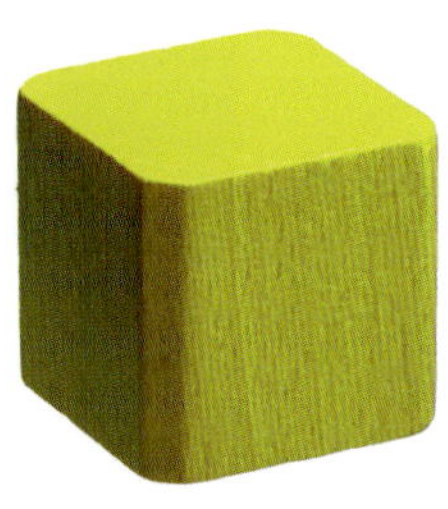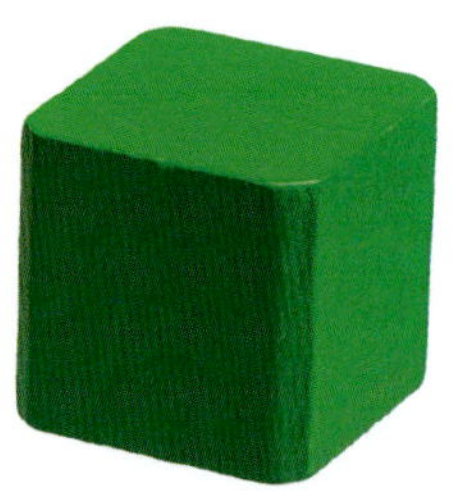

« Setting up children's building blocks so that each of three sides is shown.

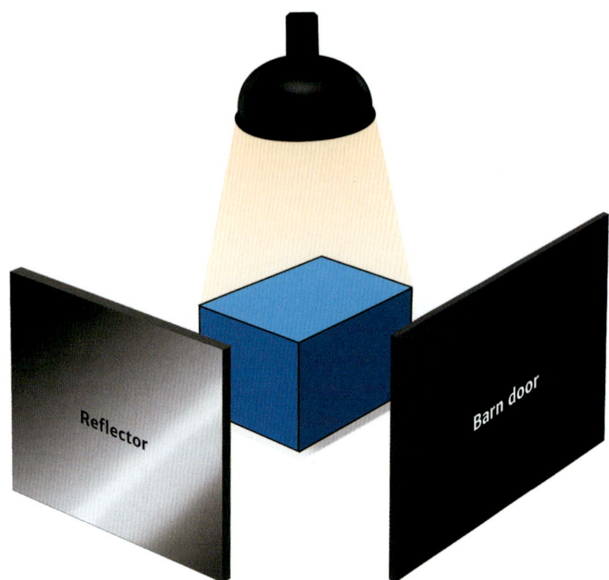

⌃ Each of the three visible sides of the parallelepiped requires a different level of lighting so that the object can be easily comprehensible within the space.

undesirable nuances in the lighting. For this reason, we generally use a different method that is easier to implement, as shown in the diagram above.

Barn Doors and Reflectors

The simplest method, and the one that I recommend, is to place a light source at a right angle to the side that you want to highlight, while making sure that its flux will reach a reflector that you have placed facing the second side, which will therefore be less illuminated than the first side, but still visible. Then, using an exposure meter, determine the distance required to make the reflected light measure between -0.5 EV and -1 EV. If the light is correctly positioned, the third side should be measured at between -1 EV and -2 EV—if the measurement is higher than that, which can happen if you are working near a bright wall or a window, you can set up a black barn door.

Dealing with Boxes

In product photography, we often have to deal with boxes. It is customary to present them open, so that the viewer can see what they are being used for. In this case, it is no longer a matter of showing three sides, but in fact, at least six, because the inside of the lid has to be visible as well as the bottom of the box, if possible.

The lighting must be positioned to illuminate this part of the box as well.

Backlighting

For glossy parallelepipeds, such as a product in a blister pack, direct lighting could potentially cause shine problems, especially if the light source is hard. Thus, we use backlighting, pointing the light source at a reflective background (usually white). The light is redirected according to the method indicated in the diagram shown at left. However, there is then a risk of getting an overly pronounced direct reflection on the top part of the object, depending on the viewing angle of the shot. We usually deal with this problem by placing black barn doors above the object (often very close to it). If this doesn't work, then we have to change the axis of the shot (by going higher up).

Cast Shadows, or Not?

The issue of cast shadows below the object is a recurring one in the world of packaging shots. We generally try to ensure that there is always a slight shadow, even against a perfectly white background, to avoid the impression that the object is floating in empty space. But depending on who or what the photo is being used for, the client may sometimes ask for there to be no shadows at all. In that case, the objects can be arranged on sheets of glass, about four inches from the support: this will make the shadow disappear, as in the shot below.

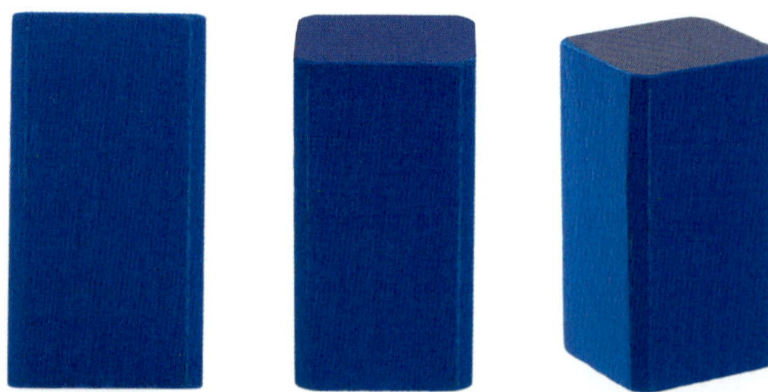

⌃ It's easy to see here why it is desirable to show three sides of the parallelepiped rather than just two or even just one.

COMPLEX SHAPES

As with parallelepipeds, shots of complex shapes must show half of the
visible sides of all polyhedrons, with a distinct luminance on each of
the sides.

Whatever the polyhedron, regular or not, it is important
for its shape to be immediately comprehensible when it
is shown in an image. The work of positioning the object
and the lighting has to do, first, with giving good visual
indications, especially in terms of shading.

Placement of Polyhedrons

Looking at the photo shown here at the right, it is impossible to determine the actual shape of the second object
from the top (no. 1)—it was photographed from the front
and we can only see six of its sides. In fact, it is the same
shape as the fourth object from the top (no. 2), of which
we can see nine sides. Even worse, object no. 1 looks like
it is a different color because the high point of the light
source is on the middle of the construction. Both of these
polyhedrons are octadecahedrons (eighteen-sided). Thus,
the placement of object no. 1 is not good because with only
six sides showing, the viewer might mistakenly believe that
it is a dodecahedron (twelve-sided). As with every shape
that we photograph, it must be placed at an angle and
photographed in cavalier perspective, such that we can see
half of the object—or even more than half, as with prisms
(where we show three out of five sides), pyramids with a
triangular base (where we show three out of four sides),
and pyramids with a square base (three out of five sides).

Hollow Polyhedrons

As with parallelepiped boxes, for hollow polyhedrons, we
need to show their interiors. We accentuate the overhead
view so as to present the maximum number of interior
and exterior surfaces possible, using lighting that will
allow the entire shape to be comprehensible.

Lighting

As much as possible, we try to give each facet of the
object its own distinct lighting. Because of the angle of
incidence of the light falling on each of the sides facing in multiple different directions, this is not actually
that hard to accomplish, and one light source is usually
enough—provided that we position the light source to
be at a right angle to one of the sides. Because the other

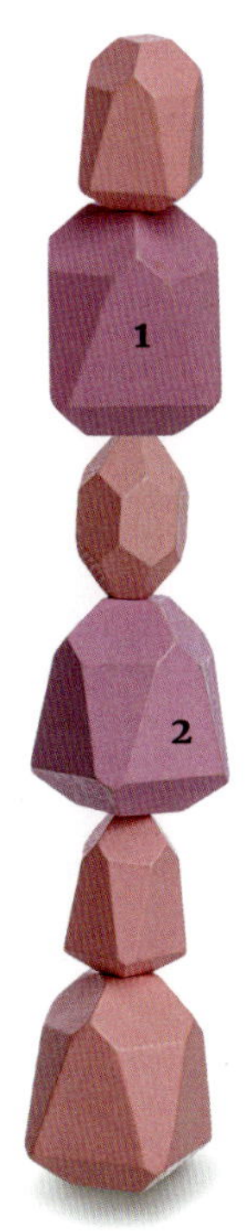

>> Make sure that each side of each
polyhedron has its own distinct
illumination to properly preserve
the sense of the shape of the body
in space.

sides are all arranged at different angles, the shading will
all look lighter or darker, which will make it easy to tell
them all apart. As with parallelepipeds, it's very helpful to position reflectors and/or barn doors while paying
attention to the angle of the primary light source and the
general reflectance of the work area.

Irregular Polyhedrons

These methods of illumination and of positioning the
light sources work well for regular shapes: I see eight
sides, and therefore I deduce that there are eight more
sides I don't see. This is obviously only a speculation,
but it's how we usually decipher the visual cues. If the
object only has one hidden side, it is easy to show it
resting on that side. If there are more than that, we can
also consider placing a mirror behind it to show what's
hidden behind.

Complex Polyhedrons

There are, of course, a host of other kinds of shapes—
regular or not, convex or not—whose positioning can be
hard to figure out. Keep in mind that you always want to
show as many sides of the object as possible. As far as
lighting is concerned, for non-convex shapes, you will
gain a lot by making slight shadows appear in order to
accentuate the sense of perspective. A light sheen on an
object's edges, especially if they are beveled, will also

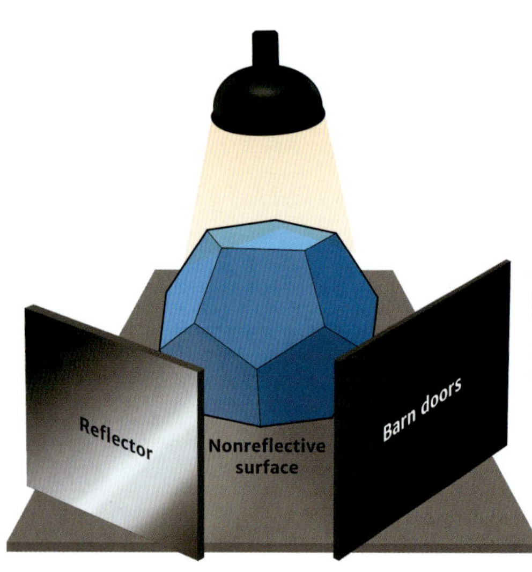

« Each of the six visible sides of the dodecahedron requires a different level of lighting so that the object can be easily comprehensible in space.

» This vase is part sphere and part cylinder.

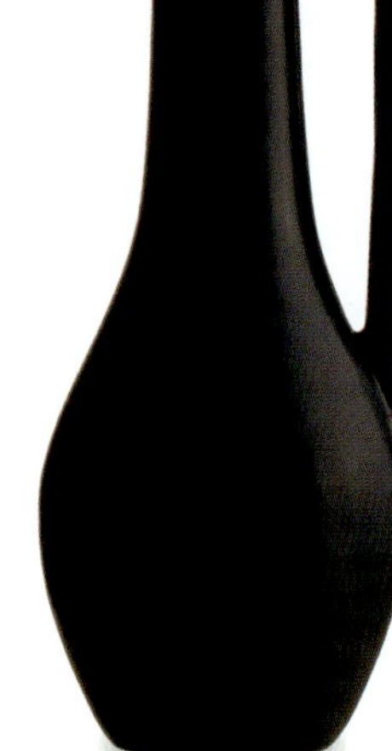

help the viewer get a more precise idea of the overall shape of the object.

Shapes and Direct Reflections

When the surface of the polyhedron is made of a glossy or satiny material, and therefore produces direct reflections, it can be a good idea to choose a very soft lighting (using a large diffusing fabric or a sheet of thick translucent paper, for example) or to use backlighting. If you do choose backlighting, you can set up the reflected light by arranging one or more reflectors at a variety of distances and angles to produce distinct lighting nuances and shades on each of the sides. You can also position one or more barn doors to accentuate the shape.

Five Large Families

All shapes can be categorized as belonging to one of five large families: flat objects (such as a painting); simple polyhedrons (such as cubes, prisms, and pyramids); complex polyhedrons; cylinders; and spheres. The vase shown above right is partially spherical (in its bottom portion) and partly cylindrical (in the top portion). For each of the shapes, you can apply the methods already described. You will see that they apply to almost all situations.

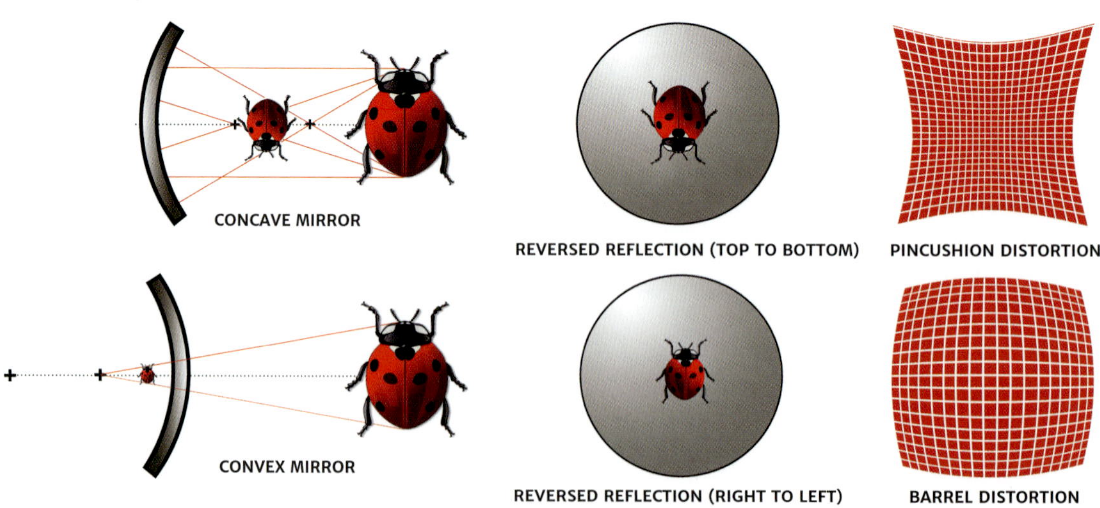

SPHERES AND ROUNDED SHAPES

Spherical and spheroid objects are among the most complex shapes to light, especially if they are varnished, like Christmas tree decorations. Whether it is a perfect sphere or simply a rounded object, the way that the laws of reflection are applied is different from the way light works for shapes with flat sides.

From teaspoons to watch faces, from coffee mugs to computer mouses, rounded shapes are everywhere. And as with spheres, the path of the reflected light rays follows a different logic here than for those we have studied so far.

The Spoon as an Example

Take a spoon, place it so you are looking at the convex side, and note: your face will appear right side up, distorted in the center, and with everything around the edges seeming to become narrower and longer. Along the edges of the spoon, you will also see elements that are very far away from you. You are dealing with the particular geometry of convex mirrors, in which what is close to the center looks rounded, and reasonably sized, while the closer you get to the edges, the more the lines appear receding and shortened, following the principle of barrel distortion (see page 86). Then, if you turn the spoon over to its other side, you will find the opposite phenomenon: you will appear upside down, and the light deviations will follow the principle of pincushion distortion: this is the geometry of concave mirrors.

Concave (or Convergent) Mirrors

The geometrical optics of spheres will help give us a better understanding of the phenomenon at work here. If we take a look at the diagram on page 86 showing what happens in a concave mirror, we will note that the actual image of the ladybug is reversed, because the light beams intersect at the focal point in front of the mirror. It appears inverted and distorted, following the rules of spherical geometry.

In other words (and looking at the diagram at the top left of page 88), when the incident ray is directed parallel to the principal axis, it is reflected on the focal point (red arrow); when it passes through the main focus, it is reflected parallel to the main axis (green arrow); and when it passes through the center of curvature, it is reflected onto itself (blue arrow).

We can use the table on page 88 to help us understand the result in terms of the image reflected by the mirror.

- When the object is located an infinite distance away, only the parallel rays are taken into consideration, and the image obtained is very small (i.e., the size of a point), located at the mirror's focal point. It looks real (non-distorted).
- When the object is behind the center of curvature, the image is smaller than the object, real (because it is on the same side as the object), inverted (because it is upside down from the object's orientation), and positioned between the focal point and the center of curvature.

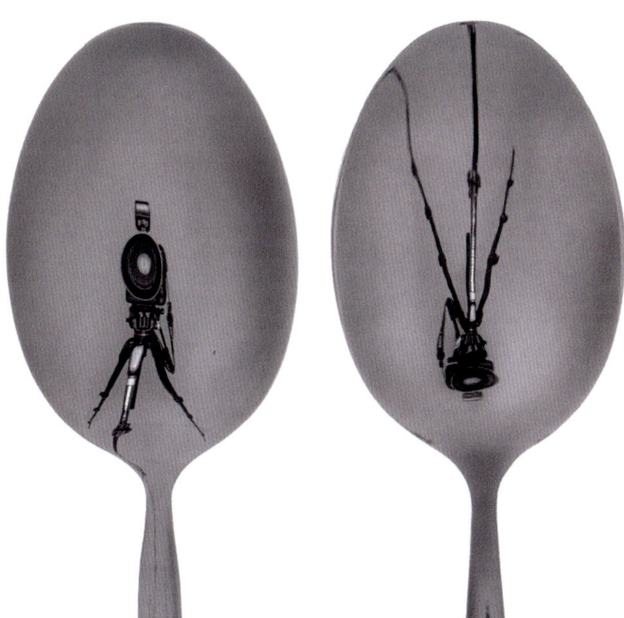

⌃ Depending on whether the spoon is photographed on its convex side (1st shot) or concave side (2nd shot), the reflections of the camera and the tripod will appear either right side up or upside down, and with either barrel distortion or pincushion distortion.

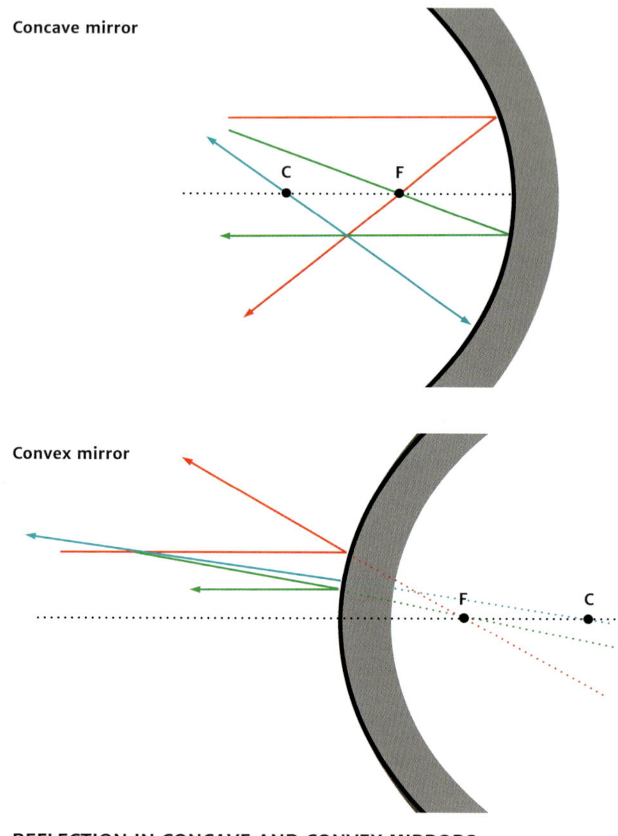

REFLECTION IN CONCAVE AND CONVEX MIRRORS

	Properties of the Image			
Position of the Object	Nature	Orientation	Size	Position
Infinity	Real	Inverted	Very small (the size of a point)	At F
Behind C	Real	Inverted	Smaller than the object	Between F and C
C	Real	Inverted	The same as the object	At C
Between C and F	Real	Inverted	Larger than the object	In front of C
F	No image			
Between F and vertex	Virtual	Right side up	Larger than the object	Behind the mirror

PROPERTIES OF THE IMAGES IN A CONCAVE MIRROR

	Properties of the Image			
Position of the Object	Nature	Orientation	Size	Position
All Positions	Virtual	Right side up	Smaller than the object	Between F and vertex

PROPERTIES OF THE IMAGES IN A CONVEX MIRROR

- When the object is at the center of curvature, the image is the same size as the object, real (because it is on the same side as the object), inverted (because it is upside down from the object's orientation), and positioned at the center of curvature.
- When the object is between the center of curvature and the focal point, the image is larger than the object, real (because it is on the same side as the object), inverted (because it is upside down from the object's orientation), and positioned in front of the center of curvature.
- When the object is located at the focal point, no image can be collected because the reflected rays cannot meet (they are parallel).
- When the object is located between the focal point and the vertex of the mirror, the image is larger than the object, virtual (because it is on the side opposite the object), right side up (because it has the same orientation as the object), and positioned behind the mirror, farther away from the mirror than the object is.

Convex (or Divergent) Mirrors

The exact opposite phenomenon is observed in the case of a convex mirror, where the focal point is behind the mirror: on page 86, the image of the ladybug appears smaller, but right side up. The shape of the mirror deflects the reflected rays after they hit the object.

When the incident ray is directed parallel to the principal axis, it is reflected in such a way that its extension is directed toward the focal point (red arrow); when the extension of the incident ray is directed toward the focal point, it is reflected parallel to the principal axis (green arrow); and when it is directed toward the center of curvature, it is reflected back onto itself (blue arrow). But the most important thing is that unlike with the concave mirror, where the position of the reflected object has a

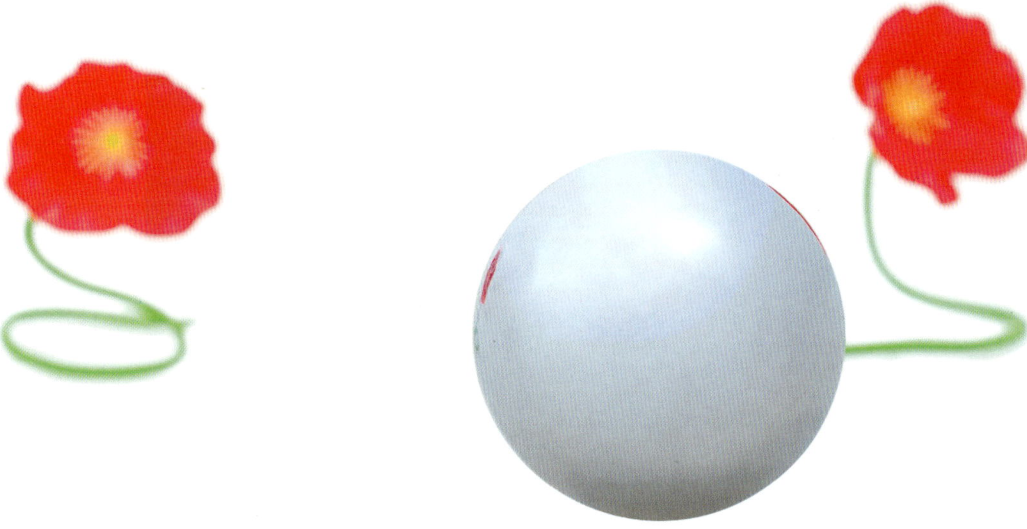

huge influence on the result in terms of the reflections, in this case, with the convex mirror, it hardly matters where the object is: the properties of the image will always be the same, in that the image will always be virtual, right side up, smaller than the object, and positioned between the focal point and the vertex, both of them behind the mirror. Note, finally, that the image appears to be closer to the mirror than the object is.

This last property will be key in most cases of lighting spheroid shapes.

Reflections in Spheres

A glossy spheroid object, whether it is a true sphere (such as a Christmas tree ornament), a circular or cylindrical object (such as a wine bottle), or even just a glossy object with rounded edges, will react to reflections in the same way as what we have just examined.

In the photo above, I placed a glossy polished-steel twelve-inch-diameter ball on a white table made for packaging shots. I then placed two plastic poppies about ten inches behind the ball, at about 140° and 220°, respectively (see the diagram at right).

When we look closely, we can see that each poppy has a reflection that appears on the respective side of the ball, with a change in proportions. The reflection appears within the sphere, even though the object creating the reflection is positioned behind it; and the reflection looks smaller, longer, and narrower. This last property will allow us to understand how to proceed in lighting spheroid objects.

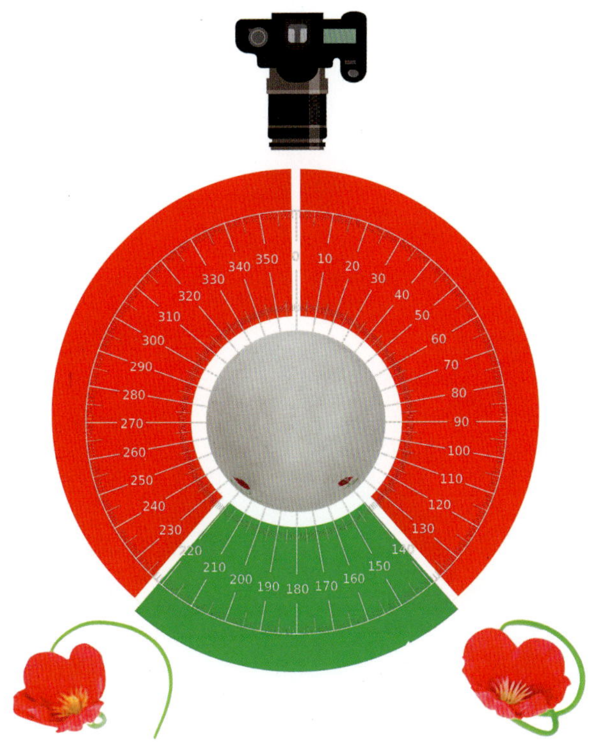

Placement of the poppies behind the ball shown in the photo above, at 140° and 220°, respectively.

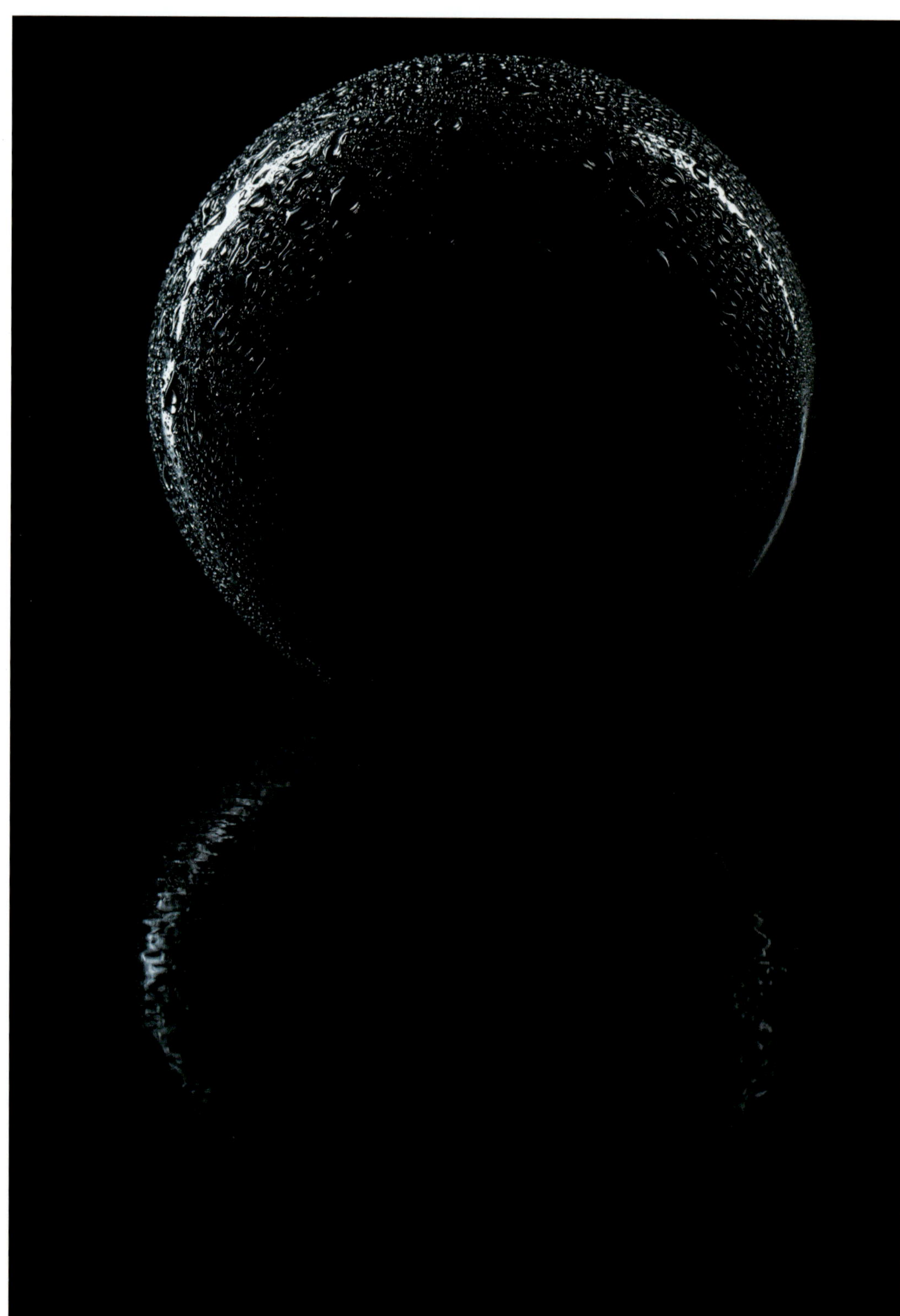

« Example of a
photograph of a glossy
sphere illuminated by
two light sources, placed
at the edge of the family
of angles. I don't appear
in the reflection, and
neither does my studio,
because I made sure
to work in the dark
with carefully directed
light sources.

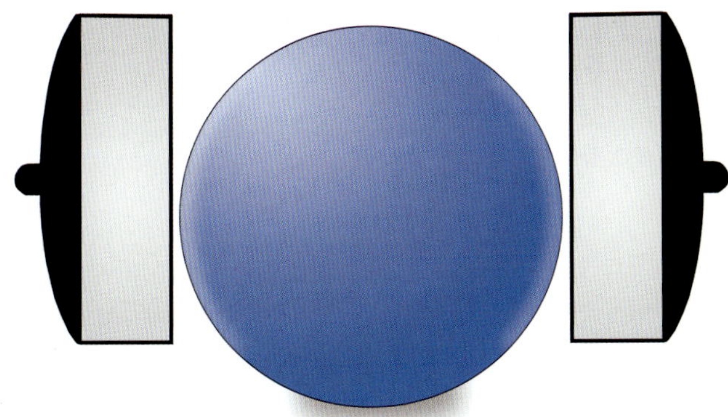

Managing the Reflections of Spheroid Objects

I want to make it very clear that spherical and spheroid glossy objects will reflect anything within their family of angles, which is about 280°: the table they're sitting on, the ceiling, the side walls, and, of course, the space in front of them. When we light this kind of object, it is thus impossible not to see our own reflection as well as the reflection of the space in which we're shooting. Therefore, it is important to make sure that there is no light source positioned in front of the sphere (to avoid direct reflection) nor anything illuminating the work space. These two principles are fundamental.

There are a thousand ways to proceed. I work in a solid-color brushed-cotton tent (this kind of fabric, brushed using a machine that gives it a fuzzy appearance, allows you to avoid all direct reflections). I am careful to hide the camera behind this piece of cloth, in which I have made an opening for the lens. If you choose black as the color, the sphere will look like the photo on the opposite page. The important thing is that the sphere be positioned in a closed, non-reflective environment of uniform color and luminance. Then, place the light sources at the edge of the family of angles, ideally at 140° and 220°—depending on the desired placement of the reflection, and depending on how spherical the object is, you could push that as far as 110° and 250°.

Lighting Transparent Spheroid Objects

So far, I have only addressed opaque spheroid objects, but we are also frequently confronted with transparent objects. This is the case for the lamp shown to the right, for bottles of white wine and rosé, and for a multitude of other objects.

The reflection issues remain the same, but the goal is usually different. We will look at ideal methods in the section on lighting glass, but the main thing to remember here is that, just like for opaque glossy spheres, the light sources can only be positioned behind the object, outside the family of angles; otherwise, reflections will appear. There are, of course, cases when that is desirable, and in those cases we can apply the methods we have described for objects of classic shapes, especially since, if the background is sufficiently illuminated, the frontal reflection will be mostly blurred and it's likely that the reflections of the space and the photographer will be very diminished. In such cases, we can use a more traditional procedure, with the sources behind the object, but without bothering with a tent.

Lighting Opaque Matte Spheroid Objects

Non-reflective objects do not pose any particular problems, but it is important to understand that even though they only produce diffuse reflections, opaque matte spheroid objects still have the same family of angles as glossy objects. Thus, we only rarely light them from the front; the light sources generally need to be positioned to the side or behind, as we will see on the following pages, in order to maintain the impression of roundness and regularity in the placement of highlights and shadows.

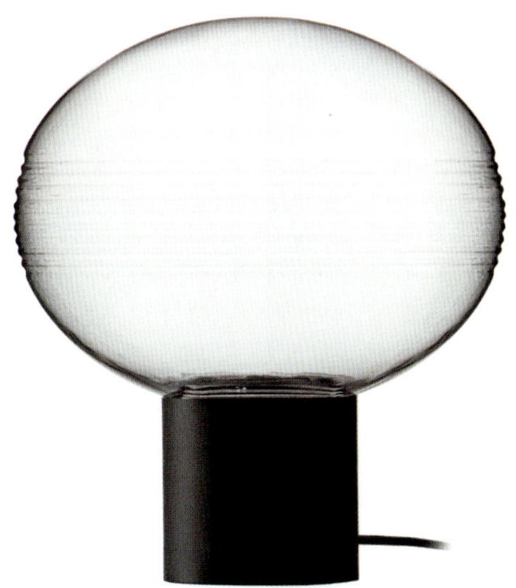

CYLINDRICAL SHAPES

Cylinders react to light the same way that spheroid objects do, but only along one axis. This greatly simplifies the lighting and the shot.

The particular shape of the cylinder, which can be found in a large number of the objects of daily life (from bottles to cosmetic vials, and including cans and some light bulbs), requires positioning the light source so as to show the shape of the object while avoiding direct reflections.

Matte Cylinders

Because matte cylindrical shapes produce only diffuse reflections, and there is no risk of direct reflections, they do not present the same kinds of challenges as glossy spheres: in other words, they do not require the light sources to be positioned outside of or on the edges of the family of angles. However, they do require that the lighting be placed in a particular way to convey a clear sense of the shape.

Unless you use special lighting for cylinders that is adapted to their shape, it will be difficult to make out what they are in the image. This is the case, for instance, for the matte plastic bottle presented below at the left: if it is illuminated from the front (which is what we do when we want to present a branded product), we lose a good portion of the sense of roundness of the visible portion, which can only be deduced from the shape of the object's silhouette. Lit by a frontal source, the cylinder could just as well be a parallelepiped presenting one of its sides. Uniform lighting will not allow the viewer to understand the shape.

To represent a cylinder accurately, you will need part of it to be in shadow and for there to be a marked difference in shading between the different parts of it, although that shading difference needs to be as gradual as possible.

Matte cylinders are generally illuminated with lateral sources. When it is positioned in that way, the light will make a shadowy section appear on the opposite side (see the diagram below), of varying size depending on how diffused and large the light source itself is.

« Illuminated from the front, we get the sense that this cylinder has a flat side; we lose any realistic sense of its shape.

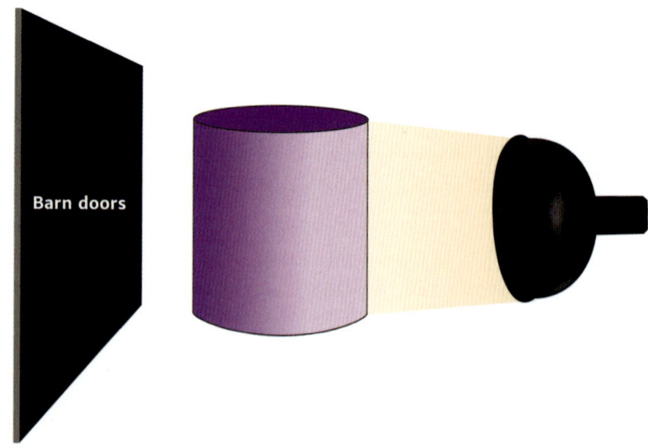

⌃ A cylinder is lit from the side. We can increase the contrast by placing a barn door opposite the light.

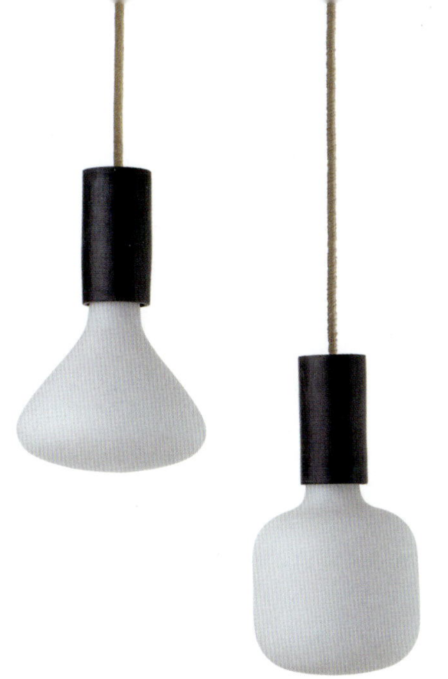

A small or distant light source provides a hard lateral light, and therefore a very pronounced shadow on the cylinder, and causes the gradualness of the shadow to decrease. This kind of lighting does not properly reflect the shape of the cylinder because it gives the impression that the shape we are seeing has two sides: one dark, one light, as with a cube. Instead, therefore, we will choose a larger and/or closer light source, so that we can create a shadow that is less dense, but more gradual, and which supports our sense of the roundedness of the object.

Similarly, we generally avoid reflectors that are placed too close because even though this would help to illuminate the shadow, it would also run the risk of distorting the viewer's perception, making it look like there is a bright facet in the area illuminated by the reflection.

As we can see in the lighting of the matte plastic ice cream cone below, all versions of lateral lighting (with or without barn doors and reflectors) result in an interesting and shape-appropriate look, with greater and lesser amounts of contrast between each area. None of the lateral lighting setups shown here is better than the others: we must keep in mind that in photography, we are appealing both to logic and to emotion, and that the luminous "feeling" that we expect from an object depends largely on the viewer's own sensibilities and the purpose of the image.

Glossy Cylinders

In terms of the reflections around its edges, a glossy or shiny cylinder positioned vertically reacts exactly the same way as the glossy spheres that we looked at in the previous section.

Before we proceed to the lighting, we first have to decide what result we want to achieve. Take the example of a wine bottle: people expect to see one or two reflections, soft and even, on either side of the bottle, along its entire length. To achieve this, we will have to place one or two light sources (depending on how many

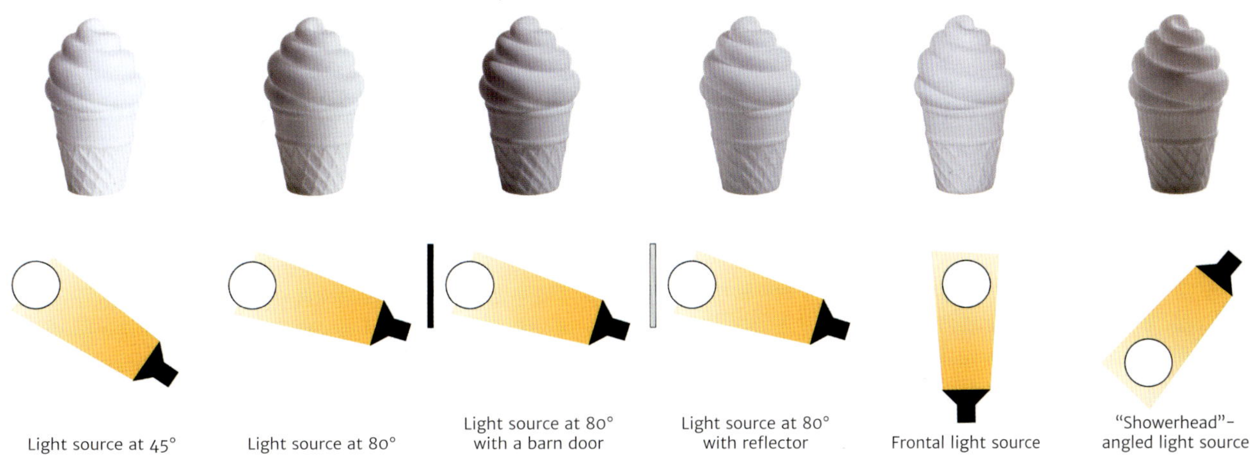

ILLUMINATION AND PLACEMENT OF SHADOWS ON A MATTE CYLINDER

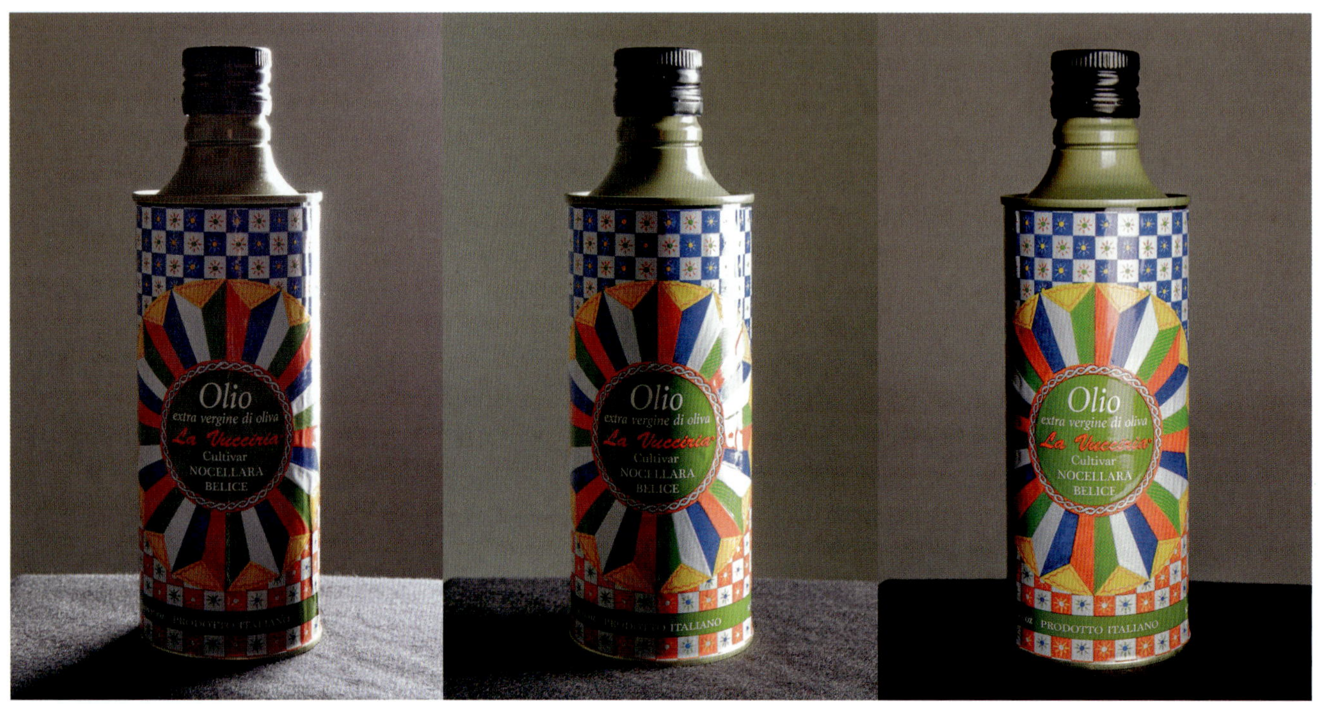

Lighting at the edge of the family of angles: the reflections appear along the edges of the glossy opaque cylinder. Lighting within the family of angles: the object has visible reflections that you can choose to keep, while making sure to shape the light sources appropriately.

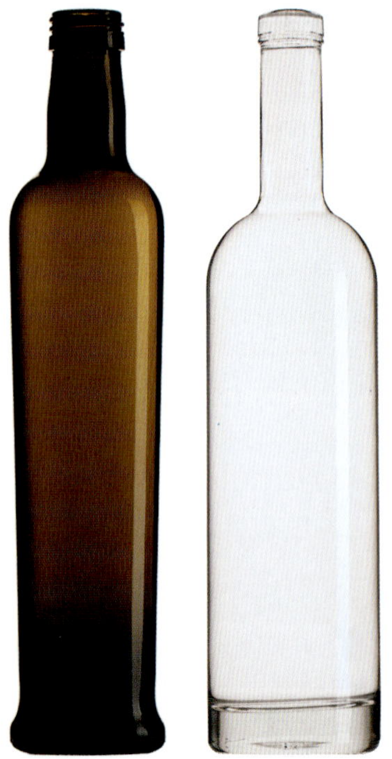

« For these two bottles, backlighting was used, with two barn doors at the edges of the family of angles, and illumination with a strip box placed in front, in order to achieve a reflection on the front part of the objects.

reflections we want) right at the edge of the family of angles (approximately at 140° and 220°; see page 89).

For soda cans, the rules are more variable, and depend on the brand and the era. Coca-Cola has long published images showing very soft reflections on either side of the can, and then two more on the front; other brands (like Red Bull) prefer to show their cans with darkened edges (using barn doors) and one or two fairly bright, narrow reflections on the visible side.

I find it to be most elegant to create a very soft reflection all across the visible side by positioning a sheet of thick translucent paper covering the entire family of angles, in which I make an opening for my camera lens. With a good backlight, the translucent paper becomes a passive source, shading the entire can. Because the reflection is smoothly present everywhere, it seems invisible, as you can see on the next page, on the right.

The main thing is to maintain the sense of the shape and to have a good understanding of where the reflections will appear, based on their placement with respect to the family of angles, which will allow you to identify what is needed in terms of lighting, diffusion, and accessories.

On the other hand, it is absolutely necessary that the reflections, if they are present, appear in the shape of bands, running up and down the entire length of the product. Little round bright spots, or any other shape of reflection, should be avoided. Rectangular light boxes or strip boxes are generally used for this purpose and will help you achieve the result you need. You can also use rectangular diffusing fabrics (or translucent paper, etc.), choosing the size based on the result you are looking for.

Transparent Cylinders

Because they react to the light exactly the same way that opaque cylinders do, we try to avoid visible reflections on the front side of transparent cylinders. Backlighting is therefore preferred here: visible backlights, if we're trying to achieve a white background (in which case the light source itself will constitute the background, usually through a diffusing fabric), or, if the background is to be black or colored, backlights arranged at either end of the borders of the family of angles so as to obtain a bright outline along the edges of the cylinder.

As with glossy opaque cylinders, you can also choose to have reflections appear on the front side of the object, making sure that they are rectangular, all one piece (not multiple small spots), and placed within the vertical axis of the cylinder.

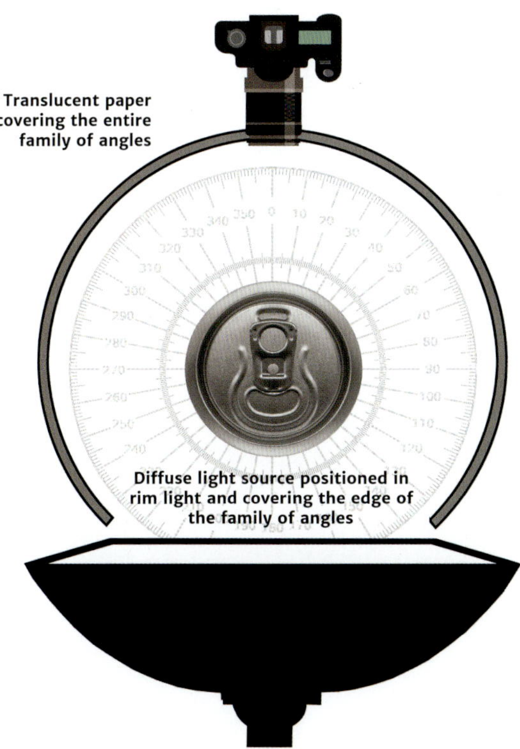

LIGHTING DIAGRAM FOR A GLOSSY CYLINDRICAL OBJECT

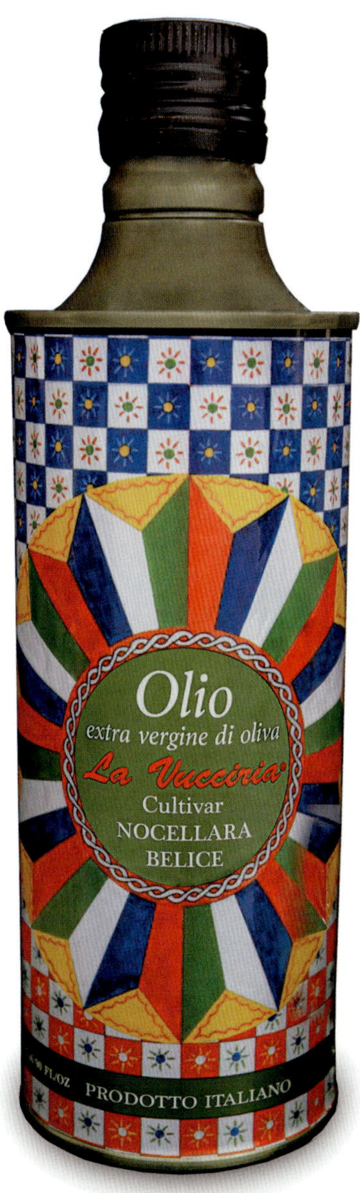

⌃ Glossy cylindrical olive oil bottle illuminated using the method of rounded translucent paper covering the entire family of angles.

LIGHTING GLOSSY METALS

Unlike raw metals, which basically produce diffuse reflections and which can therefore be lit in all different ways, polished metals require a carefully orchestrated lighting strategy.

Polished metals act like all surfaces that produce direct and specular reflections, as described by Snell's law—like mirrors and all the varnished objects we have already looked at.

Strategy

Depending on its axis in relation to the lighting, a polished steel knife can appear gray, black, or white (which corresponds to lighting on the edge of the family of angles, outside of it, or fully within it). Taken individually, none of these three kinds of reflection satisfactorily accounts for the reality of the object, because when we see a chrome-plated object it involves the simultaneous presence of all three kinds of reflection on its surface.

Like all materials that produce direct reflections, polished steel reflects what is within its family of angles: not just light, but also the environment that the object is within.

As with the cylinders we looked at in the previous section, it quickly becomes clear that it is easier to photograph the object in an environment where there is only white, black, or gray to be reflected (in other words, a tent, a light box, or a studio painted all one color), or else to place reflectors and barn doors in the places that the photographed object might otherwise reflect back.

To obtain perfect reflections that are appropriately placed, the position of the camera with respect to the object and the light source is still key.

With polished metal, unlike for most surfaces (where we try to avoid allowing reflections to appear), direct reflections are actually a key part of the visual experience. Without direct reflections, the metal looks grayish or completely opaque, just like any old matte object. Therefore, we try to present the glossiness, making sure that part of the direct reflection (which appears in the shape of a white line) appears on the object, the rest being gray or black. The glossier the object (such as with brand-new polished-steel items), the more precisely delineated the outline of the direct reflection will be. For brushed or worn steel, that border will be less distinct, with more blurring.

Thus, we make sure that the object is placed within the family of angles of the light source, by placing it so that the light source appears as harmoniously as possible in relation to the edge of the flux (which is what causes reflections to appear or not). And we make our decisions based on the shape of the object: a knife should not be

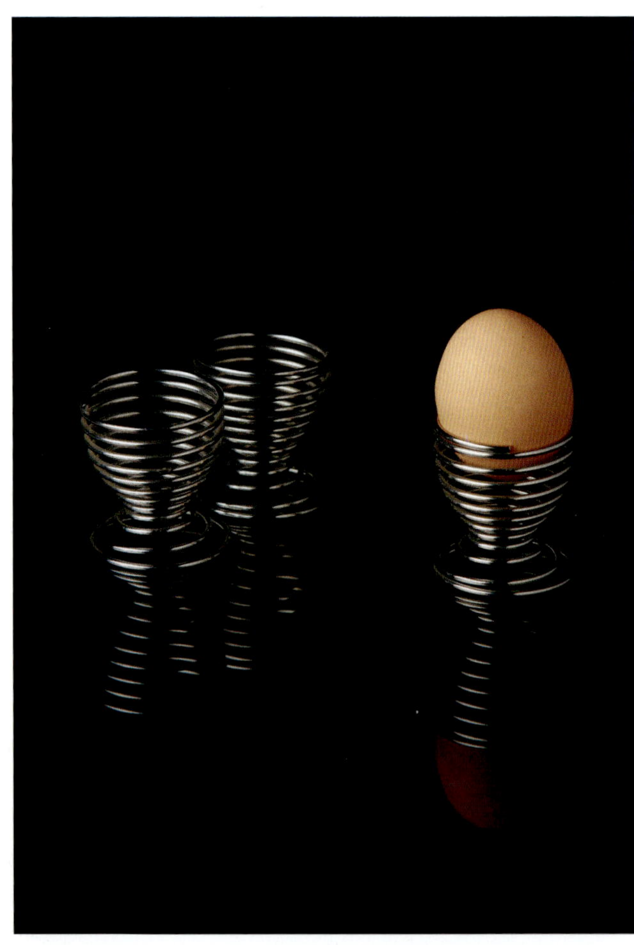

⌃ Traditional way of showing chrome-plated metals: black, white, and gray.

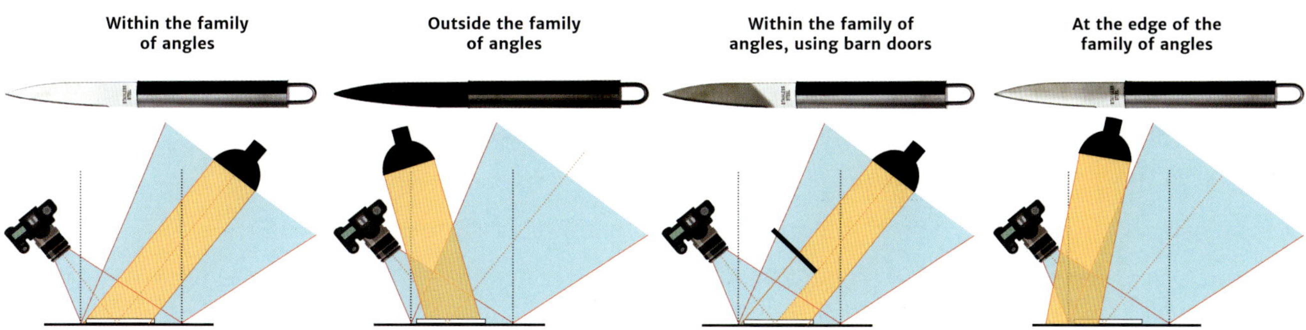

MANAGING DIRECT REFLECTIONS ON METAL

illuminated in the same way as a spoon. For a knife, we expect a direct reflection all along the length of the blade and the handle, whereas for a spoon, we try to obtain a smooth direct reflection covering the entire bowl of the spoon.

Lighting

Ambient lighting and light sources outside the family of angles have no effect on polished metal, which produces hardly any diffuse reflection. But the question of direct lighting is absolutely key. We have already seen that the luminance of direct reflections does not vary with distance: you can bring the source closer to the object all you want, but the "intensity" of the direct reflection will not change. On the other hand, the distance at which the light source is placed has a considerable effect on the base the object is sitting on: the larger or nearer the light source, the brighter the base will be the and the softer the shadow cast by the object. Conversely, the smaller or farther away the light source, the less illuminated the base will be and the harder the shadow cast by the object. To properly adjust our light sources and our camera, we perform a measurement using an independent exposure meter to define the correct exposure for the metal, optimizing the result, as always, at +1.33 EV.

Adaptations

There are as many ways to illuminate polished metal items as there are objects, each shape requiring a specific placement of the light sources. In addition, the intended purpose of the image is important. When we are creating a photograph for a high-end tableware catalog, we position the object to produce a direct reflection only on the handle, using barn doors for the blade to obtain a smooth gray. If the photograph is meant for a mass-market catalog, we will generally offer an image ranging from light to dark gray.

FOCAL LENGTH

If the framing is identical, the distance from the camera to the object will vary based on the focal length, which means that the apparent size of the direct reflection can vary considerably just because the observer is not standing in the same place and their angle of view is not the same. You will probably find it more comfortable to work with a long focal length (> 100mm), which will allow you to more accurately position the reflections exactly where you want them, because the area in which direct reflections appear will be minimized.

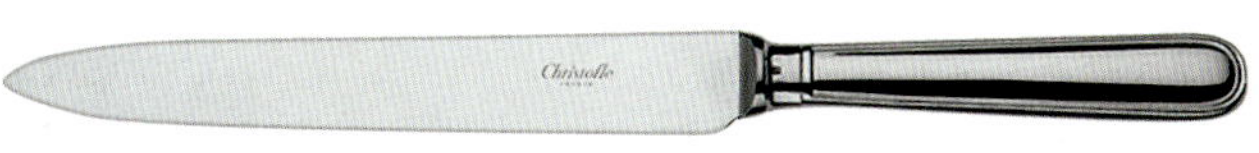

⌃ Traditional presentation of a knife for a high-end tableware brand.

LIGHTING GLASS

Glass combines two kinds of challenges that can seem extremely difficult to a novice photographer: its propensity to produce specular reflections, and its transparency. If, in addition to that, you are dealing with spheroid surfaces, such as the surfaces of wineglasses, the lighting task may seem impossible.

RULE OF THUMB

We have seen that, in order to avoid direct reflections, objects have to be placed outside the family of angles. However, if it is a spheroid object, as most drinking glasses and bottles are, we know that the family of angles covers almost 280°. Therefore, we can only illuminate the glass from behind, whether directly or in reflection. Any other approach will fail, unless the goal is actually to see a reflection.

Like polished metal, glass produces both direct and specular reflections, and if it is perfectly clean, no diffuse reflections at all. However, unlike metal, it generates polarized reflections (which vary according to the angle of incidence of the light and the shape of the glass). But even more important, when the glass is perfectly smooth, colorless, and transparent, there is no texture or surface to show.

Colored Glass

In reflections, what counts is not the color but the condition of the surface. First, therefore, we must determine whether we are dealing with opaque, frosted, or transparent glass.

Opaque Glass

Opaque glass objects, such as the bottle shown below, are some of the easiest objects to light. We use the same methods as those that are used for glossy cylinders, just

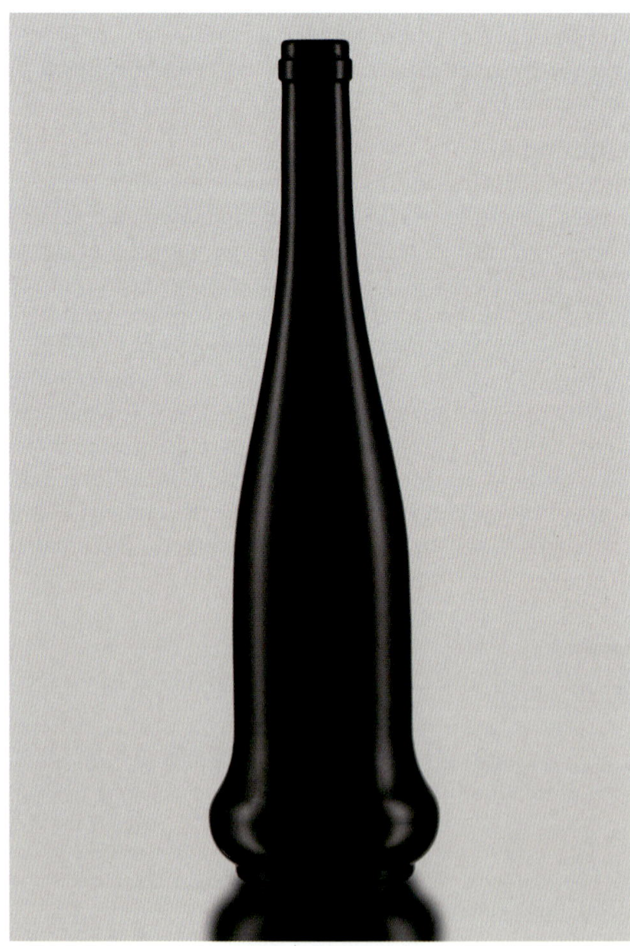

⌃ Photograph of an opaque bottle, with strip boxes positioned at 90° to either side.

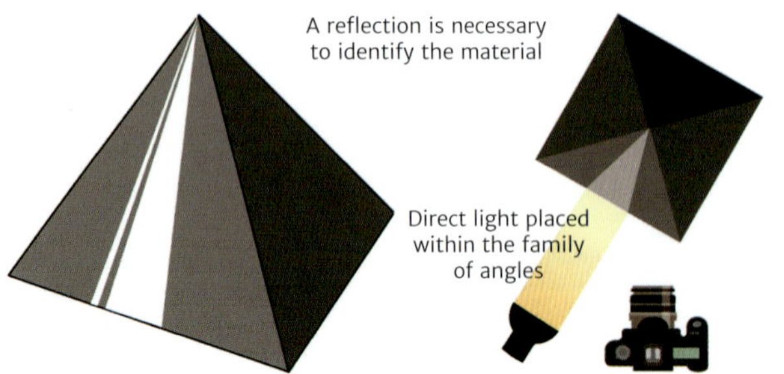

LIGHTING AN OPAQUE GLASS OBJECT

as we did for the glossy soda can. When it comes to bottles, however, tradition dictates that we cause one or two glossy reflections to appear: therefore, we position one or two strip boxes at the edges of the family of angles, or, as shown in the example on the previous page, at 90° on either side of the object (although in that case, the reflection will, of course, not be at the edge, but rather a little closer to the center of the bottle).

Frosted Glass

Unlike conventional glass objects, which produce specular reflections, frosted-glass objects generate diffuse reflections, which means that they can be illuminated however we want without running the risk of producing undesirable reflections. However, it is advantageous to light them in a broad, uniform way (using large octaboxes or large diffusing fabrics) to obtain a soft, unified rendering.

Transparent Glass

As with most glass objects, light passes through the object by simple transmission (see pages 55–56), meaning that there is none of the texture that normally allows us to "see" an object, and we can't count on diffuse light. On the other hand, glass produces specular reflections, which, while they attract the eye, do not give any information about the shape of the object or the condition of its surface. By correctly managing the quantity of light and making sure that the background does not reflect too much of it (which would cause the few shadings that we do have on the glass to disappear), it is nevertheless possible to obtain a presentable result by placing two light sources within the family of angles (see the diagram below). But the result will not be effective unless you fully understand the options and learn to carefully balance the quantities and qualities of light, as we will soon see.

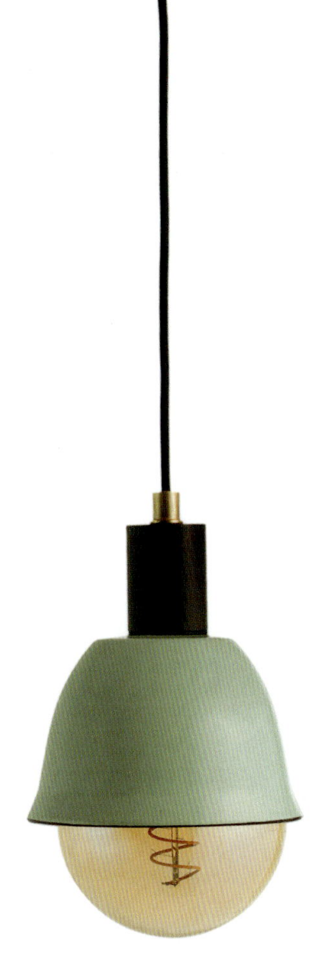

⌃ For this photo, where we needed to produce direct reflection on the metal dome and the black cylinder above the light bulb, we also end up with direct reflections on the lightbulb itself.

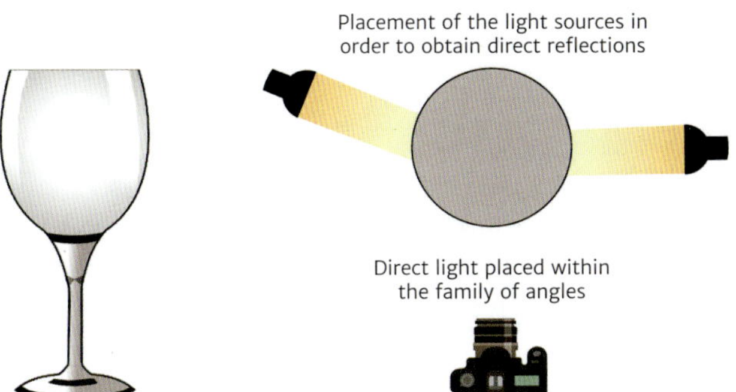

LIGHTING A TRANSPARENT GLASS OBJECT WITH REFLECTIONS

Instead of showing the object, it is better to show its shape by placing reflections along its edges. This will allow the various objects and their shapes to become clear through a play of contrasts between the light and dark areas, while eliminating direct reflections.

Snell's law has taught us that direct reflections appear when the observer is positioned within the angle of reflection of the family of angles of the source light. A source that is placed within the same axis as the observer, on a glossy surface, always produces direct reflections, which is why we always light glass from behind.

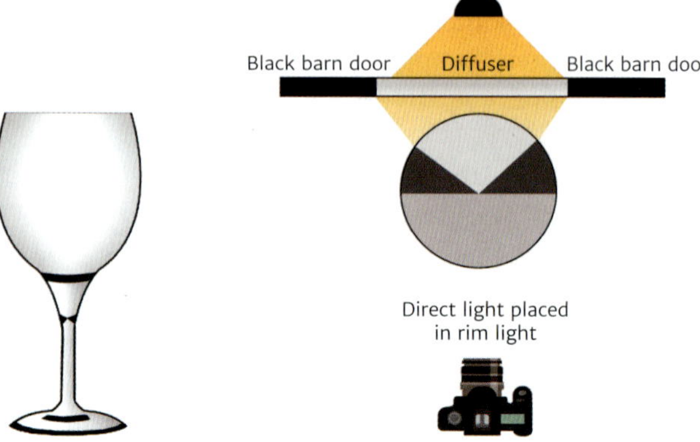

MAKING THE BLACK EDGES OF A TRANSPARENT GLASS APPEAR AGAINST A WHITE BACKGROUND

Lighting a Glass against a Light-Colored Background

The most common way to present a glass is against a white background (see illustration below). In this case, it's a matter of showing the glass's silhouette. You can find many examples of this in commercial advertising and in large retail catalogs.

Given that we do not want to see visible reflections, and that the glasses are generally spheroid, we need to adapt to the family of angles of this kind of shape, which is around 280°. The light can therefore only come from behind the object.

To achieve this result, we resort to a stratagem: because we need a perfectly white background, and we

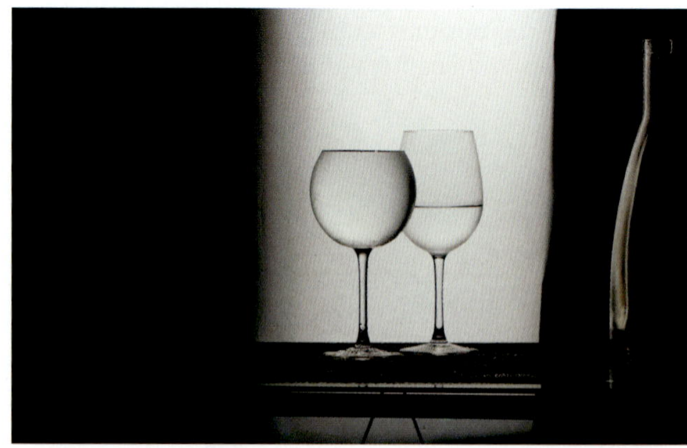

⌃ Lighting method for a glass against a white background. A strip box is installed behind a diffusing fabric. The shadowed area is positioned at the edge of the families of angles: the edges of the glass therefore look black.

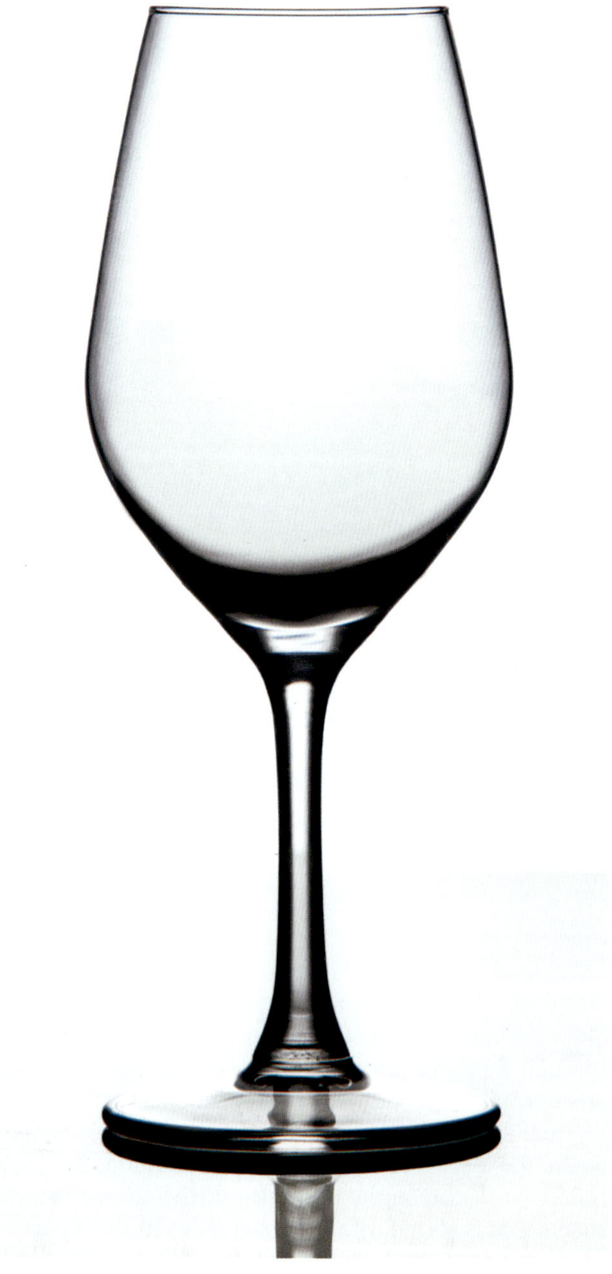

⌃ Traditional presentation of a wineglass against a white background.

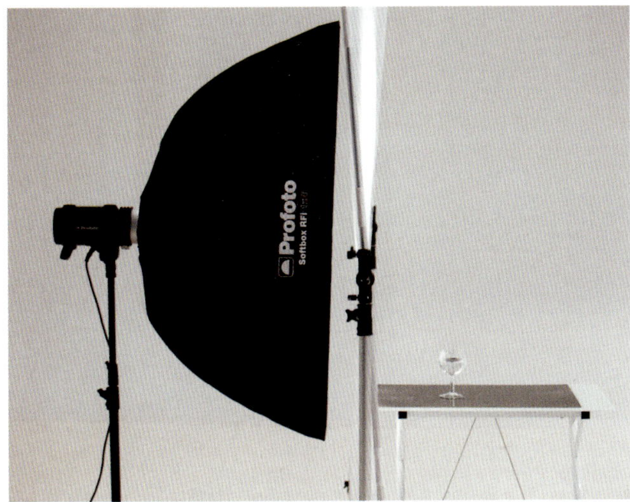

⌃ Setup for lighting a glass against a white background

also need a light source located outside the family of angles, why not combine the two?

What I like to do is place a strip box behind a diffusing fabric, close enough to make a shaded area appear around the edge of the object. It is this shaded area whose reflection we will see along the edges of the glass and which will produce the desired effect. Because the light source is placed against the light, I can adjust its strength (approximately +2.33 EV) to obtain a perfectly white background, while at the same time ensuring that there will be no undesirable reflections on the glass itself. You must be careful, however, to make sure that there is no lighting in the room except for what is directed at the glass, because otherwise reflections could appear. You could obtain a similar result by simply using the strip box, but the diffusing fabric, which you can also easily replace with translucent paper, gives the shadow of the silhouette a much softer appearance, while still maintaining a very smooth shading on the glass itself. In addition, depending on the kind and shape of glass that it is, the result can be adjusted by playing with the distances between the object, the diffusing fabric, and the strip box. This will allow you to fine-tune the density of the black, white, and gray.

Because we need to create illumination that will occupy all of the space behind the glass, so that the shot will have a white background (in other words, so that we don't have to do any retouching in our post-processing of the files), we have to make sure that the shadowed area is at exactly 140° and 220° behind the glass (see page 89);

otherwise, the silhouette will not be clearly delineated. If the lighted area is too large or overlaps too much with the family of angles, it will cause direct reflections, whereas if the area is too narrow, it will cause a black or white rectangle to appear within the glass. It's clear that the use of a strip box is appropriate for standard wineglasses but less so for decanters, for example. For something like decanters, you will probably have to cut a shape out of black cardboard to create the light shaper you need to fit the silhouette of the object.

Finally, it is necessary to place the glass at the appropriate distance so that the black reflections appear on it as clearly and sharply as possible. To make that happen, you can just move the glass back and forth until the position and the conjunction are just right.

While this method, thanks to the effects of overexposure between the quantity of light projected and the luminosity of the background (white on white), considerably reduces the problems of unwanted reflections and possible marks or smudges (from limescale, fingerprints, etc.), it does not solve the problems on the shaded or black parts. It is therefore always necessary to handle the glass with gloves and to make sure it is very clean (carefully cleaning it with white vinegar will remove the traces of limescale).

Lighting a Glass against a Dark Background

Once the method for illuminating glass against a light-colored background has been understood, it is easy to see that we can obtain the exact opposite result using a similar method. In the photo shown on the following page, we make direct white reflections appear on the outline of the glass placed against a black background.

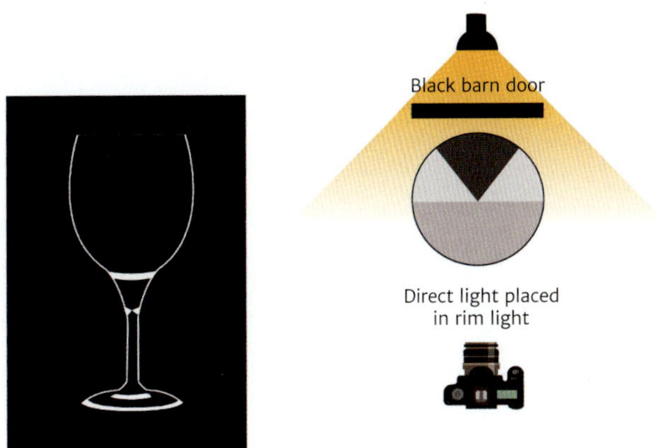

MAKING THE WHITE EDGES OF A TRANSPARENT GLASS APPEAR AGAINST A BLACK BACKGROUND

As we did with the glass against the white background, we make sure that the background (black opaque cardboard or paper) is adjusted to the outside edges of the family of angles, checking that its size and its distance from the object coincide very precisely with the place where the direct reflections are supposed to appear, as shown in the previous diagram.

If the barn door is too large, there will not be any direct reflections on the glass, which will be uniformly black; if the barn door is too small, the direct reflections will take up too much of the surface of the glass, with a very undesirable refraction on its surface.

Note that as far as the lighting is concerned, we will get better results by placing a diffusing fabric behind the black background in order to even out the light and obtain a pleasing silhouette.

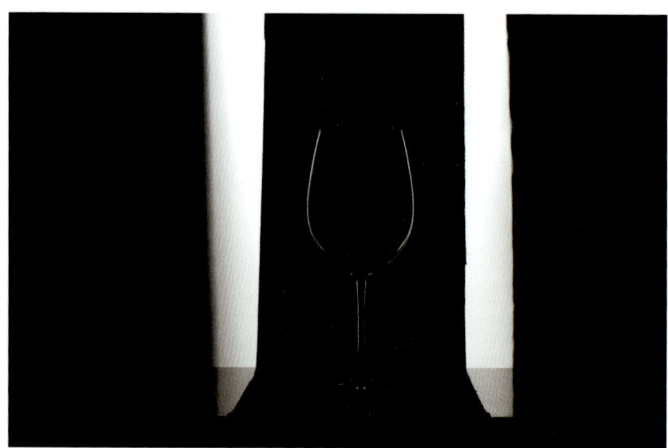

⌃ Setup for lighting a glass against a white background. A strip box is positioned behind a diffusing fabric and a black cover behind the glass. The lighted part is positioned at the edge of the family of angles, and the silhouette of the glass looks white.

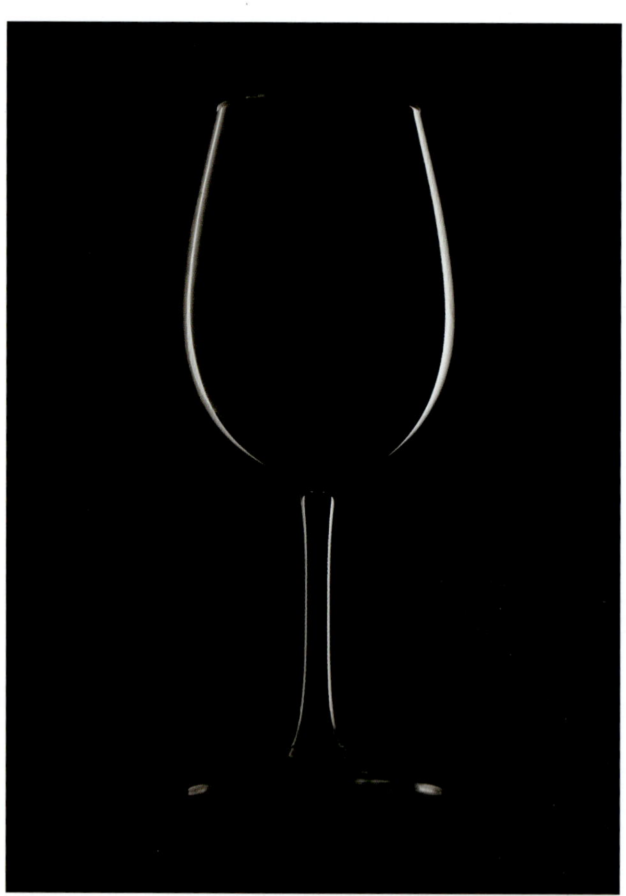

⌃ Example of a wineglass behind which I have placed a black barn door and light sources at the edges of the family of angles.

To measure the light with an independent exposure meter, we proceed in the same way as for the glass against the white background: because the direct reflections have the same intensity as the source that produces them, we measure directly on the illuminated part of the diffusing fabric, with the lumisphere directed toward the source. However, here we stick to an illumination of +1.33 EV: we are not trying for an absolute white, but rather for an even silhouette that provides some information about the material being illuminated.

Lighting a Full Glass

When it is full of liquid, a glass behaves like a biconvex lens: to reach our eyes, the light travels through air, then glass, then water, then glass again, then finally air again. Each time it passes from one material to a different one, it is refracted.

When it travels through the full glass, the light is first concentrated on its center, the image focus. But it doesn't stop there: as it passes the focal point, the light rays are inverted, and the top becomes the bottom and the right becomes the left. By inverting the light rays, we also invert what the eye perceives.

Moreover, depending on the distance between the glass and the background, the elements reflected within the family of angles will appear larger or smaller. In simple terms, if we move the glass too far away from the diffusing fabric in the example of a glass against a black background, we will see two large black bands appear on the glass. And if we place any kind of image or pattern so that it can be seen through the glass, it will appear reversed.

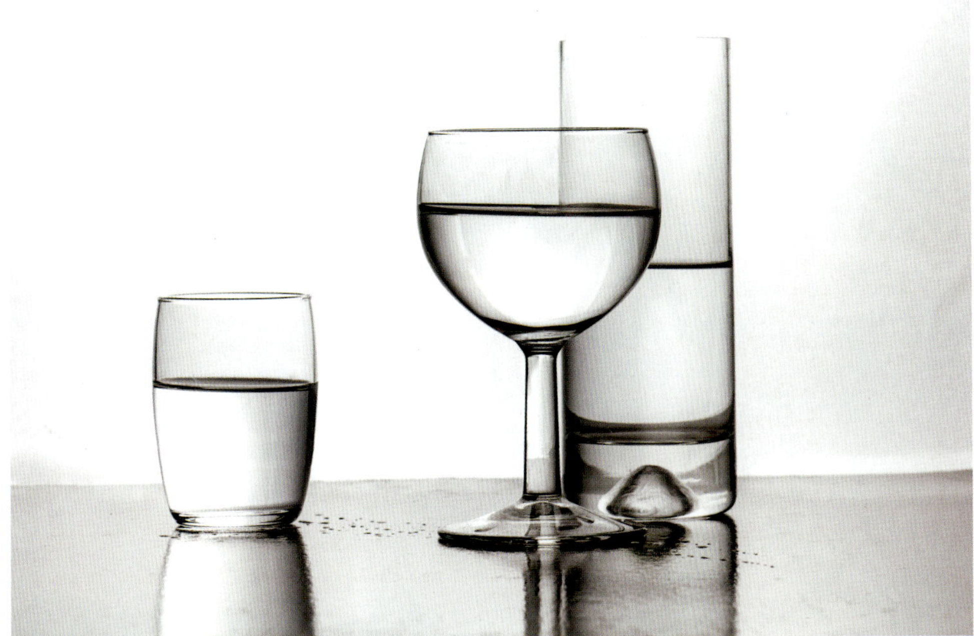

In Practice

Even though it is tempting to try to create images with very precise blacks and whites, with experience it becomes clear that using a certain amount of gray, with a gradual transition between shades, produces a more interesting result. Thus, when placing the lights and adjusting the camera, we try to obtain a slight sense of texture what will give this kind of shot realness and beauty.

You will also find that it is hard to achieve a reflection covering the entire outside of the glass.

There are three methods that tend to produce good results:
- cutting a shape out of black cardboard that closely follows the shape of the glass;
- placing the glass on a reflective black base (such as a sheet of black paper with a sheet of glass on top of it); or
- raising the glass about ten centimeters above the support.

This last method allows the glass to reflect black in all directions.

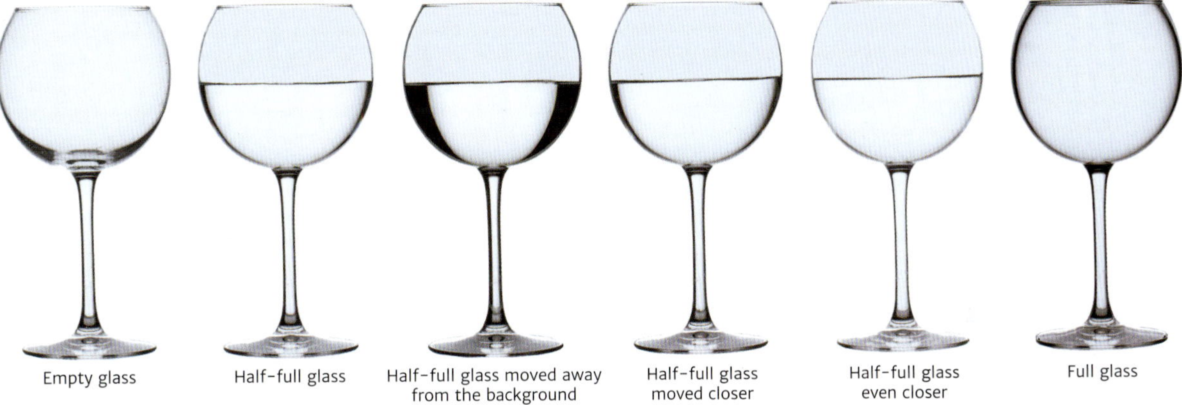

THE EFFECT OF LIQUID ON REFRACTION IN GLASS

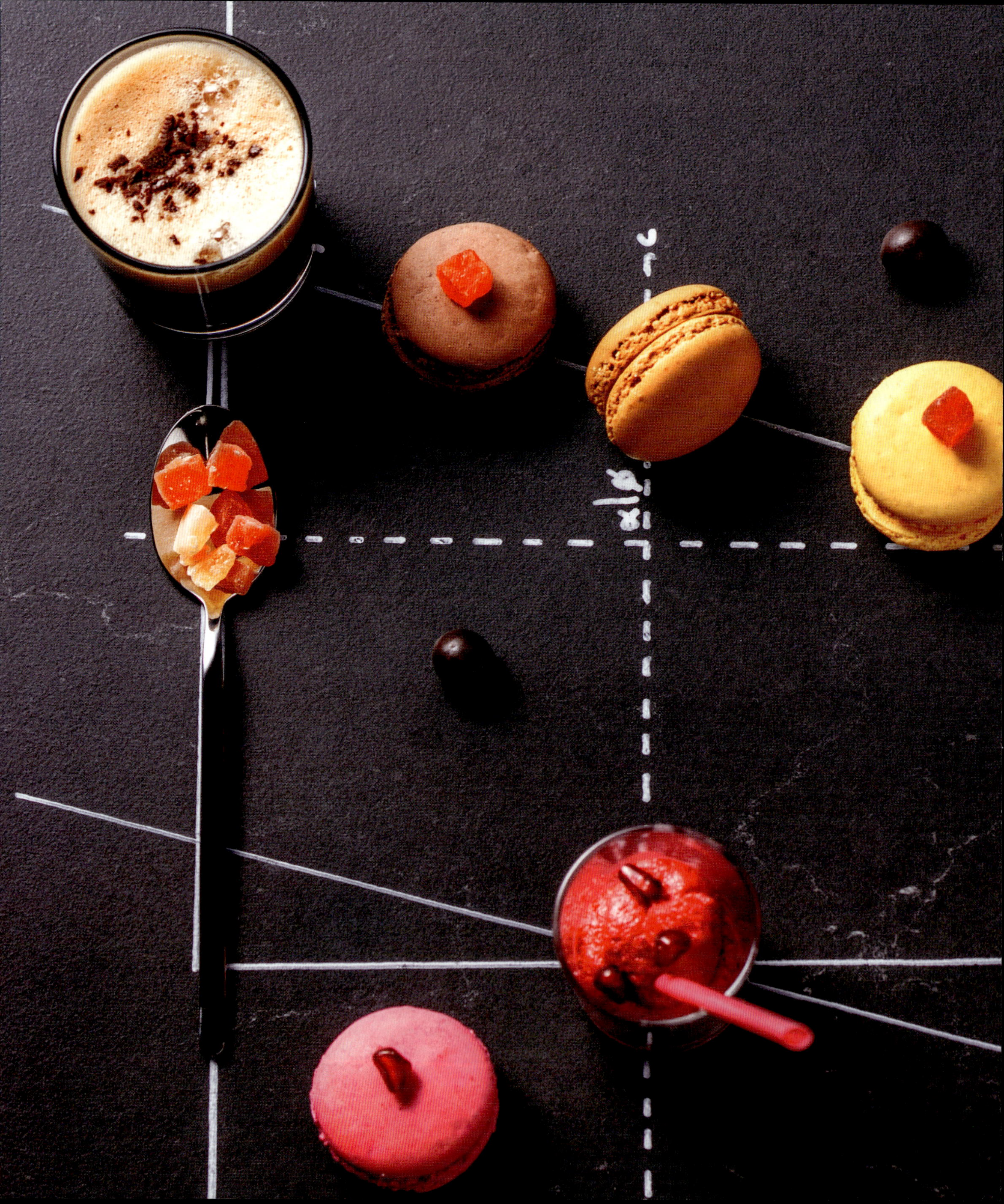

LIGHTING AND PRACTICE

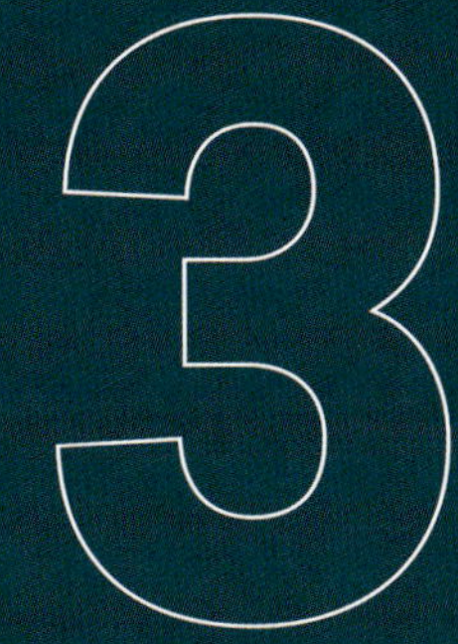

» **106** Technical Implementation
» **108** Choosing a Background
» **112** Supporting Material
» **114** Tripods
» **116** Typology of Objects
» **119** Respecting Colors
» **122** Photo Editing
» **124** Bottles of Red Wine
» **129** Bottles of Rosé and White Wine
» **132** Frosted-Glass Bottles
» **134** Empty Bottles
» **135** Lighting a Painting
» **137** Lighting a Mirror
» **139** Lighting a Pyramid
» **141** Lighting Transparent Prisms
» **143** Lighting Parallelepipeds
» **145** Lighting Cylinders
» **148** Lighting Spheres
» **151** Eliminating Cast Shadows
» **153** Lighting Food
» **158** Lighting Electronics
» **160** Lighting Jewelry
» **164** Lighting Watches
» **167** Photographing Furniture
» **169** Photographing Glasses
» **173** Make-Up and Perfume
» **178** Photographing Textiles
» **180** Photographing Clothing
» **185** Lighting Tableware
» **190** Lighting in an Aquarium
» **191** Lighting Sheet Metals
» **192** Lighting Plastic
» **193** Catalog Shots
» **196** Advertising Shots
» **199** Using Liquids
» **204** Composite Photographs

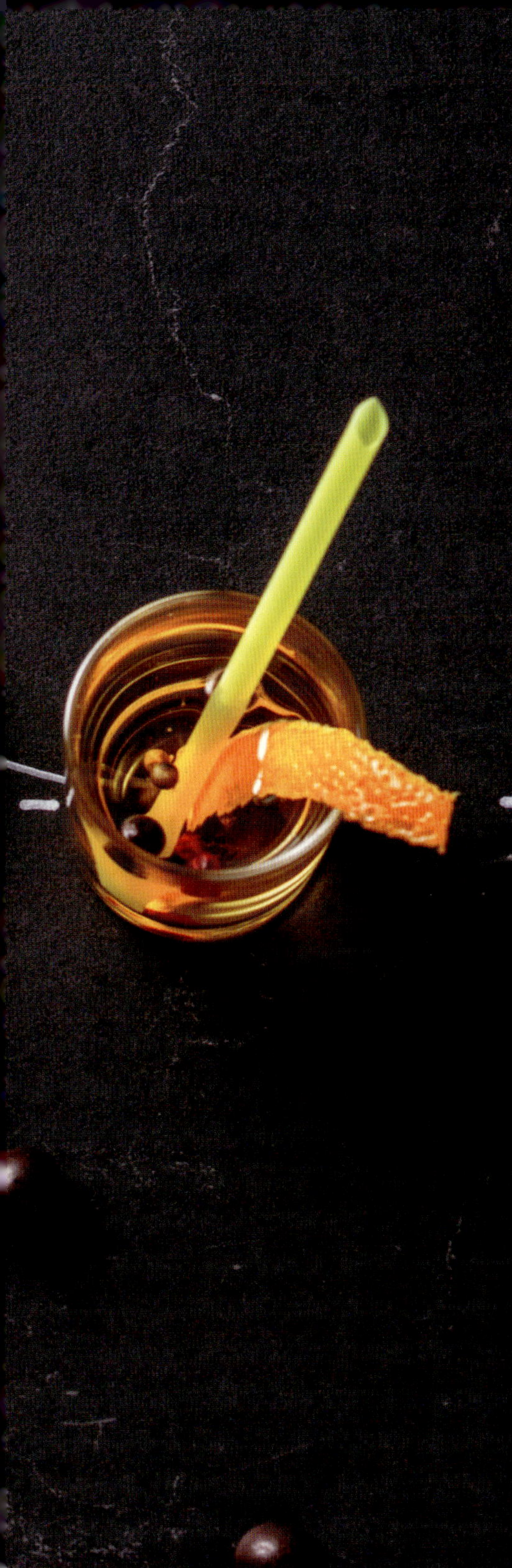

TECHNICAL IMPLEMENTATION

Stores and websites that sell photographic equipment offer a wide range of useful accessories for product photography. But each tool has its own specific use, and they are not all suitable for all cases.

One mistake many novice photographers make is to outfit themselves with a lot of accessories before they have really grasped what they are good for and how they work. In reality, every accessory has a very specific field of application, appropriate to one type of object and usually not very helpful for other kinds.

The Light Tent

The light tent, also known as a shooting tent or diffusing cube, is a cube of white diffusing fabric, held in place by piano-wire frames (which allow the cube to be folded up between uses), and whose front side can be closed up. The camera lens is then placed through a small slit in the fabric to avoid frontal reflections. These come in a wide variety of sizes, ranging from ten inches to six feet wide. They generally come with fabrics in several different colors (typically white/gray/black, but some manufacturers offer other colors) that are placed against the background and underneath the object to be photographed. This makes it possible to light the object along several different axes while maintaining an even diffusion of the light. This setup is well suited to matte and/ or slightly satiny objects that produce diffuse reflections, as well as to cylinders. However, it is completely counterproductive if you're lighting spherical objects that generate direct or specular reflections—because of its shape,

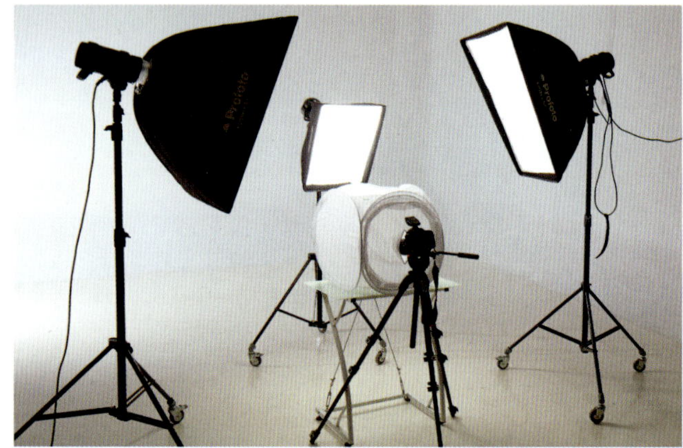

EXAMPLE OF ARRANGEMENT OF LIGHT SOURCES FOR USE WITH A LIGHT TENT

its framing wires and interior seams are reflected in the glossy objects and are visible in the photo.

As with all diffusing fabrics, it is absolutely essential to perfectly smooth out all the sides of the cube ahead of time using a steamer; otherwise, its texture could appear in the reflections. Because most commercial diffusing fabrics are lightly plastic-coated, you can't iron them.

For the lighting, we usually use four light sources: two on the side, one above the cube, and one in rim light

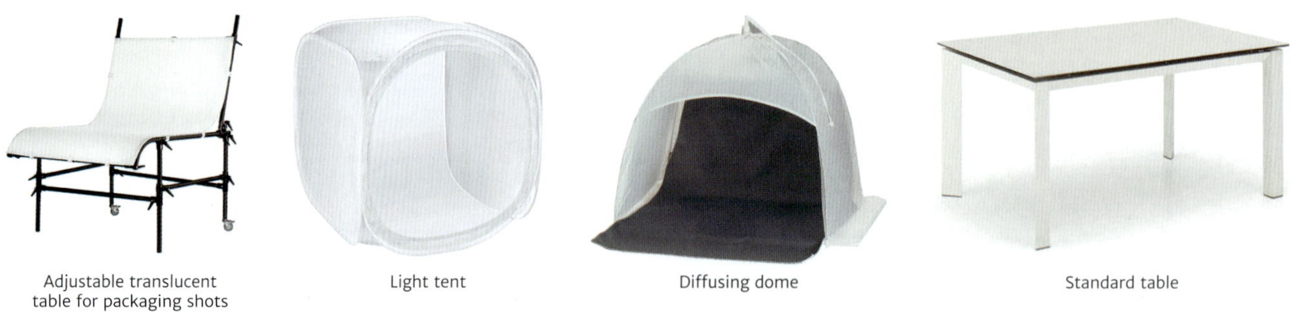

Adjustable translucent table for packaging shots

Light tent

Diffusing dome

Standard table

WORK STRATEGY

(unless a fabric has been placed to appear in the background of the image).

The front part of the cube is not specifically lit: the reflection of the light inside of it is sufficient for that. Even though the cube's fabric diffuses the light, we place softboxes on each of the light sources so that we achieve consistent, even lighting.

The light tent is perfectly suited to matte objects and to glossy cylinders, primarily polyhedrons: thus, it is the ideal tool for photographing soda cans, shoes, boxes, books, or untreated wooden toys.

The Diffusing Dome

The diffusing dome is much like the light tent, but it has the advantage of a rounded roof, which allows you to avoid any reflection of the interior seams for glossy objects that are rounded on their upper part. But it still won't work for spherical objects. It is used similarly to the tent; it works well for polyhedrons and glossy cylinders and can also be used for objects with slightly rounded tops (with a family of angles that is less than 100°).

The Packshot Table

The packaging shot table is more flexible because it gives the photographer greater freedom of movement and allows for more lighting possibilities, but it also requires more equipment to operate effectively.

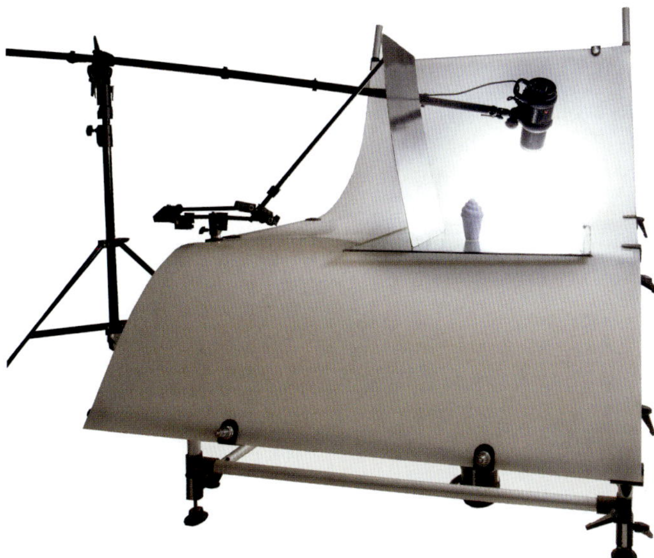

TRADITIONAL PLACEMENT OF THE LIGHT SOURCES ON A PACKSHOT TABLE

It is made out of a sheet of translucent, diffusing plexiglass (generally the Perspex brand) placed on an adjustable frame, where the angle of the background, in particular, can be manipulated. The table is generally equipped with wheels to allow it to be moved around, and with clamps to attach accessories (reflectors, diffusers, or barn doors) or light sources.

The diffusing plexiglass allows for lighting from below, and the rounded cyclorama-shaped backdrop makes it possible to obtain a perfectly uniform background behind the object (as long as it is lit with direct light rather than backlighting, which would produce a shadow on the lower part of the background). Note, however, that the lighting from below must be very precisely measured so that the lower part of the object does not show highlights. You can also avoid problems by placing the object on a transparent plexiglass base.

The final step is to set up your light sources around the object, being careful to diffuse them appropriately (see previous photo). The packaging shot table is suitable for objects of all shapes and surfaces.

The Standard Table

When the object is being photographed from above, or from a bird's-eye view, and the background does not appear in the photograph, a standard table can work fine. We shape the light by placing diffusers, barn doors, and reflectors in the appropriate places. This is the method I prefer for creating photographs of jewelry, watches, and glasses.

LED Reflecting Cube

For a few years now, manufacturers have been offering cubes whose internal wall, equipped with a reflective fabric, has LED lighting. These have the same qualities as light tents, but with less lighting flexibility because the placement of the LEDs is fixed.

The Photographer's Outfit

A product photographer usually dresses in black or dark gray. This may sound strange, but when you are photographing reflective objects, such as Christmas tree ornaments, your own reflection will often appear in the image; if you are dressed in dark colors, this is less problematic.

CHOOSING A BACKGROUND

The studio of a photographer who specializes in packaging shots—with its profusion of panels, sheets, and materials used to showcase all kinds of objects—is a veritable treasure trove.

With experience, it quickly becomes clear that the base on which the object is placed, and which will serve as a background, plays an important role in how the colors of the object end up looking and, overall, in the look of the photograph. With the exception of packaging shots for catalogs, which require a perfectly white background, you will have to think carefully about this issue.

Diffusion and Reflection

The surface on which we place the object to be illuminated can play many roles, depending on the material out of which it is made, its optical qualities, and its color.

- If it is highly reflective (such as a mirror), there is the risk that, depending on the angle of incidence of the lighting, we might get pronounced highlights on the lower part of the object. For most objects, this is a drawback, but for dark objects, it can be very effective.
- If the background is tinted, the light it reflects may color the object, which might not be a good thing for light-colored objects (first photo, next page). Thus, we generally either choose colorless backgrounds or place the objects farther away.
- Perfectly opaque and very absorbent backgrounds, like brushed cotton, prevent all reflections: they are often the best solution and are ideal for both matte and glossy objects.

Thus, aside from the effect that the background can have on the object, it is also necessary to think about its own intrinsic aesthetic qualities. It has to harmonize—in color, shape, mood, and texture—with the object being photographed. We wouldn't use the same background to present Corsican figatelli sausages, a high-tech mobile phone, or a bottle of perfume: each of these objects belongs to a different aesthetic register, and so for each one we must determine the ideal context.

Paper Backgrounds

Studio backgrounds, easy to use and perfectly matte, are made of thick high-quality paper, with a fine-toothed antireflective surface that allows you to obtain a uniform color. They are generally sold in rolls of 36 feet (the standard widths being 53 inches or 9 feet), and they are available in a multitude of colors.

You can also choose cotton-fiber art papers (like those made by Canson), which have the same characteristics and also have the advantage of already being cut into dimensions that are appropriate for photographing objects. The idea is to choose thick sheets (> 150 gsm) to avoid running the risk of folds.

You could theoretically work with all different colors of paper, depending on the scenario, but we most often end up choosing half-tones of black, gray, and beige, which work well in most situations.

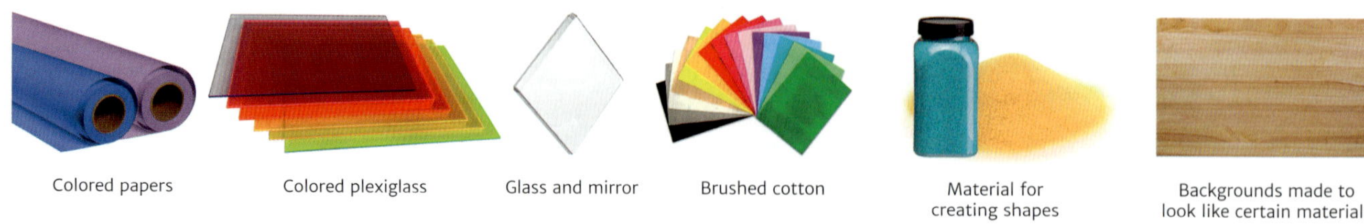

EXAMPLES OF BACKGROUNDS AND ACCESSORIES OFTEN USED IN PRODUCT PHOTOGRAPHY

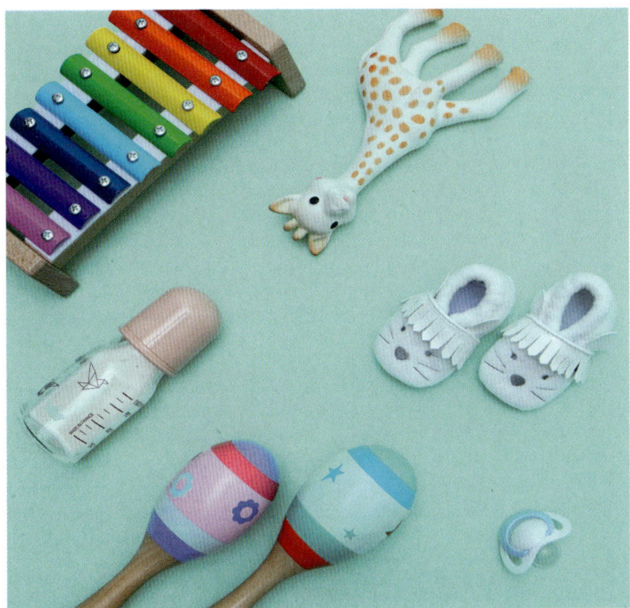

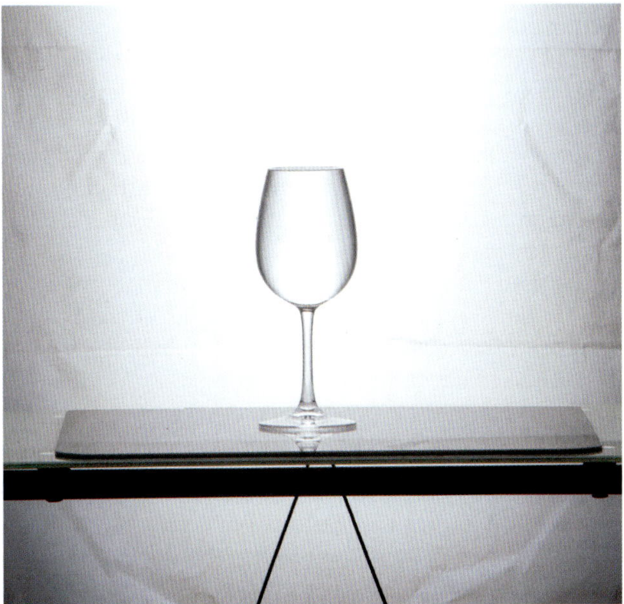

Matte Plastics

Often used for their nonreflective qualities, matte plastics are effective at avoiding reflections on objects while being easily washable (which is something we look for when we are working with fluids). The plastics are generally Trespa, HPL, or PVC, which can be found in hardware stores, home design stores, and kitchenware stores. Note that these backgrounds have a tendency to develop scratches and do not withstand heat very well, so you need to make sure to store them carefully and avoid impacts.

Glossy Plastics

Whether plexiglass, polycarbonate, Alupanel, PVC, or polyethylene, these backgrounds, once they have been lacquered, are very glossy and can occasionally serve as reflectors. They have the advantage of acting differently depending on their position in relation to the light source. Thus, a sheet of glossy black plexiglass placed within the family of angles transmits most of the light and appears white or light gray, depending on the luminous intensity—which is perfect for glassware: the background looks white but its reflection in the glass stays black, which provides well-defined silhouettes (see the photo above, right). And with glossy white plastic, we get the exact opposite effect: placed outside the family of angles, it will look completely black.

Glass

A sheet of glass placed under the object makes it possible to both play with the reflection (as with glossy plastic) and separate the shadow from the object that produced it. The farther the shadow is from the object, the softer it becomes.

This method is useful for obtaining photos without shadows, which is useful for photos that are meant to be cropped for use in catalogs, for instance. It also makes it possible to trick the viewer's gaze, giving the impression that the object is suspended in air. And because glass is less susceptible to scratching than plastic, it is used much more often—whether transparent or translucent glass, or black smoked glass.

Mirrors

Even though all the glossy materials mentioned so far act somewhat like mirrors, none of them are able to transmit all of the light they receive. When you want to make sure to get a perfect reflection of the object or light—in order to produce a perfectly white background or to reflect, for example, a computer screen—an actual mirror will be your best option. Mirrors can also be used as reflectors when the light is too weak and the reflectors can't be brought any closer without appearing in the field of vision.

Brushed Cotton

Brushed cotton (or cotton flannel) is perfect for obscuring reflections and is therefore widely used in photography. It is generally black or white, but it also exists in a wide range of colors. As its name indicates, it is a cotton fabric whose very tight weave is machine-brushed, giving it a fuzzy appearance. Its irregular surface means there is no risk that it will cause a reflection.

Brushed cotton is the ideal background material when you do not want to allow any reflections at the base at the base of an object, such as a crystal ball. It can also be used to make excellent barn doors.

Liquids

Even though liquids are not, strictly speaking, backgrounds, there has been a custom of presenting objects in water, oil, or paint. These types of setups can be photographed from above, by placing the liquids in shallow containers, such as kitchen trays or terrariums, or

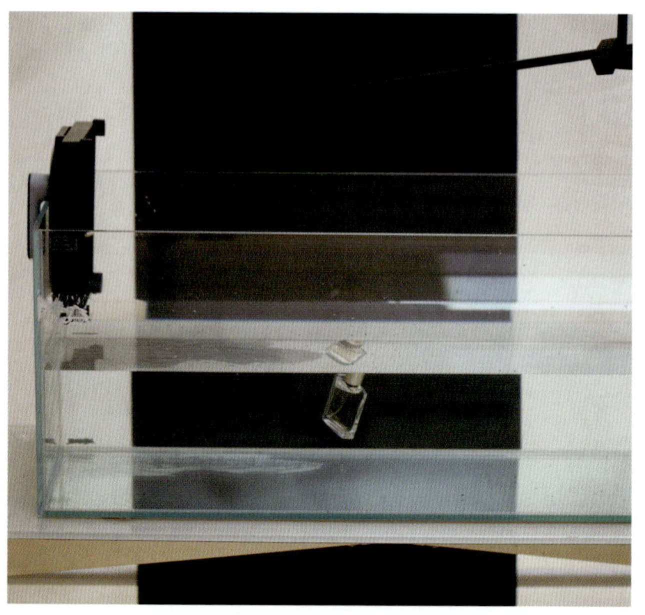

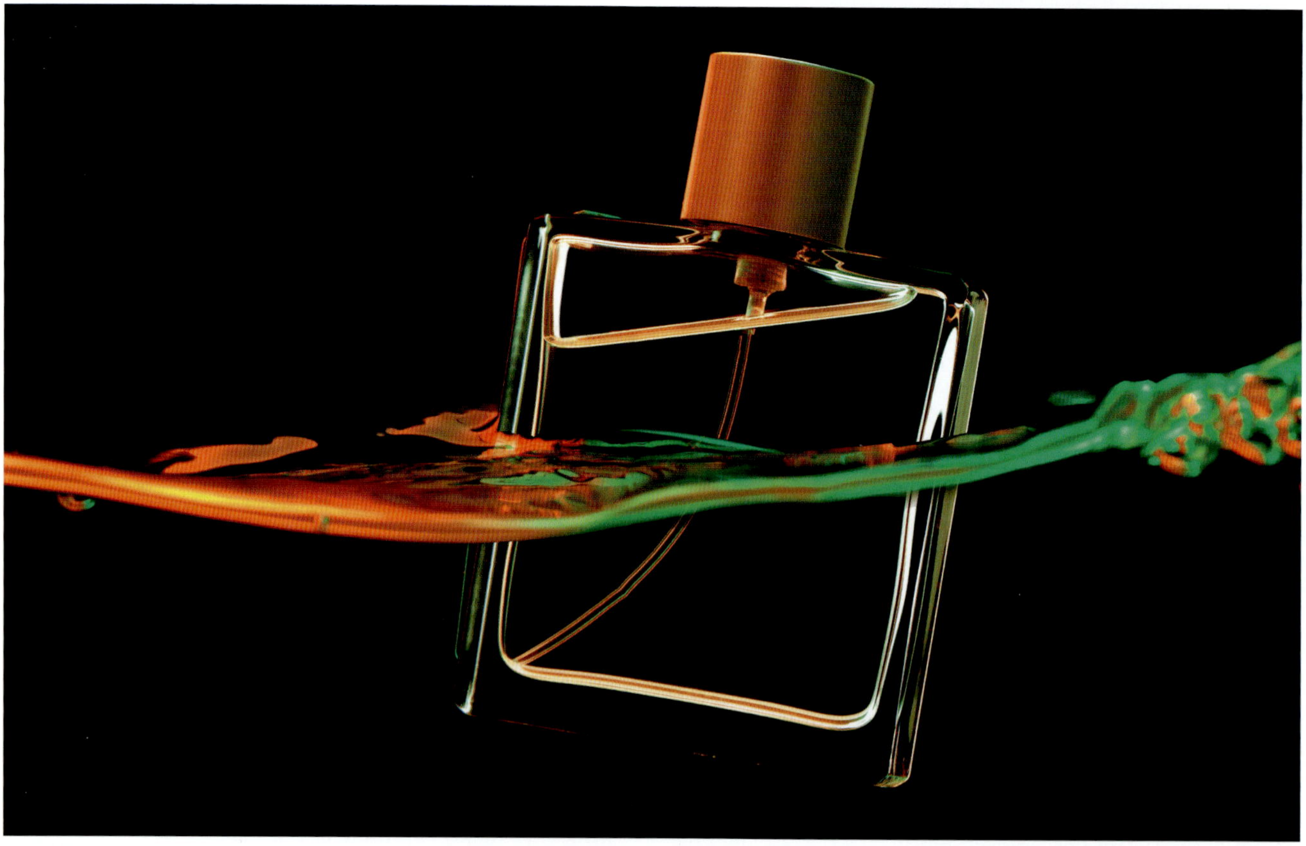

⌃ Perfume bottle suspended from a fishing line, half-submerged in the water of an aquarium. A black barn door is placed behind the aquarium, and two softboxes equipped with rust and cyan color gels are positioned in the backlight (see the staging arrangement above).

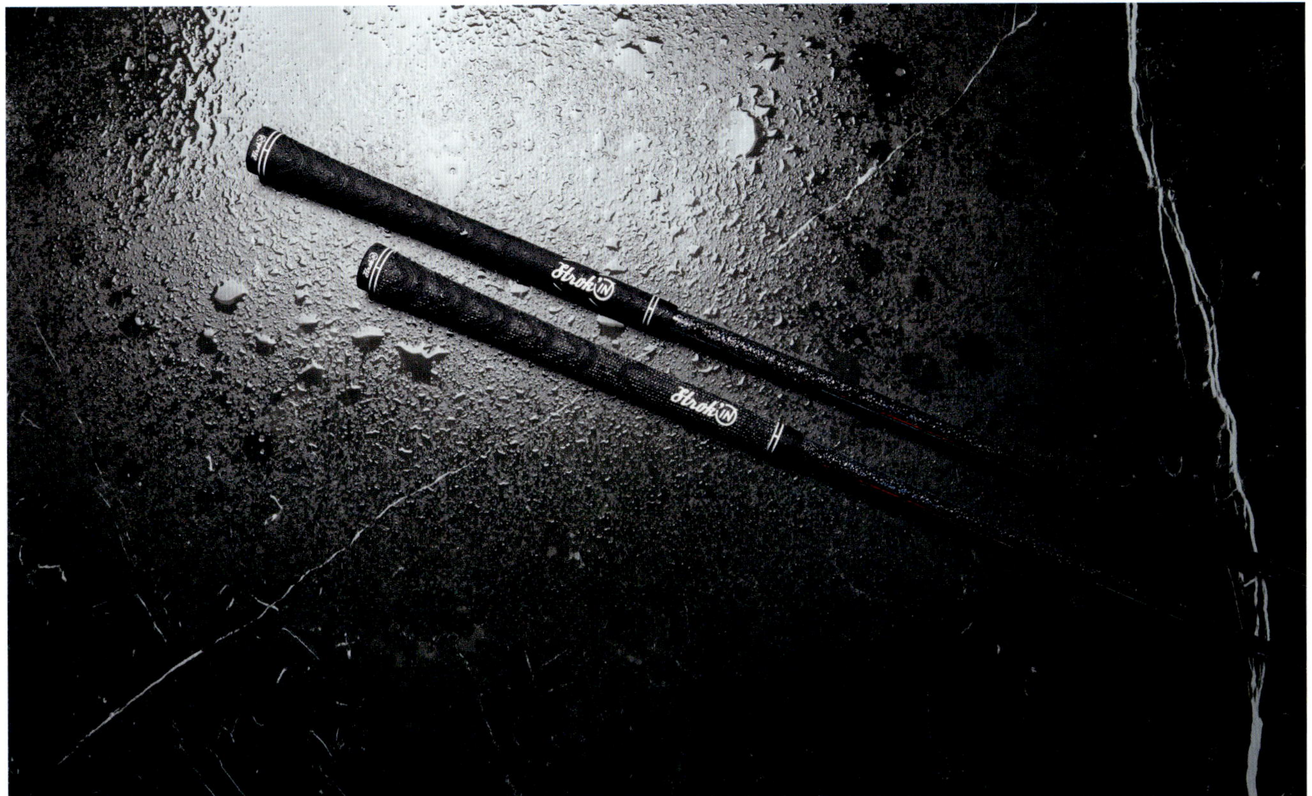

⌃ The maker of these golf club shafts chose to highlight their qualities in the rain by choosing a black marble background, moistened with a spray of water.

through a glass, like the glass of an aquarium. Liquid is only interesting as a background when it is in motion, usually with undulations on the surface (we use the kind of electric blower that is used to clean computers, or a compressed-air spray bottle), or if the object itself is in motion (see photo opposite)—but the liquid must be partially within the family of angles of the lighting so that the different undulations on its surface can be clearly distinguishable.

Textiles

Usually shown crumpled or twisted, textiles are perfect for being both background and props for the object being presented. They are widely used for watches, jewelry, and some cosmetics, for which satins and other glossy textiles are popular. Care must be taken to use them with very diffused, side lighting to give texture to their folds. One must, of course, also make sure to use fabrics that have been perfectly ironed and cleaned.

Textured Media

Most of the backgrounds mentioned so far are smooth and uniform, but there are also other kinds of backgrounds that we specifically choose for their textures or their color tones. This is the case for the marble slab in the photo above. You can also choose wooden planks or flat stones, or for an advertising shot, create entire scenes that include all different kinds of textures. People generally prefer to use noble materials like leather, wood, and metal—which are very common in packaging shots—but anything can be considered as long as the material's reflectance, mood, and color are a good fit for the object being highlighted.

Materials and Shapes

Nothing says that you have to work with flat backgrounds! You can easily make up all kinds of shapes using things like sand, fluff balls, paving stones, or foam. The only limits are, as always, the harmony of the colors, textures, and reflectance that are characteristic of each kind of material.

SUPPORTING MATERIAL

Product photography requires rigor, cleanliness, and organization. Throwing yourself into the lighting and shooting without having properly prepared the products beforehand will mean that you have to spend long hours on post-production retouching. It's a better idea to carefully plan ahead for all possibilities.

Most of the objects you will be asked to photograph are small, so small that all of the tiny defects, like scratches, dust, and fingerprints, will jump out at you once you are looking at the RAW preview on your computer screen. Incidentally, the fact that the object is so small also means that precision work is required in the placement of reflectors and barn doors. Thus, you will need to equip yourself with a series of items and devices to help simplify your work.

Preparing the Object and the Workspace

As I said at the beginning of the very first section of part 1, after carefully checking the overall cleanliness of your studio and conscientiously getting rid of almost all of the dust, you then have to make sure that the object itself is ready to be photographed. Even though we are generally presenting brand-new objects, just out of their packaging, and thus mostly free of scratches and defects, it is still sometimes necessary to remove labels (you can get rid of all traces of glue using a degreasing solvent, which you can get at any hardware store). Make sure to handle the objects with antistatic gloves to avoid leaving fingerprints, or use chamois leather (natural or synthetic) to grip them with.

If the object is made of a material that produces direct reflections and it cannot be illuminated without making the reflections appear, you can use an antireflective spray—but note that this kind of aerosol does not completely eliminate the reflections, so it is better to be careful to keep the object outside the family of angles.

For plastic objects, an antistatic spray will prevent airborne dust from settling on the object while you prepare your lighting. As a general rule, we always use an aerosol dust remover (like the ones used for computer keyboards) just before we start shooting to get rid of residual dust.

Maintaining and Arranging Backgrounds and Lighting

In addition to the standard shapers and tripods that are used for lighting, it is sometimes necessary to use a super clamp to clamp the lights as close to the object as possible; screwed to the edge of the table, this clamp is equipped with a spigot stud (a universal-sized brass cylinder that allows most studio lights to be attached to it). It may also be necessary to resort to articulated arms equipped with ball joints to position the light sources in places that are hard to reach with standard tripods and in cramped quarters—even if you often work with an extension or boom arm on your tripod. These arms are helpful not just for holding the light sources in place, but also for supporting backgrounds or accessories held up with transparent nylon fishing line. You will also need to have clamps of various sizes on hand for the different situations you might encounter.

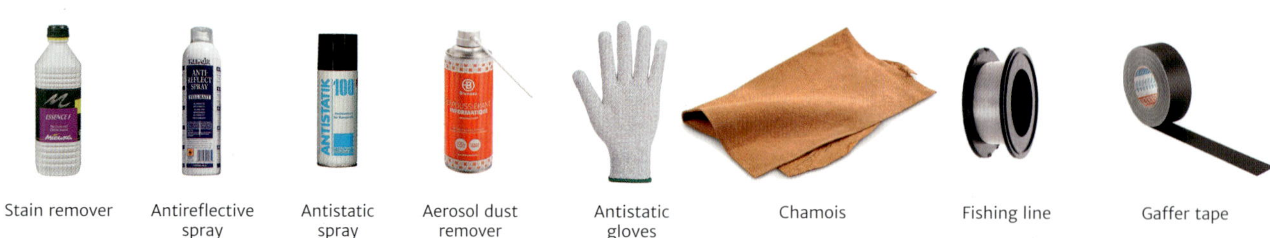

| Stain remover | Antireflective spray | Antistatic spray | Aerosol dust remover | Antistatic gloves | Chamois | Fishing line | Gaffer tape |

HANDLING, PREPARATION, AND SUPPORT MATERIALS

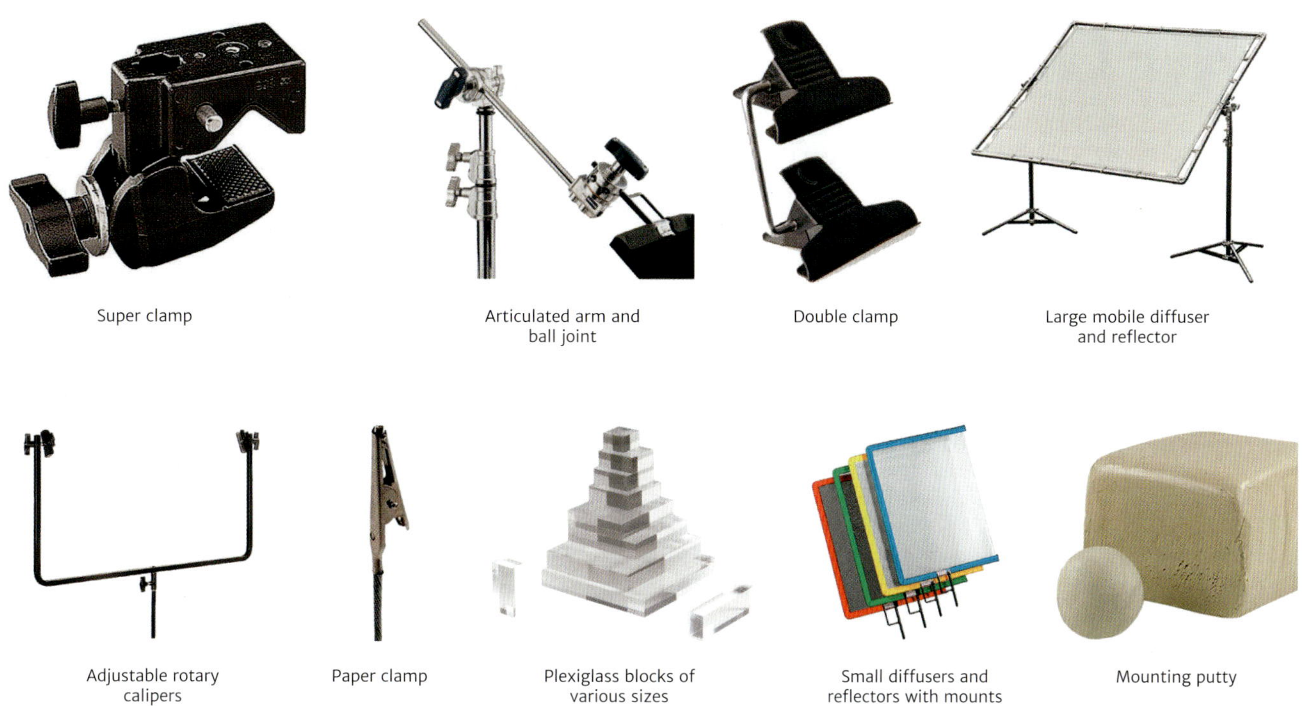

MOST COMMONLY USED MATERIALS IN OBJECT PHOTOGRAPHY

Maintaining and Arranging Diffuser Fabric

When it comes to one of the most essential accessories in product photography, namely diffusers, the offerings available from studio equipment manufacturers are actually quite poor. You will constantly need small diffusers, often arranged in circular arcs, to provide the right kind of light for rounded objects, like jewelry or soda cans. I have solved this problem by using 3-mm-thick sheets of translucent PMMA (plexiglass), which are made for diffusing LED lighting. I round them by stretching them and softening them with a thermal cleaner. Make a point of having several of these, of various sizes, on hand; they will be very useful. You can also make frontal diffusers in which you make a round opening for the camera lens, which will avoid frontal reflections on very glossy, spherical, and cylindrical objects. And finally, you can get large commercially available diffuser panels (make sure they are mobile) to even out your rear and vertical lighting; for use when lighting objects like spoons, for example.

Maintaining and Arranging the Object

The objects that we need to photograph rarely stay in the perfect position by themselves! Small transparent plexiglass blocks of various sizes and shapes can be used as wedges; these do not produce problematic shadows or reflections. For opaque objects, commercial mounting putty, which you shape into the appropriate form, can be a good solution. You can also suspend the object using a fishing line attached to a mobile bar so that the entire arrangement can be easily moved without having to retighten the line. This is a good system to use for light objects, but you will have to do some editing in Photoshop to get rid of the line.

Transparent objects, like perfume bottles, can be submerged in an aquarium filled with clean water. By limiting the phenomenon of refraction, we can obtain perfectly delineated photographs.

TRIPODS

In product photography, the tripod is an indispensable accessory. Let's look at how to choose the best one.

Whether you're shooting a cosmetics line, where every product has to be photographed at the exact same height and distance; taking several different shots for a composite photo; or just needing to position the camera at a precise spot with respect to the reflector panels, it's impossible to take professional product photos without a tripod.

Viewing Angle Accuracy

We have seen how crucial the position of the camera is in relation to the lighting, especially for the issue of reflections produced by the families of angles. It is also often necessary for the shooting equipment to be placed in a specific position at a strategic angle for the lighting and rendering of the object. This is only possible, and comfortable, if you are able to position the camera precisely, which implies the use of a tripod and a well-calibrated ball head in order to capture the ideal angle for the shot. And given that the light sources and the diffusers, sometimes even the object itself, often have to be moved slightly, it would be absurd to try to work freehand, wasting time constantly trying to reestablish the perfect angle.

Repeated Shots and Composite Photos

We often have to photograph an entire product line of related objects, such as tubes of lipstick, for example. In this case, every object must maintain the same homothetic ratio (orientation of angles) and angle of view as all the others. Thus, we work from a fixed point of view, using a tripod.

When creating a composite photo (see the section on composite photos, page 204), it is crucial to photograph the same object from the same point of view, but with different lighting each time. To simplify the editing in Photoshop and to be able to stack the layers easily, the camera must be perfectly fixed in the same spot.

Light Quantities and Long Exposures

For objects that have LED lighting or an LCD screen, there is no other choice, if you're shooting with a flash, than to lengthen the exposure time in order to be able to work in mixed asynchronous light. Again, this is only possible if the camera is completely stable.

Choosing Your Tripod

There is such a plethora of tripods available on the market that it can be difficult to know where to start. Here are the features you'll want to consider when choosing a tripod:

- How much weight can the tripod support?
- What are its maximum and minimum heights?
- Is it easy to store and transport?
- How are its legs attached?
- What shooting axes does it allow?
- What brand is it, and how much does it cost?

All manufacturers indicate the maximum weight for each model of tripod in their product sheets. Don't forget that the tripod will be holding your camera and a lens, and you don't want to let those fall! To make sure that you are getting a stable photographic tripod with an excellent weight/stability/size proportion, do the following: add up the weight of your camera and your heaviest lens and then multiply that result by 2.5.

Depending on the objects you're photographing, you will sometimes have to work very high up and other times down low, thus the tripod will need to be able to carry the camera from a height of ten inches all the way up to six or seven feet. Two elements can influence its minimum and maximum height: the presence of a center column and the legs.

For product photography, choose a tripod with a tilting center column, which you will need for radical bird's-eye views—and note that you will have to think about buying a counterweight to make sure your equipment stays stable when the column is tilted. But the most important thing is the ease that a column gives you: it is much easier to play with the height of the center column than the height of the three legs of the tripod every time you want to make an adjustment. The issue of the spacing of the legs is not critical in product photography, because we are generally working on a flat floor, but it can be an important consideration if you're working outside, where you will need to be able to adjust the spacing of the legs individually and irregularly—this is why we do not generally use tripods with a crossbar fixing the legs in place; those are mostly intended for video shots.

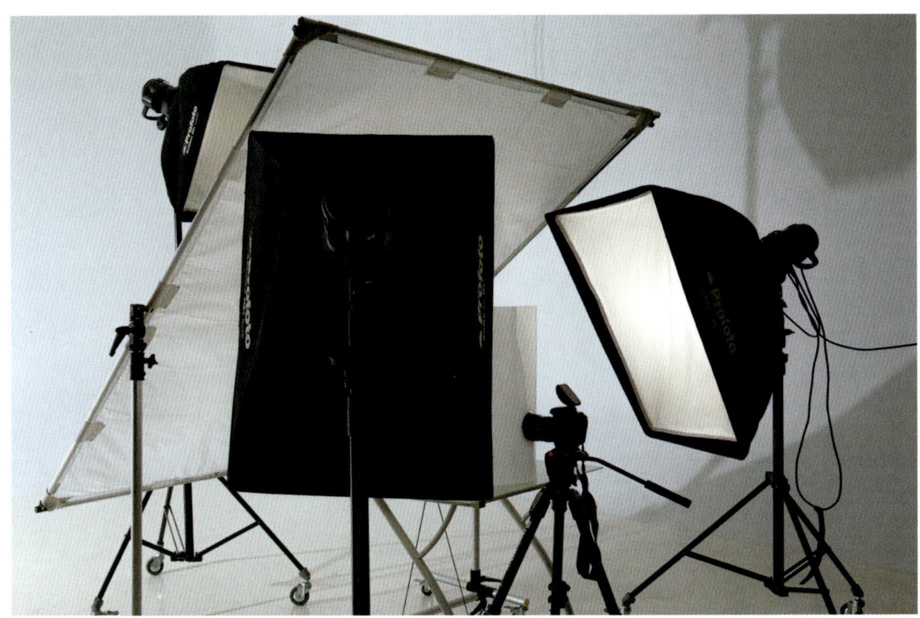

The issue of the tripod's weight is not crucial in product photography; you will rarely need to transport the tripod over long distances (of course, if you also use the tripod outdoors, the weight will become an important criterion). Heavy tripods (generally made of aluminum) are cheaper than the very light ones, which are made of carbon. If you are trying to equip a studio, then weight can be a plus, especially in terms of stability; if you are trying to limit vibrations as much as possible, then choose carbon, as it has greater absorptive power.

Choosing Your Ball Head

There is a specific kind of ball joint tripod head for every situation and every kind of photography. For ease of use, ask yourself the following questions:

- How much weight can the ball head support?
- What type of mount works with your tripod?
- What kind of mounting plate do you want to use?
- What will you use it for?
- What are your work preferences?

In terms of weight, you will need to make the same calculations as for the tripod: the weight of the camera plus the weight of the heaviest lens, multiplied by 2.5. For attaching the ball head to the tripod, the screws on the top of the foot plate are almost always 3/8-inch screws—but make sure that the ball head you have chosen conforms to this standard (if not, you can buy adapters).

The next question is the mounting plate, a small accessory that is attached to the body of the ball head and allows it to be secured to the camera. The plates usually have a 1/4-inch thread, which corresponds to the diameter of most camera mounts, but do make sure that they are compatible. Also pay attention to the size of the plates: they are not standard (some brands, like Manfrotto, make plates that only work with their own brands).

There are many different ball heads: fluid heads, 3D ball heads, pendulum ball heads, pistol grip ball heads. The fluid heads are placed on a sphere that allows the camera equipment to be tilted into all positions (vertical, horizontal, and flipping from portrait to landscape). They are well suited to product photography but sometimes lack precision (a single notch serves all the different axes).

3D, or three-way, ball heads are equipped with three knobs to determine horizontality, verticality, and tilt: this is perfect for product photography because of its precision.

Pendulum ball heads work like a pendulum (as their name implies): while they are well suited to fashion or sports photography, where you need to be able to change the angle of view quickly, they should be avoided for product photography.

Pistol grip ball heads (or joysticks) are equipped with a trigger: when you press the trigger, it releases the movement. Even though these are easy to handle, they are generally imprecise, and not well suited to product photography.

TYPOLOGY OF OBJECTS

Making a solid preliminary study of the objects you're photographing allows you to discern the right lighting and shooting strategy.

Before you even begin to decide about what lighting to use or what methods to employ, you need to establish a checklist of the particularities of the object. The more precise your checklist, the easier it will be for you to define the lighting parameters and the constraints of your shoot.

Observing the Object

The very first thing to do is to handle the object, wearing gloves, and look at it under a perfectly white, hard light. By changing its orientation with respect to the light, you will see its texture, glossiness, and flaws appear and you will be able to observe how it reacts. This will also allow you to identify its specific shape and anticipate how and at what angle you will place it on the packshot table, find out whether it is light enough for the use of fishing line, or whether it needs to be filled with liquid or have labels removed. If you do it right, this preliminary work will save you a great deal of time later on. Let's go through the various things that need to be checked.

Defining the Kind of Reflections

Handling the object under the light, you will be able to see very quickly whether it produces specular, direct, or diffuse reflections. Depending on its age (old objects are often glossy or oxidized) and its properties, it may also be that the reflections on its various parts are not all the same kind. In that case, observing the object will allow you to determine the ideal lighting with respect to the families of angles and which side is best suited to the lighting you have in mind, as well as plan what accessories you will need for lighting and shaping.

Texture

Handling an object in the light also brings out any textures (some of which can be hard to see if the light is not falling in just the right way) and will allow you to determine whether those textures are more pronounced in grazing side light or in direct reflection—in reality, it all depends on the orientation of the textures. This is true especially for leather and certain types of plastic. Then, with this information in hand, you can decide whether you want any given texture to appear.

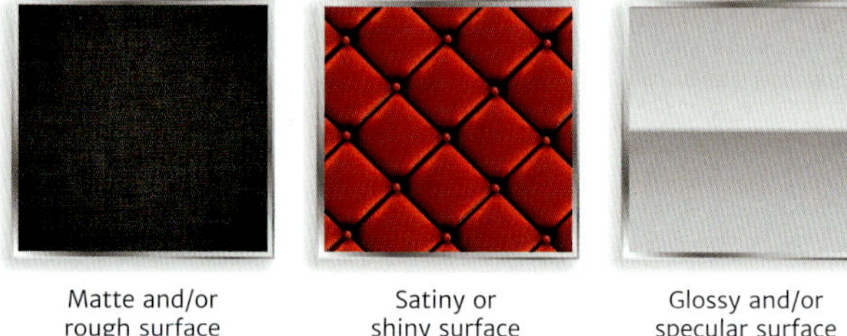

DETERMINING THE CONDITION OF THE SURFACE

Assessing the Material

Without a precise knowledge of the material that makes up the product, you run the risk of overlooking the lighting that would bring out its particular nature. A glossy black plexiglass cube looks almost exactly like a smoked glass cube or a black polished steel cube. But each of these will react very differently to light: the plastic cube will produce fairly diffused direct reflections, the steel one will create slightly wavy direct reflections, and the glass one will produce very sharp and perfectly straight direct reflections.

Defining the Transparency

When dealing with a transparent or translucent item, the material out of which it is made becomes crucial: a transparent glass bottle will not refract light in the same

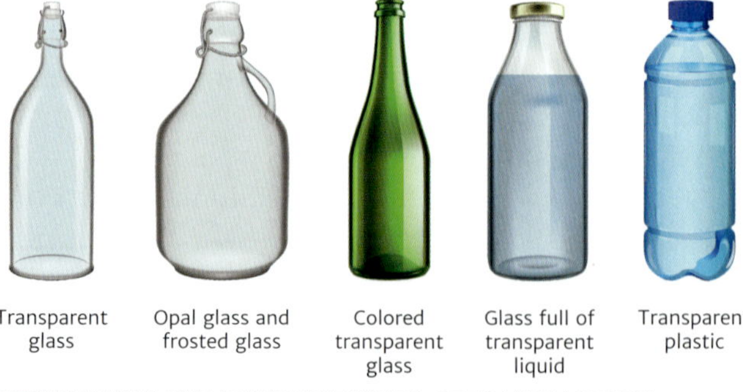

DETERMINING THE DIFFERENT KINDS OF TRANSPARENCY

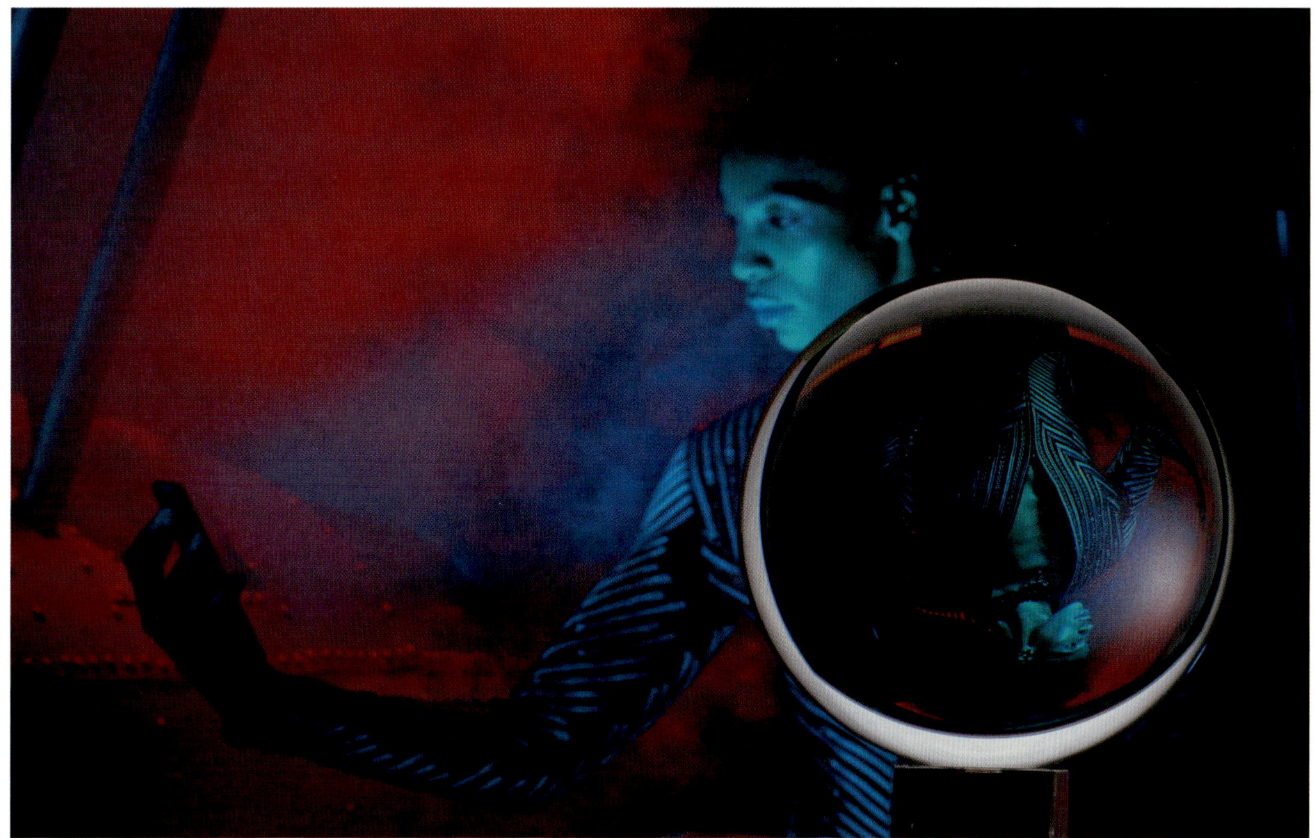

way as a crystal ball; the direct reflections generated by frosted glass will be different from those generated by a translucent plastic drinking cup.

For transparent glass, colorless or not, it is essential to use rim lighting. The refraction of the bottle's silhouette will be more pleasing if the bottle is filled with a colorless liquid (water, or better yet, transparent mineral oil, such as paraffin oil, whose refractive index is close to that of glass).

For this type of material, if we want to obtain visible reflections, we will place light sources within the family of angles, while taking care to over-diffuse the light sources (softboxes, in front of which mobile diffusers have been arranged). For frosted glass, the lighting can come from anywhere because this kind of glass essentially produces diffuse reflections. For transparent plastic, backlighting is required, but we have to use harder lights than we do for transparent glass in order to get visible reflections (generally softboxes, but without mobile diffusers). For a flat surface, such as a window, lighting at right angles will create a phenomenon of complete transmission: the glass will be invisible, but it will create visible direct reflections in all other directions.

Assessing the Shape

Finally, we need to look at the shape of the object. We know that the kind of lighting we use and where we place it will be different depending on whether the object is flat, polyhedral, cylindrical, spherical, concave, or convex, in order to give the best sense of the shape and allow it to be grasped by the viewer. Its reflections need to be correctly positioned, the differences in shading depending on the shape must be visible, and so must the differences in contrast between the protrusions and hollows if the object is concave.

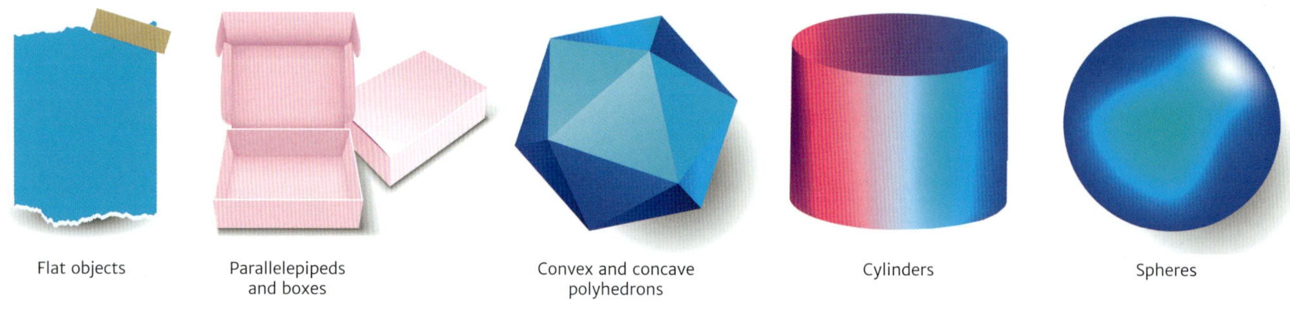

<table>
<tr><td>Flat objects</td><td>Parallelepipeds and boxes</td><td>Convex and concave polyhedrons</td><td>Cylinders</td><td>Spheres</td></tr>
</table>

DETERMINING SHAPES

Let's look at the example of the icosahedron, the twenty-sided polyhedron shown above. As shown, with its three forward faces lighter than the seven other ones, it looks convex. But if we had used a concave version of the same shape, with the light placed along the exact same axis, the result would have been the same. To make the sensation of a hollow visible, we would have had to light it from above and create a shadow on the upper part of the concave area.

Defining Colors

Next, we have to precisely determine the object's colors (see the following section), and then anticipate how they will react to the environment, light, and props being used. The color of the studio's walls, and even of your own clothing if you are working with a material that produces specular reflections, the color temperature of the lighting if it is not perfectly white, and the reflections produced by a colored mount or prop can all have an impact.

Managing Complex Objects

Of course, each object is not just cubic, glossy, or transparent. It will often be composed of materials with multiple characteristics, like the microwave oven shown below: its glass window produces direct reflections, while the rest of the object, covered in matte plastic, produces only diffuse reflections. The same is true for the blender in the illustration: the pitcher is transparent, while the base is opaque. In this type of situation, we always give priority to the material that is the most complex to light in terms of placing the light sources. For the oven, that would be the glass; for the blender, it would be the transparent pitcher.

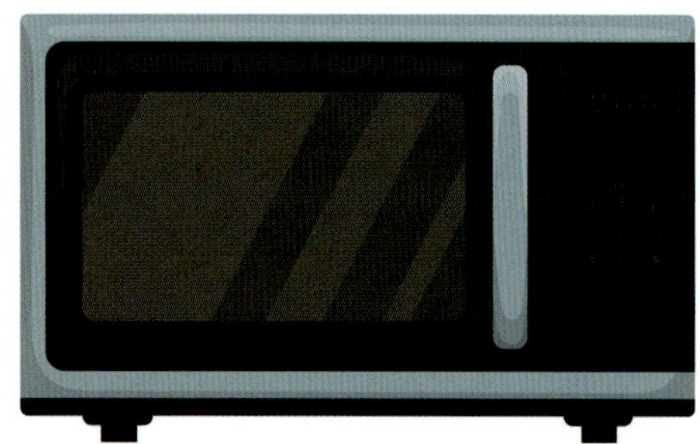

Different materials and surfaces
(here, matte plastic, polished metal, and glass)

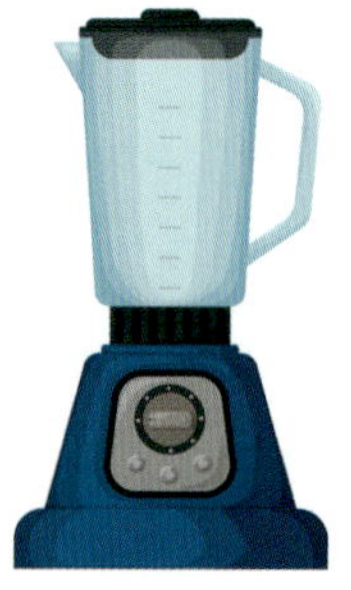

Transparent materials
and opaque materials

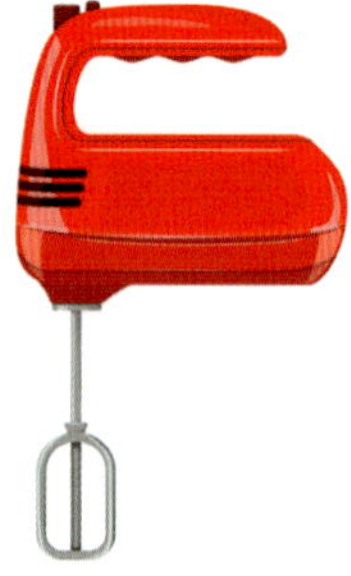

Direct reflections and
diffuse reflections

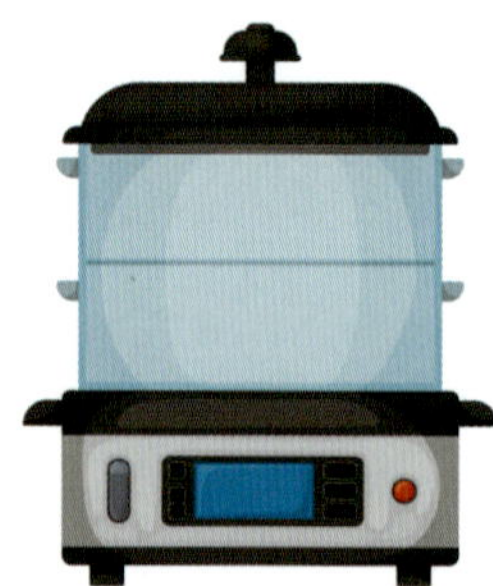

Presence of different luminances
(here, an LCD screen)

DETERMINING THE COMPLEXITIES OF THE SHAPE/SURFACE/MATERIAL

RESPECTING COLORS

In commercial photography, it is absolutely essential that the colors of an object in a photograph are faithful to the original object.

Without a rigorous calibration of the elements in the imaging chain and discipline in your working method, there is no way to obtain the exact same color in your photo as in the actual object—and a discrepancy there would, of course, be inexcusable for a catalog photo or an advertisement. Thus, you must follow a precise procedure that you reproduce every time you change the lighting.

Color and White Balance

As I discussed in the section on page 53, we perceive the color of an object because there is only one wavelength that it reflects, while it absorbs all the other colors. Thus, if we project a red light onto a green object, it will look black (having no green to reflect). Therefore, it is not so much the real color of the object that we are interested in here but the wavelengths that are present in the lighting.

Moreover, the spectrum of the light reflected by the illuminated object, which determines the nerve impulses sent by the retina, varies widely depending on the lighting, while the color that we perceive does not change. This phenomenon is called color constancy. But this is not the case for color sensors, which react according to the light spectrum that reaches them: an object illuminated by an orangish light will not produce the same signal as when it is illuminated in blue. The only way to make the color look the way it does in reality is to calibrate the camera—a procedure that will need to be repeated every time the lighting, and the ambient light, changes. We thus "inform" the camera by giving it a surface recognized as white in the main light and then weighting the signals of the colors interpreted by the sensor: this is white balance.

The Neutral Gray Card

The standard exposure calibration was set at 18% gray by Kodak in the 1930s. This is still used as the benchmark for measuring exposure and for color calibration. To standardize our white balance, then, we use a gray card.

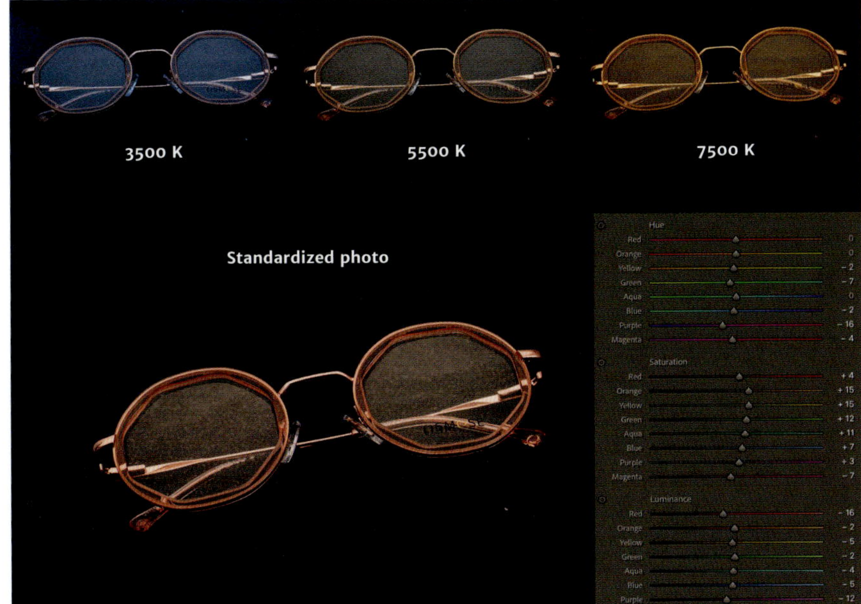

« The same object photographed at 3500 K, 5500 K, and 7500 K. A TSL (Tone, Saturation, Luminance) profile was created by photographing a palette of colors in the same lighting conditions, using the SpyderCheckr software. The screen was calibrated using a SpyderX Elite probe.

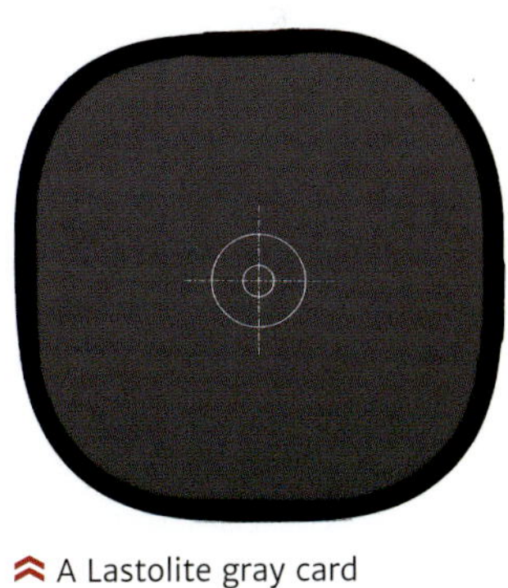

⌃ A Lastolite gray card

To simplify, a gray card reacts as if it is composed of 18% pigments that reflect light perfectly and 82% absolute black pigments. To make it clearer, we call it "neutral" gray because it includes as much red and green as it does blue: in RGB values, thus, neutral gray corresponds to a value of 118 (with a tolerance from 114 to 122), with the RGB including more levels in the dark tones than in the light ones, because human eyes are better adapted for distinguishing dark tones.

I should note that manufacturers often offer a version of these charts that includes an X for the sake of focusing.

Using a neutral gray card is very simple:

1. Place the card in the same place as the product to be photographed, under the same lighting conditions.
2. Measure the exposure using an independent exposure meter and set the camera to the measured value, without optimizing the exposure. Or proceed in reverse by adjusting the power of the light sources so that their measured illumination will correspond exactly to the camera settings. Because the photo is being taken in RAW, the white balance chosen for the first shot doesn't matter.
3. Take a photo framing only the gray card. We activate the custom white balance function of the camera by choosing this shot.
4. Take a second photo including the object, the neutral gray card, and a color reference card (following photo) side by side. This second shot will be used to finalize the calibration of the development software.

It is important to repeat this operation every time there is a change in the lighting.

Standardization in Post-Production

The RAW file format saves the values of the light received by the sensor and the adjustment of the white balance separately. The white balance adjustment performed by the camera is thus only an indicator during the post-production process, where it can be precisely corrected without damaging the file. But before calibrating the image itself, the screen that is used to view it must be calibrated.

Monitor Calibrators

This instrument is seldom used by amateurs, but it is crucial for anyone who wants to obtain perfectly true colors. High-quality calibrators are now available for under $200. You will need to go through the following

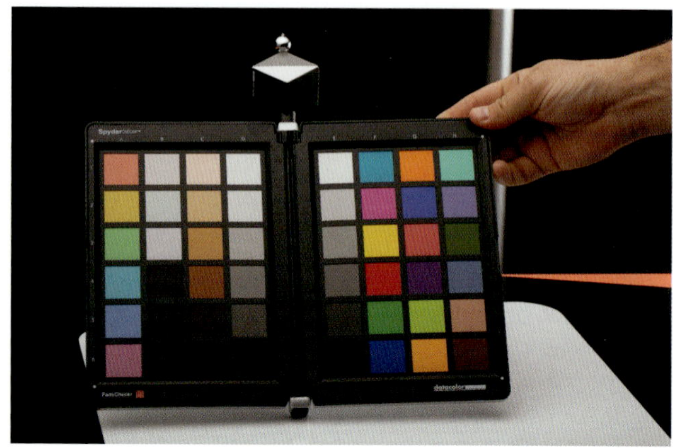

Photo of a reference palette including a neutral gray card placed in the exact same position and under the same lighting conditions as the pair of glasses on the previous page. The camera setting is what was measured with an independent exposure meter.

calibration process regularly, because screen color rendition varies depending on how long the screen has been turned on and how old it is:

1. Install the software supplied with the calibrator on your computer.
2. Position the calibrator on the screen (the calibrators usually come with an attachment system).
3. Once it has been launched, the calibration software will compare the colors of its palette with the actual display and will create an ICC colorimetric profile (a small file of a few dozen KB) that will correct the colors to keep them true.

There are automatic modes, but I suggest you carry out a complete calibration, nonetheless. You will be surprised at the quality of the result.

Creating a Color Profile for the Camera

You can save a lot of time by editing a colorimetric profile specific to your camera, using a color reference chart and the appropriate software. Simply photograph a calibrated color palette with each change in the light, and use the dedicated software to create a reference profile, which will then be interpreted by the development software. But note that this profile will only work for photos that are illuminated exactly the same way as the reference shots; every time you change the lighting, you will have to redo this operation.

Calibration Using Development Software

All development software (Capture One, Lightroom, Camera Raw, etc.) is equipped with a white balance selector tool. It is represented by an eyedropper next to the white balance editor. Simply import the photo of the neutral gray card, click on it with the eyedropper, and the software will apply the appropriate correction. Then duplicate this calibration and apply it to all of the photos that were taken with that lighting, under those conditions.

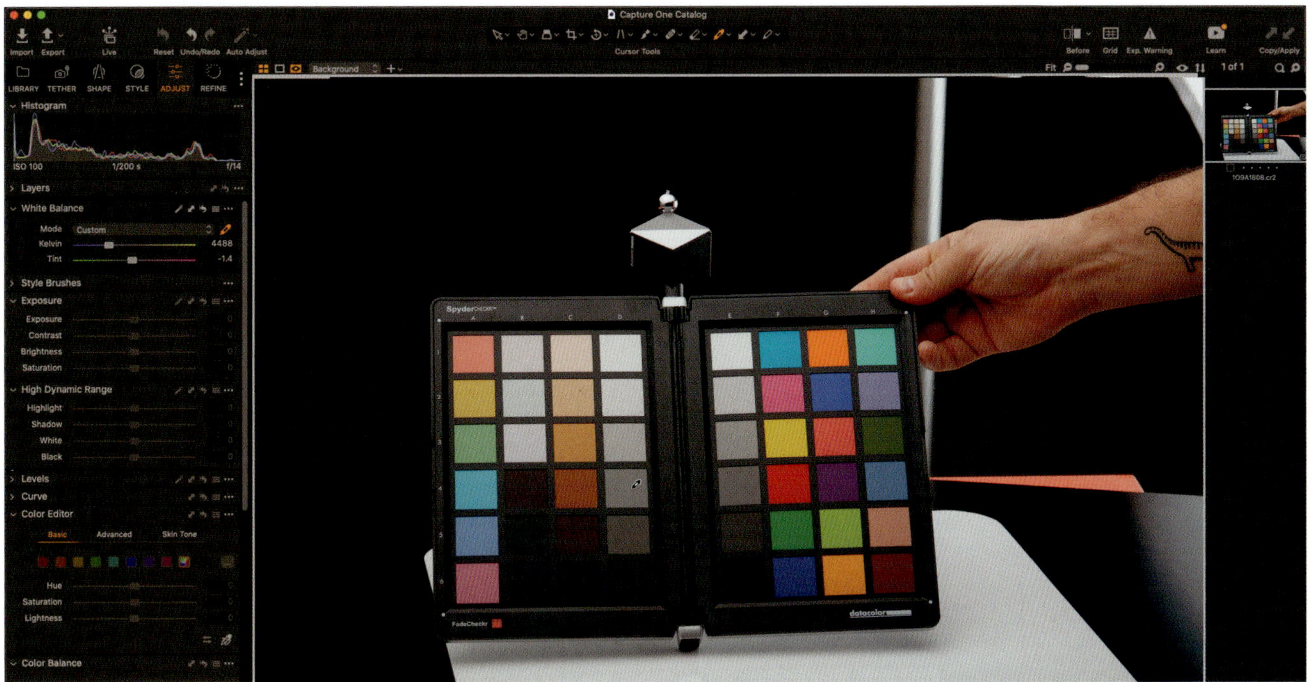

« Import the photo in Capture One (or your software of choice), select the white balance selector tool, and click on the neutral gray card. This operation will allow you to calculate the necessary white balance.

PHOTO EDITING

It is rare for photos of objects not to need any digital editing. However, we can reduce the amount of editing we have to do by carefully managing the lighting and shooting.

This book is not meant to teach you how to do digital editing, something I do little of and that is also explained in detail in many other books. My aim here, instead, is to emphasize how to prepare the shot so that any editing will be quick and successful.

What Can Be Corrected During the Shot

After years of practice, I can state that most editing for product photography can be preempted by methodically preparing the product, carefully managing the placement of the light and the measurements, precisely positioning the diffusers and barn doors, rigorously managing the imaging chain (especially in terms of color), and knowing how to control your camera.

As an example, I have used a lipstick tube placed on a transparent plexiglass wedge in front of a softbox. A reflector is placed to the right of the image. Looked at raw, before adjusting the white balance, the image shows a large number of problems, which could require dozens of minutes of editing. But most of the problems have very simple remedies: positioning barn doors to make the tube's silhouette more precise and to unify the reflections on the front section, using a gray card to calibrate the colors, handling the object with gloves, etc.

What is left are the defects that are inherent to the specific object we are dealing with here: in this case, the plastic shell is not completely smooth; the lipstick itself has miniscule nodules on its surface because the product was not stored properly; and a few fine scratches can be seen, even though the object was brand-new and in spite of the care I took while handling it.

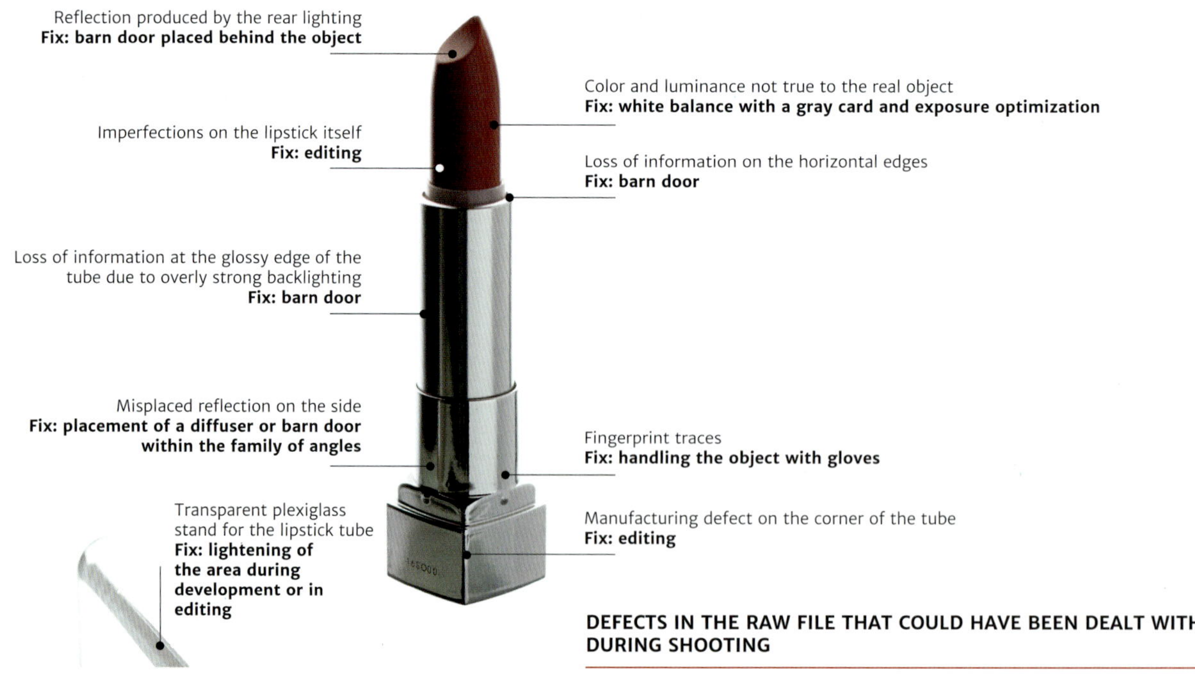

DEFECTS IN THE RAW FILE THAT COULD HAVE BEEN DEALT WITH DURING SHOOTING

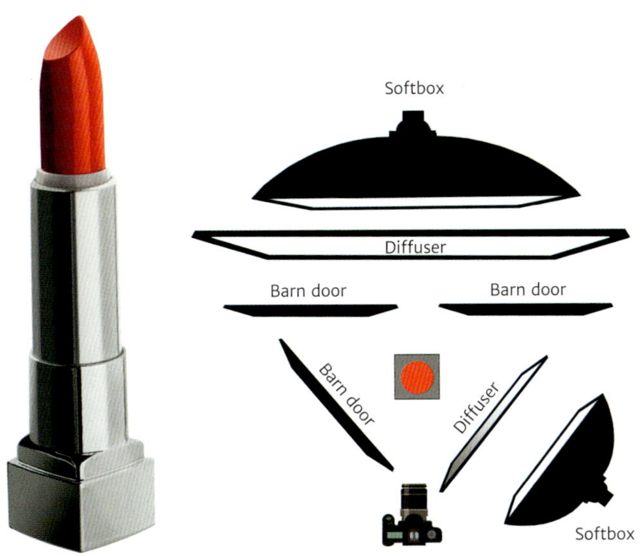

<< Here we changed the lighting of the lipstick tube by placing barn doors to either side behind the object, directed toward the front left side, while lighting from the back and from the front right using diffusers. The only editing consisted of erasing the little bumps on the bottom of the tube, the plexiglass base whose edge had been showing, and the fingerprint.

What Requires Editing

Most scratches and bumps can be corrected using the frequency separation technique. There are a lot of great, in-depth tutorials online demonstrating this technique. For now, simply note that in Photoshop, this technique will allow you to separate the image into two separate layers—one including the textures, the other including the colors—that you can edit separately. The advantage of this process over the usual correction tools (the clone stamp tool, sample source overlay, etc.) is that you can limit the editor to working on only one of the two layers. Thus, for instance, you can make a scratch disappear by duplicating a nearby, contiguous area that has no flaws in the texture layer, without affecting the color. And if the issue is a color problem, you can do the same thing in the color layer, without affecting the texture. I used this process to eliminate the scratches and irregularities on the lipstick shown above left.

For problems connected with the lighting, and with reflections that appear in the wrong place because the object has a shape defect, you can use the dodge and burn technique. In this case, on top of the layer of the image, you add a new layer filled with 50% gray (in Photoshop: Edit > Fill, and then choose 50% Gray from the Contents drop-down menu). Then, if you choose Soft Light under the blending mode option, this layer will become invisible. Using a very soft brush, set to a low opacity (less than 8%), you can then paint the areas in the gray layer where you want to fix something by applying black (to darken the areas) or white (to lighten them).

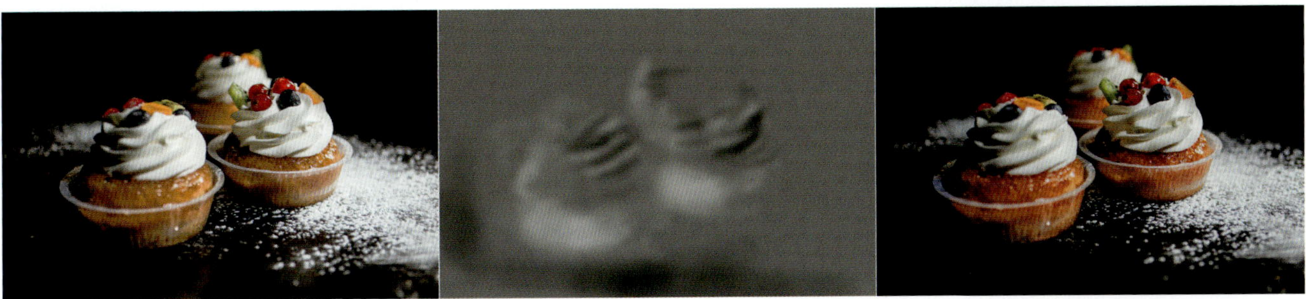

An example of dodging and burning. On the left, the original photo; in the middle, the gray layer to which we applied black and white with the brush; on the right, the photo once the gray layer was made visible using the Soft Light blending mode.

BOTTLES OF RED WINE

Lighting wine bottles is a typical assignment for product photographers. There are countless winemakers, and the vintages change every year. But photographers who truly excel in this field are rare because it is a very difficult discipline.

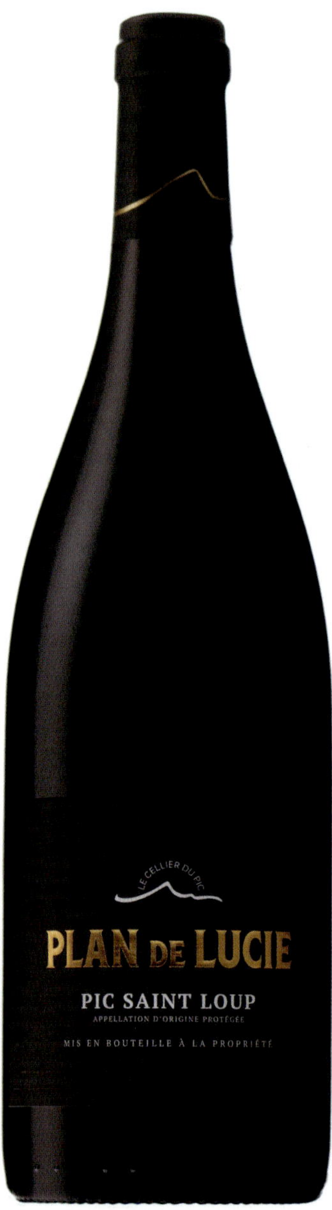

« An example of the lighting of a bottle of red wine for a catalog. This photo, illuminated using the methods laid out in this section, did not require any editing. On the golden part of the lettering, we can clearly see the influence of each light source.

In photographing wine bottles, the lighting difficulties add up: we have glossy, cylindrical glass; a matte label that is sometimes embossed and gilded; there is stenciling on the glass that produces hard-to-control direct reflections; the background must be completely white for catalogs; the management of linear reflections on the edges of the bottle; the issue of lighting the stand or holder without creating reflections on the base of the object; and so on. Everything comes together to make this a very difficult assignment. The best way to deal with it is to address the problems one at a time.

Before You Start

Before photographing a bottle, always make sure to ask the producer to choose products with no defects; they will not, however, always be able to do so. Because the bottles are packaged in industrial production lines, it often happens that the seam (the visible mold mark resulting from the press process) appears on the front of the bottle. The same is true for stains and tears on the labels and flaws in the stenciling. In each of these cases, the only solution is photo editing.

Preparing the Bottle

Before starting anything, you will need to make sure that the bottle suits the lighting you have planned for it by examining its characteristics and possible flaws, the types of reflections that can be expected, etc. This examination will also allow you to determine whether you can photograph the bottle all at once or whether there are lighting issues that are impossible to reconcile (such as the presence of a medallion that contradicts the lighting of the bands, embossing on the label that will require that it be directly lit, etc.), forcing you to create a composite photo (see page 204). Then, when you have several bottles to photograph, you will be able to organize your work so that you don't have to change the lighting for each one.

Next, you will prepare the product, making sure that it is perfectly clean (glass always attracts dust), that the capsule (protective sleeve on the neck) is well centered (you can just rotate it by firmly pressing on the neck), and that you have straightened out any folds in the label.

Setting Up the Object

Bottles are generally photographed on commercial pack-shot tables, but you could obtain a similar result by placing a sheet of translucent plexiglass over two trestles arranged in front of a white background. Just be careful that the space behind the arrangement, as well as on both sides of it, is wide enough for you to be able to set up your diffusers and light sources.

It will make things much easier if you shoot in a place where there is no lighting other than what is intended for your product, with a black background behind you, and wearing black yourself: glass's highly reflective surface works like the glossy sphere we discussed on page 87, where everything within the family of angles that is light-colored or luminous will show up.

The ideal setup is to position the object on a stand solid enough that the lighting meant to illuminate the lower part of the image is not reflected on the bottom of the bottle. I use four-inch-high matte-black cylinders, with a slightly smaller diameter than that of the base of the bottle. Make sure that it stays perfectly straight.

The stand can then be removed in post-production, using a linear filter in Lightroom if the bottom of the bottle is flat, or using an area selection tool in Photoshop if the bottom of the bottle is serrated.

Lighting the Background

Start by placing a light source directed toward the background, in rim light, so that the entire space behind the bottle is white. It doesn't matter whether the light is soft or hard, but it's a good idea to use a zoom bowl equipped with barn doors to direct the light properly.

The light on the background is then measured at +3.33 EV in relation to the camera setting (or more if the object

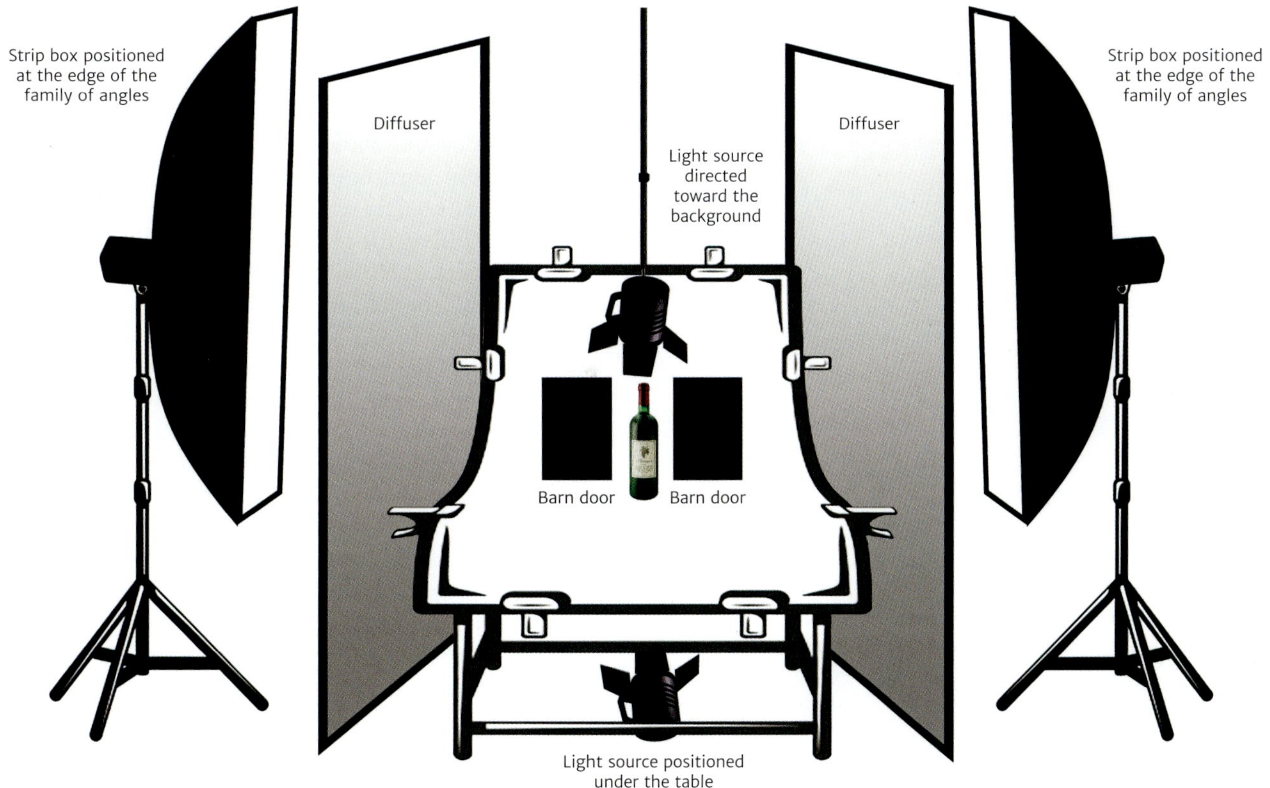

STANDARD METHOD FOR LIGHTING A BOTTLE OF RED WINE

is very far from the background). For example, when the lighting of the background is measured at f/18 for a camera setting of f/5.6, the background will be completely white. Of course, with this much light, there is also the risk that the edges of the bottle will be massively overexposed; but this can be mostly dealt with by making sure that the background is as far away from the product as possible.

Lighting the Base

Proceed in the same way by positioning a light source under the table to accompany the reflection of the rim light. This light should not be very strong, since the table is very close to the bottle; this light is only meant to accompany the rim light, which already produces a significant reflection on the table (see diagram on page 125). The main issue here is to even out the light on the bottom of the image and give a little light to the label.

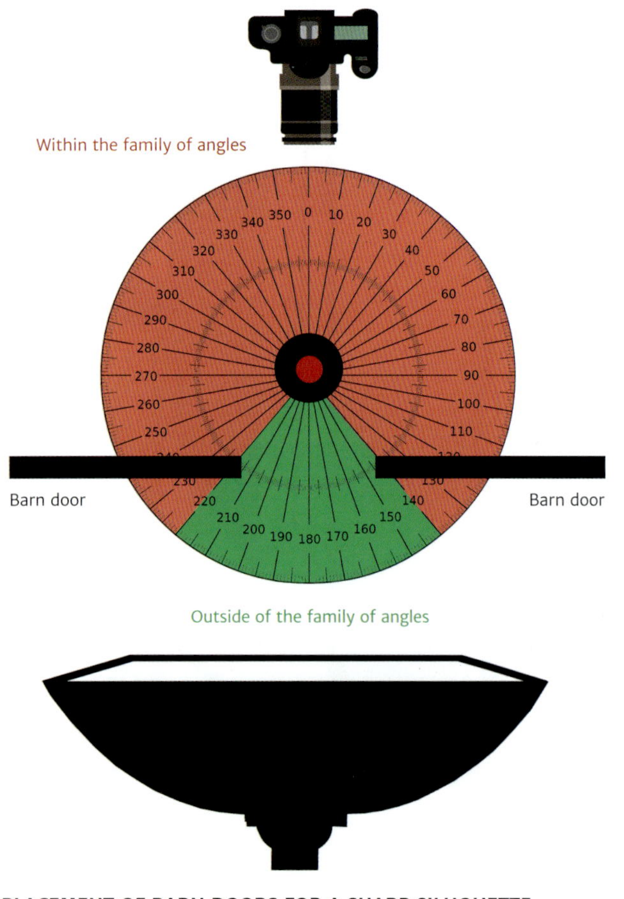

PLACEMENT OF BARN DOORS FOR A SHARP SILHOUETTE

This light, nicely diffused by the plexiglass of the table, will join the two side strip boxes to even out the lighting on the label. It should be adjusted (using the power measured on the table, with the lumisphere directed toward the light source) to the same value as the camera setting. Add +0.3 EV if the label is dark or black.

Producing a Sharp Silhouette

We have already noted that when the backlighting is strong enough to create a perfectly burned-out background, there is a risk that its reflection will create an unappealing fade-out effect on the edges of the bottle. To avoid this, and to produce clean, well-defined edges, you will need to position two barn doors behind the object, one on each side (see diagram at left). Given that glossy cylindrical objects have a family of angles of 280°, like spheres, the barn doors will have to be positioned outside the family of angles—at least at 220° and 140°. They will, of course, appear in the photograph, but the bottle will be perfectly illuminated, and you can just crop the photo to remove them.

Producing Even Reflections on the Edges

In Europe, the tradition is that in lighting bottles of red wine, you must have one or two bands of direct reflections, more or less subdued depending on the category of wine, on at least one of the two sides of the bottle. The number of bands of reflection and their quality will vary depending on the grape variety, the appellation, the winemaker, and the photographer (see photo on following page), but the fact remains that for fine wines, very soft reflections are created, and for lesser wines, slightly harder reflections.

There is no kind of light shaper that is perfectly suited to projecting these reflections, which must be long, narrow, and extremely diffused. You can use reflected lights, projecting the light from two strip boxes onto reflectors placed at 260° and 100°: the light quality will be perfect, but the width of the bands will be hard to correct. My advice is that you use two strip boxes behind two large diffusers instead (see diagram on page 125), both of them positioned in the same way, which will avoid climaxes in the reflections. By playing with the distance between the strip box and the diffuser, you can easily manage the quality of the reflections and comfortably decide on the result you would like to attain. One of the main advantages of this arrangement is that, along with the lighting positioned under the table, it allows you to illuminate the label as well. With two reflections, the

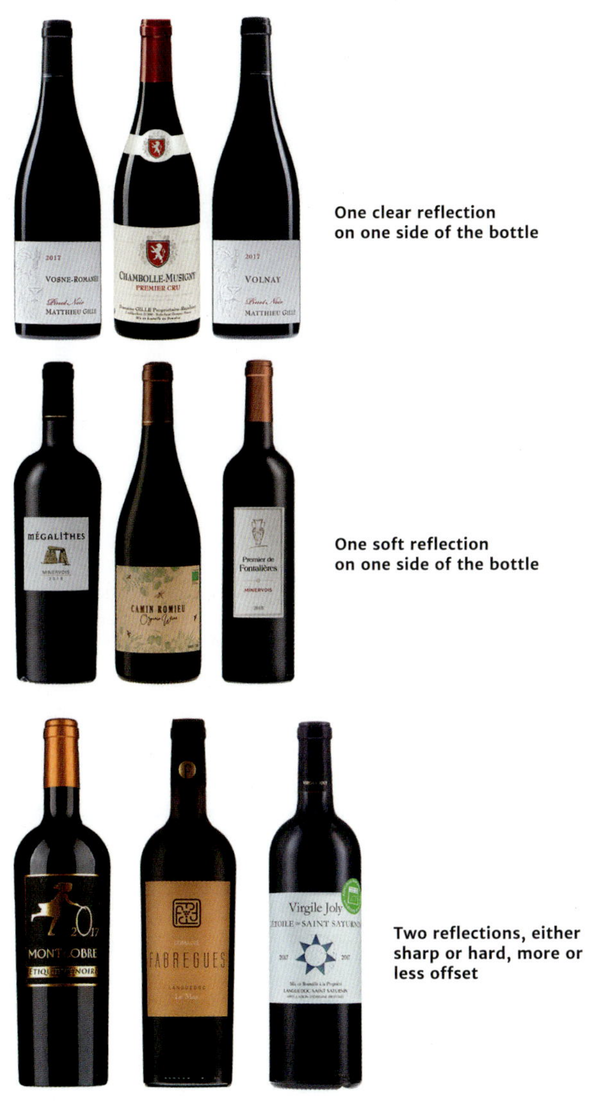

POSSIBILITIES FOR LIGHTING BOTTLES OF RED WINE

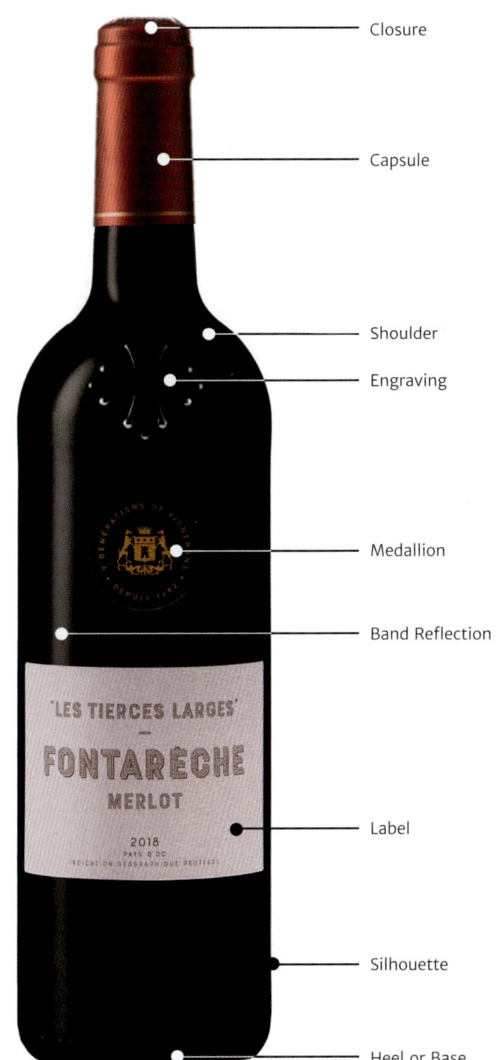

VOCABULARY

light on the label is evened out and will not need any intervention in post-production (i.e., dodge and burn; see previous section).

Lighting the Label

The label does not generally need its own dedicated lighting. However, if it is embossed or has glossy lettering (usually gold or silver), you may need to place a light source along one of the frontal axes, which will produce an unsightly reflection in the glass. Then you will have to take two shots: one arranged as described above and

one in which you only light the label. The two photos can then be combined in Photoshop, with only the label selected for the second shot.

Lighting the Engraving

The cylindrical shape of the bottle allows for radical "showerhead" lighting. (By "showerhead" lighting I mean the light is positioned like a showerhead in relation to the product; see the illustration on page 93). When the bottle also includes engraving (usually a coat of arms, such as the Occitan cross or cross of Languedoc for wines

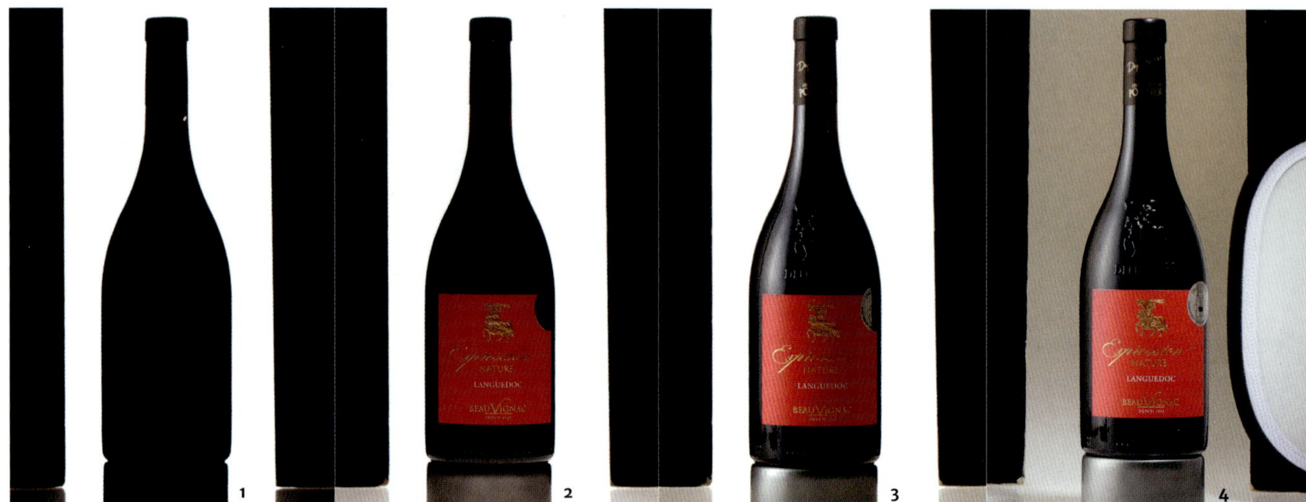

⌃ Example of steps for positioning the lighting: 1. Place a light source directed toward the background and two barn doors within the family of angles. 2. Set up a light source underneath the table to light the bottom of the bottle and, to some degree, the label. 3. Place a strip box on one side of the bottle, at an angle of approximately 100°. 4. Arrange a diffuser in front of the strip box and a small white reflector at around 100° to direct the light onto the medallion. For this shot, because the presence of the diffuser and the reflector will give too much light to the engraving, the medallion will need to be addressed with a third photo.

from southern France), you will have to light that separately, as you do for label embossing.

Because of the shape and the material of engravings, they are unable to produce diffuse reflections. No matter what the lighting, you will never achieve even lighting across the entire engraving. Therefore, you will need to use a snoot, equipped with a honeycomb grid and positioned in a vertical showerhead position, directed toward the engraving. This will produce direct reflections onto all of the convex surfaces situated within the same angle, leaving the rest in shadow. You just need to be careful to make the ray of light narrow enough so that it does not also light the bottle's shoulders.

Lighting the Capsule

When the capsule is light-colored, no additional lighting is needed, but for black capsules you might need to plan for more lighting. If the light is narrow enough (using a snoot equipped with a honeycomb) and directed horizontally at the level of the capsule, the result can be satisfactory. You can also place a barn door below to avoid possible reflections on the glass.

Lighting the Medallion and the Cardboard Sleeve

Some bottles have a medallion, either awarded by an agricultural competition or indicating some special feature of the wine and meant to attract the consumer's attention. These are stickers that are generally positioned between the capsule and the neck of the bottle, and they are often gold or silver. A medallion requires the same kind of lighting as the capsule, but the medallion is often too low for it to be lighted without risking creating reflections on the glass. Thus, a separate photo must be taken and then integrated as a layer in Photoshop.

Likewise, there are often cardboard sleeves (printed cardboard placed on the bottle's shoulders and wrapping around its neck). They usually do not cause any problems, because they react to light the same way the label does. If not, they should be treated like the capsule.

Color and Preparation of the Shot

Most bottles of red wine look opaque, in which case the color of the liquid is not crucial. But for light red wines, such as a Beaujolais Nouveau or a Bordeaux Clairet, the shot will have to be carefully calibrated using a gray card. Every wine expert will tell you that the color of the wine is both a commercial tool and the identity of the product. Also make sure not to oversaturate the colors in post-production.

BOTTLES OF ROSÉ AND WHITE WINE

Even though the container is not that different from what is used for red wine, because of their greater transparency, rosés and white wines react differently to light. The question of color, therefore, takes on greater importance.

While the lighting of bottles of rosé and white wine seems simpler, because you need fewer light sources, it also requires greater precision, especially in the management of tones and nuances.

Delicate Lighting

Unlike for the bottles in the previous section, here the challenge is to make the color of the liquid look as good as possible—it needs to be harmonious, true, and even. The lighting of the back of the bottle is no longer just a matter of lighting the background, but also of providing the luminance and color that match the wine itself.

The light source, therefore, is no longer directed from the front to the background, but rather behind the background, so that the light is as diffuse as possible. If you don't have a standard packshot table available, you can achieve a similar result by placing a diffusing fabric behind the bottle and then, behind that, arranging a light equipped with a relatively large light box. Make sure that the light measured on the diffuser (with the lumisphere directed toward the light source) is +3.33 EV, as with the bottles of red wine. This arrangement will ensure that you have a very soft, even lighting, while limiting the appearance of localized highlights.

As usual, you will need to arrange two barn doors at the edge of the bottle's family of angles to ensure a well-defined silhouette. Also pay attention to making the reflection of the black bands at the edges of the bottle as fine as possible by positioning the covers very precisely. You can make the positioning more exact by moving the bottle to the ideal distance. Think of the edges of the bottle looking as though they had been drawn with a well-sharpened gray pencil.

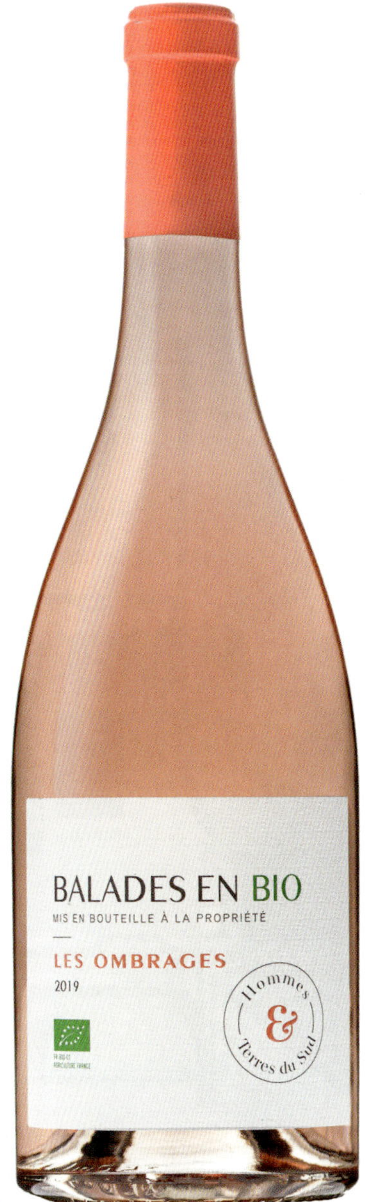

» Example of lighting of a bottle of rosé for a catalog.

Reflections or No Reflections?

You do not need to light the bottle so as to produce bands of reflections on either side of the front of the bottle; some winemakers, however, will ask for that.

The presence of the bands has the advantage that it solves the problem of lighting the label, while keeping the bottle from looking like it is made of frosted glass (see next section).

If you're trying to produce a shot without visible reflections, you will need to use the method for lighting cylinders: a rounded diffuser placed in front of the bottle, with a hole in it for the camera lens to pass through. This will position the backlighting to reflect on the diffuser, so that the front of the bottle is globally illuminated, without any reflections appearing on it—there will, in fact, be a reflection, but since it covers the entire visible surface, it can't be distinguished. And if, by any chance, the result ends up looking a little foggy, you can just apply a 10% or 15% Dehaze filter in Lightroom.

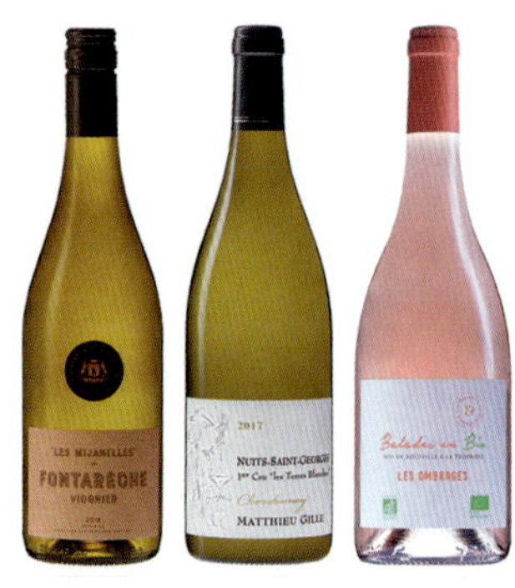

One clear reflection on one side of the bottle

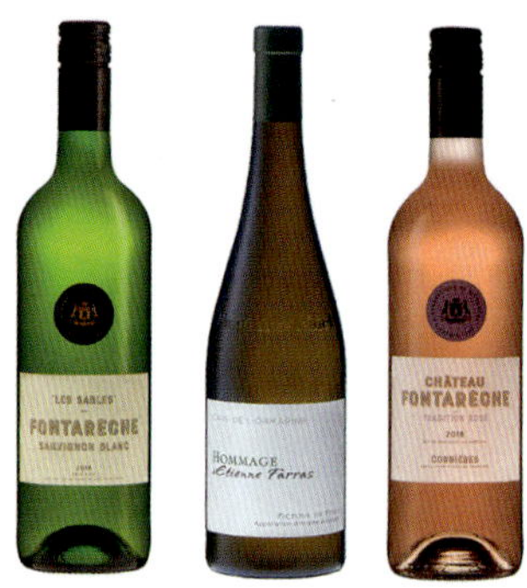

One soft reflection on one side of the bottle

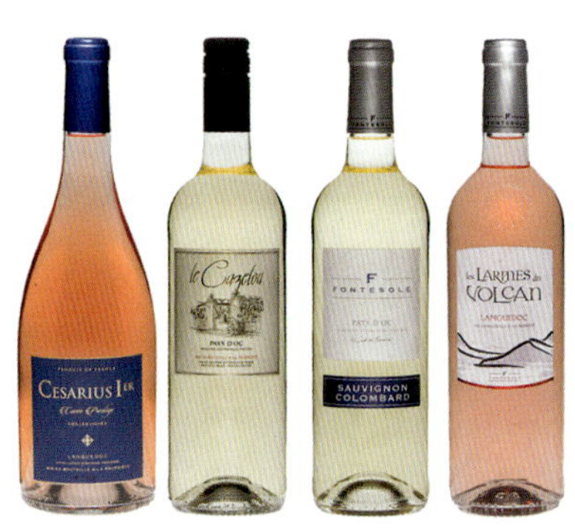

No reflections

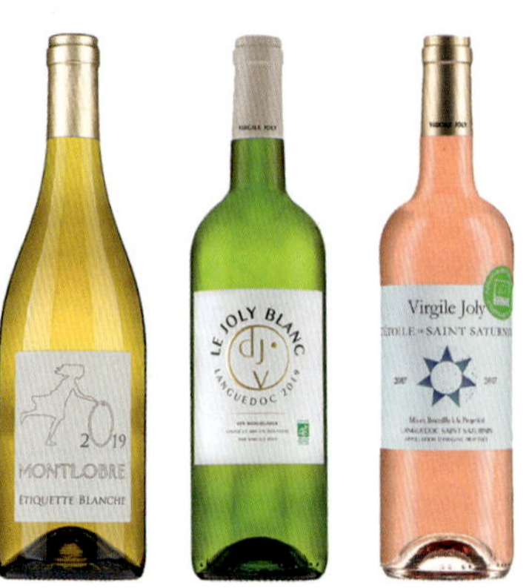

Two reflections, sharp or hard, more or less offset

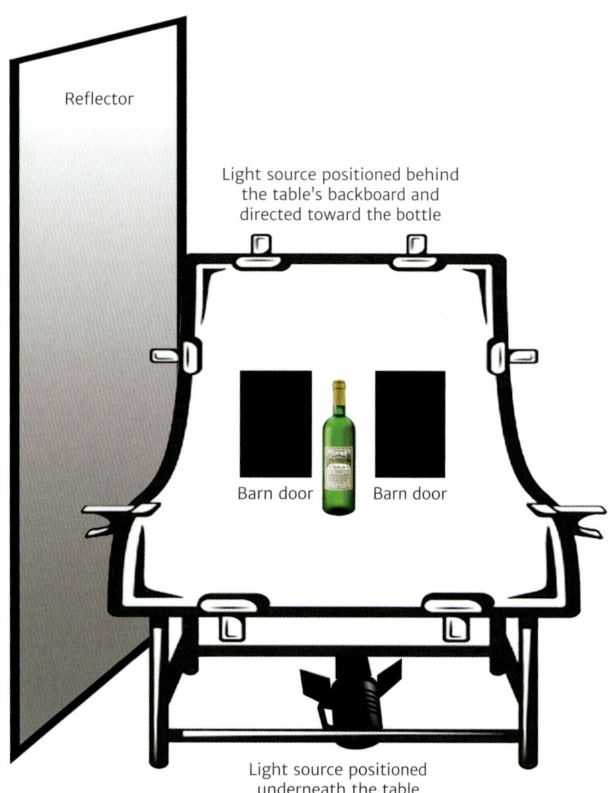

STANDARD METHOD FOR LIGHTING ROSÉS AND WHITE WINES

POSSIBLE WAYS OF LIGHTING ROSÉS AND WHITE WINES

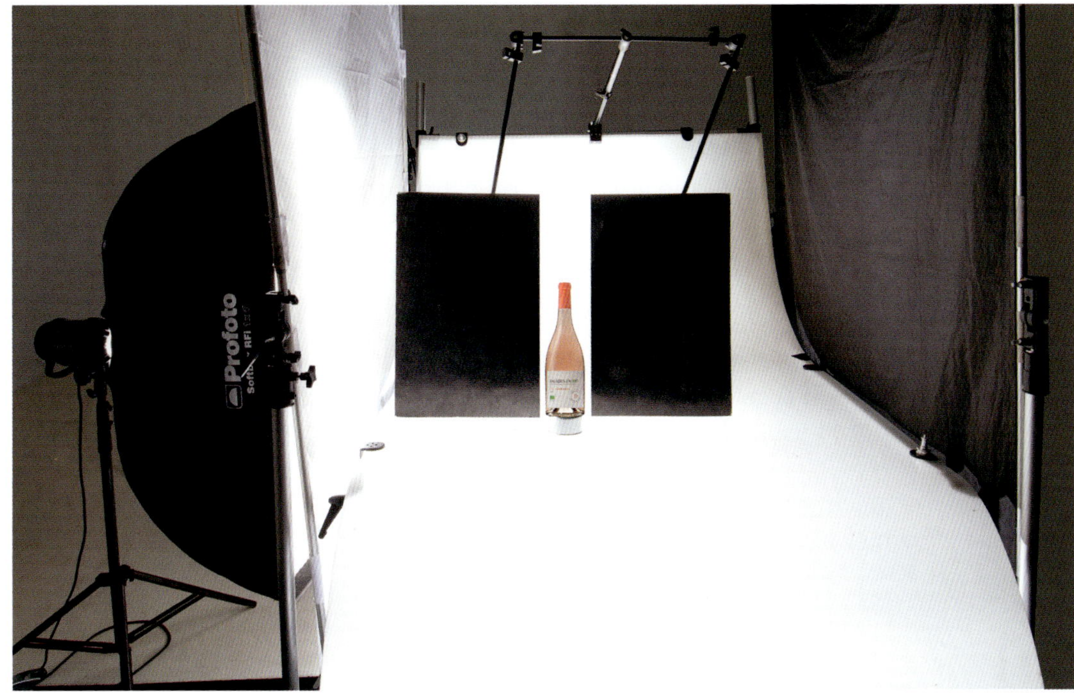

« A behind-the-scenes view of the lighting of the bottle shown on page 129. Three light sources were used: a bowl fitted with a barn door and placed behind the table's backboard, using backlighting through the plexiglass; a light source on the ground, underneath the table, directed vertically toward the bottle; and a strip box behind a large diffusing fabric, to the right of the bottle. Two barn doors were placed behind the bottle, and a third one to the left of the bottle.

If you decide to include visible reflections, then just use the method that has been outlined for red wine, while playing with the dimming as much as possible: move the light source away from the side diffuser so that its luminous flux covers all of it, or even move the diffuser away from the bottle if the light source is too close to it (because the diffuser is not fully illuminated, the source will look smaller, from the point of view of the bottle, than if it were fully lit).

Wine All the Way to the Top

Some winemakers and some labels want their bottles of rosé and white wine presented so that the surface of the liquid cannot be seen, so it looks as though the bottle is filled all the way up to the cork. Of course, there is no such thing in reality, because the empty space left underneath the cork at the neck of the bottle prevents the wine from escaping if there is a change in temperature and a resulting increase in pressure. In these cases, therefore, you have no choice but to edit the photo in Photoshop. You can duplicate the color of the wine in the area above the label (which is the most even area in the photo) and then paste it into the empty space, using a layer mask. Then, all you need to do is pass the eraser tool, set to a low opacity, over the area as much as is needed to fill the empty space.

Color and Post-Production

White wines and rosés are textbook cases of the need to calibrate the camera using a well-suited colorimetric profile and the use of the gray card and the colorimetric probe described on pages 119–120. The color of the wine is not a coincidence, but rather is the result of meticulous work on the part of the enologist, who has chosen to blend several different wines according to their taste qualities, of course, and the result they desire in terms of color.

Rigorous management of the imaging chain and rigorous control of the lighting will ensure that the final color is true, but you must also be careful not to saturate the colors that you obtain in the final phase of post-production: this would have the effect of "pinking" white wines, which is considered to be a flaw associated with poor winemaking—purists would think they looked like "stained" wines, which are wines contaminated by the presence of red wine anthocyanins. In addition, note that the fashion, originating with wines from Provence, is to present ever paler rosés, to give the impression that they are lighter and fresher.

FROSTED-GLASS BOTTLES

Frosted-glass bottles, generally used for white wine and rosé, are becoming more and more common. To illuminate them properly, the light must be extremely diffused.

This kind of bottle is produced using a technique called *satinizing*, in which the bottle is immersed in an acid bath that attacks the surface of the glass, giving it a frosted or sandblasted look (depending on how long it is in the acid). After that, the lighting plays an essential role in emphasizing the impression of a silky finish.

Diffuse Reflections

After it has been attacked by the acid, the surface of the bottle is no longer smooth, and it can no longer produce direct reflections, only diffuse ones. Thus, there is also no longer any risk of producing poorly positioned highlights. You might therefore reason that any light source, placed anywhere, would work just fine. And this would be true if you were photographing a bottle filled with something opaque, but the challenge here, as in the previous section, is to light the bottle while making the contents look as good as possible, in terms of both light and color.

In addition, even though the bottle only produces diffuse reflections, there is still the risk, if you use lighting that is too hard or too localized, that shiny spots might appear, which would then require editing work. As with all translucent objects, therefore, you need to have a solid strategy for the lighting.

Evenness in the Color of the Wine

The management of the light here involves producing very even lighting behind the bottle so that the color of the wine will be as constant as possible, while also maintaining the tonality that we expect from a cylinder (a gradual change in lighting across the various parts of the shape).

As always in such cases, you will need to make sure that you have perfectly calibrated your screen and adjusted your white balance using a gray card, as well as a colorimetric profile on a palette. It's essential to get the right shade.

After that, you will have to place your light sources so that they are well centered—the laws of refraction mean that this positioning will ensure that the light is well distributed across the bottle, and will avoid the presence of discolored or grayish areas along its edges.

Lighting Strategy

As with all transparent glass, the strategy of backlighting is a necessity here. To achieve the softest and most even light possible, use the following steps:

1. Position the rim light, equipped with a softbox, behind the bottle, then place a diffusing fabric far enough away from the softbox that it will be lit up over its entire surface.

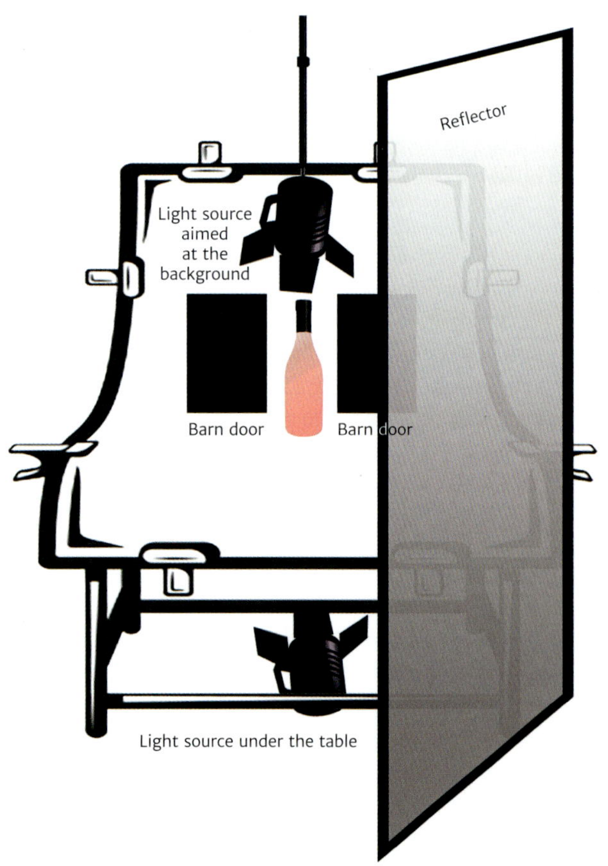

STANDARD METHOD FOR LIGHTING FROSTED-GLASS BOTTLES

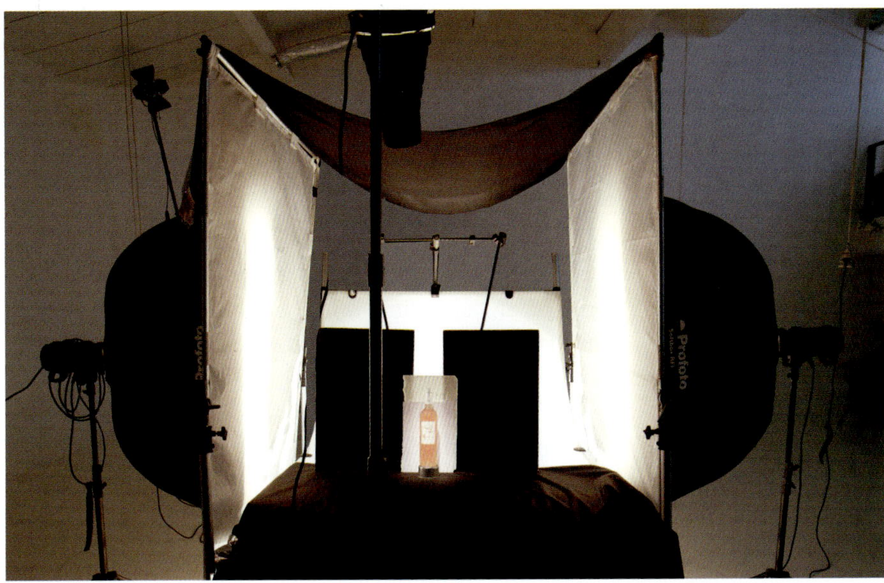

A behind-the-scenes view of the lighting of the bottle at right. The front of the bottle and the label are illuminated using a snoot equipped with a honeycomb grid positioned frontally at 70°, from above. A brushed cotton sheet is placed under and over the bottle to avoid reflections from above and below, and a sheet of translucent paper is positioned behind the bottle to even out the lighting of the wine.

The rim light can also be placed in reflection, as in the diagram on the previous page: pointing backward from the front, it is reflected on the panel located behind the bottle. The light is soft and even, and the setup will therefore be simpler.

2. Arrange two barn doors, one on each side of the bottle, to create a sharp silhouette. Place a sheet of translucent paper in the center (see the behind-the-scenes photo above) to harmonize the lights and give a sense that the color of the liquid has been smoothed.

3. Place two strip boxes along the two sides, behind diffusers, not to create reflections (as would be the case for smooth glass bottles), but to avoid creating areas of low light along the edges, and, especially, to illuminate the label and the capsule.

4. Because this kind of bottle is quite sensitive to grazing side light, do not light up its base from below. We generally place the bottle on a fabric that absorbs light, such as brushed cotton.

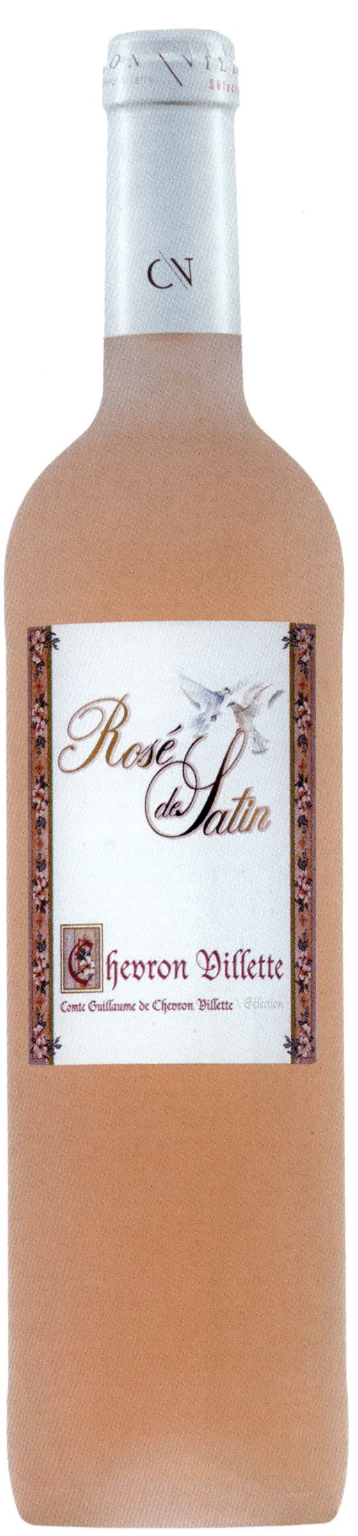

Example of lighting of a frosted-glass bottle of rosé for a catalog.

EMPTY BOTTLES

Glass bottles generally have a lot of flaws, particularly ones due to uneven thickness of the glass and the presence of opaque particles or air bubbles.

We have seen that it is advantageous for a glass container to be shown full, because the presence of a transparent liquid has the effect of evening out the light through refraction. This is true for all the bottles we have looked at so far. But the problem must be addressed anew when we photograph empty bottles.

Flaws

Glassmakers have a rich vocabulary for describing flaws in bottles: streaks, refractive index gradients, inclusions, bubbles, chips, stones, tears, etc. It is clear that laborious editing work will be required to produce a high-quality shot that you can present to your client.

Filling the Bottle

The best way to solve the problem is to play with the refraction of light: filled to the brim, the bottle will behave like a magnifying lens, and all the flaws on the interior surface will disappear. You can use water for this, but for an optimal result you will find that a transparent mineral oil, like paraffin oil, works best.

You can take this even further: by submerging the bottle in an aquarium filled with water, you can also eliminate the flaws on the outside of the bottle. In this case, it is the whole apparatus of aquarium, water, and bottle taken together that works as a magnifying lens.

Of course, flaws related to the inclusion of particles and air bubbles will still be visible because their refractive indexes are very different from that of glass, but most defects will be corrected.

Lighting

As with the wineglass, we proceed using backlighting (a strip box placed behind a diffusing fabric). This light alone may be enough, as with the photo of the flask below, but glassmakers often require there to be a pronounced reflection on the front of the object: to make that happen, a strip box is placed at 90°. This kind of reflection makes it possible to emphasize how polished the glass is while also showing off the bottle's specific shape.

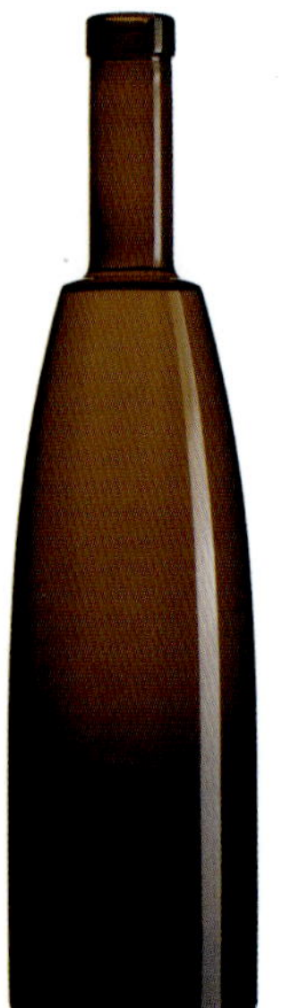
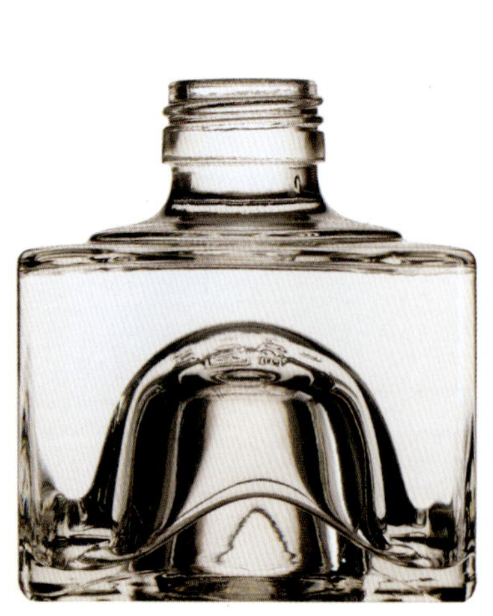

« Three bottles, with different shapes and colors, filled with water and photographed using backlighting.

LIGHTING A PAINTING

Creating photographic reproductions of pictorial works is a common commercial activitiy for object photography studios. It is easy to see that, more than in any other area, this activity requires absolute fidelity to the original.

Reproductions meant for museums, photographs for exhibition catalogs or posters, certificates of authenticity—the list of areas in which a photographer is required is a long one, and provides regular work for professionals. It demands rigorous attention to fidelity in terms of both colors and proportions.

Preparation

The very first thing you have to do is make sure that the orientation of angles (homothety) in the shot is perfect. You do this by placing the camera lens at the level of the center of the painting, at a perpendicular angle to it. This requires setting up the camera on a tripod at the necessary distance to maintain an average diagonal angle of view of 24°. Thus, for a 12-inch painting, we use a 135mm lens at sixty inches away; for a 6.5-foot work, we use a 50mm lens with the camera 10 feet away (see the table on page 49). These precautions will allow you to guarantee that the proportions of the work are reproduced perfectly, matching the artist's original work.

Lighting

The lighting is arranged so as to achieve the most even and largest light possible, while keeping its contrasts as minimal as possible. To do this, very diffused lighting is placed more than 6.5 feet away from the object—traditionally, this light consists of two light boxes at 45° on either side of the painting. For textured paintings, we shall see that we have to add diffusing fabrics to minimize certain localized shadows. But hard lighting (bowls, lenses, shapers without diffusion) cannot be used at all. As a rule, you should also avoid frontal lighting, which could allow the shadow of the camera (and of the photographer, if you aren't using a remote control) to appear, and could generate very uneven lighting—the central climax area could cause highlights to appear on the painting.

Issues with Texture

Most of the works that photographers are asked to reproduce include material effects that you will have to try to render in the shot, while trying not to allow the shadows that they might produce to distort the image. To do this correctly, you will have to understand some things about painting.

Watercolors allow the grain of the paper to show through, and they accentuate it, so the grain must therefore be visible in the shot. Some paints are mixed with extenders (most often gypsum, kaolin, or lime); these are used to add dimensionality to the painted surface, and you can make them show by adding a third light box at 90°—in other words, a grazing side light meant to bring out the textures through slight shadows. The same is true for oil paints or acrylics mixed with sand, sawdust, shavings, or undercoats of coarse canvas or crumpled paper (as used by the Surrealists). For other techniques, such as the palette-knife paintings that were common among the Impressionists and, earlier, Fragonard, or material work using sponges or brushes, it may sometimes be necessary to slightly lower one of the two light sources in the standard arrangement (by 0.1 to 0.3 EV) to make the technique visible. When the texture of the canvas or the paper on which the work is painted plays an important role, as in Kandinsky's and Egon Schiele's watercolors, you will obtain a more elegant and more precise result by using a camera without a low-pass filter, such as the Canon 5DSR or the Nikon D5300. This kind of equipment, which

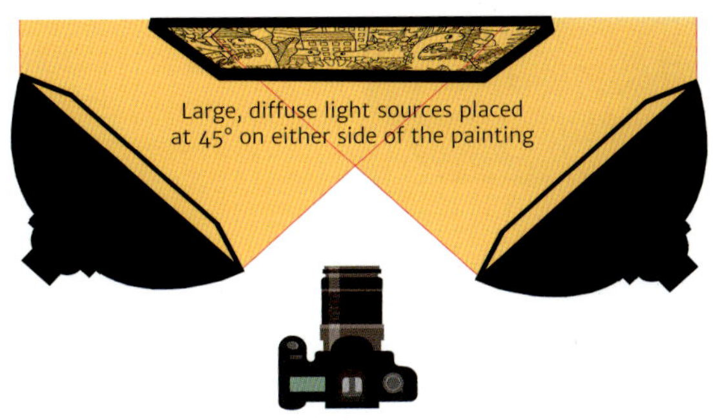

STANDARD METHOD FOR LIGHTING PAINTINGS

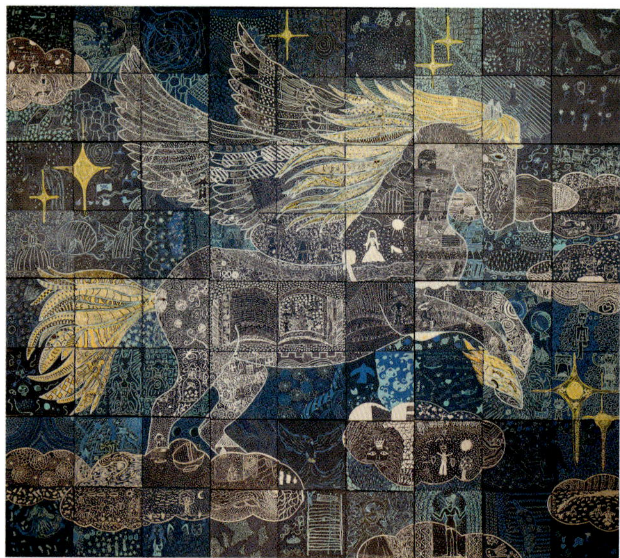

Particular Shapes and Materials

Many of the works that need to be photographed come in a variety of shapes. Collages, triptychs, stacked frames, 3D effects—the possibilities are endless. I remember, for instance, a painting by a Russian visual artist: it was red all over, and the very tightly woven cotton canvas was stretched in the center over a wooden pyramid, creating very different material effects depending on where you stood in relation to the work. In cases like this, you will need to use the lighting methods adapted to each kind of shape, as we discussed earlier: one of the two light sources will have to be somewhat minimized so that a slight shadow can indicate the presence of the pyramid.

Faithfulness to Colors and Reproduction

An accurate calibration to the color palette is crucial, especially if the photo is meant for reproduction or is being used for a certificate of authenticity. You will need to pay attention to the perfect measurement of your lighting (optimizing it during shooting, and correspondingly underexposing it during development), a good white balance using a gray card, the creation of a photographic reference on a color palette, and the precise calibration of your screen using the monitor calibrator. Remember that if the work includes materials that produce direct reflections, you will do well to wear black to avoid creating your own reflection as well.

allows you to represent high-frequency information such as repetitive patterns (the screen of a canvas or the grain of a paper) without an anti-aliasing filter reducing the sharpness of the image, will provide good results.

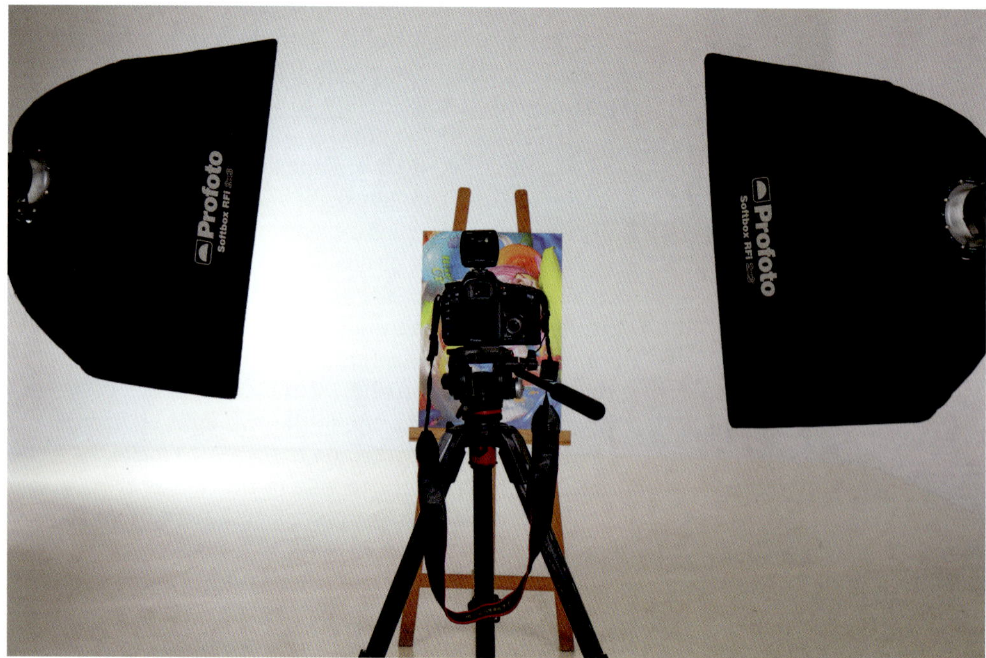

« A behind-the-scenes view of the lighting of a painting.

LIGHTING A MIRROR

Presented for their own sake or as part of another object, mirrors can be found in many situations. What I want to give you here is not so much a lighting method as a philosophy of photographing.

In photography, a mirror is essentially nothing but a reflection. It is up to us to decide what it is going to reflect. Thus, even before we think about what kind of lighting we use, we need to decide what we want to see appear in the image.

Preparation

More than any other object, a mirror must be perfectly cleaned before it is photographed. Fingerprints, static dust—everything will be visible in the final shot. To clean the mirror, I suggest spraying it with a mixture of hot water and white vinegar (lemon juice also works well), and then wiping it off with a microfiber cloth, using horizontal strokes from top to bottom.

Strategy

What you need to do now is determine what kind of result you'd like to obtain (see diagram below). If the camera is placed entirely within the family of angles of the light source, the mirror will appear completely white; if outside, it will appear completely black; if it is between the two, it will be partly black and partly white.

Mirrors are traditionally shown progressing gradually from white to light gray. To create this effect, position a light source whose reflection is larger than the total surface of the mirror, usually by setting up a large reflective fabric so that the edge of the family of angles coincides with the edge of the object. In photo shown below left,

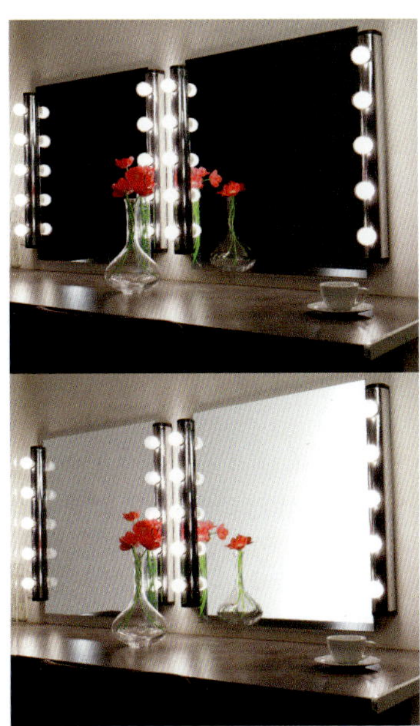

The same mirrors, lighted along different angles. The lighting in the bottom photo does the best job of showing that this is a reflective surface.

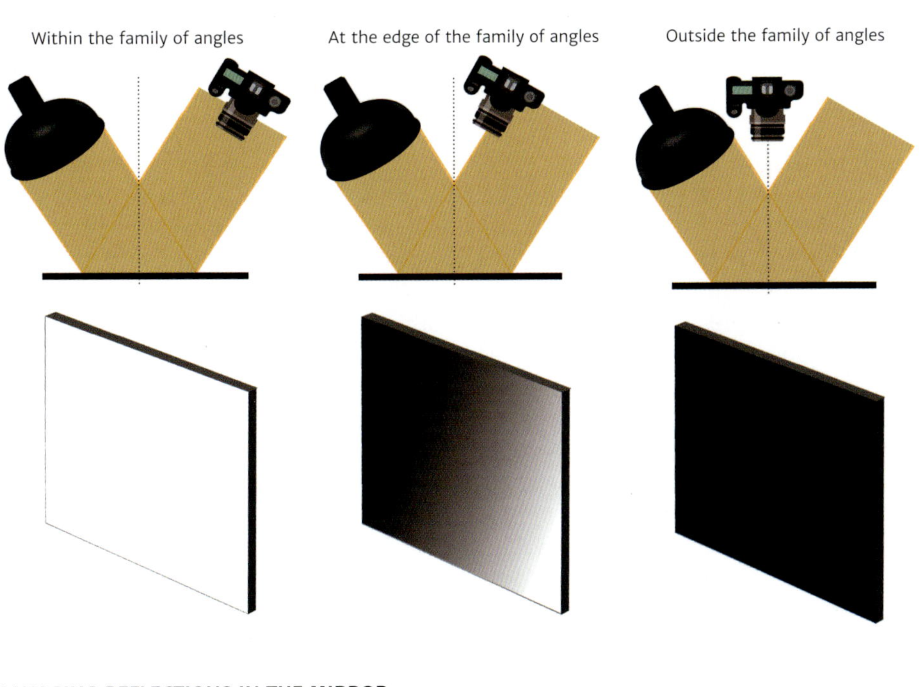

MANAGING REFLECTIONS IN THE MIRROR

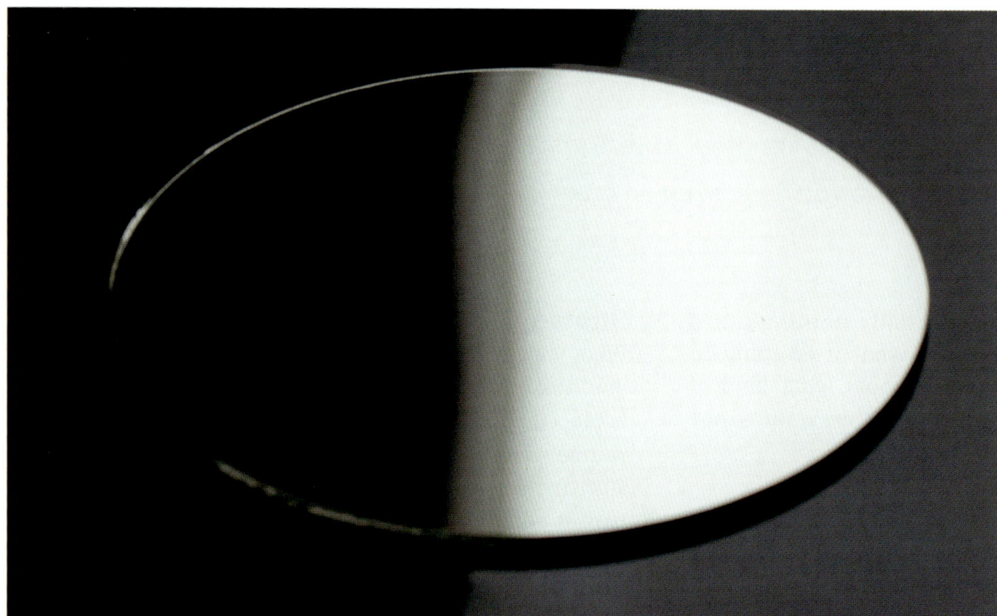

for example, a large diffusing fabric was stretched and backlit at an angle to obtain the gradual white-to-gray effect that was desired.

More and more often, however, we see mirrors shown with a clear line between the light and the dark reflections (as in the photo above). To achieve this, use lights with barn doors set up to clearly delineate the difference between the two reflections. This more modern approach is what most manufacturers now prefer.

Light and Barn Doors

For mirrors, as with all reflective surfaces, you will usually need to avoid hard light sources or lights that are too localized. Instead, you can increase the lighting surface by using either large shapers (octaboxes or umbrellas) or diffusing fabrics. Sometimes both. Another good solution is to aim the light toward a large white wall and then use its reflection to light the mirror. If it is placed far enough away to reveal what needs to be visible, this arrangement provides very even lighting, ideal for a mirror or any surface that produces direct and specular reflections. If you're trying to produce very segmented lights, alternating between black and white, you can also use barn doors; a black piece of cardboard works just fine. But you should be aware that because of the particular conformation of mirrors, you will not be able to produce a perfectly clean break between the reflection and the unaffected area: there will always be

a gray band that appears because of the refraction in the thickness of the glass covering the mirror; the thicker the glass, the wider the band.

Accessory or Base

In product photography, mirrors are often used as a base for the objects being photographed. They make it possible to obtain clearly drawn reflections, which are very useful when the presence of reflections is required. If the glass of the mirror is very thick, a very clear outline will be visible at the base of the object. In fact, the thickness of the glass leaves a small margin of direct reflection in the place where the object is placed, while its reflection appears a little farther away: it's useless to try to outline it with a pen.

Mirrors are also used as reflectors. They are much more efficient than normal photographic reflectors because they reflect about 95% of the light. When you need to set up complex lighting arrangements, or if space is tight, you can always use small mirrors to help you light or unblock one area or another. They are widely used in jewelry photography, where you need to call on a large number of light sources to create light effects on as many facets of the jewelry as possible (for example for precious stones).

And finally, as bases for objects to be photographed, mirrors make it possible to provide a faithful accompaniment for the projection of a particular subject (see page 197, backlighting method using a computer screen).

LIGHTING A PYRAMID

In theory, the problems posed by pyramids should not be that different from the problems of parallelepipeds. As with parallelepipeds, it should be a matter of showing half the sides, with different lighting, but it is not that simple.

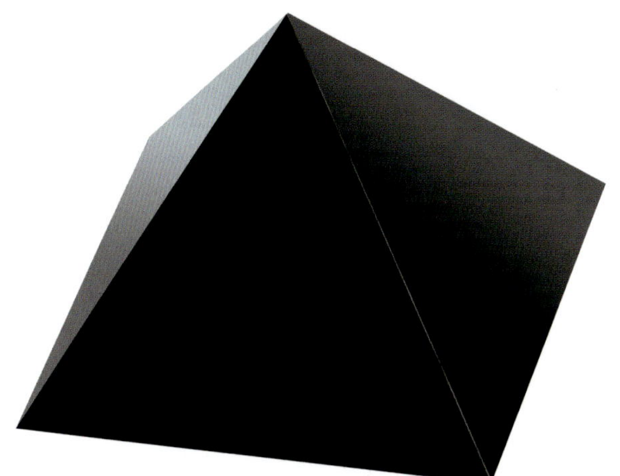

The only good way to show three sides of a pyramid with a square base is to photograph it from a bird's-eye view.

Let us begin by recalling that there are two main kinds of pyramids: pyramids with triangular bases, which have four sides; and pyramids with square or rectangular bases, which have five sides. For triangular pyramids, the exercise is easy enough: only two sides must be shown, and any angle of view will be effective. For square pyramids, on the other hand, the particular layout of the shape means that the only way to show three sides is if the photographer works from a bird's-eye view. If the photographer is placed any lower, the third side will only appear at the very edge, thereby rendering the shot much less effective. The pyramid is thus an exception to the rule that says that for every shape, you have to show half of the sides.

Matte Pyramidal Objects

As with most objects that produce diffuse reflections, the lighting of matte pyramids is pretty simple: one of the two faces is lit up locally, leaving the other in shadow. Any kind of lighting can be used, but you must make sure to avoid having too great of a contrast between the high and low lighting if the object is large. Nevertheless, it is customary to use beams of light that are larger than the exposed side, placed perpendicularly so as to obtain even lighting.

Satiny or Glossy Pyramidal Objects

Glossy or polished pyramids are usually lit using indirect lighting, especially if they are small, like the obsidian pyramid shown below, which is only two inches high. The goal is to obtain a soft but gradual lighting, to give a nuanced sense of the material. The easiest way is to direct a narrow source, such as a snoot or a small honeycomb, toward a reflector, which you place to the side so that it will reflect the light toward the lateral side. It is usually the front face that is left in shadow, but nothing says you can't do it the other way around.

The advantage of having a narrow, reflected source is that it avoids making the pyramid look too artificial, because the variation in lighting is easy to handle (all you have to do is rotate the reflector slightly to obtain more or less pronounced differences in tone), while also allowing you to show the material the object is made

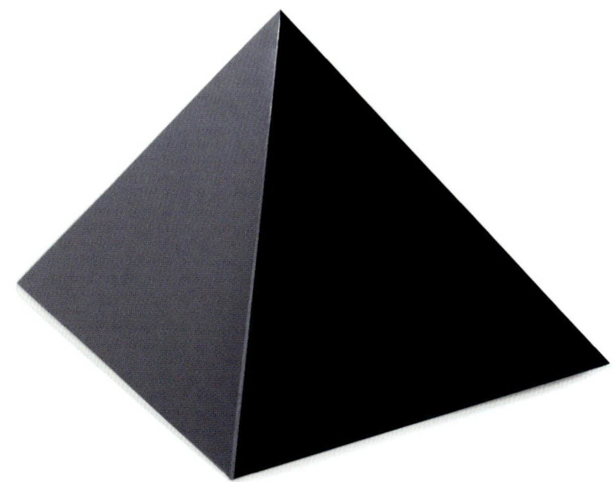

Example of lighting for a pyramid with a square base in glossy obsidian.

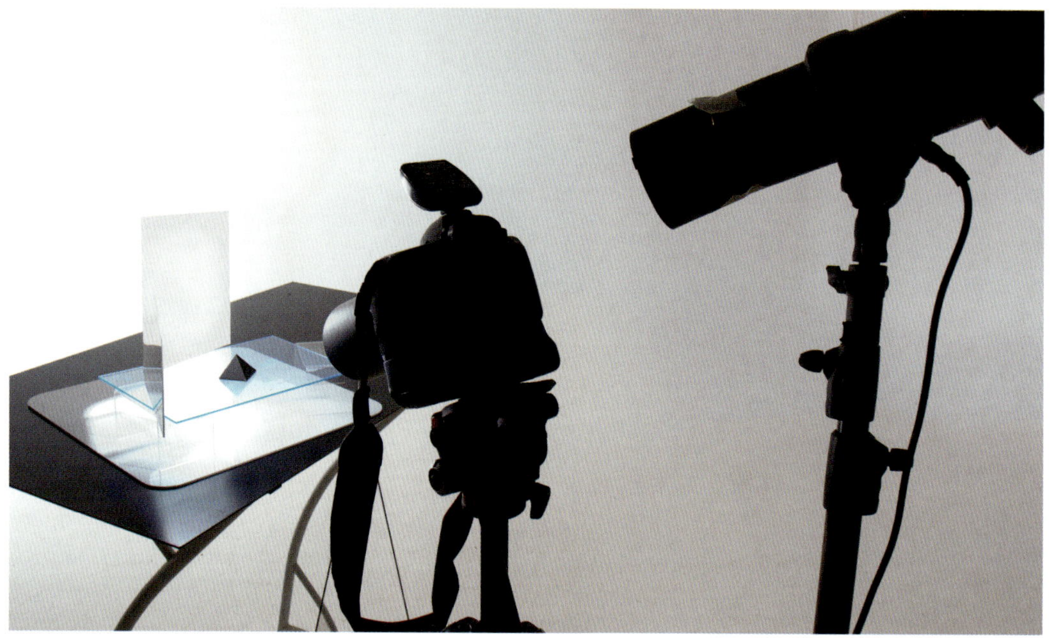

from. Marbles, brushed metals, and wood benefit greatly from being lit in this way.

Transparent Pyramids

Transparent pyramids, made of glass or crystal, act like prisms (see the following section): the refraction of the light and the particular angle of the sides of this shape create multiple internal reflections, resulting in a pretty chaotic outcome. To obtain a photo that is more pleasant to look at, you need to work in a controlled environment (for instance, inside a light tent), while making sure to use a black surface on one of the two sides to create a contrasting effect between them: one side will look black, and the other gray, which will allow the viewer to better comprehend the shape.

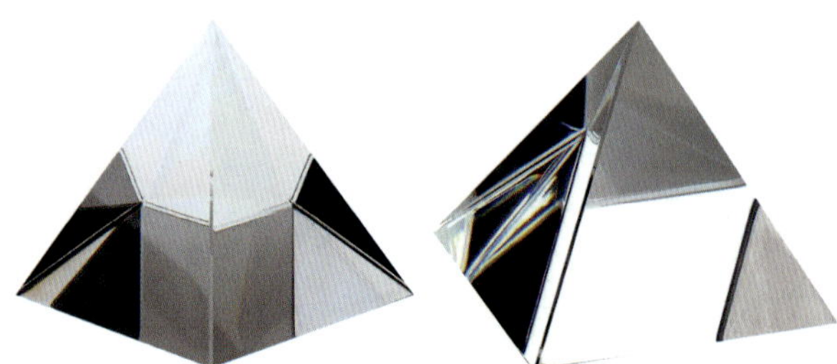

Transparent pyramids act like prisms. To avoid refractions going every which way, like those shown here, it is advisable to photograph these shapes inside a light cube.

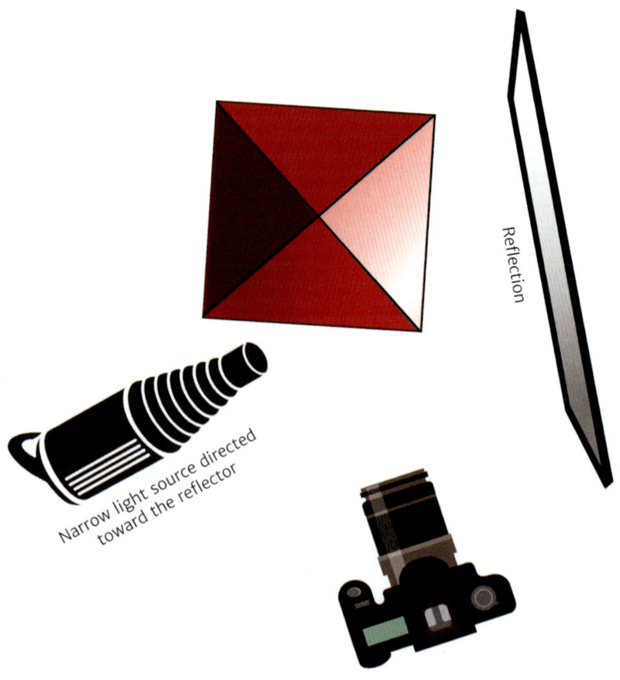

STANDARD METHOD FOR LIGHTING PYRAMIDS

LIGHTING TRANSPARENT PRISMS

Transparent prisms are among the most complex shapes to light. Ideally, each of the three faces should show a different shade, but without a contrasting surface (as with the printed page shown at right), the project will be unsuccessful.

Transparent prisms can be easy to light when it is a question of showing the breakdown of light into the rainbow. A beam of polychromatic white light crossing the prism will be refracted and break up into beams of seven colors, from violet to red. All you have to do is direct a very narrow light source, like that of a flash or flashlight equipped with a gobo with a very small aperture, toward one of the sides of the prism: the light will be refracted on the opposite side and the ray that is produced reveals a spectrum of seven colors.

When it comes to lighting the prism itself, however, the situation is more complex.

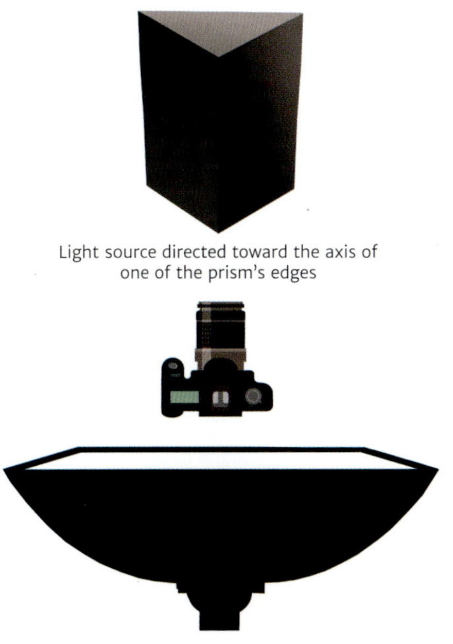

Light source directed toward the axis of one of the prism's edges

LIGHTING A PRISM WITHOUT REFLECTIONS

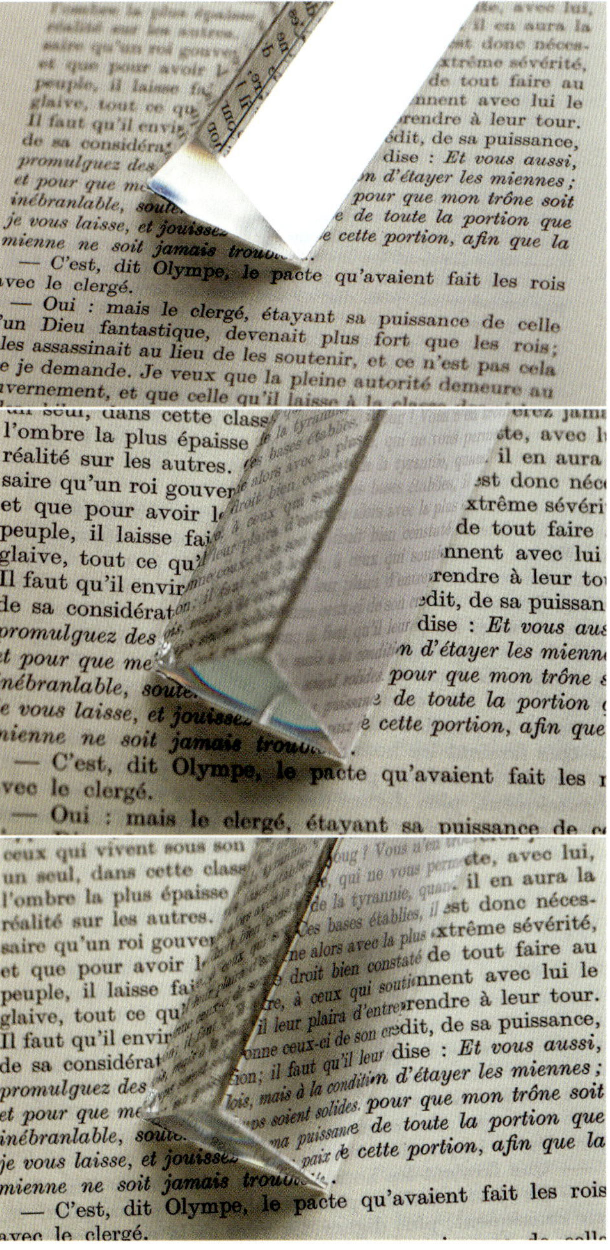

⌃ Transparent prisms can only be lit without reflections by placing the camera and a light source exactly within the axis of one of the prism's edges.

Prisms without Reflections

To fully understand the shape of the object, it is generally desirable for there to be a direct reflection on one of the sides. But there are times when this won't work, as in the illustration on the previous page where the text needed to be as precisely legible as possible. The only solution in this kind of situation is to arrange the light source and the camera within the exact same axis as one

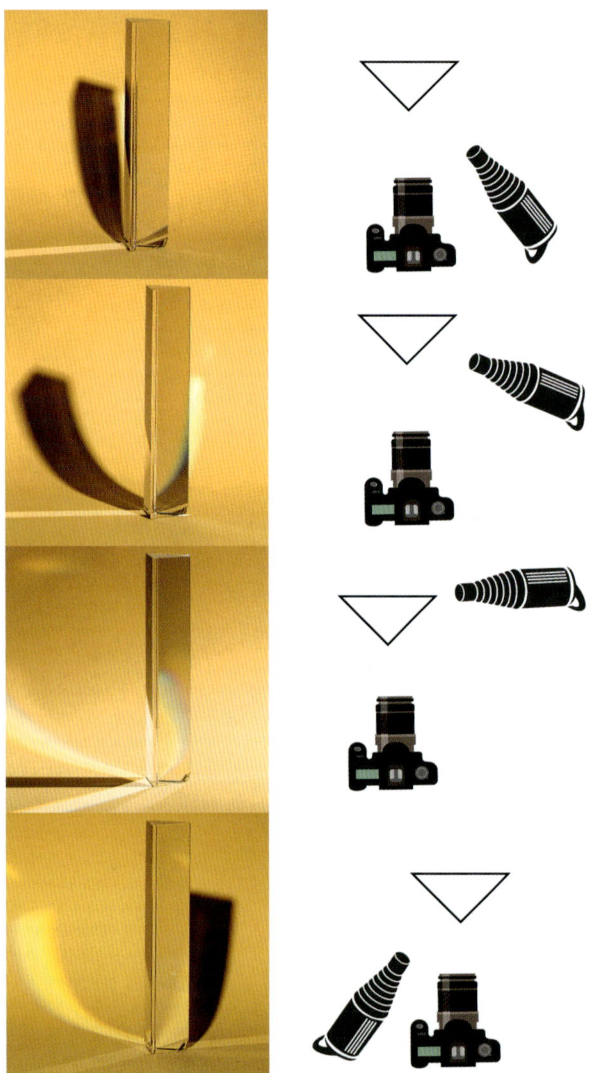

▲ The transparent prism refracts light within the angle of each of its sides. Thus, it produces three rays of light, and a shadow that is always opposite the incident light source.

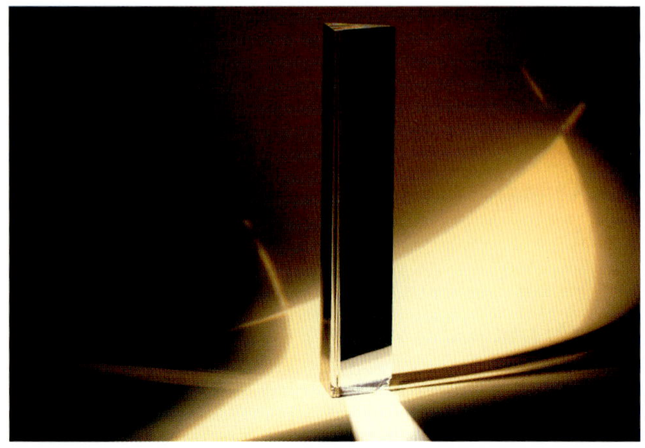

EXAMPLE OF LIGHTING A PRISM USING AN OPTICAL SHAPER EQUIPPED WITH A TRIANGULAR GOBO

of the edges of the prism: the light will refract so that no direct reflection appears.

Using Refracted Rays

However, since what is interesting about a transparent prism is the way in which it refracts light, it is often presented so that we can see its effect on the light. The smaller the light source, the easier this is to see. In the examples shown at left, I used a Profoto Spot Small optical shaper. You can see that the shadow is always exactly opposite the incident light. It can easily be made to disappear by placing the prism on a glass surface elevated above the base (see the section "Eliminating Cast Shadows" on page 151). Three light beams of varying intensity (depending on their angle with respect to the incident light source) appear elsewhere, within the axis of each of the sides.

You will notice that the prism reflects the light in its environment. If you want the light on all the visible sides to be uniform, place the prism inside a light cube, or else arrange solid sheets of cardboard vertically to either side of the object.

LIGHTING PARALLELEPIPEDS

An product photographer is constantly dealing with articles whose general shape
is close to that of cubes, slabs, or rhombohedrons. While lighting them does not
usually create major difficulties, it is important to have a good grasp of the logic
of the lighting.

In the section devoted to the theory of parallelepiped
lighting, we saw that it was necessary for at least three
of the visible sides to be lighted in different ways to
properly anchor the shape in space. In practice, however,
there are a few pitfalls that may occur.

Mixed Shapes

It often happens that the object to be photographed is
made up of multiple sections of various shapes, like the
medium-format Hasselblad shown here: while the camera is cube-shaped, the lens is cylindrical. We could, of
course, try to light each of the two shapes with its own
dedicated light source, or else take two photos that would
be combined in post-production, but an image produced
using one light source would be more natural and more
pleasing to the eye than a composite photo.

Because the assignment here is to make a promotional
photo in which the name of the brand needs to appear,
the cubic shape of the camera itself will be given more
weight. By placing the major light source (a 24 x 16-inch
softbox behind a diffusing fabric) within the axis of the
lens, we can simultaneously light the front surface of the
lens and the front side of the cube. The multiple reflections within the lens are due to the presence of several
glass layers. This lighting is measured at +1.33 EV with a
flash meter placed level with the front of the lens.

A second light source is placed to the side to illuminate
the right side of the camera. It is measured at +0.4 EV.

The last side of the cube, finally, is not lit, but the
metallic elements (accessory shoe, shutter, etc.) benefit
from the main lighting.

Satiny or Glossy Shapes

When you want to light a parallelepiped that is glossy
(such as a lacquered cube) or satiny (such as a box that
is varnished but not polished), you must decide whether
or not you want there to be visible reflections, and if so,
what kind.

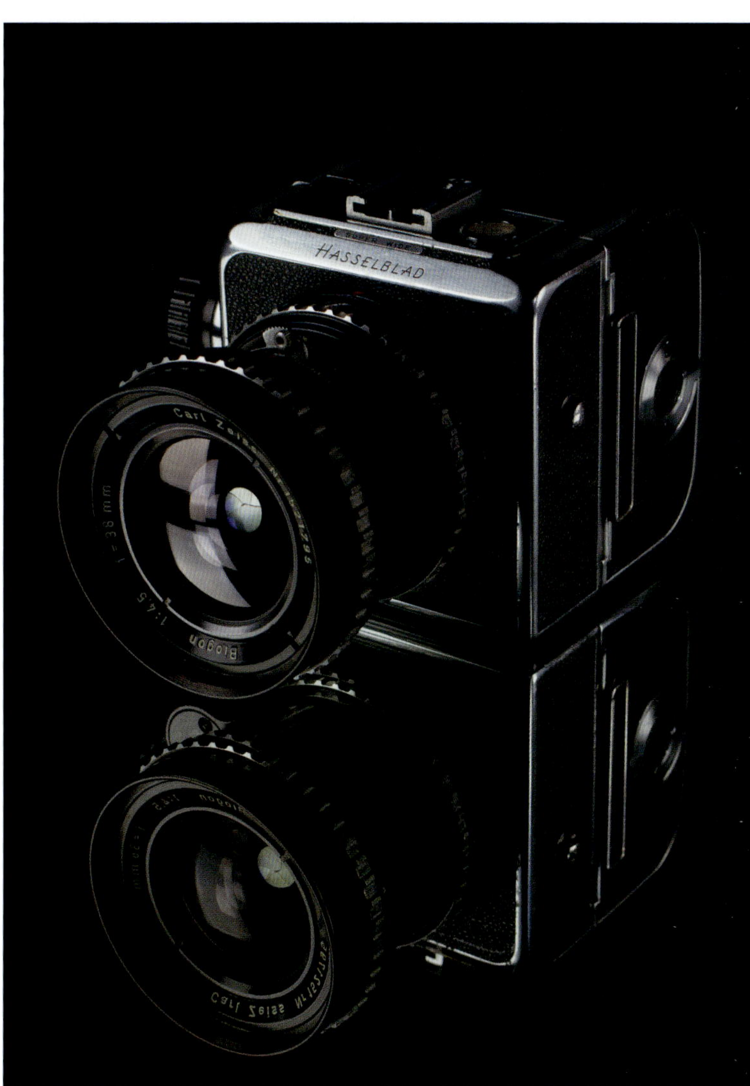

⌃ In this photo, the lighting for the (cubic) camera itself was
emphasized over the (cylindrical) lens, with different levels of
lighting on each of the three sides.

For perfectly smooth shapes, like polished steel or glass cubes, you would usually use hard (bowl-type) light sources and barn doors in order to get contrasting black and white reflections, with a quick transition from light to dark, for a lacquered effect. For practical reasons, you will normally emphasize the side closest to the incident light source, but if there is a particular detail of the object that needs to be highlighted, you can choose a different side, lighting it with a different source.

Generally, you will use only one light source, positioned toward one of the sides. The climax is measured at +1.33 EV on that side, and then one of the other two sides is lit with a reflector. Because reflected light is always weaker than direct light, you can be absolutely sure that the lighting of the second side will be consistent with the presentation of the shape.

Boxes

Most of the parallelepipeds that we are asked to photograph are boxes. It is always a good idea to light their interior, with the lid raised.

The method is simple: arrange a showerhead light source, usually a snoot or a bowl with a honeycomb, to avoid having the light "drool" onto the side edges of the box; then direct a second light, usually a softbox, laterally toward one of the other two visible sides of the object.

If the box is shallow, like an empty sardine can, for example, you can use one showerhead light source, and one of the other two sides can be lit with a reflector, as shown in the diagram below.

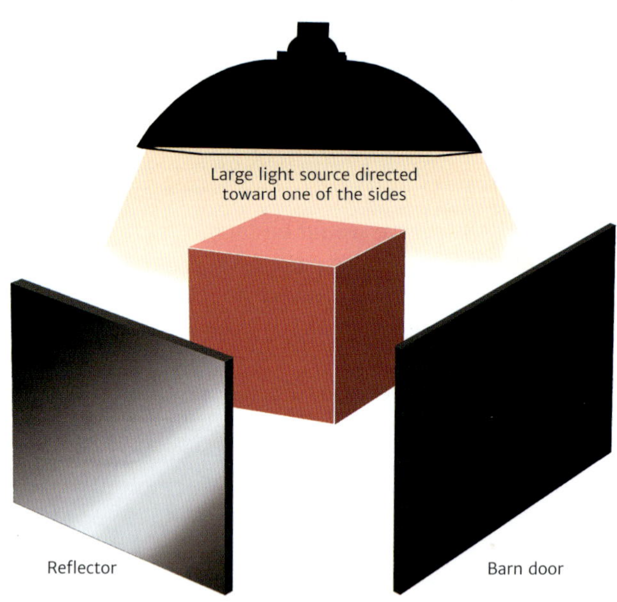

STANDARD METHOD FOR LIGHTING PARALLELEPIPEDS

⌃ Example of lighting a cube using a single light source placed at 45°. Based on the axis of the source light, each side looks different.

LIGHTING CYLINDERS

Cylinders come up a lot in packshots and advertising, especially because of the large number of sodas and other kinds of drinks that come in cans. Cylinders require precise and perfectly controlled lighting.

We have seen that cylinders, like spheres, have a family of angles of approximately 270°. This means that we will get direct reflections as soon as a light source is placed anywhere other than directly behind the object itself. Fortunately, this ability to produce direct reflections only applies around the perimeter, and cylinders can be lit from above and below with no fear of reflections.

Matte Cylinders

The shape and reflectance of tires, wooden rolling pins, candles, and such make these objects easy to light as soon as you place the incident light source to one side or the other of the cylinder. The important thing is to create a very gradual light and half-light, using very soft light sources such as large softboxes, lighting reflected off of light-colored walls, or very diffuse light sources. You can then control the gradient by changing the orientation of the light source and/or by modifying it using a reflector placed across from it. You will see that some objects

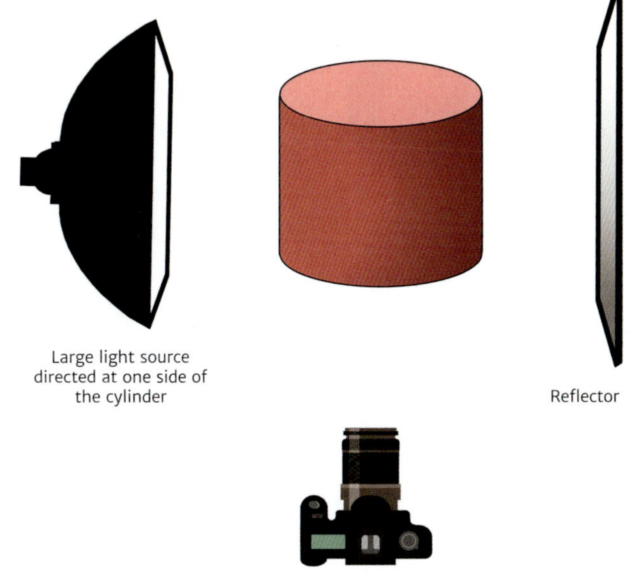

STANDARD METHOD FOR LIGHTING MATTE CYLINDERS

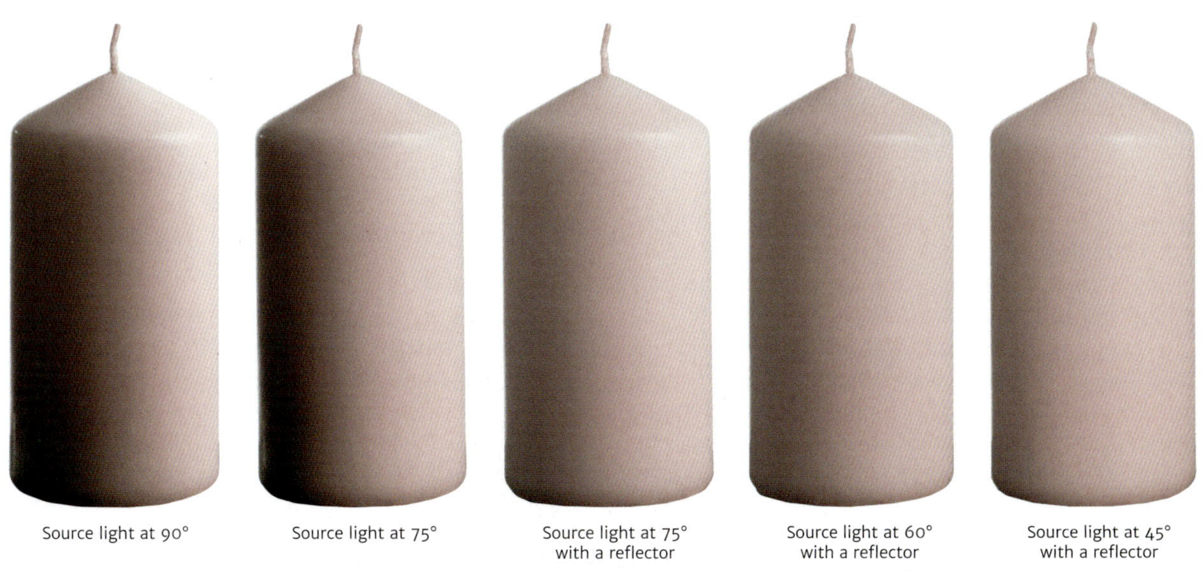

Source light at 90°

Source light at 75°

Source light at 75° with a reflector

Source light at 60° with a reflector

Source light at 45° with a reflector

⌃ Several possible ways to illuminate a candle.

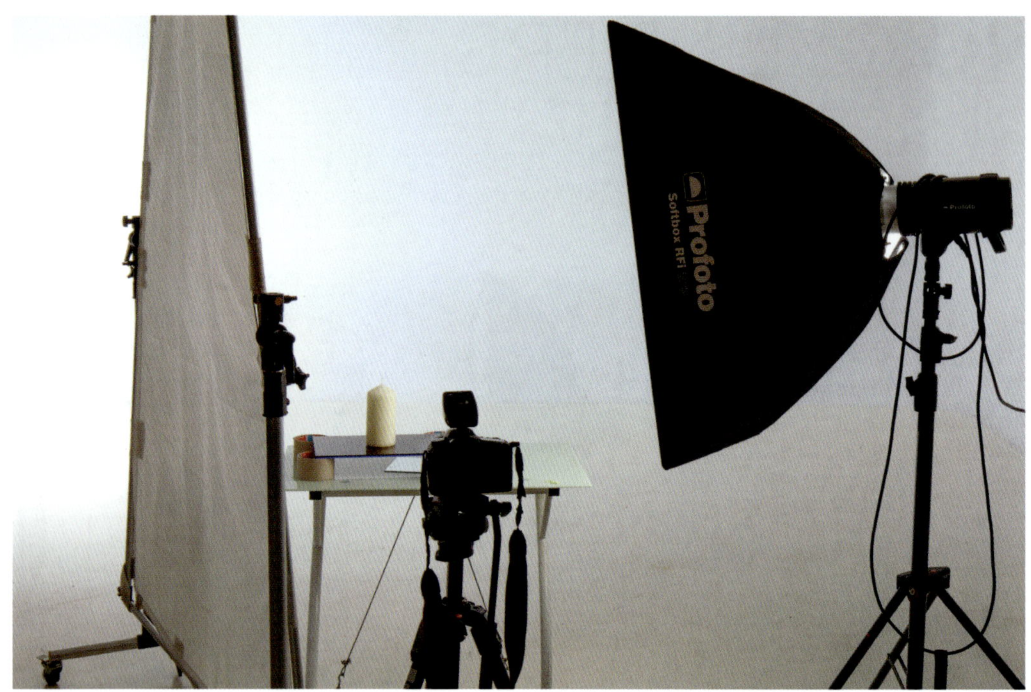

« A behind-the-scenes view of the illumination of the candle.

benefit from showing more or less pronounced gradations of light and shadow. But we try to avoid hard light sources, which erase the sense of the object's roundness and suggest a flat side, like that of a parallelepiped, by showing a shadow that is too localized.

Remember that a cylinder needs to be lit so that the light is as gradual and diffuse as possible. In the five photos shown on the previous page, the two candles at the left suffer from having an overly pronounced area of shadow and a too-narrow area of half-light.

Satiny and Glossy Cylinders

Things get more complicated again with glossy cylinders. Without reflections, they look very dark and insubstantial; using standard lighting, like light boxes, the only reflections you will get are narrow bands. Of course, you need to avoid overly localized light sources, like bowls or snoots, which will only cause reflections in the shape of very obnoxious little circular highlights. This is due to the cylinders' families of angles, which make it necessary to use very large light sources, arranged at very different angles, in order to produce reflections that will look much like what we tried to obtain with matte cylinders. You might think that a strategy like the one I have already mentioned, consisting of illuminating a large wall, would

be enough to fill the entirety of the cylinder's family of angles, but that would not work here. The only way to light a glossy cylinder and to cover most of the family of angles is to place a rounded reflector in front of the object (see the behind-the-scenes view on the following page). I use 3-mm-thick sheets of translucent plexiglass (PMMA), rounded with a heat gun. The cylinder reflects the reflector itself, and you can modulate the lighting, as we did with the candle, by choosing to place the light source on one side or the other of the diffuser, in order to vary the gradation from light to dark. You can use one rounded reflector or several, the important thing being that they cover the entire family of angles.

Soda Cans

The soda can, the most common example of cylindrical product photography, can be lit in many different ways. There are multiple lighting options using strip boxes, characterized by several parallel lines of lighting of variable intensities. The technique is simple: place at least three long, narrow light boxes on each side of the camera (traditionally at 30°, 150°, and 300°), pointed toward the soda can, but make sure that their lighting strengths are not the same (from +1.3 to +0.5 EV depending on the color of the can and the desired effect). The result is a "pop" look that emphasizes the glossiness of the product, but it plays down the writing and doesn't allow for nuances in the photography.

I find it much more elegant, and much simpler to carry out, to set up the lighting via a rounded diffuser. A single light source is sufficient for lighting the front of the object. If it needs to be presented against a white background, then a second light source can be placed, either directly (as in the behind-the-scenes view shown below) or else as a directed reflection toward a light-colored background, measured at +3.33 EV. Note that you can also arrange two light boxes for direct lighting on either side of the camera, directed toward the diffuser, if the surface of the object is not perfectly reflective, as is the case with certain brands of beer and some tea-based beverages.

You can also play up the contrasts on the can by arranging a black barn door on one of the edges to diminish the reflections on one side of the object.

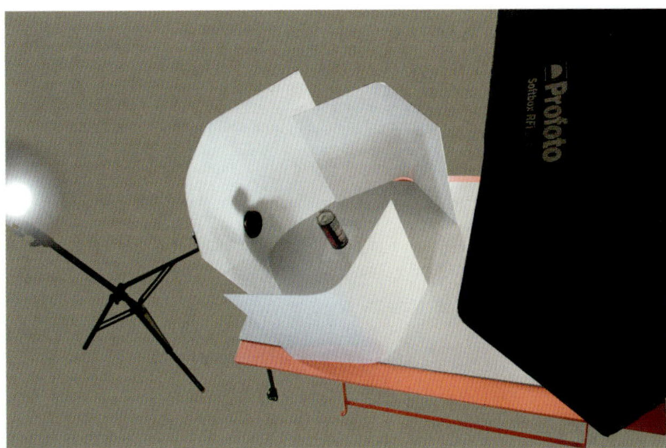

⌃ A behind-the-scenes view of the lighting of a soda can according to the method indicated on page 95.

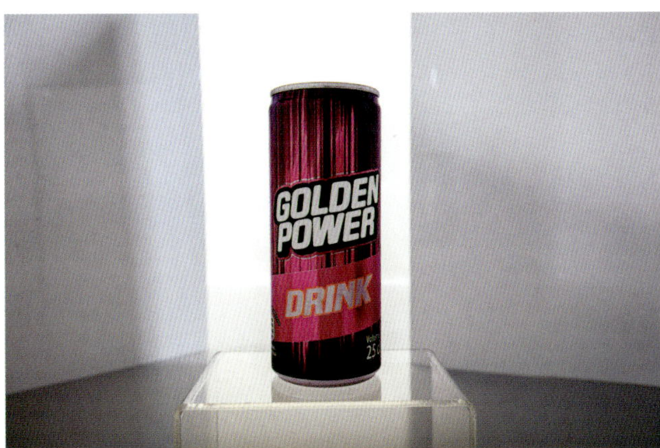

⌃ A behind-the-scenes view of the same scene from a different axis.

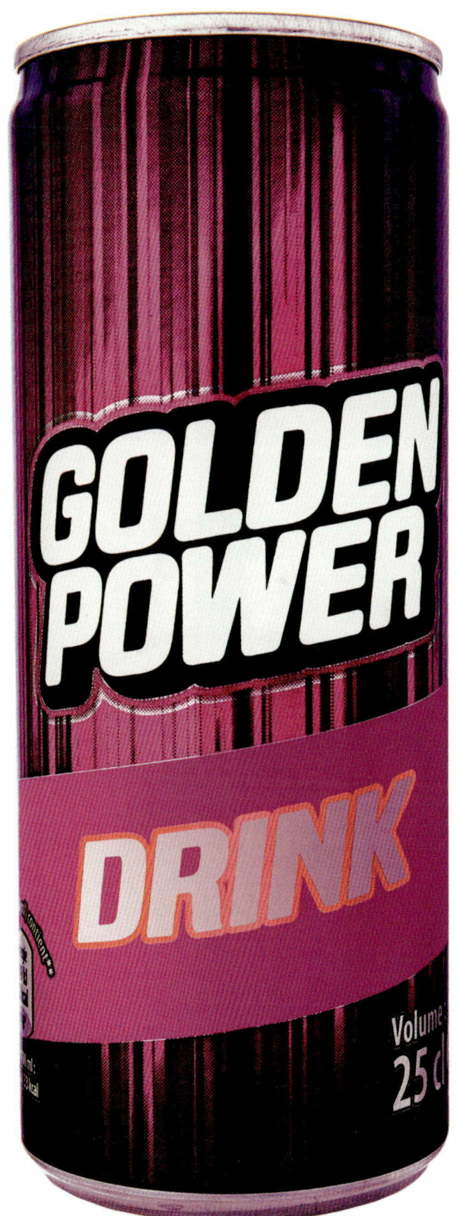

⌃ Final photo of the soda can.

LIGHTING SPHERES

As with mirrors, photographing spherical objects has more to do with a philosophy of shooting than with the practice of lighting—because it is not so much the sphere itself that we are photographing, but the reflections that it produces.

Whether a sphere is matte or glossy, opaque or transparent, the challenge is always the same: presenting the roundedness of the shape through an even transition from light to dark and as soft of an ending as possible. This can only happen if you work with very large, very diffuse light sources, at the very outside edges of the family of angles.

Photographing a Matte Spheroid Object

Even though matte objects are not going to produce the problem of throwing direct reflection, it is nevertheless true that frontal lighting, especially if it is localized, creates an effect of small round highlights, which is not a

harmonious look. Depending on the desired effect, you can light spheres the same way that you light matte cylinders, using a very large light source positioned behind a large diffusing fabric, within the family of angles (from 100° to 140°), while also placing a reflector opposite it to help with the transition in the light and to soften the terminator.

The most effective solution, however, involves the method presented in the diagram below left. Position a large light source (such as a light box) behind the sphere, and a large, rounded diffuser, occupying the entire family of angles, in front. Then place a white reflector below the structure to cover all of the family of angles, and in that reflector create an opening for the camera lens. The backlighting will serve both as background light, by presenting a light-colored backdrop (or a white one, if it is measured at +3.33 EV), and as a key light, by reflection against the rounded reflector.

Photographing a Satiny or Glossy Spheroid Object

Spherical and spheroid objects reflect all of the elements and lights that are present in their family of angles. However hard you try, you will always find the space behind

STANDARD METHOD FOR LIGHTING SPHERES

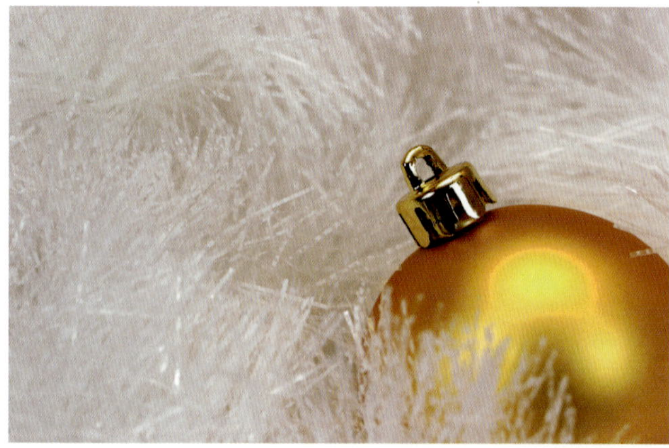

⌃ A Christmas tree ornament photographed using the unfocus technique.

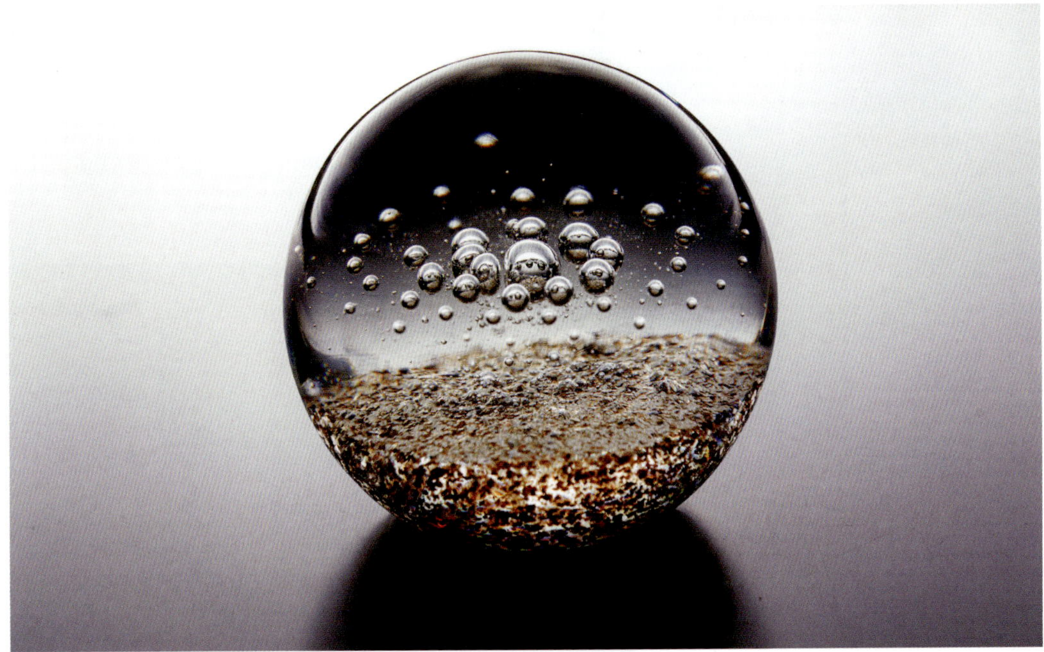

you, the ceiling, the walls, and your camera appearing on the surface of the sphere. The idea, therefore, is to create a space whose reflection on the object will be compatible with the image that you want to produce.

Thus, to obtain a perfectly black sphere (as in the photo on page 90), simply lit along its upper edge, you need to place both a light source in rim light and the object on a black surface. If the studio is large enough, you can turn off all the lights and take cover under a black cloth (because as the photographer you are closer to the object than the studio walls are, the backlighting will otherwise illuminate you): then, because the sphere has nothing to reflect except for the backlighting, it will look black.

To obtain a completely white sphere with a slight gradation toward light gray, the only possible procedure is to photograph it inside a light tent, with a light source placed to the side, but the result will not be perfect: you will see the rounded reflection of the tent's interior seams, which you can only get rid of with editing software.

The most common technique for photographing this kind of object (such as a Christmas tree ornament), however, is to make a composite shot using the *unfocus* technique: Position one or more direct light sources pointing at the sphere and place the camera on a tripod. Take a first shot focusing on the ball (basically on the edges, or on the loop at the top), and then a second one using a focus that blurs the reflections of the light sources. To create the photo on the previous page, all you have to do then is open up the two images in your image-processing software and combine the two images, keeping the blurred part of the reflections, along with the sharp focus on the edges of the ball, the plastic loop, and the elements around it (in this case, the needles of an artificial white Christmas tree).

Photographing a Transparent Spheroid Object

Crystal balls and other spherical transparent glass paperweights are reasonably easy to light. You just need to make sure that the rear lighting is intense enough to keep the frontal reflections from appearing. Let's analyze the setup for the lighting of the crystal sphere photographed above (the behind-the-scenes view is on the next page). One light source is positioned on the ground, aimed at a white reflector placed at a 45° angle behind the sphere. As with the drinking glasses presented earlier, the lighting here has the effect of clearly defining the silhouette of the object, while maintaining a pronounced lightness of color on the interior. The reflector also spreads the light so that a direct reflection appears on the upper part of the sphere. The rest of the elements (air bubbles, sand, etc.) are lit by continuous refraction, with a pretty white-gray-black gradation: this is simply the image of the reflector's white-gray-black lighting.

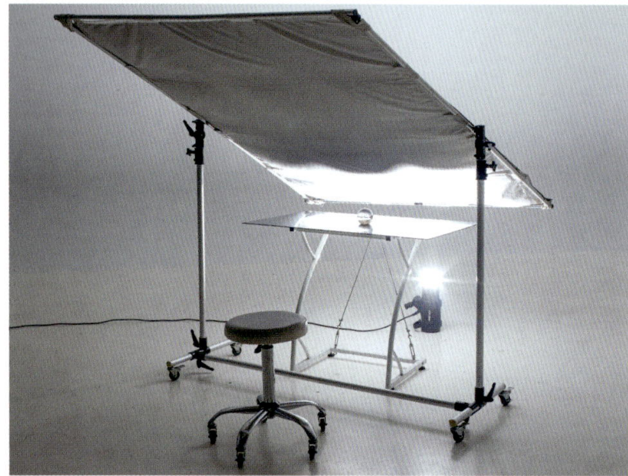

Photographing a Complex Spheroid Object

These ideas can be extrapolated to complex spheroid objects, such as the plaster skull covered in glossy silver paint, at right. Its general shape, especially with the ridges formed by the bone structure of the eye sockets, nose, and jaw, make it impossible to use just one light source—the small photos show what a single light source would show, depending on its placement.

In addition, overly uniform lighting would cause an object like this to lose much of its power. Instead, I suggest using lighting consisting of three sources (see the behind-the-scenes view below): one placed to the right

side to light the frontal bone, nasal bone, teeth, and the front of the lower jaw; a second one to the left at a 55° angle to light the sphenoid bone, temporal bone, and lower jaw; and finally, a third one, at 140° behind the skull, at the edge of the family of angles, to light the parietal bone.

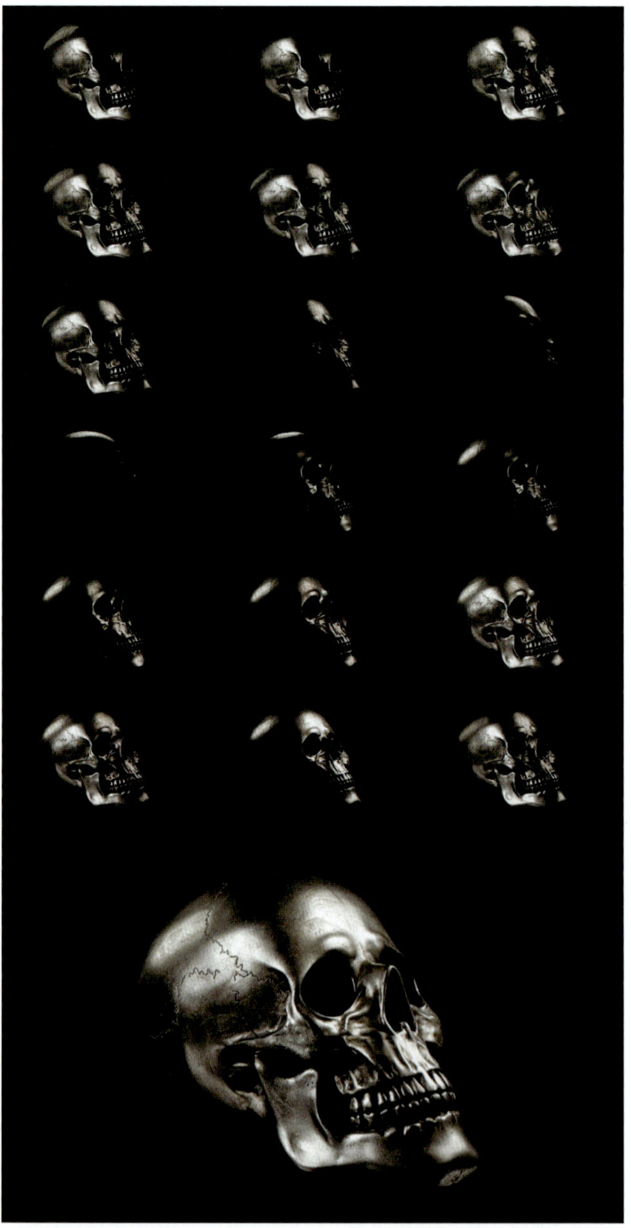

This plaster skull, covered in metallic paint, can look very different depending on the number and axes of light sources.

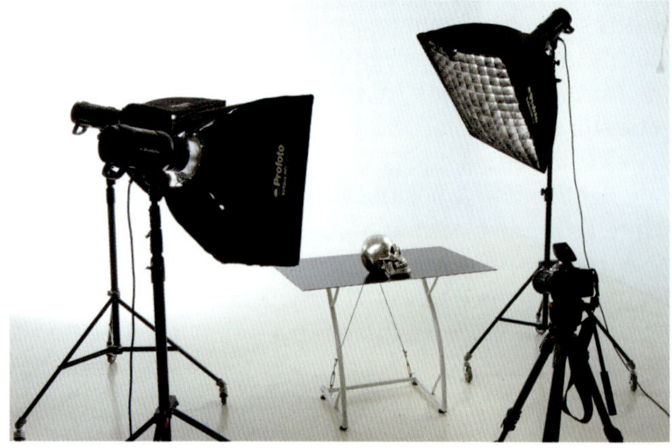

The skull in the large photo at right was lit with three light boxes equipped with honeycombs so that the background would stay black.

ELIMINATING CAST SHADOWS

Even though, in most cases, we want to show a shadow because it gives a sense of the relationship between the object and its environment, there are often times when graphic professionals require images without shadows. In this section, we'll discuss the easiest way to achieve this type of image when photographing.

If you are a professional in the visual arts, you have probably already had clients ask you for "cutout" photos. These are shots, generally delivered in PNG format, in which only the photographed object is present, without any background or shadows. You can, of course, obtain this kind of result in post-processing by using an object-selection software tool: a pen, lasso, color picker, etc. But there is a technique that is as old as photography that works very well, and which the profession appears to have forgotten—this book is a chance for me to refresh their memory.

Direct Transmission

We have already seen that as long as it is at a right angle to a sheet of glass, light is transmitted perfectly, without producing reflections. Everything that is placed on the glass therefore seems to be floating in the air. The shadow cast by an object is usually directly underneath it, where it touches the surface it is sitting on, and the closer you are to the object, the darker it is. But in this particular case, the shadow of the object does not appear right where it connects, but instead is seen lower down, on the opaque surface underneath the glass sheet.

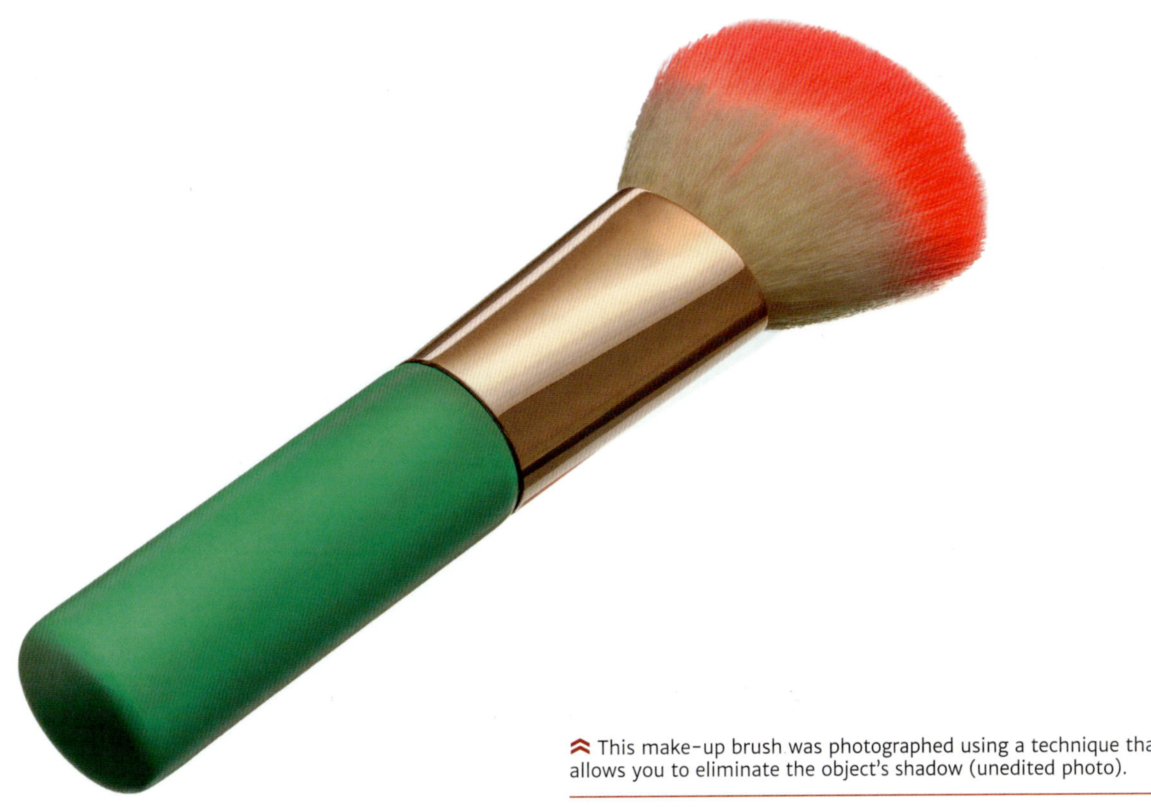

⌃ This make-up brush was photographed using a technique that allows you to eliminate the object's shadow (unedited photo).

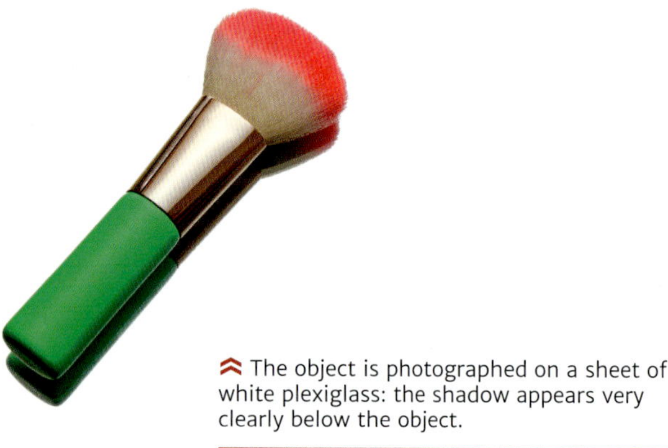

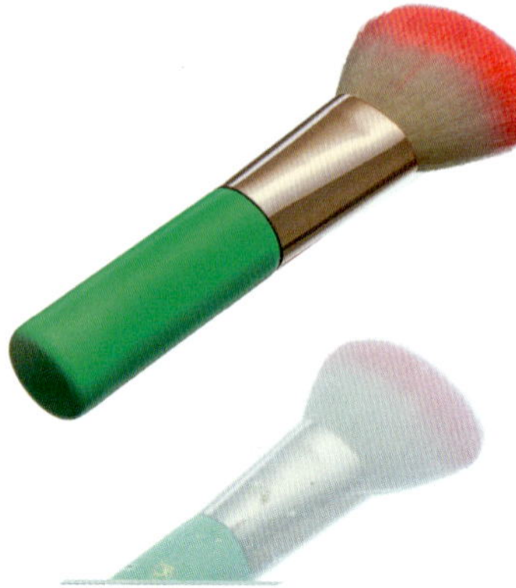

If you separate the sheet of glass from its support with wedges, the object's shadow may appear very distant from the object that generates it. I used this peculiarity of light to create the photo of the flying cup on page 237. By framing the shot to keep the shadow outside of the frame, you can give the impression that there is no shadow at all.

To make it possible to understand the process better, I placed a mirror about four inches below the glass sheet (see the photo below of the behind-the-scenes view and the photo above on the right). This arrangement allowed me to get a good sense of where the shadow would have appeared if I had chosen a sheet of opaque paper instead of the mirror. In this way, depending on the angle that I choose for the shot, I can make the reflection or the shadow appear in the position I want it to.

This method allows you to eliminate the cast shadow or, if the framing does show it, give the impression that the object is floating. This arrangement can be used to avoid undesirable reflections on glossy objects, like eyeglasses where the shadow that the glasses casts might appear in reflection on the glasses themselves.

You could also choose to stack up several sheets of glass, using wedges to create different spacing between them, to give a sense of depth and segmentation to multiple objects.

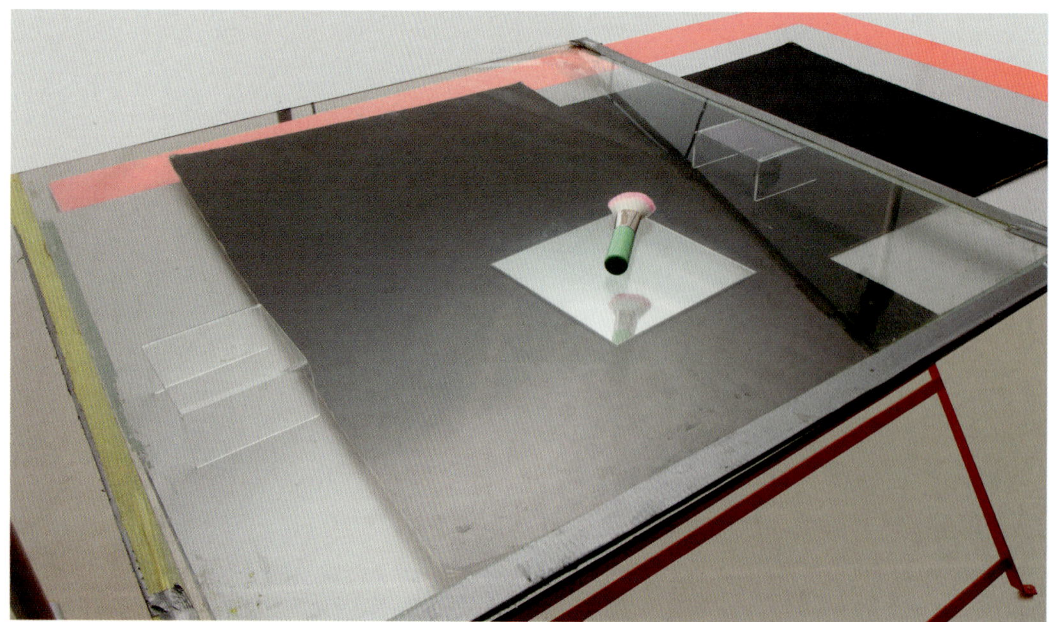

LIGHTING FOOD

It would be easy to dedicate an entire book just to food photography alone. This field has taken on such importance in product photography over the last few years that it is essential to discuss it here. Let's start by returning to the fundamentals.

Despite the preconceived notions that you can find on many blogs, to understand food photography, you must begin with a good understanding of the basic foundations of the laws of optics: primarily reflection, refraction, and the idea of the family of angles.

Fundamentals of Lighting

There is no difference, in terms of lighting, between a tomato covered in olive oil and a Christmas tree ornament. Both are spherical, opaque, and glossy. Their families of angles cover about 270° and in both cases we will see visible reflections if the incident light is placed anywhere other than at the rear. Beginning with this information, and with the fact that most foods are glossy, shiny, and vaguely rounded, it becomes clear that the primary lighting must be positioned as backlighting or, possibly, on the side.

Most dishes presented on social media are lit by a large window or outside on a veranda. A diffusing fabric is placed in front of, behind, or next to the table that the food is on. This is not a surprise: a large, very diffuse source is required for all glossy objects. As usual, we adjust the camera by optimizing it to +1.33 EV in relation to the light measured at the peak.

We then clear away the shadows generated by this main light source using a reflector (gold-colored for most food, silver for fish and other seafood) or, sometimes, with a second light source set at 1.5 EV weaker, in order to maintain the contrasts.

Of course, we then vary this lighting depending on the dishes or the food being photographed. If we are trying to create an atmosphere around a complex winter dish, such as a beef bourguignon, we'll choose a dark, rich background, with strong contrasts in the light (+1.33 EV for the key light and −0.5 EV for the fill light), whereas if it is a summery fruit salad, we might choose a very light background, lessening the contrasts between the two light sources (+1.33 EV for the key light, +0.6 EV for the fill light).

The Standard Shot

Most food compositions are photographed from the front, at a slight angle from above (5° to 20°), so that the traditional axis of a seated diner can be maintained. The main dish and the accessory elements (ingredients, spices, cutlery, etc.) are arranged to keep the eye's interest, and therefore the fill light is augmented somewhat, adjusting it to be no more than 1 EV lower than the key light.

This type of shot, however, though it is still prominent on restaurant menus and advertising posters, is starting to go out of fashion.

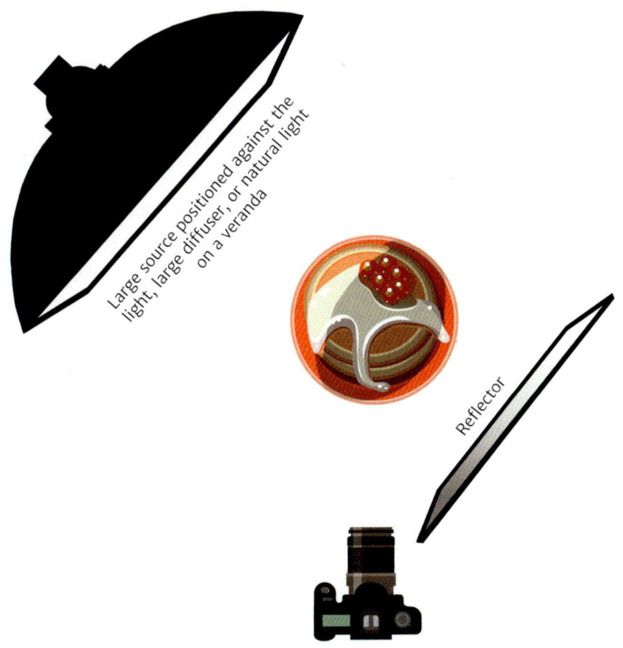

STANDARD METHOD FOR LIGHTING FOOD

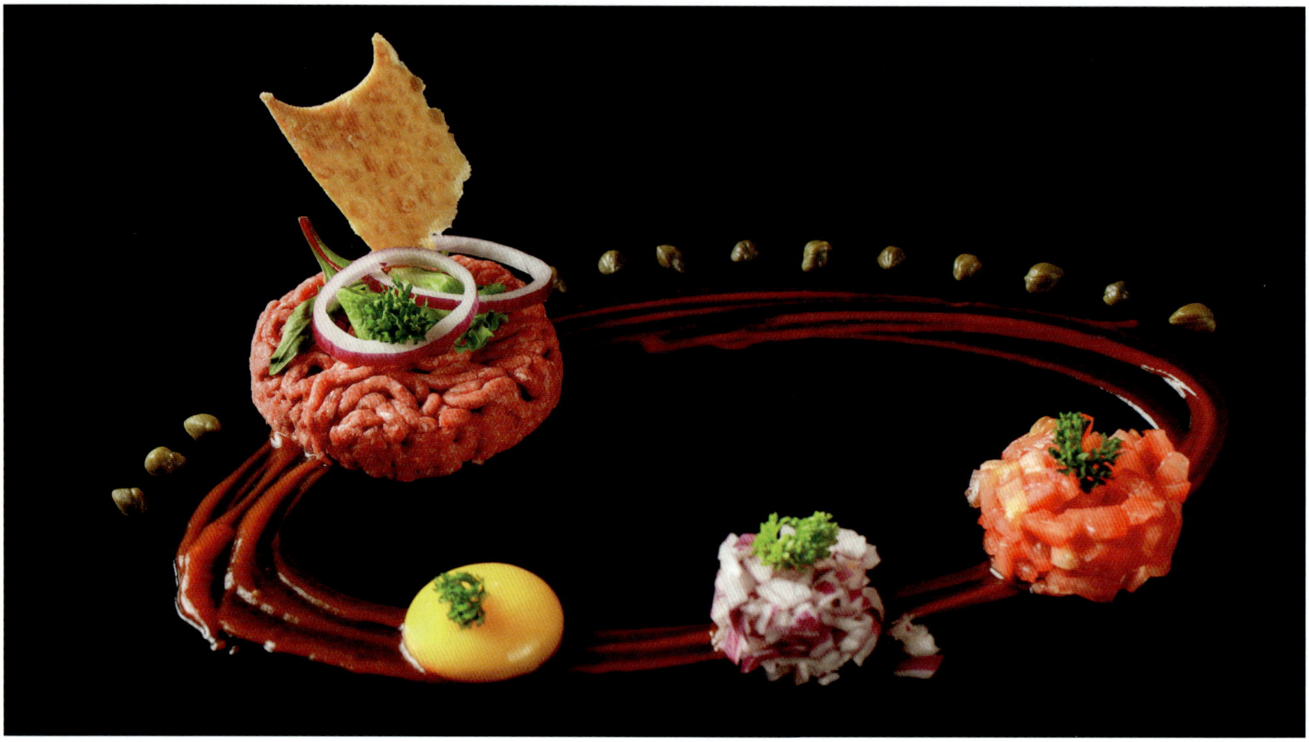

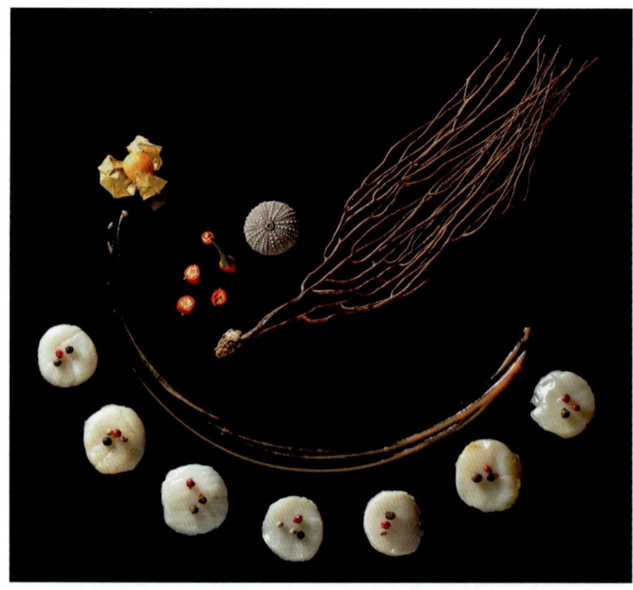

Traditional angle of shot. Most of the food items are spheroid and glossy, like the red fruits seen on the next page. Thus, they are treated like glossy spheres, with a soft, even light positioned within the edge of the family of angles.

Shooting from a Radical Bird's-Eye View

Over the past several years, it has become more and more de rigueur to shoot dishes and foods from a radical bird's-eye view. The new wave of set designers and other food preparers prefer to emphasize the visual aspect of the food and the composition work, setting themselves apart from the traditional, old-fashioned kind of representation, which does less justice to the textures. This is done by reducing the intensity of the fill light or even doing away with it entirely to reinforce the visual contrast in the image and accentuate the graphic aspect of the presentation.

In truth, more than the light or the angle, it is the composition of the scene that is most important, and that catches our eye, in this kind of image.

Composition in Three Layers

In composing the shot, we generally use layers, which allows us to give depth to the image while emphasizing the shapes, colors, or textures. Let's take the example of the photo on the next page, with a first layer made up of a sheet of white plexiglass, a second layer of ground

A radical bird's-eye-view shot is becoming more and more popular in culinary photography.

paprika raked with a serrated putty knife, a third layer made up of the scattered fruit, and a fourth of small glass jars filled with fruit. I want to note that this is a method of composition, not a "rule," as some writers put it. By borrowing organizational methods from classical painting, comic strip drawing, and even the movies, we can take advantage of many different methods of composition, as we will see in the section devoted to this subject (on page 208). For the image to work, we have to carefully manage the empty and full areas, the color harmonies, the geometry of the various elements, and the contrasts. But you will see that the further you progress in composition, the "lighter" your images will become.

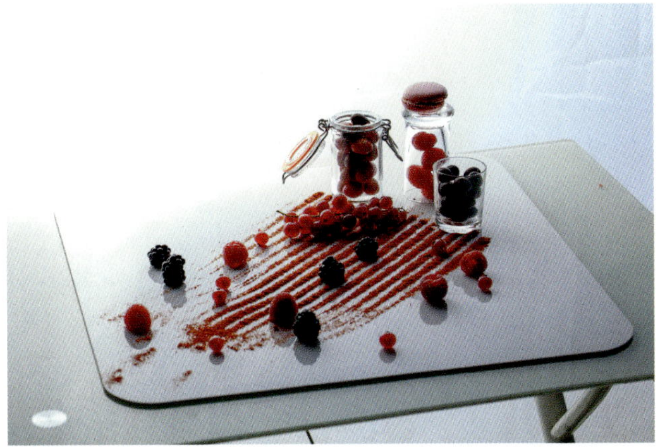

A large 24 x 55-inch softbox was placed in backlight, behind a diffusing fabric.

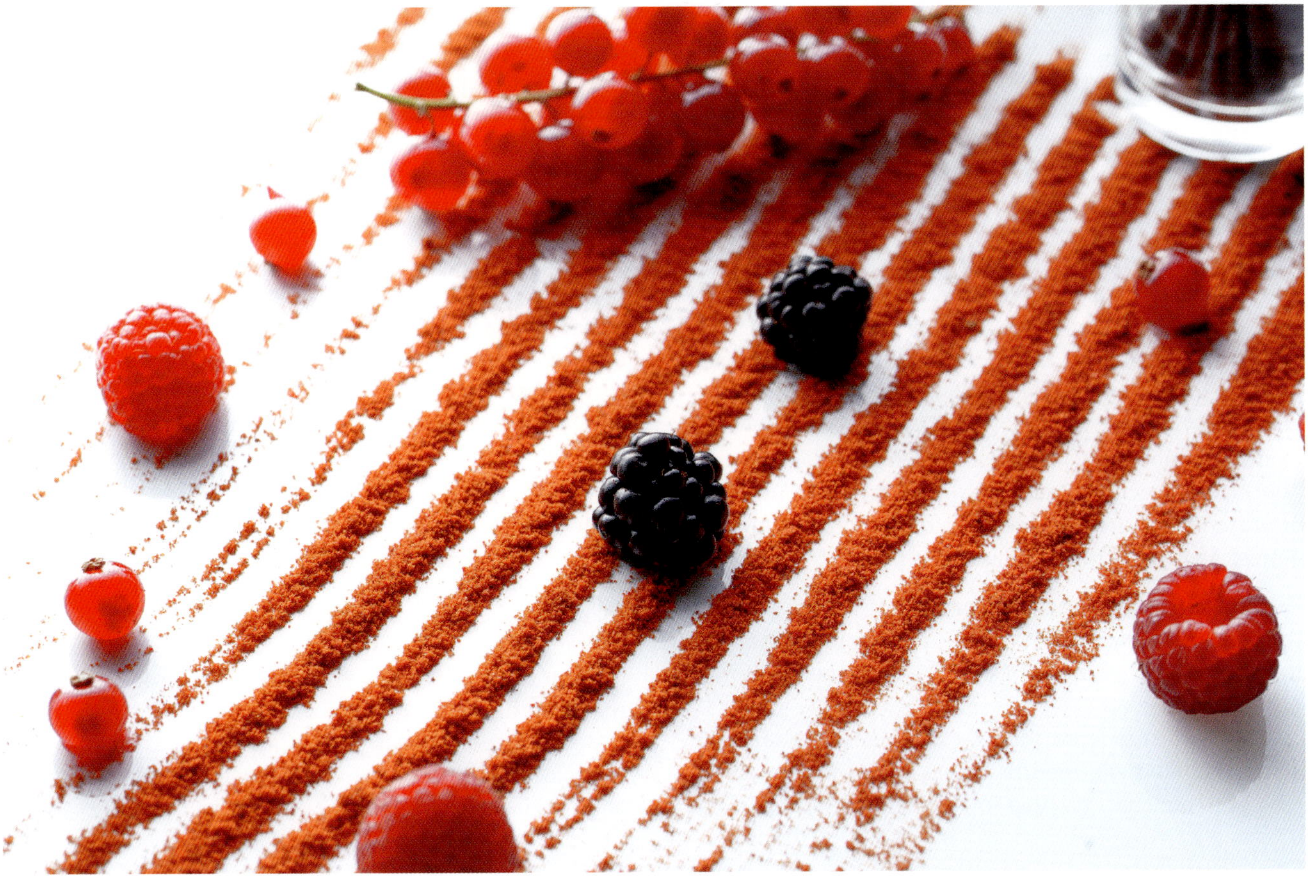

Bird's-eye-view shot. The fill light is adjusted to be less intense than in a traditional shot to maintain a nicely contrasting effect.

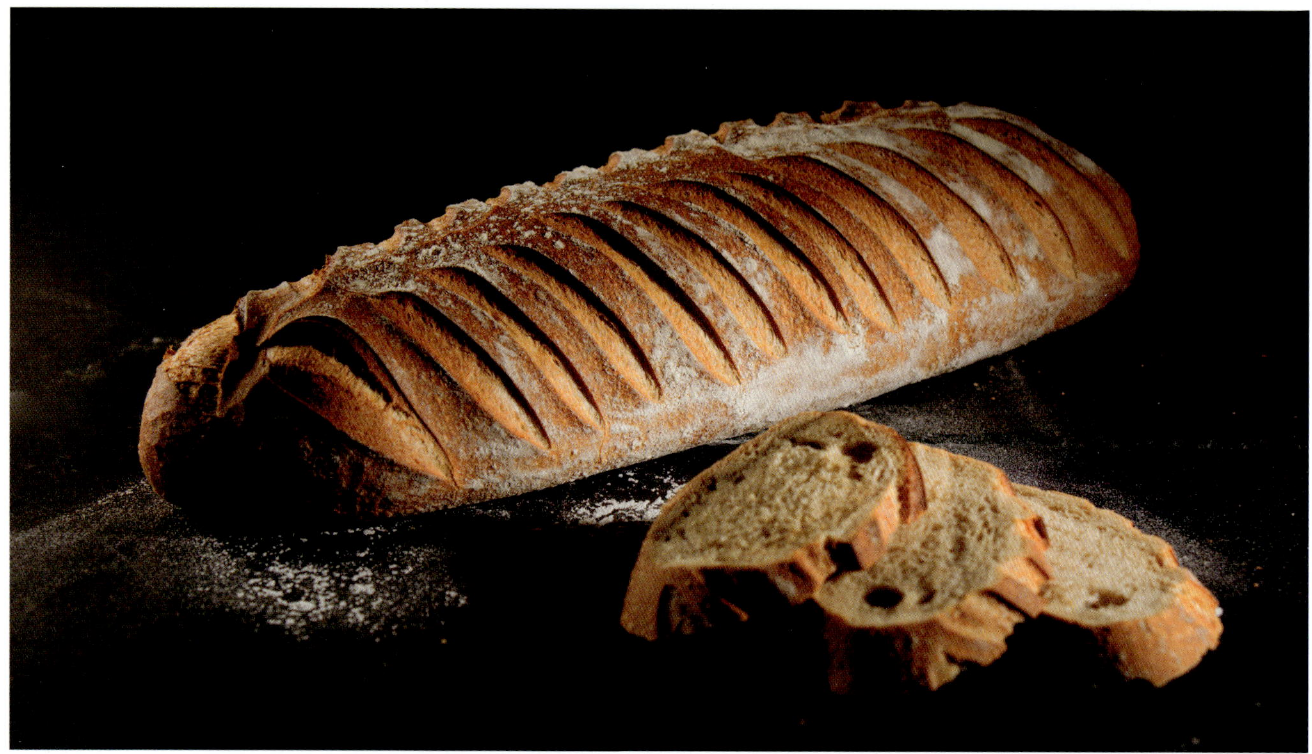

⌃ It is often a must to have lighting that brings out textures—for instance, on a loaf of bread.

Moving Outside the Framework

You do not have to present food on a flat surface, not even on a table. The advertising of the last forty years has taught us to think of food in highly varied contexts: being thrown into liquid (such as breakfast cereal being poured into a bowl of milk), explosions (a common way to show hamburgers, showcasing each ingredient), syrup pouring over waffles (see pages 238–239) . . . All kinds of presentation are possible, with or without editing, but almost always with the main lights placed in backlight.

Set Design and Preparation

In food photography, what is more important than the lighting or the managing of the camera is the art of preparing the dishes.

The first step is to identify a dynamic, a series of geometric elements and/or colors that will give you a reason to arrange the food in a certain way—the basics of these techniques can be found in the section on composition (page 208). The idea is to highlight a food using either contrast or harmony: for contrast, we can look for opposing geometric shapes, different textures, contradictory orientations, etc.; for harmony, we can try to find similar or complementary shapes and colors to go along with the shape and color of the food.

Finally, and this is certainly the biggest issue for novices, you are not trying to photograph what tastes good but what is the most visually stimulating to the appetite. If you pour maple syrup over steaming hot pancakes, by the time you press the shutter, the pancakes will already have absorbed the syrup! But if you substitute motor oil for the syrup, the syrup will look more real than life. And it will be easier to arrange for a more effective visual impact. This is also true for milk, which is replaced with white glue in ads for breakfast cereals and for many other foods.

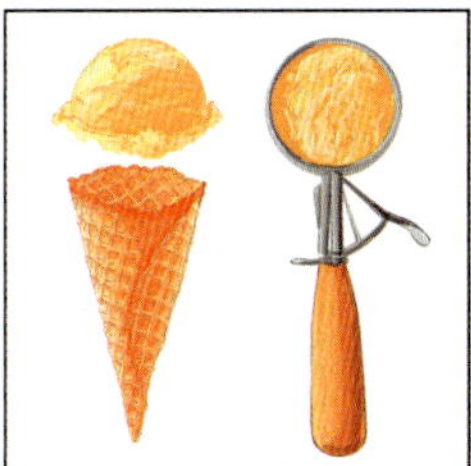

Ice cream. Because this kind of product tends to melt quickly, losing the texture we expect to see, it is replaced with mashed potatoes, flattened with a fork, and then colored with pigments.

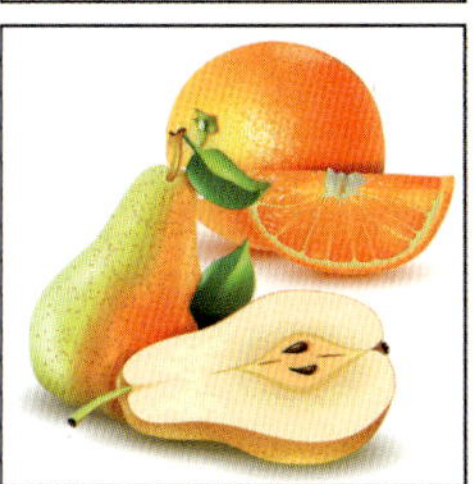

Fruit. To make fruit properly glossy, you can use hairspray or a spray deodorant. Either of these will create tiny glossy bubbles on the surface of the fruit, giving a sense of freshness.

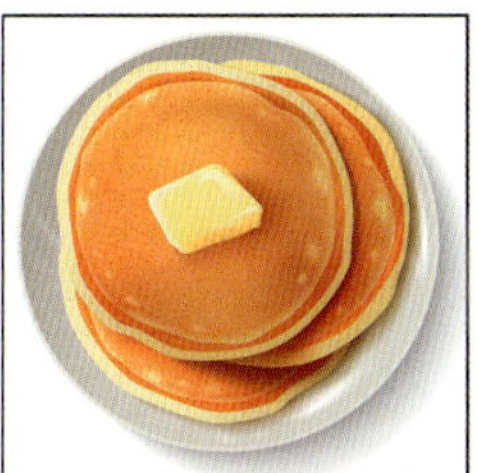

Crepes and pancakes. Maple syrup and honey tend to be absorbed very quickly, so they are replaced with motor oil. Alternatively, you can keep the syrup from being absorbed by spraying the pancakes with a fabric water repellent.

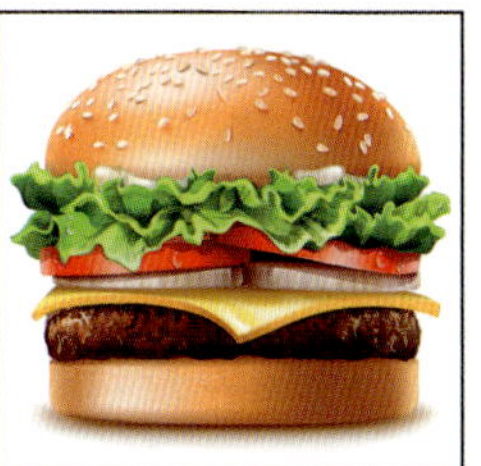

Ground beef. The meat has to be almost raw to maintain its shape and texture. It can be colored using a mixture of gouache paint and shoe polish. Grill marks can be made with hot chopsticks.

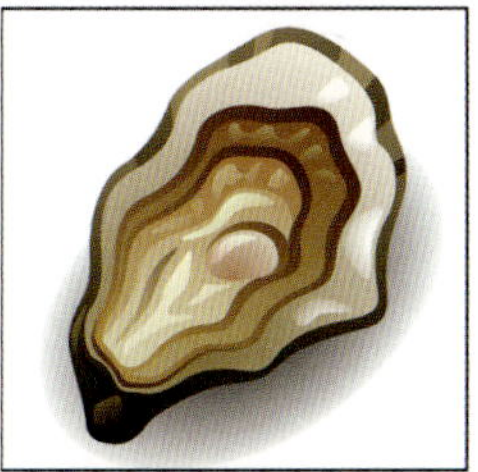

Seafood. If it is exposed to the air too long, seafood tends to curl and dry up. It can be coated with glycerin, using a brush, to maintain its glossy, liquid look.

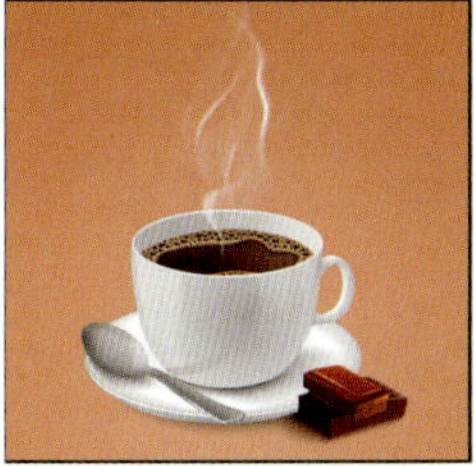

Heat. To give the impression that a dish or drink is hot, hide an incense burner behind the dish or cup, or hide cotton balls that have been moistened and then heated in a microwave.

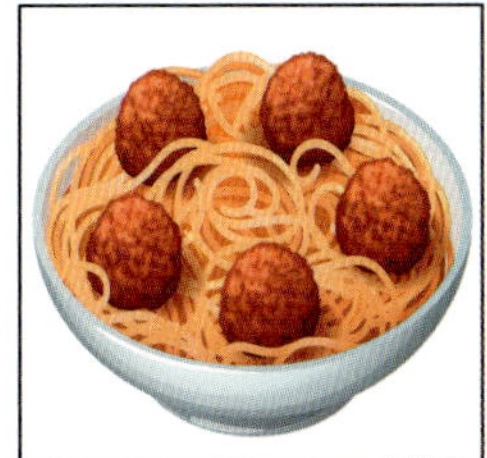

Pasta. Pasta tends to dry out quickly and absorb sauces. Spray it with a mixture of water and glycerin right before the shoot.

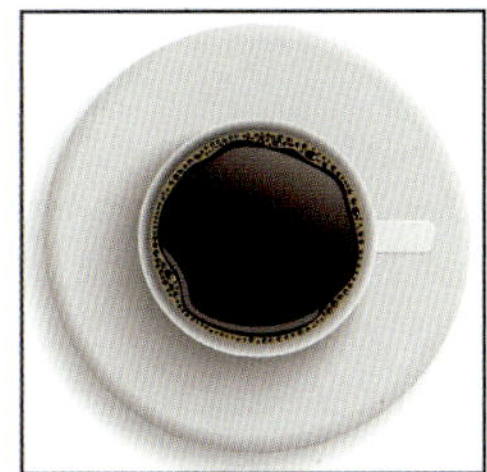

Foam. For foam on top of hot drinks like coffee, steamed milk, or hot chocolate, we mix some of the drink with liquid dish soap, and pour that on the surface of the drink just before shooting.

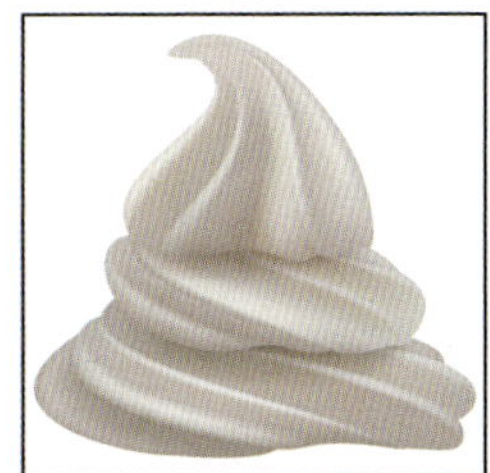

Whipped cream. To help whipped cream keep its shape longer, mix it with shaving cream ahead of time.

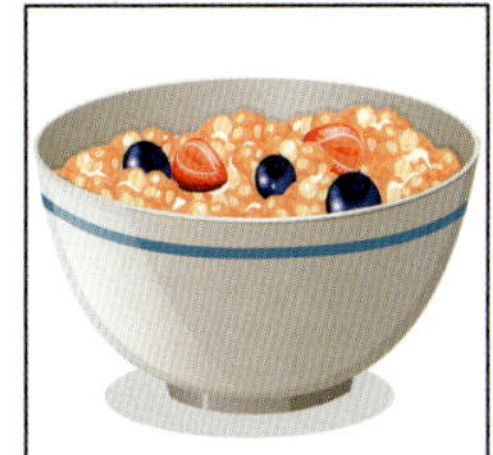

Milk. When we need to show an arrangement that includes milk (such as breakfast cereal), we substitute liquid white glue for the milk. This allows the cereal to stay on the surface without getting wet or changing its appearance.

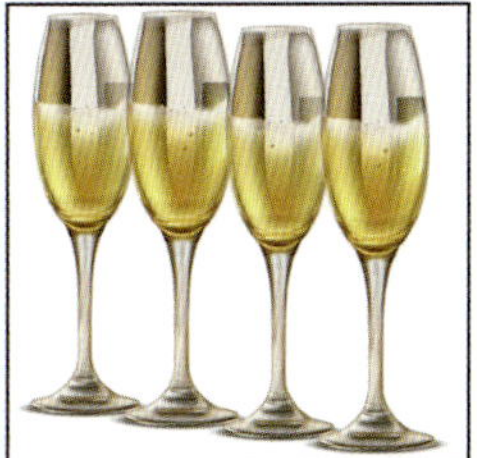

Bubbles. To keep bubbles in a glass longer, we mix some of the liquid with an effervescent tablet, and then pour that into the glass at the moment of the shoot.

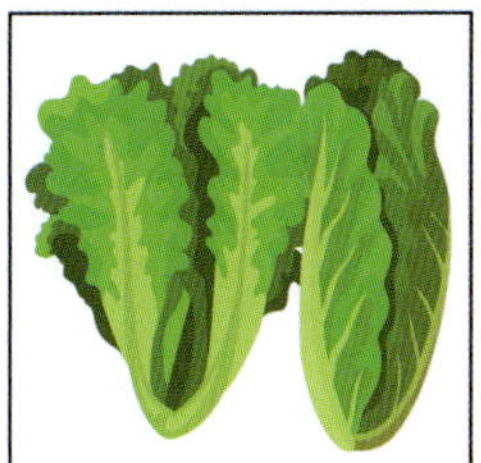

Green vegetables. To reinforce the color of green vegetables, we immerse them in a bowl of water filled with ice cubes. The very cold temperature keeps them nice and green.

PREPARING FOOD TO BE PHOTOGRAPHED

LIGHTING ELECTRONICS

Whether we're talking about smartphones, computers, food processors, or electronic gadgets, it is crucial to manage the light to give the overall impression of innovation and technology.

Every new laptop that comes onto the market has to relegate all the ones that came before to an old-fashioned past, making has-beens out of them. This needs to show in the photograph. Thus, in terms of both lighting and staging, we must be able to offer a new vision, often one that is inspired by science fiction, which regularly comes up with new ways of seeing modernity.

Preparation

Electronic objects are dust traps because of the static electricity inherent in the material they are made from, usually glossy plastic for their shells. It is therefore necessary to perform a very thorough cleaning of the workspace, as well as dust with an antistatic spray, wearing gloves.

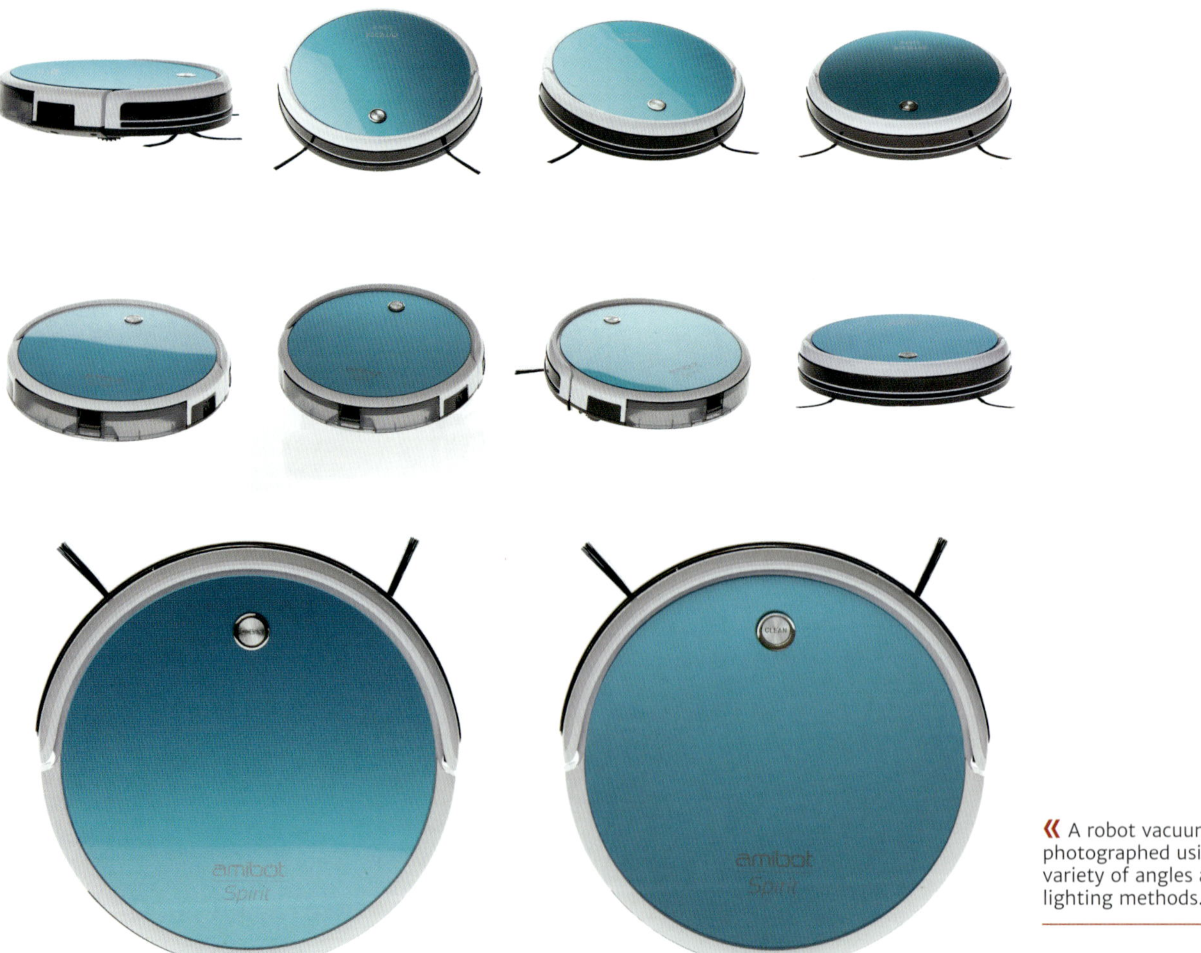

« A robot vacuum cleaner, photographed using a variety of angles and lighting methods.

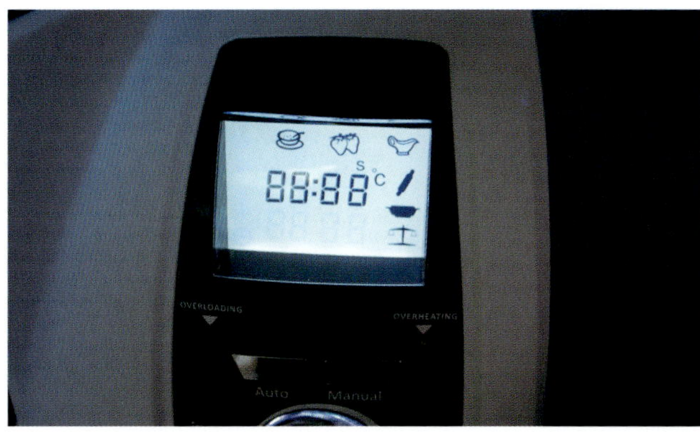

Lighting

Electronic objects, which are often very glossy, do well if they are photographed along very precise lighting angles in order to bring out the direct reflections that will emphasize their shape in the appropriate places. I propose here a study of this process, using the ten photos on the previous page of the Amibot Spirit robot vacuum cleaner as an example. Depending on the angle of the incident light (a sixty-inch octabox, placed about three feet above the vacuum cleaner) to the surface of the robot, the impression that the direct reflection will give of the object's shape will change, as will the look of the material. Even the power button looks different.

There is no one best way to light a product like this because each angle allows us to show a particular aspect of the shape, the technical specifications, or the texture. It's up to you and your client to agree on what should be highlighted.

Managing LCD Screens and Other Product Lights

Most current electronic devices have screens and other lighting features, such as power and status lights, that must be shown in the photograph. The best practice is therefore to light the object with a flash, following the methods of asynchronous lighting.

A flash delivers a considerable amount of light over a very small period of time (on the order of 1/1000 of a second), while the product's lights themselves produce very weak but continuous lighting. You just need to work in a very dark space and measure the light of the flash so that it is optimized to +1.33 EV relative to the camera setting: for example, a flash measured at f/8 for a camera set to f/5, 1/200 s, ISO 100. At this point, if you release the shutter, the device's lights or the LCD screen will disappear, but the object itself will be perfectly lit. Then, you simply need to change the exposure time, for instance by adjusting the camera (on a tripod) to 1/3 s, for the device's lights to increase by 6 EV and to become 64 times more intense.

Using this value, most products' lights will be properly illuminated, but if the light seems too weak, there is no reason not to lengthen the exposure time even more. The power of the flash will remain constant: because the flash lasts a very short time, the exposure time doesn't matter to it. In a case like this, make sure to work in the dark, and, of course, be sure not to leave the pilot light of the flash on: its continuous light would mess up the calculation.

Catalogs and Staging

Because of online sales sites, it is now customary to present objects against a uniformly white (color value 255) background, in a square format. But for the purposes of demonstration, we also continue to take situational shots, like with the vacuum cleaner presented below. People expect to see its specifics, its practical functioning, or its design aspects in one image. Thus, the image we produce must correspond to the object's style and colors: it would be very silly to show this vacuum cleaner underneath a Louis XV dresser or in front of 1950s floral wallpaper! The space must be organized to correspond to the environment that people want to see in combination with the product.

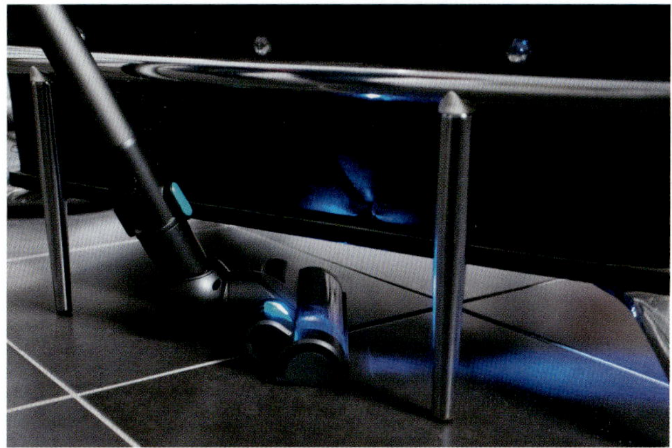

LIGHTING JEWELRY

For anyone just starting out, lighting and shooting jewelry, especially if it is metallic and has shiny or glossy stones like diamonds, can seem impossible without hours of post-production work. But careful management of the lighting can allow you to get a good result with the unedited shot itself.

Because most jewelry is small, we always end up working close-up with macro lenses. Thus, even the smallest bit of dust and tiniest imperfections will be visible. It is essential to give the jewelry a good dose of antistatic spray and to handle everything with gloves. The jewelry itself is fixed into place with small pieces of sticky putty.

The Lighting Philosophy

Because of the size of the objects being photographed, we will, of course, have to use very small diameter light sources. I usually use snoots equipped with honeycombs,

STANDARD METHOD FOR LIGHTING JEWELRY

but many others in the profession often work with small directional LED lights, which are very effective when you need to manage the lighting on precious stones.

No matter what kind of lighting you are using, the jewelry will need to have each of its parts lighted using different angles, quantities, and qualities of light. For the example of the rings shown here, we can distinguish three different areas:

- The inside of the rings require fairly large diffuse lighting, enough to cover about half of its diameter. Typically, small light boxes are used for this, placed behind diffusing fabric. But depending on the size and shape of the object, a snoot behind a diffuser may also do the trick.
- Then the edge of the rings needs to be lit (see photos below) because the roundness of the ring is an essential element for understanding its shape. To achieve this, a light source is placed at right angles to the edge (a diffused snoot works well).
- Finally, the stones need to be lit so that as many flashes of reflection appear as possible. The way in which diamonds are cut—to allow total refraction—causes them to return most of the rays at a right angle. We therefore have a narrow and very hard light source at a right angle to the stone. If there are several stones, as on the ring on page 162, we can think in terms of arranging several light sources in a corolla shape to illuminate the stones that are located at different angles.

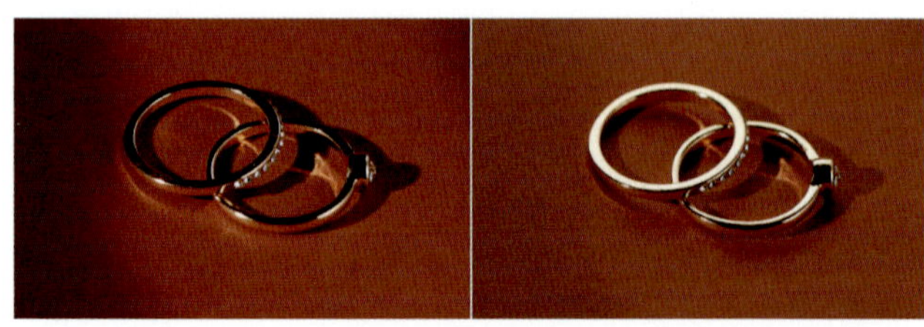

⌃ In the first photo, the lighting is localized on the front edge. In the second photo, the rings are backlit using a large diffusing fabric.

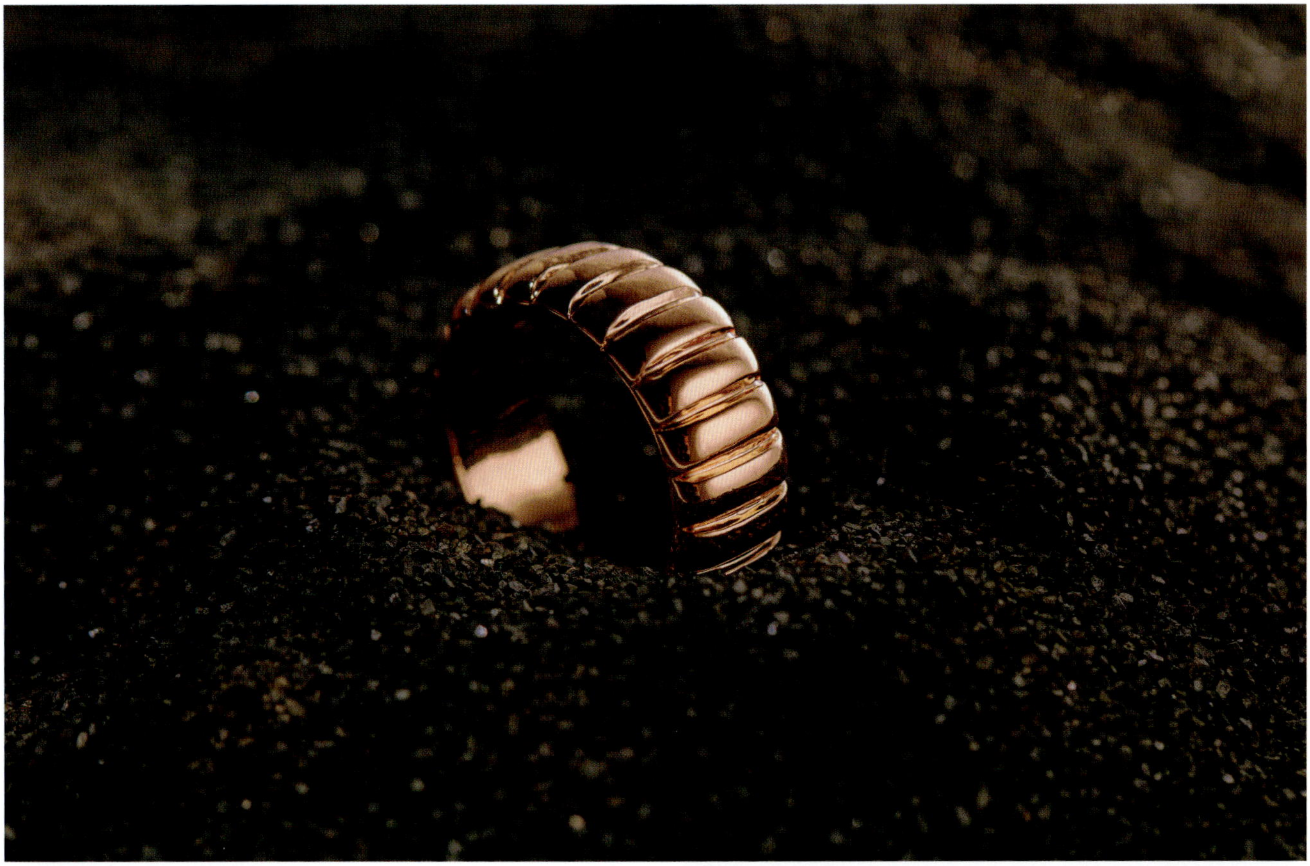

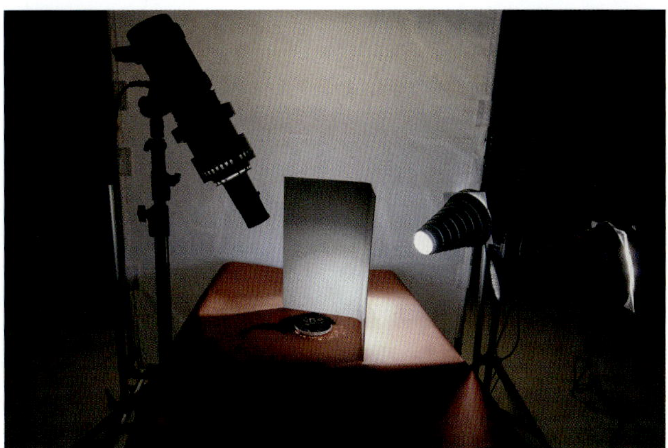

LIGHTING EXAMPLE FOR JEWELRY

Implementation

The simplest procedure is to arrange rounded sheets of PMMA plexiglass along the axes that correspond to the desired lighting. Then install the snoots at the necessary positions for lighting the edge, the stones, and the inside and outside faces of the ring. I will just note here in passing that some objects, like simple bands (such as wedding rings), can be lighted using a simple arrangement of light boxes positioned to the side and above the object, but that for most other cases, the lighting will have to be more precise. The lighting of objects this small also requires a good number of very small adjustments of the angles: I recommend that you attach the ring to a mobile background, such as a piece of cardboard, so that you will not have to move every single light source every time you make an adjustment. Then, make sure that every part of the jewelry is well lit by scrupulously observing each of the reflections.

⌃ A behind-the-scenes look at the lighting for the ring shown above.

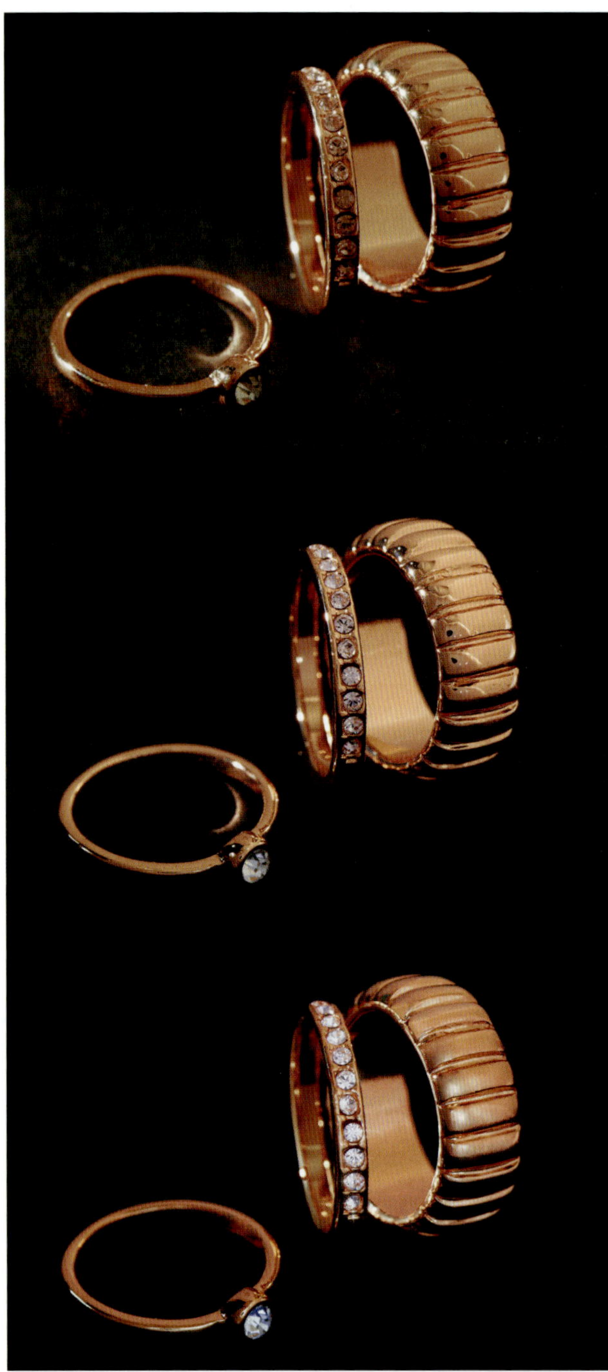

Shines and Colors

Jewelry is often made of glossy metal: generally rounded, it acts somewhat like the Christmas tree ornaments we looked at earlier, and it reflects the entire workspace. Thus, you need to make sure that there is no light source coming in to interfere with your lighting arrangement, so it's important to work in a dark studio. If you are presenting several pieces of jewelry at the same time, you will also have to make sure that they do not reflect each other by choosing an angle of placement outside the families of angles.

It is essential to take the colors of the metals and stones into account; therefore, you need to undertake a complete calibration, using a gray card and a color palette, before shooting. I recommend that you repeat this operation every time the lighting changes or anytime you decide to introduce new accessories or different backgrounds into your image.

Catalogs

For catalogs, the fashion now is to have a white background and present the object in a square format. Rings are generally placed at an angle, balanced on the side using a small plexiglass wedge that is placed as far back as possible from the gemstone (this can easily be erased in post-production). But the presentation can vary depending on the brand, the style, and the medium where the images will be displayed. In the figure on the next page, you can see the most commonly requested angles.

We look for the lighting to be as even as possible, with no pronounced shadows and no environmental reflection—the smoothest possible light. This is why we use diffusers so much, as close as possible to the piece of jewelry. Glossiness is also a requirement, with regular reflection lines across the entire piece of jewelry, and without any jaggedness or changes in texture.

Advertising

There are countless ways to highlight a piece of jewelry in advertising. People are always trying to come up with ingenious new ones, but there are five common methods we can list:

- Jewelry worn by a model, in a lifestyle context. With careful staging, you create an atmosphere by evoking emotion and belonging to a social group. Think, for example, of Fabergé's 2018 campaign entitled "The Russian Seasons."

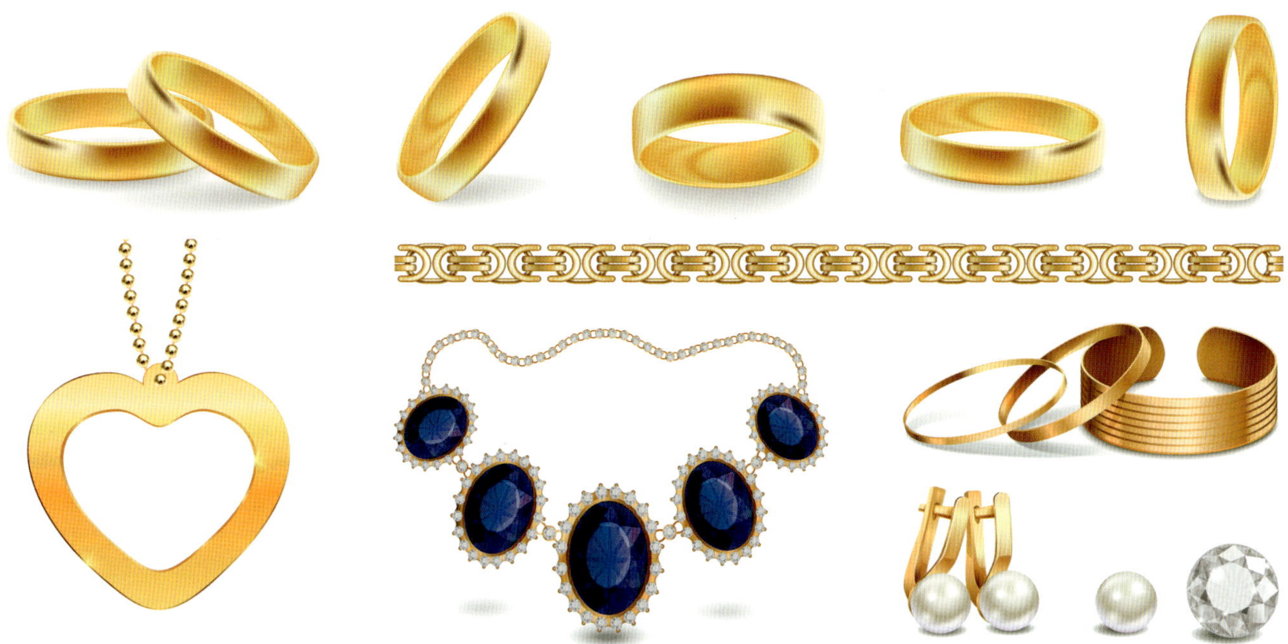

- Portraits of models against a plain background, as in Chanel's 2016 advertising campaign with Keira Knightley photographed by Mario Testino, or Piaget's 2018 advertisements. The focus here is on the jewelry and the model's posture.
- Close-ups of a model (a hand wearing a ring, or a cheek and an ear with an earring, etc.), as in Fred Joaillerie's 2018 campaigns or in most of Djula's advertisements, which have made this look one of their trademarks.
- A packshot of the piece of jewelry presented by itself, stripped of any other context, sometimes in extreme close-up, as in Cartier's 2019 "Trinity" campaign, where the triple ring was presented as a diptych: once in its entirety and once in a very tight close-up of the upper part of the object.
- A staging of the piece of jewelry, as in the 2016 Akillis ads, in which a ring embellished with rhinestones was placed on a charcoal sphere, which was in turn posed on a stand lined with gray sand, all against a black background. Or the 2019 Chopard campaign, in which two rings were suspended from a black ribbon against an anthracite background.

LIGHTING WATCHES

The lighting methods used for watches combine the methods used for jewelry, fabrics, and eyeglasses.

As with jewelry, lighting a watch—emphasizing the outline of the case and giving body to the crystal face without allowing overly visible reflections to erase its inscriptions and hands—requires very precise, well-directed lights and careful management of the diffusions.

Lighting Philosophy

Here, too, we work with great precision, with carefully directed light sources, generally snoots and small honeycombs. To avoid the direct reflections and highlights that tend to come with this kind of lighting, we arrange diffusing screens on each of the sides to be lit. Rectangular cases can be lit just like standard parallelepipeds, with lights generating differences in tone on each of the three sides of the case, while round cases can be lit just like cylinders, with a single light source placed to create a regular gradient along the edge.

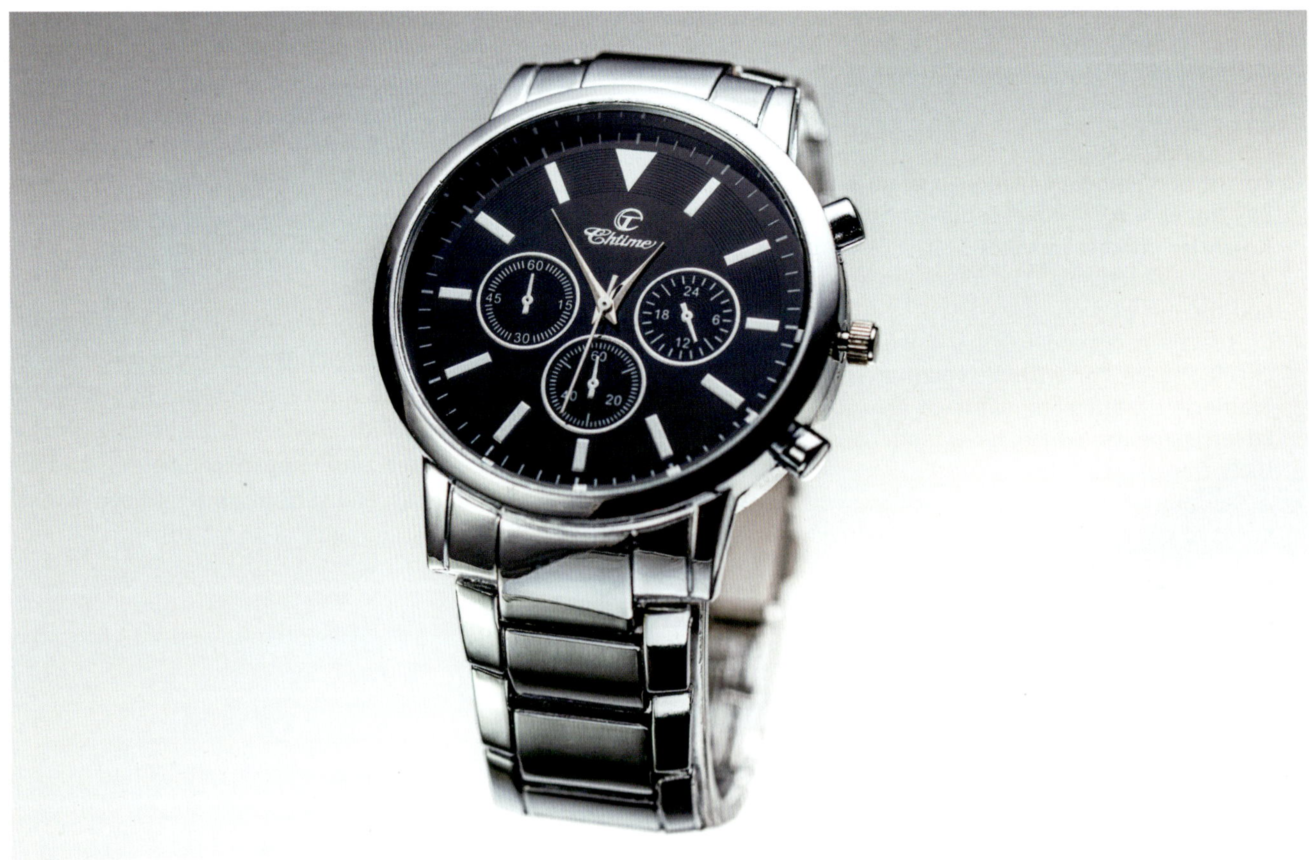

Plexiglass display stand used to hold the watchband closed for the photo setup.

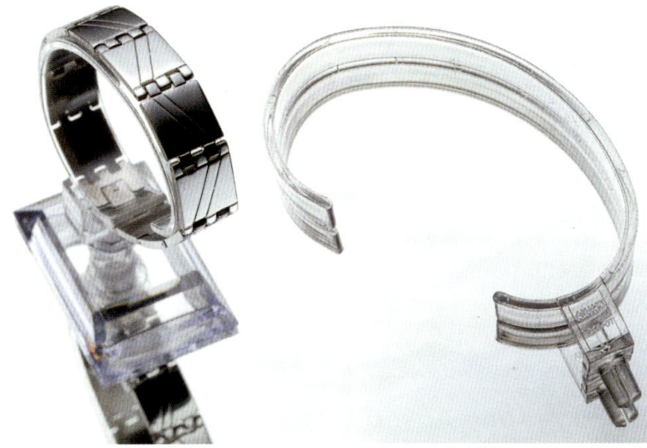

⌃ Example of lighting on a watch.

As for the glass, there are different schools of thought. Some prefer to light it so that it disappears: they take advantage of the phenomenon of direct transmission by placing the light source at a right angle to the glass and photographing the watch from an angle. Others, however, including myself, prefer to manage the lighting so that a very slight, soft, gradual reflection appears on the glass. In such a case, you have to position yourself at the extreme edge of the family of angles of a very large and diffuse light source (such as a large octabox arranged behind a diffusing fabric).

Preparing the Watch

While dusting the watch, the hands are also adjusted so that they do not overlap with any of the inscriptions on the dial (which generally include the brand, the model, and the technical specifications). They are traditionally placed at 10:10, and the second hand at 40 seconds. Pay special attention to the knobs and to the mechanism, if it is visible: they tend to catch dust and small hairs, but a burst of compressed air will get rid of those easily. The watch can be held in a closed position by attaching it around a plexiglass form (see image above). There are also display units equipped with a plexiglass bracelet strap, a clip, and a base to hold the watch in the air, which makes it easier to light.

Lighting the Glass and the Hands

It is easy to make the glass disappear, since all you need to do to make that happen is place the light source outside of the family of angles, but then shadows may appear on the dial, underneath the hands, and on any embossed elements. A better strategy is to place the light source in direct transmission and the camera outside the family of angles: this way the dial and the hands will be perfectly lit, but the glass will not be visible.

The glass can also be lit at the edge of the family of angles with a large diffusing source. This will have the most attractive effect if the dial is black or very dark: the glass will appear just slightly, without any strong reflections that would make the inscriptions illegible.

While the hands do not generally pose any kind of problem, they occasionally have a particular shape (with beveling, inlays, engraving, etc.) that requires lighting that is contradictory to what the glass requires, generally a grazing side light. In a case like this, we can create a composite photo using one lighting arrangement for the glass and one for the hands, putting it all together at the end using editing software.

Lighting the Bezel and the Edges of the Case

Unless you are creating a composite photo, the bezel (the ring or rectangle that holds the glass front of the watch in place) will of necessity be illuminated at the same time as the glass. Thus, it will look different depending on whether or not you have decided to make the glass invisible. And therefore, the look that you want to give to the bezel ends up taking priority. For large metallic bezels, such as those on men's watches, lateral lighting is usually used to give a sense of chiaroscuro; in that case, you would light the dial and the glass in reflection, in order not to spoil the effect. For narrower bezels, direct lighting is appropriate.

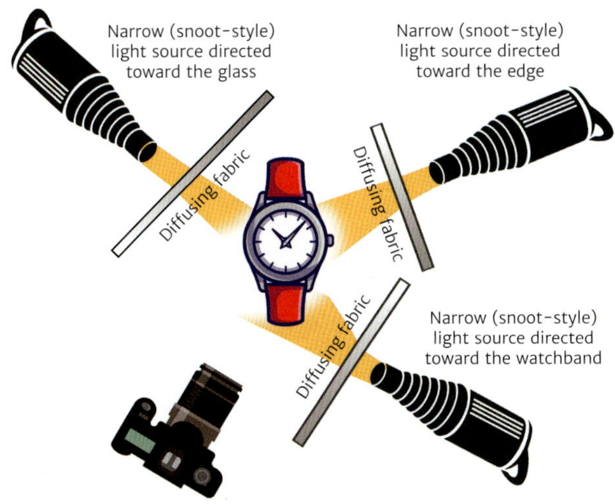

STANDARD METHOD FOR LIGHTING WATCHES

Lighting the Wristband

Most photographers agree that backlighting is the most effective way to light the wristband. It is appropriate for most materials, from metal to leather to textured plastic. Simply place the light source in rim light or behind the wristband, within its axis, at a grazing angle. To obtain an even gradient, however, wristbands made of smooth plastic, like the wristbands on Swatch watches, will benefit from being lit with a very diffuse source, placed at right angles to the edges of the family of angles.

Lighting the Details

For luxury watches with diamonds or other precious stone inlays, we use the method described for jewelry: direct light sources, slightly diffused (in this case, snoots equipped with honeycombs placed behind diffusers), directed toward the stones. If this ends up clashing with the lighting for the glass or the watch hands, then it will be necessary, again, to create a composite photo.

Catalogs and Advertising

Since the early 2000s, catalogs have presented most watches in the same way: with the dial facing forward and the wristband closed around a rounded support stand (as shown on the preceding page). This method is replacing the previous standard, which involved showing the watch photographed flat, with the wristband open or folded over, from a bird's-eye view.

In advertising, we use the same techniques as for jewelry: the watch can be displayed on a model's wrist in a lifestyle context (in which case, a packshot image is also included in the ad as a reminder), as in the French ad for the 2015 Rolex master goldsmith Cellini model; or in a close-up on a model's wrist, as in the ad for the 1995 Rolex Oyster Perpetual GMT master II, where a tight frame showed the watch on the arm of a man in a suit photographed in a subjective shot, as if the viewer was James Bond himself.

Most campaigns, however, are centered on the object itself, staged with other items, as in the 2010 advertising for the Khésis watch by Chaumet (in which the object was posed on folded origami paper flowers), or else presented alone, as with the FO 264/1 from Festina (a gold watch photographed closed, from the front, against a midnight-blue background in a wide shot close-up, to show the diamonds on either side of the dial).

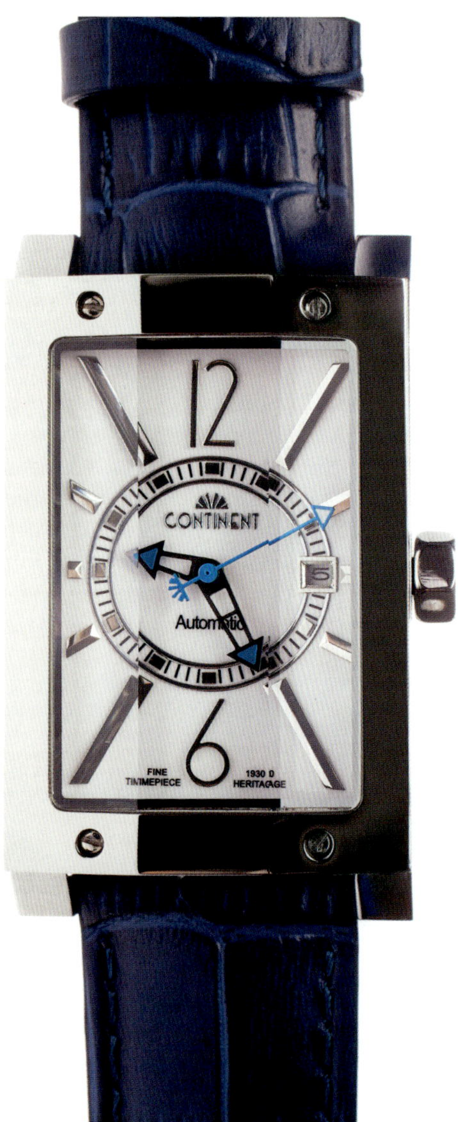

EXAMPLE OF THE LIGHTING OF A WATCH

PHOTOGRAPHING FURNITURE

Furniture photography was totally revamped at the beginning of the 1990s, with more dynamic images than the traditional presentations on location that had been produced up until then.

In the late 1980s, brands like Ikea completely overhauled the concept of furniture, and thus the way pieces of furniture were presented in photography. Until then, furniture was exhibited in its traditional environment. But after that turning point, the entire context was staged in the studio, with the creation of miniature sets, usually consisting of a foamboard background to which paintings or shelves could be attached, and a removable floor (floating flooring, carpet, linoleum, etc.). This technique makes it possible to produce visuals more quickly by allowing the sets to evolve as the scene is rearranged. And for packshot images against a plain background, here, too, the standard is now white (color value 255) with a square-format presentation.

Lighting Philosophy

Except in unusual cases, furniture is lit using very large light sources, as diffused as possible, which are arranged quite far away to avoid overly pronounced contrasts; in this case, that would be large octaboxes or umbrellas placed behind diffusers, or, more simply, light sources directed toward the walls, in reflection. Take care to ensure that there is a very light-colored and diffuse shadow underneath the object, to give it some "lift" while not attracting too much attention. There is no need to add an extra light source to attenuate the shadow, because that would cause problematic reflections on the piece of furniture; simply make sure that the light is as soft and as even as possible.

Catalogs

For photographs meant for a catalog, the object is presented along several axes: front, three-quarter view, potentially from the back, and if the piece of furniture has doors, they are shown both open and closed. We also take "usage shots" by adding accessories or graphic elements: a television set on a TV stand, the dishes set out on a dining room table, a computer on a desk, clothes hanging from a clothing rod, etc. These situational shots are not insignificant at all; they allow the consumer to project themselves into the space and visualize whether the clothing rod they are thinking of buying will be large enough for the number of coats they want to store there, for example.

The whole thing is lighted in the same way as individual pieces of furniture: large diffuse sources, perfectly white and low-contrast light, precise color calibration.

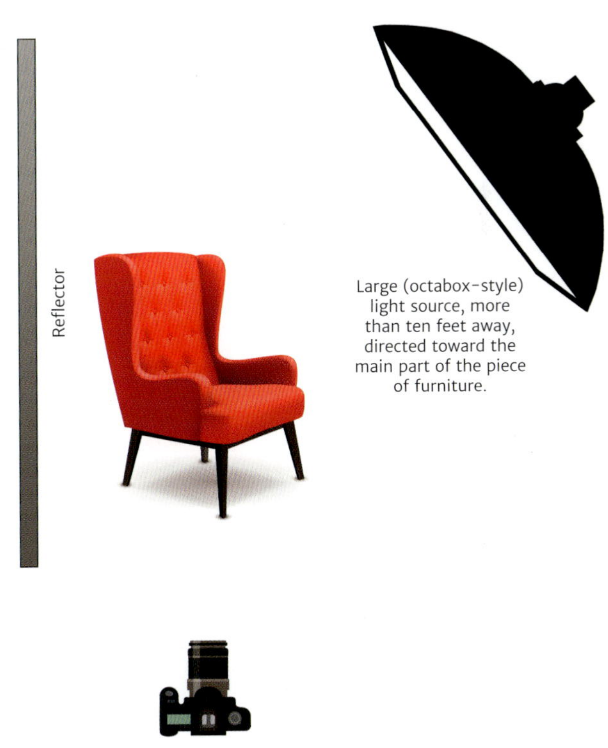

STANDARD METHOD FOR LIGHTING FURNITURE

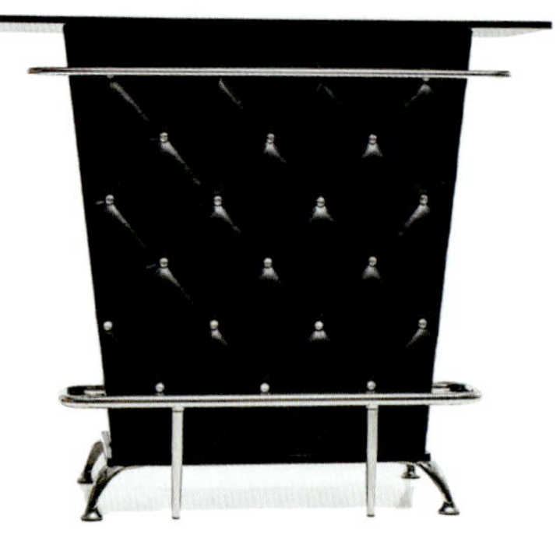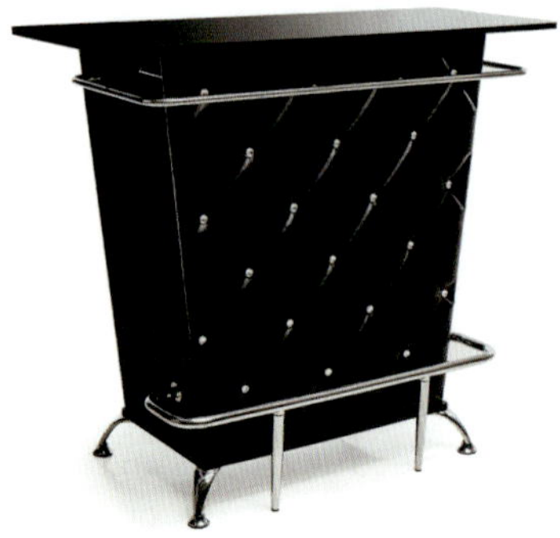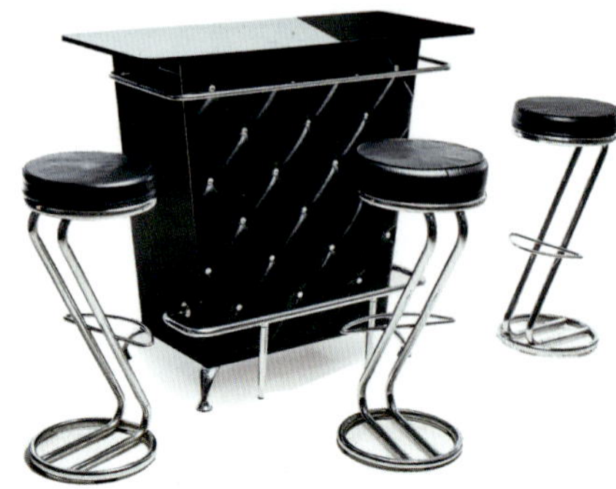

⌃ Several presentation options for a bar set, and two lighting choices for the countertop. The countertop in the center image was lit using a large diffuser, and the one to the right with a softbox placed at the edge of the family of angles so as to emphasize its glossiness.

Viewing Angle

We usually choose a viewing angle that is close to that of a person of average height facing the furniture being shown: horizontal for cupboards and bookcases, and at a slight downward angle for tables, desks, or beds. The only exception is that chairs and armchairs, when presented alone, are photographed from a horizontal angle.

Because most other items of furniture are shaped approximately like a parallelepiped, they are presented in three-quarter view, taking care for the light to be more pronounced on the part that is naturally the most important: the tabletop for a table, the front side for a cupboard, the seat for a chair or a couch, etc.

Contextualizing

When it comes to putting the piece of furniture in context, the trend is to keep it simple: we don't want to overload bookshelves with books and tchotchkes, we only put one category of objects on a table, and we present a limited number of frames and accessories on a wall. In the same way, we work in undersaturated interiors, with (monochrome) colors that harmonize with the piece of furniture. Think in terms of light mouse gray, beige, taupe, and ecru for all elements of the environment: carpets, curtains, wall art, lighting, etc.

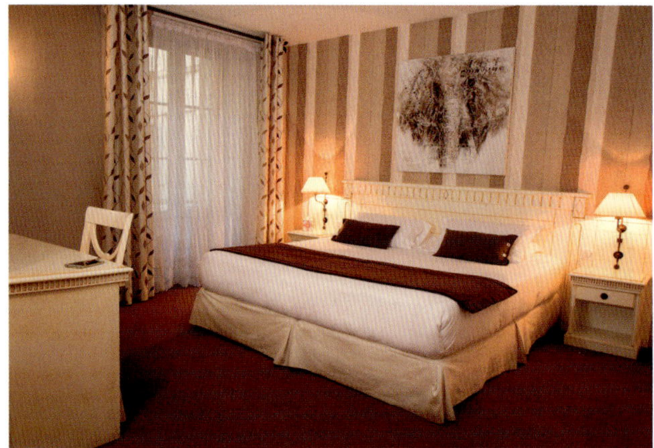

⌃ Example of the presentation of a bedroom set on location. A flash equipped with a sixty-inch umbrella was installed on the left and the exposure time was managed so that the light from the lampshades represented 40% of the total light, using a flash meter measurement. You can also create an interior design in the studio to present a piece of furniture in context.

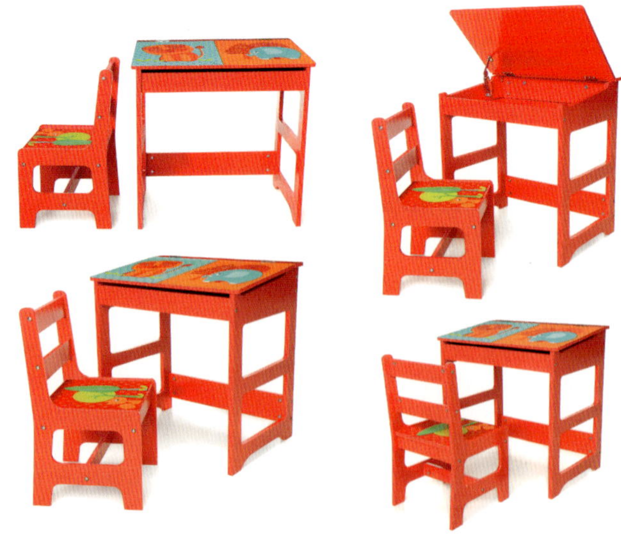

PRESENTATION EXAMPLE FOR A CHILD'S DESK

PHOTOGRAPHING EYEGLASSES

In this sector, where competition has increased over the last fifteen years with frames changing much more frequently than before, there is also a constantly increasing demand for photography. Let's review lighting and shooting methods.

Once you understand the laws that govern reflection on surfaces that produce direct reflections, a pair of glasses is not very difficult to light. But the common misconception that there should not be any reflections robs many of the images of life and of nuance. The current trend, on the contrary, is toward showing a slight veil over the lenses, which produces much livelier photos.

Lighting Philosophy

Before beginning to arrange the light sources, the project needs to be defined: whether or not the lenses should appear (for prescription glasses; this question does not arise for sunglasses); how the frames should be placed;

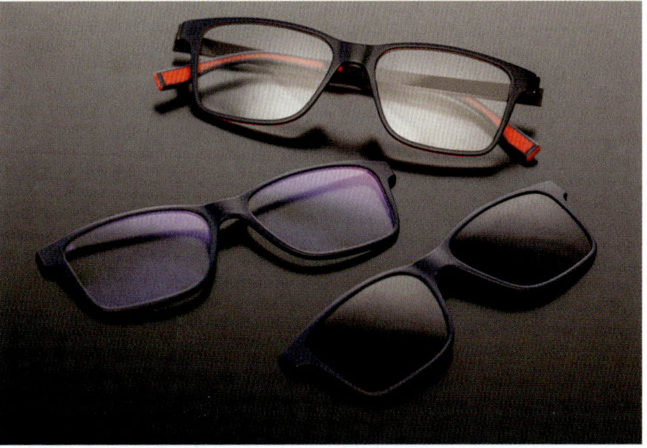

EXAMPLE OF PRESENTATION FOR PRESCRIPTION GLASSES AND SUNGLASS CLIP-ONS

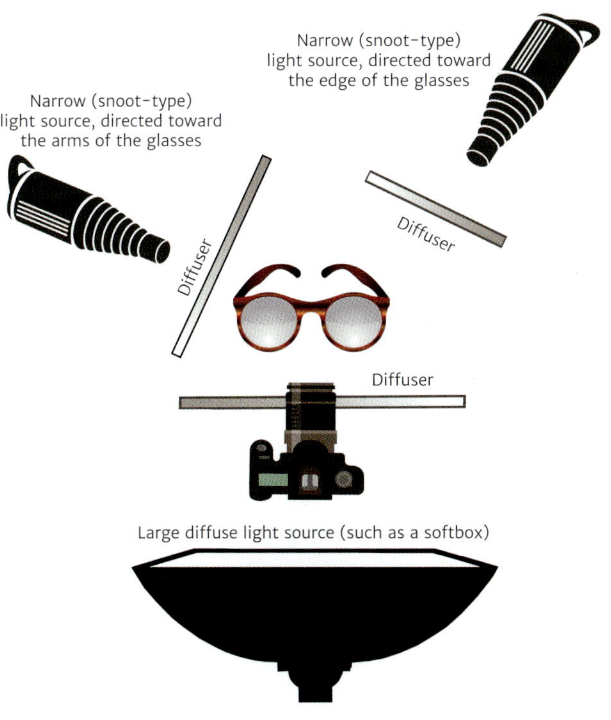

STANDARD METHOD FOR LIGHTING PRESCRIPTION GLASSES WITH FLAT LENSES

whether or not the arms (technically called the temples) should be folded; which specific material or color should be emphasized; etc. For prescription glasses, we usually work with a large diffused light box for the lenses and small diffused sources for the temples and edges (see diagram at left). For sunglasses, we usually use back-lighting, with a large light source (such as a light box), and a reflection, with a rounded reflector placed in front of the frame, so as to best showcase the lenses with a very even reflection.

Until the mid-2000s, we generally showed glasses frames without lenses in them, which had the advantage of solving the main problems of reflections. Today, however, the tendency is to not only leave the lenses in, but to highlight them. Of course, you still need to avoid overly pronounced or localized reflections; these would draw too much attention, overshadowing the temples and the internal parts of the glasses, such as nose pads, which need to be made visible when this kind of object is presented. This is why we try to obtain a very even reflection that is weak enough in terms of luminous intensity that it is possible to see through the lens.

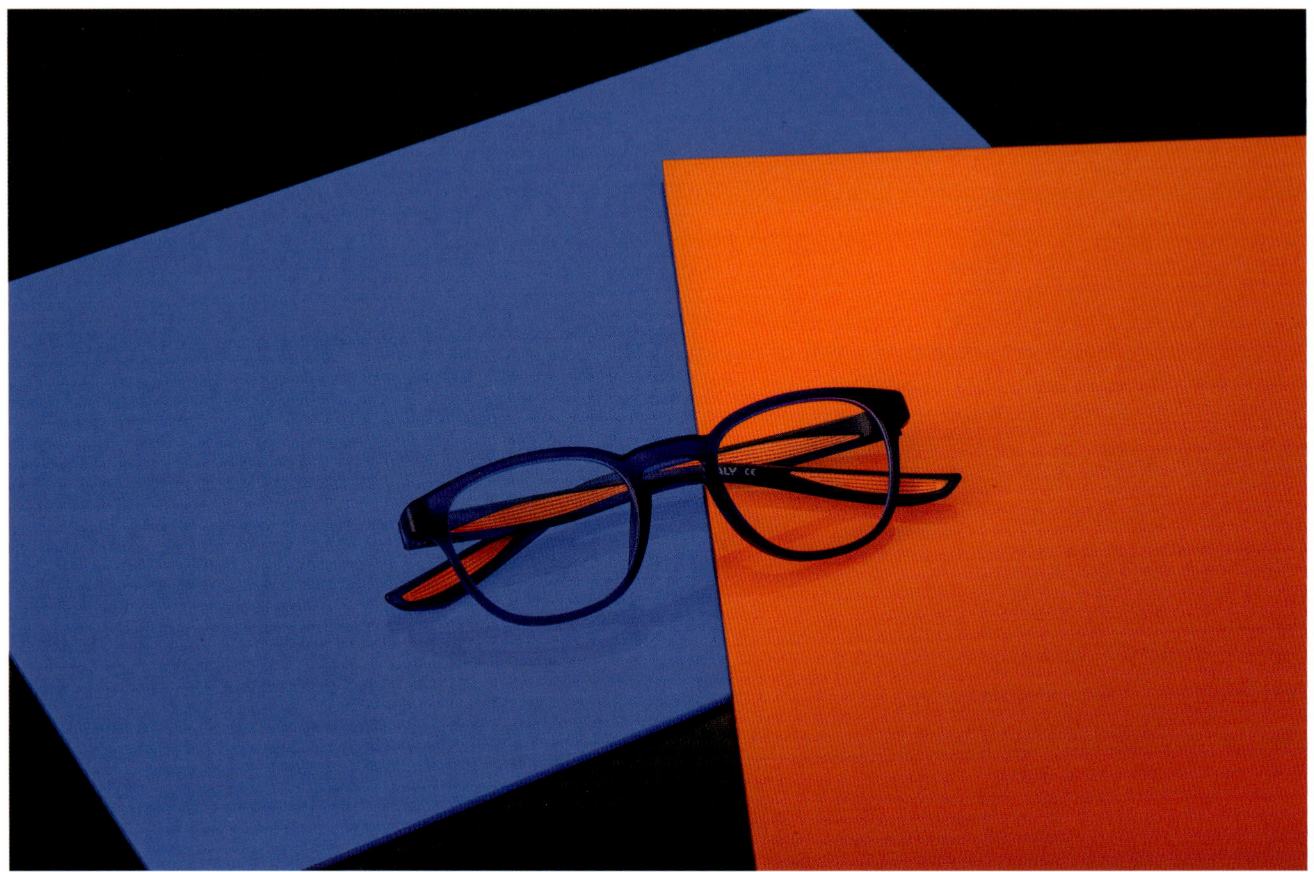

⌃ In glasses photography, it is very important to show the frame and its basic characteristics, while also providing tools for understanding the quality of the lenses, which can only be obtained through rigorous management of the reflections and the associated graphic elements. In this shot, we arranged the light source outside the family of angles of the lenses, which almost do not appear at all.

We use very large lights that cover the entirety of the glasses' family of angles: 180° for flat lenses and up to 250° for curved lenses (for ski goggles, that can go up to 300°). For the photos presented in this book, I worked using a sixty-inch octabox placed approximately three feet from the frame, behind a 98 x 60-inch diffusing fabric.

For the kind of curved lenses that you find on sunglasses, and on certain lenses for correcting astigmatism, a flat diffusing fabric would not be enough to produce a reflection that covers the entire family of angles. The strategy here, then, is different: we use rounded diffusers that we place very close to the pair of glasses, making a hole in a diffuser for the camera lens.

Sunglasses

Because sunglass lenses are usually opaque, we don't try to show what could be seen through them (which would be possible using backlighting); instead, we simply highlight the look of the lenses and frames.

Thus, the lighting work consists of giving substance to the front of the glasses, which we light using a rounded reflector (see photo page 147). An elegant lighting arrangement will show an even but lightly gradated reflection, which implies that the light source placed at a slightly descending angle (of about 10° to 20°). For sports glasses and protective glasses, you can also play with a direct reflection trimmed by a barn door, which emphasizes the high-tech aspect that the brands who market this kind of product are looking for.

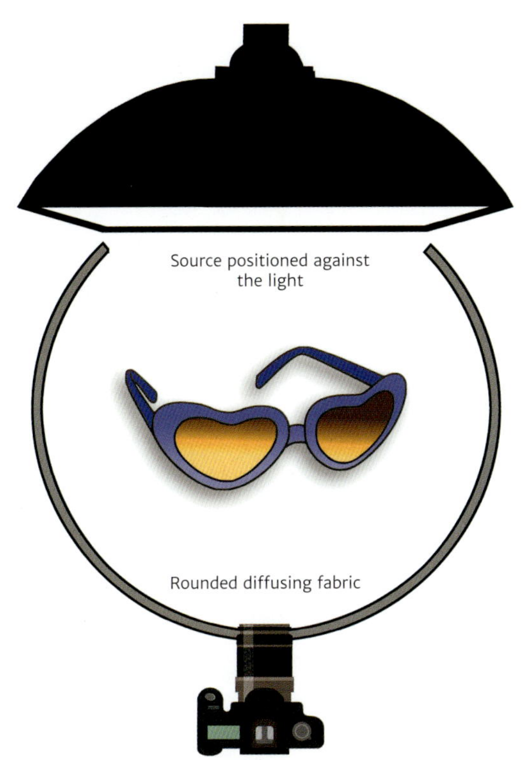

**STANDARD METHOD FOR LIGHTING SUNGLASSES OR
PRESCRIPTION GLASSES WITH CURVED LENSES**

Viewing Angle and Catalogs

Most eyeglass frame manufacturers now use a slightly descending angle (about 15°) for the shots, showing the frames unfolded in three-quarter view. However, a horizontal shot with the frame shown from the front (sometimes without the temples, though this is considered less than ideal by American and Asian brands) is beginning to become standard, especially for photos meant for non-European markets. Some brands also require other kinds of presentations (see next page, bottom). These are most often photos against a uniformly white (color value 255) background, in a square format, meant for e-commerce.

Unlike most objects, which we light to create a slight shadow cast by the object, eyeglasses are shown in catalogs without a shadow, and in order to manage that, the glasses are placed on an elevated sheet of glass (see the method outlined on pages 151–152).

Obviously, with this technique, the reflection on the lenses disappears, but for the catalogs this is not a problem; in fact, it's quite the contrary.

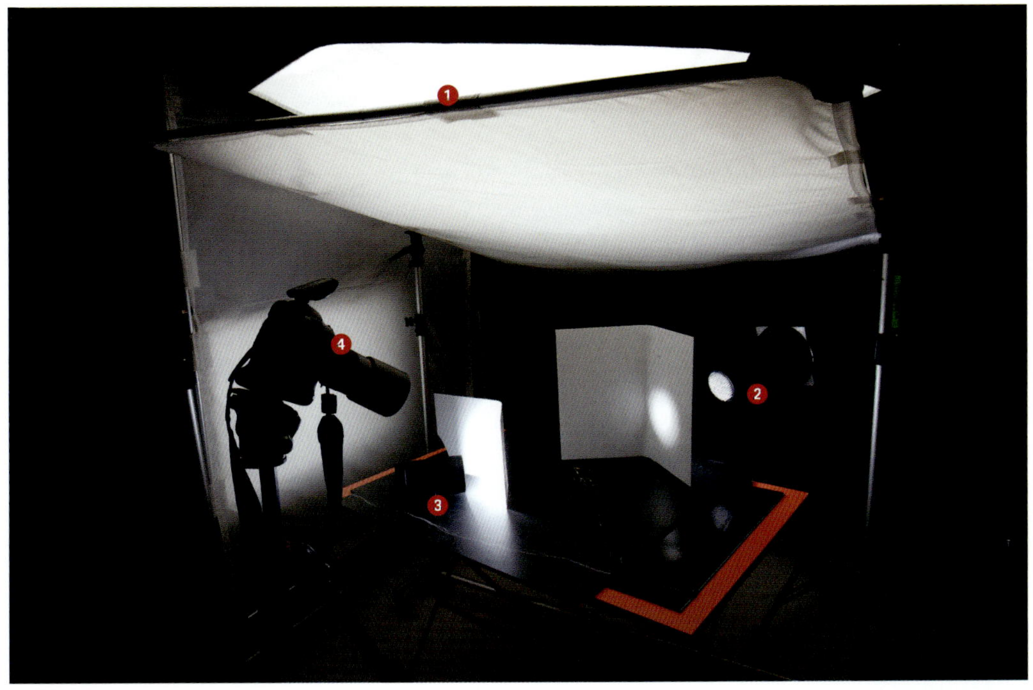

« To produce the photo on the following page, I used four light sources. **1.** An octabox at a showerhead angle above the scene, with a large diffuser placed to create an even reflection on the lenses. **2.** A snoot in backlight behind a sheet of translucent plexiglass to light the marble slab. **3.** A small flash, uncovered, behind another sheet of translucent plexiglass, to eliminate the shadows cast by the snoot. **4.** A light box, at the left, behind a large diffuser, to even out all the light.

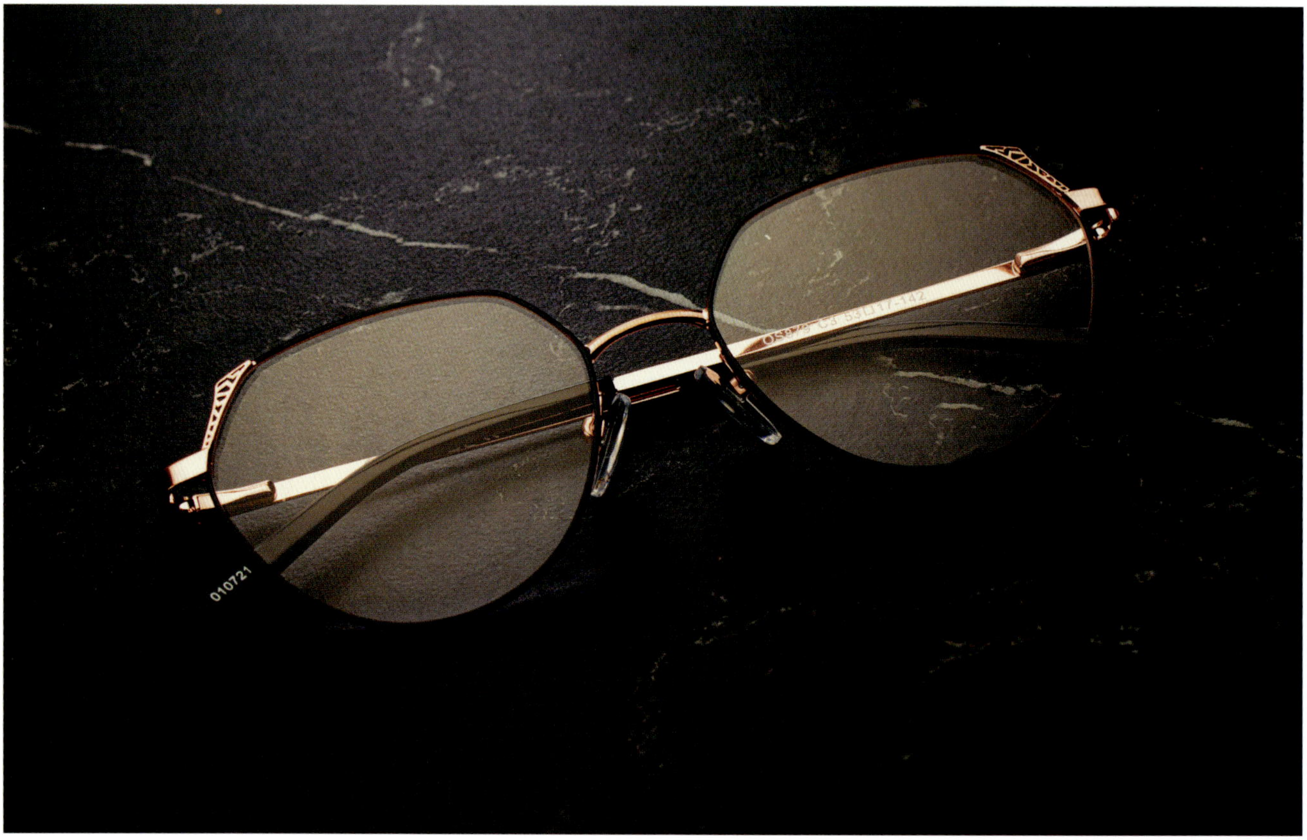

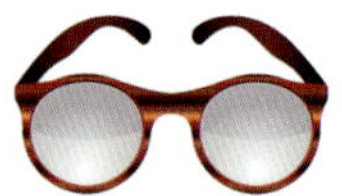

⌃ The final photo (setup on the previous page), presented without any editing.

Advertising

Advertisements usually show the glasses being worn by a model. Except for certain sunglasses frames, the object is seldom shown on its own or in a staged scene (that kind of photo is generally intended instead for a website or printed catalog).

As for framing, it has been done in every possible way: from close-ups, as in the 1992 Krys campaigns, to the wide shots of the 2011 Atol campaign using Adriana Karembeu, by way of the medium shots of the 2015 advertisements for Optic 2000. The goal is more to show a lifestyle than it is to show the frame itself.

Finally, in terms of lighting, what is required is often the kind of high-key lighting that we use for cosmetics, with large, very soft and diffuse light sources, in very clear-cut environments, demonstrating that "glasses are made so that you can see better."

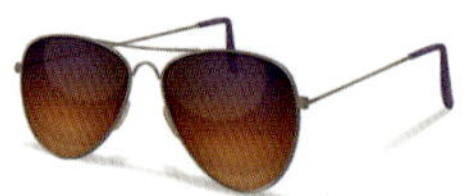

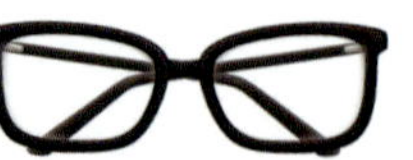

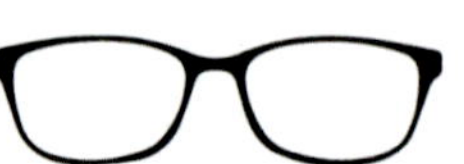

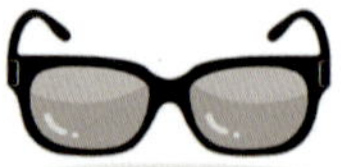

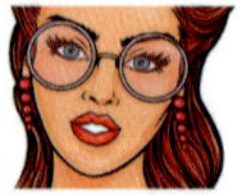

| From the front, unfolded | Three-quarter view, unfolded | From the front, folded | From the front, without temples | Suspended | Worn by a model |

STANDARD PRESENTATIONS FOR EYEGLASSES

MAKE-UP AND PERFUME

Whether we're talking about lipstick, mascara, eye shadow, perfume, or skincare cream, make-up photography has obeyed very strict and mostly unchanging rules for lighting since the mid-1980s. What follows is an overview of those rules.

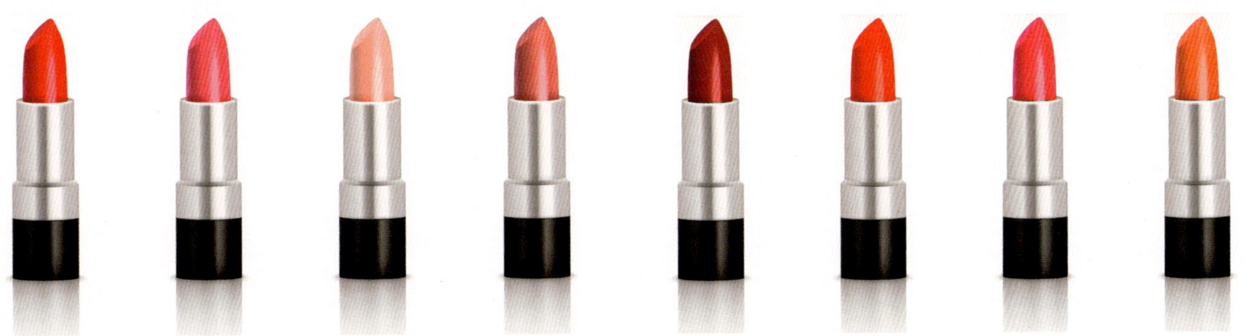

⌃ For this line of lipsticks, it is easy to understand why the color calibration needs to be precise.

Nothing has really changed in the lighting of products intended for body care, hygiene, and beauty for long enough now that their standard presentations have become firmly anchored within photographic practices.

Lighting Philosophy

The rule is simple: when the cosmetic product is inside its tube, bottle, or jar, we begin with the lighting practices appropriate to the container depending on its shape and/or its ability to transmit light. Thus, a tube of lipstick, generally cylindrical, needs to be lighted from the side to create a band of reflection that covers both the tube and the lipstick itself. When the product itself is being shown, however, the lighting depends on the reflectance and the textural effects we want to obtain. Looking at the cold cream on page 175 it is easy to understand that the priority in this image is to show the texture, both liquid and stable, of the cream—which has been prepared to give this impression and which has been lit from the side with a grazing light. And yet, beyond the simple question of the lighting, there is the question of the intended use: a mascara meant for beauty, a moisturizing cream for body care, or a shampoo meant for grooming will not all be presented with the same effects. Even if a tube of concentrated milk and a tube of toothpaste have the same shape, we would never think of staging or lighting them in the same way.

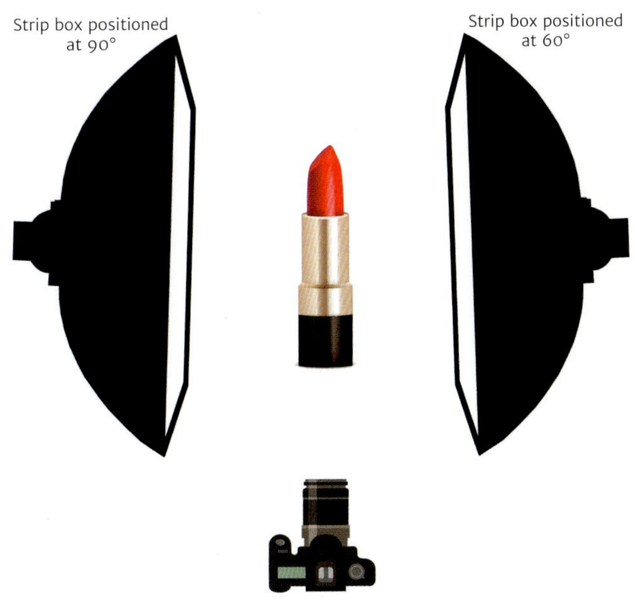

STANDARD METHOD FOR LIGHTING LIPSTICK

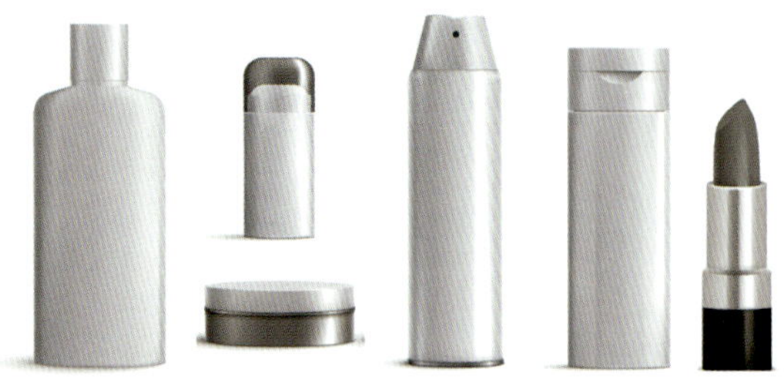

Bottles, can, tubes, and jars made of plastic or opaque metal
Lighting based on the lighting principles for cylinders (see page 92)

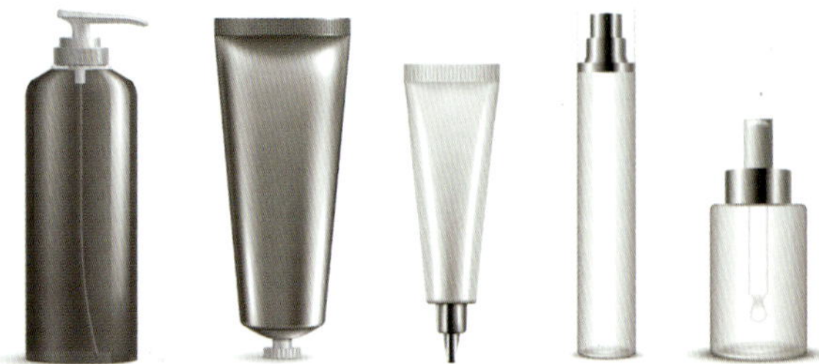

Bottles and tubes made of tinted translucent plastic
Lighting based on the lighting principles for cylinders (see page 92),
and backlighting to allow light to appear in transparency

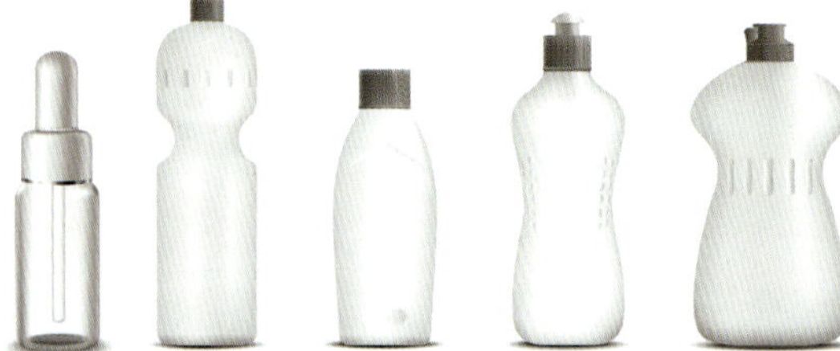

Bottles made of clear translucent plastic
Backlighting based on the lighting principles for glass (see page 98),
and optional lateral light source to create a soft reflection

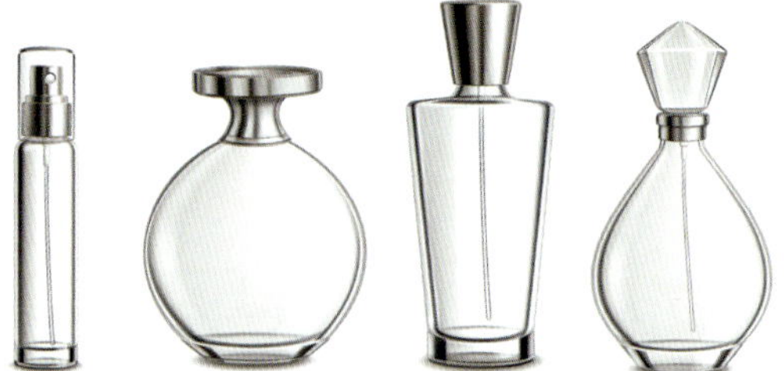

Bottles made of transparent glass
Backlighting based on the lighting principles for glass (see page 98)

METHODS FOR LIGHTING THE MAJOR CATEGORIES OF COSMETIC PRODUCTS

Glossy Tubes

Glossy tubes (made of either plastic or metal) are generally used for lipsticks and are often lighted to obtain a "glitzy" effect. Instead of using the rounded reflector method that is now used for soda cans, it is customary to arrange one or two light sources within the cylinder's family of angles in order to allow a glossy line all along the length of the lipstick tube. We do this by placing two strip boxes, one at 90° and one at 60°. The tube is presented with the lipstick extended, so that the flat part of the top of the lipstick can be seen from the front or in a three-quarter view. This presentation makes it possible to distinguish the differences in shading and to better understand the color of the product.

Depending on the brand, we might choose one light source or two. In luxury and haute couture brands, the general preference is for one single, fairly narrow band, with a light source at 90°, but it is not uncommon to see two or even three bands, sometimes exaggeratedly wide. Lipstick is photographed horizontally, with the camera at the level of the center of the object.

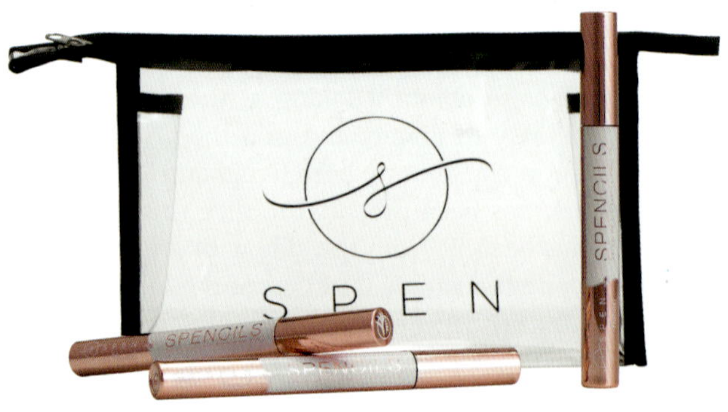

⌃ Example of the staging of a cosmetic product and its packaging.

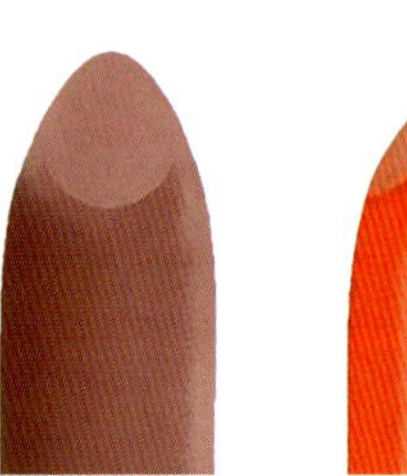

« Customary angles for positioning the top of the lipstick; the flat part should be visible.

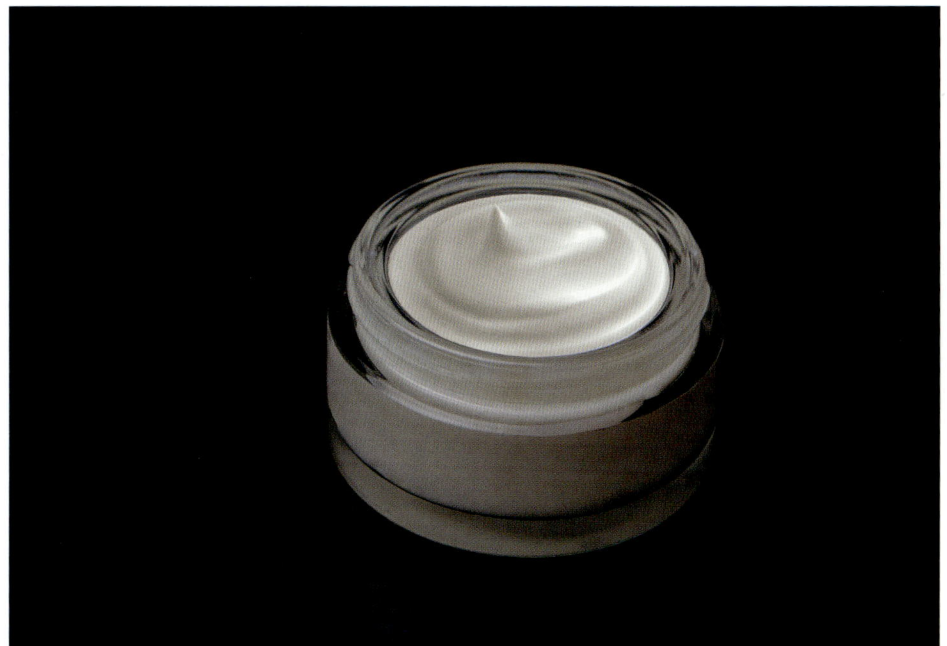

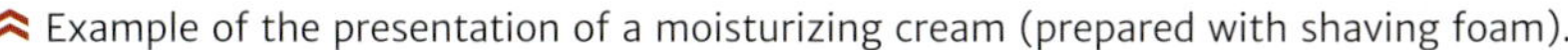

Example of the presentation of a moisturizing cream (prepared with shaving foam).

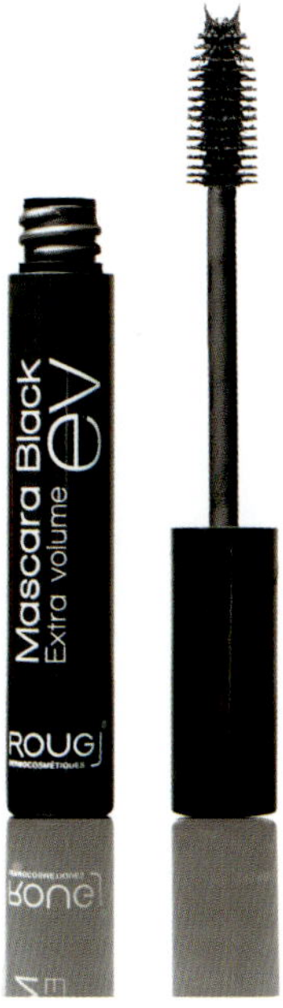

Example of the presentation of a tube of mascara.

Metallic tubes are sometimes also used for mascara. They are lighted in a similar way: with one or two bands of glossy light, usually placed along the edges.

Matte Plastic Tubes and Jars

Matte plastic tubes and jars are generally used for health-care and hair care products. They are presented either standing vertically, with a shadow at the cap, or lying down, with a shadow along the whole length of the tube. They are cylindrical, and are sometimes illuminated with two bands, using the same method as for glossy tubes, but the more usual tendency is toward even lighting using a diffuser: a softbox-style light source is placed on one of the two sides in order to produce a lighting similar to that used for candles, shown on page 145. If the object being photographed is a healthcare product, like a mois-turizing cream or a serum, the effect is softened using a reflector on the opposite side.

Glass Jars

Glass jars are usually made opaque by their contents, a cream that does not let light through. They are there-fore treated the same way as glossy tubes. However, it is the reflectance of the lid that is going to dictate the choice of lighting: a metallicized plastic lid will benefit from showing reflections, while a matte cover deserves gradual, even lighting. In the first case, we use direct light sources (like strip boxes) placed within the family of angles; in the other case, a large and very lateralized light source is preferred, arranged behind a large diffus-ing fabric to obtain the usual gradual lighting.

For several years now, however, the fashion has been to present the jar open, with the lid either visible or not, to show the texture of the cream—a very important element in encouraging the actual act of purchasing, because some creams are unpleasant to apply. For it to be a "seller," the jar is presented as shown above. Because creams are often too thick or too runny, shaving foam of the same color as the cream is mixed in with the cream (I discussed this on page 157). This mixture is put into the jar using a piping bag like those used for whipped cream in pastry.

Metal Jars and Cups

The metal jars that powders and blushes come in are seldom presented from the front. Here, a radical bird's-eye view is preferred, or a 45° angle, with a large, dif-fuse showerhead light source, like the light provided by octaboxes. The object is presented open, so that its con-tents can be seen.

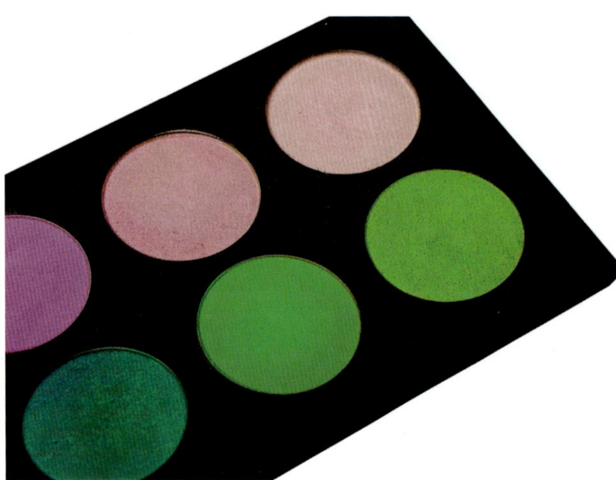

For powder, the color and texture are both crucial, and therefore the light source is arranged more from the side to provide more density to the texture. Blushes, meanwhile, require only direct, diffuse light; it is only their color that matters.

Tinted Translucent Plastic Tubes

Tinted transparent or translucent plastic tubes, like the ones that are used for serums and oils, benefit greatly from being backlit. This allows the consistency of the product, along with any pigments or glitter that it might contain, to be seen. A light source within the family of angles is usually added to show a reflection on one of the two sides of the tube, which gives a sense of radiance that is appropriate to the product being offered.

Transparent Plastic Tubes

We light transparent tubes the same way we do glass vials: with a single light source, very diffused, in rim light. Reflections are very seldom desired, but if they are desired they can be obtained by placing a strip box within the tube's family of angles.

A marketing trend launched in the 1980s involved giving the sense that the product is "clear," that it includes no chemical products or toxic additives—that it is as pure as water. The way we translate this idea into lighting involves handling the artificial lighting and composition effects very soberly, drawing as little attention as possible to the container. The light should be managed by staying close to the optimization of +1.33 EV, without darkening the grays, the objective being for the viewer to guess at the tube more than actually see it.

Transparent Glass Bottles

This type of container, usually reserved for body oils and perfumes, is always lit from behind to avoid badly aimed direct reflections on the front of the object. If certain brands require a visible reflection, we place a light box aimed directly at one of the sides: for rounded vials and bottles, between 100° and 120°, and for parallelepiped bottles, at 70°.

The general preference, however, is to avoid visible reflections. A single backlight, through a diffusing fabric, not only illuminates the bottle while outlining its silhouette, as in the two following photos, but also has the advantage of revealing the liquid that it contains, along with its color. You must take great care to ensure that the luminance does not distort the color of the product.

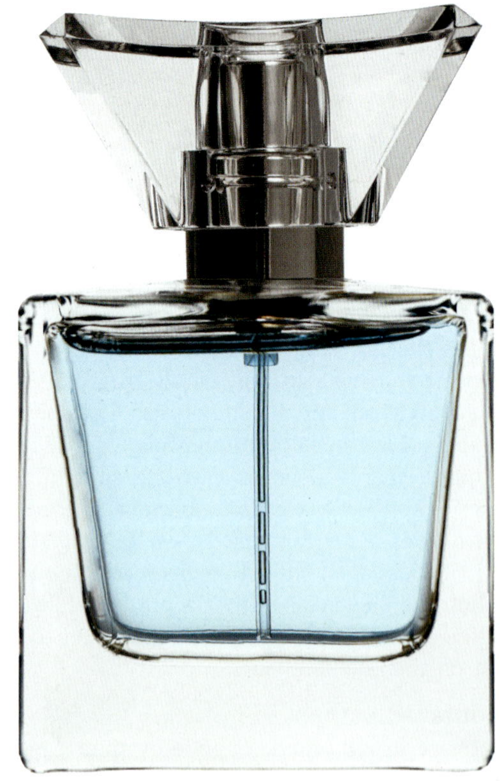

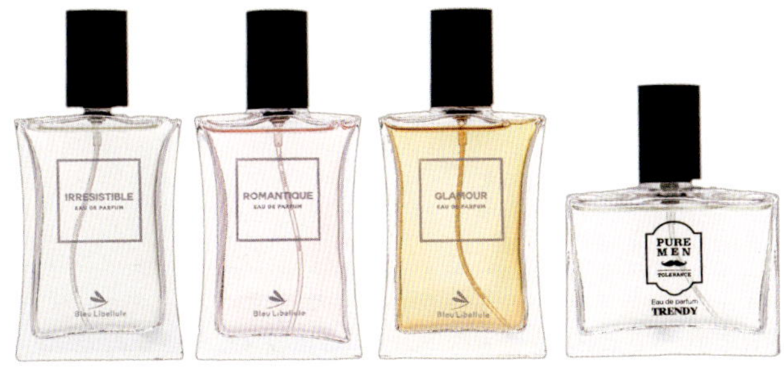

⌃ Example of the presentation of a line of perfumes.

For opaque liquids, such as glittery oils and thick lotions, you can choose between:

- backlighting with a light box placed in rim light behind a diffusing fabric, and a reflector positioned behind the product; or
- backlighting with a light box placed in rim light behind a diffusing fabric, and a light source occupying the entire family of angles of the visible side of the bottle (with a softbox set up behind a flat diffuser if the object is a parallelepiped, or a rounded diffuser if the object is cylindrical). Be careful to adjust the light source to only +0.6 EV for a soft, even reflection.

Advertising

For cosmetics, the job of the advertising photograph is to present either the product, for what it is supposed to contain (a tube of skincare cream containing peach milk in the middle of a basket of peaches, for example, as in Clarins' 2020 Milky Boost Cream campaigns), or the effect that it is supposed to cause (satiny reflections on skin, for example, as in the Nuxe campaigns for its "Huile prodigieuse," running since 2016).

Perfume, on the other hand, occupies its own special position. The object itself is not directly featured; it usually appears only as an inset packshot on large posters that otherwise feature a live model for the purpose of conveying a particular concept. Think, for example, of Givenchy's campaigns for L'Interdit, where we see a young woman in an evening dress stealthily taking the Paris metro to an underworld party. However, there are some campaigns that prefer to focus on the product itself, alone, such as the campaigns for Jean-Paul Gaultier's Scandal perfume, where the bottle is presented on a torn poster that the perfume seems to be blowing up.

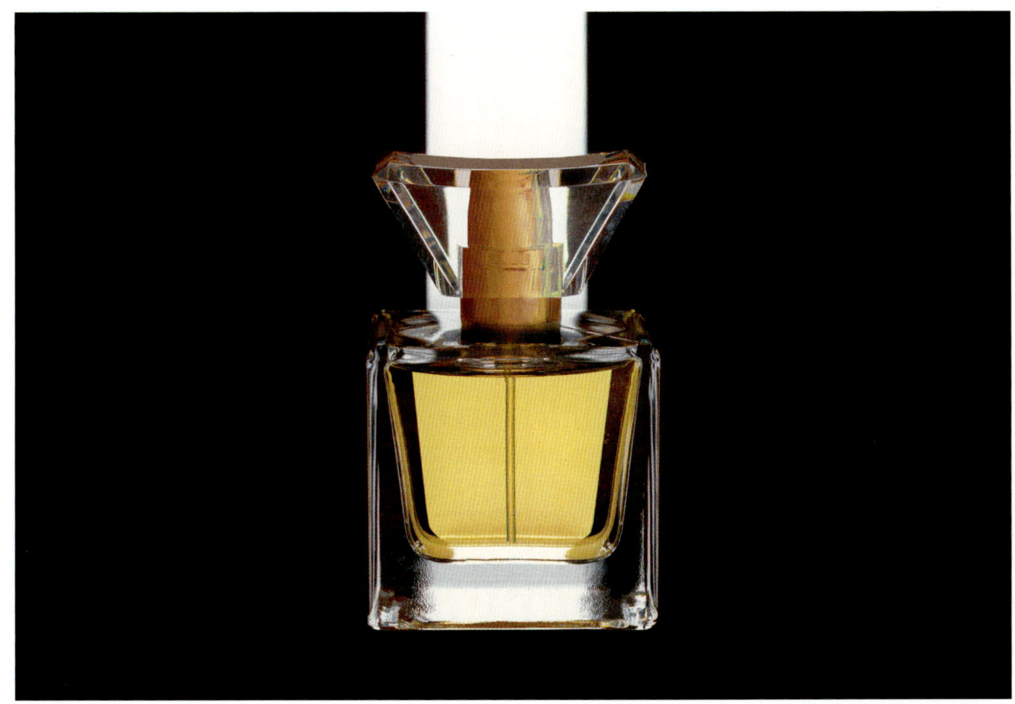

« Example of staging for a perfume advertisement.

PHOTOGRAPHING TEXTILES

Most textiles are very easy to light, but they require good technique in the preparation and a lot of ingenuity.

Except for very glossy textiles used in particular shapes—things like polyester satin cushions or metallic Lycra cushions—which require special lighting, most textiles, which do not produce direct reflections, can be lighted any way you like, as long as the width of the light beam that is used covers the entirety of the surface being photographed. On the other hand, when the textiles are presented in those particular shapes, such as cushions or hangings, the lighting strategies will have to be specifically adapted.

Matte Textiles

Matte textiles, like cotton, linen, wool, and viscose, are usually illuminated using large diffuse sources, like softboxes, placed at a right angle to the mesh of the fabric. Fabrics are usually shown flat, but sometimes you might be asked to show them crumpled, or in a compass-rose pattern—that doesn't happen often, though.

Glossy Textiles

When the material of the textile needs to be emphasized, or for a fabric that looks different depending on the angle of the light, you will have to place your source at an oblique or grazing angle: the goal is to allow the textures and reflections to show. Here, too, you will want to use large light sources, like octaboxes.

Textiles in Use

When they are presented as upholstery—for instance, covering cushions—textiles have a tendency to fall into lots of folds and rarely present an elegant silhouette. To avoid hours of post-production work (continuous-knit textiles are very hard to retouch because of their moiré effects), the product can be firmly held in place using a thin wire cable or piano wire stuck to the hidden side of the object with gaffer tape. The same thing can be done for hats and purses. For hollow objects, like pencil

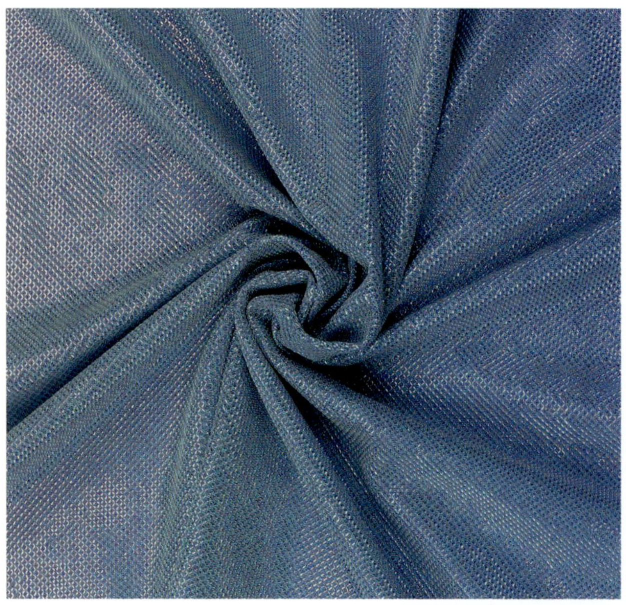

⌃ Traditional presentation in the form of a "compass rose," used for glossy textiles (in this case, polyester).

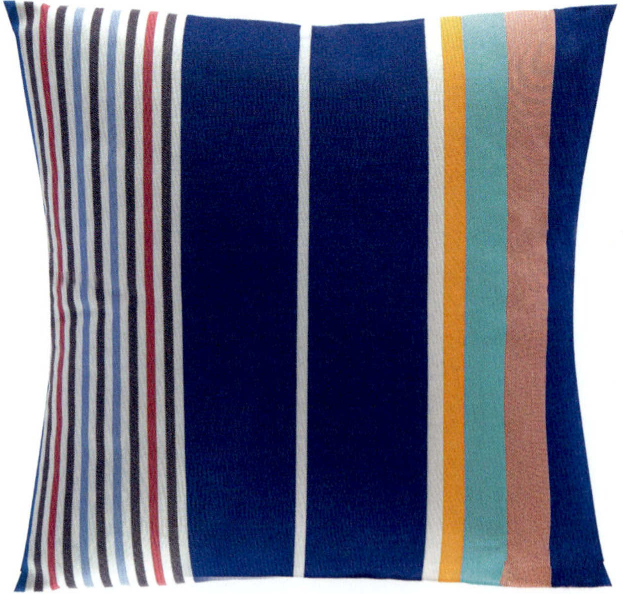

⌃ To achieve a good result, it is essential to smooth the fabric using a wire stretched across the hidden side of the cushion.

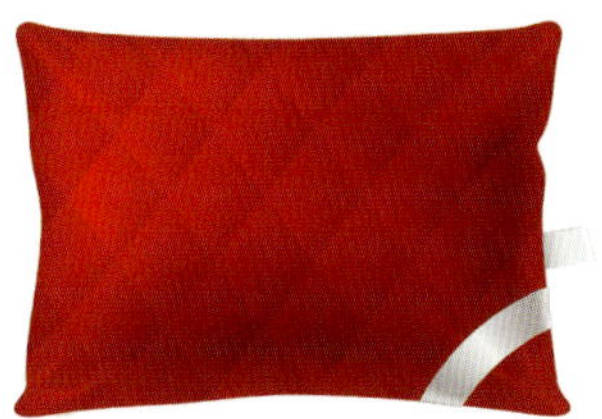 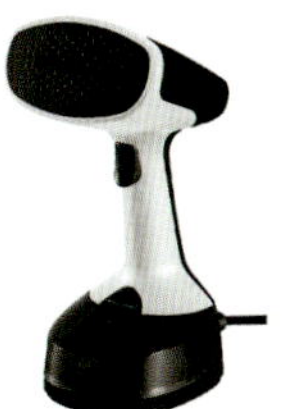

Steamer for filled textiles and drapes

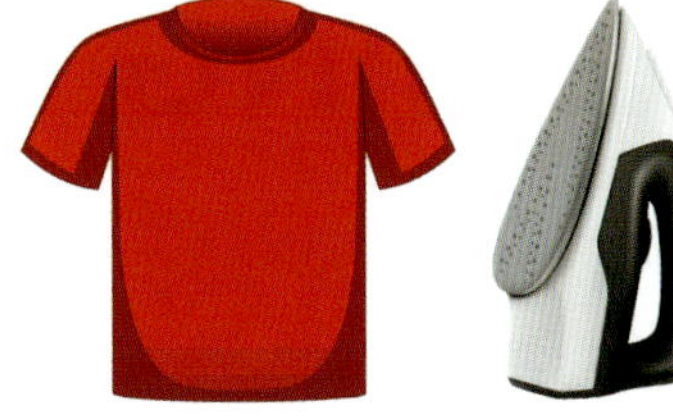

Iron for flat textiles

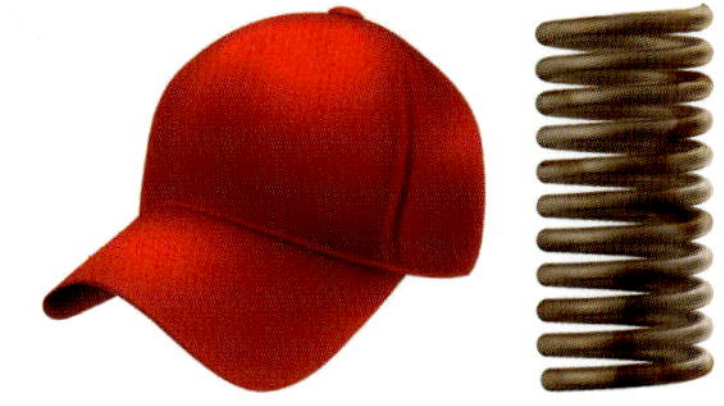

Recreating shapes using wire

PREPARING TEXTILES

cases, you can stuff them with cotton—avoid newspaper, because it creates little bumps that will be visible in the photo, especially with oblique lighting.

Drapes and Hanging Fabrics

When you have to photograph fabrics in context, like curtains or drapes, you will need to use a steamer. Unlike an iron, which is useful for small-sized textiles, a steamer can be used on shaped objects (like cushions) or objects already in position: a large drape that was ironed on a table would crease again before it was even installed on a rod. A steamer can also be used for textiles that are attached to frames (like the fabric on the chaise longue below), which cannot be ironed.

Presenting the Materials

Matte fabrics are usually shown flat (or rolled up), after having been prepared with an iron. They must be positioned to highlight the specific qualities of the fabric that produce lighting or textural effects, as with metallic Lycra, lamé, jersey, organza, embroidered fabric, satin, and all glossy, satiny, or textured textiles. There are two standard techniques for these: crumpling and the compass rose:

- To achieve a crumpled presentation, lightly fold the fabric using accordion folds and then let it fall so that the folds look natural, while creating effects of light and shadow that make it possible to see how the fabric behaves in the light. This technique, which requires an expert hand, is used less and less.
- A compass rose presentation involves placing a stick in the middle of the fabric and then rotating it while pressing down hard: the fabric will then take the shape of a corolla. This is the technique that is currently more popular.

One last technique, which is, for now, used basically in the Asian market, is to place a rounded object underneath the fabric to suggest the effect it will have when it is worn as clothing.

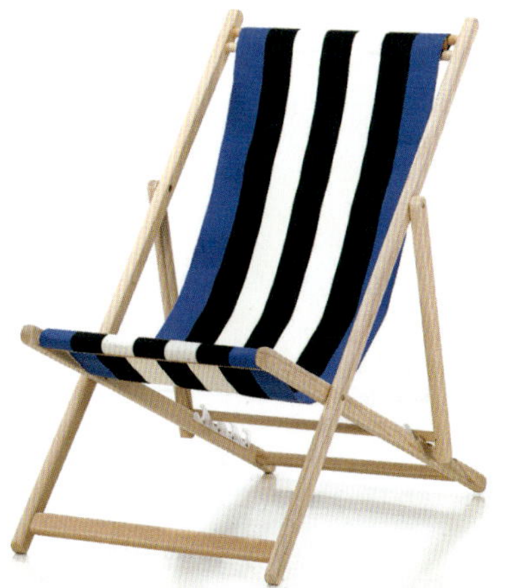 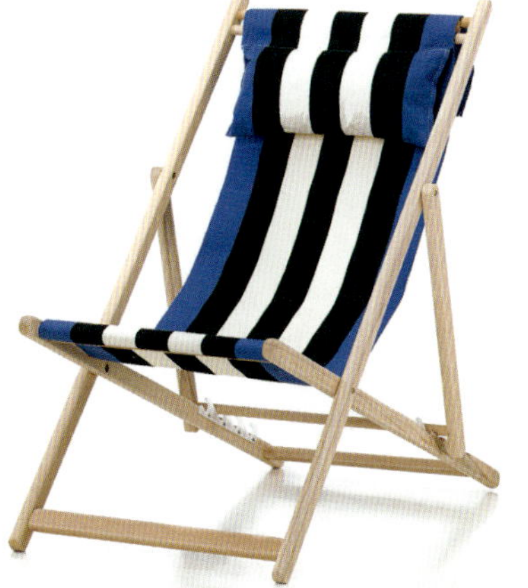 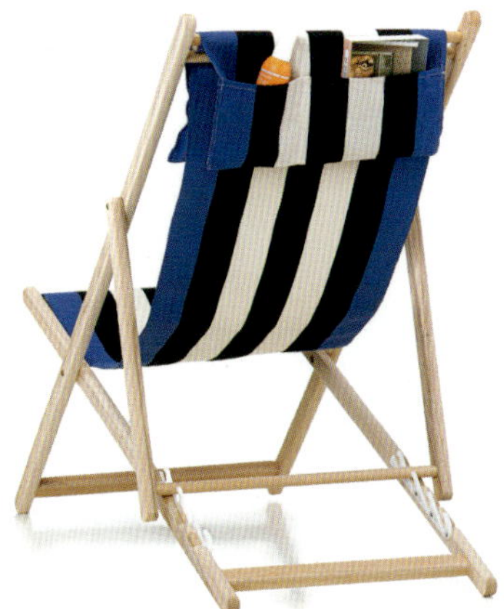

⌃ Example of various presentations of a textile element on a folding chair.

PHOTOGRAPHING CLOTHING

If there is one area where fashions, and therefore also photographic techniques, evolve quickly, then it is definitely the area of clothing. And yet, the basics of the most important techniques haven't changed; they are just sometimes updated and tweaked a bit.

This is typically an area where skill and experience make the difference. While the techniques of lighting, as with textiles, continue to be fairly simple because most materials produce diffuse reflections, the issues of preparation and staging do call for some in-depth study.

Lighting Philosophy

Basically, we use large diffuse shapers, placed more than six feet away, in an axis at right angles to the product, in order to avoid overly pronounced contrasts in the materials that would distort the texture of the item of clothing. And yet, if the item is made from a glossy fabric (a satin boxing robe, for instance) or a textured one (like an Irish cable-knit sweater), the lighting might need to be closer up or more oblique.

Traditionally, we work with large octaboxes or umbrellas. With rare exceptions, shapers like bowls or lenses are not used.

Preparing the Product

We never photograph an item of clothing that has not been properly smoothed with a steamer and possibly brushed with a lint brush. Some fabrics, such as furs, velvets, and the thick wools used for winter coats, will also benefit from being cleaned of dust with a can of compressed air. This is especially important for dark garments or highly textured ones, on which dust is very visible.

Flat Presentation

T-shirts, polo shirts, and (more rarely) button-up shirts are usually shown flat, on a large table. It's important to make sure that all the important elements (the brand label, logo, any stitching, embroidery, etc.) are clearly visible and that nothing sticks out from the fold. For this type of presentation, we set up an octabox six feet above the item of clothing and the camera in a radical bird's-eye view within the same axis. After calibrating with the color palette and gray card, and optimizing the measurement at +1.33 EV, we can then start shooting.

Folded Presentation

For a T-shirt, polo shirt, or button-up shirt, what the potential buyer is mostly interested in is the shape of the collar, the shape of the neckline, the stitching, and any details on the sleeves; in other words, everything that is on the upper part of the garment. Thus, it is possible to present it folded and ironed, with the lower part hidden. This arrangement is often chosen to show the range of colors an item is available in. For the lighting and setup, you can proceed as with the presentation of flat items.

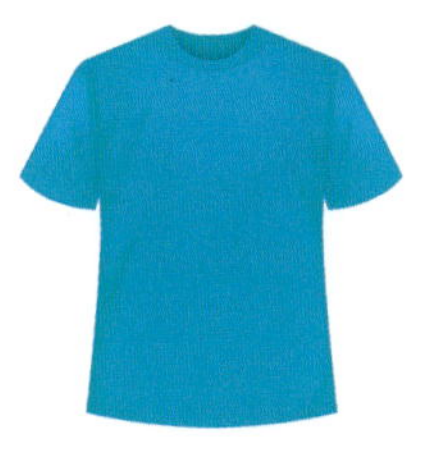

Flat

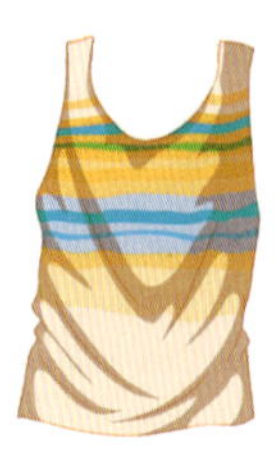

On a hanger

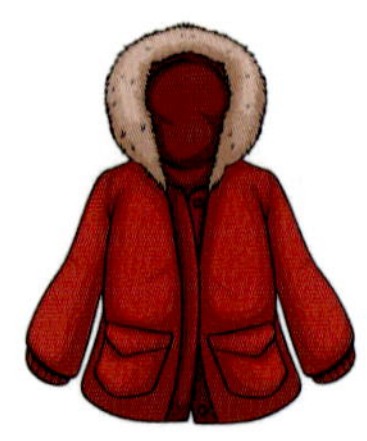

Crumpled

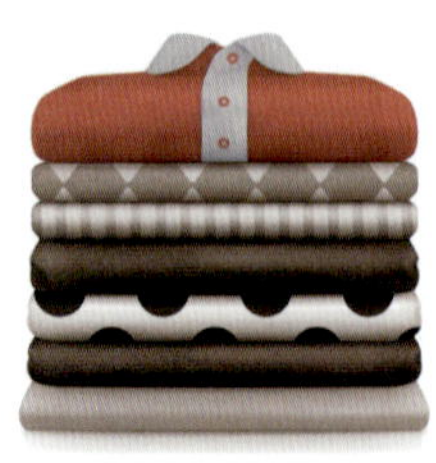

Stuffed

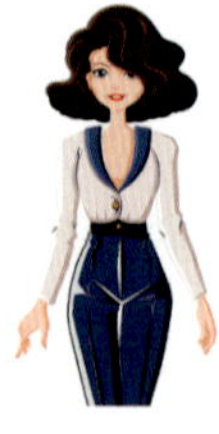

Folded

Worn

THE SIX STANDARD WAYS OF PRESENTING CLOTHING FOR A CATALOG PHOTO

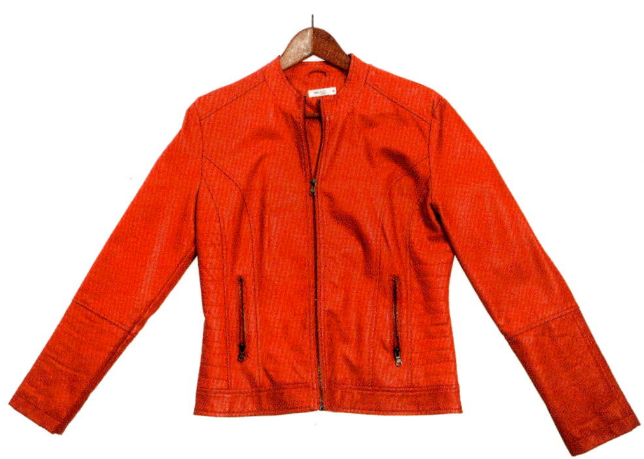

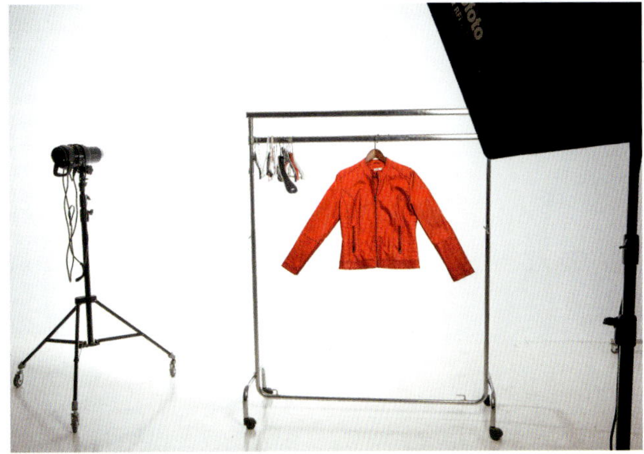

⌃ Example of presentation on a hanger.

⌃ A behind-the-scenes view of the presentation on a hanger.

On the Hanger

This is a trend that is taking hold in the mass market and in e-commerce (Asos, Charmkpr, Shein, etc.). Putting the garment on a hanger has the advantage of speed for the shot and avoids the splayed-out look that can sometimes be a downside of presenting clothing flat. The hanger should be a solid color, darker than the item of clothing (usually gray or cream-colored, to harmonize best with the color of the clothing). The photo is presented without showing either the hook or the rod that hold up the hanger. As always, the garment must be properly dusted and ironed beforehand. It is lit with a large octabox located about six feet away.

Crumpled

The crumpled way of presenting a piece of clothing, very trendy from 2000 to 2015 under the influence of fashion magazines that adopted it as a way to promote sportswear-style looks for young adults, shows the garment on a flat base, from a bird's-eye view, without any of the ironed or rectangular look of the traditional flat presentation. Here, movement and the "pop" effect of the product are emphasized, and it is laid out in a way that brings it to life: the sleeves are folded as though the garment were out running, the interior folded down as if there were a gust of wind, etc. To highlight the sense of dynamism, the composition also often includes other elements, like coordinated shoes, or a T-shirt slipped into a jacket. This kind of presentation, lighted the same way as clothes presented flat, is still used by some sellers, such as LightInTheBox or Etsy.

Stuffed

Photography where the clothing is essentially "worn" by a ghost, a style that arrived in Europe in the mid-1990s, involves giving the item of clothing a shape. Thus, the consumer can visualize what the garment will look like when it is worn, while still seeing its interior—as if it were on a transparent model.

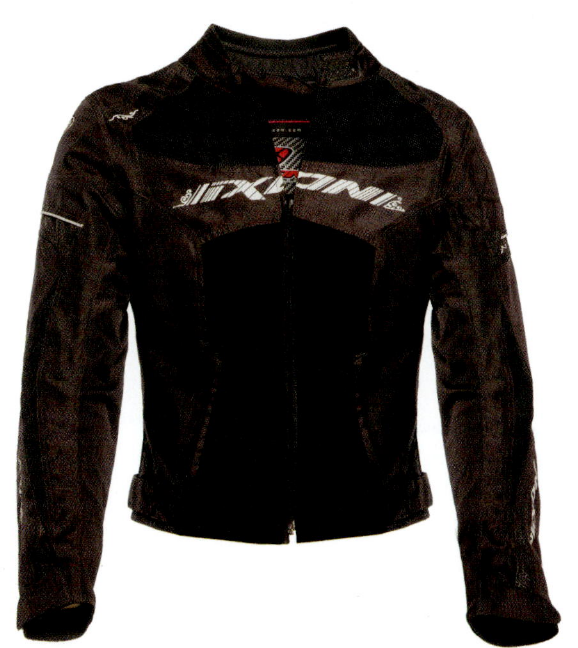

⌃ Example of a jacket shown stuffed (worn by a ghost).

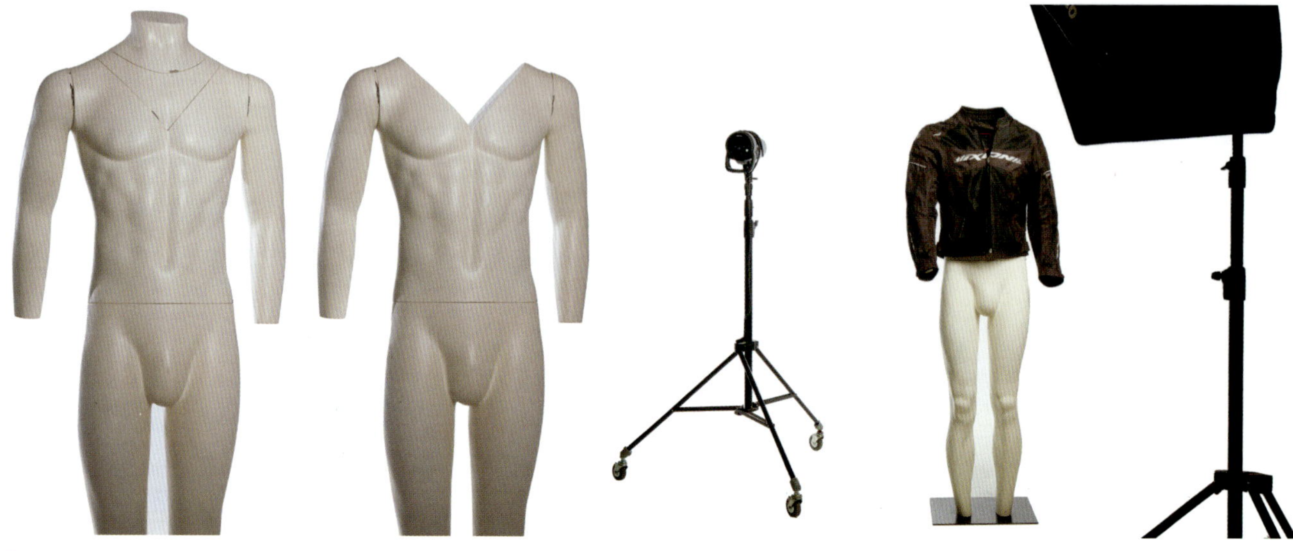

⌃ A behind-the-scenes view of a photo of clothing worn by a ghost mannequin.

Note that some photographers do still use composite photography and post-production editing here (photographing the item first with and then without a model, to capture, in several photos, the background elements hidden by the model, and then make the model disappear)—a terribly time-consuming technique that has become unnecessary. Plastic mannequins that can be disassembled were created especially for this process. The piece of clothing is put on the mannequin, from which everything that is not necessary to hold up the clothing and that could be visible is removed: the neck for T-shirts, the neck and the top of the throat for scoop-necked dresses, the arms for tank tops, etc. A large light source is positioned tilting slightly downward (by 5° to 15°), from the front or very slightly to the side (but not by more than 20°). The colors must, of course, be scrupulously calibrated and the measurement perfectly optimized. It should be that the manufacturers of these "ghost" mannequins also offer a wide range of stands for motorcycle helmets and hats (a dome held up by a metal rod).

A photo taken this way usually does not require any editing, though the openings cut in the mannequin sometimes require a little bit of trimming: the shoulders for straps, the bottom of the thigh for skirts, etc.

The Lighting and Presentation of Shoes

Shoe photography could justify an entire section of its own because there are so many possibilities and techniques. While the most common technique involves showing only one of the two shoes in profile (the right shoe if the front of the shoe is pointing right, the left shoe if the front is pointing left), there are actually seven standard ways to choose the angle and arrangement of shoes.

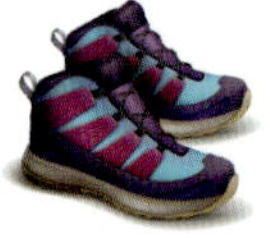

Pair of shoes in three-quarter view

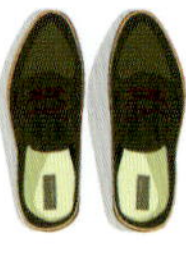

Pair of shoes in bird's-eye view

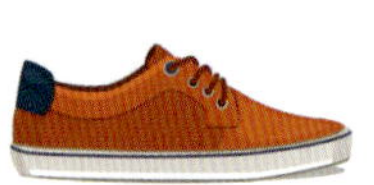

Shoe in profile

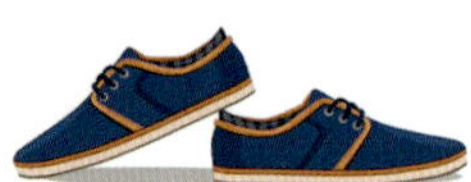

Overlapping pair

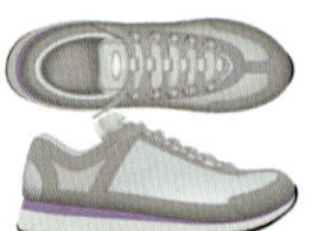

Pair from above and in profile

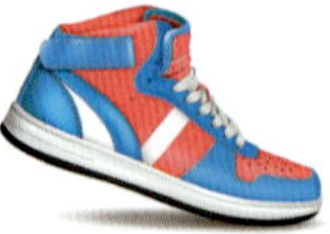

Shoe in movement and with contact

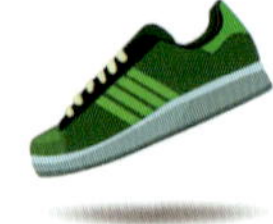

Suspended shoe

CUSTOMARY WAYS OF PRESENTING SHOES FOR A CATALOG

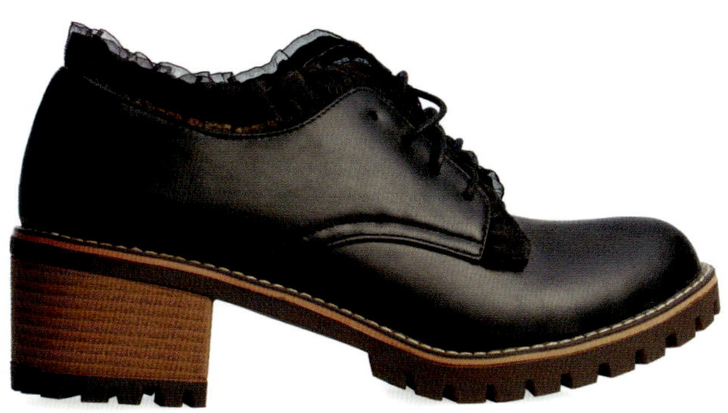

Presentation of a shoe in profile.

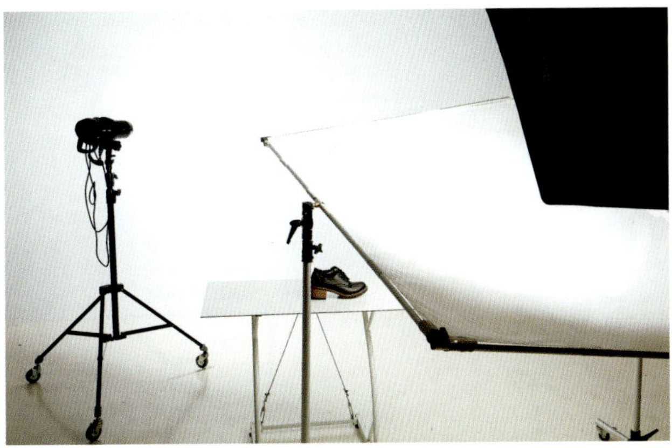

A behind-the-scenes view for the photo at left.

For matte, fabric, or felted leather shoes, every kind of lighting is possible. The preference is usually for a light box above the product, with a reflector placed at an angle toward the back of the shoe (and if you leave the heel slightly in shadow, it makes it look like the shoe is smaller, which sells it better). For glossy or partly glossy shoes, especially athletic shoes, you should instead use localized sources for the purpose of creating direct reflections on the most important elements: the toe cap, the reinforcements, the heel cup, the upper, and the tongue. This is the method I used for the sneakers shown below.

The tendency now, especially for sportswear shoe brands, is to show the shoes in motion. They are suspended with nylon thread to give the impression of walking or running. For more traditional shoes, most manufacturers continue to present them in pairs, in a three-quarter view or just in profile.

Lacing

Managing laces, whether they are shoelaces or corset laces, requires the use of best practices in preparing for the shot: if it is poorly prepared, the visual impact will likely be less effective. Straight lacing is generally preferred, but consumers expect to see ladder lacing or commando (military-style) lacing on safety shoes, for example. If you decide to work in this field, I can only recommend that you learn all the codes and practices of this specialty.

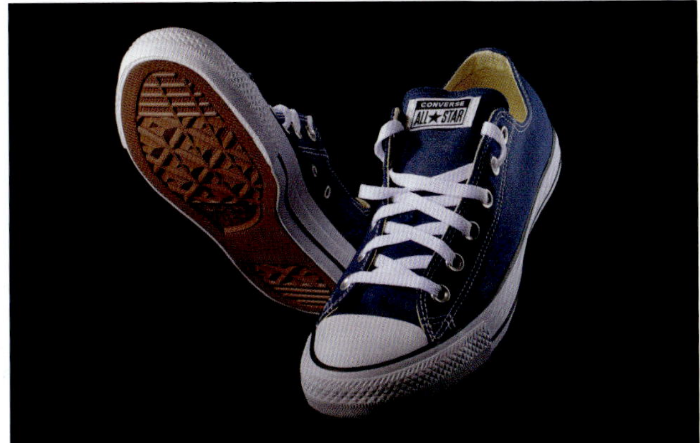

We try to create a sense of movement, even for catalog shots.

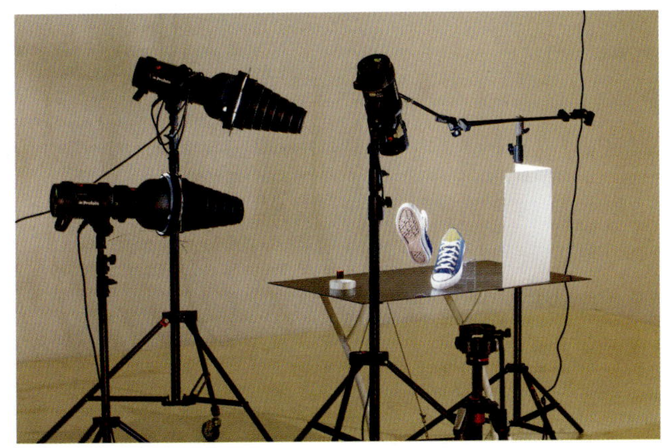

A behind-the-scenes view for the photo at left.

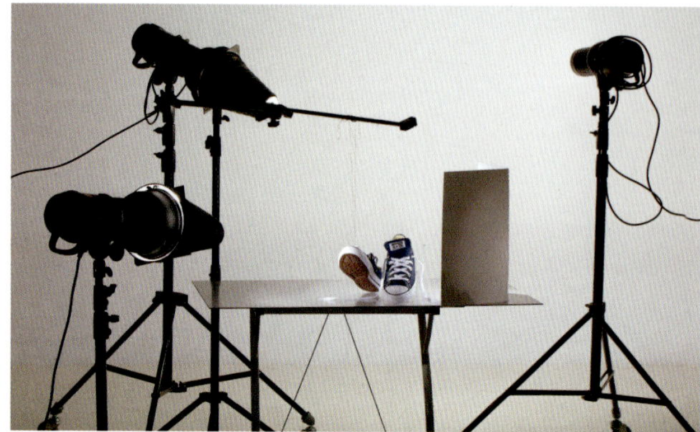

⌃ A behind-the-scenes view for the photo below.

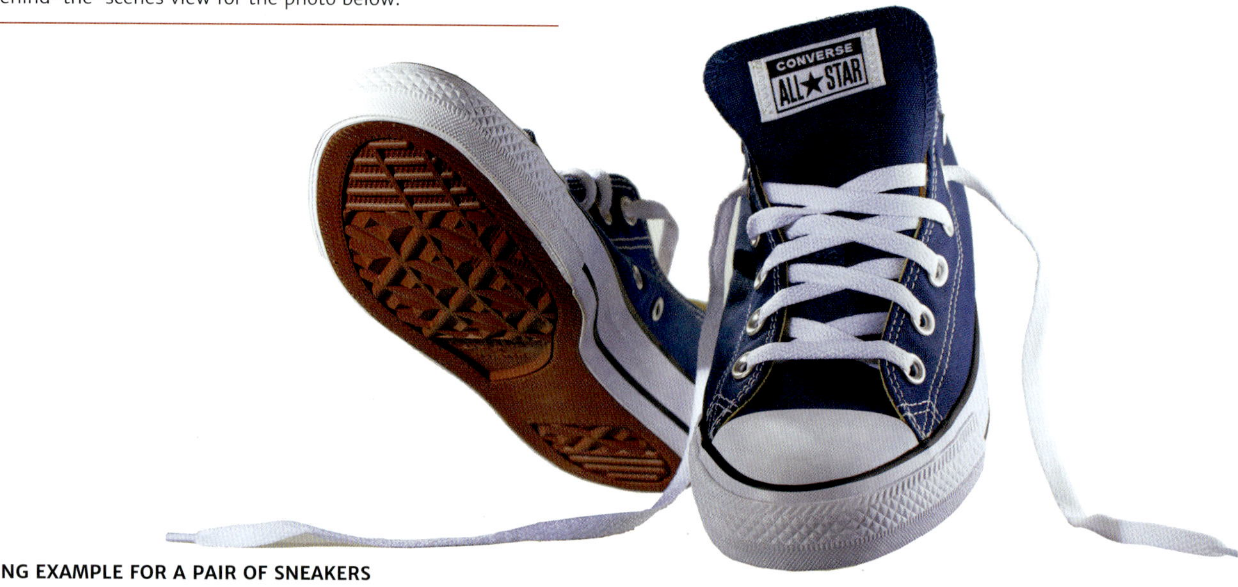

LIGHTING EXAMPLE FOR A PAIR OF SNEAKERS

STRAIGHT LACING TECHNIQUE

Widely used in shoe packshot photography, straight lacing provides an orderly appearance that is very pleasing to the eye.

- Pass each end of the lace through the first pair of eyelets, from the outside in.
- Make sure that both ends of the shoelace are the same length.
- Insert the left end into the eyelet just above on the left, from the inside outward, and then into the eyelet opposite it.
- Run the two shoelace ends that are now on the right from the inside to the outside, making each one skip an eyelet and come out two eyelets higher.
- Repeat each of these last two steps until you reach the last eyelets. Please note that this technique only works with shoes that have an even number of eyelets.

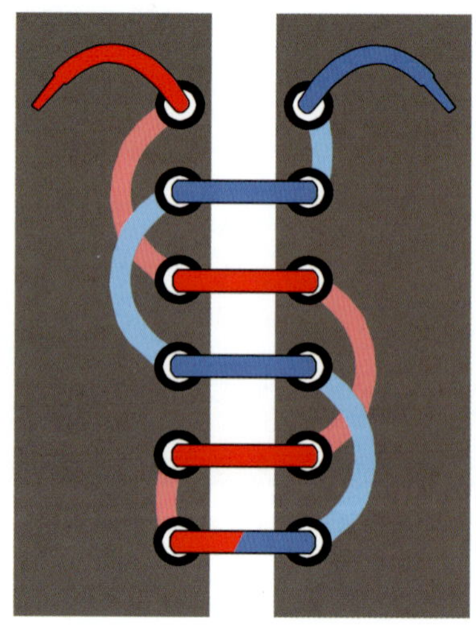

« Straight lacing

LIGHTING TABLEWARE

Although they look simple, spoons, forks, and glasses are very difficult to light. They require a solid understanding of the specificities of lighting on rounded or transparent surfaces.

Every time I give a student a spoon to photograph, I watch their face, which is so confident at first, gradually fall as they discover the depths of complexity in lighting something that is actually nothing more than a concave mirror (or a convex one, depending on how the spoon is placed). Without a knowledge of the laws that govern the family of angles of spheroid surfaces (see page 87), it could take hours to find a lighting arrangement that really enhances the object. Let's look at how to arrange high-quality lighting for these everyday objects.

Lighting Flat Metal Objects

It is fairly easy to arrange the lighting for knives and all the flat metal objects that can be found on a table. We have seen that the reflection in a plane obeys elementary rules: the angle of incidence is equal to the angle of reflection. Thus, all we have to do is decide how much of the reflection we want to see on the object and then position ourselves accordingly, either inside or outside the family of angles.

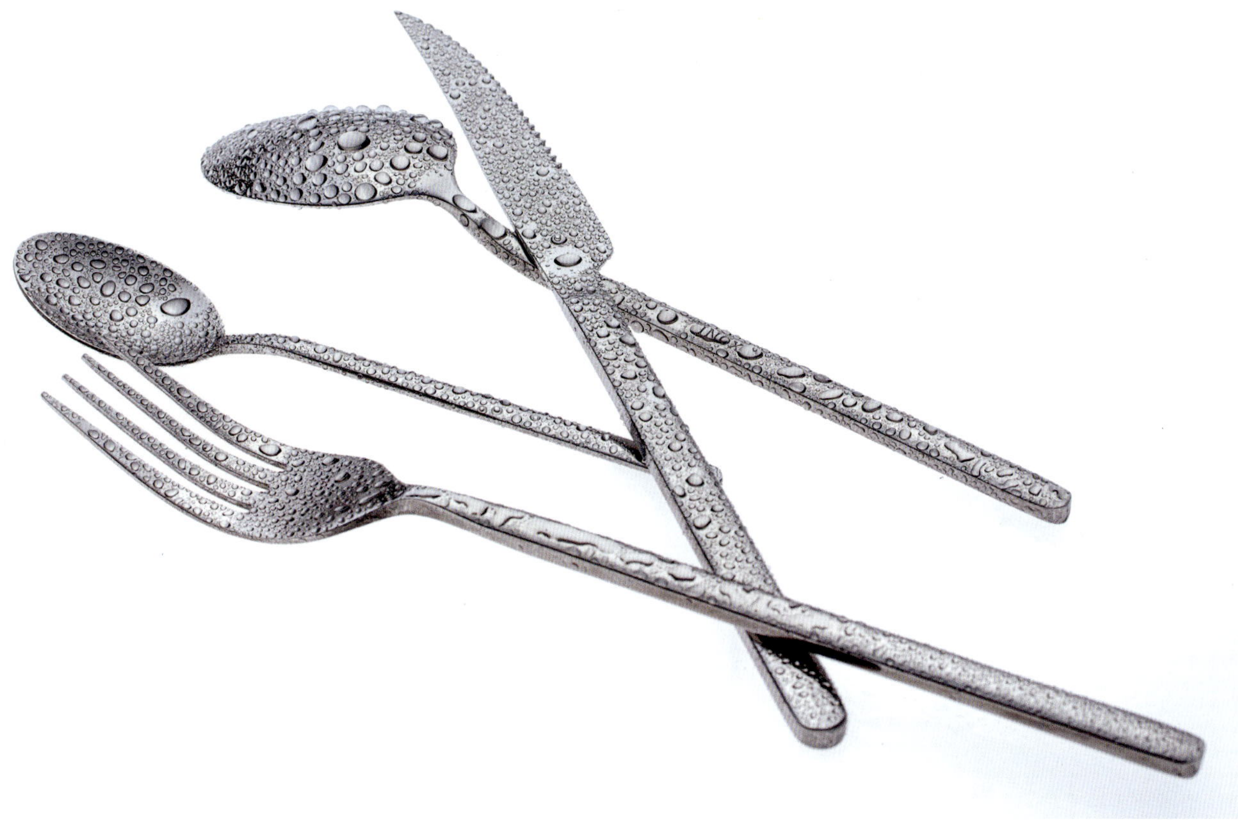

⌃ Every piece of cutlery has its own particular shape, generating different reflections. If we photograph all the pieces together, we have to choose very large, even lighting, with an orientation that is relatively angled with respect to the light source, in order to obtain a contrast.

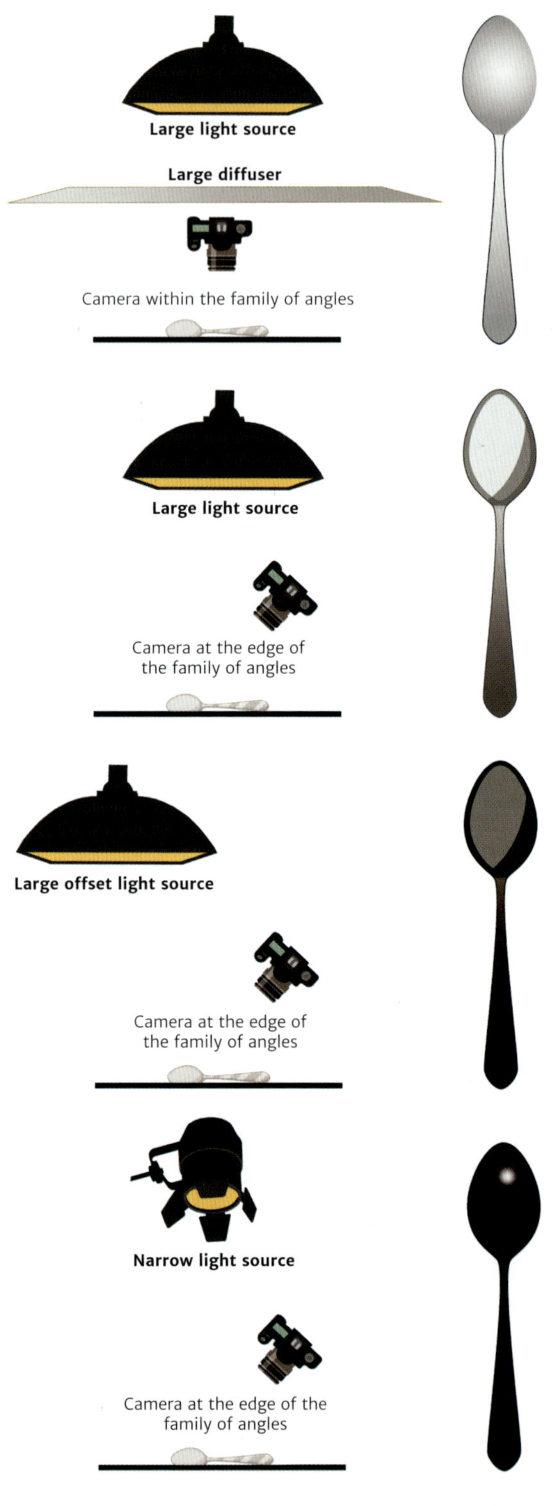

MANAGING THE REFLECTIONS ON A SPOON

We generally place ourselves at the edge of the family of angles to obtain a reflection over 90% of the object while leaving a darker edge. We can also put the object right in the center of the family of angles and then insert a barn door between the object and the light source to create a more pronounced shadow, which is desirable on carved knives. On this type of product, the shadow of the barn door gives substance to any inlays or engravings, whether protruding or hollowed, by generating a contrast between the lighted part within the axis of the light source and the part that is darkened by the shadow of the barn door.

Lighting Rounded Metallic Objects

Things get more complicated when we start trying to light forks, spoons, ladles, or any other kind of glossy rounded object. Now we are working in spherical geometry—it is impossible to get a good result if the illuminating source is only present on one axis.

In this case, we need to set up a lighting arrangement that comes from several directions at the same time, with axes spread out over at least 200°; otherwise, the reflection will not be even or gradual over the entirety of the object. The surface of the lighting is greatly enlarged by placing a very large diffuser very close to the spoon, or

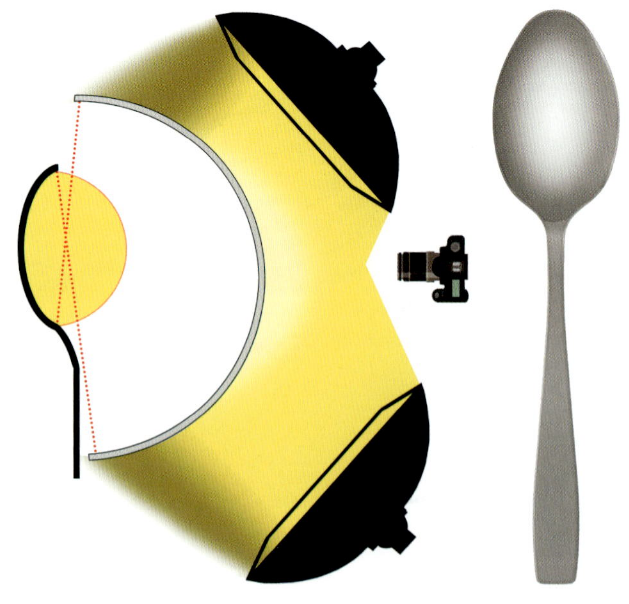

⌃ The lighting of a spoon.

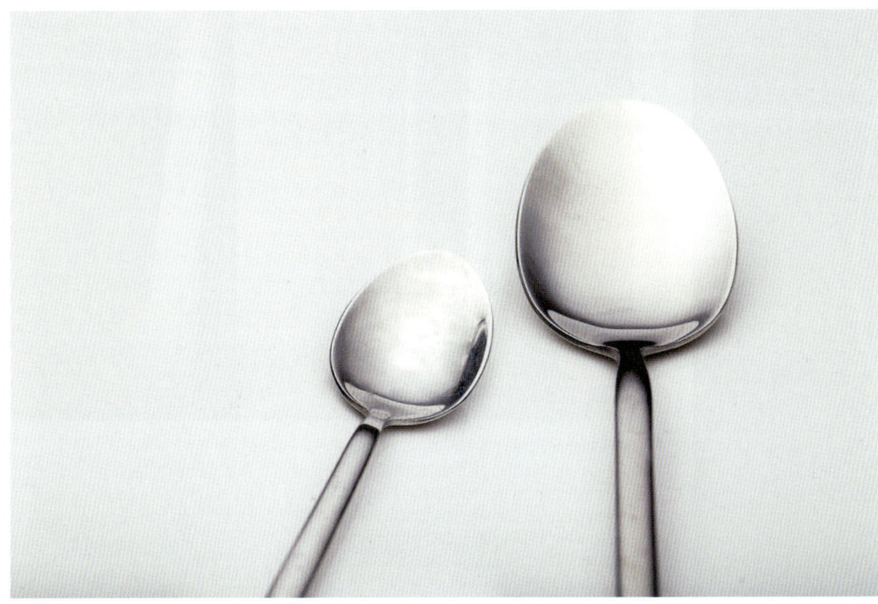

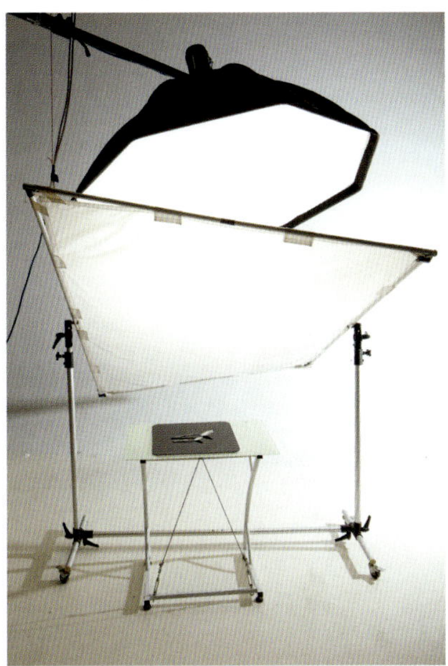

even better, by setting up a rounded diffuser between the object and the light source. In truth, the size does not matter: the only thing that really matters is that the light comes from enough directions at the same time to be able to light the entire surface.

The more rounded the object (like a ladle, for instance), the larger the family of angles that needs to be covered. This problem can be resolved by bringing the diffusing fabric closer or by positioning a diffuser to cover a larger angle, as in the behind-the-scenes photo above.

The goal is to obtain a gradation in the light, brighter in the center of the spoon, then becoming darker at the edges—a more or less rapid gradation depending on the effect you are looking for. Of course, you do not want any reflection to appear from any of the elements of the environment (parts of the studio, reflections of the

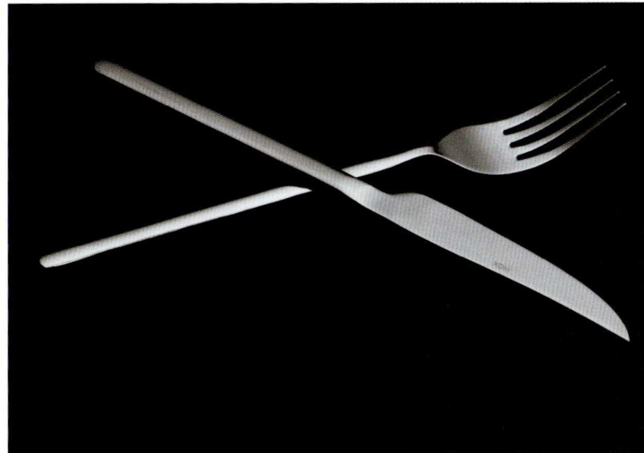

⌃ Lighting example for a knife and fork.

⌃ Detail of a fork.

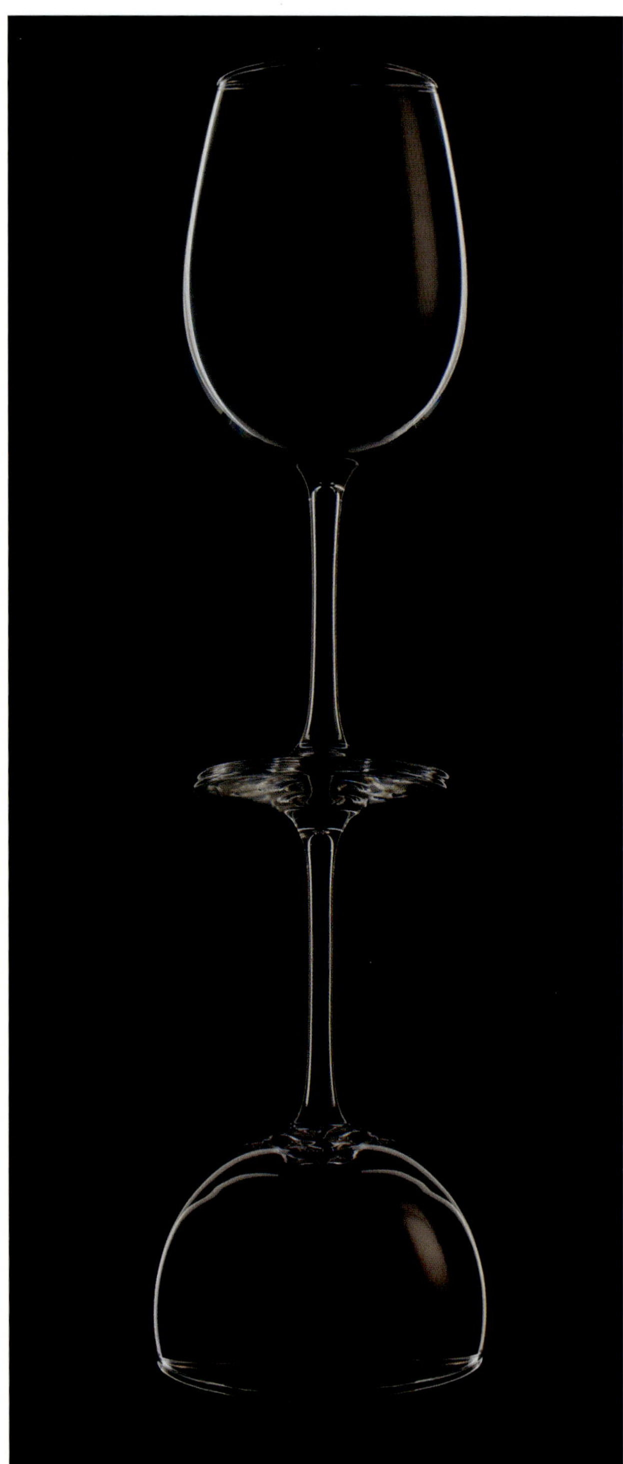

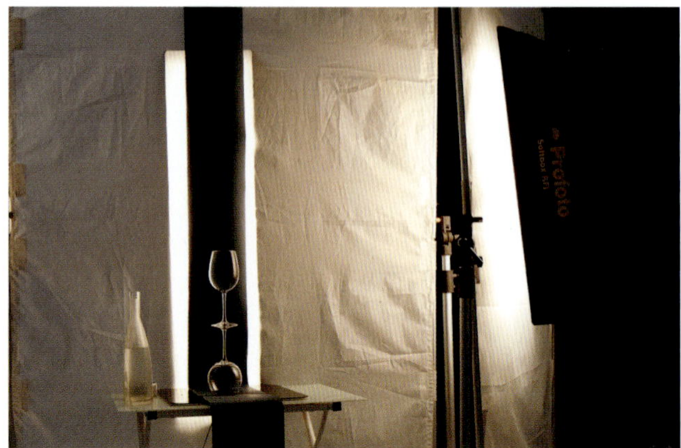

⌃ A behind-the-scenes view of the photo at left. A strip box is set up behind a diffusing fabric on which a band of black paper has been placed to cause the silhouette of the glasses to appear. A second strip box is positioned at 60° to the right, behind a diffusing fabric to obtain a reflection.

photographer, etc.), which means that the diffusing panel needs to be very close to the spoon or ladle, and the angle of the shot needs to be as close as possible to the center of the family of angles.

Lighting Glasses

I will not repeat the methods for lighting glass (see page 98). However, you may encounter difficulties if you try to create a composition that includes both glass and rounded objects—for instance, spoons—which will often happen when you are photographing a set table. In this case, two strategies are possible:

- If you want each of the objects to be lit perfectly, plan for individual lighting for each of them, and then work on a composite photo.
- More often, the lighting is determined based on which object has the larger family of angles. Here, that would be the glass, if it is round, and therefore we place a backlight behind a diffusing fabric in a dark studio. Of course, the lighting will not be perfect on the spoon, but the lack of lighting in the family of angles only means that black areas will appear (because the environment is not illuminated), which will produce a more coherent, and thus more visually pleasing, composition and lighting than the composite photo would.

⌃ Properly lighting the glass makes it possible to get effective results from the moment of shooting.

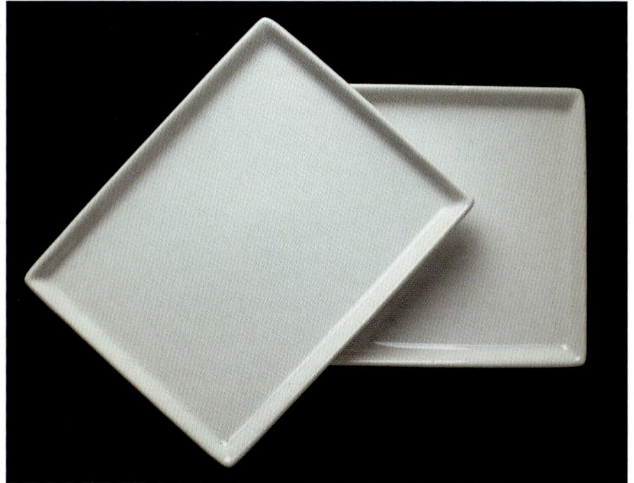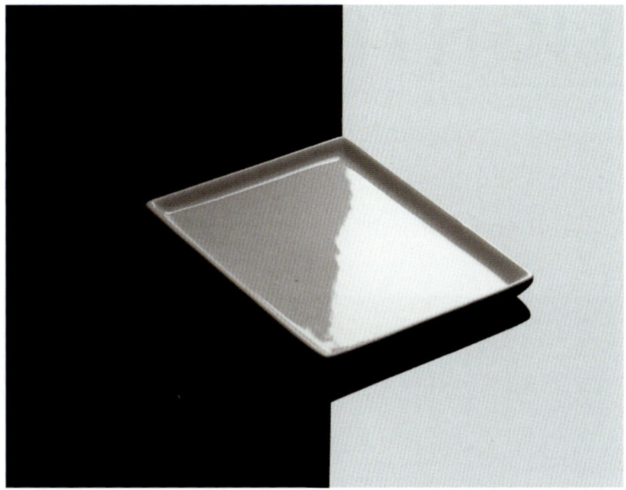

Lighting Spheroid Objects

Our experience with lighting objects like cylinders and spheres makes it easy to resolve the problems posed by cups, mugs, and bowls.

This kind of object is lighted by placing a single light source on one of its two sides, changing the intensity of the shadow on the other side by using a reflector. Then we add a light source at a radical showerhead angle to light the interior of the object (the single lateral light will not be enough here), generally with a slightly higher intensity (on the order of 0.3 EV)—because this light source is the key light, it will be the one we measure at +1.33 EV, and the lateral source will therefore be set to about +1 EV.

Very glossy bowls—for instance, new porcelain or polished steel bowls—which produce direct reflections, must be lighted with very large and diffuse light sources, covering extended families of angles. Because it produces no diffuse reflections (or only very few), a pointed light source here would only result in a burst of light, without illuminating the object itself.

Lighting Plates and Platters

Lighting a plate at a right angle (from a radical showerhead angle if the plate is set on a table, for instance) would cause us to lose most of the information about the edges and the shape (hollows, rounding, texture, etc.). A slightly lateralized lighting (as in the illustration above) is therefore required. The ideal is to obtain a direct reflection that emphasizes the curves and light shadows. We use light boxes that are large enough to cover the entire family of angles (which is about 20° for a standard plate): a sixty-inch octabox, placed at a 30° angle, slightly offset, six feet from the object, is more than enough.

Including Contents

Even though tableware is usually presented empty, elements are sometimes added to give the image a little more life: wine in the glasses, a piece of fruit on a plate, coffee in a cup, and so on. Because the element being added is a subordinate one, the strategy is to choose an element that will react in the same way as the container: a transparent liquid in the glass will force us to change its distance from the light source (because of the refraction in the liquid); a rounded piece of fruit is preferred if the lighting for the plate has been placed behind (as on the photos above), etc.

LIGHTING IN AN AQUARIUM

When shooting transparent, liquid-filled objects, such as perfume bottles, the laws of refraction make it possible to obtain very precise shots with well-constructed lighting through the water of an aquarium.

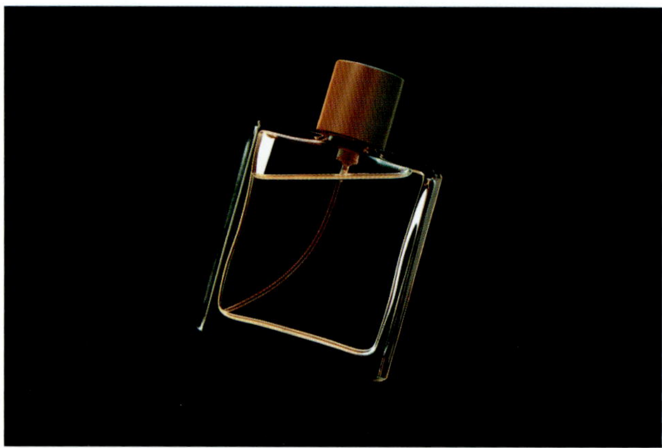

⌃ Immersed in water and photographed through the aquarium glass, transparent objects filled with liquid produce reflections that are better distributed, smoother, and more visually pleasing.

With a minimum of effort, the aquarium technique yields well-lit photos that require no digital editing (or very little of it). The water around the object transmits the light and evens it out, and it also makes it possible to reduce the difference in the refraction coefficient from the liquid in the bottle.

The only reason we don't use this method for bottles of white wine and rosé is because of their paper labels: the water darkens the print while also revealing the veins of the paper, and there would be more post-production editing work than with the technique discussed in the section on page 129.

Preparation

You must, of course, make sure that the water and the glass surfaces of the aquarium are completely clean, and that all the air bubbles produced by filling the aquarium and submerging the object are gone. Also pay attention to the water temperature: if it is too cold, it will cause a problematic fog on the surface of the glass.

The object must be completely submerged, but not touching the bottom (which would require you to edit the lower part of it afterward): it can be suspended using a fishing line (as in the photo opposite) or placed on a transparent glass base (avoid plexiglass, which tends to float).

Lighting

Because the aquarium is made of glass, the only way to light it is with backlighting (if the lighting were in front, we would see a reflection that would mask the object). Therefore, proceed with the method for lighting transparent glass (see page 99).

Finally, we need to work on the look of the background. If we want it to be black, we put a piece of black cardboard behind the aquarium and one or two light sources on either side of the cardboard; if we'd rather have it light-colored, we set up a diffuser behind the aquarium and a light source behind that (usually with a light box).

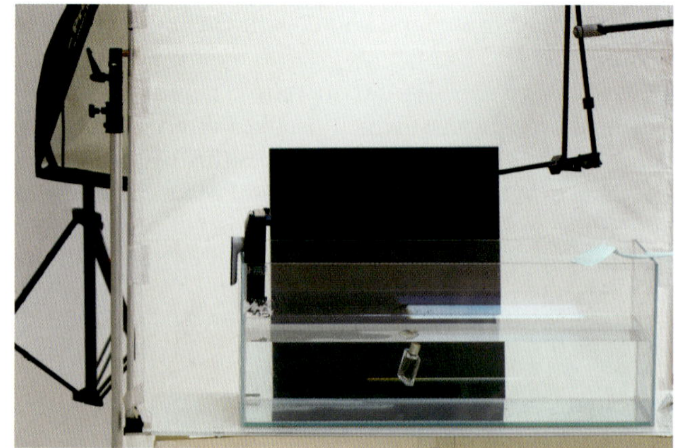

⌃ A behind-the-scenes view of the photo above at left.

LIGHTING SHEET METALS

Lighting gold, silver, or palladium, whether plated or not, presents the same difficulties as lighting any glossy metallic surfaces, but when it is applied in thin leaf form, it poses an additional problem of texture.

I have often had to deal with the problem of illuminating sheet metals. If the metal has been applied using the traditional method (using rabbit skin glue, red ocher, and oily mixtures), a gilded surface tends to react in unexpected ways to direct reflections: because every leaf (usually available in an 3 x 3-inch format) is applied separately, you run the danger of seeing the striated effect that can be observed in the photo on the left below.

Cause and Remedy

Because the gilded surface is not completely smooth or even, the direct reflections look irregular, creating unexpected material effects. But the metal we are showing is one whose surface usually looks smooth, and we expect the reflections to be harmoniously distributed and the color to be precise. Below, the world map created with gold leaf by Mickaël Lelouche, a gilder from Hérault, has been lit in two different ways: In the first shot, a 16 x 24-inch light box was placed to the right of the image. The color gradient suggests that the gold is appropriately glossy, but the angle that allows us to see that (about 60°) also brings out the texture of the gold leaf process. In the second photo, the light is directed toward the wall of the studio to illuminate about fifty square feet, and allows the angle of reflection to cover about 30° of the board. Because the lighting surface is much larger, the light is also softer, the angle of incidence more oblique, and the weave of the gold leaf less obvious—a much more pleasing result.

Gold Leaf on a Non-Flat Surface

On a surface that is not flat, like the draped fabric in the statue below, the issue of the texture is less problematic than properly rendering the look of the gold. It is necessary to generate a certain number of direct reflections so that some areas will appear in highlight, with other darker areas, even completely black ones, in juxtaposition. Here, too, we use diffuse lighting with light boxes arranged obliquely, and ensure that the colors are well calibrated to obtain the exact shade of the metal.

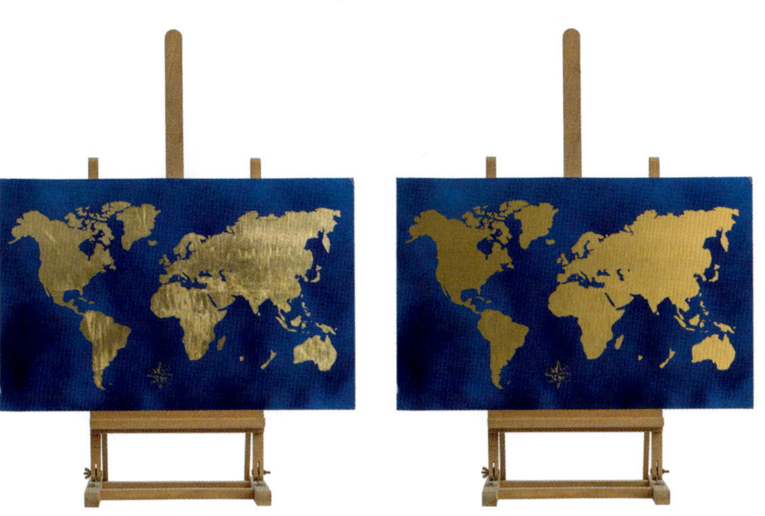

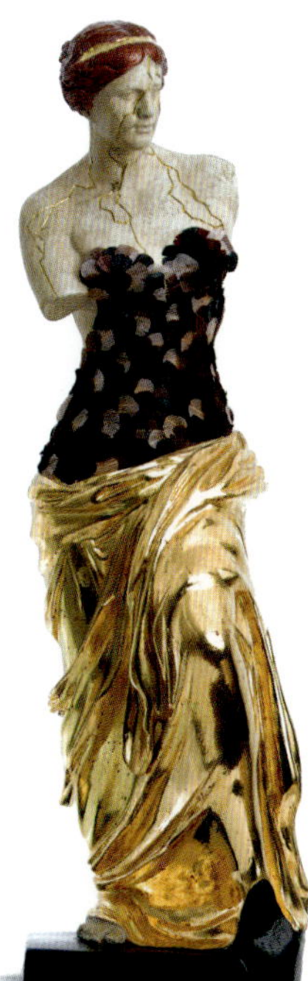

« Gold leaf applied to a flat surface always produces a striated effect. A large diffuser with a very lateralized light source can minimize this effect.

» Lighting of a gold-colored draped fabric.

LIGHTING PLASTIC

Smooth plastic produces soft direct reflections. For the material to be properly appreciated, those soft reflections must be brought out without allowing them to become too strong.

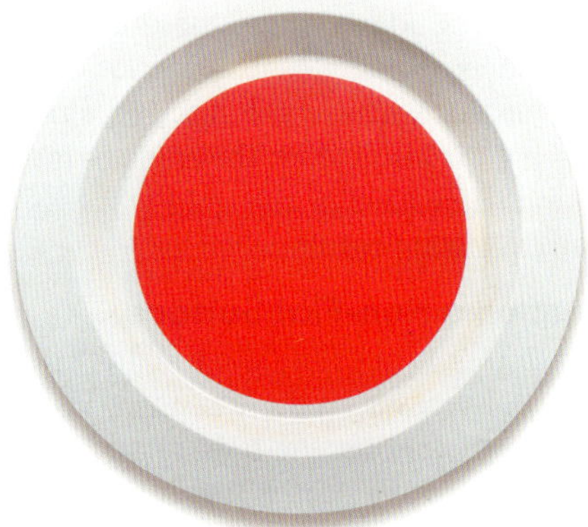

⌃ Example of lighting for a plastic plate.

Commercial plastic materials, which are smooth enough to make direct reflections appear, are nevertheless not smooth enough for those reflections to be well positioned or precisely defined.

Molded Plastics

As with other glossy materials (glass, metal, etc.), we completely avoid the use of lights that are too pointed or too hard: they would produce reflections in the form of individual bursts, which are not very helpful for accentuating the silhouette of the object. This is why here, too, we use light boxes, sometimes softened with diffusing fabrics. The problem lies in the fact that these objects, which are often imperfectly molded, can generate direct reflections at a variety of angles, which gives the sense of a less precise shape than what we want to show. For instance, for the plate presented above, when lighted from the bottom up, it displays a reflection that makes it look like there's a bump (which fortunately disappears when we light it in the other direction).

Soft Glossy Plastics

Soft plastics, like the waterproof cover of the stroller opposite, always look wrinkled when you take them out

of their box. They absolutely must be smoothed before being photographed. You can get good results by placing them flat in a heated space for a short time (between 95° and 105°F). Sometimes they also need to be stretched briefly, using weights, to smooth out their folds. The same is true for plastic bags and other soft wrappings.

Once the material is nicely smoothed, the positioning of the light will be easier, even if you still need to be prepared for a few scattered direct reflections (at least those reflections will give the viewer a reasonably good sense of the kind of material it is).

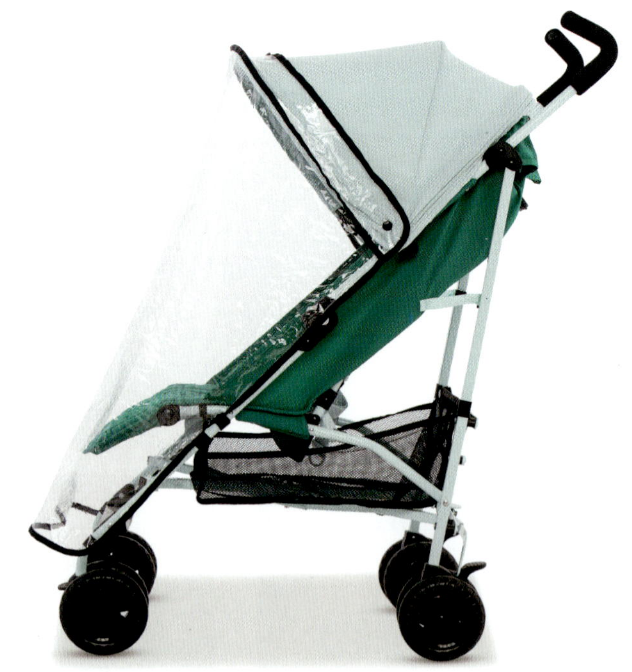

⌃ Soft transparent plastic can be prepared by using a hair dryer to limit the number of folds and achieve a smooth glossiness, like on a mirror-smooth water surface.

CATALOG SHOTS

Most of the shots that are ordered from professional product photographers are meant for catalogs. The lighting, framing, and angle of view are standardized to achieve a result that is easily understood and that sells.

Intended for presentation in a printed or online catalog, packshot photographs require a rigorous work mode, organization, and standardized procedures.

Methods

Before launching into the preparation for lighting, you need to identify the products to be photographed and decide on a lighting that will be appropriate for all of them—or, if that is impossible (for instance, if there are both transparent glass bottles and opaque cubes), then you will need to organize the objects into categories in order to limit the lighting changes and avoid mistakes in colorimetry, viewing angles, or presentation angles. This preparation will save you a lot of time, especially if you are shooting a large number of objects.

As with all objects, you need to make sure to carefully dust everything, remove the rear labels from transparent bottles, position caps on the correct axis, etc.

Standardization

Your client expects standardized shots: you can't have photos of similar objects, taken at different angles, with different lighting and varied framings, next to each other in the catalog. Thus, you need to use a tripod, making sure that the lens is perfectly horizontal and placed at the object's center of gravity, at a sufficient distance to

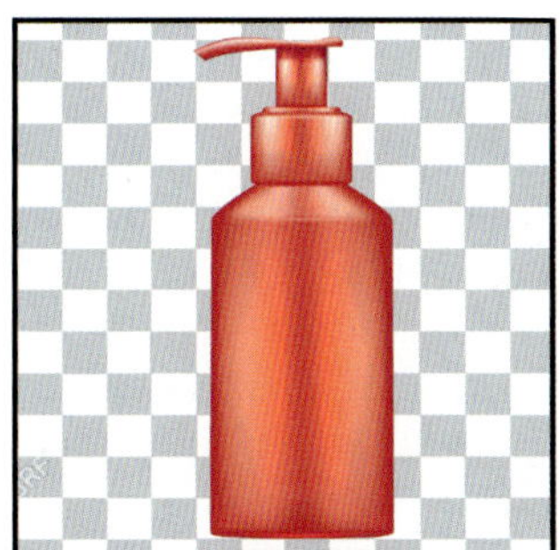

Transparent PNG

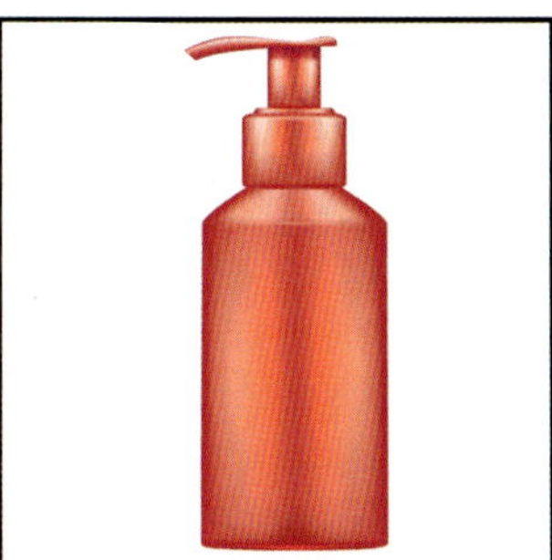

Against a white background

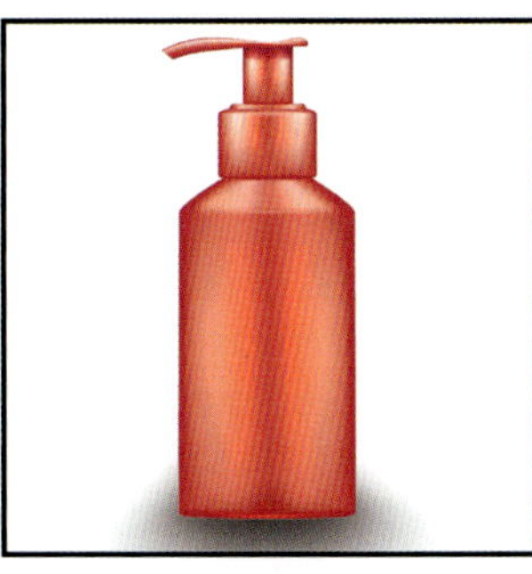

Against a white background
with shadow

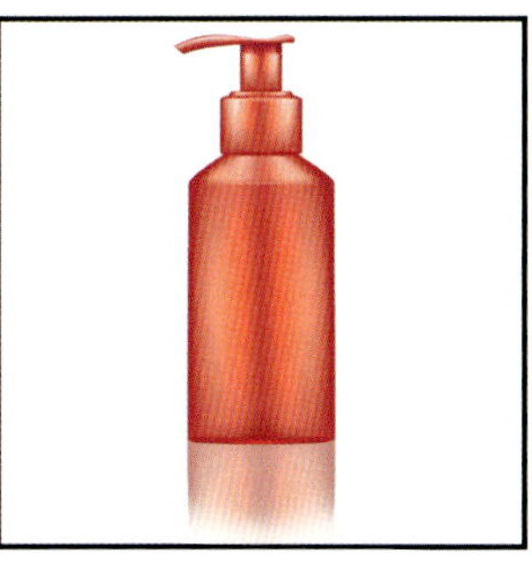

Against a white background
with reflection

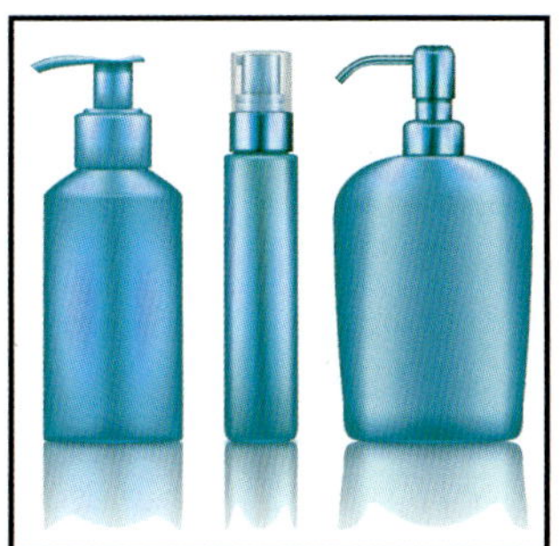

Showing a line of products

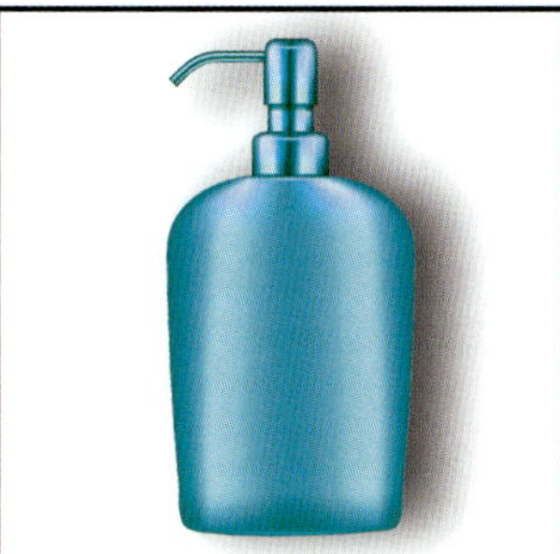

Flat

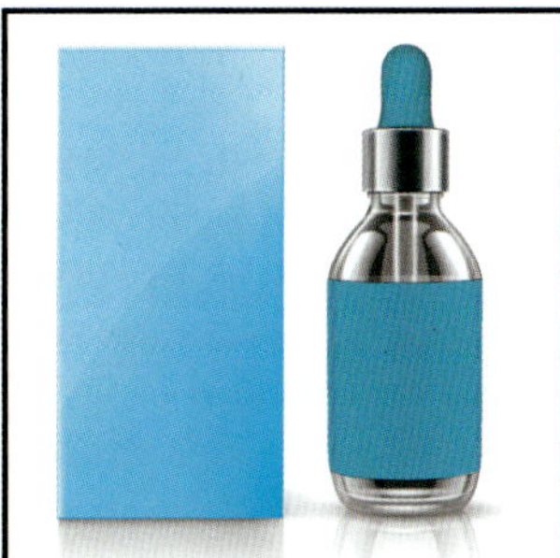

With packaging

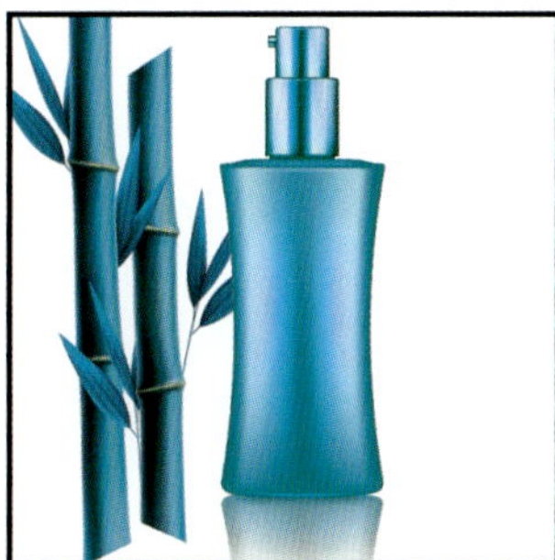

Staged

PRESENTATION METHODS FOR CATALOG PHOTOS

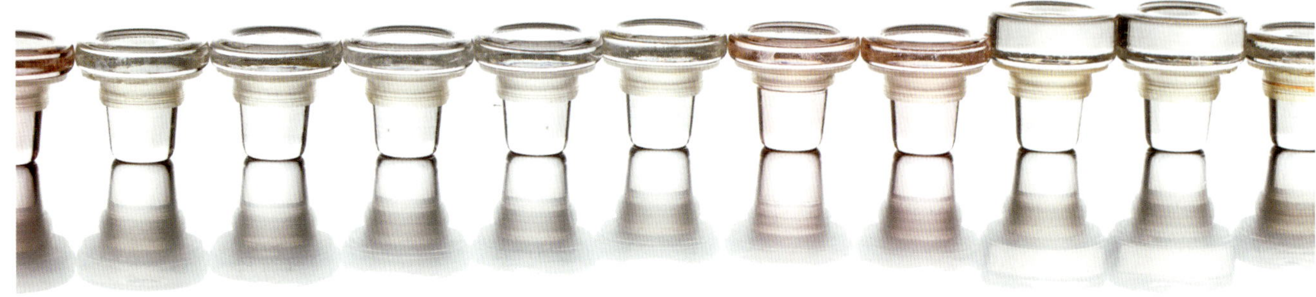

⌃ For this collection of bottle stoppers, the client chose a white background and visible reflections cast onto the base.

remove the sense of perspective. For a twelve-inch-tall object, for example, you will position yourself at sixty inches, with a 135mm lens (see page 49).

As usual, you need to perform a rigorous color calibration, using the method of identical gray card, color palette, file calibration, screen calibration, and color space on all the instruments being used.

The images must be delivered with identical framing of objects with the same homothetic ratios. Even if they are objects of very different sizes, like a small container of mustard and a large bottle of whiskey, they need to be shown at the same size and in the same proportions since they will be appearing in the same catalog.

You also need to maintain the same presentation method: if an object is shown with a cast reflection (see diagram on previous page), all the others must be as well. You will therefore have to maintain the same kind of base and overall approach to the lighting (even if you then need to adapt it to the shape and surface reflectance of each category of object).

And, finally, the lighting must be standardized not only in terms of colors, but also in quality, quantity, and angle of light for each product category.

Standard Presentations

There have traditionally been eight ways to present objects for catalogs: against a transparent background; against a white background with no cast shadows; with a cast shadow; with a cast reflection; as part of a product line (with or without packaging); flat; and in context.

Presentation against a transparent background is achieved in post-production with editing software. This is where a very even lighting of the background, without any reflections on the edges of the product, is most useful. By positioning barn doors to avoid a reflection on either side of the back of the object, and by measuring the reflected light at less than +0.3 EV on its silhouette, we can make the silhouette perfectly sharp and clearly distinguished from the background. The object can be outlined in Photoshop, without any loss or "nibbling away" of the silhouette, using a simple selection tool—an infinitely faster operation than outlining it with a pen tool. Then all that needs to be done is to erase the background and save the file as a transparent PNG.

The method for presenting the object against a white background is exactly the same, but without the need to use editing software. We simply need to make sure that the background is perfectly white (RGB color code 255/255/255) by exposing it at +3.33 EV and ensuring with the exposure meter that the lighting is identical over the entire framed area.

To manage the cast shadows without any editing required, the objects are placed on sheets of glass, maintained at a good distance from the support so that the shadow will not appear in the framed area (see pages 151–152). Please note that this method only works with objects that can be lighted at a perfectly right angle to the sheet of glass.

When we need to get shots with cast reflections, there are a couple of ways to proceed:

- Use a sheet of glass in the same way as in the previous case, but place the key light in a frontal axis to the product.
- Use a mirror or, my preference, sheets of plexiglass or acrylic.

With a black or white base, and depending on the angle of incidence of the lighting, we can obtain a more elegant cast reflection that is slightly blurred, appropriate

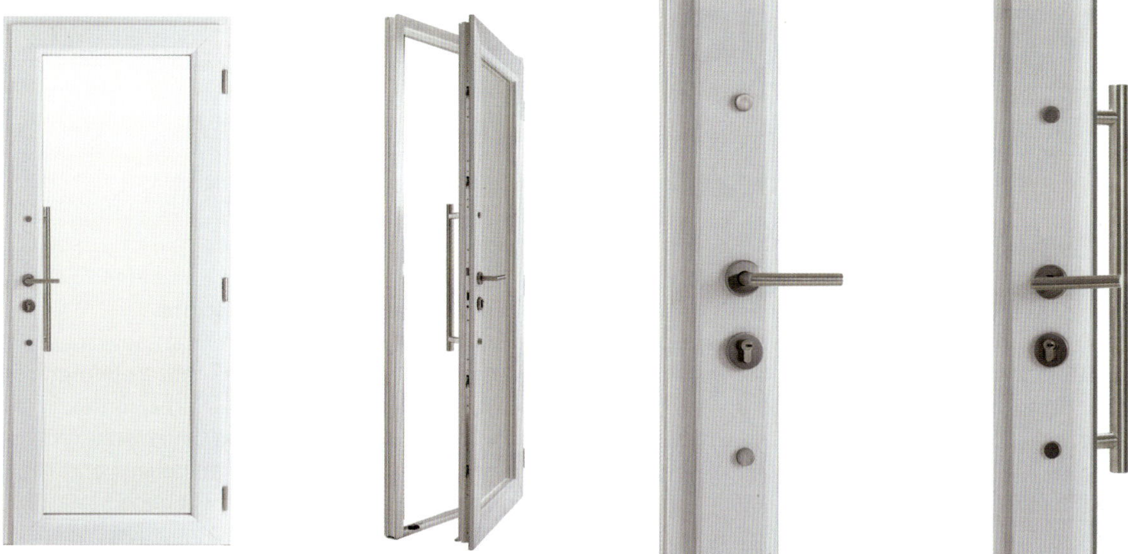

for commercial imagery. With a light source placed within the family of angles of a black plexiglass base, the reflection that appears on the base will look white (or light gray, depending on the intensity of the lighting), but with respect to the object, it will retain the characteristics of a barn door: it will not produce any reflections on the object and it will give depth to the low lights, unlike mirrors or sheets of glass.

For a flat presentation, the object is placed lying down and the camera is positioned above in a radical bird's-eye view. For matte objects, the lighting is placed above the camera (for obvious practical reasons, we then use a remote control to release the shutter). When photographing glossy objects, the lighting will be arranged to the side or, when we are dealing with transparent glass, as backlighting—in which case it is necessary to use a light table or at least a translucent base (such as PMMA), underneath which a light source is installed.

Other Kinds of Presentation

Depending on the brand and the kind of product, you will also see many other ways to highlight the functionality of the objects, their variations in shape and color, their options, their content, etc. Sometimes they will be shown with the same framing, as is done for the stroller below, or with close-ups of certain details, as in the door shown above. The important thing is to show the same characteristics of lighting, colors, depth of field, and sharpness, even while the framing and angle of view can vary greatly. Remember that all these shots will be presented in a coherent manner in the same space, and sometimes even as animated GIFs online (as was the case for the stroller shown below).

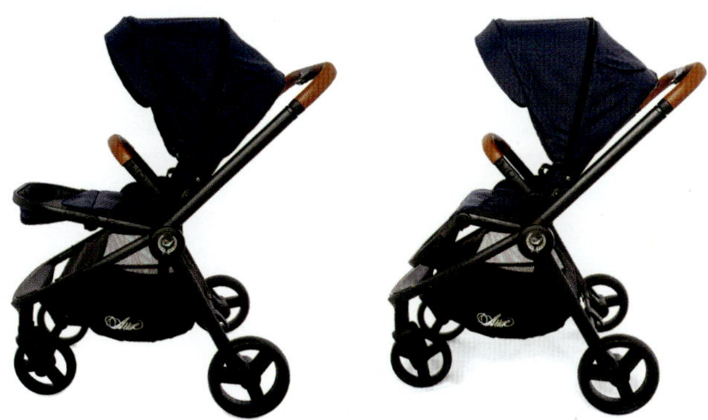

Brands usually ask for photos that allow the consumer to visualize the different ways the product can be used.

ADVERTISING SHOTS

In advertising, the aim is not so much to give a realistic representation of the product as it is to create an image that arouses desire by using a variety of different psychological techniques.

In most cases, it is up to the brand's art director or the advertising agency to decide what image will be produced. However, you may find yourself directly in contact with the client, with no intermediary, and end up having to carry out the visual creative work yourself from scratch: from developing a concept to post-production, including the shooting itself, of course.

From Concept to Mood Board

It would be wrong to think that an advertising image is just the result of a "good idea" that a photographer came up with alone in their studio. On the contrary, the image is the result of a project that is constructed through a series of exchanges between the client and the creative agency, using a creative tool: the mood board.

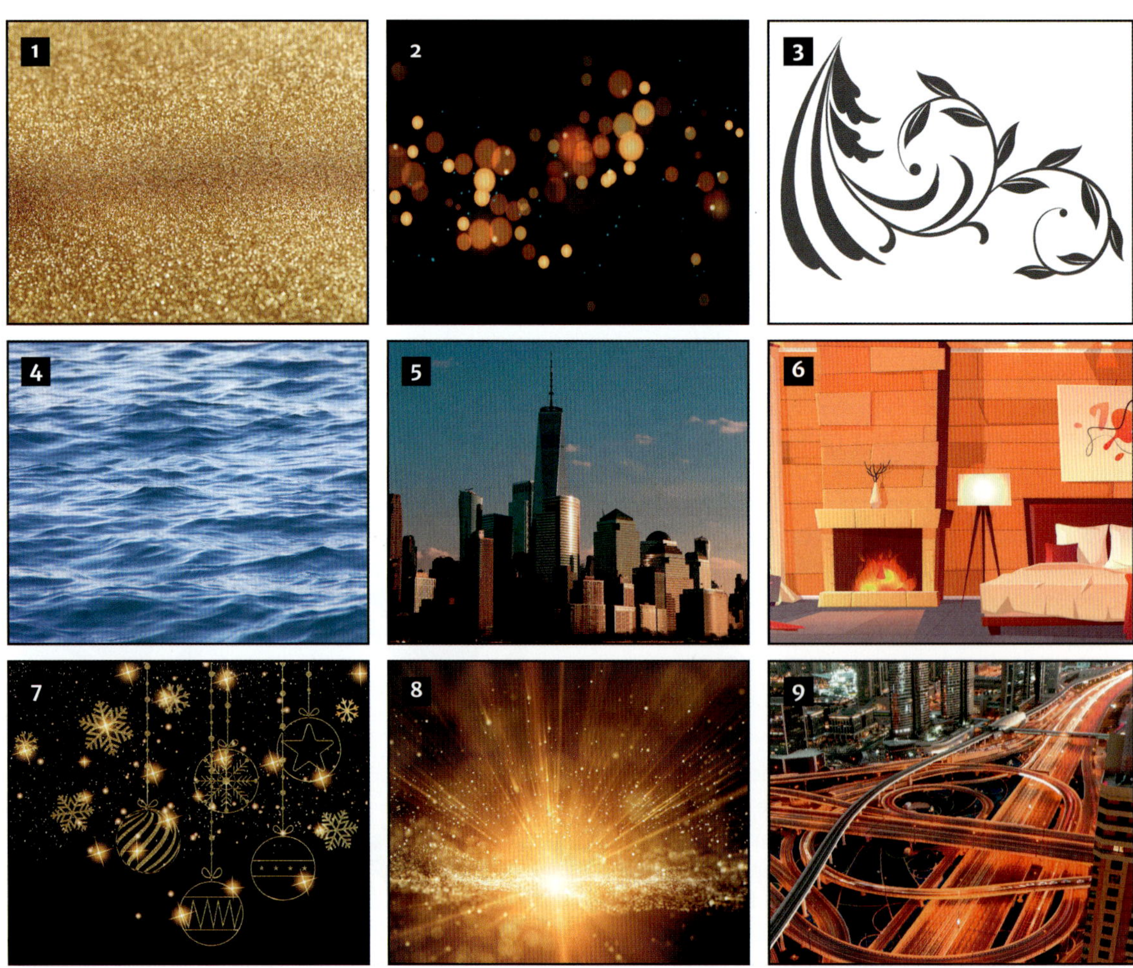

EXAMPLE OF A MOOD BOARD

Words, which are subject to interpretation, are not enough on their own. Because we are dealing with images here, we operate using photography and drawings. There are a thousand different ways to represent a concept as diffuse as liberty, for example, in images: a kite in the sky, a figure on horseback in distant mountains, a barefoot dancer in the streets of New York—the list goes on.

Initially, everything depends on the marketing strategy of the brand and its agency, which defines a series of concepts based on the target audience and market research. Then, a series of images is collected showing architecture, patterns, shapes, objects, textures, and colors that allow a dialogue to begin between the photographer and the client. After a few exchanges, which usually result in one or more images being changed, we arrive at a definitive mood board, like the one shown on the opposite page, a bridge between the concepts defined by the agency and the visual creation.

The creative work then consists of developing a branding proposal, made up of several mood boards that are meant to describe, as effectively as possible, the universe of the final photograph, as well as defining a budget.

A well-designed mood board makes it possible to identify all the requirements, and therefore all the costs, for a project: the locations where the shooting will be done if the photo is going to be taken outdoors (for instance, for a car ad), the elements and colors of the environment, the accessories and materials that need to be added, the desired lighting atmosphere (which will determine the time of day when the photo needs to be shot if it's an outside or location shot, or the type of shapers to be collected if it's a studio shot), and, finally, the "spirit." The creative developer then brings all of these disparate elements together to design the image as a whole.

Note that this technique is used in advertising, but that it can be transposed into all aspects of graphic creation. There are several different online platforms (like Pinterest) that make it easy to create mood boards, and you can also find extremely intuitive brainstorming and design tools (including gomoodboard.com and mural.co) to help in the creative process.

Mood Boards and Creation

Let's learn to read and use the mood board on the previous page:
- Images 7 and 8 correspond to the "spirit" of the project—in this case, Christmas and fireworks.

- Image 6 shows the desired atmosphere: a warm, enveloping interior.
- The spirals and the luminous traces of car headlights on twisting roads in images 3 and 9 indicate the geometric elements and shapes that are wanted for the shot.
- Image 4 serves as a graphic underpinning for adding parallel lines, like those of a swell at sea.
- Images 1 and 2, showing gold and yellowish-orange colors and glitter effects, give a sense of the background effect.
- Image 5, finally, indicates the placement of the objects to be promoted.

Implementation of the Shot

There were thousands of images that could have been produced based on such a mood board. I have chosen to show you a method that is found more and more often in product photography for advertising, using the creation of the shot of the perfume bottles on the next page.

We create an illustration that uses the key graphic elements (colors, geometry, etc.) and we display it on a computer screen. We then put the computer on a table, making sure to put a mirror (or a sheet of glossy black plexiglass) over the keyboard.

We then arrange the bottles on the surface, based on the architectural order that has been decided on (such as the buildings of Manhattan). We set up the camera on a tripod within the axis corresponding to the photographic project, with the appropriate framing, after having carefully chosen the distance of the camera and the focal length of the lens to achieve the desired perspective. We

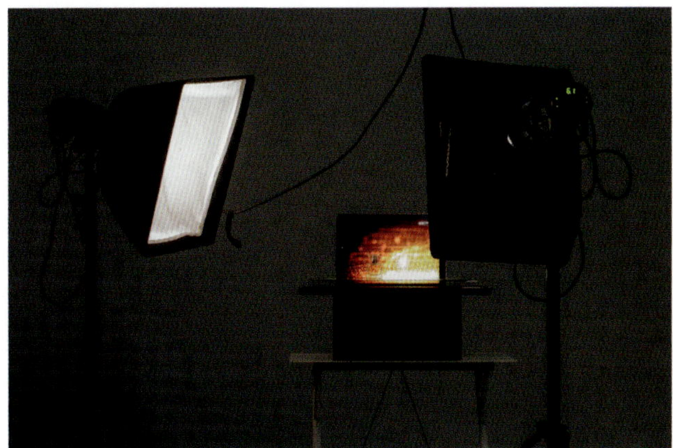

A BEHIND-THE-SCENES VIEW OF THE PHOTO ON THE FOLLOWING PAGE

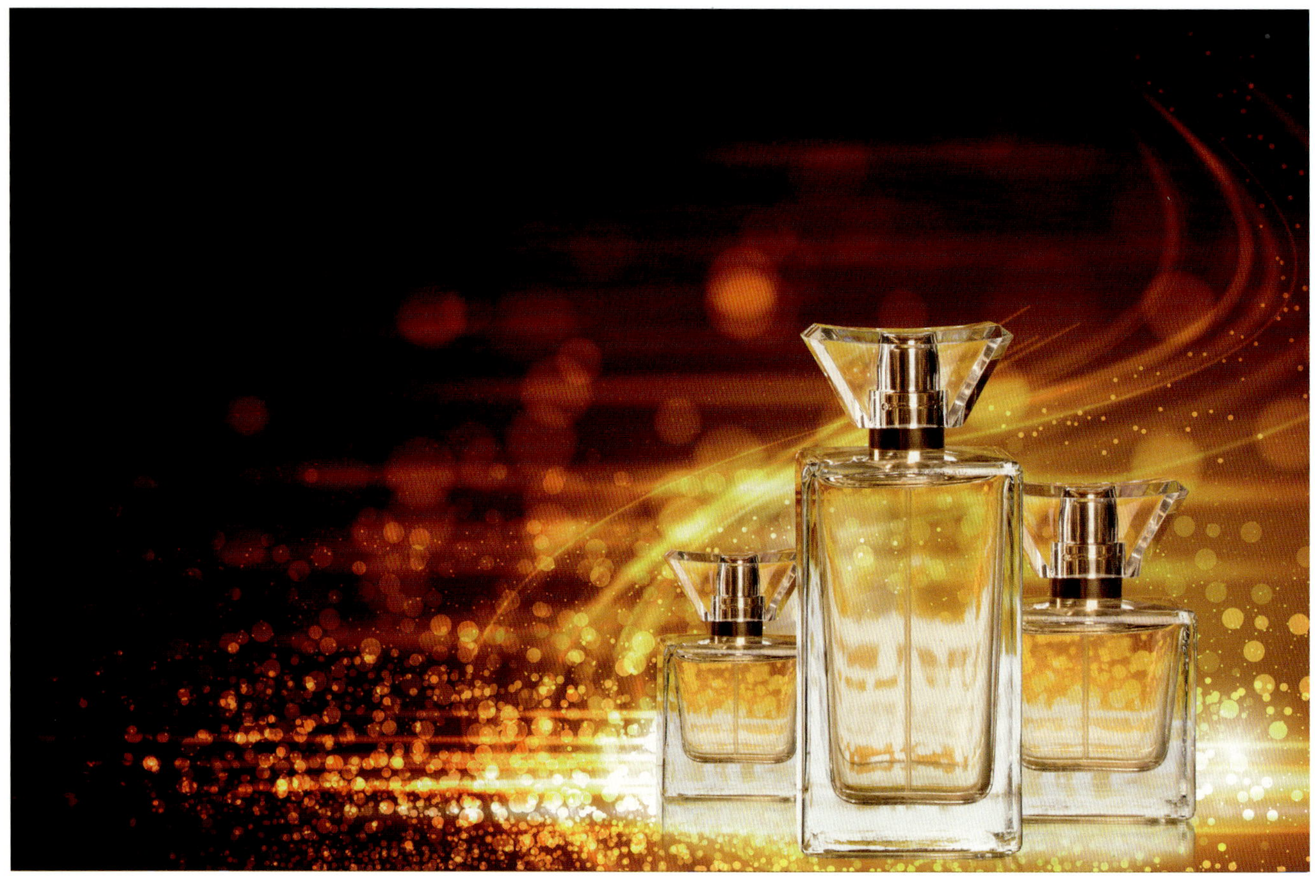

PHOTO CREATED BASED ON THE MOOD BOARD ON PAGE 196

then place one or more flashes in the positions that are best suited to presenting the shape of the objects, while avoiding unwanted reflections, and finally, we add the appropriate diffusers.

Once everything has been set up, we go on to measure the light produced by the screen (which we have set to the maximum so that we can be more flexible in adjusting the camera), using an independent exposure meter with the lumisphere in position and directed toward the screen. Using the built-in calculator, we modify the exposure time until we have reached the aperture we want to use on the camera. For example, if I measure the screen at 1/125 s, ISO 100, f/1, I will need to adjust my camera to f/8 to achieve the depth of field I want: by changing the exposure time on the exposure meter, I get f/8 at 1/2 s. I adjust my camera to that value (1/2 s, ISO 100, f/8), while making sure that there is no other light in the room where I'm working.

The flashes are then adjusted—to produce the same amount of light, for example—and checked with the flash meter. Don't forget to turn off the flashes' guide lights because their light would be added to the light of the screen.

Now all we have to do is release the camera shutter with a remote control (to prevent any jiggling of the camera in such a long exposure). The flashes will go off at the beginning of the shot, lighting the objects for a very short period. The rest of the exposure time will be devoted to recording the continuous light from the screen. The final photo is as you see it here.

USING LIQUIDS

Once you have mastered the laws of optics and the methods of lighting objects thematically, it is time to start creating some dynamism and movement in objects that are, by their nature, inanimate. Nothing works better for this than the fluidity of liquids.

Splashes of water, gouache paints, cream, or colored powders produce the most beautiful effects when it comes to staging an object. They suggest movement and liven up the shot, producing striking effects. But it isn't easy to know how to do this at first.

Liquid and Contrasts

By nature, water is colorless and transparent. To make it visible in photography, we need to work the same way we do when lighting glass. Backlighting works very well, as long as you create some contrast by including a dark area around the edges of the light; as with transparent glass against a white background, the liquid will reveal itself in gray-and-white material effects and darker borders. To do this, we place a diffusing fabric behind a transparent tray full of water, and against that, a flash equipped with a light box. Then we just release the shutter a fraction of a second after the object has pierced the surface of the liquid.

For opaque liquids, like milk, cream, or gouaches, the lighting has to be placed within the family of angles of the projection, usually at a shallow showerhead angle (60° to 70°), or laterally (60° to 90°), depending on how many direct reflections we want to show. Note that thick or viscous liquids have the benefit of reacting slightly more slowly than water does, which makes it easier to time the shutter release when you're working manually.

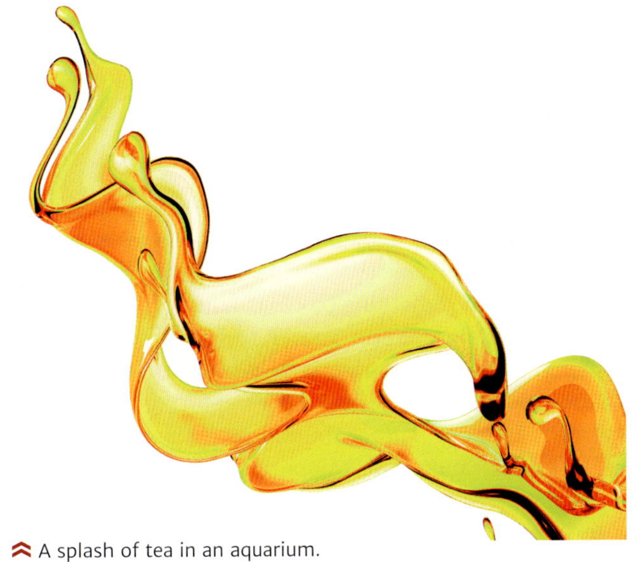

A splash of tea in an aquarium.

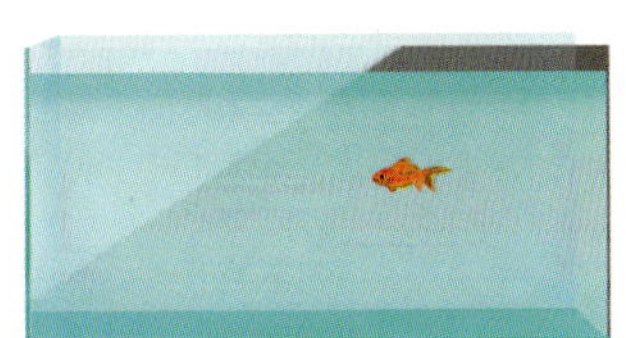

Fill an aquarium, while making sure to leave some empty glassed-in space at the top.

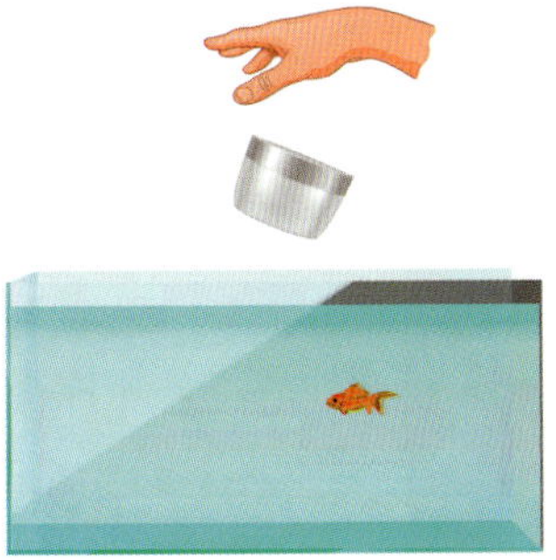

Drop the object from above.

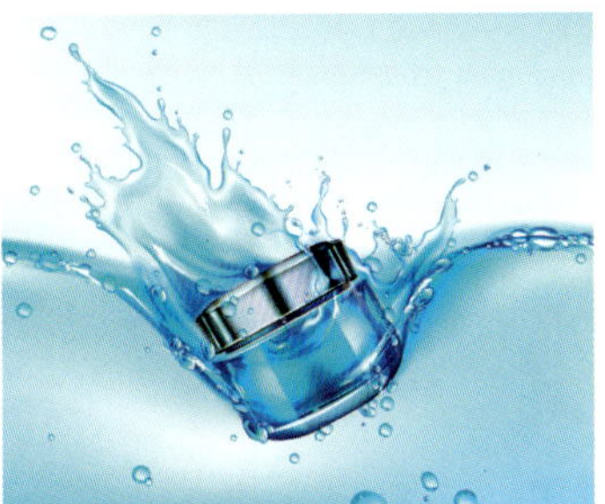

Release the shutter at the moment the object pierces the surface of the water.

PHOTOGRAPHING AN OBJECT PIERCING THE SURFACE OF THE WATER

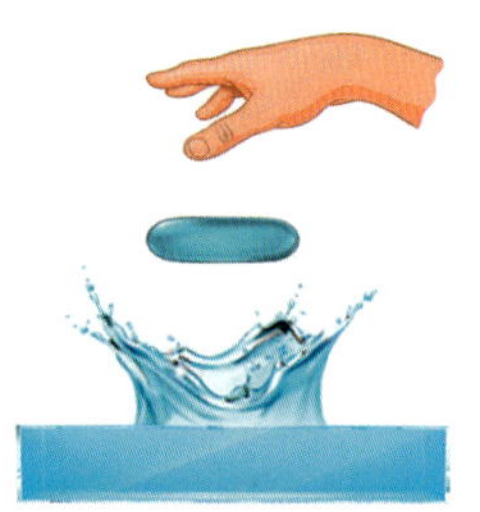

Drop a flat
transparent object.

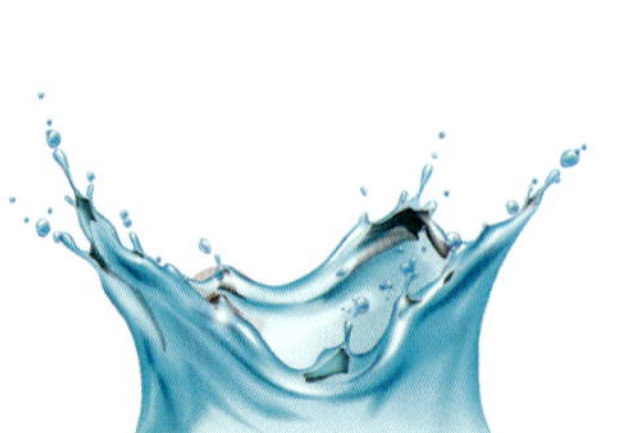

Select the splash.

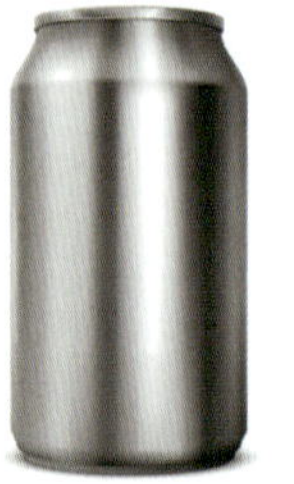

Light and photograph the can.

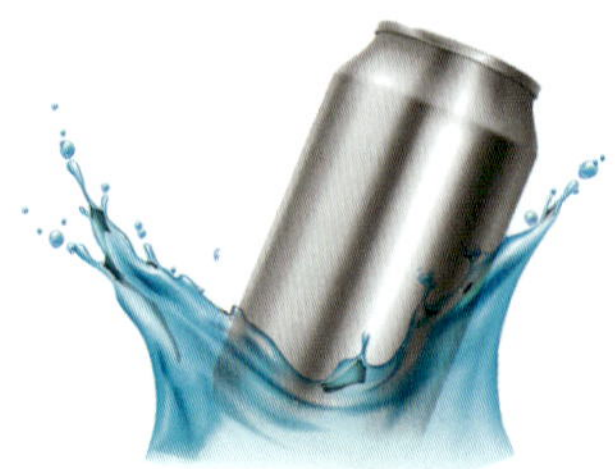

Combine the two shots, playing
with the transparencies.

PHOTOGRAPHING A DRINK CAN THROWN INTO THE WATER

Laser Release

The fashion for photography using liquid in motion has prompted manufacturers to offer automatic release solutions. These electronic systems plug into the camera and trigger it when something (such as liquid) trips the laser beam that they produce. The Pluto brand was the first to market this kind of accessory, which also works with sound (making it very useful for capturing the precise moment when a balloon bursts or a firecracker goes off). Other brands, like Miops Smart, also offer triggers connected to microvalves and computerized Mariotte siphons, making it fairly easy to photograph water drops, or drops colliding.

Real and Composite Splashes

The most common technique consists of dropping an object into an aquarium half-filled with water and taking the photo at the moment the object pierces the surface of the liquid.

The procedure is as follows: place a flash equipped with a light box behind a large diffuser, which is in turn set up behind the aquarium. If you want a black background, arrange a piece of black cardboard behind the aquarium and two light sources, one on either side of the container. Make sure that the walls of the aquarium are completely clean, without any fogging, and that the space above the liquid is large enough for the framing of the photo and the splashing that you expect.

Set up the camera on a tripod, at the distance that will allow the framing to cover an area one-third below and two-thirds above the water surface. Place a target in the center of the aquarium as a way to focus on the spot where the object will be dropped. Block the focus. Then release the shutter at the right time, using a remote control, usually a fraction of a second after the object has hit the water. Of course, you will need several attempts to time this moment perfectly. Remember to set up plastic sheeting on the ground and to protect your lighting and camera equipment against splashing.

While this technique is very good for rendering the liquid photographically, it does not take the appearance of the object itself into account, which is why many object photographers prefer a composite method. In that case, you follow the same procedure, except that what you

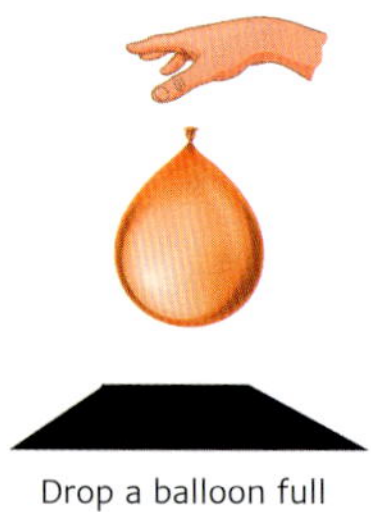

Drop a balloon full
of paint.

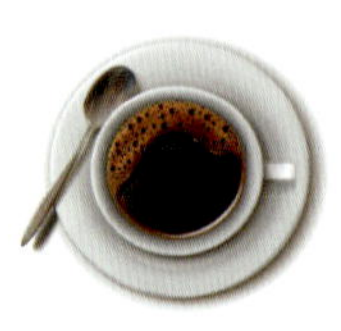

Photograph the surface.

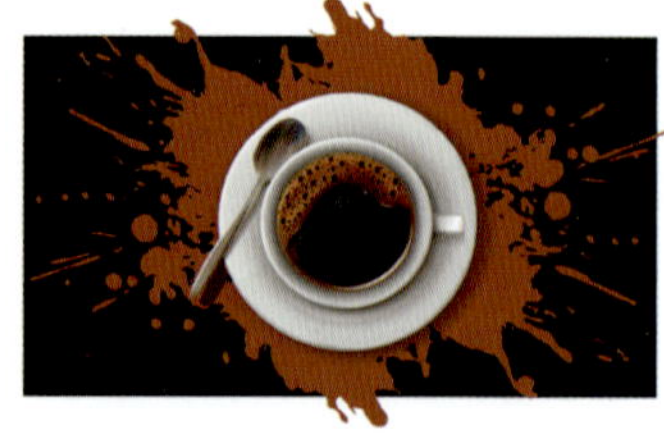

Prepare the object.

Place the object on the
splattered surface.

SIMULATING A SPLASH

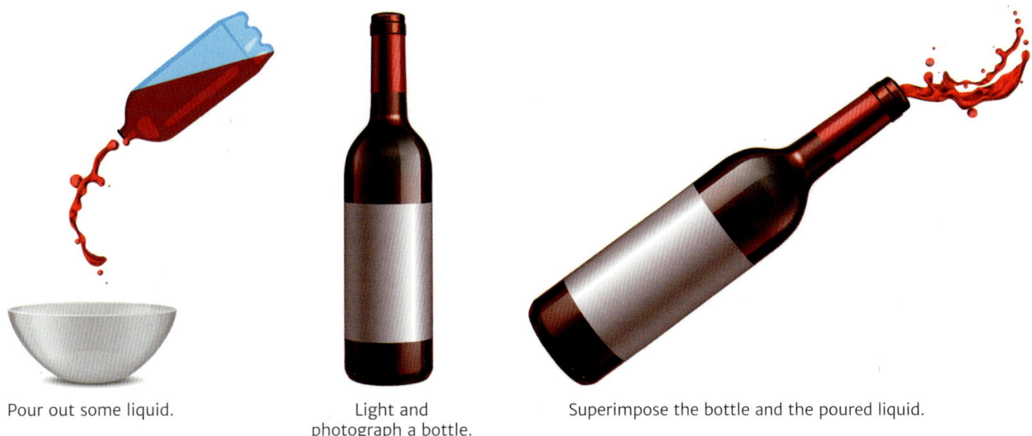

BRINGING A BOTTLE OF WINE TO LIFE WHILE MAINTAINING THE DESIRED REFLECTIONS

drop into the water from above is a transparent object with a diameter similar to the one you are going to photograph. Then, in Photoshop, that placeholder object will be replaced by the actual object, as shown in the diagram above. This technique has the advantage of avoiding lighting that is unsuitable for the product, but it is very time-consuming to integrate the image of the product into the aquarium image using layer masks and differentiated transparency effects.

You can also create the impression of a splash by simply playing with its after effects. For example, you can drop a balloon full of paint onto a plain surface and then set the object to be photographed on top of the paint splashes (see diagram at bottom of page 200).

Splashes

The fashion is also for liquids to be presented in streaks or streams. As in the illustration above, we can simply empty a bottle and photograph the liquid as it flows out. Excellent results can be achieved by poking a 3/4-inch-diameter hole in the bottom of a bottle and then plugging it up with a piece of gaffer tape. Then fill the bottle with a liquid that has the desired characteristics, such as wine, plug the neck with your thumb, and turn the bottle upside down. At the appropriate time, remove the gaffer tape from the base, and after also removing your thumb, swing the bottle back and forth a little in a slight pendulum movement so that the flow of the liquid as it pours out will not be too straight. The hole pierced in the bottom of the bottle will keep it from emptying in spurts and jerks. In terms of lighting, proceed as in the case of the splashes shown on the previous page.

From the resulting photo, choose the part of the liquid that you find most interesting and merge it with another shot, taken with the appropriate lighting.

Waves

More simply, we can present an object in a shallow tray, like a cafeteria tray or a backing tray, into which we have poured a 1/2 or 3/4 inch of water. We place a large diffuser behind the arrangement so that the surface of the water is in the middle of the family of angles. It will then look uniformly gray or white, depending on the intensity of the lighting. Then, simply create a wave using a blower or an anti-dust spray and take the picture. The

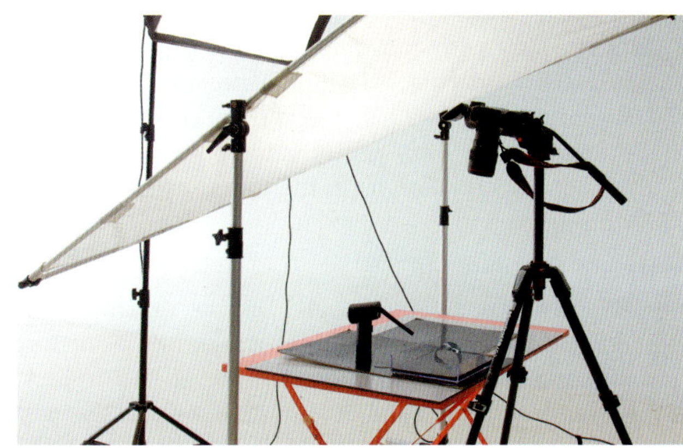

⌃ A behind-the-scenes view of the photo on the following page: the watch is arranged in a black plexiglass tray in which water has been placed. Compressed air is blown onto the surface to create waves. A very diffused light source is placed at a 45° angle overhead.

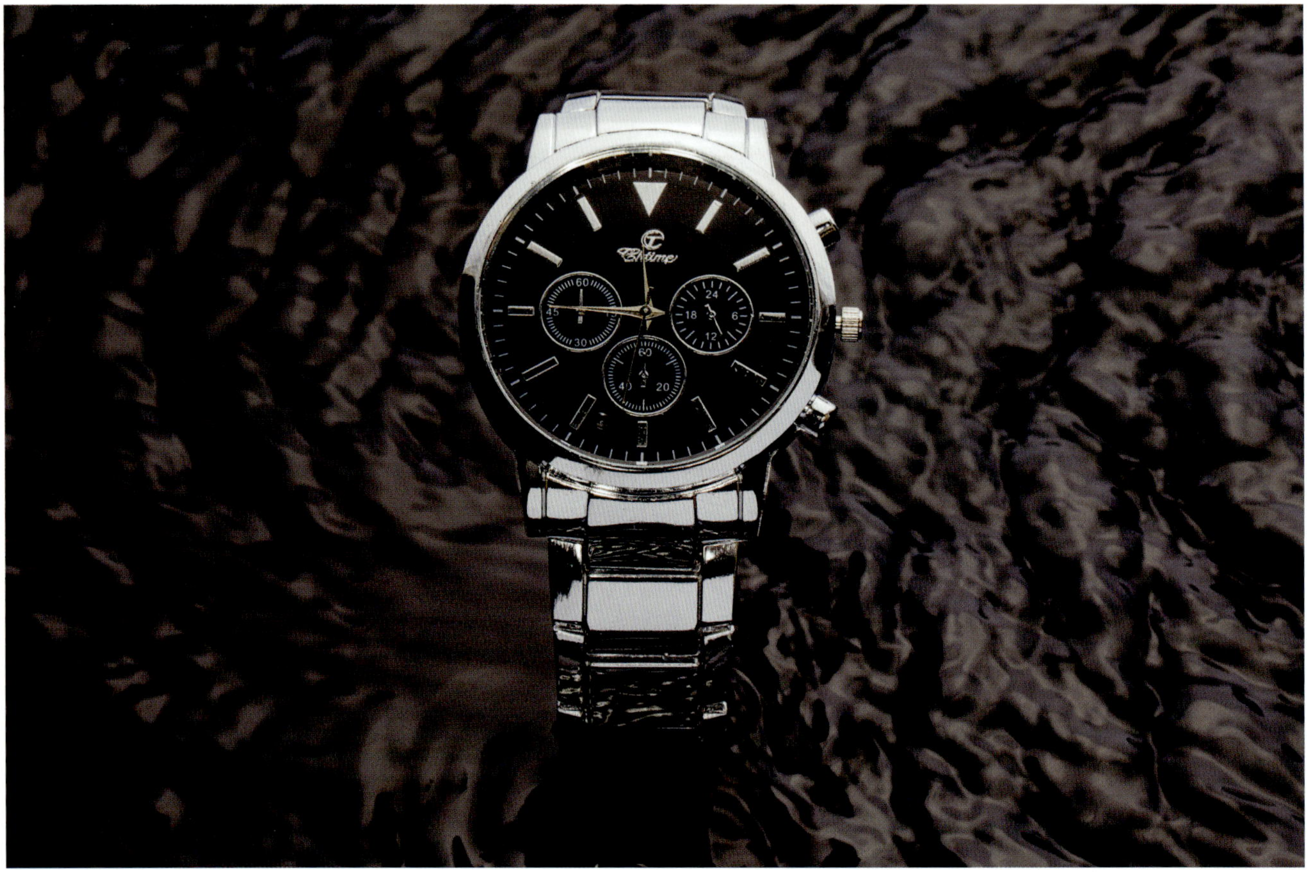

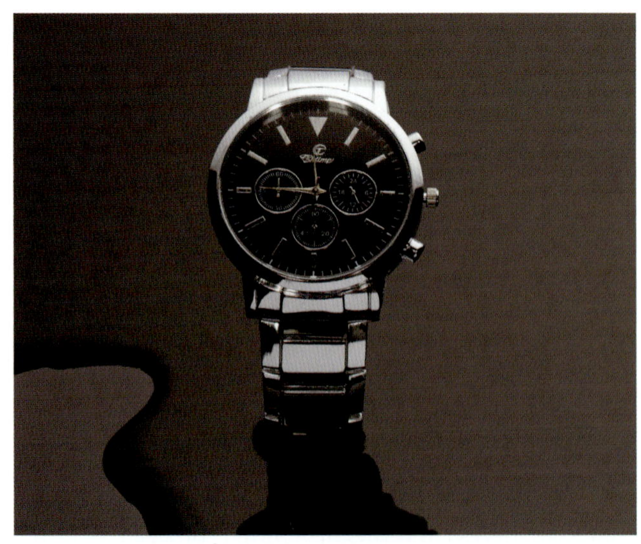

⌃ Using waves to highlight an object.

result will be similar to that of the picture of the watch shown above.

We can play with movement in a similar way; for instance, with a necklace. Hang the necklace on a lever so that the medallion is just above the water. Then start the lever swinging, very gently, and you will get beautiful concentric undulations in the water, as seen on the following page.

Without Movement

At rest, the thin layer of water in the arrangement explained in the previous section works like a mirror, but with a smoothness that a mirror never has. In fact, if the water is spotless and dust-free, it will have a very clean look and produce very soft light, well suited to the presentation of metal and glass objects. In this kind of arrangement, we place a small glass wedge at the surface of the water, smaller in diameter than the object to be photographed, and set the object on the wedge.

⌃ The same watch as before, shown on water at rest.

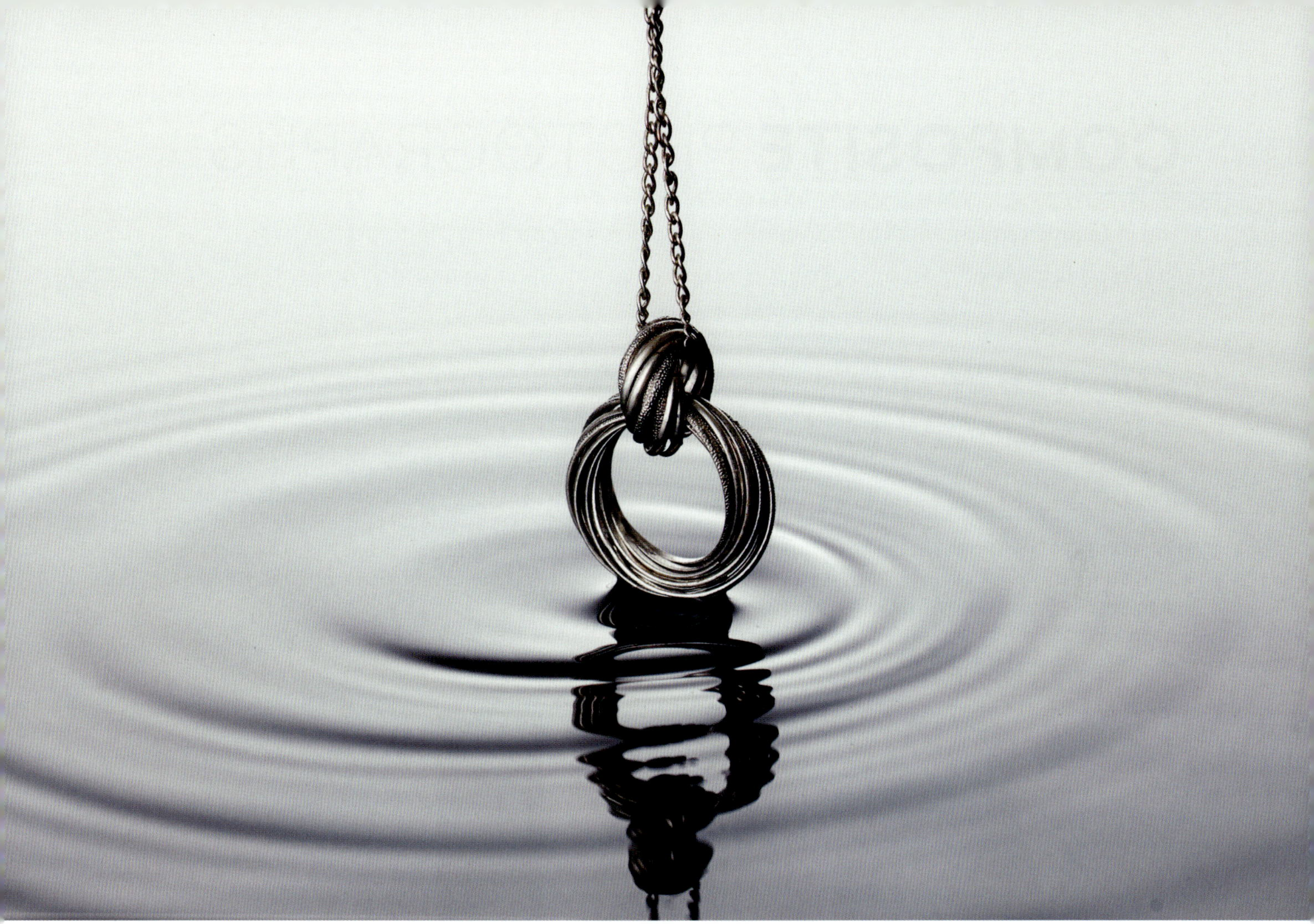

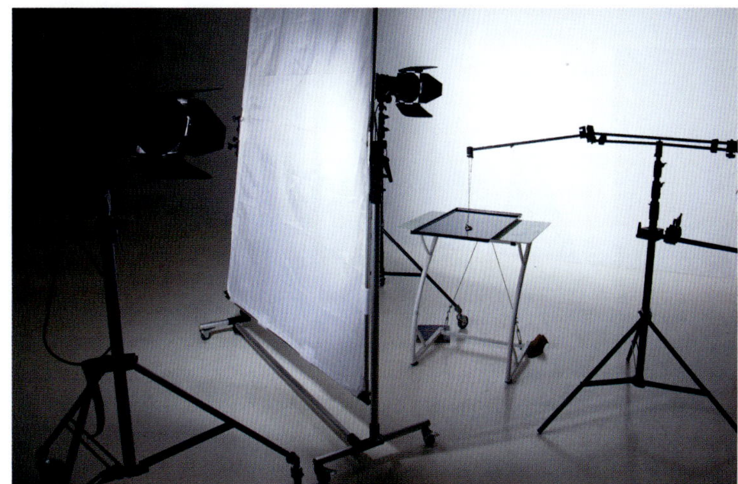

» A behind-the-scenes view of the photo above. A source (with zoom bowl and a barn door) is directed toward the rear to illuminate the wall and create a uniform reflection over the entire surface of the water. A second, similar source is set up behind a diffusing fabric and directed toward the front of the necklace to light it.

COMPOSITE PHOTOGRAPHS

The industry's requirements for packshots are increasingly pushing photographers to create composite photographs. This is a way to save time, limit editing, and present variations on a product.

With the rise of e-commerce and the growing demand for photographs of objects, it has become necessary to become more efficient in our work by using the composite method, especially because of the increasing number of variations in the same product.

Increasing Efficiency

Imagine that you need to present the same plastic duck in twenty different colors. You could, of course, photograph each object, one after the other. But you could also just photograph one of them, with the light falling just right, then photograph the rest of them with good color calibration, and finally successively apply each color to your original model in Photoshop.

In the same way, because there is not an infinite number of shapes of wine bottles, you could choose to make perfect shots of the twenty existing models, the fifteen most common engravings, and the ten most commonly used capsules. Once you have compiled this catalog, all that is left to do is to photograph the labels and then

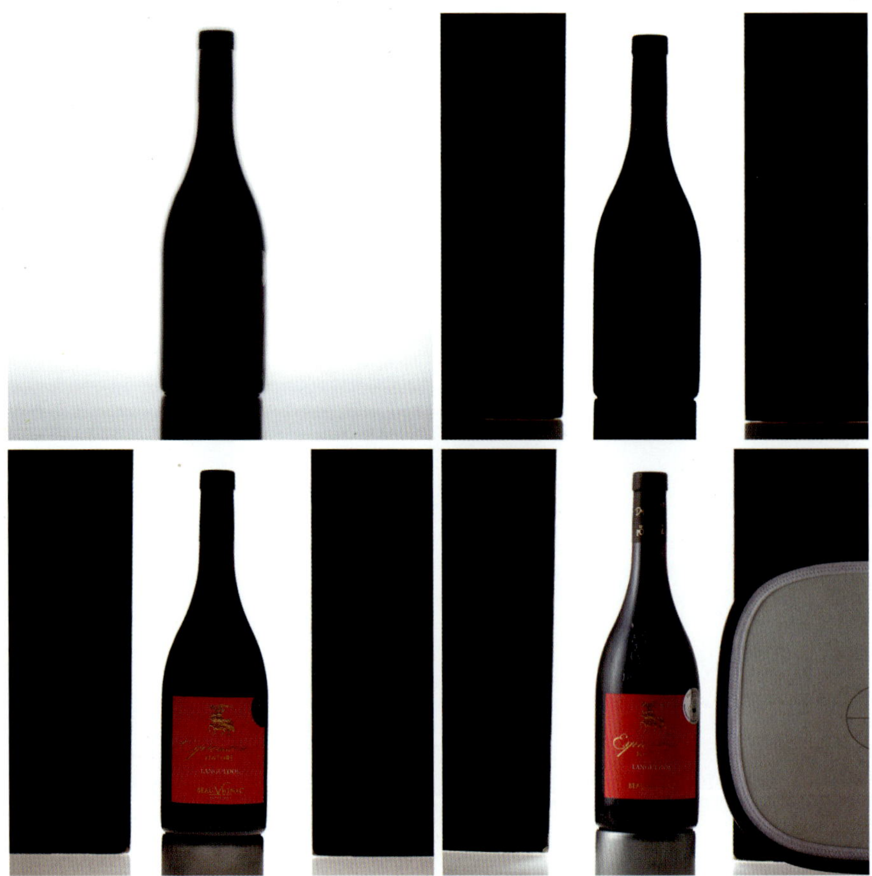

« Example of the production of a photograph of a bottle of wine using the composite method. Each photo is lit so that it will add a particular detail to the assembled photograph.

attach them to the appropriate files. This kind of practice is more and more common in major studios that specialize in this area.

Composite Lighting Management

As we have seen, the lighting of a bottle of wine involves the perfect positioning of at least three light sources, and many more than that if there are engravings, capsules, medallions, or sleeves to take into account. And this entire operation must be completely reproduced every time there is a new bottle.

But we can also proceed differently, separately and selectively illuminating each of the elements to be highlighted. Care must be taken to ensure that the camera does not move at all and that the lightings do not overlap. Then all we have to do is group all the shots together, as layers, in Photoshop, and select each aspect of the object that we're interested in on each particular shot, while erasing the others. This is the procedure often followed for wine bottles and perfume bottle caps.

Photographing a Product Line

Most of the compositions shown in packaging photos are also created using a composite method. For instance, if we need to photograph thirty tubes of lipstick that all need to be presented together, it is a safe bet that not all of the tubes will be perfectly lit, given that they are not all in the same position with respect to the lighting and that they can also cast shadows on each other. Thus, we photograph each one of them separately; if it is only the color of the lipstick that changes, then we proceed in the same way as with the plastic ducks mentioned on the previous page. Then we place each of the different images into one file, where we can move the various elements around at will, depending on the client's needs and the requirements of the layout.

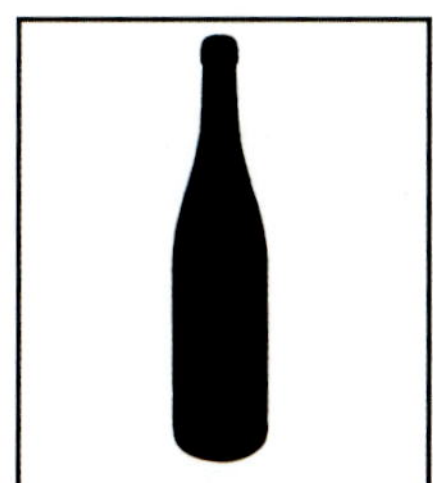

Backlighting with a barn door to obtain a clear silhouette.

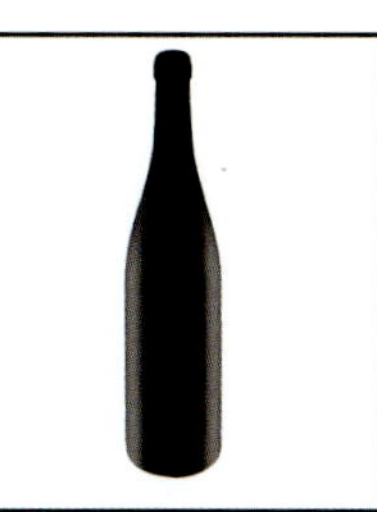

Lighting of the edges of the bottle using two large reflectors at the edge of the family of angles.

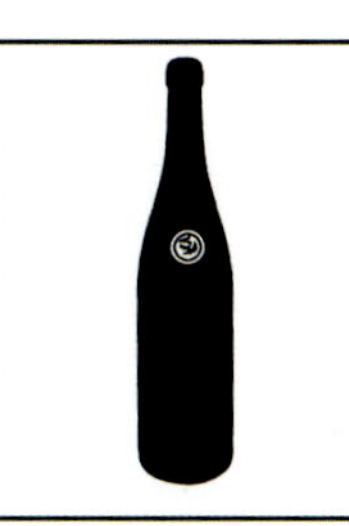

Lighting of the stenciling using a softbox at a showerhead angle.

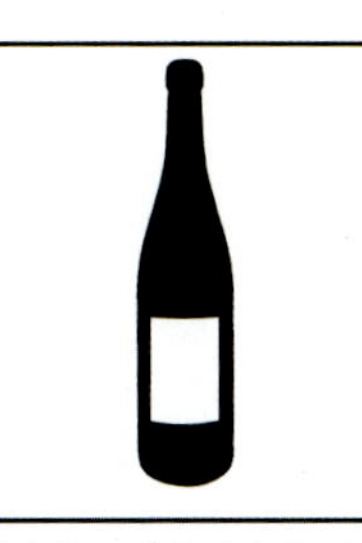

Lighting of the label using a large frontal softbox.

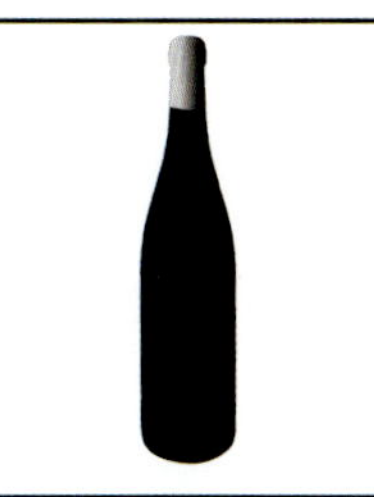

Lighting of the capsule with a softbox placed at the same height.

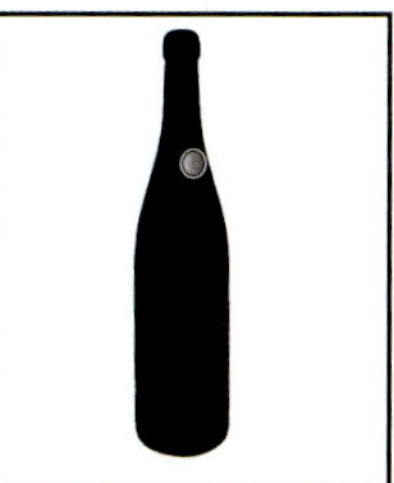

Lighting of the medallion using a softbox placed at the same height.

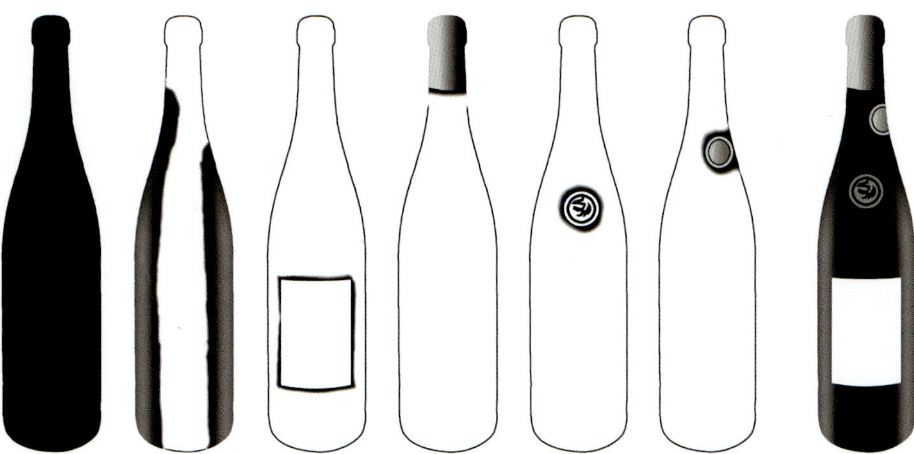

Using editing software, we pick up each of the locally lighted areas to place it on the photo of the silhouette, making sure to create blurred edges so that they will fit in well with the image.

STEPS IN THE CREATION OF A COMPOSITE PHOTO OF A BOTTLE OF WINE

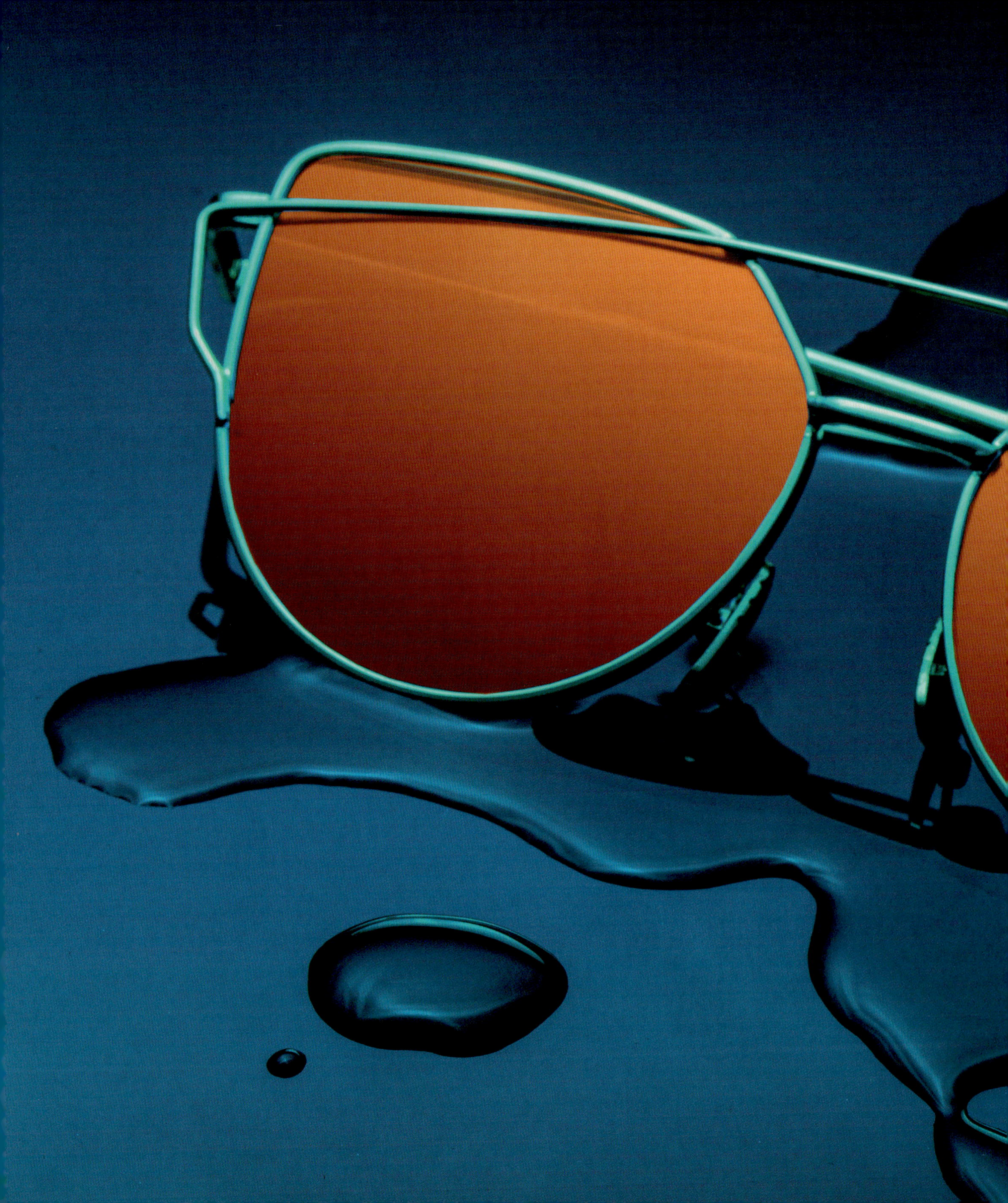

4

COMPOSITION
AND PROBLEM RESOLUTION

» **208** Composition and Contrasts
» **214** Staging
» **217** Artistic Visions
» **221** No Object Is Perfect

COMPOSITION AND CONTRASTS

Many books have been written about how to produce interesting images. Whether we are talking about objects or people, the methods are approximately the same; for objects, however, the idea of contrast is key.

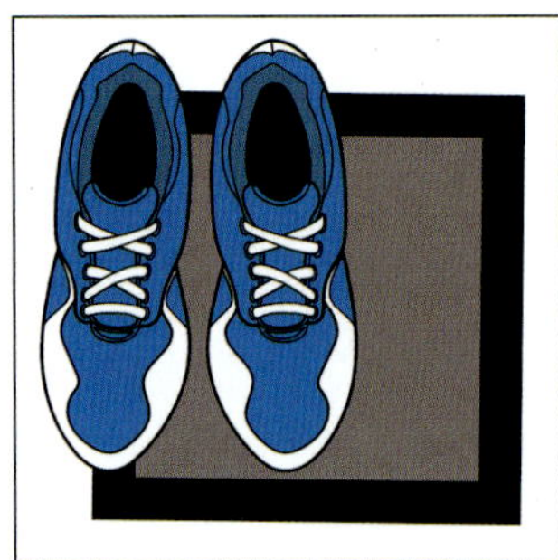

Contrasting Shapes
Different geometrical elements
(for instance circles and squares)

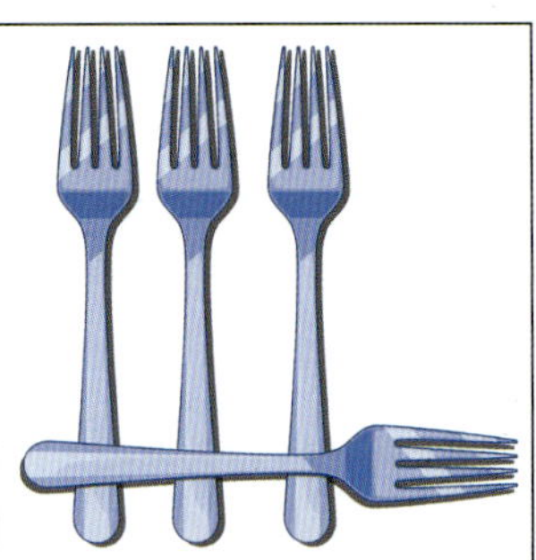

Contrasting Directions
Objects placed along
different axes

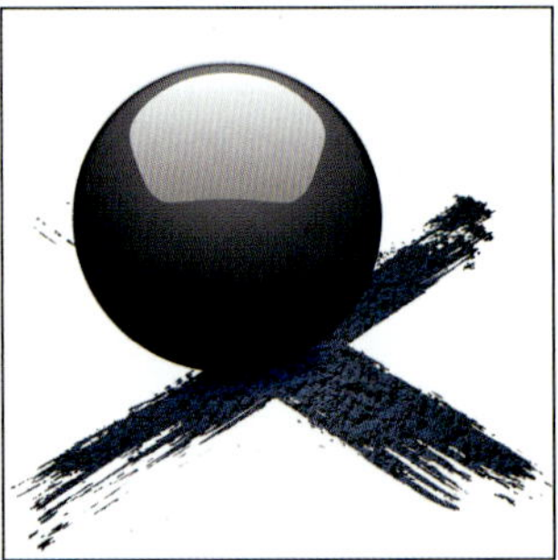

Contrasting Surfaces
Juxtaposition of objects with
contradictory surfaces

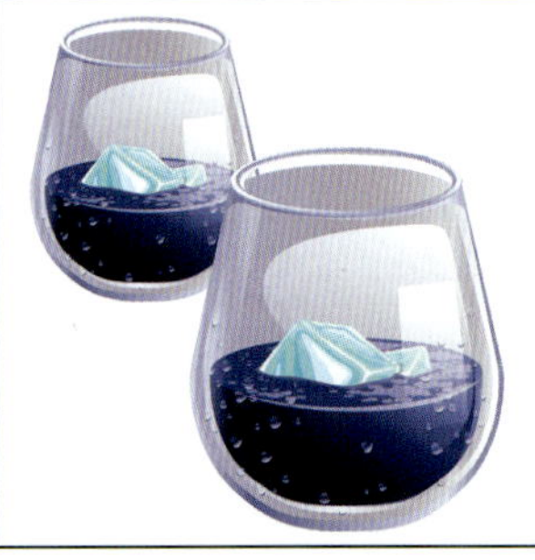

Contrasting Planes
Objects placed at
different distances

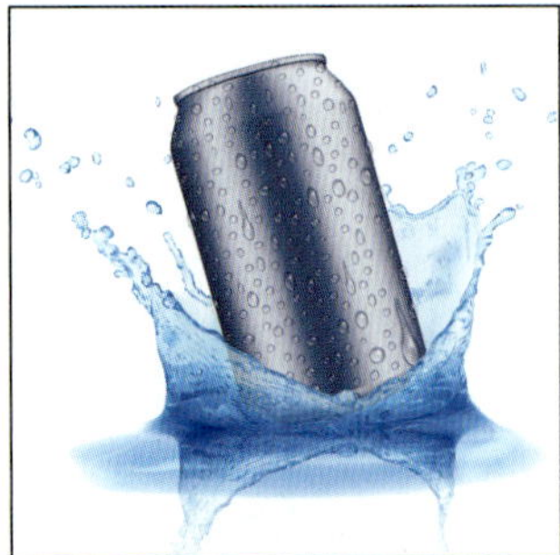

Contrasting Movement
Juxtaposition of fixed elements and
elements in motion

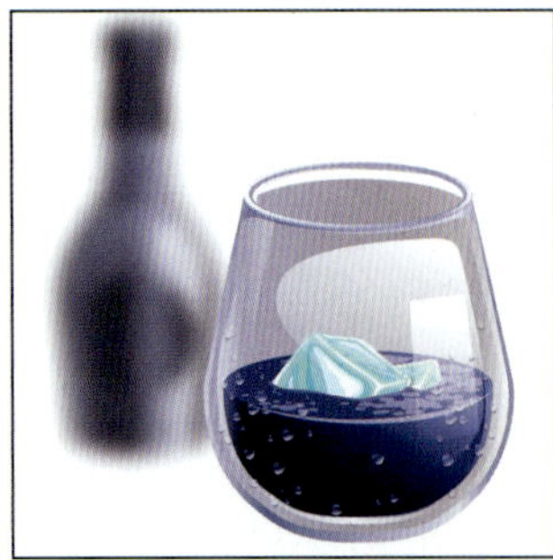

Contrasting Sharpness
Highlighting an object by playing with
depth of field

CONTRASTS BETWEEN OBJECTS

Whatever the environment or context in which you choose to place an object to be photographed, you must never lose sight of the fact that the object itself is the important thing compared to everything surrounding it, even while you create a visual dialogue among all the elements. It is through this play with contrasts and harmonies that you will be able to create a successful composition.

COMPOSITIONAL CONTRASTS

In a photograph, an object only exists because of the lighting and the shooting angle, but what gives it a greater or lesser degree of importance in the image is its arrangement in space and its position in relation to the other elements around it. Let's review some of the most common methods of composition to help you decide which accessories and which materials will provide the best accompaniment for the object that you want to present.

Contrasting Shapes

Let's start with one of the most obvious aspects of composition: the shape of the object. Imagine that you have to photograph a round wineglass: its roundness will be perfectly highlighted if you place it in front of a square shape or in front of horizontal or diagonal lines.

Contrast through Repetition

Going the opposite direction, we can accentuate the presence of an object by repeating its shape multiple times (see the photo on the next page). The repetition can be simple, but one of the objects can also be arranged a little bit differently from the others to focus attention on that one object.

Contrasting Directions

Another method consists of placing (similar or dissimilar) objects in a different axis from the one on which we want the viewer to focus. For a better effect, we can set up a very regular placement, potentially even using

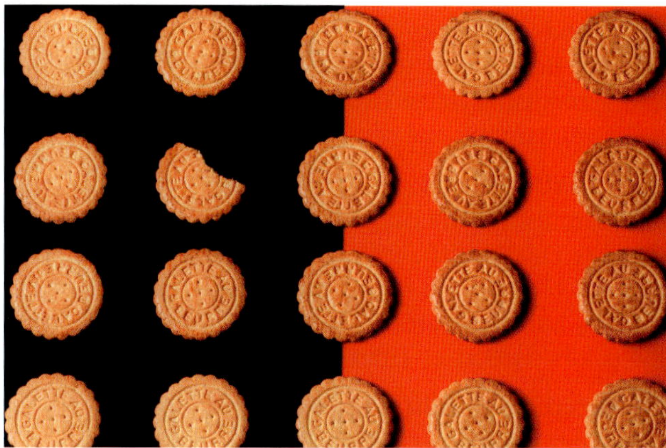

⌃ An example of contrast through repetition, using Petit Beurre cookies. This image was created to draw the viewer's eye to the one cookie that has been nibbled on.

a ruler to create a very precise layout. In the diagram on the previous page, I presented three forks aligned vertically, all equidistant from each other: the viewer's gaze is then drawn to the one fork that is horizontal.

Contrasting Surfaces

The interplay between material effects, such as soft and rough, is used a lot in advertising for cosmetics, and is very effective. A jar of moisturizing cream presented on a dry, rough surface, such as cracked earth, will appear infinitely smoother and softer than if it was posed on a piece of satin.

Contrasting Planes

The objects can also be arranged on different planes. This method provides perspective and lends depth to the shot.

Contrasting Movement

Objects, which are inanimate by nature, benefit greatly from being presented with an appearance of movement. This concept is often taken up in advertising by using objects thrown into the air, sprays of powder, and other "suspended" compositions.

Contrasting Sharpness

Frequently used in culinary photography, contrasts in sharpness inevitably draw the viewer's attention to the object that is in focus. Depending on the depth of field we choose, all of the other objects that are at a different distance will appear more or less blurred; they are chosen not so much for their shape as for their color, because that is what will be most visible in the overall composition.

COLOR CONTRASTS

The theory of color contrasts—formalized by Johannes Itten, the great Bauhaus theoretician, between 1919 and 1923—plays an essential role in compositional choices in all of the graphic arts. Having a good understanding of the relationships that arise between associated colors will allow you to properly choose the background and an accessory color.

Hot and Cold

Because they relate to our perception of reality—cold is associated with nighttime and ice, and heat with sun and fire—we experience blue and green as cold colors and red and yellow as warm ones. Putting them together in one shot creates a good and very graphic visual impact. A

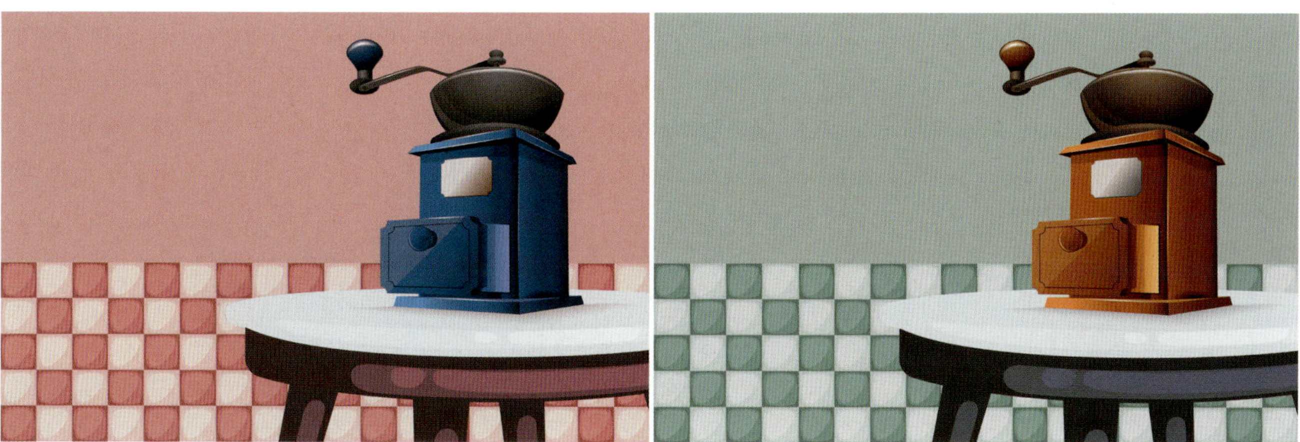

TEMPERATURE CONTRAST (HOT/COLD)

turquoise cup against a reddish-orange background will thus assure an excellent result (in addition to the fact that these two are complementary colors).

Light/Dark Contrast (Chiaroscuro)

The chiaroscuro effect is very useful in color photography, but is absolutely necessary if you are producing a black-and-white photo. This notion, which is often misunderstood, is one of the primary driving forces behind many modern compositions (think of "Les Poissons Noirs" by Georges Braque [1942] or "The Old Guitarist" by Pablo Picasso [1965]). It involves pairing two colors that don't look different in terms of their luminance but that are distinguished by a strong contrast in how light they are. Yellow, for instance, is very light, and loses its luminosity when it is darkened; a chiaroscuro contrast will connect these two yellows.

Try this experiment in Photoshop: Take a blue (RGB 66/92/164) and a green (RGB 82/91/41), which are fairly close, and desaturate the image—the contrast will be obvious. But then, if you take two very different colors, like a reddish-orange (RGB 198/51/53) and a sky blue (RGB 58/171/229), the contrast disappears.

Contrasting Hues

This contrast requires at least three pure, luminous colors that are clearly differentiated from each other. Yellow, red, and blue are the strongest expressions of color contrast by hue. Its expressive force diminishes the further the colors used stray from the primary colors.

Contrasting Quality

This contrast is expressed in the degree of "purity" of a color, its intensity. The contrast opposes a pure and luminous color with a dull color, often the same one mixed with white, black, gray, or its complementary color (as soon as a pure color is lightened or darkened, it loses luminosity). Thus, we can place a pure-colored object against a background of the same color that has been dulled by being mixed.

Contrasting Quantity

Contrasting quantity allows us to determine the proportions of the colors with respect to each other. So, for instance, if we decide to place a yellow banana against a purple background (yellow and purple being complementary colors), we need to frame that so that the proportion between the two colors is identical to the proportion of luminosity between the colors. As a reference: yellow to orange is 1/4 to 3/4; red to green is 1/2 to 1/2; orange to blue is 1/3 to 2/3.

Simultaneous Contrast

The law of simultaneous color contrast, stated in 1839 by the chemist Michel-Eugène Chevreul, can be summarized as follows: "The tone of two ranges of color appears more different when we observe them in juxtaposition

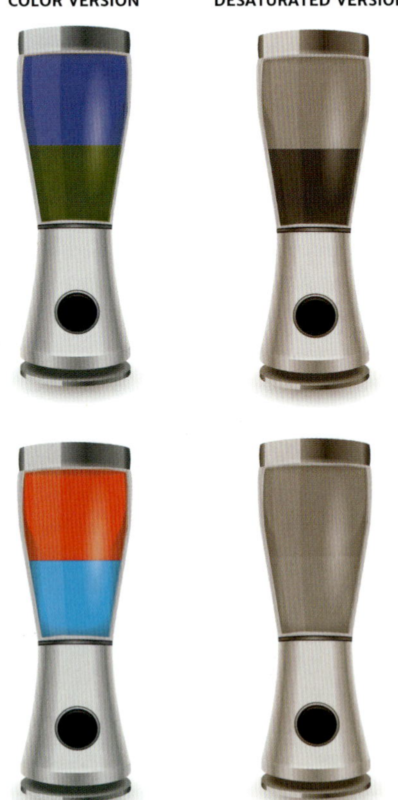

CHIAROSCURO CONTRAST

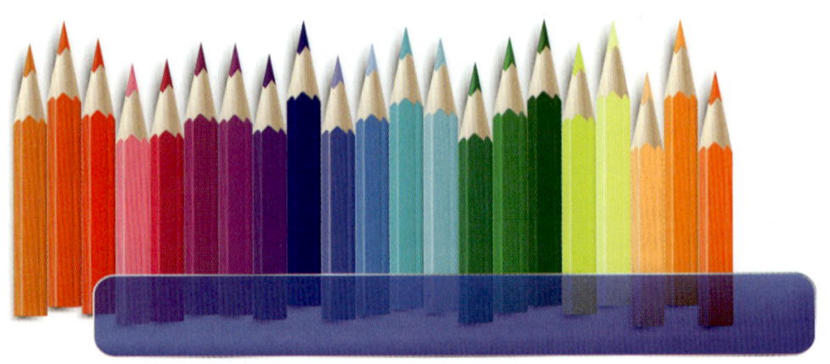

OVERLAPPING CONTRAST

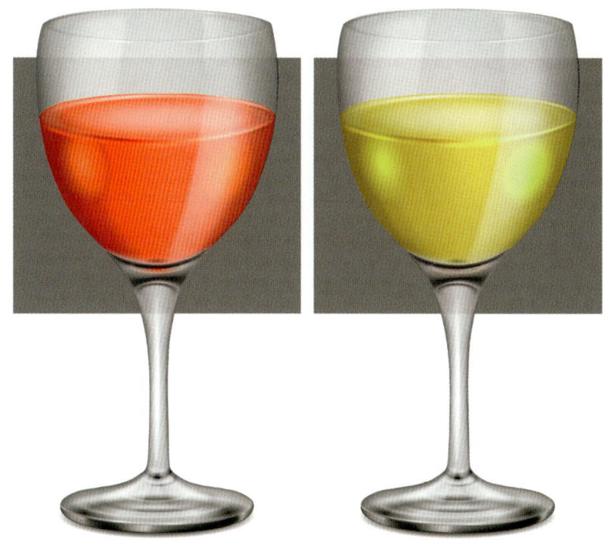

light background that we often produce in the studio, but it requires more work on the lighting in terms of contrasts to give more substance to the object.

For any given color, the eye requires its complementary color at the same time, and produces that color itself if it is absent. This phenomenon is more and more pronounced the longer we look at a color and the brighter it is.

The simultaneous effect can happen between a gray and a pure color, but it can also take place between two pure colors that are not totally complementary.

In the presence of a chiaroscuro contrast, the simultaneous effect is harder to obtain.

COLOR HARMONIES

To emphasize how important they are, I explain these rules of harmony in all my books; in product photography, they are absolutely crucial.

BASIC RULES OF HARMONY

Except for monochromes, where we can play with colors of identical or similar shades, we try to preserve similar saturation levels in the colors we put together, thus choosing either only pastel tones or only bright shades. Similarly, we always frame a shot so that there is a hierarchy in terms of the space occupied in the image by each of the colors presented.

TONE ON TONE (MONOCHROME)

It is quite easy to produce monochrome presentations of objects, and it has become very popular in the last few years (be careful not to confuse monochrome with black

than when we observe them separately, against a common neutral background."

This method was an important inspiration for the Impressionists, such as Vincent van Gogh. It works very well, especially with images against the kind of uniform

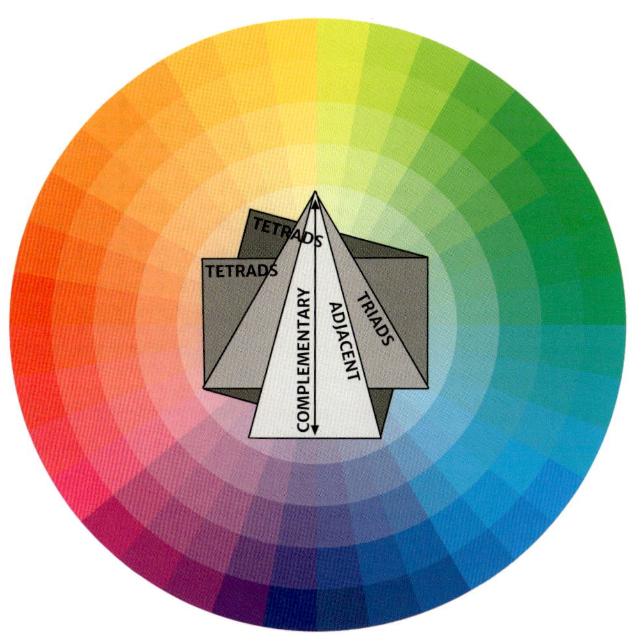

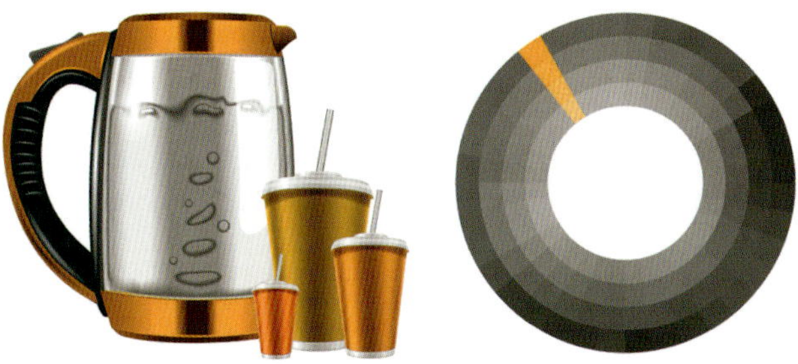

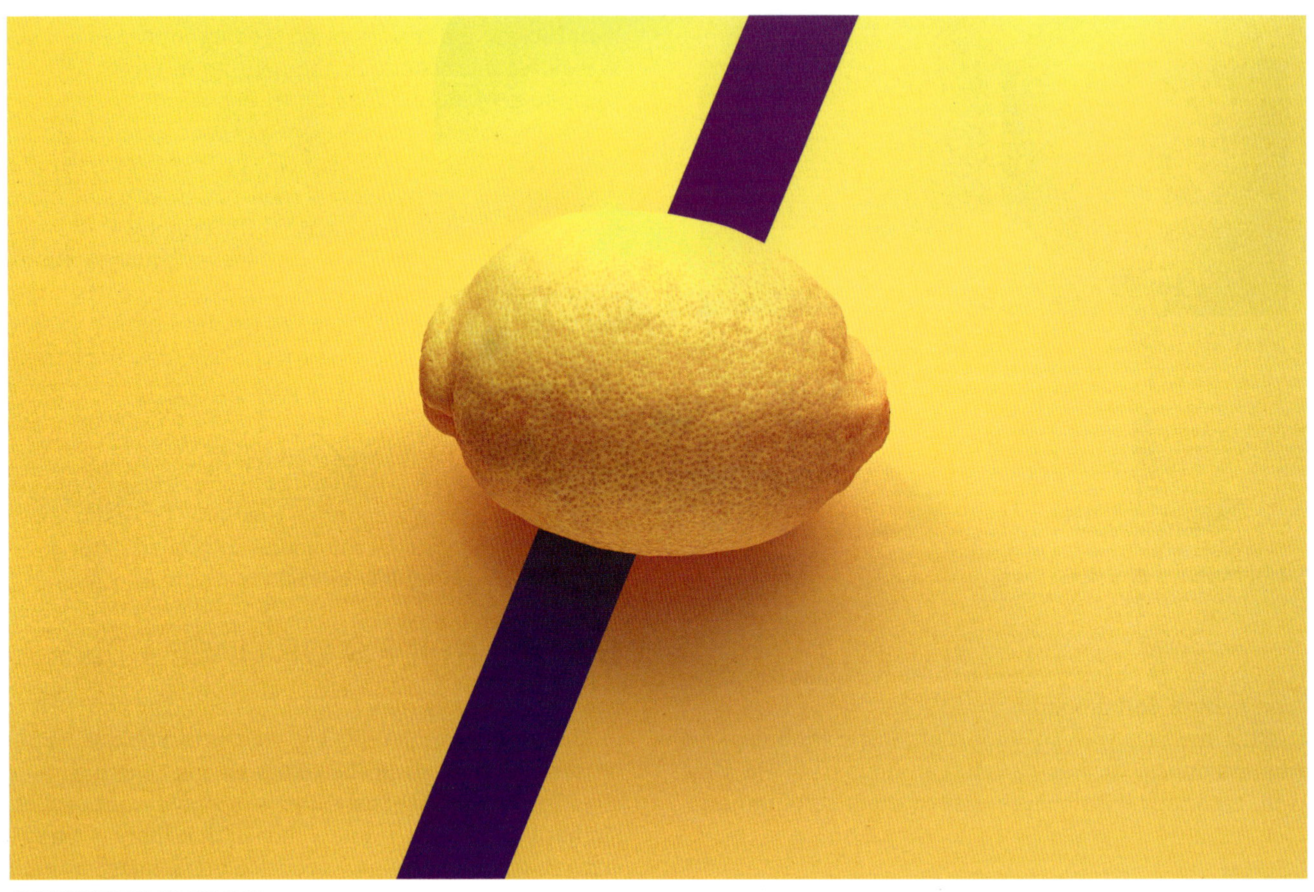

and white, which is just a monochrome of black). We observe the color of the object that is to be presented, and then we set it up in an environment (or simply against a background) that is made up of the same color tone— see the red peppers against a red background on page 255. The elements, or the backgrounds, have the same shade, but they are more or less luminous, or more or less saturated. This is the only case in which varying the saturations can work.

This kind of harmony is used for technological objects, perfume bottles, glassware, watches, gilded objects, luggage, and sometimes for eyeglasses.

Direct Harmony

The most common kind of color harmony is direct harmony. This involves bringing together in the same photograph a color and its opposite on the color wheel (its complementary color). In additive synthesis (the process of generating colors in photography), complementary colors are colors that, when mixed together, produce a neutral gray. The juxtaposition of two complementary colors creates a very visually interesting contrast effect: the colors support each other, and each one makes the other livelier and more intense.

This kind of harmony produces very pop-like visuals. It is often used for presenting plastic objects or objects meant for adolescents or young adults: T-shirts, sneakers, mugs, and other small everyday objects.

Adjacent Colors

Harmony using adjacent colors makes it possible to bring in a third color. To make this happen, we associate a color with the two colors that are on either side of its complementary color on the color wheel. This kind of harmony, which is still within the slipstream of direct harmony, gives us access to a wider, more elegant, and richer range of colors, but with less tension, because the third color acts as a buffer.

As with direct harmony, harmony using adjacent colors makes it possible to create warm or cold atmospheres (since there is always at least one warm shade and one cold one), which present an increase in subtlety, even though this involves shades that can seem very distant from each other.

This kind of harmony can be found in advertising for soft drinks, beers, household products, low-end cosmetics, and food industry products.

Colors in a Triad

Triad color harmony also involves three colors, but these three are all equidistant from each other on the color wheel. This produces a slightly more pronounced, higher-contrast result than harmony using adjacent colors.

Triad color harmony is often used in pop culture and generates a powerful contrast among the different shades, while ensuring that the warmest color will predominate. Thus, this arrangement only works well if the product has a warm color—otherwise, the environment or the accessories will end up providing the visual focus.

This kind of harmony is generally used for institutional advertising aimed at young people, such as fast food, desserts, or summery snacks.

Colors in a Tetrad

Tetrad color harmony involves four colors that are equidistant from each other on the color wheel. It is actually a conjunction of two pairs of complementary colors. Comprising two warm colors and two cold colors, this kind of harmony allows us to construct very colorful and very lively images, with radical contrasts, and it evokes the colors of childhood. It can be used for toys, candy, and pop accessories.

Monochromes

Monochrome harmony is made up of a set of colors that are very close to each other on the color wheel. This kind of harmony is very similar to tone-on-tone harmony, but it involves more colors, giving the shot greater visual depth. There are variations in how wide or narrow the range of colors is: it could be red / reddish-orange / orange, for example, or just reddish-orange / orange.

Monochrome composition is pleasant and discreet. It is often used for perfume, cosmetics, alcohol, and, in particular, luxury eyeglasses.

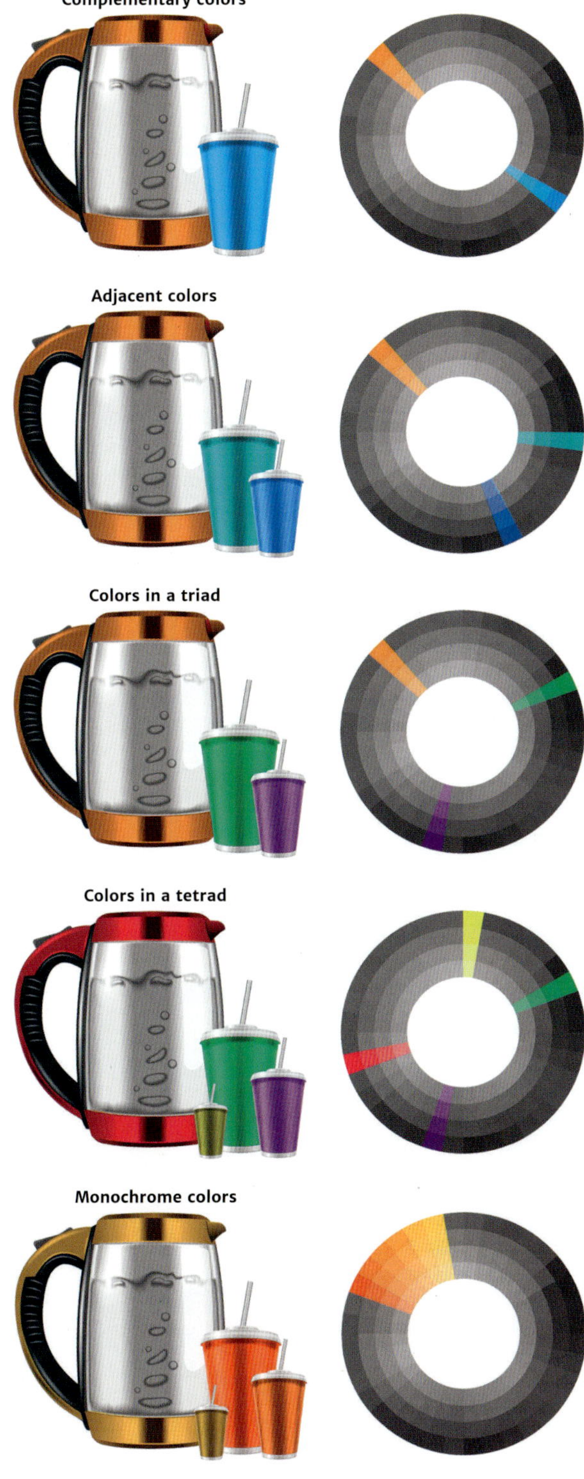

STAGING

For a better understanding of the composition methods detailed in the previous section, I thought it would be a good idea to show you how to use them by applying them, in turn, to the same type of objects.

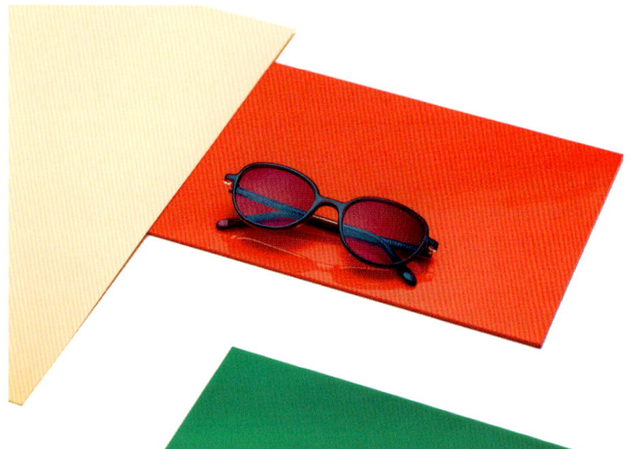

CONTRASTING SHAPES

I took advantage of the production of a catalog for a manufacturer of eyeglass frames to illustrate how objects can easily be put into context.

Object and Shape

To stage a pair of very rounded eyeglasses with black frames, in this first example, it was simple to choose a shape that was fundamentally different and to play with straight lines. I therefore used small 8 1/2 x 11-inch sheets of plexiglass, colored in complementary colors (red and green), and cream as a supporting color. The frames could have been positioned in several other places: straddling the cream-colored sheet and the red one; between the red and green sheets; or within the same axis and between the cream-colored and green sheets, perpendicular to the red one.

Object and Direction

For the second pair frames, in gold metal with leopard temple tips, I opted for a chiaroscuro contrast and an arrangement based on contrasting directions. The gold asserts itself nicely against the teal blue, creating a lovely and very elegant contrast. Positioned diagonally, the frames stand out perfectly from the blue sheet.

Object and Texture

To make a contrast with the soft and very feminine look of the rounded, black-and-gold third pair of frames, I wanted to play with a rough look and diagonal lines. I chose a supporting surface of red sand (a color that produces a nice proximity with the gold), raked with a parquet putty knife. To keep it in harmony with the other photos, I retained an overall rectangular look, using the sand on the sheet of black plexiglass.

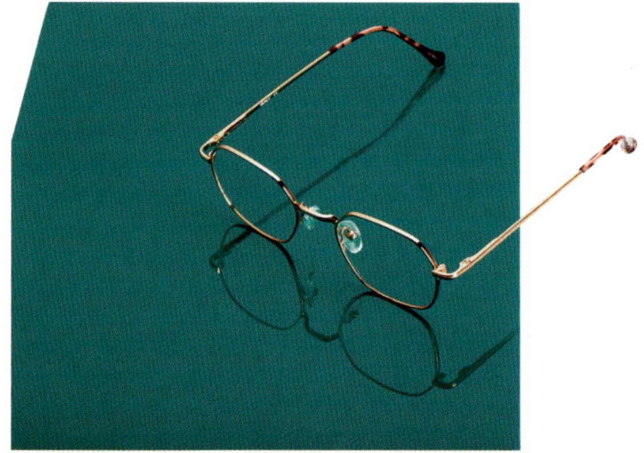

CONTRASTING DIRECTIONS

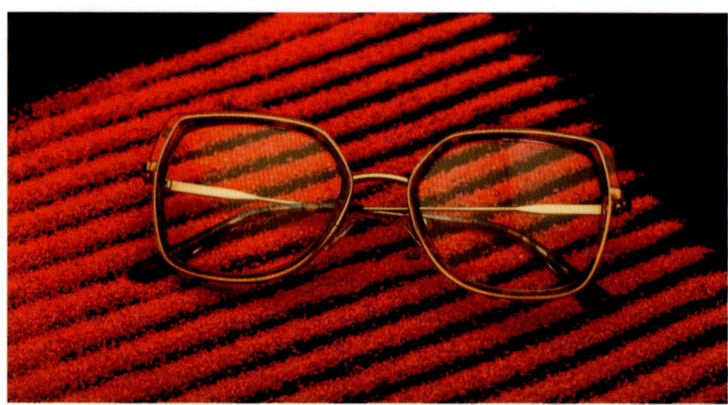

CONTRASTING TEXTURES

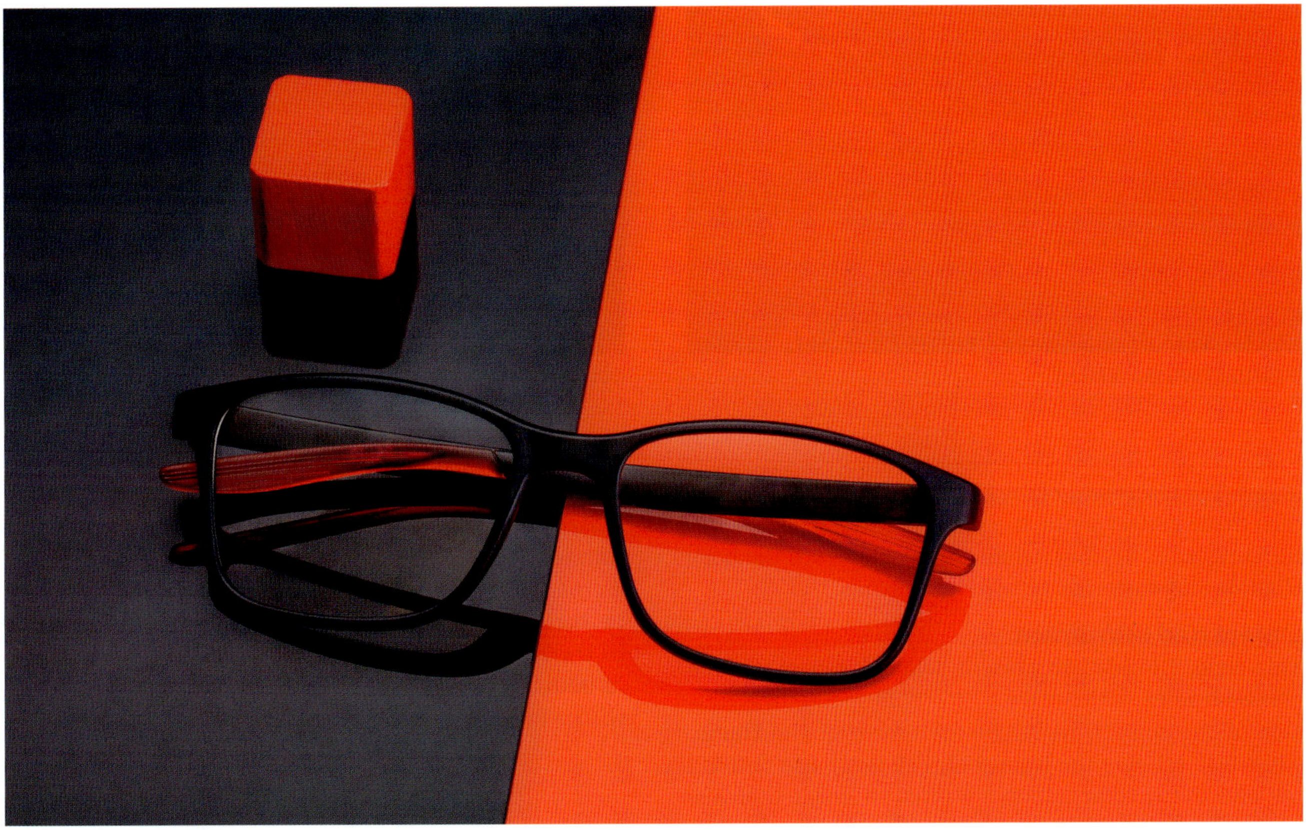

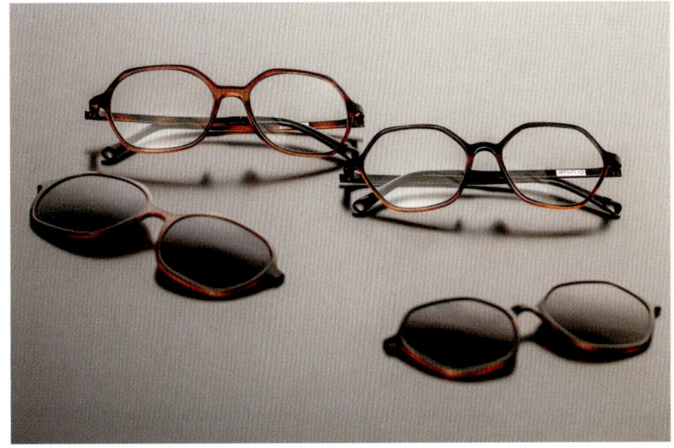

CONTRASTING COLORS

Object and Color

The next pair of frames was black and red, but more masculine and less rounded. The easiest thing was to pick up the same color code, placing the temples so that they stood out well against each of the two sheets, arranged slightly on a diagonal to add dynamism. I also added a small red cube on the black sheet to slightly unbalance the effect.

Object and Plane

To present these prescription glasses that turn into polarized sunglasses, there were a number of possible staging setups I could have imagined. But because I needed to show two variations of the frames, adding accessories or colors would have made the image hard to decipher. I therefore chose to present the two frames and the clip-on sunglasses on a sheet of gray plexiglass, backlit at a slight angle for a gradual transition to half-light. This kind of lighting also produces a nice gradient on the sunglass

CONTRASTING PLANES

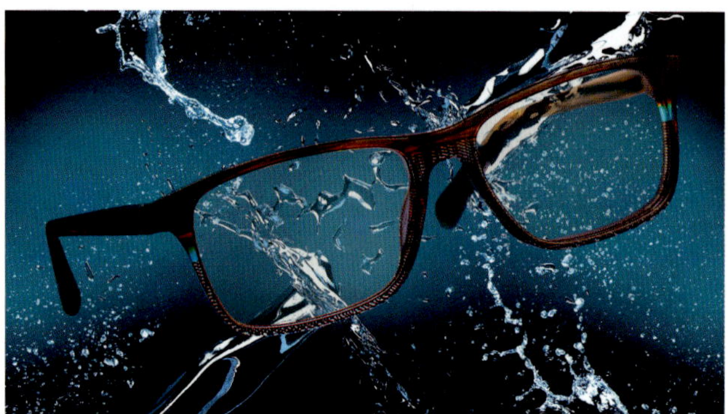

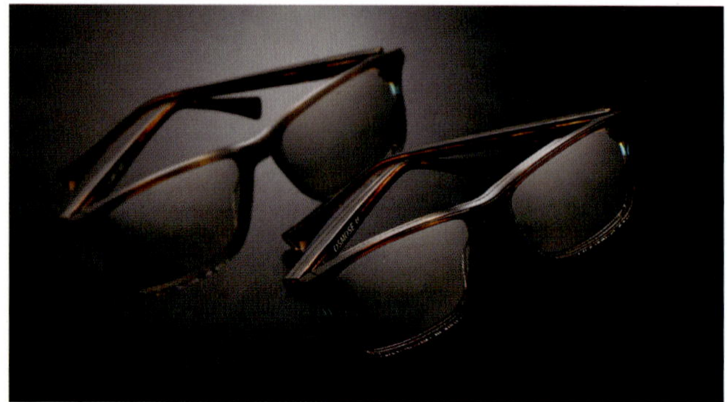

lenses. The placement of the objects in contrasting planes then made perfect sense: the prescription glasses behind, the sunglasses in front, while also playing with the horizontals and diagonals to add dynamism.

Object and Movement

This time, I needed to present some brown masculine glasses frames, which have a little blue spot on the outside of the rim. To highlight the brown of the frame, while also echoing the little spot, I chose to use nothing but blue in my composition. I wanted an image that was relatively dark, but dynamic. We placed the camera on a tripod, suspended the frames over a plastic dish with nylon fishing line, and hung a piece of translucent paper behind the arrangement. We installed a flash equipped with a Spot Small Profoto with an M-shaped gobo and a blue gel behind the translucent paper. Then we sprayed water from below, while releasing the camera shutter with a remote control.

The image shown above is a composite consisting of the first shot without the water spray (so there would not be any little drops on the lenses) and the two other shots with splashes.

Object and Sharpness

The next task was to show a relatively massive-looking pair of glasses with green flakes, emphasizing their masculinity. It felt natural to choose a dark background, with a burst of light to attract the eye to the image and a slightly graduated reflection on the glass. To better show the frames in perspective, and to create a contrast in sharpness on them, I placed a second pair of the same glasses behind the first pair and used a shallow depth of field.

Object and Repetition

Finally, my client wanted us to present many different frames together. Even though it isn't new, the repetition method, playing on a diagonal effect that was put forward by the Dutch photographer Edwin Westhoff, seemed to fit the bill perfectly. I set up the frames on a light table, lit both from below and from a showerhead angle above, with a large 60-inch octabox.

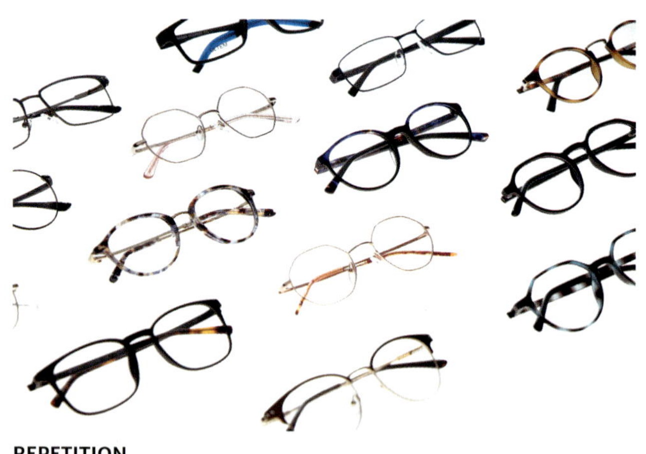

ARTISTIC VISIONS

We do not just photograph objects for commercial or advertising purposes; we can also repurpose them to create poetic or playful images.

Far removed from the traditional representation of objects to elicit desire and provoke a purchase, many artists, including the Spaniard Chema Madoz and the American Brock Davis, present objects that have been repurposed from their original function in amusing and creative compositions.

Working creatively with objects and accessories is an excellent activity for photographers specializing in product photography: it gives you new ideas, opens up new perspectives, and allows you to discover new ways of doing things. And because it has nothing to do with any commercial obligations, it turns into a privileged moment of photographic pleasure and joy.

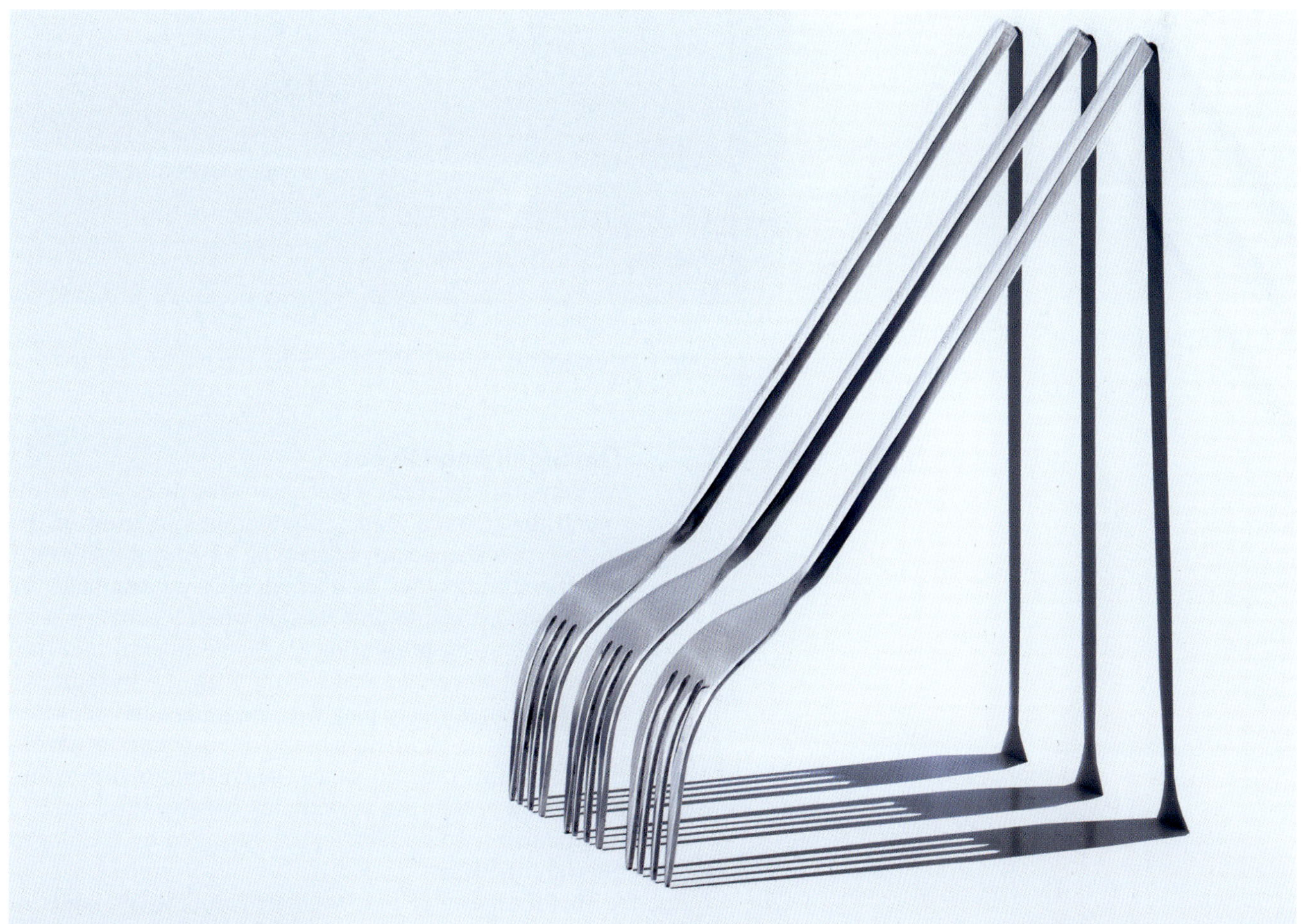

THREE FORKS PLACED AT A 45° ANGLE AGAINST A SHEET OF WHITE CARDBOARD, LIT WITH AN OPTICAL SHAPER

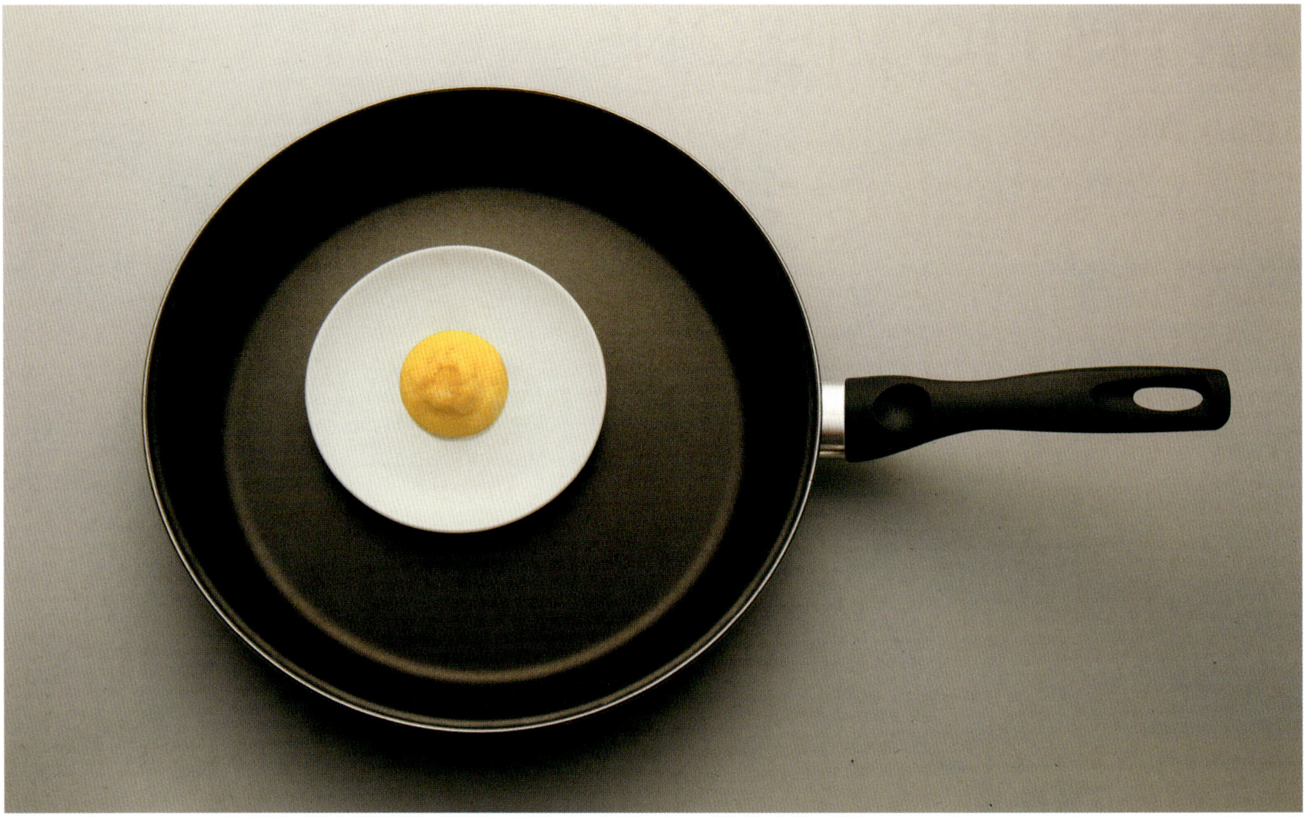

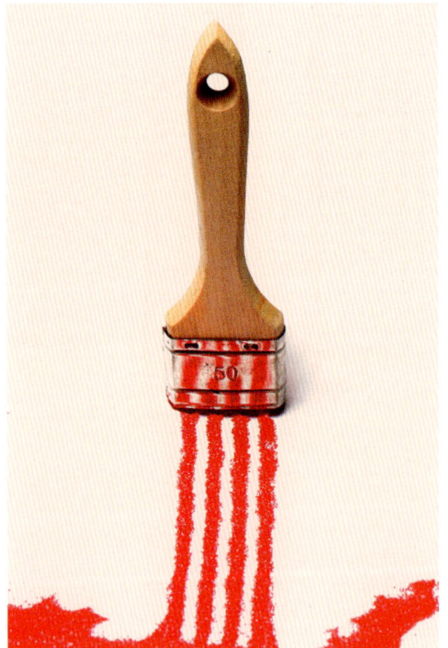

⌃ A frying pan, a saucer, and half of a lemon.

« Red sand raked with a putty knife, and a brush with its bristles cut off.

The Signifying Object

We can start with the object for what it is: the burnt match that Chema Madoz photographs in front of the knot of a wooden board, suggesting a flame, doesn't represent anything other than a match. Or we can make the object suggest something else, as when Madoz evokes a thermometer by presenting the same match, laid flat, framed by two vertical scales from 0° to 40°. In short, we can allow ourselves to play with meanings and alienated usages, like the McIlhenny brand in 2019 with its advertisements for Tabasco sauce, suggesting a fire extinguisher by presenting the famous bottle with a hose, a thermometer, and a handle, accompanied by the slogan "Beware the Heat."

In this spirit of play we can combine all kinds of objects in our compositions, making sure that our visual cues allow the viewer to quickly grasp the joke. The photo of the "fried egg" above would not be that interesting if it wasn't obvious that it was fake.

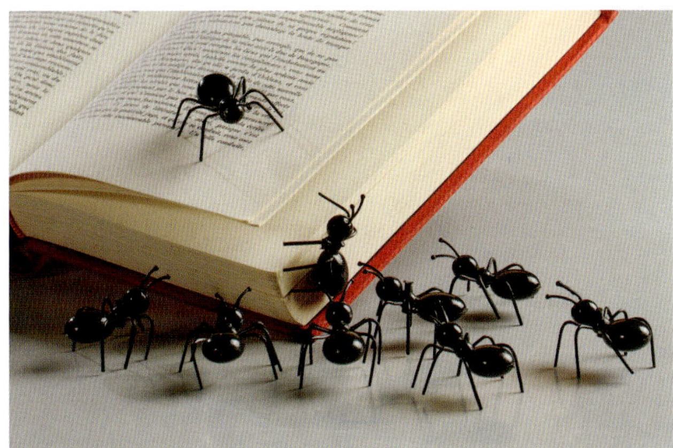

You can also play with the absurd by transforming objects, as in Jacques Carelman's catalog of unfindable objects, with his famous kangaroo rifle (a rifle with a wavy barrel) or his bathtub with a door. Or you can work with retouching. The Californian Randy Lewis likes to mix objects with living creatures: a rolled-up garden hose with a snake's head, a cabbage with a sheep's head, an umbrella whose handle is the neck of a swan. There is an infinite number of ways to play with creating burlesque compositions.

Shape, Volume, Color

More generally, the starting point for every creative project is a reflection on the object's shape, color, and volume. Let's take the photos presented on the next page for our examples.

1. Start with the Tabasco bottle: We need a vermilion red background, of the same Pantone color as the sauce. Because it is spicy, we look for hot peppers in the same color. That provides a preliminary image.
2. Take away the bottle and just keep the hot peppers. Take a second shot.
3. Add a second sheet of a nearby color—here, an orangish-yellow. Reorganize the peppers so that the cayenne pepper sticks out onto the yellow sheet. Third image.
4. Take away the peppers, keep only the yellow sheet, and find an object of the same color: a yellow lemon.
5. Take away the lemon and substitute the cayenne pepper.

Each photo works, and has its own aesthetic interest, and they can also all work together.

This is the procedure we follow now whenever we want to produce a creative project: we start with one idea and, step by step, change one or more elements, playing with the shape, angle of view, light, appearances and meanings, and mixing genres, as in the photo below—where a cable with a jack plug is rolled up on a fork, as if it were spaghetti.

A good way to avoid lighting problems is to always start with the lighting rules that apply to the object based on its shape and the condition of its surface, and then deduce what accessories will be compatible. For the fork below, which produces direct reflection, the choice of a cable that generates only diffuse reflections was a way to avoid the risk of problematic lighting on one of the two elements.

Once you have assimilated the laws of optics and their use based on the typology of objects, a whole world of possibilities will open up to you.

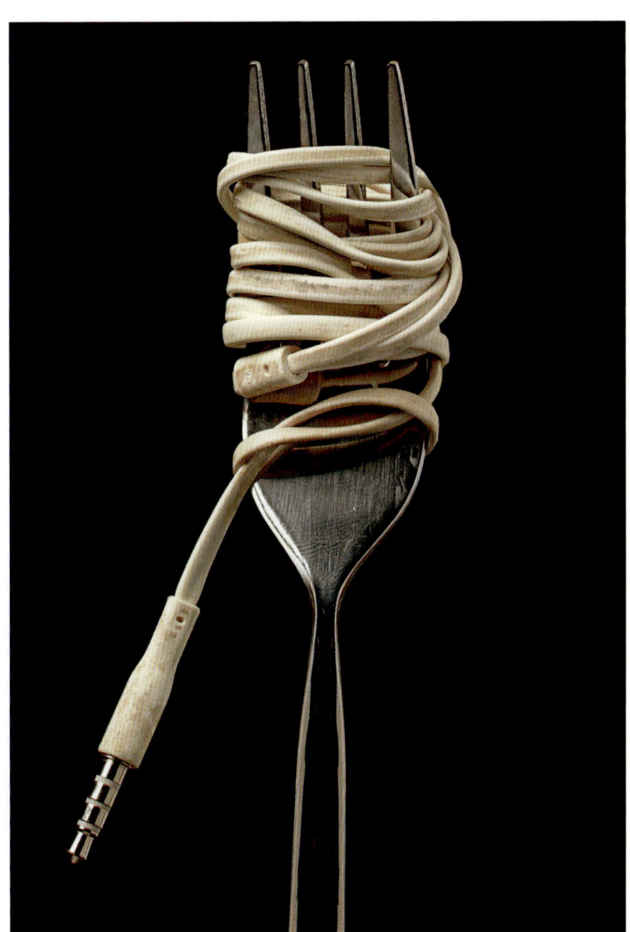

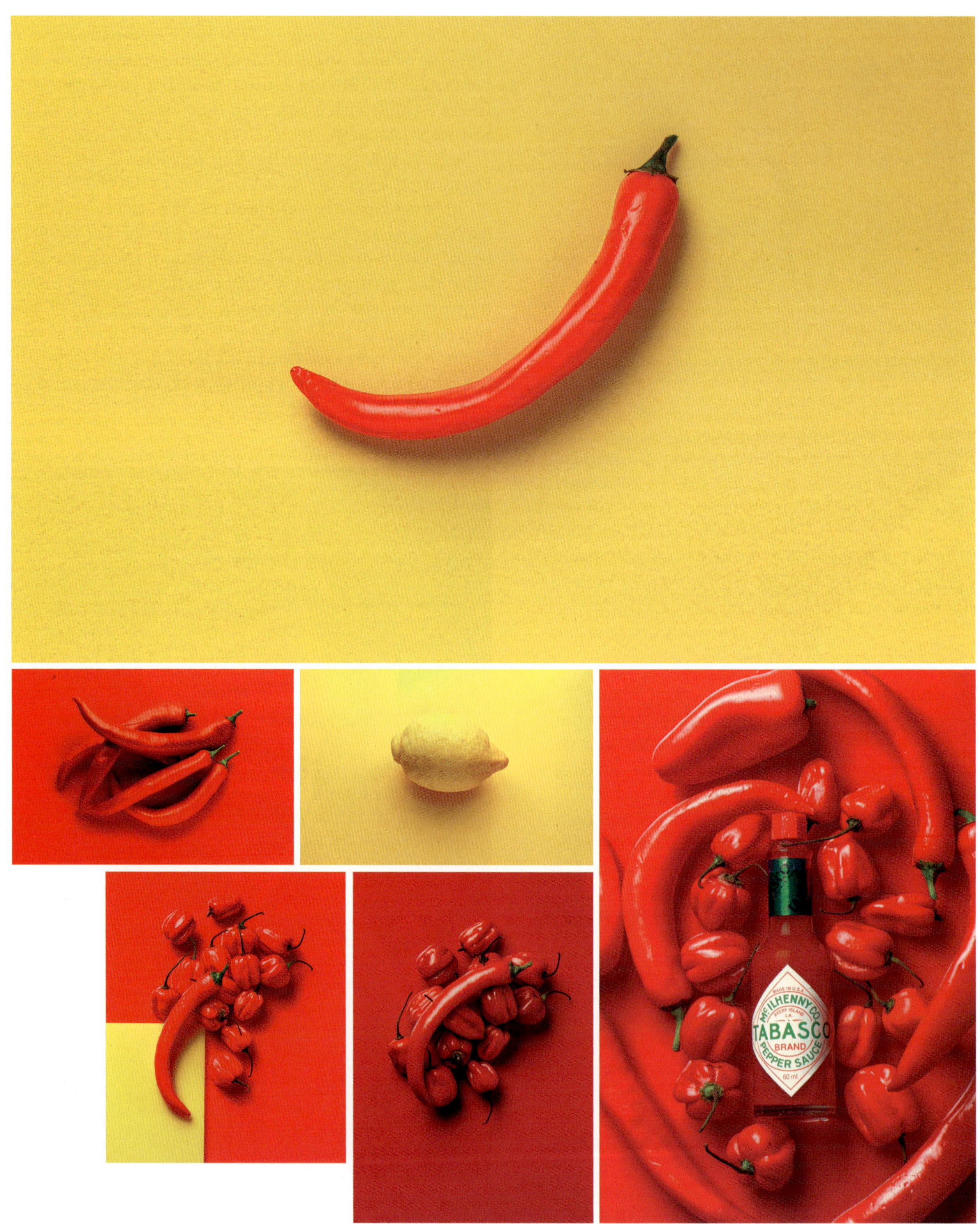

NO OBJECT IS PERFECT

Scratches, irregularities in glass, faulty molding, rough spots due to poor polishing, incorrectly positioned or torn labels, air bubbles—there is always some kind of defect that will require post-production work.

In my entire career, I have never seen an object that did not have at least one defect: a scratch, dust embedded in the glass, imperfect molding, an irregularity in the glass, etc. Even though I am always careful to spare myself the work of post-production editing by using appropriate lighting and properly preparing the objects, it is clear that in product photography, we will always end up having to edit our photos to some extent. Indeed, we often photograph from very close-up, using macro lenses: the tiniest little fault, invisible from a greater distance, therefore looks enormous. And yet, if everything has been prepared according the rules, the editing will be very quick. Let's take a brief look at some photographic tips that can help you avoid (or limit) your post-production editing.

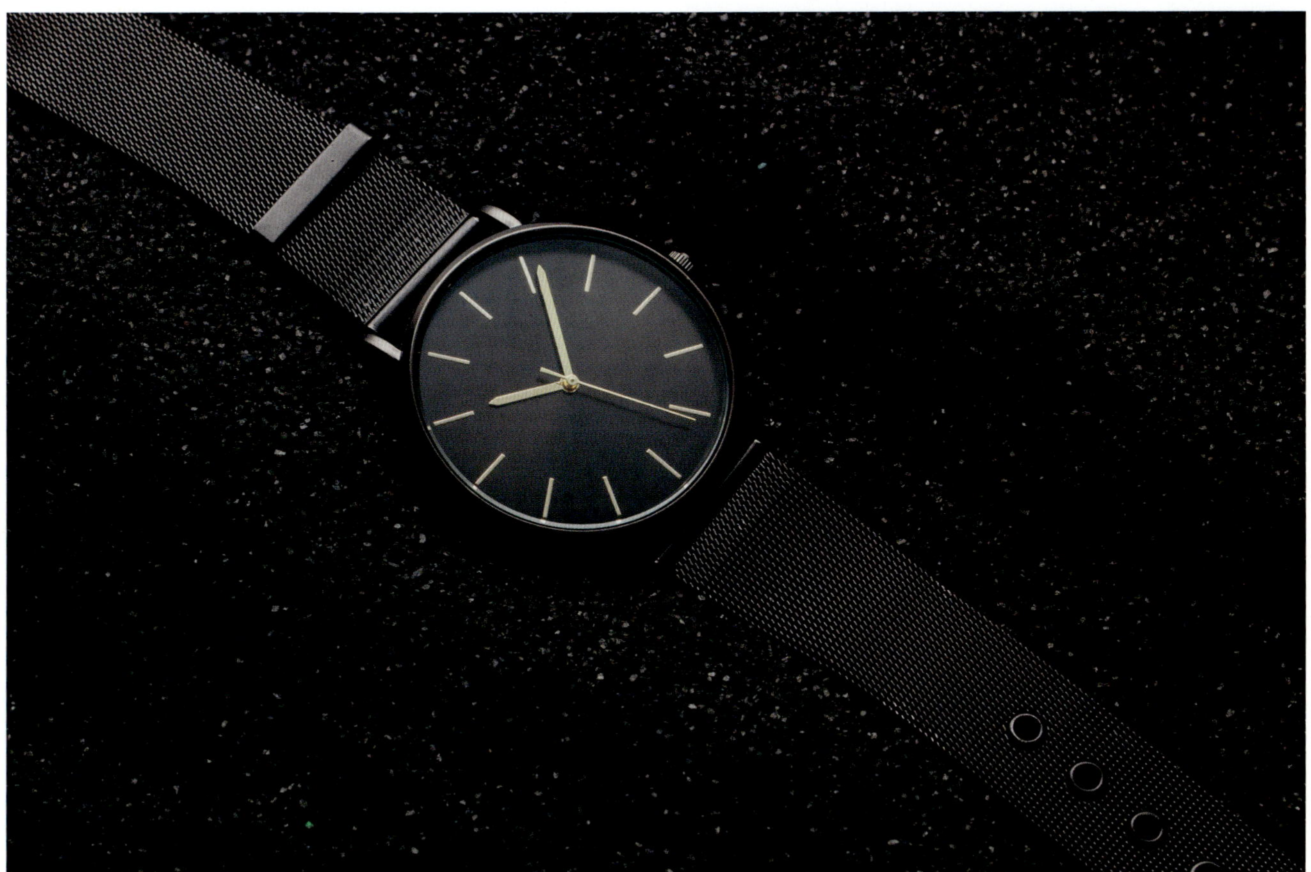

⌃ Even though it is new, the wristband of this watch has tiny scratches on it that look like little white dots, mainly in the lower part. Unfortunately, they are very visible under the lighting that is appropriate for the dial.

Overly Dark Bottle Labels

Many brands of wine and spirits use black or very dark labels, making it impossible to light the bottles using the method suggested on page 124. There are two possible solutions that will allow the label to show up better:

- lighting it with direct light using a diffuse source, then imbedding it into the composite photo in post-production;
- positioning a light source at the lowest point, or increasing the intensity of that source if it is already in position (the cylindrical shape of the bottle means that it is possible to light it along this axis without running the risk of reflections).

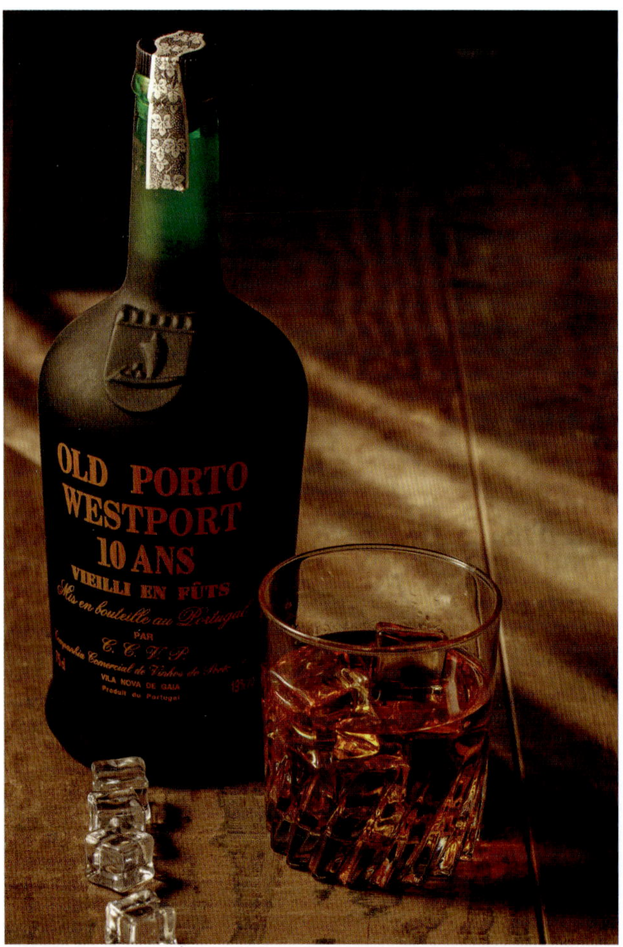

⌃ The certification label on the cork was torn when it arrived from the supplier. The only option was to remove it before taking the final photograph.

Rear Labels Shining Through

A recurring issue with transparent or translucent liquids (white wine or rosé, whiskey, rum, etc.) is that the rear label (a label placed on the back side of the bottle, often including legal information and a description of the product) poses two major problems: it is very visible because of the backlighting required by this kind of object, and it prevents the light from being well-distributed over the liquid. The only solution is to remove the label: soapy water will usually do the trick, but any traces of glue can be removed using a degreasing solvent. Make sure to carefully protect the front label while you are doing all of this.

Glossy Labels

Some products, mainly cosmetics and body-care products, have a laminated or varnished label meant to protect it from drops of water, which are present in bathrooms where these items are often used. But such labels will, of course, produce direct reflections as soon as they are lit within their family of angles. Here, too, there are a few simple solutions to the problem:

- lighting behind a large, rounded diffuser, as in the method suggested for lighting cylinders (pages 95 and 145): a reflection will appear, but it will be so even and uniform that it will not offend the eye, and it can also be reduced using the Dehaze tools in either Lightroom or Capture One;
- making a composite photo, as in the case of an overly dark wine bottle label.

In all cases, it is crucial to avoid direct frontal lighting. However, because most labels for cosmetics and body-care products are light-colored, a simple reflector redirecting the lateral lights will usually be enough.

Embossed Labels

Embossed labels, which are often gilded or silver-plated, and frequently varnished as well, are common in the world of wine and spirits and have caused problems for generations of photographers, starting with the question, "How can I show that the label is embossed and gilded without contradiciting the appropriate lighting for the bottle?"

To tell the truth, there is no satisfactory solution within the shoot itself. If you light the bottle according to the rules (backlighting and lateral lights), the embossing will not be visible; if you place a light source on one side of the label, the inscription will be white, gold, and then black (see the bottle of Japanese whiskey on the page opposite). We find the same problem when we want to light gold, but here, the rounded shape makes things even more complicated.

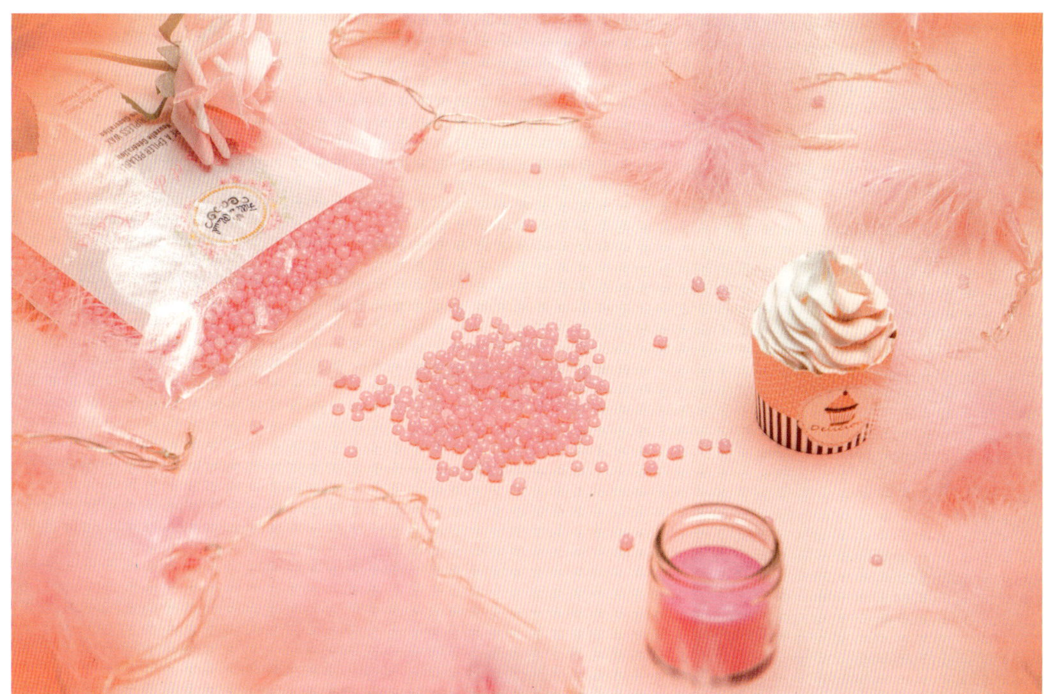

The best solution is to use the same rounded diffuser that we use for cylinders. It produces a harmonious lighting, well suited to gold, with a gradual passage through the family of angles: the gold has its usual familiar appearance, shifting from yellow to a very dark yellow, with a very soft direct reflection on the most exposed part. But while this arrangement is perfect for the embossing and the label, it is less so for the bottle, especially if we want to create bands of visible reflections along the edges, as is usual for wine. In this case, we could consider a composite photo, with one shot for the label and the other for the rest of the bottle.

Textures and Contradiction

When labels are made out of textured paper (as in the image at left), the lighting that is required for the bottle disproportionately accentuates these material effects, to the point where they are more prominent than the words. In this case, there is no other solution than to use heavily diffused frontal lighting behind a rounded diffuser, and to create a composite photo.

Dust

Dust settles everywhere. It is easy enough to get rid of using a compressed-air canister for the brief moment when the shot is being taken, but sometimes there is also dust present within the object; for instance, under the glass of the watch dial seen on the next page. In such cases, we then have to open the back of the case, take out the movement retainer (which is usually white), delicately remove the winding stem by pressing with the

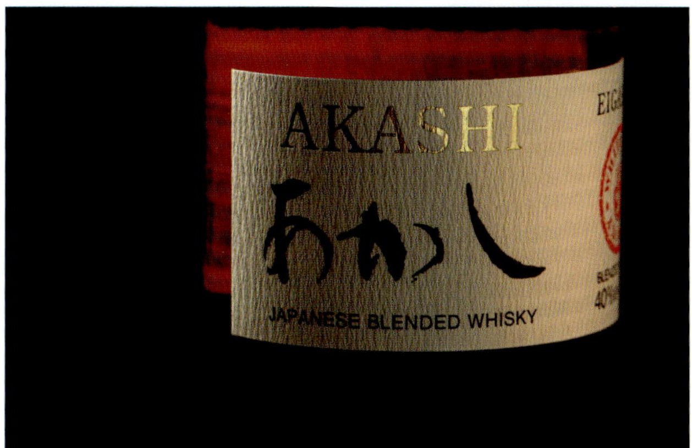

⌃ The brand mark, in gilded embossing, and the texture of the paper are incompatible with the lighting that is expected for the bottle; you will have to choose.

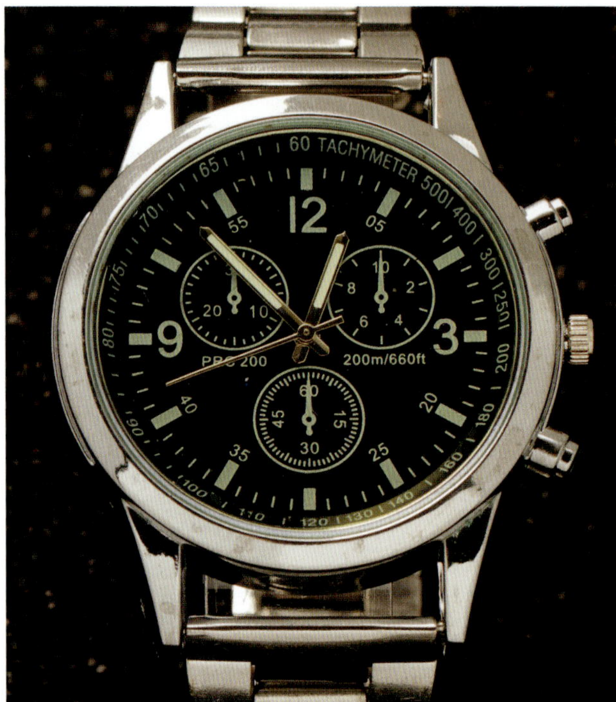

⌃ This watch, even though it is new and just removed from its protective packaging, includes dust under the glass and a little bit of oxidation on the case and the bezel.

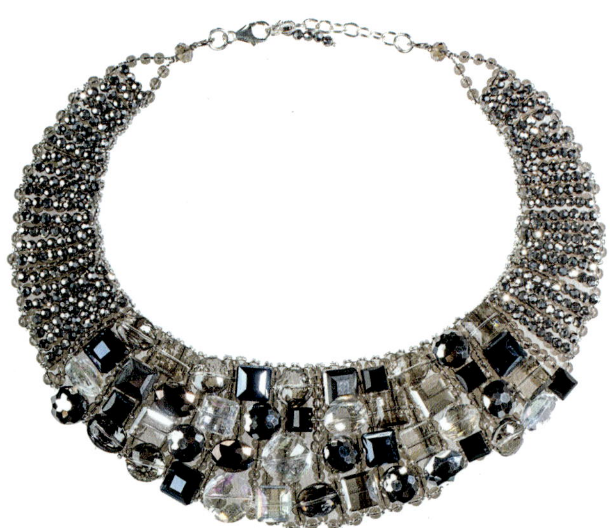

⌃ Example of poor lighting (with insufficiently diffused light sources) of a necklace with a large number of reflective surfaces. A diffuser should have been put in place, and the intensity of the lighting should have been lowered.

tip of a pair of small pliers, and then dust the dial and the glass with a blower, before reassembling it all again. This kind of operation is essential when the dial includes repetitive textures, raised areas, or glossy spots. If it is a simple dial and/or there is not much dust, a little bit of detail editing in Photoshop will be sufficient.

Defects in the Glass

Recurring problems in glassware, especially for bottles and flasks produced industrially in large quantities, include cords (cord-shaped dark areas), refractive index gradients (iridescent flat spots that appear in the light), and all kinds of inclusions (air bubbles, chips, blisters). All of these defects diminish the visual effect of good lighting, which we expect to show regular transparencies and reflections. There is nothing to be done about these in terms of lighting or shooting; these defects can only be eliminated with digital editing.

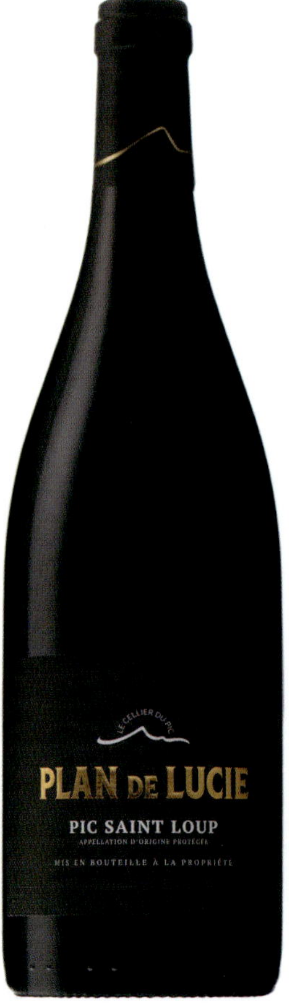

« On this bottle of wine, the seam of the glass is located at the very edge of where we have positioned the reflection. If the reflection had been wider, or more offset to the left of the image, the seam would have been very visible.

Bottle Seams

All wine bottles have a seam, which can be seen up and down the entire length of the bottle: this is the trace of the mold that was used to form the glass. When the bottle is filled, sealed, and labeled, the seam can be found just about anywhere: it's totally random. If it is on the back side, it is often not visible because the backlighting leaves it in shadow. The problem becomes thornier when it is on one of the edges. Because the lighting that is meant to produce the reflective bands hits the edge of the bottle at a grazing angle, it makes the seam very visible. It can be eliminated in several different ways:

- by placing the reflective band in front of or behind the seam (previous image);
- by not lighting the side where the seam is visible;
- by producing a composite photo of the label and the bottle rotated on its axis, so that the seam is positioned behind the bottle.

Scratches and Dents

Scratches and dents are common defects in plastic or thin metal objects, like aluminum cans, and they become highly visible under grazing side light. This can be remedied by placing a very diffuse light source from the front. This will often be enough, but more pronounced defects are only fixable in post-production.

Molding Defects

As with seams in bottles, we often find all kinds of molding defects, especially in objects made of injection-molded plastic. These include shrinkage (shallow bumps or depressions on the surface of a molded item), warping (a part designed with walls that are too thin for the target material, which is thus at high risk of crinkling), burrs along the weld lines, and swirling (a color defect linked to the use of several dyes). These problems can be addressed in two ways:

- using very diffuse, non-grazing lighting, for shape defects (shrinkage, warpage, and burrs)—a frontal lighting arrangement behind a diffusing fabric is usually the solution;
- with post-production editing when the issue is swirling or other discolorations of the plastic (unless you can turn the object to show a side that is free of the issue).

Creases in Soft Plastic

This is a recurring problem on all the soft plastic surfaces of bags and protective wraps. The material is not completely

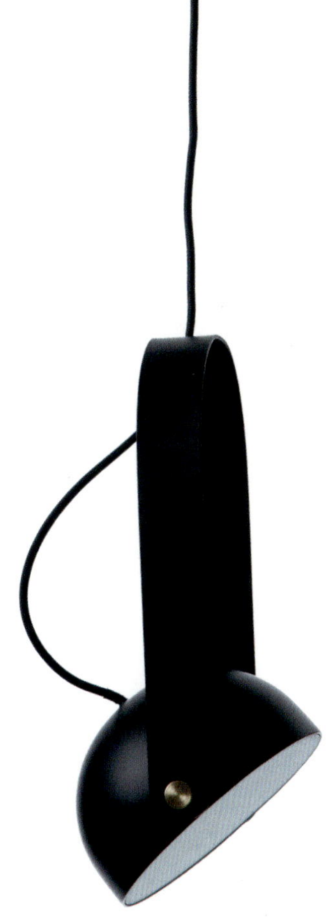

⌃ This suspension cable has just been unwound, making little waves appear. As with some other plastics, it needs to be placed under slight tension, near a heat source.

smooth, and it produces erratic, omnipresent direct reflections, which can only be dealt with in two ways:

- making the bag partially disappear so that all we see of it is its contents and the label (this is of course only possible if the plastic is transparent)—we use rim lighting for this;
- flattening and smoothing the surface of the plastic by placing the object near a heat source (not more than 100°F) and stretching it using gaffer tape or tongs. This is the most judicious solution. Let the heat act for about twenty minutes, then let the object cool back down. At room temperature, the reflections will still be present, but there will be fewer of them and they will be more pleasing to the eye. We do the same thing for electric cables.

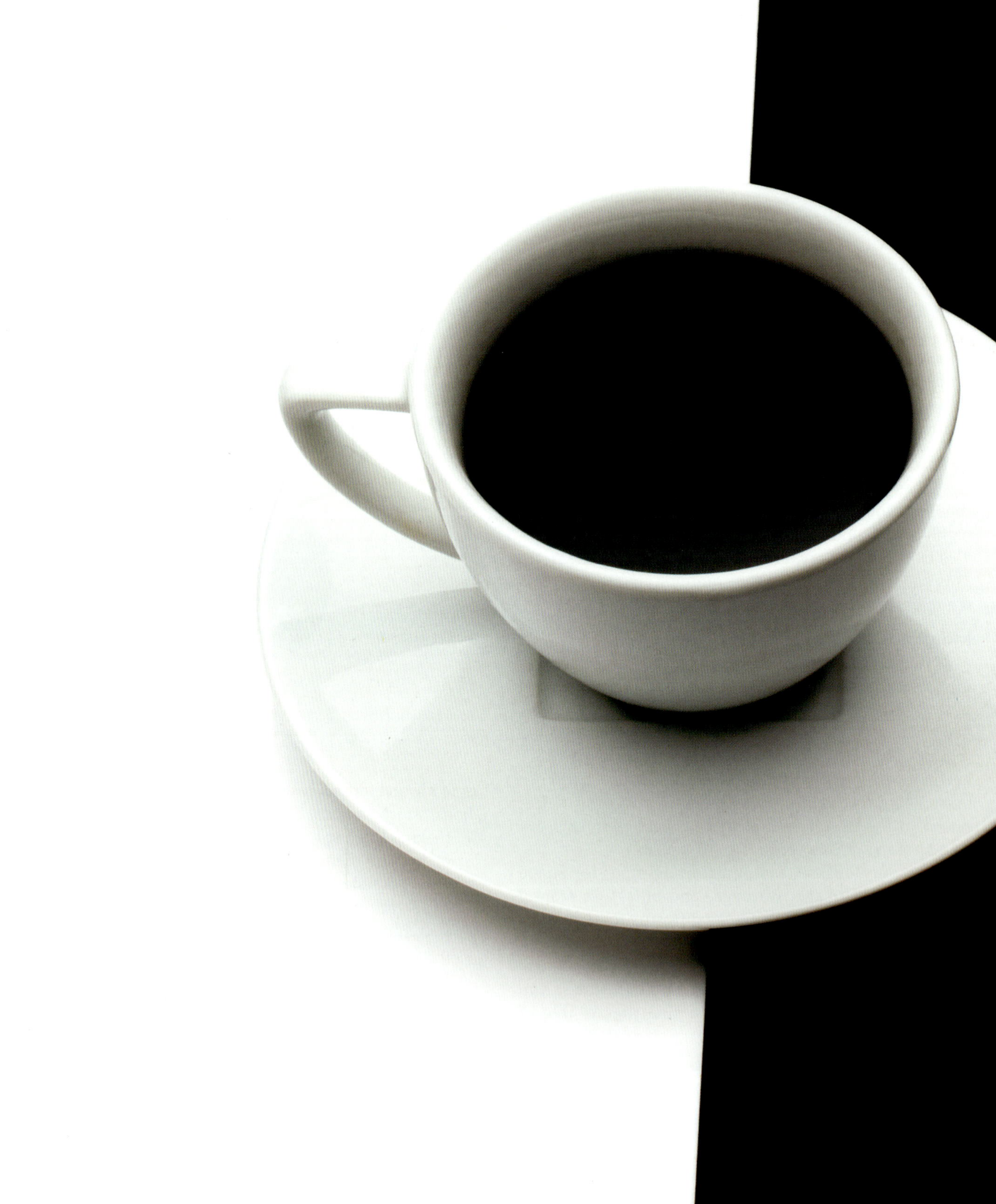

IMAGE ANALYSES AND LIGHTING SETUPS

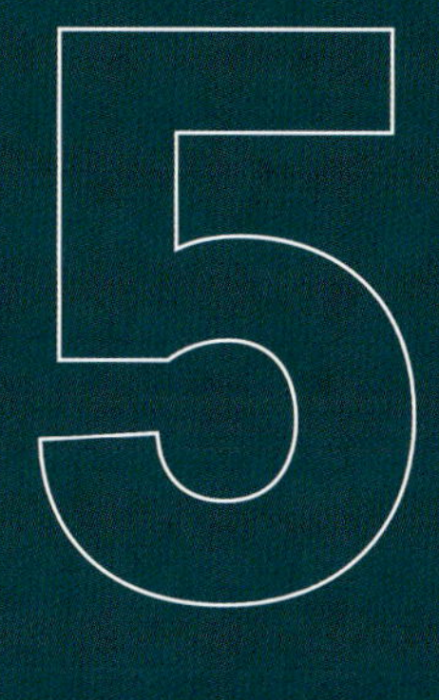

» **228**   Practical Exercises

» **230**   A Study of Rings

» **232**   Sneakers Rock

» **234**   Fragrance Diffuser

» **236**   Flying Teacup

» **238**   Waffles with Honey

» **240**   Blue Orange

» **242**   Into Orbit

» **244**   Floating Perfume

» **246**   Ants with Watch

» **248**   Old Port

» **250**   Freshness and Fruit

» **252**   Jar of Moisturizing Cream with Splashes

» **254**   Red Chili Peppers

» **256**   A Watch and its Impact

» **258**   Anatomy of a Hamburger

» **260**   Exploding Whiskey

» **262**   Upside-Down Levitation

PRACTICAL EXERCISES

We will now study seventeen different photographs of objects to understand how to obtain a variety of results, in terms of both lighting and art direction.

The photographs presented in this final chapter were taken with flashes; flashes are more comfortable to work with, but we could have obtained similar results with continuous lights, as long as the shapers were identical. What matters is the quality of the lights as well as the harmony between the strength of the light sources and the settings of the camera.

Harmony

The most important thing in lighting an object is not so much the actual power of the light sources as it is their proportions to each other. What is the use of knowing that one flash is measured at f/5.6 and another one at f/11 if no one explains that what makes the shot interesting is precisely the fact that the second source is projecting a light that is 2 EV more powerful than the first one? Understanding the mechanics of a lighting arrangement will allow you to make much more progress than if you were just following the steps of a recipe, of which there are large numbers to be found, without an understanding of its deeper meaning.

Thus, I invite you, in the following exercises, to try to understand the harmonies that exist among the various sources, their respective roles, and the artistic goal that underlies each arrangement. It is by completely immersing yourself in this way of thinking about light that you will learn to truly master it. The range of photos shown here is, of course, subjective, but they cover a large number of the lighting situations that you might face in the course of your practice.

Concrete Applications

Rather than give you the actual measurements of each light source in the lighting plans for the photos on the following pages, I have chosen to indicate the proportions with respect to the camera settings, along these lines: "flash directed toward the back of the cup (+1.33 EV)." This makes it possible to apply these lighting scenarios to every kind of situation and every setting.

For every example, you will also find the distance, the type of shaper used, and the angle of placement of the light sources. These are crucial pieces of information

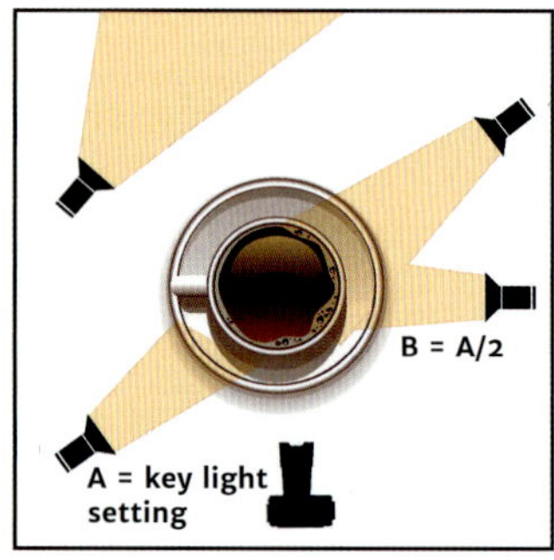

We begin by setting up the following harmony: B is half of A, C is twice A, and D is three times A—for example, a model illuminated in Rembrandt lighting against a perfectly white background, with a pronounced Hollywood hair light and a softened fill light. The idea is to transpose this setting by changing the type of lighting.

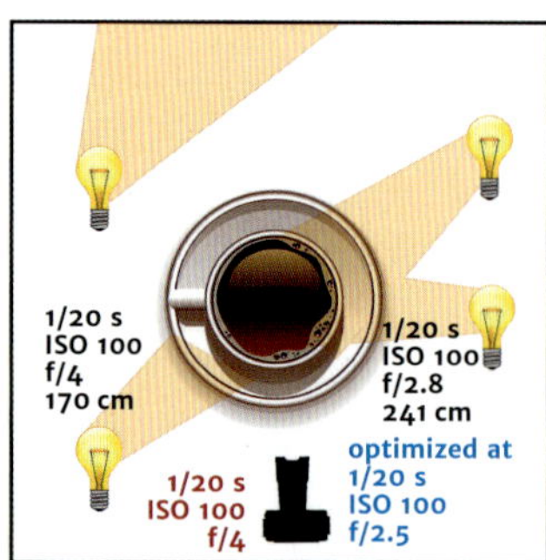

1. The measured strength of a bulb A, based on 1/20 s at ISO 100, is f/4. From that we can deduce that B = f/2.8, C = f/5.6, and D = f/8. Since we cannot vary their intensity, we will have to play with their distance by applying Newton's inverse square law, and adjust the camera while maintaining the same exposure time of 1/20 s.

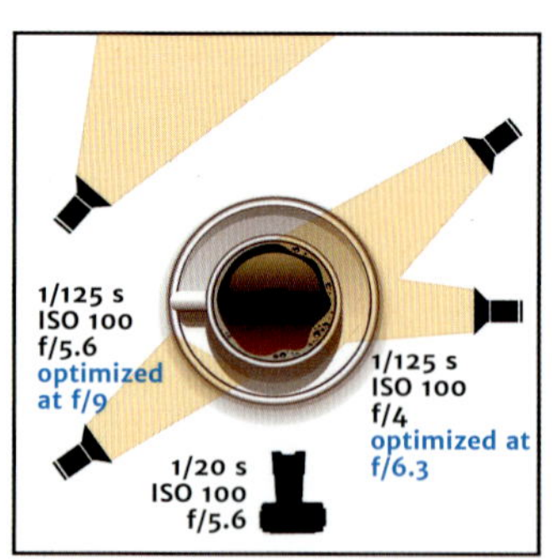

2. We're working with a flash. There are a few limitations on the strength, thus we choose the camera setting at the outset—for instance, on the basis of 1/125 s, ISO 100, f/5.6. We optimize the strength of the flashes while keeping the proportions defined by the beginning harmony, so as not to have to change the camera settings.

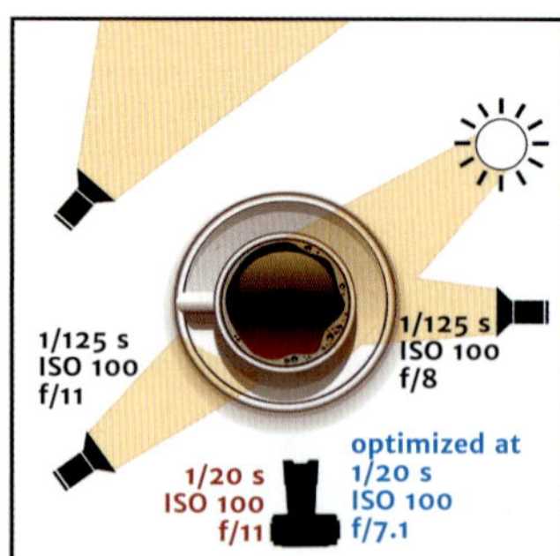

3. Here we're photographing in the sunlight. We have no choice: we have to start with its measurement and keep the same exposure time. We can optimize the camera settings (1/20 s, ISO 100, f/7.1) or change the flash to the exposure time proportions (which will also modify the apparent strength of the sun and make the calculation a little more complicated, but it is simple enough).

UNDERSTANDING AND APPLYING LIGHT STRENGTH HARMONICS

that will allow you to understand the placement of the light and shadows, and therefore the effects produced by the objects being lit. To say that a source is placed "at a showerhead angle" above the coffee cup is not at all useful if it isn't spelled out whether the light source is completely vertical above the subject or whether it is at a 30° angle with respect to the vertical. The specific angle changes everything: in the first case, we would obtain a direct reflection on the entire surface of the coffee, whereas in the second, the edge of the cup would create a visible reflection on the liquid.

Application

It is relatively easy to apply the harmonies (in other words, the balance between each of the sources and the camera setting) onto all of the lighting systems (see diagram on previous page). Of course, this will require a little bit of mental gymnastics, but it is easy to understand that you get the same exposure at f/4, ISO 100, 1/100 s as you do at f/5.6, ISO 200, 1/100 s, or at f/5.6, ISO 100, 1/50 s.

Practicing

I invite you to reproduce the shots on the following pages after gaining an understanding of the steps of placement, light quality and quantity, art direction, and color harmony. Also make sure to spend some time studying how the light is diffused on each of the objects that you will be shooting to determine what the best lighting is in each case. This is not about releasing the shutter: trust your eyes and learn to look.

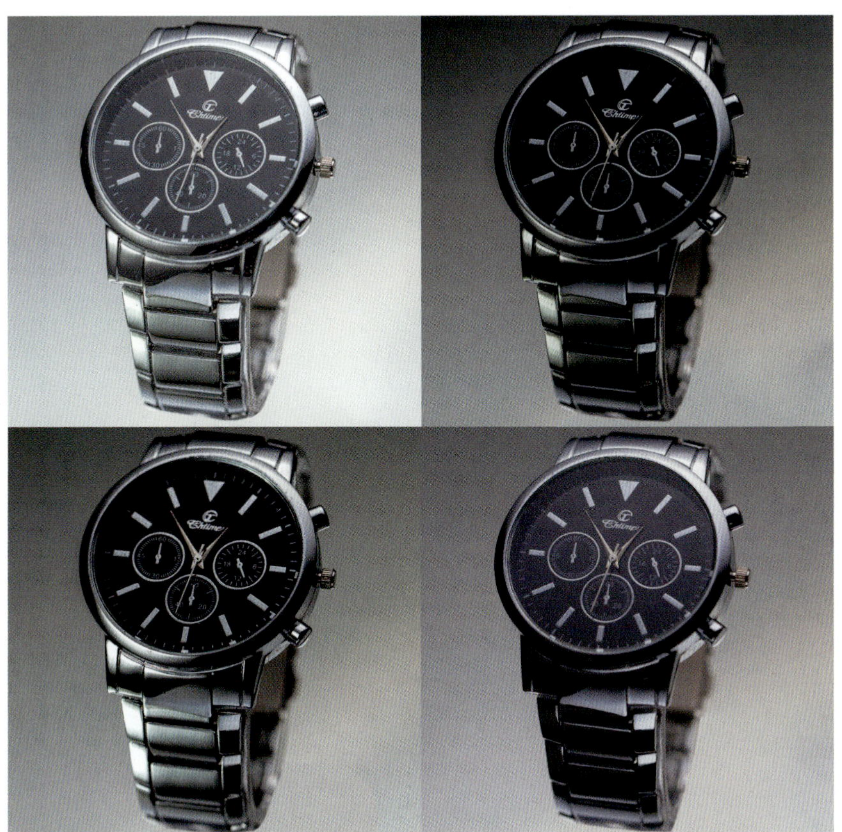

« Study involving several kinds of lighting on the same watch, with different diffusions and intensities.

A **STUDY** OF RINGS

Jewelry is probably one of the most difficult realms in product photography. The objects are small, which makes the lighting of their various parts complex and requires precision. This is why we often use very narrow light sources, like snoots, usually fitted with honeycombs.

Diffusion and Direction

The fact that most pieces of jewelry are rounded means that we need to use diffusers that are also rounded, in order for the lighting to faithfully follow the curves without jerkiness. In the lighting scheme I propose here, flash no. 1 is positioned very close to a rounded PMMA plexiglass diffuser, which is itself very close to the jewelry, so that the lighting of the interior of the large ring is smooth and even. It is easy to see what happens if the lighting is not diffused this way in the three small shots at the top of the next page.

We proceed the same way in lighting the diamonds on the small ring: they will not appear in all of their splendor unless we use a slightly lateralized lighting, whose flux is enlarged and pointed in directions compatible with the arrangement of the stones, so that they are all illuminated and produce little bursts of light. Here, too, we use a rounded diffuser. Finally, we place a snoot equipped with a honeycomb, using Paramount lighting, still behind a rounded diffuser, to light the outside of the two rings and cause reflections to appear on each of the ridges.

TECHNICAL DATA SHEET

Camera: Canon 5DS R
Lens: EF 100mm f/2.8L Macro IS USM
Focal distance: 100mm
Aperture: f/11
Speed: 1/160 s
Sensitivity: ISO 100

❶ **Flash:** Profoto D1 equipped with a snoot and a honeycomb, directed toward the interior of the ring through diffuser no. 5. Set to +1 EV.

❷ **Flash:** Profoto D1 equipped with a Spot Small directed toward the rear of the ring. Its flux is constricted by the barn doors (no. 8). Set to +0.8 EV.

❸ **Flash:** Profoto D1 equipped with a honeycomb, directed laterally toward the diamonds through diffuser no. 6. Set to +0.4 EV.

❹ **Flash:** Profoto D1 equipped with a snoot and honeycomb, directed toward the base of the ring through diffuser no. 7. Set to +1.33 EV.

❺, ❻, ❼ **Rounded diffusers**

❽ **Barn doors:** Two small black barn doors for directing the light of flash no. 2.

Staging

To accentuate the sense of these shapes and make the rings stand out from the black background (a sheet of Canson anthracite paper, because black is hard to light correctly), I placed a small optic shaper in backlight, with two small barn doors meant to create a rather thin ray of light between the objects.

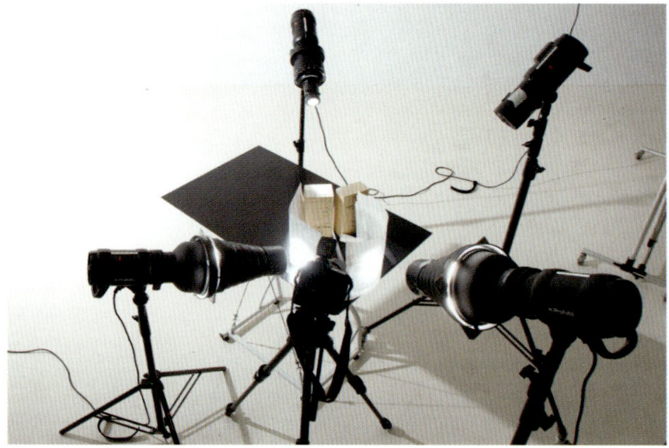

⌃ A behind-the-scenes view of the production of the shot on the following page.

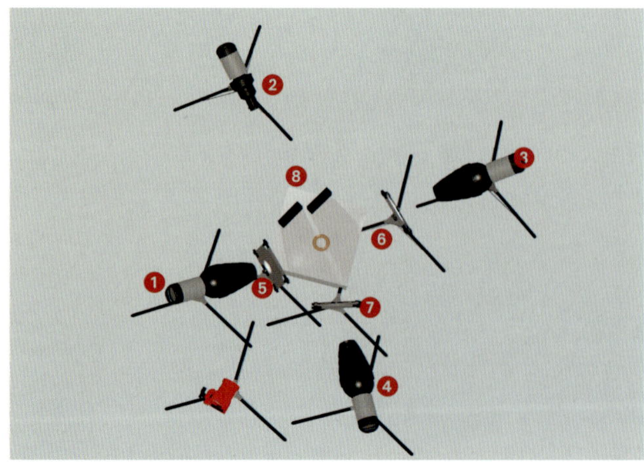

LIGHTING DIAGRAM

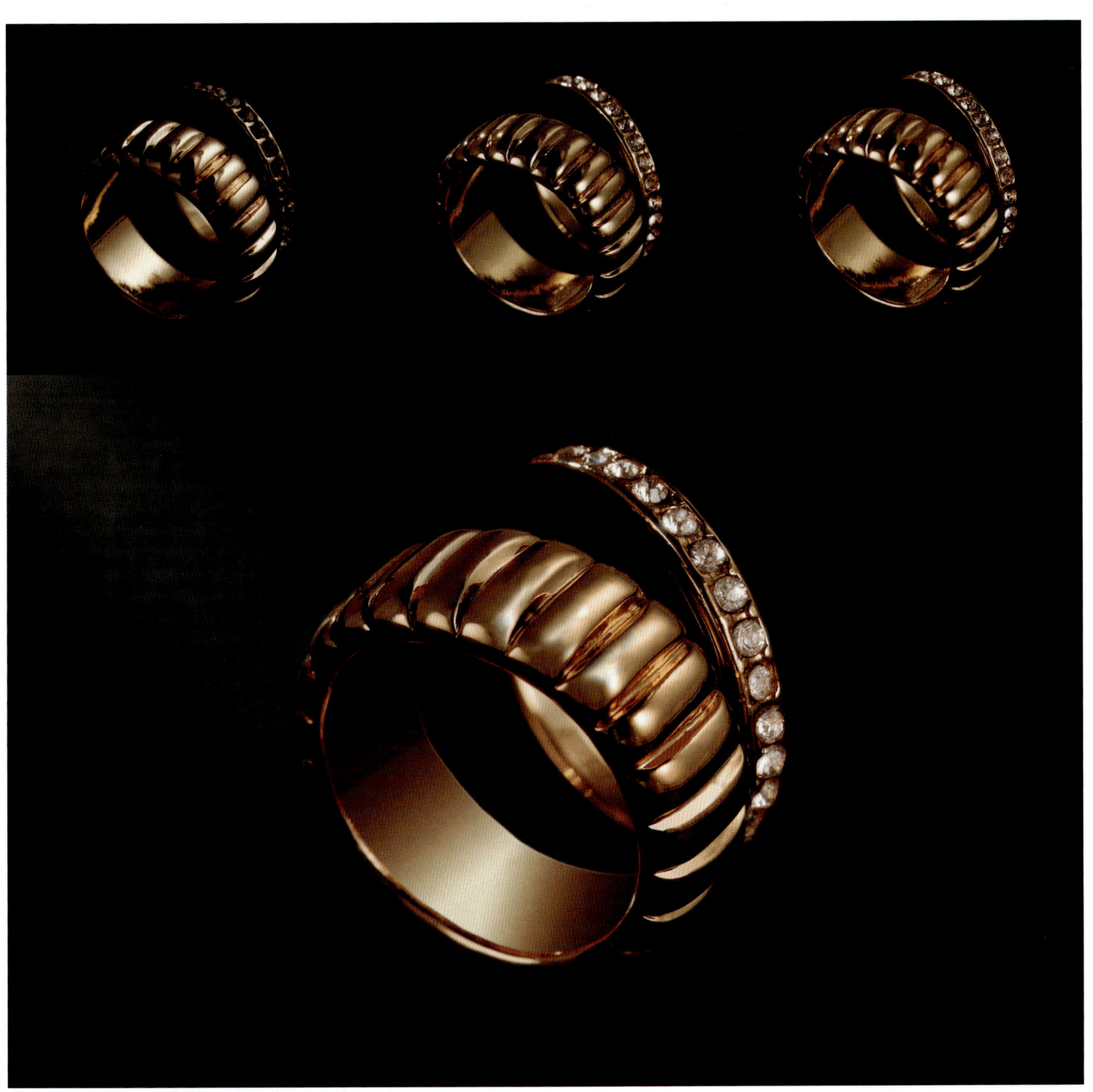

3 LIGHT SOURCES + 1 REFLECTOR
SNEAKERS ROCK

For this ad for a pair of sneakers, I wanted a somewhat vintage atmosphere. I therefore chose a black marble base that had been previously dirtied up with anthracite and mouse-gray paint, rubbed with a sponge. The goal was also to present the shoes the way they might be found at the foot of a teenager's bed, one shoe halfway on top of the other. Therefore, it was important to play with the lighting to create a dynamic scene, while also making a point of the sneakers' material and texture.

Implementation

The sneakers are first positioned on the prepared, and thoroughly dried, marble slab. A rim light (a flash equipped with a snoot, positioned high and directed down at an angle) is used to create a spot of rounded light around the shoes, also lighting the back of the shoes at the same time. This flash is set for optimized metering at +1.33 EV.

A second source, of the same kind as the first one, is placed laterally to simultaneously light the upper part of the shoes (including the laces), the sides, and, by reflection on reflector no. 4, the opposite side of the shoes.

The third source (flash no. 1) is placed in the front, angled at about 45°, to light the front of the shoes (especially the soles). A measurement of +0.3 EV is sufficient (the reflector also redirects some of the light of the other flashes).

Artistic Choice

In the vintage spirit, we wanted to bring out the sense of a shoe that had been worn, to use the lighting to avoid making the textile too smooth, but without that getting in the way of what we wanted to communicate. This is one of the roles of backlighting: hitting the edge of the sneakers at a grazing angle, it brings out the hollows and bumps of the fabric, which gives more substance to the final image.

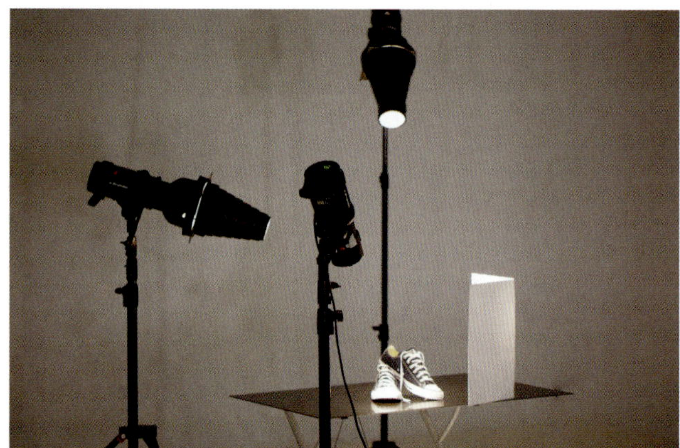

⌃ A behind-the-scenes view of the production of the shot on the following page.

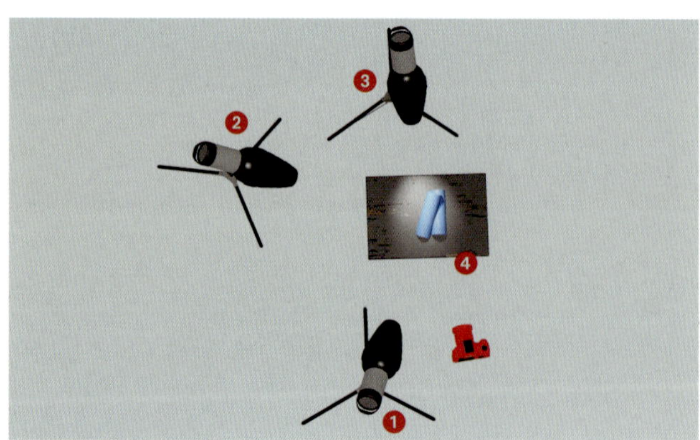

LIGHTING DIAGRAM

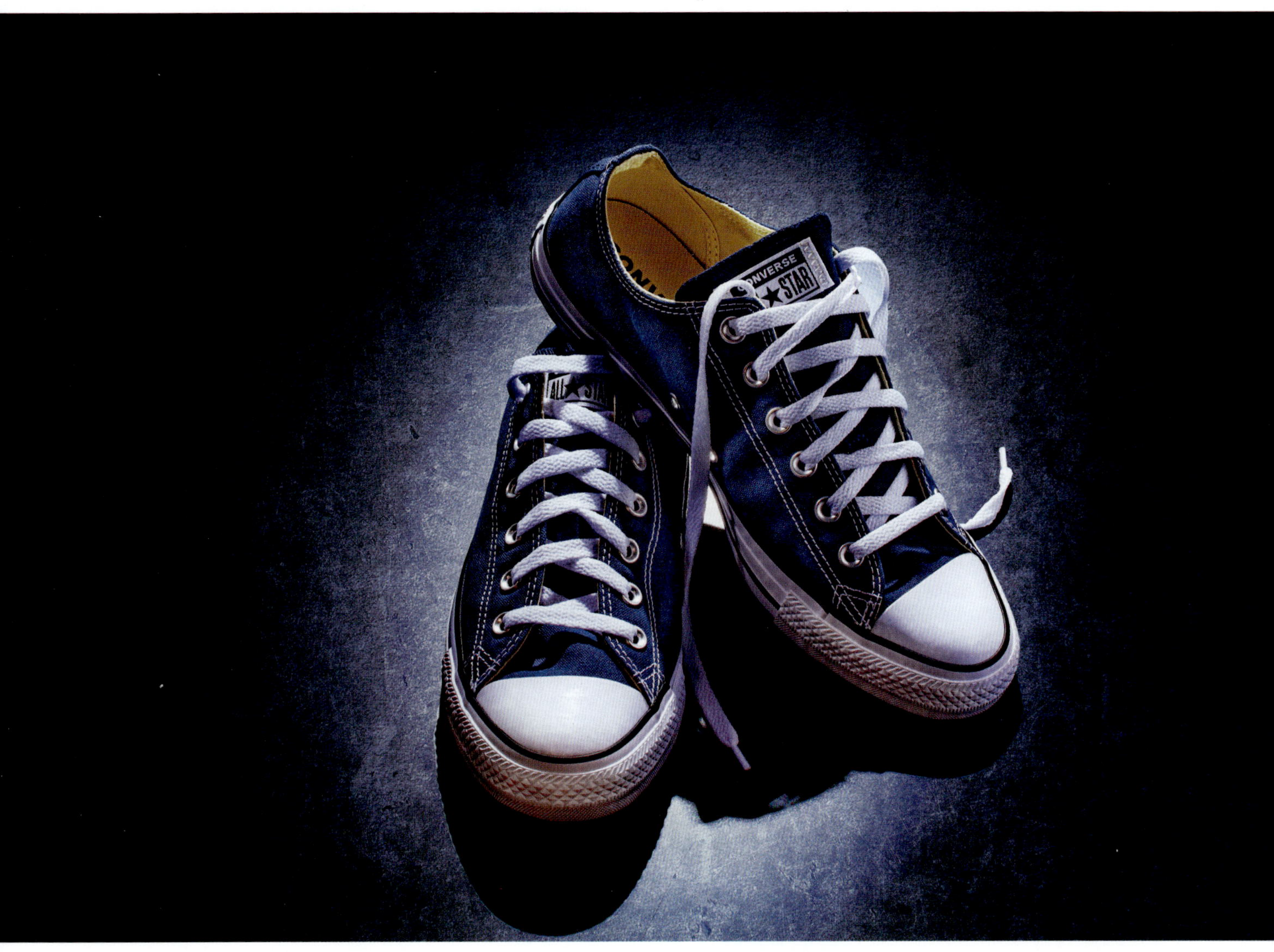

FRAGRANCE DIFFUSER

To present this home fragrance diffuser, we wanted to play with verticals. We had noticed that underneath a rear lateral lighting, the light refracted into a multitude of parallel vertical lines in the thick glass fragrance bottle, which worked well with the two stoppers and the cotton rod that we wanted to place horizontally, in counterpoint.

Setup and Reflected Light

A black metal base is placed underneath the bottle to create a dark foundation for the image—but the lighting will partially brighten this surface. The verticalities are accentuated by the glossy base, which shows the reflections of the flask and the stoppers. In terms of light, we have seen that we always need to light transparent glass bottles from behind, even more so if the liquid they contain is also transparent. But rather than proceeding with direct backlighting, we thought it would be fun here to light the background with reflection. Therefore, a reflector is placed behind the fragrance bottle and a light source is positioned on the ground, directed toward the reflector. The aim is for the interior of the bottle to be illuminated along with the background, with localized highlights.

A second source, equipped with a light box, is placed laterally, in a feathered position, to light the edge of the cylinder without creating any direct reflections, so that the metal label is nicely legible, with the rest of the light beam dying out against the reflector while brightening the background.

Camera: Canon EOS 5D MARK IV
Lens: EF 100mm f/2.8L Macro IS USM
Focal distance: 100mm
Aperture: f/6.3
Speed: 1/125 s
Sensitivity: ISO 100
❶ Flash: Profoto D1 equipped with a 24 x 36-inch light box, directed toward the edge of the family of angles of the bottle, in a feathered position. Set to +1.33 EV.
❷ Flash: Profoto D1 equipped with a zoom bowl, placed at on the ground and directed toward the reflector positioned behind the flask. Set to +0.1 EV.
❸ Reflector

Organization of the Objects

There were several possible scenarios for the organization of the four elements: centering the bottle or not; placing the stoppers in a stepped arrangement (what was finally chosen); or placing the small black stopper closer to the bottle. The cotton rod could also have been presented vertically, or even diagonally, but the arrangement that was finally adopted has the benefit of giving center stage to the most important object: the bottle.

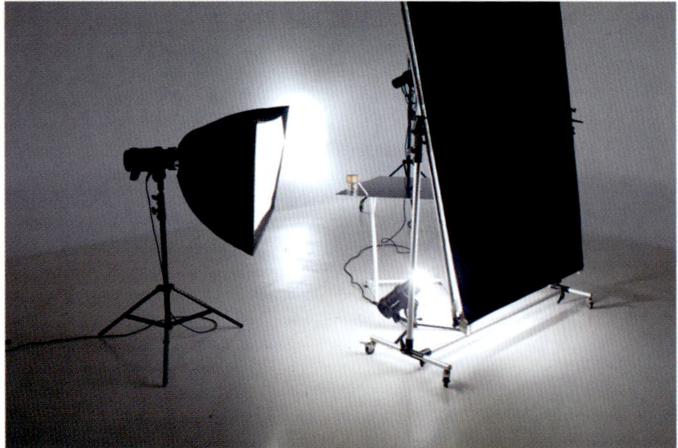

A behind-the-scenes view of the production of the shot on the following page.

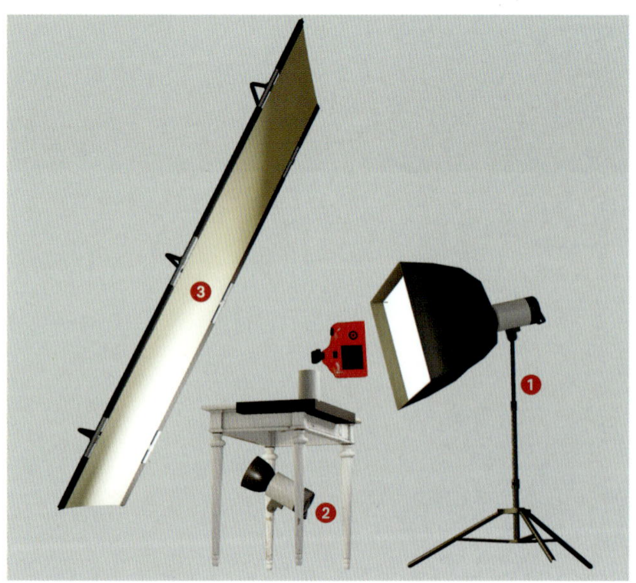

LIGHTING DIAGRAM

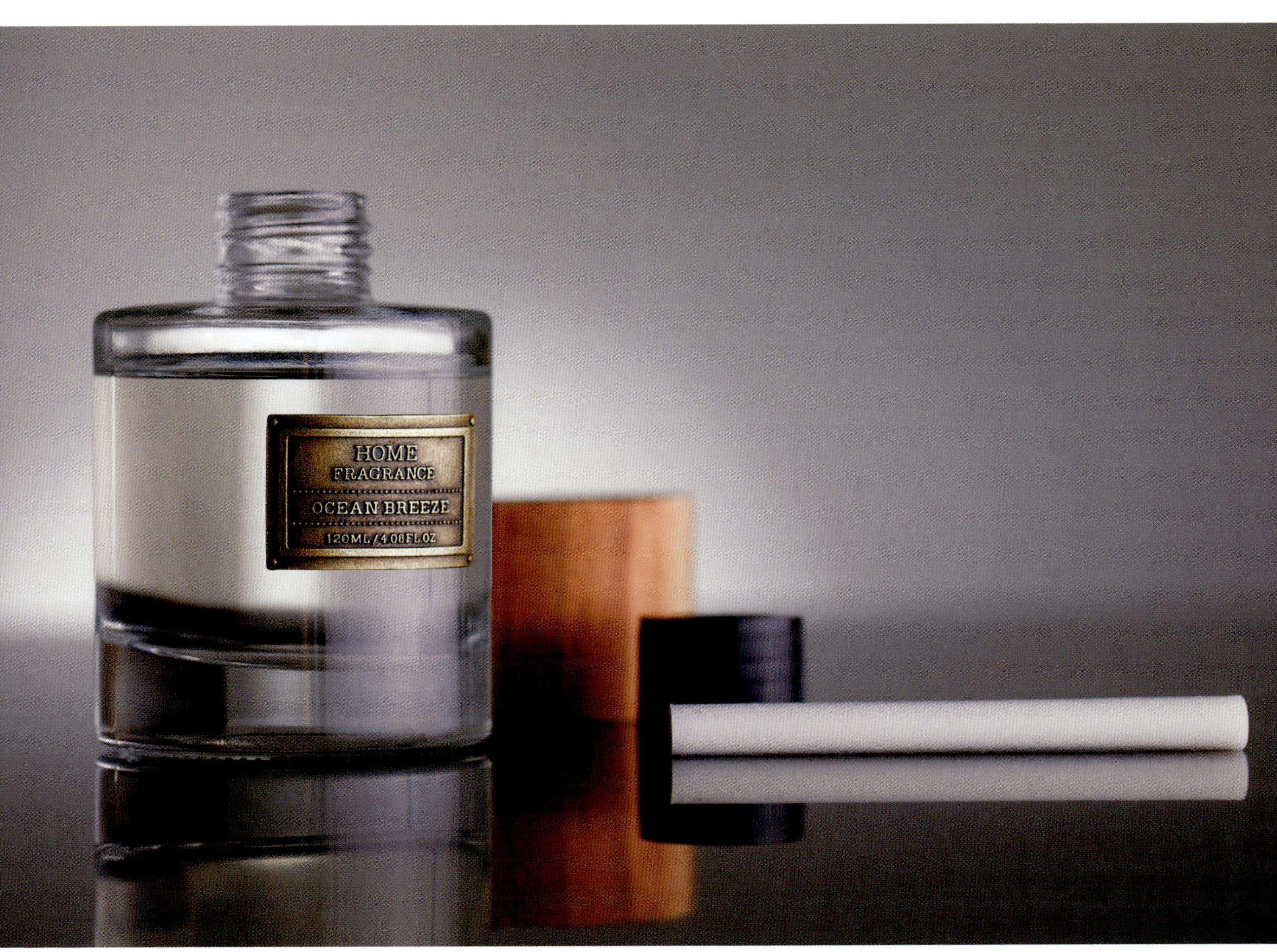
HOME
FRAGRANCE
OCEAN BREEZE
120ML/4.08FL OZ

2 LIGHT SOURCES + 1 DIFFUSER + 1 SHEET OF GLASS
FLYING TEACUP

The phenomenon of direct transmission is ideal for making shadows disappear or, even better, shifting them to where you want them, depending on the height you've chosen for the sheet of glass in relation to an opaque base placed underneath it, and the angle of the light source. This arrangement allows you to create all sorts of illusions and bring many different images to life.

Implementation

A saucer is placed on a translucent sheet of plexiglass (in this case, a packshot table), lit from below using a placed vertically flash, whose beam is directed toward the saucer.

A sheet of glass is positioned across two wedges, holding it in place about ten centimeters above the saucer. On the glass is a cup filled with black gouache diluted with water (more aesthetically pleasing in a photo than actual coffee): its shadow should appear on the saucer to accentuate the impression of levitation. A flash equipped with a large octabox is placed vertical to the entire arrangement to illuminate the cup and the saucer and create a shadow of the cup on the saucer. In connection with the lighting under the table, this lighting will allow us to even out the light on the translucent plexiglass. Photographed outside of the family of angles of the reflection of the glass, that reflection will disappear. That's it.

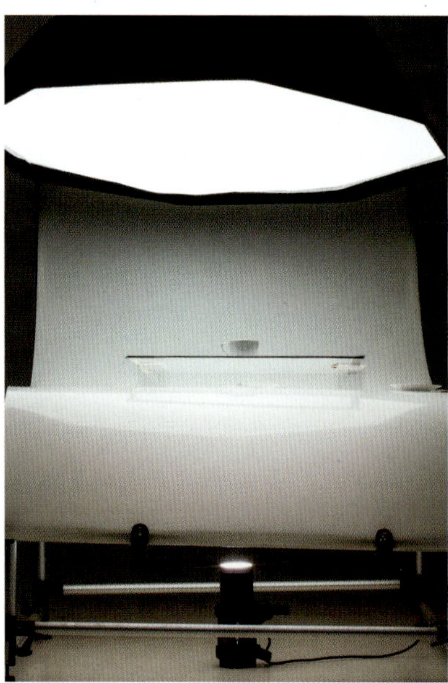

« A behind-the-scenes view of the production of the shot on the following page.

TECHNICAL DATA SHEET

Camera: Canon 5DS R
Lens: EF 100mm f/2.8L Macro IS USM
Focal distance: 100mm
Aperture: f/13
Speed: 1/200 s
Sensitivity: ISO 100

❶ **Flash:** Profoto D1 equipped with a 60-inch octabox, placed at a showerhead angle above the cup at about 32 inches. Set to +1.33 EV.

❷ **Flash:** Profoto D1 equipped with a zoom bowl, placed on the ground to light the diffuser positioned below the saucer. Set to +0.4 EV.

❸ **Sheet of glass:** To hold the cup about four inches above the diffuser.

❹ **Diffuser:** To hold the saucer and to spread the light of flash no. 2.

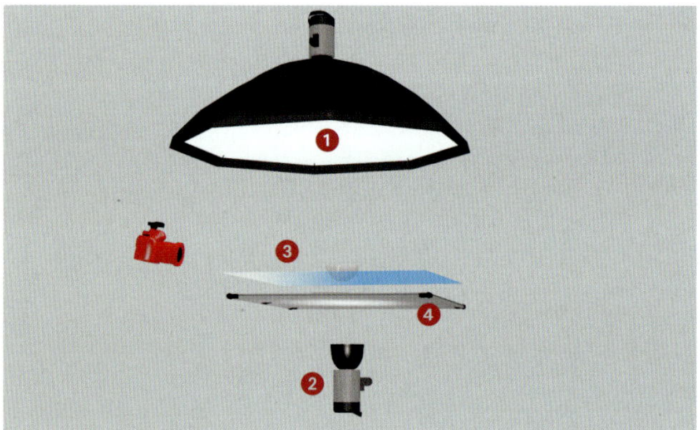

LIGHTING DIAGRAM

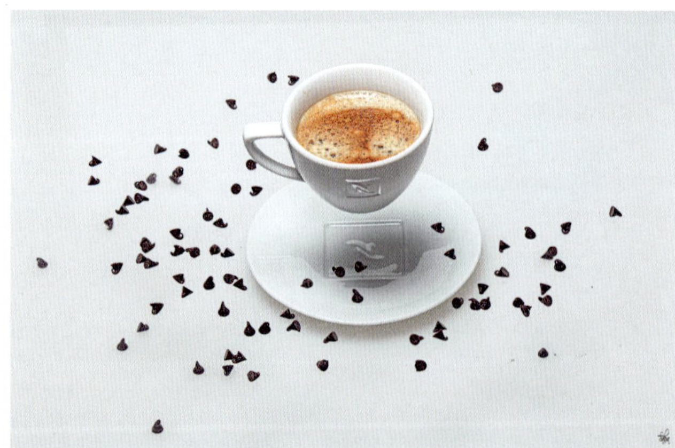

⌃ Version staged according to the same principle.

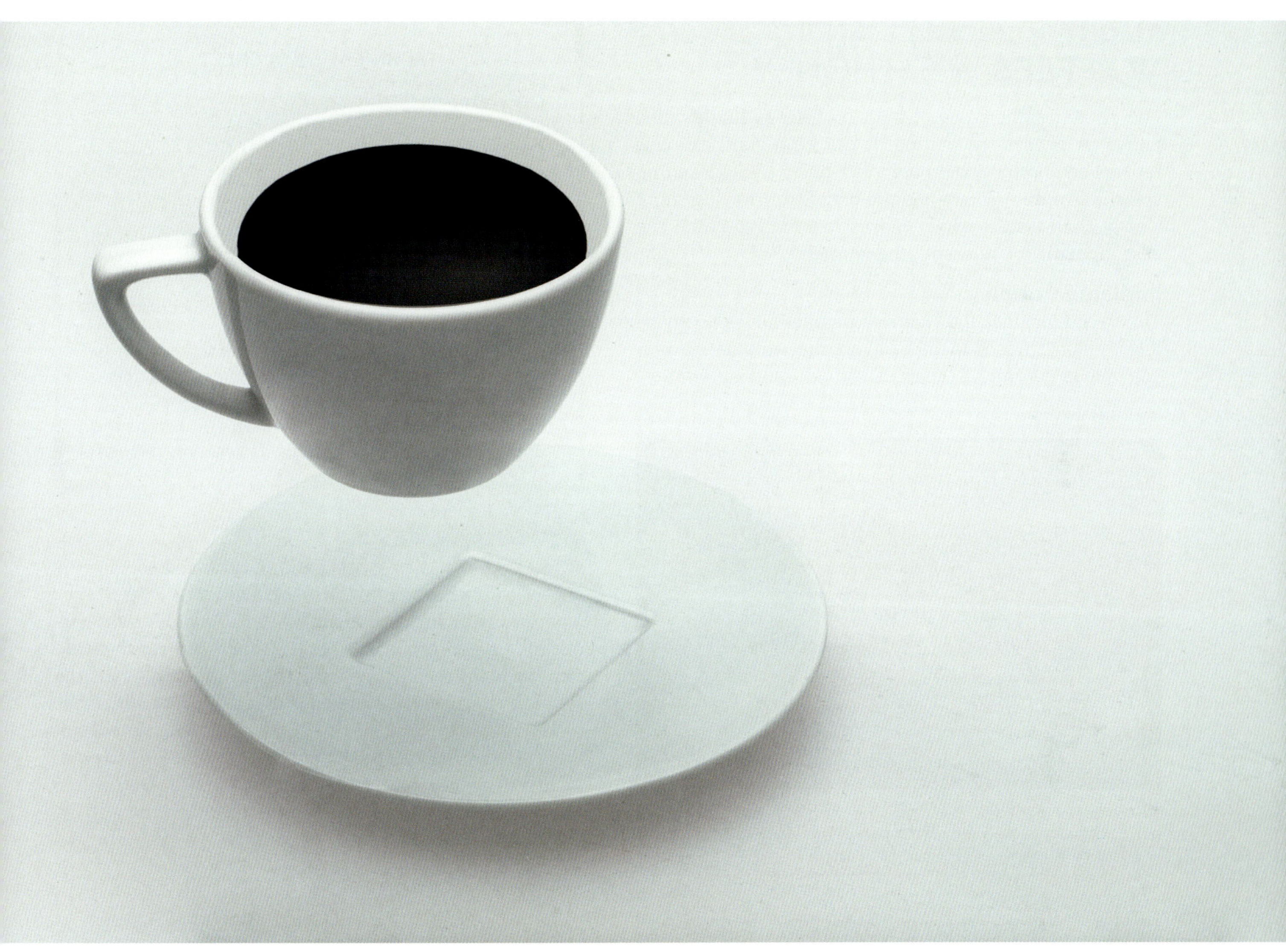

3 LIGHT SOURCES + 1 SHEET OF GLASS
WAFFLES WITH HONEY

The photographic study of light on viscous liquids, like honey, is always fascinating. It can be a good exercise for novice photographers before they try photographing splashing water. Honey has the benefit of flowing more slowly than water, which makes it easier to catch the best moment for releasing the shutter.

Implementation

This setup includes four pairs of parallel lines of "invisible" nylon thread, installed with the threads of each pair about two inches apart. They will hold up waffles,

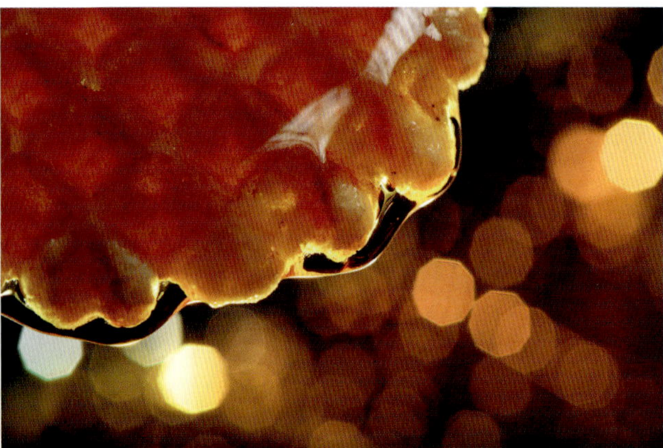

The honey that has dripped onto the sheet of glass, lit by flash no. 3, produces a lovely out-of-focus bokeh effect, with a shallow depth of field.

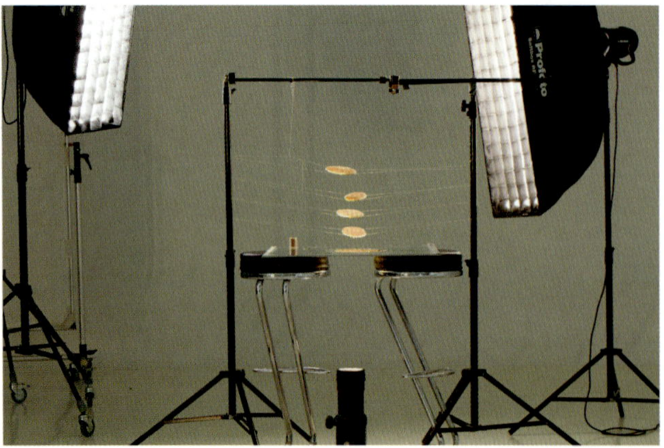

A behind-the-scenes view of the production of the shot on the following page.

suspended in the air, with lighting arranged so that the viewer can believe the waffles are levitating. Two flashes equipped with strip boxes are placed at two different levels: the first is responsible for lighting the top of the waffles, while the second lights the edge of the waffles and the side of the waffles tilted toward that flash. A third flash is placed on the ground, vertically, to light the lower edge of the waffles as well as the honey that we are going to pour. To avoid any possible splashes of liquid onto that flash, a sheet of glass is placed between the flash and the waffles.

Then all that is left to do is pour the honey, preheated so that it pours easily.

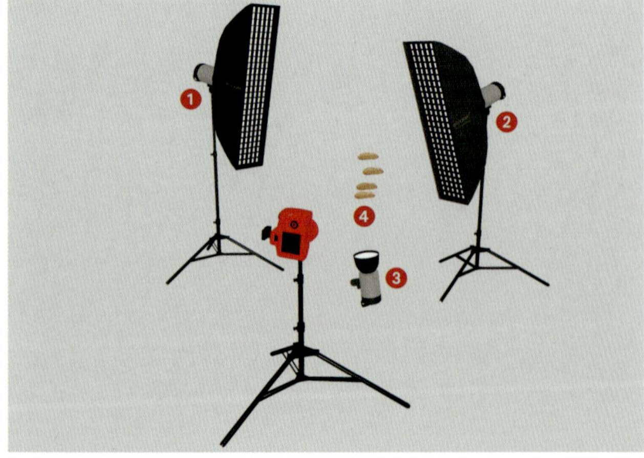

LIGHTING DIAGRAM

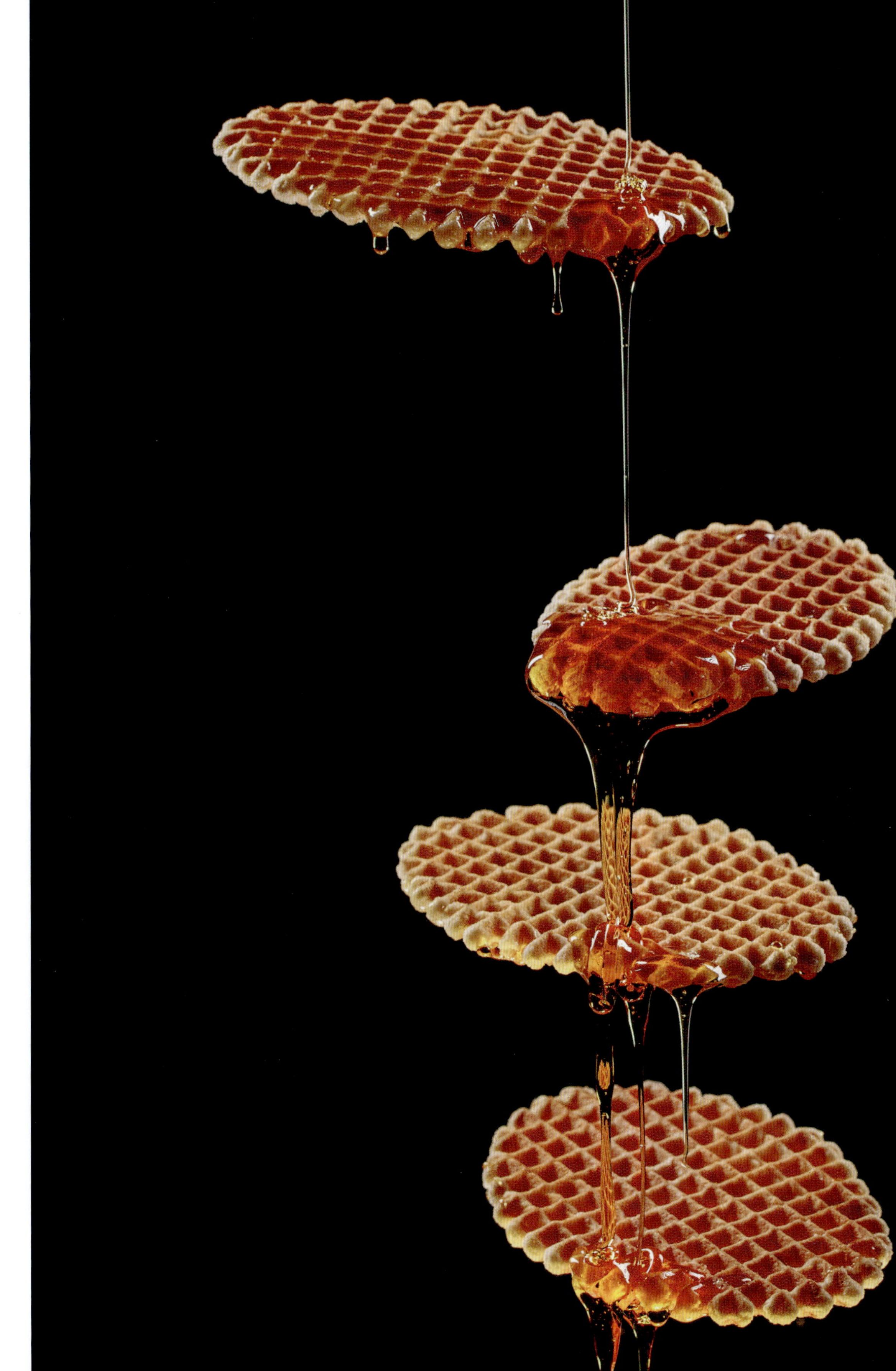

BLUE ORANGE

This shot is more of a creative study of complementary colors than it is a complex study of lighting, but I think it's interesting to show that we can get very elegant results with few resources and good art direction.

Art Direction

This image is meant to amuse the public while playing with color. An orange, its leaf, and its stem are painted blue. Once dry, the fruit is cut cleanly in half so that we can see the orange color and the juiciness of the inside. The mismatch between the blue and orange colors echoes the contrast between the lushness of the fruit and the roughness of its peel and the paper (in the same blue color) placed beneath it. The glossiness of the orange is accentuated by painting it with a little bit of peanut oil.

Setup

The lighting is very simple to manage, with one light source, as soft as possible—in this case, a 60-inch octabox placed in backlight and tilted down at an angle (130° in relation to the camera). A white reflector installed laterally six inches from the fruit is responsible for redirecting part of the lighting as fill light, to clear the shadow and light the front part of the peel.

TECHNICAL DATA SHEET

Camera: Canon 5DS R
Lens: EF 100mm f/2.8L Macro IS USM
Focal distance: 100mm
Aperture: f/11
Speed: 1/200 s
Sensitivity: ISO 100
❶ **Flash:** Profoto D1 equipped with a 60-inch octabox, directed toward the orange and tilted down at an angle. Set to +1.33 EV.
❷ **Reflector:** Placed opposite flash no. 1 in passive fill light.

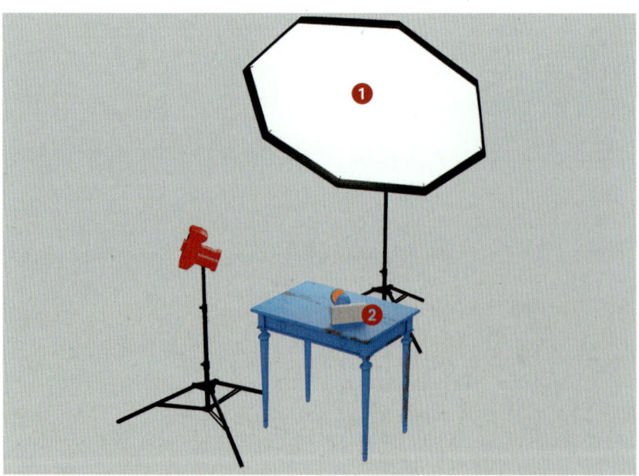

LIGHTING DIAGRAM

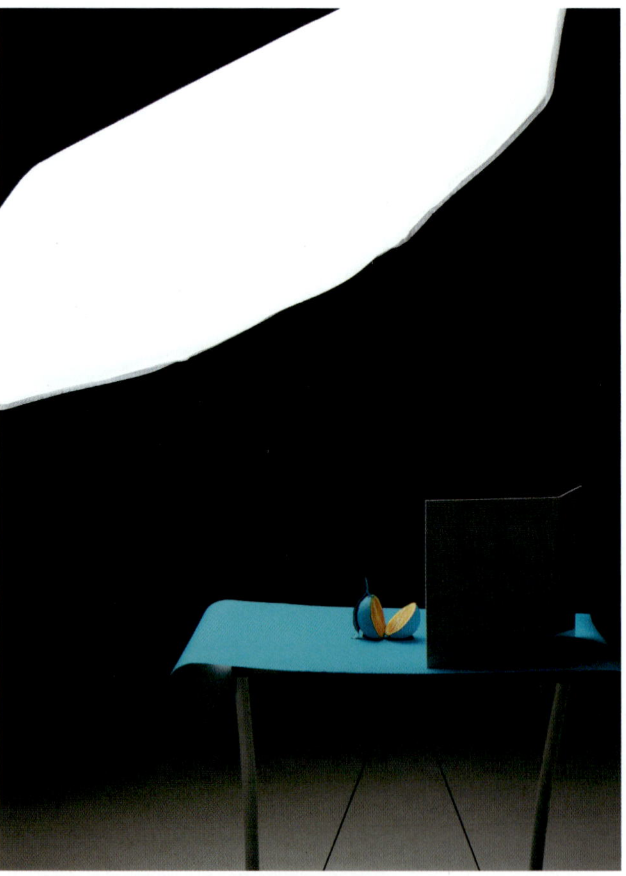

⌃ Behind-the-scenes view of the production of the shot on the following page.

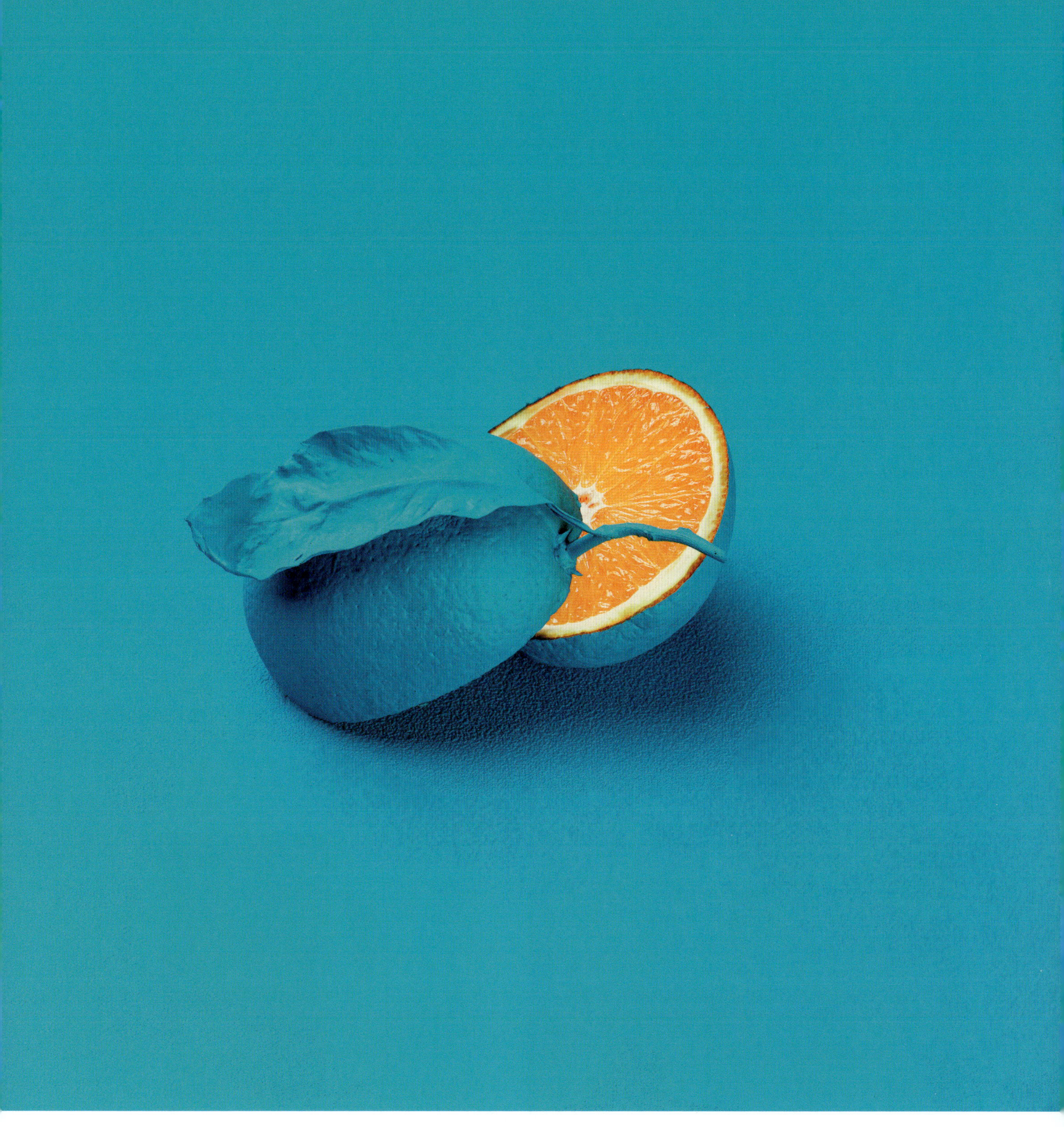

INTO ORBIT

Most ads for soda and beer cans are created using composite photography and require quite a bit of work. For this exercise, I wanted to play with perspective and angles by photographing this beer can from below, as if it were flying into the sky and I was watching it from the ground.

Implementation

It is easy to imagine photographing the bottle by suspending it with nylon thread, for example, but there is the danger that the threads might give way and the can, which is pretty heavy, could fall on the photographer or the flash. To be safer, a sheet of glass is positioned across two bar stools, acting as trestles, and the can is placed on top of the glass.

The easiest way to light the object is with a backlighting that will produce two nice bright lines on the edges of the can, and to place a rounded reflector in front of it to distribute the light evenly and regularly across the visible part of the can. A large barn door is set up to avoid flare and keep the background of the composition perfectly black.

This lighting arrangement is perfect for highlighting the front of the can, but it leaves the back of it in shadow. Therefore, a flash equipped with a small honeycomb is placed on the ground, positioned vertically and directed toward the sheet of glass. Thanks to the phenomenon of direct transmission, there is no risk of reflections, as long as the angle of the shot is properly situated outside the family of angles.

TECHNICAL DATA SHEET

Camera: Canon 5DS R
Lens: EF 100mm f/2.8L Macro IS USM
Focal distance: 100mm
Aperture: f/11
Speed: 1/200 s
Sensitivity: ISO 100

❶ [and] ❷ **Flashes:** Profoto D1, each equipped with a 12 x 48-inch strip box, directed in backlight to the edge of the can's family of angles. Set to +1.33 EV.
❸ **Flash:** Profoto D1 equipped with a honeycomb and placed on the ground, directed toward the back of the can and the ice cubes. Set to +0.5 EV.
❹ **Barn doors**
❺ **Sheet of glass:** To hold up the can and the ice cubes and allow us to shoot from below.
❻ **Reflector:** To redirect the light of flashes no. 1 and no. 2 toward the front of the can.

Once all of the lights are set up, it turns out that the sensation of flight will be more pronounced if ice cubes are arranged on the sheet of glass (actually cubes of acrylic glass, to avoid traces of melted ice). Then all that remains is to photograph the composition while making sure that the barn door, which has been tilted, takes up all of the background of the photo, and that we do not see the reflector.

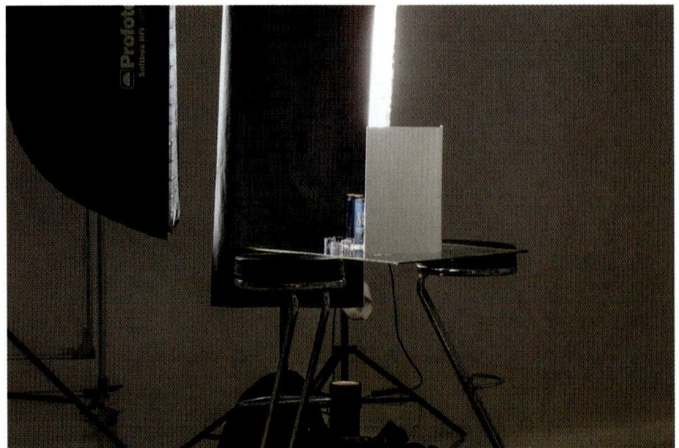

⌃ A behind-the-scenes view of the production of the shot on the following page.

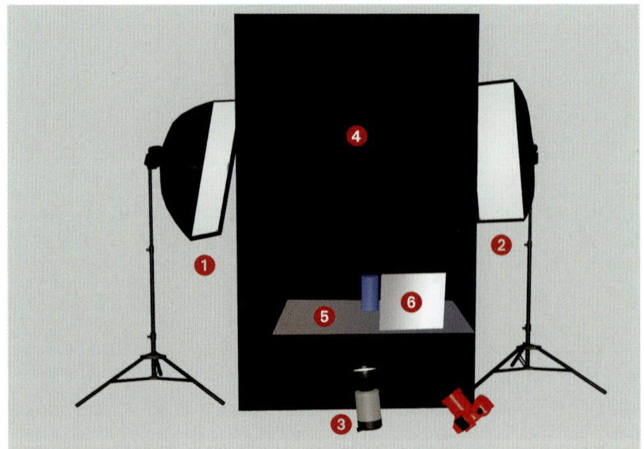

LIGHTING DIAGRAM

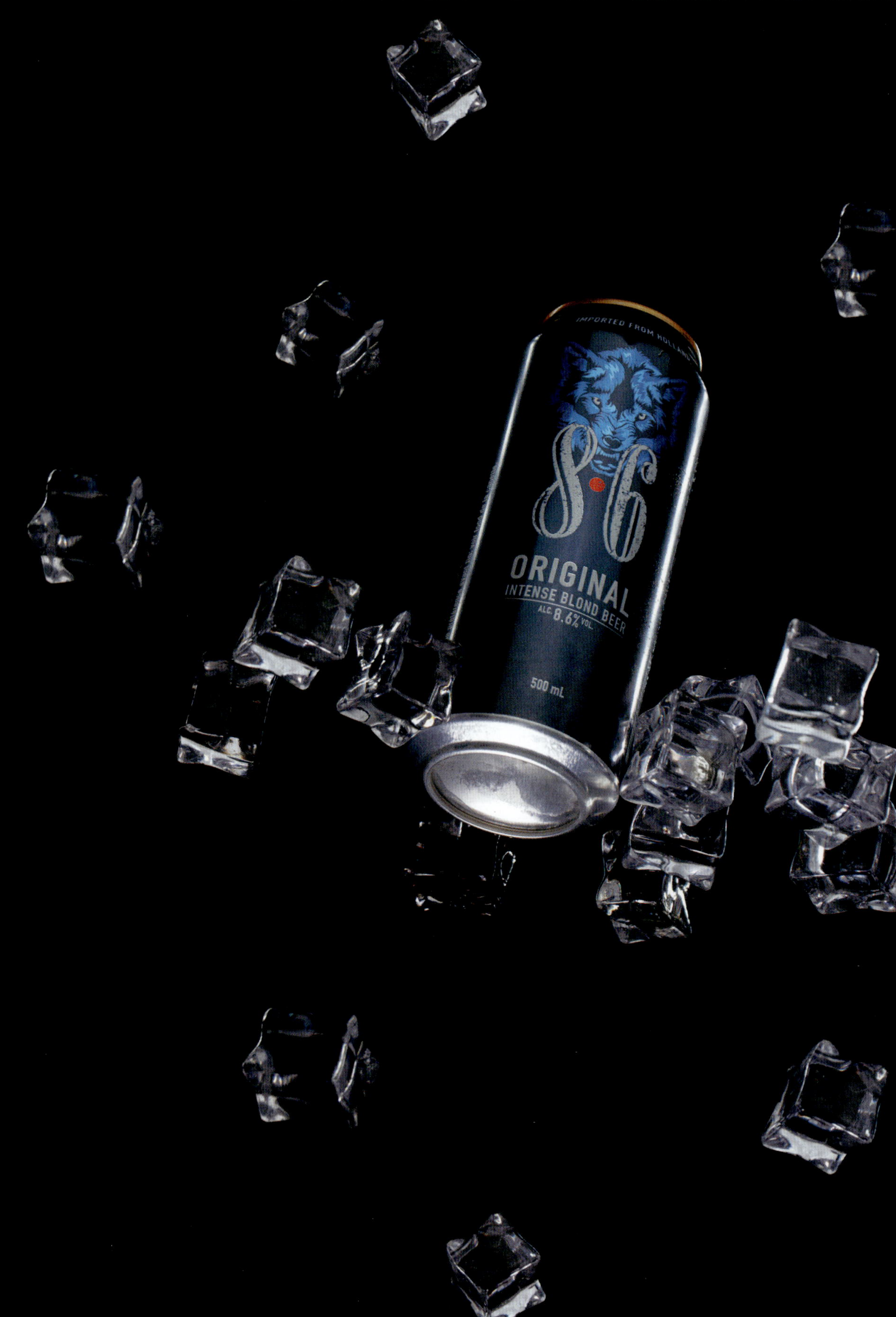

IMPORTED FROM HOLLAND
8.6
ORIGINAL
INTENSE BLOND BEER
ALC. 8.6% VOL.
500 mL

FLOATING PERFUME

Water in motion is always fascinating to light. It also has the advantage of harmonizing well with the objects that we want to stage. Here is a way to successfully create this kind of image, which has been common on social media ever since product photographer Frank Castillo, based in Florida, started the trend.

Implementation and Lighting

A shallow waterproof container (because the ideal for this photo is for it to be uniformly black, I suggest a black cafeteria tray) is filled with water to at least half an inch deep. The perfume bottle is positioned so that its key parts are out of the water (if necessary, a small transparent glass wedge can be slid underneath). Note that this only works with objects whose shape can be shown with backlighting.

A large diffuser is placed behind the tray, angled so that the light falling on it provokes a direct reflection over the entire surface of the liquid—in other words, at about 60°. A large, soft light source is also added to the setup—for instance, by using a large light box behind. The idea is for the entire diffuser to be lit so that an even reflection appears on the water.

Finally, the camera is positioned at a radical bird's-eye view above the tray to obtain a framing that includes the product and the water.

TECHNICAL DATA SHEET

Camera: Canon 5DS R
Lens: EF 100mm f/2.8L Macro IS USM
Focal distance: 100mm
Aperture: f/8
Speed: 1/200 s
Sensitivity: ISO 100
❶ Flash: Profoto D1 equipped with a 24 x 36-inch light box, directed down at an angle through a diffuser. Set to +1.33 EV.
❷ Diffuser
❸ Tray of water: To produce small waves under the influence of an electric blower.

A blower (ideally a wireless electric dust remover with a directional nozzle made for computers; see the behind-the-scenes view below) is used to project air (from a good distance away to avoid splashing water on the bottle) onto the surface of the liquid, which will then be covered with small waves. Then it's time to shoot.

You can get interesting results by using paraffin oil instead of water, or by substituting a transparent back-lit tray.

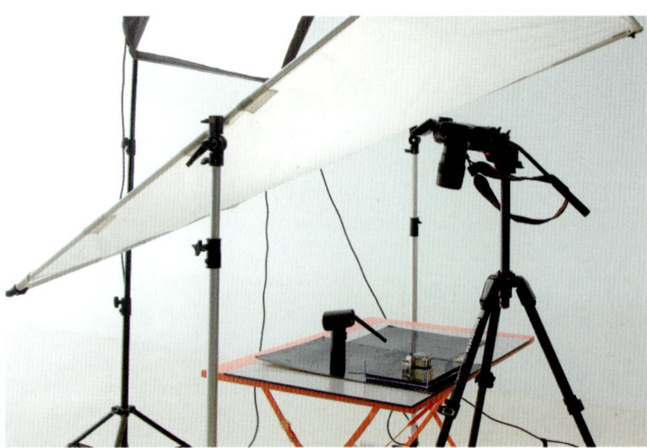

⌃ A behind-the-scenes view of the production of the shot on the following page.

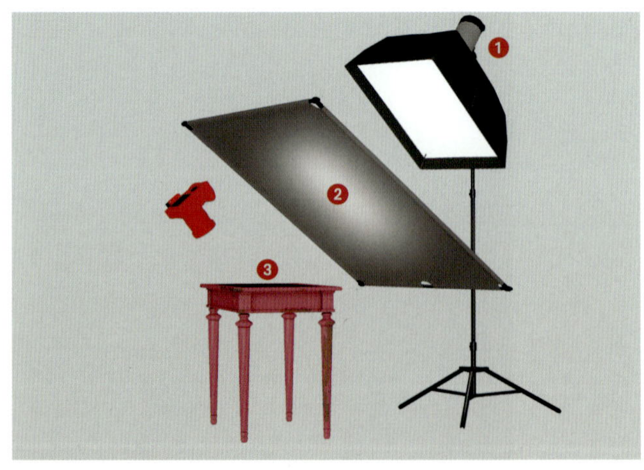

LIGHTING DIAGRAM

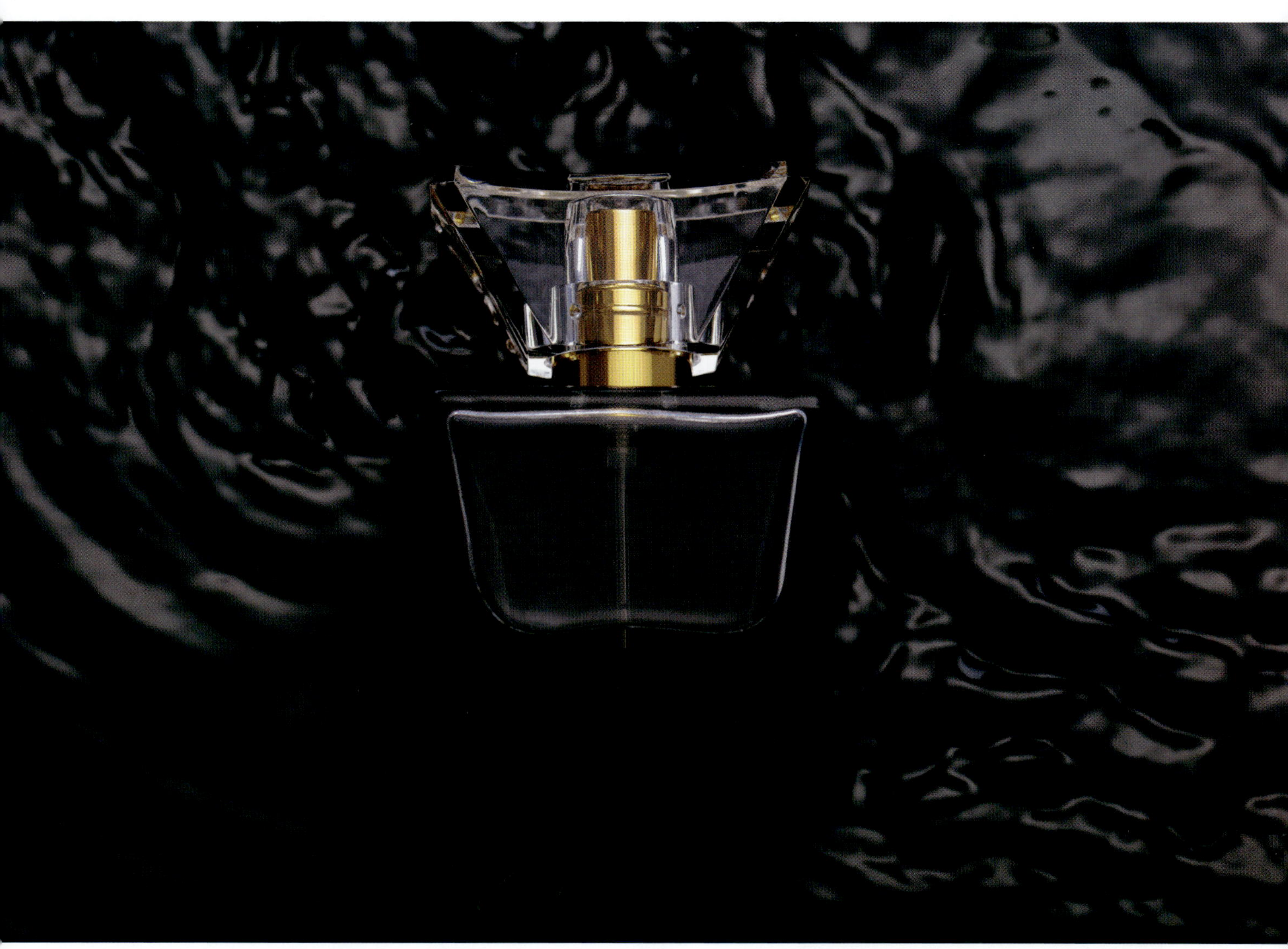

ANTS WITH WATCH

For this little scene staged around a polished steel watch, I needed some accessories that would be dark enough not to draw too much attention but amusing enough to be interesting. They would also have to react correctly to the required lighting for the watch. Online, I found some small satiny black plastic ants that would work well.

Staging and Lighting

A sheet of anthracite Canson paper is arranged on the table and a transparent plastic supporting bracelet is placed inside the wristband of the watch so that it will stay in place during the shot. The watch is set to 11:05 to allow the brand logo and the three round screens to be perfectly visible and not hidden by the watch hands.

The ants are arranged around the watch as if they had found a very attractive object, like a pile of sugar.

Two diffusing panels are set up behind the watch and to the side, with a flash equipped with a light box behind each of them. The rear diffusing panel (no. 4 on the diagram) is sufficiently tilted so that the light is also diffused across the dial. The function of flash no. 1 is to illuminate the front of the wristband, the dial, and the ants. The second flash, placed laterally behind a diffuser (no. 3), serves to light the inside of the wristband, the ants, and the paper support.

To avoid having the front of the wristband stay in shadow, a mirror is placed in front of it to redirect the light produced by the backlighting (flash no. 1). The angle of the mirror, tilted toward the camera (see the photo of the behind-the-scenes view), makes it possible to maintain black areas on the lower part of the wristband frame, adding visual interest to the image.

TECHNICAL DATA SHEET

Camera: Canon 5DS R
Lens: EF 100mm f/2.8L Macro IS USM
Focal distance: 100mm
Aperture: f/10
Speed: 1/200 s
Sensitivity: ISO 100

❶ **Flash:** Profoto D1 equipped with a 12 x 16-inch light box, placed in backlight to light the rear part of the wristband through diffusing fabric no. 4. Set to +1.33 EV.

❷ **Flash:** Profoto D1 equipped with a 24 x 36-inch light box, placed laterally to light the ants, the left edge, and the interior of the wristband, through diffusing fabric no. 3. Set to +0.5 EV.

❸ [and] ❹ **Diffusing fabrics**

❺ **Mirror:** Positioned to reflect the light of flash no. 1 toward the front of the watch and dial.

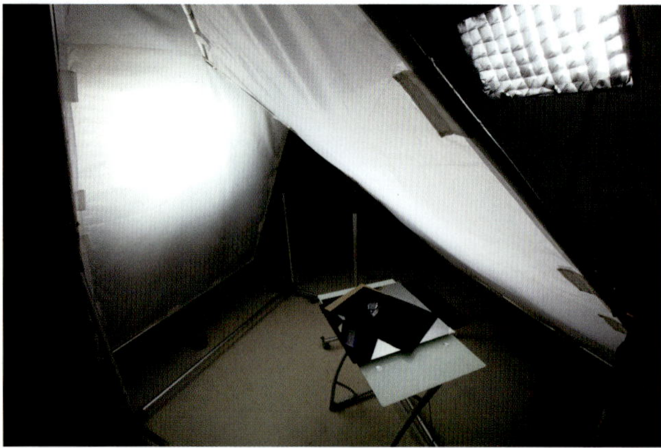

A behind-the-scenes view of the production of the shot on the following page.

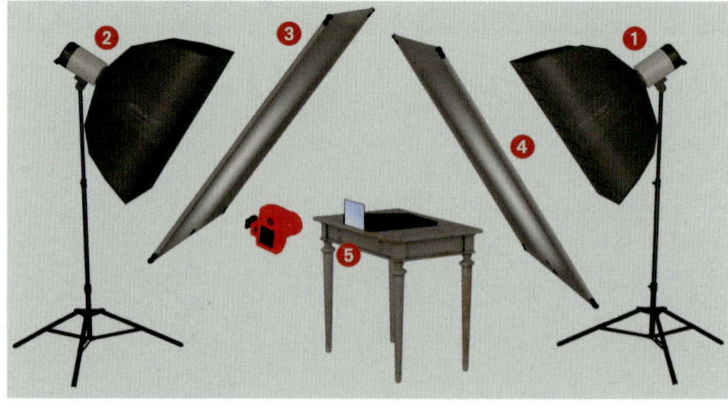

LIGHTING DIAGRAM

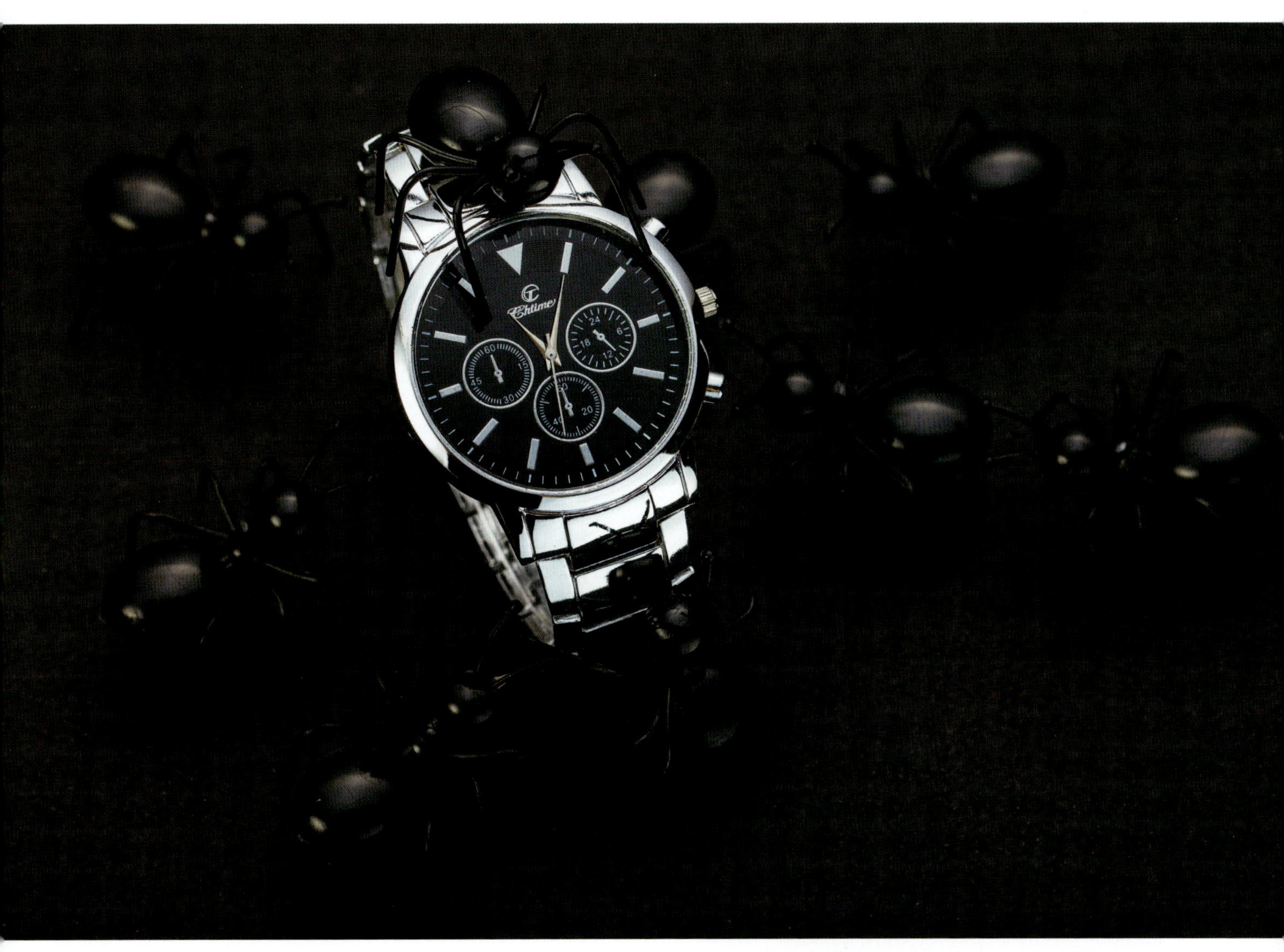

OLD PORT

This bottle of port required a traditional presentation, with wood, warm colors, and a subdued interior atmosphere.

Implementation and Lighting

Some strips of old parquet flooring in oak tones are arranged on a table, in a color similar to the inscriptions on the bottle. To keep the southern spirit, an optic shaper (no. 2 in the diagram) is placed as backlight, equipped with a gobo cut into the shape of a window blind, to dress up the background and strengthen the sense of an interior scene.

The bottle is turned slightly toward the left of the image (because it is a nostalgic image), a glass filled with port is positioned on the right side of the image, and an open book is placed in the background—its pages are held in the air by two small wedges, arranged so as not to appear in the shot.

All that's left to be done is to light the objects on the table. A flash equipped with a light box is placed as backlight on the right side to light the book, the glass, and the right edge of the bottle. For the bottle itself, the method is simple: because it is made of frosted glass, it cannot produce very unpleasant direct reflections, as long as a very diffuse, yet focused light is used, so as not to overwhelm the scene. Thus, a flash equipped with a snoot is directed downward from above, toward the bottle; this angle has the advantage of nicely highlighting the embellishment of the boat, the little half-spheres, and the base of the crest, while also lighting the inscriptions. Because this lighting alone still produces a few direct reflections on the bottle (it was rather old and had not been preserved under the best of conditions), we set up a diffuser (a thick sheet of translucent paper) to limit the reflections and even out the lighting.

TECHNICAL DATA SHEET

Camera: Canon 5DS R
Lens: EF 100mm f/2.8L Macro IS USM
Focal distance: 100mm
Aperture: f/13
Speed: 1/200 s
Sensitivity: ISO 100

❶ **Flash:** Profoto D1 equipped with a snoot, directed toward the front of the bottle through a sheet of translucent paper. Set to +1.33 EV.

❷ **Flash:** Profoto D1 equipped with an optic shaper and a gobo projecting the shadow of a window blind in backlight. Set to +0.5 EV.

❸ **Flash:** Profoto D1 equipped with a 24 x 36-inch light box, placed in backlight at the edge of the bottle's family of angles. Set to +0.6 EV.

❹ **Translucent paper**

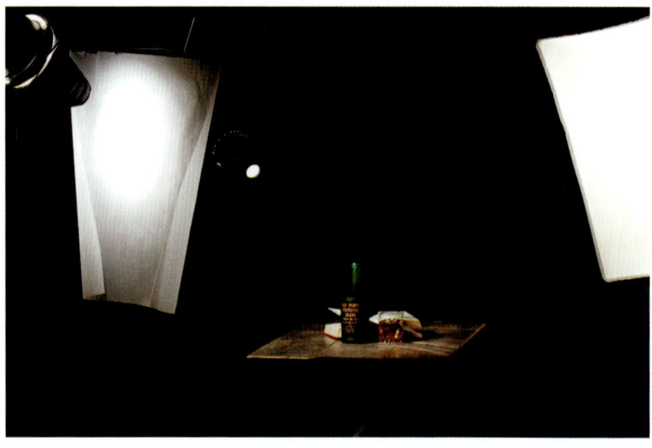

⌃ A behind-the-scenes view of the production of the shot on the following page.

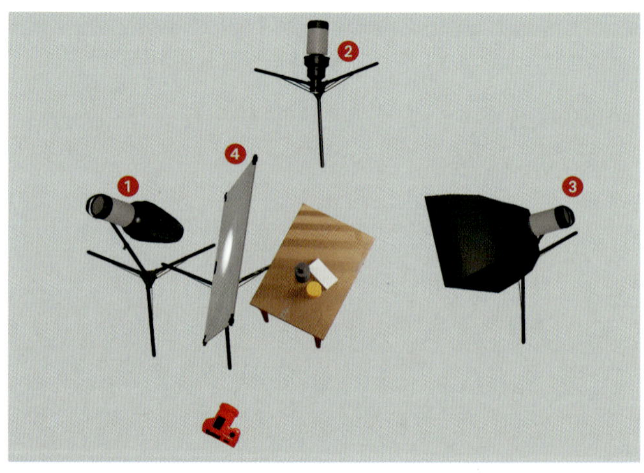

LIGHTING DIAGRAM

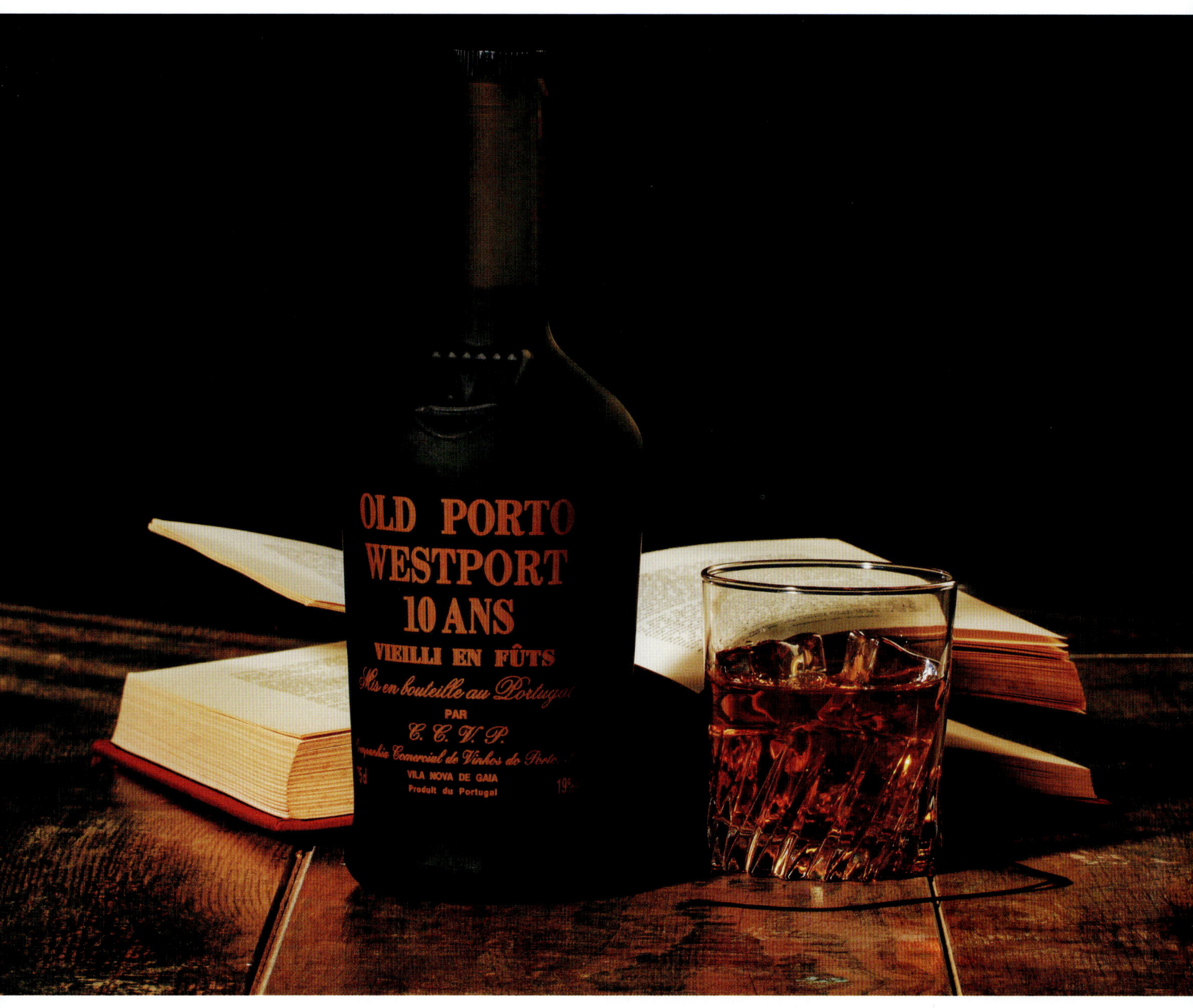

OLD PORTO
WESTPORT
10 ANS
VIEILLI EN FÛTS
Mis en bouteille au Portugal
PAR
C.C.V.P.
Companhia Comercial de Vinhos do Porto
VILA NOVA DE GAIA
Produit du Portugal

3 LIGHT SOURCES
FRESHNESS AND FRUIT

For this composition, fresh and colorful, I wanted to be able to quickly change the look of the background (from black to white, in this case) while still keeping the same optical effect on the water.

Implementation and Lighting

The initial arrangement consists of a fork planted in a Granny Smith apple and small wooden toothpicks connecting a red pepper, a tangerine, a lime, and a yellow pepper. The fork is kept in place with gaffer tape on a plexiglass wedge and a tray is positioned to catch the water below. For the lighting, an octabox is arranged in backlight to light the back of the fruit and spotlight the water. A second flash, equipped with a small light box, is set up at a slight bird's-eye view for a lateral lighting. A third flash equipped with a light box is directed toward the white wall behind the scene. Once the flash has been set to +3.33 EV in relation to the camera setting, the wall looks uniformly white; when the flash is off, the wall is completely black. Now all that's left to do is pour water over the yellow pepper, let gravity do its work, and release the shutter at the right moment.

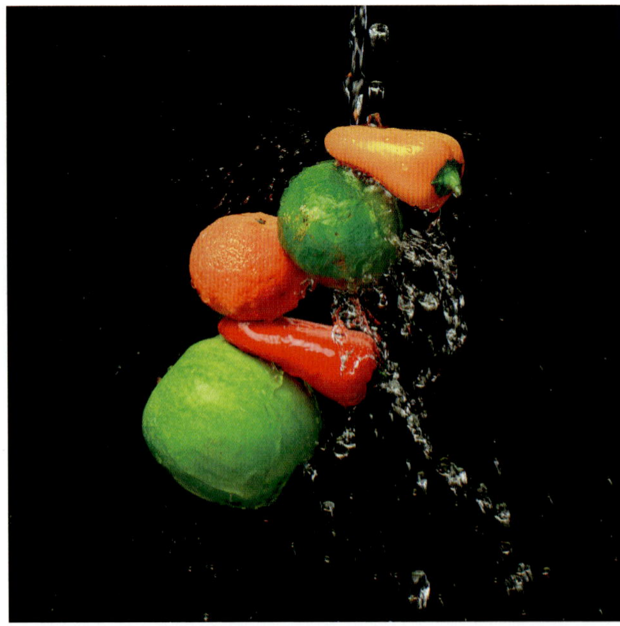

In this photo, we did without flash no. 3.

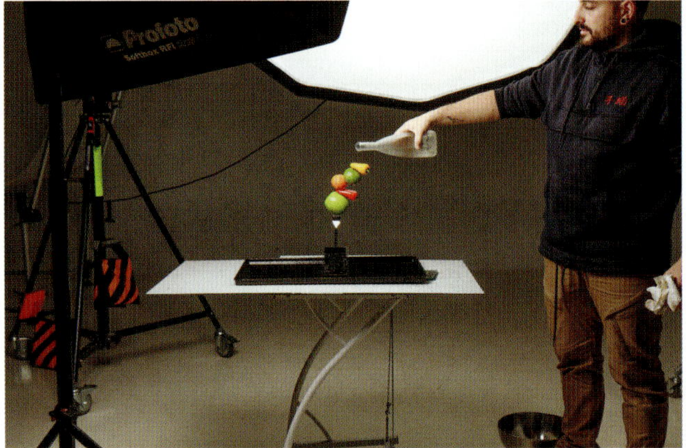

A behind-the-scenes view of the production of the shot on the following page.

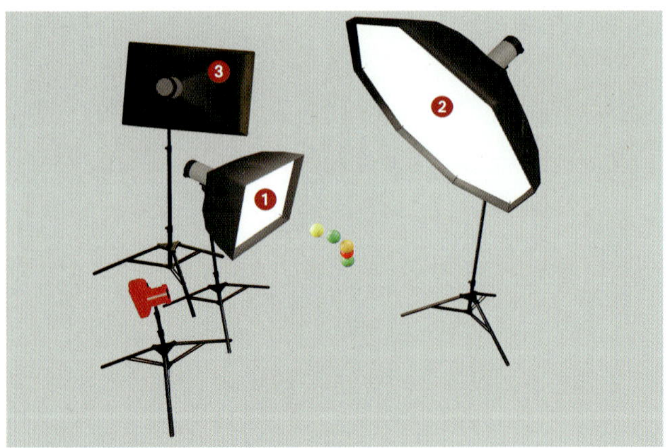

LIGHTING DIAGRAM

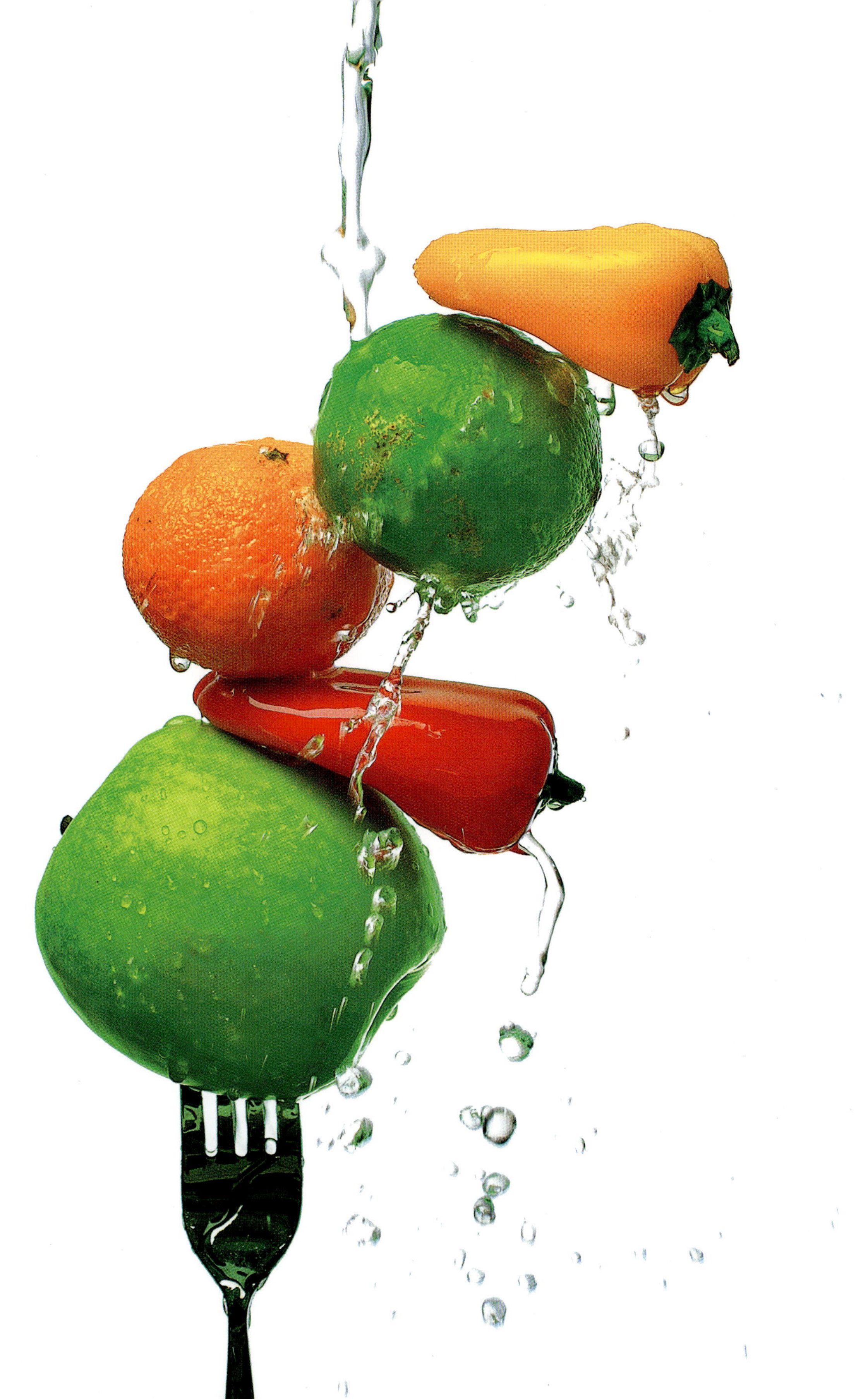

JAR OF MOISTURIZING CREAM WITH SPLASHES

Photos of glass objects submerged in the water of an aquarium are always delightful. When they are underwater, objects always look better lit, cleaner, and have more pronounced contrasts. And the submersion produces splashes that are always interesting for this kind of shot.

Implementation

The aquarium is placed on a table that is sturdy enough to support the weight of the water. The bottom third of the tank is filled with water, so that there is a large enough frame and we can catch the splash behind the glass without seeing the edge. Two flashes equipped with light boxes are arranged in backlight, one on either side of the aquarium, to light the glass jar appropriately and give substance to the water when it splashes. Then a bare-head flash equipped with a blue gel is directed toward the back wall so that the color of the background will be in harmony with the darker blue of the jar of moisturizing cream.

Now we just need to drop the jar into the water and take the shot when the splash looks best. Of course, this will take several tries, especially for finding the axis along which to drop the object (here, a light rotation of 20° turned out perfect for the splashes to be just right).

Unfortunately, there is a downside to this arrangement: when the water splashes, there is a projection of little drops that hit the inside of the glass wall of the aquarium. We could, of course, erase them in post-production, but I suggest instead that you make them disappear by pouring water on the glass wall. This will only take a few seconds, whereas the post-production editing would take infinitely longer, especially in areas where the splash and the water droplets overlap.

TECHNICAL DATA SHEET

Camera: Canon 5DS R
Lens: EF 100mm f/2.8L Macro IS USM
Focal distance: 40mm
Aperture: f/11
Speed: 1/200 s
Sensitivity: ISO 100
❶ [and] ❷ **Flash:** Profoto D1s, each equipped with a 24 x 36-inch light box, placed in backlight at the edge of the jar's family of angles. Set to +1.33 EV.
❸ **Flash:** Profoto D1, bare head and equipped with a blue gel, directed toward the wall behind the aquarium. Set to –0.3 EV.
❹ **Aquarium:** One-third filled with water.

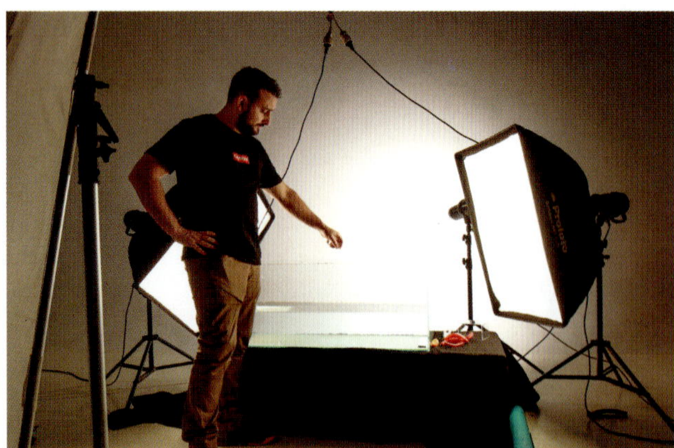

⌃ A behind-the-scenes view of the production of the shot on the following page.

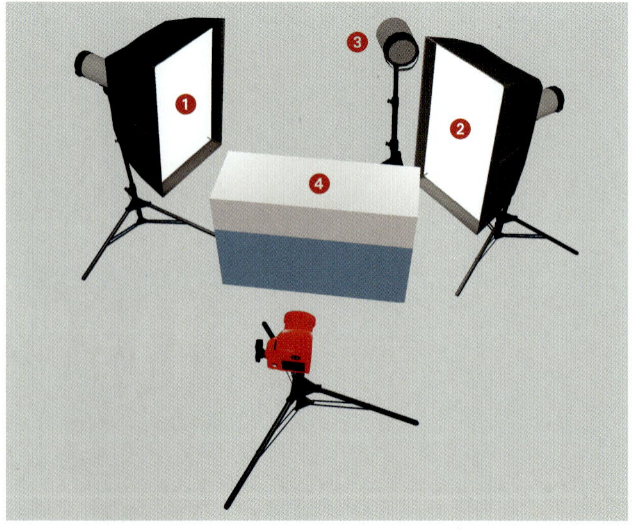

LIGHTING DIAGRAM

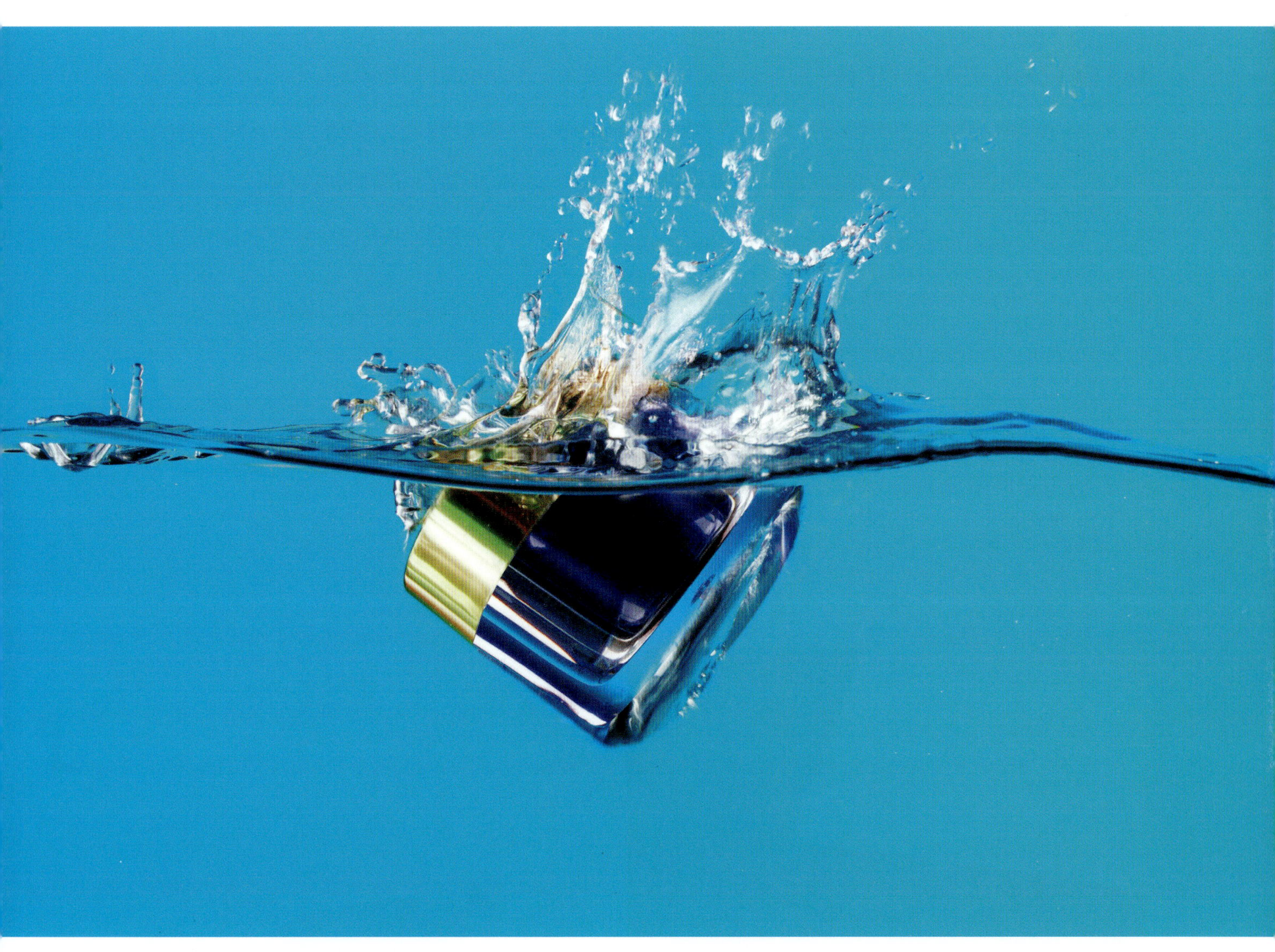

RED CHILI PEPPERS

As with the blue-colored orange, this exercise has more to do with playing with the aesthetics and organization of and among objects than with studying complex lighting.

Art Direction

Here, we are presenting different kinds of red chili peppers (cayenne peppers and West Indian hot peppers), chosen for their similarity in color and surface condition, which looks lacquered under direct lighting.

To obtain a perfect monochrome, the peppers are arranged on a base of the same color: a sheet of glossy red plexiglass. The difficulty is in making the reflections appear on the peppers but not on the plexiglass, which would look white or pink if we placed a light source within its family of angles.

One light source is enough, as long as it is large and diffuse enough. A 24 x 36-inch light box is set up 20 inches from the peppers, in backlight, at a lightly feathered angle, so that the light will reflect on the peppers but not on the plexiglass.

Now the shadow produced by that light source needs to be cleared. A rounded reflector placed in fill light makes the light softer and better distributed, and offers a more effective result than a flash, which would produce overly localized direct reflections on the peppers.

> ## TECHNICAL DATA SHEET
>
> **Camera:** Canon 5DS R
> **Lens:** EF 100mm f/2.8L Macro IS USM
> **Focal distance:** 100mm
> **Aperture:** f/10
> **Speed:** 1/200 s
> **Sensitivity:** ISO 100
> **❶ Flash:** Profoto D1 equipped with a 24 x 36-inch light box, placed in backlight and directed toward the peppers. Set to +1.33 EV.
> **❷ Reflector:** Placed in fill light to clear the shadows produced by the flash.

⌃ A behind-the-scenes view of the production of the shot on the following page.

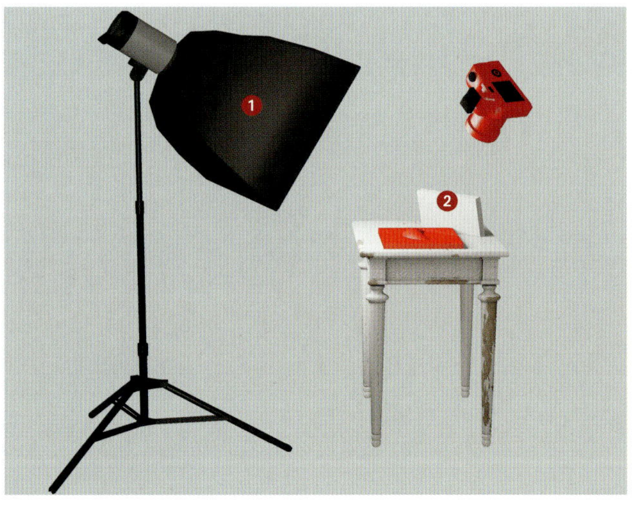

LIGHTING DIAGRAM

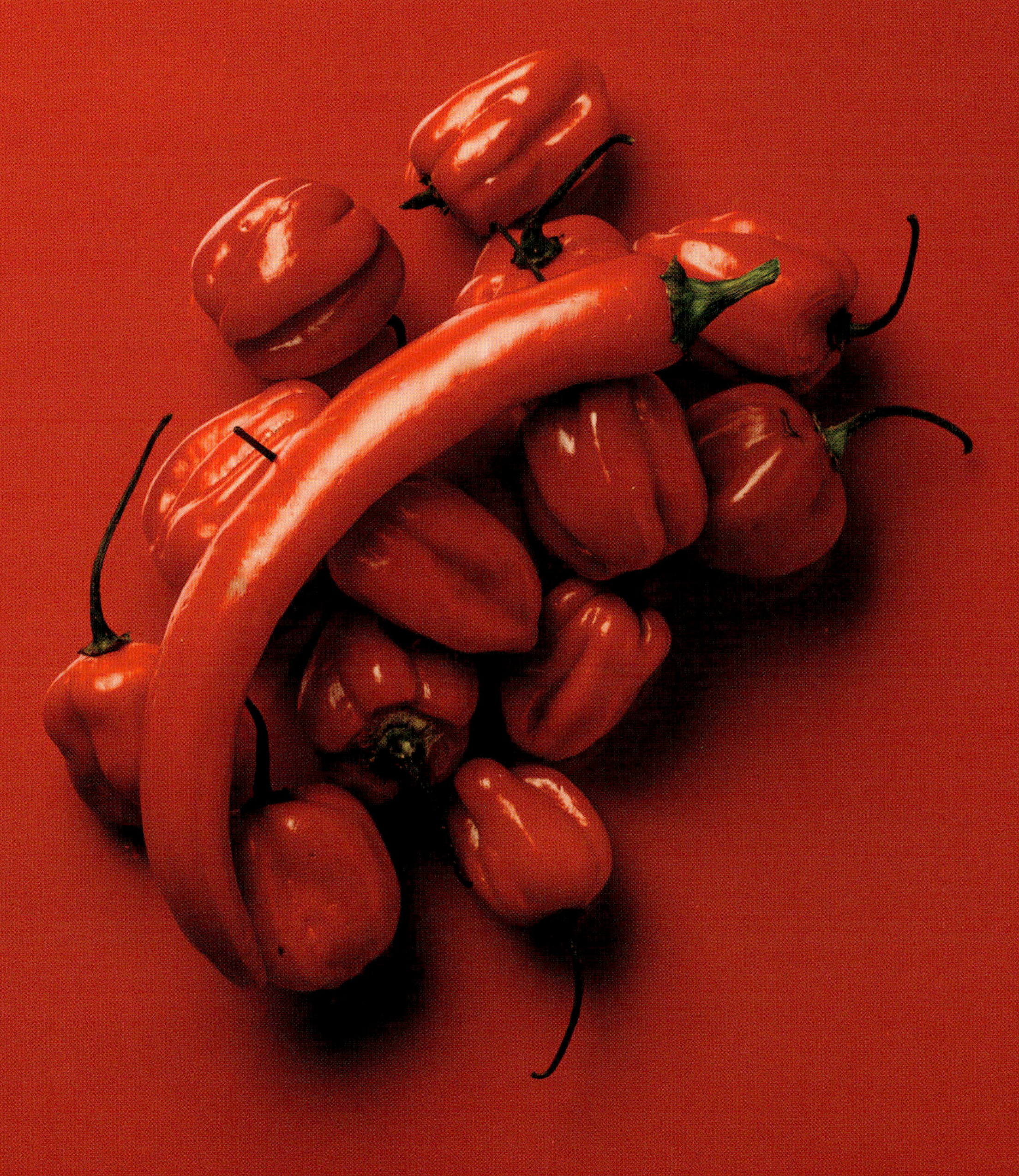

A WATCH AND ITS IMPACT

In advertising, visual impact is the most important goal. So why not suggest an actual physical impact, like that of a meteorite, or any object heavy enough to dig a crater and crack the ground?

Art Direction and Implementation

To get this effect, sixteen cups of white flour are poured into a Pyrex dish, then tamped down using a board the size of the dish. To dig the crater, a round bowl is placed in the center of the dish and pressed down on: the flour cracks all around the crater, as we see in the image below and the one on the following page. Then the bowl is carefully removed.

Next, the watch is placed in the center of the crater, with the wristband already rounded with the help of a transparent plastic support bracelet.

In terms of lighting, the usual backlighting is used, which is perfect for very glossy objects like watches: a flash equipped with a 24 x 36-inch light box is placed about 8 inches behind a large 78 x 60-inch diffusing panel, which in turn is positioned about 24 inches behind the dish.

A rounded reflector in is positioned in front of the dish to redirect the backlighting to light the watch dial.

Note that these two lighting arrangements, both at grazing angles with respect to the surface of the flour, allow us to accentuate the textural effect, especially on the cracks.

TECHNICAL DATA SHEET

Camera: Canon 5DS R
Lens: EF 100mm f/2.8L Macro IS USM
Focal distance: 100mm
Aperture: f/8
Speed: 1/160 s
Sensitivity: ISO 100
❶ Flash: Profoto D1 equipped with a 24 x 36-inch light box, placed behind the diffuser. Set to +1.33 EV.
❷ Diffuser
❸ Reflector: Placed in fill light to clear the shadows produced by the flash.

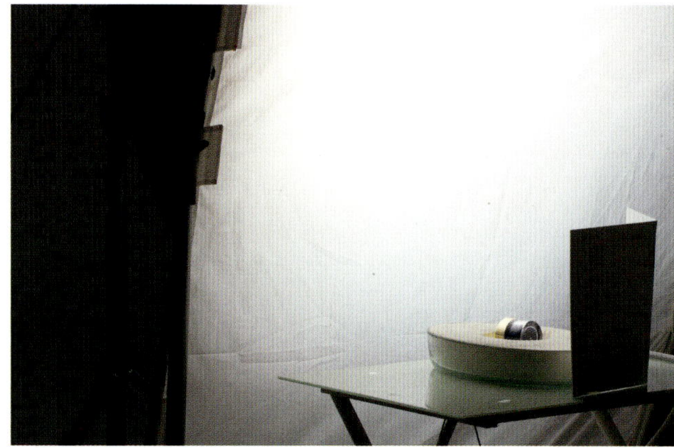

⌃ A behind-the-scenes view of the production of the shot on the following page.

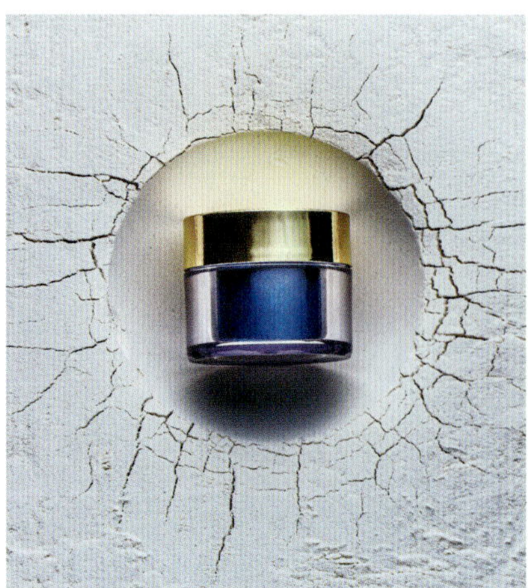

《 In this shot, we have replaced the watch with a glass jar of moisturizing cream, which gives us a better view of the effect of the light.

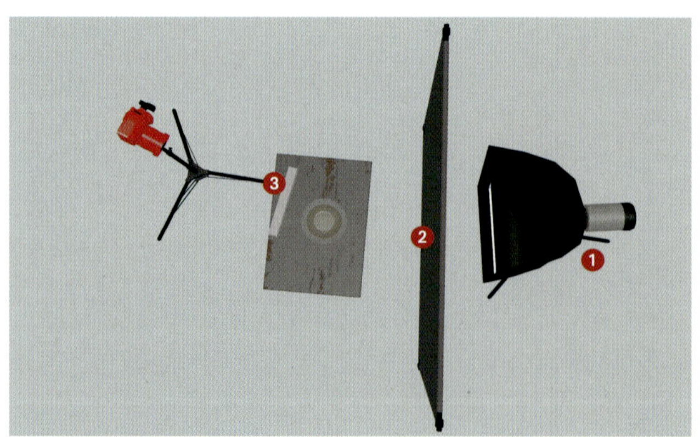

LIGHTING DIAGRAM

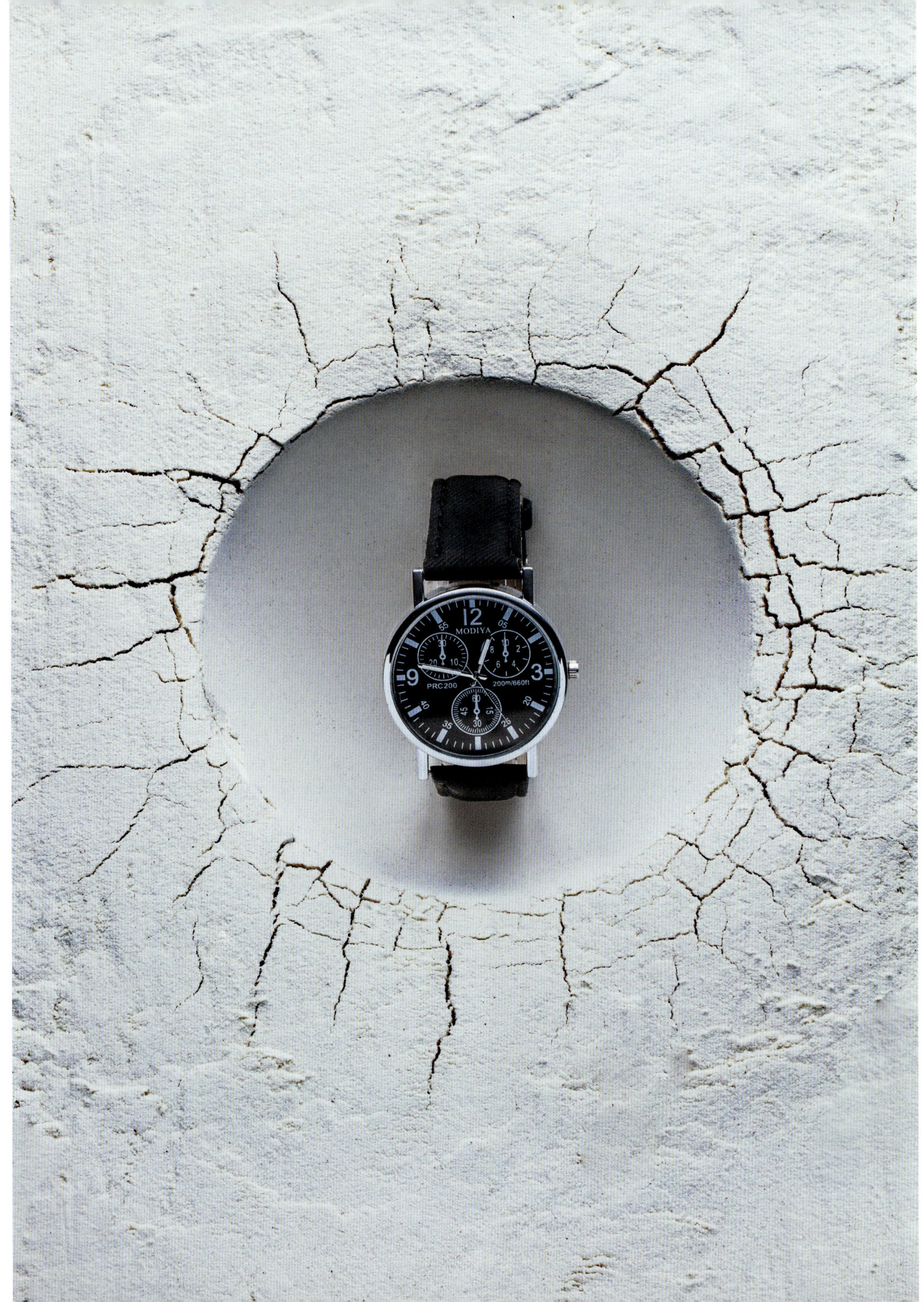
12
9
3
MODIYA
PRC 200
200m/660ft

ANATOMY OF A HAMBURGER

Over the last few years, we have seen thousands of examples of this kind of shot, created with Photoshop, on social media. The idea here was to show that we could obtain a similar result in the shoot without later editing.

Setup and Lighting

We operate the same way here as we did for the waffles with honey on pages 238 and 239, stretching paired sets of "invisible" nylon thread between two tripods. Two lateral flashes equipped with small light boxes (12 x 16 inches) and honeycombs are set up so that the light will only illuminate the food and allow us to get an unlit background, which will look black in the shot. The flash on the right is placed higher than the top half of the bun, so that the main light is descending. The difference between the light on the top and bottom halves of the bun should be no more than 0.4 EV (+1.33 EV on the top half and no less than +0.9 EV on the bottom half, in other words), with the angle of the flash corrected if necessary to make sure that happens. The second flash only serves as a fill light, and is set to approximately +0.4 EV. Then, taking care to make sure that none of the objects knocks over any of the ones below it, each of the elements that is supposed to make up the burger is suspended from the nylon threads: the sesame buns, the tomatoes, the onions, the cheddar cheese, the leaves of lettuce (first dipped in ice water to bring out their color), and the hamburger patties (cooked only on the surface).

A little sauce is poured on one of the patties—here, we used barbecue sauce diluted with water so that it would be more liquid. And then the camera shutter is released. Depending on the angle of incidence of the flashes, the nylon threads might appear in places: this is something we can easily erase in Photoshop. But if the flashes are pointing in the right directions, and are placed so that their beams go in the same direction as the threads and the background is black, the threads disappear.

TECHNICAL DATA SHEET

Camera: Canon 5DS R
Lens: EF 16–35mm f/4L Macro IS USM
Focal distance: 35mm
Aperture: f/8
Speed: 1/160 s
Sensitivity: ISO 100

❶ Flash: Profoto D1 equipped with a 12 x 16-inch light box equipped with a honeycomb, placed in backlight. Set to +1.33 EV.

❷ Flash: Profoto D1 equipped with a 12 x 16-inch light box equipped with a honeycomb, placed laterally at 80° to the camera. Set to +0.4 EV.

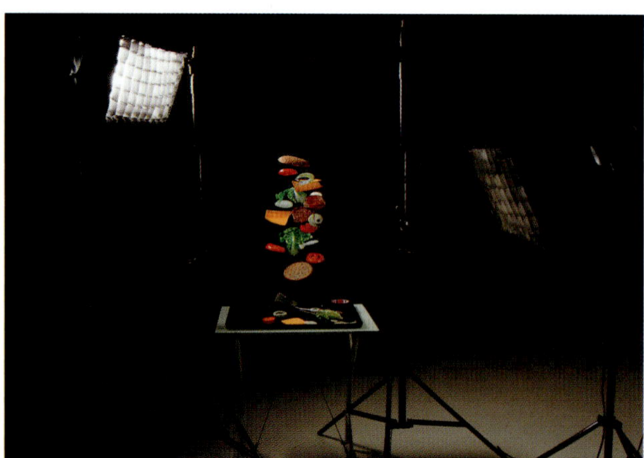

⌃ A behind-the-scenes view of the production of the shot on the following page.

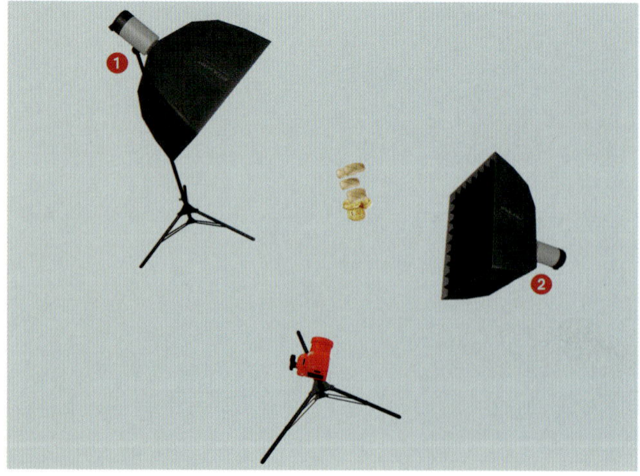

LIGHTING DIAGRAM

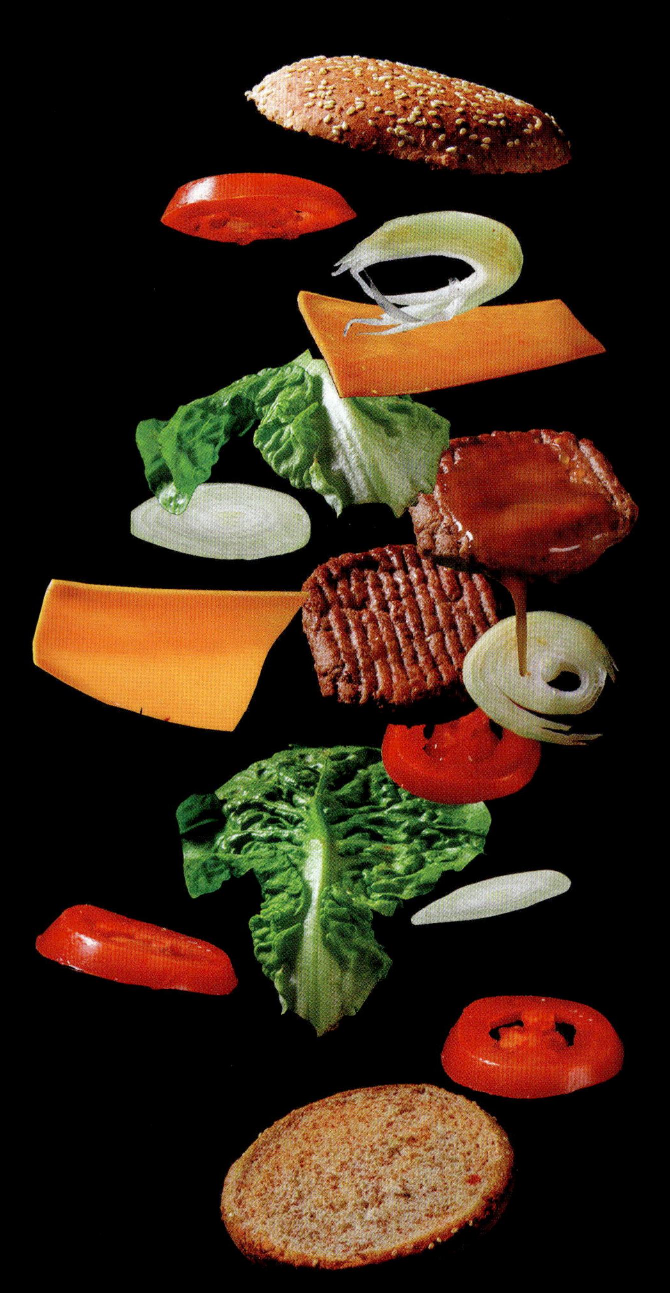

EXPLODING WHISKEY

For this exercise, what we want is coherent lighting for the glass and its contents, a harmony of complementary colors, and a dynamic composition.

Implementation and Art Direction

A sheet of blue plexiglass is arranged on the table so that it extends beyond the edge of the table (a piece of gaffer tape is used to keep it in place). A glass filled with whiskey and acrylic glass ice cubes are balanced on the edge of the sheet of plexiglass.

Nylon threads are hot-glued to some other acrylic glass ice cubes, which are then suspended from a bar above the glass so that they seem to be levitating around it.

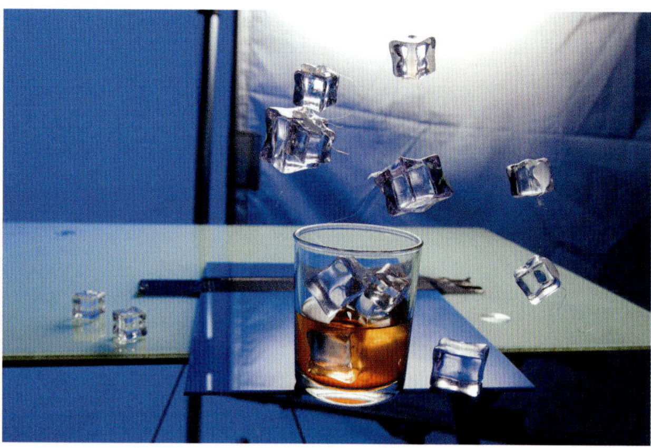

⌃ Detail of the lighting on the glass and the arrangement of the trick.

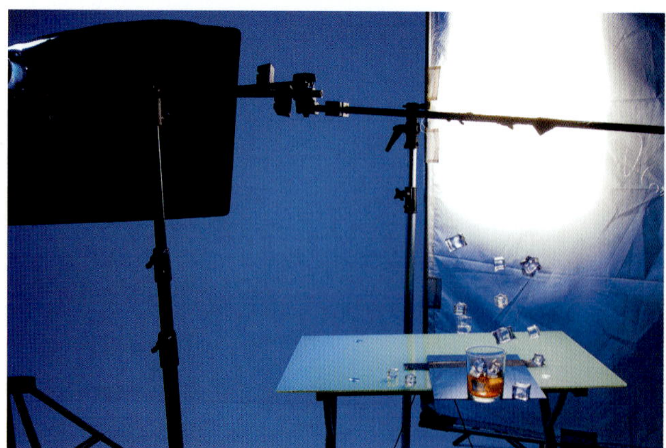

⌃ A behind-the-scenes view of the production of the shot on the following page.

TECHNICAL DATA SHEET

Camera: Canon 5DS R
Lens: EF 100mm f/2.8L Macro IS USM
Focal distance: 100mm
Aperture: f/7.1
Speed: 1/160 s
Sensitivity: ISO 100
❶ Flash: Profoto D1 equipped with a 12 x 16-inch light box and a blue gel, directed toward the wall behind the glass. Set to +0.1 EV.
❷ Flash: Profoto D1 equipped with a 12 x 16-inch light box, placed in backlight behind the diffuser. Set to +1.33 EV.
❸ Diffuser

For the lighting, a large 78 x 60-inch diffuser is placed behind the table, and a flash equipped with a 12 x 16-inch light box is placed behind that. They are positioned so that the glass is lit from behind, without direct reflections. A second flash, equipped with a blue gel that matches the blue of the plexiglass is directed toward the white wall behind the composition.

Then we lie on the ground and photograph the glass from below. Note that given the angle of flash no. 1 and the fact that the background is light-colored, a small touch-up in Photoshop will be necessary to erase some of the threads that become visible.

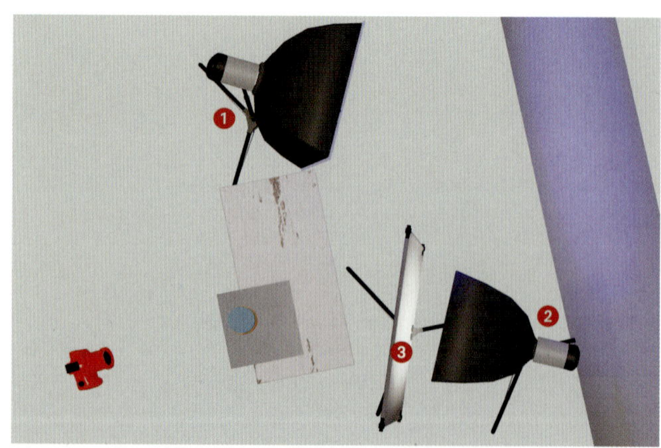

LIGHTING DIAGRAM

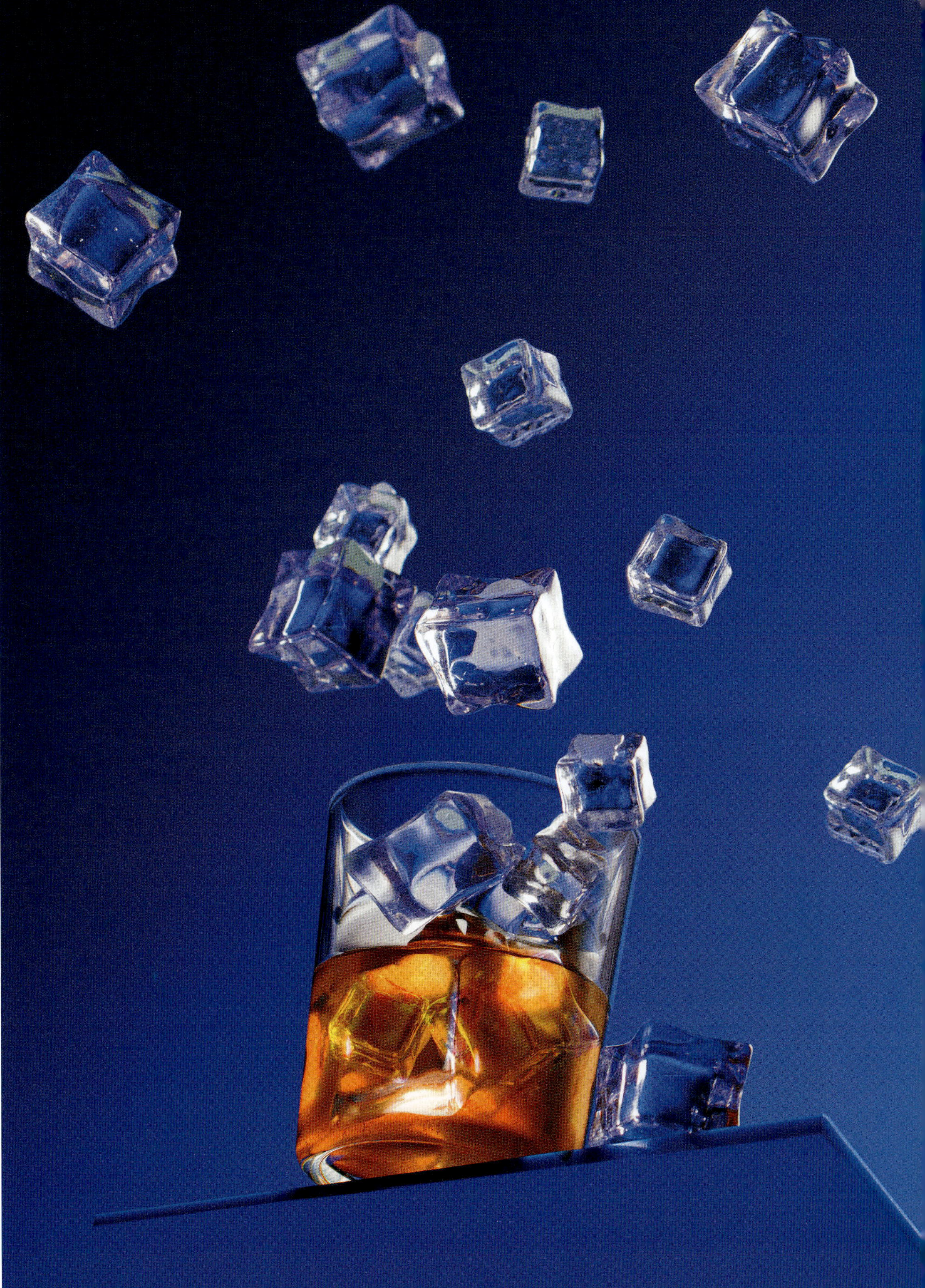

UPSIDE-DOWN LEVITATION

I produced this shot during a master class on product photography at Studio B612 in Lavérune in 2020. I wanted to show what we can do to obtain shots that are theoretically impossible to create without digital editing. Because my purpose here is to show that the laws of optics, along with a little bit of ingenuity, are usually enough to resolve photographic problems, this is the method that I suggested to my trainees there.

Trickery and Lighting

A saucepan containing cold water, agar, and grenadine syrup is brought to a boil for 30 seconds, and then while the mixture is still hot, it is poured into a wine glass (which has been preheated to avoid thermal shock, which could shatter the glass). This is allowed to cool until the preparation is sufficiently gelled that it will not move when the glass is turned upside down. (We can reclaim the glass later by reversing the procedure: agar becomes liquid at approximately 185°F.) The glass full of agar and grenadine is hung upside down with a nylon thread attached to a bar. Finally, a second glass, identical to the first one but empty and right-side up, is placed on a sheet of white plexiglass.

Now the setup is ready, we just have to proceed with the lighting.

Here, we use the standard method, which involves setting up a large diffuser behind the glasses and a flash, equipped with a strip box, behind the diffuser. Lighted outside the family of angles, the glasses will be devoid of reflections, while the shadow caused by the proximity of the strip box and the diffuser will cause lovely dark lines to appear all along the the silhouettes of the glasses.

TECHNICAL DATA SHEET

Camera: Canon 5DS R
Lens: EF 70–200mm f/2.8L USM
Focal distance: 200mm
Aperture: f/5.6
Speed: 1/160 s
Sensitivity: ISO 100
❶ **Flash:** Profoto D1 equipped with a 12 x 48-inch strip box, placed in rim light behind a diffuser. Set to +0.33 EV.
❷ **Diffuser**

A behind-the-scenes view of the production of the shot on the following page.

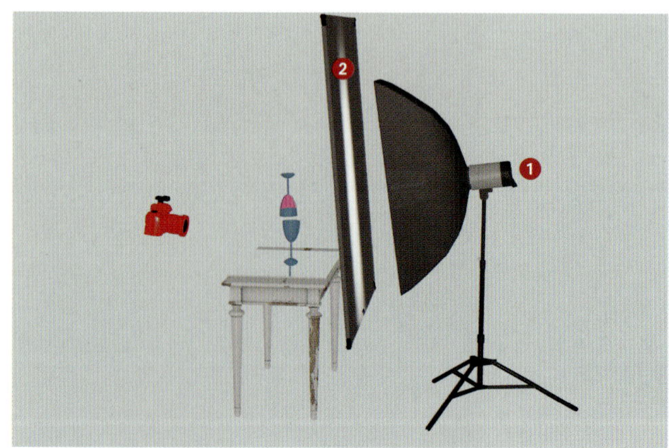

LIGHTING DIAGRAM

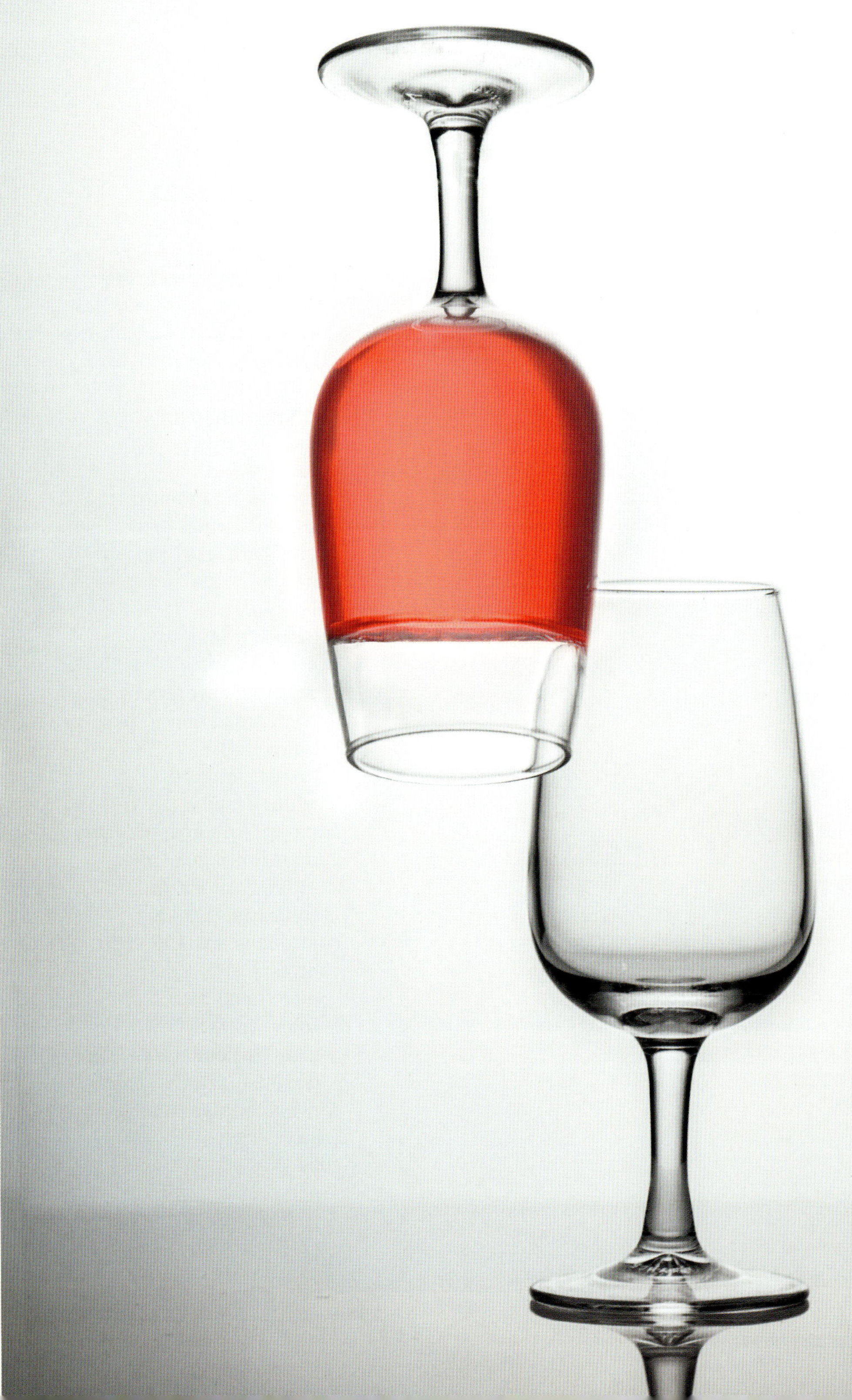

INDEX

A

absorption of light, 52–53
Adelson, Edward, 41
advertising photos, 196–198
aerial perspective, 45
ambient light, 22
angle of view, average, 49–50
antistatic gloves, 16, 112
aquariums, 190

B

background, 108–111
  absorption, 108
  brushed cotton, 110
  diffusion, 108
  glass, 109
  liquids, 110
  maintaining, 112
  mirrors, 109
  paper, 108
  plastic, 109
  reflection, 108
  textiles, 111
  textured, 111
background light, 22
backlight, 22
  parallelepipeds, 84
barn doors, 53
bottles
  defects, 224–225
  empty, 134
  example, 248–249
  frosted glass, 132–133
  labels, 222
  seams, 225
  wine, 124–131
boxes
  lighting, 144
  positioning, 84

C

cans, 147, 242–243
Capture One, 26
case studies, 230–263
catalog photos, 193–195
central linear perspective, 44
checker-shadow illusion experiment, 41
clean work space, 16, 112
clothing, 180–184
clothing, photographer's, 107
collapsing planes, 49
color, 119–121
  calibrating monitor, 120
  contrasts, 209–211
  gray card, 119–120
  harmony, 211
  light, 21
  monochrome, 211
  profile, 120
  selective absorption, 53
  standardization in post-production, 120
  temperature, 21
  texture and, 79
  white balance, 21, 119–120
composite photos, 81–82, 204–205
composition, 208–220
  artistic, 217–220
  contrasts, 208–213
continuous artificial light, 28–30
contrast
  directions, 214
  color, 209–211
  compositional, 208–213
  textures, 214
convex/concave mirror, 86, 87–89
creases, 225
cube
  perspective, 45
  positioning, 83

cutlery, 185–188
cylinders, 92–95
    glossy, 93–95, 146
    lighting, 145–147
    matte, 92–93, 145
    transparent, 95

D

defects, 221–225
dents, 225
depth, representing, 44–50
diffraction, light, 57
diffusion, 19, 32, 56–57
    diffusing dome, 107
    light tent, 106
    shadows, 32–33
dispersion, light, 55
distance
    camera to object, 71–73
    object to light source, 73
dust, 16, 112, 223

E

editing photos, 122–123
    reducing editing, 122
electronics, lighting, 158–159
equipment
    background, 108–111
    cleaning, 112
    handling objects, 113
    lighting, 106–107
    setup, 106–107, 112–113
example setups, 230–263
exercises, 228–229
exposure meter, 19, 24–26
    display, understanding, 25
    lumisphere, 25–26
eyeglasses, 169–172

F

families of angles, 67–73
    distances and, 70–73
fill light, 22
flash, 30
    shutter speed and, 25
    X-sync, 25
flash meter, *see* light meter

fluorescent tubes, 30
focal length, recommended, 49–50
focus stacking, 57
food, 153–157
    composition, 155
    examples, 238, 240, 250, 254, 258
    lighting, 153
    preparation, 156–157
    set design, 156
    shooting angle, 154
fragrance diffuser, 234–235
furniture, 167–168

G

glass, 98–103
    background, 109
    colored, 98
    dark background, 101–102
    defects, 224–225
    frosted, 99, 132–133
    full glass, 102
    light background, 100–101
    liquid and, 102–103, 260–261
    opaque, 98
glasses, *see* eyeglasses
glossy objects, 61
    cylinders, 93–95, 146
    direct reflection, 63
    metals, 96–97
    spheres, 148
gold leaf, 191
gray card, 21, 119–120

H

half-light, 19, 31–36
halogen lamps, 29
handling products, 112
HMI lights, 29
hot-shoe flash, 30

I

illuminance, 18
incandescent light, 29
incident light, 18
independent light meter, *see* light meter
inverse square law, 22, 74–75
irregularities, 221–225

J

jewelry, 160–163
  example, 230–231

K

Kelvin scale, 21
key light, 22

L

labels, 222
LED lights, 30
LED reflecting cube, 107
lenses, 17
  refraction and, 58
light
  absorption, 52–53
  ambient light, 22
  amount, 18–19
  angle, 23
  background light, 22
  backlight, 22
  basics, 18–23
  climax, 24
  color, 21
  continuous artificial, 28–30
  contrast, 20
  controlling, 28–30
  diffraction, 57
  dispersion, 55
  distance of source, 22, 74–75
  fill light, 22
  flash, 30
  hard, 31
  incident, 18
  inverse square law, 22, 74–75
  key light, 22
  measuring, 24–27
  meter, 19, 24–26
  natural, 28
  point source, 31
  polarization, 53–54
  primary source, 22
  quality, 19–20
  reflected, 18
  reflection, 58–66
  refraction, 58
  rim light, 22
  roles, 22
  secondary source, 22
  selective absorption, 53
  soft, 31
  tent, 106
  texture, and, 78–82
  transmission, 55–57
  white balance, 21
light meter, 19, 24–26
  display, understanding, 25
  lumisphere, 25–26
light tent, 106
lights, product, 159
liquid
  aquariums, 190
  background, 110
  contrasts, and, 199
  glass, in, 103
  splashes, 200
  still, 202
  waves, 201
luminance, 18, 59
lumisphere, exposure/light meter, 25–26
lux, 24

M

makeup, 173–177
matte objects, 61
  cylinders, 92–93, 145
  spheres, 148
measuring light, 24–27
metal
  glossy, 96–97
  lighting, 191
mirrors
  convex/concave mirror, 86, 87–89
  lighting, 137–138
modifiers, light, 17
molding defects, 225
monitor calibration, 120–121
monolight flash, 30
mood board, 196

N

natural light, 28

O

objects, typology, 116–118
oblique perspective, 44
overexposure warning, 27

P

pack-and-head system flash, 30
packshot table, 107
paintings, lighting 135–136
parallelepipeds, 83–84
    lighting, 143–144
penumbra (half-light), 19, 31–36
perfume, 176–177
    example, 244–245
perspective, 44–50
    aerial, 45
    central linear, 44
    changing, 46
    collapsing planes, 49
    horizon and, 48
    oblique, 44
    shooting distance and, 47
photovoltaic effect, 52
plastics, lighting, 192
point source, 31
polarization
    light, 53–54
    reflections, 65
polarizing filters, 66
polyhedrons, 85
post-production, 122–123
practical application, 228–263
preparation, work space and objects, 16, 112
primary light source, 22
prisms, transparent, 141–142
problems, resolving, 221–225
product lights, 159
pyramid, lighting, 139–140

R

RAW file calibration, 26
real-world examples, 228–263
red wine, 124–128
reflected light, 18
reflection, 58–66
    accentuating, 66
    complex shapes and, 86

diffuse, 61, 64
direct, 63, 75
families of angles, 67–73
light quality and, 68
overlapping, 69
polarization and, 54
polarized direct, 65–66
specular, 62, 64, 75
spheres, 89–91
surface conditions and, 61
texture and, 79
refraction, 58
    liquid, effect on, 103
    refraction index, 58
rim light, 22
ring flash, 30
rosé, 129–131

S

satiny objects, 61
scratches, 225
secondary light source, 22
selective absorption of light, 53
shadows, 31–43
    angle of light and, 38
    background distance, 33
    contradictory, 40
    dark, 31
    diffusion and, 32–33
    direct light and, 34–35
    eliminating, 151–152
    eliminating, 35
    half-light, 19, 31–36
    hard/soft, 31, 40
    light, 31
    multiple, 40
    placement, 38
    position, 37
    quality, 30
    reflected light and, 34–35
    shapes and, 37–43
    source light and, 31
    surfaces and, 38
    terminator, 39
    texture, 78–82
    transition to light, 19

shapes
    complex, 85–86
    cylinders, 92–95
    illumination, 41
    parallelepipeds, 83–84
    perception of, 41
    representation of, 41–43
    shadows and, 41
    spheres, 87–91
shapers, light, 17
shoes, 182–184
    example, 232–233
silverware, 185–188
size, perception of, 47
sneakers, *see* shoes
Snell's law, 58, 59
soda cans, *see* cans
specular reflections, 61
speedlights, 30
spheres, 87–91
    complex spheroid, 150
    convex/concave mirror, 86, 87–89
    glossy, 148
    light on, 39
    lighting, 148–150
    matte, 148
    reflections in, 89–91
    spheroid, 150
    transparent, 149
splashes, creating, 200, 252–253
staging, 214–216
studio flashes, 30
sunglasses, 170
surface condition (of object), 42
    glossy objects, 61
    matte objects, 61
    matte, 91
    mixed, 81–82
    opaque, 91
    satiny objects, 61
    texture, 78–82
    transparent, 91

T

table
    packshot, 107
    standard, 107
tableware, 185–189
    example, 236–237
teacup, 236–237
terminator (shadow), 38
textiles, 178–179
texture, 78–82
    color and, 79
    light orientation, 78
    light quality, 78
    mixed surfaces, 81–82
transmission, light, 55–57
transparent objects
    cylinders, 95
    glass, 99
    prisms, 141–142
    spheres, 149
tripods, 114–115

V

vanishing lines, 44
vanishing point, 44

W

watches, 164–166
    example, 246–247, 256–257
water, *see* liquid
waves, creating, 201
wedges, 17
white balance, 21, 119–120
white wine, 129–131
wine, lighting
    red, 124–128
    rosé and white, 129–131
work space, preparation, 16